COMMERCIAL LAW

D1334927

AUSTRALIA
Law Book Co.
Sydney

CANADA and USA
Carswell
Toronto

HONG KONG
Sweet & Maxwell Asia

NEW ZEALAND
Brookers
Wellington

SINGAPORE and MALAYSIA
Sweet & Maxwell Asia
Singapore and Kuala Lumpur

COMMERCIAL LAW

Sweet & Maxwell's Textbook Series

7th edition

Paul Dobson
Barrister of Lincoln's Inn
Visiting Professor of Law at Anglia Ruskin University

Dr Robert Stokes
Lecturer in Law, The Liverpool Law School

THOMSON
™
SWEET & MAXWELL

7th edition
(2008) Commercial Law

Published in 2008 by
Sweet & Maxwell Limited of 100 Avenue Road,
http://www.sweetandmaxwell.co.uk
Typeset by Interactive Sciences Ltd, Gloucester
Printed and bound in Great Britain by
Ashford Colour Press, Gosport, Hants.

No natural forests were destroyed to make this product;
only farmed timber was used and re-planted.

British Library Cataloguing in Publication Data

A CIP catalogue record for this book
is available from the British Library

ISBN 9780421901308

PREFACE

This edition sees a change to the title of this book which until now was published under the title "Sale of Goods and Consumer Credit". Over successive editions its content had expanded to include topics not strictly within the meaning of that title, including a lot of the growing body of law concerned with consumer protection. For this edition I determined that the topics covered should be further expanded, to include the law of agency. The book is thus re-titled and rather larger than previous editions. Some material in consumer credit has been removed—most of it of little relevance in most commercial law courses. Nevertheless, the book still contains what I think is the most extensive coverage of consumer credit to be found in a student book on commercial law. I am absolutely delighted that Dr Rob Stokes of Liverpool University agreed to join me for this edition. He has undertaken virtually all the work. I have, however, reviewed every chapter with him and we both take the blame for any errors or solecisms which may appear.

Developments and changes in the law have of course been incorporated in this edition. Thus the effect of the Consumer Credit Act 2006 has been fully taken in, as also has the effect of the Consumer Protection from Unfair Trading Regulations 2008 (which implemented the European Directive on Unfair Commercial Practices). We have managed at the last minute also to include coverage of the new regulations dealing with the consumer's right to cancel an agreement made during or following a trader's visit to a consumer's home—regulations which do not confine that right to the situation where the trader's visit to the consumer's home is unsolicited, but which extend it to cover also the situation where the visit is a solicited one.

We trust that this book will continue to be useful to those studying consumer law, sale of goods and consumer credit, as well as now to those whose studies also include the law of agency.

We have stated the law as we believe it to be on September 1, 2008.

Paul Dobson
Woodford Green

ACKNOWLEDGMENTS

The publishers and authors would like to thank the following bodies for permission to reprint material from the following sources:

The Incorporated Council of Law Reporting: Extracts from Law Reports Queen's Bench, Weekly Law Reports, Law Reports Appeal Cases, Law Reports King's Bench.

LexisNexis Butterworths: Extracts from the All England Law Reports (Reproduced by permission of Reed Elsevier (UK) Limited trading as LexisNexis).

Oxford University Press: Extract from Medical Law Review: Goldberg, "Paying for bad blood: strict product liability after the hepatitis C litigation" [2002] Med. Law Rev. 165.

NI Syndication: Extract from Times Law Reports: *Genn v Winkel* (1911) 28 T.L.R. 483.

Informa Law: Extracts from Lloyd's Law Reports.

CONTENTS

TABLE OF CASES

TABLE OF STATUTES

TABLE OF STATUTORY INSTRUMENTS

TABLE OF EUROPEAN LEGISLATION

Part I

SALE OF GOODS

Part 1

SALE OF GOODS

Chapter 1

INTRODUCTION AND DEFINITION OF CONTRACT OF SALE OF GOODS

WHAT THIS BOOK IS ABOUT

This book is about domestic commercial law. Commercial law is the body of rules applied   **1–001** to commercial transactions. These rules cover many diverse areas of law including the sale of goods; the law of agency; corporate law; banking law and the regulation of consumer sales including trade descriptions law and consumer protection and the regulation of credit in consumer transactions. Given the vast scope of the term "commercial law" many have questioned whether commercial law should even be regarded as an area of law, or whether it is merely an amalgamation of various distinct areas of law.[1]

This book is concerned primarily with three areas within commercial law: the sale of goods, the law of agency and consumer credit. These areas form the core areas of law covered by undergraduate and analogous courses. This book is intended to offer a clear and concise doctrinal account of these areas of law whilst also offering an analytical approach in scrutinising and critiquing the law.

The sale of goods is the most common of type of commercial transaction. The term "sale of goods" embraces agreements which are apparently very different. For example, the sale of a newspaper for 30p from a stand in the street, the sale of industrial machinery for millions of pounds to a large company and the sale of aircraft to the government are all equally contracts (i.e. agreements) of sale of goods. Although this area of law developed through the law merchant it is now clear that there is a growing divide between consumer and non-consumer cases. Issues such as remedies under sale of goods contracts, satisfactory quality and the passing of risk are now determined in no small part by the consumer status, or otherwise, of the buyer.

---

[1] See, for example, the discussion in Goode, *Commercial Law* (2004), pp.8–10.

1–002   The bulk of the first part of this book is devoted to the contractual relationship between the buyer and seller, i.e. the rights and duties between them. A clue to these will often be found in the Sale of Goods Act 1979. Reference will constantly be made to sections of this Act.

The second part of this book is concerned with the regulation of consumer credit, an area which has undergone considerable reform in recent years, driven no doubt, by the vast increase in the use of credit in recent times.

The third part of this book is devoted to the law of agency which is a fundamental aspect of commercial law. The role and importance of agency law within commercial law is considered below.

1–003   It must be remarked at the outset that it is principally between the buyer and seller that rights and obligations exist. These arise out of their bargain (i.e. their contract of sale). It is commonly thought, but wrongly so, that the buyer's best legal rights exist against the manufacturer. This common misconception is fostered and perhaps shared by a great many retailers. Of course, a manufacturer does enjoy the rights and incur the obligations of a seller but these exist as between himself and the person(s) to whom he sells his goods. Similarly, he has the rights and obligations of a buyer as against the person from whom he purchased his raw materials. A manufacturer does have some obligations which arise independently of his position as buyer or seller. Reference will be made to manufacturers as well as to auctioneers who also have liabilities (and rights) distinct from those of the seller and buyer.

One matter in particular will not figure too much in Pt I. This is where goods are taken on hire-purchase, credit sale or conditional sale terms. These types of agreement will be considered in Pt III.

HISTORICAL DEVELOPMENT OF SALE OF GOODS LEGISLATION

1–004   Before the definition of a contract of sale of goods is considered, something must be said of the history and sources of the law relating to sale of goods. The Sale of Goods Act 1979, only the second such Act to have been passed in this country, replaced the original Sale of Goods Act 1893. The original Act had been amended in the years before 1979 by such Acts as the Misrepresentation Act 1967, the Supply of Goods (Implied Terms) Act 1973, the Consumer Credit Act 1974 and the Unfair Contract Terms Act 1977. These amendments, though significant, were principally changes of detail and not substantial in extent. Thus the 1893 Act remained largely in the form in which it was originally enacted. The current Act, the Sale of Goods Act 1979, did not seek to make further changes in the law, but was a consolidation measure which reproduced (with a few technical amendments) the provisions of the 1893 Act as amended. Thus the provisions of the 1979 Act are in large part the very same ones as those originally passed in 1893. Indeed, the majority of the section numbers are the same as they were in the 1893 Act. The 1979 Act has itself been amended, principally by the Sale and Supply of Goods Act 1994 and the Sale of Goods (Amendment) Act 1995. Nevertheless, it is still true to say that much of the law of sale of goods today is basically the common law, i.e. the law stated over the years by judges in the process of deciding cases before them. The 1893 Act was intended, not to effect radical changes in the law, but to codify it, i.e. to put the common law into one statute to which it was easy to refer.[2] The 1979 Act once again put

[2] See Arden, "Time for an English Commercial Code?" (1997) 56 C.L.J. 516.

the law into one statute by incorporating all the amendments which had been made in the original Act. However, decided cases still have to be referred to in two situations. The first is where the Act is silent or ambiguous on any given point and the second is where the court in a decided case has given a particular interpretation to a section of the Act (or to the same section in the original Act of 1893). In the case of a conflict between the pre-existing common law and any statute, the latter always prevails. In this book references to sections of the Sale of Goods Act are references to sections of the current Act, the Sale of Goods Act 1979.

THE ROLE OF AGENCY IN COMMERCIAL LAW

Given the broad areas of law which fall under the umbrella of "commercial law" it is not **1–005** surprising that the relationship between agent and principal can play a significant role in many, if not all, of these areas. Moreover, this relationship is not merely predominant within the realm of business-to-business transactions. Consumers will from time-to-time have dealings with an agent, whether as principal or otherwise (though they may not realise it). For example, when purchasing a car an individual may act as principal where another (e.g. a car dealer) agrees to find a specific vehicle for his buyer. Equally, the consumer may be purchasing the car from an agent of a (possibly) undisclosed principal (i.e. the owner of the car). On the other hand, the car dealer may be advertised as an "Approved Agent of Vauxhall" when in law, that "agent" is buying and selling goods in his own right, i.e. there is no agency relationship and the contact of sale of goods will be between the customer and the dealer. It is clear that within commercial law countless transactions are conducted by agents. The role of agency, therefore, within commercial law should not be underestimated.

Moreover, as will be seen throughout the text, many legal problems (and solutions) hinge upon agency law. For example, the ability of a purchaser to claim good title to goods bought from a non-owner will, in certain circumstances, depend upon whether the buyer purchased the goods from an agent. The passing of property in a sale of goods contract may well depend on the role of warehousemen acting as agent, whether for the buyer or for the seller.

THE SALE OF GOODS

Definition

Section 2(1) of the Sale of Goods Act defines a contract of sale of goods as: **1–006**

> "a contract whereby the seller transfers or agrees to transfer the property in the goods to the buyer for a money consideration, called the price."

Three elements in this definition require explanation: "property", "goods" and "money consideration".

"Property" means ownership. Selling is the most common method by which ownership is transferred from person to person. Sometimes the contract provides that ownership will be transferred at some later date. Such a contract is termed "an agreement to sell" but it is still a contract of sale within the definition because of the words in s.2(1), "agrees to transfer". Of course, a contract which lacks any agreement to transfer property (ownership) at all, will fall outside the definition, e.g. a contract where one person simply agrees to borrow or hire the another person's goods. This type of contract, i.e. where possession, but not ownership, is agreed to be transferred, is altogether different and is called a contract of bailment.

"Goods" is defined by s.61 to include "emblements, industrial growing crops and things attached to or forming part of the land which are agreed to be severed before sale or under the contract of sale". Thus, a contract to sell crops which are growing or to be grown—whether they mature within a year (e.g. wheat) or not (e.g. timber)—is a contract of sale of goods. The only exception to this is when the crops are sold along with the land on which they are growing or to be grown. In this case the crops are not "agreed to be severed before the sale or under the contract of sale".

1–007   Things, other than crops, which are "attached to or form part of the land", are "goods" only if they are identifiable as being distinct from the land. *Morgan v Russell & Sons*[3] concerned the sale of some slag and cinders which were lying on a particular piece of ground. They were not in identifiable heaps but had melted into the soil. It was held that the slag and cinders were not distinct from the land itself and therefore were not "goods".

Other things which are not "goods" are "things in action and money".[4] Things in action include cheques and stocks and shares. Although money is not normally "goods", a coin which is sold as a curio piece and not as currency, is regarded as goods: *Moss v Hancock*.[5] Apart from the exceptions mentioned, "goods" include "all chattels personal",[6] i.e. all tangible moveable things.

The third element of the definition is "money consideration". A contract of barter, i.e. where goods are exchanged for other goods, lacks this element and is not a contract of sale. However, where goods are exchanged for a combination of money and other goods, the contract is one of sale of goods. In this case there is a money consideration even though goods are also given. In *Dawson v Dutfield*,[7] two lorries worth £475 were to be paid for by a combination of two "trade-in" lorries worth £250 and the balance in cash. It was held that there was a contract of sale of goods and that the sellers could sue for the outstanding balance of the price.

1–008   Whether there was a "money consideration" was in issue in *Esso v Commissioners of Customs and Excise*.[8] Esso devised a petrol sales promotion scheme whereby a World Cup coin was given away at Esso petrol stations with every four gallons of petrol purchased. Posters displayed at petrol stations read "Free World Cup Coins" and "One coin given away with every four gallons of petrol". There could be no doubt that when a garage proprietor sold petrol to a customer he made a contract of sale (i.e. of the petrol) with the customer, since the customer agreed to pay a "money consideration", the price. Did the garage proprietor also make a contract of sale in relation to the World Cup coins? If he did, then Esso

[3] [1909] 1 K.B. 357.
[4] Sale of Goods Act 1979 s.61.
[5] [1899] 2 Q.B. 111.
[6] s.61.
[7] [1936] 2 All E.R. 232.
[8] [1976] 1 W.L.R. 1.

were liable to pay purchase tax (since abolished) in respect of all the World Cup coins they had produced. Esso advanced two arguments. First, they claimed that the garage proprietor made no contract at all with the customer in relation to the World Cup coins. The coins had small intrinsic value and therefore the offer in the posters could not have been intended to create a legally binding relationship (i.e. a contract) between the garage proprietor and the customer. The majority of their Lordships rejected this argument and held that it had been intended that a customer who accepted the offer by buying four gallons would thereby become entitled in law to have a World Cup coin. Esso's second argument succeeded. It was held that the contract in relation to the World Cup coins was not a contract of sale. There was not just one contract made between the garage proprietor and the customer. There were two. Beside the contract for the sale of the petrol there was a separate collateral contract relating to the World Cup coins. The posters amounted to an offer by the garage proprietor to supply a World Cup coin if the customer would buy four gallons of petrol. That offer was accepted by the customer making a contract to buy four gallons. The consideration which the customer gave for the garage proprietor's promise to supply a World Cup coin was the making of the contract to buy four gallons of petrol. The making of a contract to buy four gallons of petrol was not a "money consideration".[9]

Sale Distinguished From Other Transactions

We have already examined the difference between sale and barter. More can be learned about the nature of a sale from a comparison of it with other contracts.   **1–009**

Contracts for Labour and Materials Supplied

These contracts are not uncommon. Take an example: a builder sub-contracts the job of putting the roof on a house which he is building. The sub-contract requires the sub-contractor to supply the tiles. This is not a contract of a sale of goods because its principal object is the provision of services: *Young & Marten v McManus Childs*.[10]   **1–010**

The words in s.2(1), "transfers or agrees to transfer the property in goods to the buyer", have been interpreted by the courts to require that the transfer of ownership to the buyer should be the main object of the agreement. If the main purpose is something else (e.g. the provision of labour) then the agreement is not a contract of sale. This is so even though an incidental or ancillary object of the contract is the transfer of ownership in some goods. In *Robinson v Graves*[11] the Court of Appeal held that a contract whereby an artist agreed to paint a client's portrait for him was not a contract of sale of goods. Even though, when finished, the canvas would be transferred to the buyer's ownership, the substance of the agreement was the provision by the artist of his skill and labour. If, on the other hand, the client selected from the artist's studio a finished painting and agreed to pay for it, that agreement would be a contract of sale of goods. In that case the artist would be agreeing, not

---

[9] For a further discussion of this case and of contracts of barter, see paras 8–003 and 8–004 below.
[10] [1969] 1 A.C. 454.
[11] [1935] 1 K.B. 597.

to provide his skill and labour, but simply to part with the ownership of a finished canvas, the fruit of his past efforts. The substance of such an agreement is the transfer of ownership.

It is not always easy to decide what is the substance of the contract, the provision of services or the transfer of ownership. It may be helpful to know that the courts have treated the following as contracts of sale—contracts: to make and supply ships' propellers according to a specification, *Cammell Laird v Manganese Bronze & Brass*[12]; to prepare and supply food in a restaurant, *Lockett v A. & M. Charles Ltd*[13]; to compound and supply animal foodstuff according to a formula setting out the ingredients and their proportions, *Ashington Piggeries v Hill.*[14] A borderline case, *Samuels v Davis*[15] came before the Court of Appeal in 1943. It concerned a contract to provide a made-to-measure set of teeth and it arose because they did not fit. The Court sidestepped the question of whether it was a contract of sale or for services, by holding that, whichever it was, there was an implied term of the contract that the goods should be reasonably fit for the purpose for which they were intended. The seller was therefore liable.

Contracts to Supply Computer Software

1–011   Here the contract may or may not involve the transfer of goods. Thus if the software is transferred by simply being downloaded on to the purchaser's machine from the internet or from a disk temporarily supplied by the software supplier, the contract is not one of sale of goods, since the program or software, not being tangible, does not amount to "goods", *St Albans DC v ICL.*[16] Nevertheless, if the program is intended by the parties to enable a computer to achieve specified functions, there will be an implied term at common law that the program is reasonably fit for this purpose. If, however, the software is supplied on a permanent medium, such as a disk, the contract will be one of sale of goods. It is then no different from a book (or video or audio cassette). In that case there will be the statutory implied terms that the goods will be of satisfactory quality and reasonably fit for their purpose. According to the *St Albans* judgment, the statutory implied obligations extend not only to the physical disk, book or video but also to its contents. Thus supplying an instructional manual containing wrong instructions would amount to a breach of these terms, as would supplying a disk with defective software.

Such an approach has been criticised for placing greater emphasis on the nature of the conveyance to the end user of the product than it does on the properties of the product being conveyed. In *Beta Computers (Europe) Ltd v Adobe Systems (Europe) Ltd*[17] Lord Penrose criticised the notion that where software is supplied on a permanent medium, such as a disk, the contract will be one of sale of goods and no different, for example, to a sale of a book[18]:

---

[12] [1934] A.C. 402.
[13] [1938] 4 All E.R. 170.
[14] [1971] 2 W.L.R. 1051.
[15] [1943] K.B. 256.
[16] [1996] 4 All E.R. 481.
[17] 1996 S.L.T. 604. For commentary on this decision, see Gretton, "Software: binding the end-user" [1996] J.B.L. 524.
[18] 1996 S.L.T. 604 at 608–9.

"This reasoning appears to me to be unattractive . . . It appears to emphasise the role of the physical medium, and to relate the transaction in the medium to sale or hire of goods. It would have the somewhat odd result that the dominant characteristic of the complex product . . . would be subordinate to the medium by which it was transmitted to the user in analysing the true nature and effect of the contract".

A further issue which has caused difficulty is the legal nature of the conveyance under which the software is supplied. This problem is based upon the situation when software is not sold, but rather is licensed.[19] In *Watford Electronics Ltd v Sanderson*[20] it was held that since the software had not been sold but had been supplied under licence the Sale of Goods Act 1979, and therefore the statutory implied term as to quality, were inapplicable.[21] The Court was prepared, however, to import the same obligation through the common law.[22] What can be said with certainty at this time is that the issue remains unresolved by the courts and that this "lack of clarity surrounding the legal approach to software is both commercially arbitrary and commercially inconvenient".[23]

Contracts of Hire-Purchase

It is the hallmark of a contract of sale that seller and buyer each enter a commitment that there will be a transfer of ownership from the seller to the buyer. A hire-purchase agreement lacks this. Under a hire-purchase agreement the hirer undertakes to hire the goods for a specified period at a specified rent and he is given an option to buy the goods when he has paid all the specified rent. Since he has only an option and does not legally commit himself to buy the goods, the contract is not one of sale: *Helby v Matthews*.[24]   **1–012**

In reversing the decision of the Court of Appeal, Lord Macnaghten sitting in the House of Lords suggested that[25]:

"The contract . . . on the part of the dealer was a contract of hiring coupled with a conditional contract or undertaking to sell. On the part of the customer it was a contract of hiring only until the time came for making the last payment. It may be that at the inception of the transaction both parties expected that the agreement would run its full course, and that the piano would change hands in the end. But an expectation, however confident and however well-founded, does not amount to an agreement . . . ".

Consider the emergence in modern times of a new species of hire-purchase agreement: the "Lease Purchase" or "Personal Contract Purchase" commonly used within the motor industry to finance sales of new motor vehicles. Rent is payable throughout the agreement

[19] In the majority of cases, this is correct.
[20] [2001] 1 All E.R. (Comm) 696.
[21] This view has received support, see for example *Benjamin's Sale of Goods*, but for a convincing argument to the contrary, see the discussion in Green and Saidov, "Software as Goods" [2007] J.B.L. 161 at 174–5.
[22] This being less problematic than the finding that the contract would fall under the Supply of Goods and Services Act 1982 as a bailment under s.6(1).
[23] Green and Saidov, "Software as Goods" [2007] J.B.L. 161 at 161.
[24] [1895] A.C. 471.
[25] [1895] A.C. 471 at 482.

period and is calculated on the amount of depreciation likely on the vehicle. At the end of that period, the lessee has the option to purchase the vehicle for a sum calculated to be the capital/residual value of the vehicle. What is the economic objective of such a contract? Clearly it is distinct from that of a hire-purchase agreement, which is in effect a secured sale.[26] That much is self evident from the nature of the instalment payments being calculated on the estimated depreciation of the vehicle (or goods) over the contract period. This however, may be contrasted with the payment structure of a typical modern hire-purchase agreement, where the option is frequently to buy the goods at the end of the contract period for only a nominal fee, which is certainly not representative of the estimated value of the goods at the end of the contract period. The courts have not yet had the opportunity to determine the legal classification of this new form of instalment contract. Since, however, the lessee has only an option and not a commitment to buy, it appears not to be a contract of sale of goods.

Contracts of Agency

1–013   Sometimes X sells goods to Y who in turn sells them to Z. Sometimes however, Y acts as X's agent in selling to Z. In the former case Z buys his goods from Y and if they are not delivered or are defective Z can look to his seller, Y, and if necessary can sue him for breach of contract. In the latter case Z buys from X through X's agent Y; it is with X that he has made his contract and if things go wrong, he can look to his seller, X, for a remedy. The answer to the question "who sold to Z?" depends upon whether Y was a buyer and reseller or whether he was merely an agent for X. The answer is not helped by the fact that people who are in fact buyers and resellers are often termed in the trade "agents". As previously noted, car dealers, for example, may be called "Vauxhall agents" but they are not necessarily agents for the manufacturer. They themselves buy new cars and resell them to members of the public. The true nature of the transaction can be ascertained only by examining the terms of the contract between X and Y. If it is clear that Y is buying the goods for himself, albeit with a commitment or intention to resell, then Y is a buyer and reseller.[27]

The problem can arise acutely in a situation where Y takes goods from X on "sale or return" terms. Is Y a buyer and reseller or is he X's agent? In either case he does not run the risk of being left with the goods; if he cannot find a purchaser he can return them to X. The answer is that he is X's agent if under the terms of his contract with X he has no right himself to buy the goods but can only sell to a third party: *Weiner v Harris*.[28] Contrariwise, if he has the right himself to buy the goods he is a buyer and the contract between X and Y will be one of sale of goods and not one of agency: *Weiner v Gill*.[29]

The problem can also arise where Y takes goods from X under a sale of goods contract which contains a retention of title clause, i.e. a clause stating that Y is not to become the owner unless and until he has paid for them and that if Y resells them before paying for them, X's ownership is to transfer from the goods to the proceeds of the resale received by Y.

---

[26] Indeed, this fact is responsible for the number of cases involving the sale of goods by a non-owner. In many instances, a hirer under a hire-purchase agreement sells the goods due to the (mistaken) belief that he is entitled to do so.

[27] See generally, Pt III, below.

[28] [1910] 1 K.B. 285.

[29] [1906] 2 K.B. 574.

Suppose Y sells the goods to Z before he has paid X for them. Clearly, although he is not yet the owner of the goods, he has the authority of the owner, X, to resell them. In this situation is Y a buyer and reseller or is he merely X's agent for selling the goods to Z? This question will be important if Z wishes to sue his seller for breach of contract (e.g. if the goods are defective) or if Z fails to pay the price. Whom can Z sue and who can sue Z? To put it another way, who is the other party to the contract by which Z purchased the goods? Who is the seller who sold the goods to Z? The answer is twofold. First, as between X and Y, Y is acting as X's agent in selling to Z; secondly, as between Y and Z, Y is selling as principal: *Aluminium Industrie Vaasen BV v Romalpa Aluminium Ltd.*[30] Thus, although Y owes X the duties which an agent owes to his principal, it is Y who as seller can sue Z for the price and be sued by Z for the breach of the contract of sale.

Contracts of Hire

Hiring, or bailment, is the transfer of possession of goods by the bailor to the bailee on   **1–014**
condition that the goods shall be returned to the bailor under the terms of the contract. It is easily distinguishable from a sale of goods on the basis that the objective of a bailment is to transfer only physical possession of the goods. The objective of a sale of goods is to transfer the property within the goods.[31]

A contract of bailment can take the form of an instalment contract and can be regulated under s.15(1) of the Consumer Credit Act 1974 (as amended) which defines a "consumer hire agreement" as:

"an agreement made by a person with an individual (the 'hirer') for the bailment or (in Scotland) the hiring of goods to the hirer, being an agreement which:

(a) is not a hire-purchase agreement, and
(b) is capable of subsisting for more than three months".

Where a contract to supply goods is properly regarded as a contract of hire, and not of sale, the Supply of Goods and Services Act 1982 imports similar implied terms into the contract of hire as the Sale of Goods Act does into a contract of sale.

The Importance of the Definition

Contracts other than contracts of sale of goods are not governed by the provisions of the Sale   **1–015**
of Goods Act 1979. Although they will often be governed by some other Act of Parliament, none of them is governed by an Act which is as comprehensive as the Sale of Goods Act. Later in this book, some of these other Acts of Parliament are considered, including the Supply of Goods (Implied Terms) Act 1973 (Chapter 23) and the Supply of Goods and Services Act 1982 (Chapter 8). Another important statute, the Consumer Protection Act 1987, which deals with manufacturers' liability, is also considered later (Chapter 9).

[30] [1976] 1 W.L.R. 676. For a fuller account see para.3–042, below.
[31] See *Chapman Bros v Verco Bros & Co Ltd* (1933) C.L.R. 306.

Chapter 2

FORMATION AND CANCELLATION OF THE CONTRACT

FORMATION OF THE CONTRACT

A contract of sale is an agreement by which the seller and buyer undertake mutual obliga-   **2–001**
tions. At the very least the seller agrees that the buyer shall become the owner and the buyer
agrees to pay the price. Often there are more obligations that just these. The number and
extent of the obligations can be ascertained only by reference to the terms expressly agreed
in the contract and to those extra terms which the law automatically implies into it. These will
be discussed later.[1] At present we are concerned with what amounts to an enforceable
agreement (i.e. a contract). If there is no contract or it is unenforceable, then neither the buyer
nor the seller can complain that the other has broken it.

Time of Making the Contract

It is important to know exactly when a contract is made because until that time either party   **2–002**
is free to back out. An agreement is made when one person makes an offer to another and
that other accepts it. Until there is an offer which is accepted, there is no contract. An offer
is something which is clearly intended if accepted to form a binding agreement. Thus it has
been held that the display of goods on the shelves of a self-service shop is not an offer:
Pharmaceutical Society of Great Britain v Boots Cash Chemists.[2] The customer who takes
them from the shelf therefore does not accept an offer. Rather, the offer is made by the
customer when he takes the goods to the cash desk and it is accepted by the assistant at the

---

[1] See Ch.7.
[2] [1952] 2 Q.B. 795.

cash desk. At any time before that, either party can back out. In particular the customer can restore the goods to the shelf and will be under no obligation to pay for them.

Similarly, the display of goods in a shop window does not amount to an offer: *Fisher v Bell*.[3] The person who enters the shop and asks to buy the goods displayed in the window does not therefore accept an offer. He in fact makes an offer which the shopkeeper is free to accept or reject. The display of goods in the shop window or on the shelves of a supermarket is an invitation to treat, i.e. an invitation to members of the public to make an offer to buy. The acceptance of an invitation to treat does not make a contract.

The difference between an offer and an invitation to treat can most clearly be seen in auction sales. The auctioneer asks for bids. He may receive quite a lot of bids and will usually accept the highest. When the auctioneer asks for bids he is making, not an offer, but an invitation to treat. Each bid is a separate offer and a contract is not made until the auctioneer accepts one of them. Thus s.57(2) of the Sale of Goods Act reads:

> "A sale by auction is complete when the auctioneer announces its completion by the fall of the hammer, or in other customary manner; and until the announcement is made any bidder may retract his bid."

2–003   Another problem which has sometimes exercised the minds of academics is, "At exactly what stage is the contract concluded in the case of a purchase from an automated vending machine?" Is it when the purchaser puts his money in or is that merely an offer which the machine accepts? Some words of Lord Denning M.R. in *Thornton v Shoe Lane Parking*[4] are helpful in this context. The case actually involved a contract made between a motorist wishing to park his car and the proprietor of a car park with an automatic entrance barrier. His Lordship, however, also spoke about a machine which issues railway tickets and his comments would appear to apply equally to a machine selling goods. Referring to the customer, he said[5]:

> "He was committed at the very moment when he put his money into the machine. The contract was concluded at that time. It can be translated into offer and acceptance in this way: the offer is made when the proprietor of the machine holds it out as being ready to receive the money. The acceptance takes place when the customer puts his money into the slot."

It seems then that the display of goods in an automatic vending machine—unlike that in a shop window or on the shelves of a supermarket—is not merely an invitation to treat but is an offer.

Once an offer can be identified there is not usually any difficulty in ascertaining whether it has been accepted. The general rule is that an acceptance takes effect when it is actually communicated to the offeror: *Entores v Miles Far East Company*[6]; and *Brinkibon Ltd v Stahag Stahl*.[7] There are, however, two or three exceptions to this. First, in circumstances

---

[3] [1961] 1 Q.B. 394.
[4] [1971] 2 Q.B. 163.
[5] [1971] 2 Q.B. 163 at 169.
[6] [1955] 2 Q.B. 327.
[7] [1983] 2 A.C. 34.

where the post is expected to be used as the means of communication between the seller and buyer, an acceptance takes effect when it is posted. Thus there is still a contract even if the letter of acceptance is lost in the post: *Household, Fire & Carriage Insurance Co v Grant*.[8] Secondly, where the offeror expressly or implicitly waives the need for acceptance to be communicated to him, the acceptance will take effect when the acceptor does whatever act is necessary to indicate his acceptance. The vending machine situation provides a good example of this. The contract is complete when the customer puts his money in the slot. He is certainly not expected to telephone or to write a letter to the proprietor of the machine.

Even if the offeror waives the need for communication to him, there must always be some act to indicate acceptance. The offeror cannot say "if you do nothing you will thereby accept my offer!" In *Felthouse v Bindley*[9] the offeror wrote to his nephew offering to buy the latter's horse. In the letter he said, "If I hear no more about him, I consider the horse mine". The nephew sent no reply and the court held that no contract was made. A contract is an agreement. It follows that one person cannot impose a contract upon another. If, on the other hand, the person to whom an offer is made says, for example, "If you do not hear from me within a week, you can assume that I have accepted your offer", then that will amount to an acceptance unless he communicates otherwise within the week. In *Re Selectmove Ltd*,[10] Gibson L.J. said[11]:

2–004

> "Where the offeree himself indicates that an offer is to be taken as accepted if he does not indicate to the contrary by an ascertainable time, he is undertaking to speak if he does not want an agreement to be concluded. I see no reason in principle why that should not be an exceptional circumstance such that the offer can be accepted by silence".

There may be a third exception to the general rule that an acceptance takes effect when it is actually communicated to the offeror. In *Brinkibon Ltd v Stahag Stahl*[12] the House of Lords confirmed the decision in *Entores v Miles Far East Co*,[13] that normally in the case of a telephone conversation or a telex communication the postal exception does not apply and therefore the acceptance takes effect when (and where) it is actually communicated to the offeror. Their lordships did, however, state that a different result might apply to a telex message which was not a direct communication in office hours between the acceptor and the offeror, e.g. if it was sent at night or was sent or received through telex machines operated by third persons. In such a case the acceptance could take effect upon dispatch or upon communication to the machine at the receiving end of the telex link or upon actual communication to the offeror. A court would have to decide that issue by reference to the intention of the parties, to sound business practice and to its own judgment as to where the risk should lie.

[8] (1879) 48 L.J.Q.B. 577.
[9] [1863] 1 New Rep. 401.
[10] [1995] 1 W.L.R. 474.
[11] [1995] 1 W.L.R. 474 at 478.
[12] [1983] 2 A.C. 34.
[13] [1955] 2 Q.B. 327.

Sales Via the Internet

2–005   Doubtless, the advertising of goods (or indeed services) will normally amount to no more than an invitation to treat. Someone responding to such an advertisement and submitting an order via an email may then be making what is in law an offer. If so, the advertiser is free to accept or not. Assuming that the advertiser accepts by email, there will presumably be the same uncertainty as to when the contract is made, as was expressed in the *Brinkibon* case about the position where the parties were not in direct telex communication in office hours. It would seem absurd, however, for the result to be that the contract is not made until the offeror decides to log on and check his emails (perhaps a week more or later?). In one widely publicised instance in 1999, Argos, a catalogue shopping company, advertised on its website a television set for £3 instead of £300.[14] Apparently many orders for these televisions were placed via the internet before the company realised its mistake. For those people who had not received any confirmation of their order, it seems reasonably clear that there was no contract. Apparently, however, some had received confirmation by email. This was, arguably, an acceptance. This unfortunate incident gave rise to no reported decision.[15] It seems probable however, that the contract was unenforceable by any of the buyers since they surely must have known that the bargain (a television for £3) was not intended by the seller and the law does not allow one party to snatch a bargain which he knows is not intended by the other: *Hartog v Colin and Shields*.[16]

Unsolicited Goods and Services

2–006   Goods are sometimes sent without prior request.[17] The recipient might become worried if successive letters then come threatening that action will be taken to obtain the price. Clearly, the recipient who does nothing does not enter into a contract to buy the goods and therefore is not bound to pay. In spite of the lack of any right to payment, some unscrupulous firms have in the past found it profitable to market their wares by sending them out unsolicited. This had two undesirable results. One was that some members of the public were unaware that they need not pay and gave in to the pressure of successive threatening letters. The other was that the goods, if they were not purchased by the recipient, still belonged to the sender. Therefore the recipient did not dare to throw them away and was in effect forced to give them house room. The Unsolicited Goods and Services Act 1971 tackled both of these social problems. Section 2 makes it a criminal offence to make demand for a payment for unsolicited goods without reasonable cause to believe that there is a right to it. Section 1 provided that after six months, unsolicited goods were deemed to be an unconditional gift to the recipient.

---

[14] See for example *http://news.bbc.co.uk/1/hi/business/the_economy/441740.stm* [Accessed July 4, 2008]. In 2002 Kodak mistakenly advertised a digital camera at £100, and not the intended price of £329. It is questionable whether the contractual intent argument would be applicable in this situation. However, it appeared that the customers who had placed orders had received confirmation emails, and in any event, Kodak honoured the orders. See *http://news.bbc.co.uk/1/hi/sci/tech/1795624.stm* [Accessed July 4, 2008].
[15] See generally, Capps, "Electronic Mail and the Postal Rule" [2004] I.C.C.L.R. 207.
[16] [1939] 3 All E.R. 566.
[17] This is called inertia selling.

Section 1 of the 1971 Act has since been repealed and replaced in order to bring it into line with art.9 of the Distance Selling Directive.[18] This was achieved by the Consumer Protection (Distance Selling) Regulations 2000.[19] Regulation 24 now deals with inertia selling, and applies where three requirements are satisfied:

(i) The unsolicited goods[20] must be sent to a person with a view of his acquiring the goods.[21]

(ii) The recipient has no reasonable cause to believe that the goods were sent with a view to being used for business purposes.[22]

(iii) The recipient has not agreed to either acquire or return the goods.[23]

Where these stipulations are met, reg.24(2) provides that the recipient may "use, deal with or dispose of the goods as if they were an unconditional gift to him".[24] Moreover, reg.24(3) expressly provides that the rights of the sender are extinguished. Thus the previous requirement under s.1 of the Unsolicited Goods and Services Act 1971, namely that unsolicited goods will become an unconditional gift after six months, is no longer valid: under the Regulations, there is no such time limit.

Section 2 of the Unsolicited Goods and Services Act 1971 now applies only in the case of **2–007** goods sent for the purposes of the recipient's trade or business. In other cases, criminal sanctions relating to inertia selling are now to be found in reg.24(4) and (5). Regulation 24(4) makes it an offence for any person who, without reasonable cause to believe that there is a right to payment, makes a direct demand for payment (or asserts a present or prospective right to payment) in respect of unsolicited goods or services not connected with the business of the recipient.

Regulation 24(5) makes it an offence for any person who, without reasonable cause to believe that there is a right to payment, indirectly pressures the recipient for payment in respect of unsolicited goods or services not connected with the business of the recipient. This indirect pressure may take one of three prescribed forms:

(a) threatens to bring any legal proceedings, or

(b) places or causes to be placed the name of any person on a list of defaulters or debtors or threatens to do so, or

(c) invokes or causes to be invoked any other collection procedure or threatens to do so.

For coverage of recent legislation relevant to internet sales, e-commerce and distance selling, see Chapter 16 below.

---

[18] Directive 1997/7.

[19] Consumer Protection (Distance Selling) Regulations 2000 (SI 2000/2334), as amended. The Regulations came into force on October 31, 2000.

[20] "Unsolicited", for the purposes of reg.24, is defined by reg.24(6), as "goods sent or services supplied to any person, that . . . are sent or supplied without any prior request made by or on behalf of the recipient".

[21] reg.21(1)(a).

[22] reg.21(1)(b).

[23] reg.21(1)(c).

[24] Though only as between the sender and the recipient, i.e. third party rights are unaffected.

Form of the Contract

2–008   The law on this is very easy and is contained in s.4:

> " . . . a contract of sale may be made in writing (either with or without seal), or by word of mouth, or partly in writing and partly by word of mouth, or may be implied from the conduct of the parties."

In this respect contracts of sale of goods are different from contracts for the sale of land. Whereas there are no particular formalities for the former, a contract for the sale of land can only be made in writing incorporating all the terms on which the parties have expressly agreed and signed by or on behalf of each party.[25] The distinction between goods and land is therefore important.[26]

Capacity

2–009   Certain persons lack the legal capacity to make a contract. Thus contracts are not generally binding on the following people: persons who at the time of making the contract were either minors, or so insane or drunk as not to know what they were doing. Such a person can enforce the contract against the other party but cannot generally himself be sued. An exception to this, however, is found in s.3:

> "(1) Capacity to buy and sell is regulated by the general law concerning capacity to contract and to transfer and acquire property.
> (2) Where necessaries are sold and delivered to a minor or to a person who by reason of . . . drunkenness is incompetent to contract, he must pay a reasonable price for them.[27]
> (3) In subsection (2) above 'necessaries' means goods suitable to the condition in life of the minor or other person concerned and to his actual requirements at the time of the sale and delivery."

In one case a minor undergraduate bought 11 fancy waistcoats: *Nash v Inman*.[28] It was held that the tailor could not sue for any money because the goods were not necessaries; the minor was already well supplied with waistcoats. The result of this decision was that not only was the minor under no obligation to pay for the waistcoats but also, apparently, he could keep them! Now, however, the law is different. Section 3 of the Minors' Contracts Act 1987 empowers the court, where it would be "just and equitable" (i.e. fair) to do so, to require the minor to return property which he has acquired under a contract which is unenforceable against him.[29]

---

[25] Law of Property (Miscellaneous Provisions) Act 1989 s.2.
[26] See para.1–007, above.
[27] s.3(2) used to provide for the situation where necessaries are supplied to someone who is incompetent to contract by reason of mental incapacity. That situation is now dealt with similarly by the Mental Capacity Act 2005 s.7.
[28] [1908] 2 K.B. 1.
[29] The Family Law Reform Act 1969 reduced the age of majority to 18 so that only people under that age enjoy the privileged status of minor.

Not surprisingly some traders are reluctant to deal with minors on any basis other than that the minor pays cash before taking the goods away. On the other hand, to refuse to give credit can be to turn away valuable business. Thus sometimes a trader will agree to give credit to a minor providing an adult (usually a parent) signs a document guaranteeing the minor's debt. Until 1987, however, a guarantee was no safeguard because the legal nature of a guarantee is that it is subsidiary to, and dependent upon, the contract which is guaranteed. If the latter was void, then the trader had no recourse against the guarantor: *Coutts & Co v Browne-Lecky*.[30] If, on the other hand, the adult had signed a contract, not of guarantee, but of indemnity, that contract could be enforced against the adult even if the minor's contract was void: *Yeoman Credit Ltd v Latter*.[31] Thus the difference between a contract of guarantee and one of indemnity was vital. Now, however, where a contract is unenforceable against someone merely because he is a minor, a contract of guarantee is enforceable against the guarantor.[32]

THE PRICE

The Amount

Section 8 provides: **2–010**

> "(1) The price in a contract of sale may be fixed by the contract, or may be left to be
> fixed in a manner agreed by the contract, or may be determined by the course of
> dealing between the parties.
> (2) Where the price is not determined as mentioned in sub-section (1) above the
> buyer must pay a reasonable price.
> (3) What is a reasonable price is a question of fact dependent on the circumstances
> of each particular case."

The price is normally a basic part of the agreement and normally it will be expressly agreed. It might appear from s.8(2) that, if no price is agreed and there is no method of ascertaining it, a reasonable price is automatically payable. This is not necessarily so. The price is so basic that, if the parties have expressly left it over for later agreement, the court may well conclude that the parties did not intend to make, and have not made, a contract. This was the conclusion of the House of Lords in *May & Butcher v R*[33] where an agreement for the purchase of government tentage provided that the price, the manner of delivery and dates of payment were to be agreed upon from time to time. If the contract had simply failed to mention these items, they could have been resolved by applying the provisions of the Sale of Goods Act. Equally, if the contract had provided for the price to be fixed by the seller (or buyer), that would have been binding. However, the contract expressly left the price and other items over for later agreement. That being so, and the items being so basic, their Lordships

[30] [1947] K.B. 104.
[31] [1961] 1 W.L.R. 828.
[32] Minors' Contracts Act 1987 s.2.
[33] [1934] 2 K.B. 17.

held that the parties had not intended to make a contract but simply had agreed to agree. There was therefore no contract.

If, however, a relatively minor matter is left over for later agreement it does not necessarily follow that there is no contract. It is perfectly possible in law for parties to make an interim agreement for the sale of goods which requires further negotiation to iron out the less important details of the transaction: *Pagnan S.p.A. v Feed Products*.[34] All the circumstances must be examined to see whether they intended to make a binding contract, albeit one with some details outstanding. In *Foley v Classique Coaches Ltd*[35] the defendants bought some land from the claimant and it was a condition of the purchase that the defendants agreed to buy petrol (for their coach business) only from the claimant. The agreement provided for the price of the petrol "to be agreed by the parties from time to time" and, failing agreement, to be settled by arbitration. It was held there that the parties had made a binding contract, albeit with the price still outstanding.

Clearly if there is no contract, as in *May & Butcher v R.*,[36] no price is payable and s.8 is irrelevant. If there is a contract the price is ascertained by the relevant method in s.8 (in *Foley's* case by arbitration, the manner agreed in the contract).

Valuation

2–011   Valuation by a third party is one method the parties can stipulate for ascertainment of the price. Section 9 provides that where he cannot or does not make the valuation, the contract is avoided. In that case there is no obligation on the seller to deliver the goods and none on the buyer to pay. Section 9 has one exception to this:

> " . . . if the goods or any part of them have been delivered to and appropriated by the buyer he must pay a reasonable price for them."

Section 9(2) provides that where the valuation is prevented by the fault of one of the parties, the other may maintain an action for damages against the party at fault. Where the valuer makes the valuation, then, unless the valuer was acting fraudulently in connivance with one of the parties, the valuation will be binding as between the parties. If, however, the valuation was arrived at negligently, the victim (i.e. the buyer or seller, depending upon whether the valuation was too high or too low) will have a claim in negligence against the valuer: *Arenson v Casson*.[37]

Deposits

2–012   It is not uncommon for the buyer to pay part of the price at the time of making the contract to buy. This payment could be either a deposit or mere part payment. The effect of a deposit

[34] [1987] 2 Lloyd's Rep. 601.
[35] [1934] 2 K.B. 1.
[36] [1934] 2 K.B. 17.
[37] [1975] 3 W.L.R. 815.

or mere part payment is a matter of agreement between the parties. In the absence of any agreement to the contrary, a deposit is generally forfeited by the buyer if the sale falls through because of his fault. A mere part payment, however, is returnable. A deposit is, in the words of Lord Macnaghten in *Soper v Arnold* "a guarantee that the purchaser means business".[38] It is a security for the completion of the purchase.

As so often, the law endeavours to discover the intention of the parties. It examines all the circumstances to see whether they intended the money to be a deposit or merely a payment on account. If the parties actually use the word "deposit", then unless there is evidence to the contrary it will be assumed that that is what they meant: *Elson v Prices Tailors Ltd*.[39]

Of course, if the seller has a claim against the buyer either for the price or for damages[40] he will in making his claim have to bring into account any money already received—whether as deposit or merely as a part payment. The seller cannot expect on the one hand to be fully compensated for the sale falling through and on the other to be allowed in addition to retain a deposit already received.

CANCELLATION

Cancellable Agreements

The general rule is that, once a contract is made, neither party is free to back out. To that rule there is an exception created by the Cancellation of Contracts made in a Consumer's Home or Place of Work etc. Regulations 2008.[41] These Regulations give effect to the Doorstep Selling Directive[42] and replace the Consumer Protection (Cancellation of Contracts Concluded away from Business Premises) Regulations 1987[43] with effect from October 1, 2008. Broadly speaking, the 2008 Regulations give a cooling-off period of seven days to a customer who enters into a contract (to buy goods or services) as a result of doorstep canvassing. The customer is given the right to cancel the contract during that cooling-off period. This gives him an antidote to the high pressure selling techniques sometimes employed by door-to-door salesmen. The Regulations are intended to protect ordinary consumers and therefore do not apply where the customer is making the contract for business purposes.

The 2008 Regulations simplify and extend the law relating to doorstep selling and apply when the customer makes the contract during either an unsolicited or solicited visit[44] by the trader (or his representative) to the customer's home, to someone else's home or to the customer's place of work.[45] An unsolicited visit might occur where the trader (without the customer having requested him to do so) has telephoned the customer indicating that he is willing to make a visit. The trader's subsequent visit will be unsolicited. Similarly, if the trader makes an unsolicited visit during which he indicates that he is willing to make a further

2–013

[38] [1889] 14 App.Cas. 429 at 435.
[39] [1963] 1 W.L.R. 287.
[40] See Ch.12.
[41] SI 2008/1816.
[42] 85/577/EEC.
[43] SI 1987/2117.
[44] Defined in reg.5(a).
[45] reg.3(1)(a).

visit to the customer, the trader's subsequent visit will also be unsolicited. A solicited visit might occur after a consumer has completed and returned a reply-paid card thereby requesting the visit. It might similarly occur after a consumer has visited, say, a carpet shop and whilst there has agreed to a representative calling in order to measure the consumer's lounge and issue a quotation for supplying and fitting a carpet. The distinction laid down by the 1987 Regulations between solicited and unsolicited visits (with only the latter falling under the scope of the 1987 Regulations) no longer applies. The Cancellation of Contracts made in a Consumer's Home or Place of Work etc. Regulations 2008 will apply to both solicited and unsolicited visits with effect from October 1, 2008.[46]

We have seen that a contract *made* during an off-trade premises visit is cancellable. This will be the case where an offer is made by one side which during the visit is accepted by the other. It could occur, however, that the visiting salesman gets the customer to complete an application or proposal form (i.e. an offer to buy) and that the salesman takes the form away saying that the customer will receive a reply letter. If a few days later the salesman's firm sends his customer a letter accepting the customer's offer, the contract is made, not during the visit, but a few days later. Nevertheless the Regulations still apply to such a contract.[47]

2–014　In addition to the contracts mentioned so far, the Regulations also apply to contracts made during an excursion organised by the trader away from his trade premises.[48] This is a trading practice (more common on the Continent than in the United Kingdom) whereby a trader organises a coach or boat trip and then during the trip gets travellers to buy or offer to buy goods or services. The resulting contracts are cancellable under the Regulations. This does not, however, apply to a contract made by someone visiting, say, the Ideal Home Exhibition and making a contract at a trader exhibition stand. Even if such a customer is on an excursion, it is not one organised by the trader.

Excepted Contracts

2–015　There are some important exceptions to what has been said so far. Certain contracts are excepted and are therefore not cancellable under the Regulations, namely any contract:

(1) where the price (including VAT) is £35 or less[49];

(2) for the supply of food, drink or other goods intended for current consumption by use in the household and supplied by regular roundsman[50];

(3) of insurance[51];

(4) for any "relevant regulated activity" defined by Sch.3, para.8, including investment agreements governed by the Financial Services and Markets Act 2000.[52]

---

[46] For a more detailed explanation of the distinction between solicited and unsolicited visits and also the 1987 Regulations, the reader may be directed to the 6th edition of this text.
[47] This is made clear by reg.5(c).
[48] reg.5(b).
[49] Sch.3, para.6.
[50] Sch.3, para.2.
[51] Sch.3, para.4.
[52] Sch.3, para.7.

Also excepted are contracts for the construction, sale or rental of immovable property or a contract concerning other rights relating to immovable property unless such a contract is for[53]:

(i) the construction of extensions, patios, conservatories or driveways;

(ii) the supply of goods and their incorporation in immovable property; or

(iii) the repair, refurbishment or improvement of immovable property.

There is a further exception for certain mail order (and other) "catalogue" agreements which give the customer equal rights.[54] Such a contract is excepted if three conditions are satisfied:

(i) its terms are set out in a catalogue which is readily available to be read by the customer in the absence of the salesman before a contract is made;

(ii) there is to be a continuing contact between the trader (or his representative) and the customer; and

(iii) the contract expressly gives the customer the right to return any goods within seven days of receiving them and to cancel the agreement.

Finally, a contract is excepted if it provides credit of £35 or less (unless it is a hire-purchase **2–016** or conditional sale agreement).[55] This last exception leads to an absurdity whereby a contract (say, to install new kitchen units for a cash price of £2,000 payable immediately on completion of the work) which would otherwise be cancellable, will be excepted if it contains a term that £35 of the price is not payable until, say, six months after completion.

Cooling-off Period

Where the Regulations apply, they give a cooling-off period entitling the customer to cancel **2–017** the agreement at any time within the cancellation period which is defined by reg.2 as "7 days starting with the date of receipt by the consumer of a notice of the right to cancel".[56]

The Regulations require the trader to give the customer a notice of his cancellation rights and a detachable form must also be provided for the customer's use. These must be in the form required by the Regulations and must be given to the customer during the trader's visit (or during the excursion). If the trader fails to comply with these requirements, he is not allowed to enforce the agreement against the customer.[57]

The customer is entitled to cancel the agreement by giving the trader written notice of his intention to cancel the contract within the cooling-off period. He does not have to use the

---

[53] Sch.3, para.1.
[54] Sch.3, para.3.
[55] Sch.3, para.5.
[56] reg.7(1).
[57] reg.7(6). He also commits a criminal offence under reg.17 where such a notice is not provided.

detachable form provided by the trader.[58] If the customer posts (or emails) his notice of cancellation, it will be effective to cancel the agreement provided it is *posted* (or the email is sent) within the cooling-off period, i.e. even if it does not reach the trader until later or even if it never reaches him.[59]

Effect of Cancellation

2–018   Broadly speaking, the customer is entitled to be repaid any money he has already paid before cancellation and must return any goods he has received. He need not, however, transport the goods but can wait for the trader to come and collect them. The customer's duty to take care of the goods ceases 21 days after he cancelled the agreement, unless before then he has received from the trader a written signed request to hand them over.[60]

By way of exception, the Regulations create a new category of specified contracts which may be cancelled under reg.8 but where the consumer will be still liable to pay for goods or services supplied before the cancellation, i.e. such contracts are not subject to the normal position whereby the consumer is to return any goods received and receive back any money paid. A "specified contract" is defined by reg.9(4) as any contract for:

(a)   the supply of newspapers, periodicals or magazines;

(b)   advertising in any medium;

(c)   the supply of goods the price of which is dependent on fluctuations in the financial markets which cannot be controlled by the trader;

(d)   the supply of goods to meet an emergency;

(e)   the supply of goods made to a customer's specifications or clearly personalised and any services in connection with the provision of such goods;

(f)   the supply of perishable goods;

(g)   the supply of goods which by their nature are consumed by use and which, before the cancellation, were so consumed;

(h)   the supply of goods which, before the cancellation, had become incorporated in any land or thing not comprised in the cancelled contract;

(i)   the supply of goods or services relating to a funeral; or

(j)   the supply of services of any other kind.

The consumer has to pay for goods (and services) supplied under a specified contract.

After cancelling any other cancellable contract, the customer is entitled to be repaid any money he has already paid.[61] He is also given a lien on any goods which he is himself

---

[58] reg.8(3).
[59] reg.8(5). This principle is extended to a cancellation notice sent by electronic mail through reg.8(6).
[60] reg.13.
[61] reg.10(1).

supposed to return.[62] This entitles him to refuse to hand them over until he has been repaid the money repayable to him.

If as part of the cancelled contract the customer has traded in goods in part-exchange, the trader must return those goods (in substantially the same condition) to the customer within 10 days beginning with the date of cancellation.[63] If he does not, the customer is entitled to their part-exchange allowance instead. The customer can use his lien to enforce this; he can refuse to hand over any goods which are returnable by him until he receives the part-exchange allowance.[64] **2–019**

Relationship with Cancellation Provisions of the Consumer Credit Act

A number of contracts cancellable under the Regulations will also be cancellable under the Consumer Credit Act 1974. The latter provisions are fully explained in Pt II of this book at para.22–040 onwards. The rules are very similar, the main difference is that in most cases the cooling-off period under the Consumer Credit Act will be longer. From the trader's point of view the position is straightforward. If the contract is cancellable under the Consumer Credit Act as well as under the Regulations, it is only the provisions of the former with which he must comply—i.e. provisions as to giving the customer notice of his cancellation rights. **2–020**

It should also be noted that in the case of some excepted contracts (i.e. where the Regulations therefore do not apply), there will be provisions of the Consumer Credit Act giving protection to the customer. Thus a contract for house repairs or improvements which is secured by a mortgage of the house will normally be subject to a compulsory pre-contract consideration period.[65]

Relationship with Distance-selling Provisions

Where a contract is made exclusively by distance communication, the consumer is given a right of cancellation by the Consumer Protection (Distance Selling) Regulations 2000. These provisions are fully explained at para.16–005 below. Since the 2008 Regulations cannot in practice apply unless there has been some face-to-face contact with the consumer, there is no chance of a contract being cancellable under both the 2008 and 2000 regulations. **2–021**

---

[62] reg.10(2).
[63] reg.14(2).
[64] reg.14(3).
[65] See para.22–034, below.

Chapter 3

THE PASSING OF PROPERTY AND RISK

INTRODUCTION

A contract of sale is made in order to transfer ownership from the seller to the buyer. This **3–001** transfer of ownership is called by the Sale of Goods Act "the Transfer of Property". It often takes place on the very instant that the contract is made. However, it can occur at almost any time from the making of the contract onwards—perhaps months or years later. Until it does so, the goods remain the property of the seller. The word "property" as used in the Sale of Goods Act is generally taken to mean ownership[1] and is defined by s.61 as "the general property in the goods". When considering the passing of property from the seller to the buyer, we are therefore dealing with something different from the physical handing over, (i.e. delivery) of the goods. The transfer of ownership and the transfer of physical possession often do not occur simultaneously. Thus, sometimes a seller will find himself still in the possession of goods after the ownership in them has passed to the buyer. Equally, it is possible for goods to be delivered to the buyer some time before they become his property.

Contrary to common belief, the buyer's right to obtain possession of the goods does not depend upon him being the owner. Unless the parties agree otherwise, he has the right to take delivery upon payment of the price and to do so irrespective of whether property has passed to him. Why then does it matter at what point in time the property passes? The answer is that four important things depend upon the passing of property.

---

[1] The curious approach of the Sale of Goods Act in distinguishing concepts of "property" and "title" in Pt III has been subject to much academic thought. See for example, Atiyah, *The Sale of Goods*, 11th edn, 315–320; Ho, "Some Reflections on 'Property' and 'Title' in the Sale of Goods Act" (1997) 56 C.L.J. 571. For a compelling analysis of the relationship between "property" and "title" within the Sale of Goods Act, see Battersby, "A reconsideration of 'property' and 'title' in the Sale of Goods Act" [2001] J.B.L. 1.

(i) Unless the parties agree a different time for payment, the seller can sue for the price only after property has passed—s.49.[2]

(ii) Unless and until the buyer has the ownership in the goods he cannot transfer that ownership on to any further person. This rule is subject to a number of exceptions.[3]

(iii) Risk, prima facie, passes with property—s.20. The risk of accidental damage is borne (unless otherwise agreed) by the owner. This rule is of questionable merit. It would seem sensible to link risk with possession rather than with ownership, because the person in possession of the goods is in the best position to see that they come to no harm. Still, s.20 represents the law and we shall return to it later.

(iv) In the event of either the seller or the buyer becoming bankrupt (or, in the case of a company, going into liquidation), the rights of the other party over the goods may well depend upon whether property has passed to the buyer.

CLASSIFICATION OF THE CONTRACT

3–002   We cannot pinpoint the exact time that property passes without first classifying the contract. It will be one of two types, being either (i) for the sale of specific goods, or (ii) for the sale of unascertained goods.

Specific Goods

3–003   These are defined in s.61 as "goods identified and agreed upon at the time a contract of sale is made and includes an undivided share, specified as a fraction or percentage, of goods identified and agreed as aforesaid". If, at the time the contract is made, it is possible to point out the particular goods upon which the parties have agreed, then those goods are clearly "identified and agreed upon" and therefore specific. For example second-hand car deals are usually contracts for the sale of specific goods. At the time of the contract the parties know which particular car is being sold and bought. They have "identified and agreed upon" that car. Similarly, most contracts made in supermarkets are purchases of specific goods. At the time of the contract (i.e. at the cash desk) the parties have identified and agreed upon the goods (i.e. those brought by the customer to the cash desk).[4]

   Kursell v Timber Operators[5] concerned the sale of timber which at the time the contract was made was still growing in a Latvian forest. The buyer was to fell and take away the trees for himself. The trees which he was entitled to fell and remove (i.e. which he was buying) were described in the contract as "all trunks and branches of trees, but not seedlings and young trees of less than six inches diameter at a height of four feet from the ground". They

[2] See para.12–003, below.
[3] See Ch.5.
[4] Contrast the position of groceries bought online via the website of the same supermarket.
[5] [1927] 1 K.B. 298.

were to be measured at the time of felling and the buyer was given 15 years in which to do the felling. Until the time for felling, it therefore could not be said which trees were within the contract. They were not "identified" at the time the contract was made. It was held that they were not, therefore, specific goods.

An agreement to sell some unspecified goods out of a larger specified quantity, as in *Kursell v Timber Operators*, is not a contract for the sale of specific goods. The goods actually being sold must be identified. Contracts to sell the following are therefore not contracts for the sale of specific goods: "a bottle of port from the seller's stock"; or, "12 of the seller's stock of 13 bottles of port". This description does not tell us which out of the 13 are being sold. *Re Wait*[6] involved a contract to sell 500 tonnes of wheat out of the cargo of 1,000 tonnes in the ship *Challenger*. The 500 tonnes were not specific goods because, in the words of Lord Hanworth M.R., "There was no ascertainment or identification of the 500 tonnes out of the cargo in bulk".[7] Even if the 500 tonnes were subsequently separated from the bulk of the cargo, and thereby identified, this would not make them "specific goods". The relevant time is when the contract is made. Only if they are at that time identified and agreed upon will they be specific goods. This is clear from the definition in s.61.

Suppose a seller with just 12 bottles of port in stock agrees to sell 12 bottles of port to a **3–004** particular buyer. Even this may not be a contract for the sale of specific goods. Even if the seller has every intention of supplying the buyer with the 12 bottles currently in stock, it still may not be a contract for the sale of specific goods. In order to determine whether it is, the terms of the contract must be examined and, if necessary, construed (i.e. interpreted). If the terms are such as to leave the seller free, if he should wish to do so, to obtain more wine of the same description for delivery to the buyer, then the contract goods have not been identified and agreed upon at the date of the contract and the contract is not one for the sale of specific goods: *Re London Wine Co (Shippers)*.[8] There is a difference between a contract to sell "12 bottles of port" and one to sell "the 12 bottles of port which I now have in stock". The former is not a contract for the sale of specific goods, whereas, if the seller has just 12 bottles of port in stock, the latter *is* a contract for the sale of specific goods.[9]

The words in the definition of specific goods referring to "an undivided share, specified as a fraction or percentage, of goods identified and agreed as aforesaid" deal with the position where what is sold is a share in goods which are identified. A typical example would be the sale of "a 10 per cent share in the race horse White Rum". The horse, White Rum, is identified and agreed upon at the time of the contract. Provided (a) that it is an *undivided* share that is being sold (e.g. not the right back leg!) and (b) that the share is expressed as a fraction or percentage, the contract will still be one for the sale of specific goods.

Unascertained Goods

The Sale of Goods Act does not give a definition of unascertained goods. If the contract is **3–005** not for the sale of specific goods however, then it must be for the sale of unascertained goods,

---

[6] [1927] 1 Ch. 606.
[7] [1927] 1 Ch. 606 at 617.
[8] [1986] P.C.C. 121.
[9] Consequently goods purchased online will generally be sales of unascertained goods, irrespective of whether the online seller has only one such item in stock at the time of contracting.

i.e. goods which are not identified and agreed upon at the time of contracting. This was the position in both *Kursell v Timber Operators*[10] and *Re Wait*.[11] However, within the category of unascertained goods the Sale of Goods Act distinguishes between two types:

(i) A specified quantity of unascertained goods out of an identified bulk—e.g. "500 tonnes of wheat from the cargo of 1000 tonnes on the *Challenger*."

(ii) Purely generic unascertained goods—e.g. "500 tonnes of wheat".

In the former the seller can fulfil his contract only by delivery of 500 tonnes from the specified cargo, whereas in the latter he can fulfil his contract by supplying 500 tonnes from any source. This difference, however, does not alter the fact that both are contracts for the sale of unascertained goods.

Having been told that there can be a contract for either the sale of specific goods or for the sale of unascertained goods, one might ask, "Is there not a third category? Can there not be a contract for the sale of ascertained goods?" The answer is that there is no third category. If at the time the contract is made, the goods are ascertained (i.e. identified and agreed upon), then the contract is one for the sale of specific goods. If they become ascertained only after the contract was made, the contract at the time of its creation was for the sale of unascertained goods. The time for classification is when the contract is made. Therefore there are only two possible categories of contract, for the sale of specific goods and for the sale of unascertained goods. The word "ascertained" is used in the Sale of Goods Act to mean goods which become identified and agreed upon only after the contract is made.

Future Goods

3–006   Section 5(1) reads:

"The goods which form the subject of a contract of sale may be either existing goods, owned or possessed by the seller, or goods to be manufactured or acquired by him after the making of the contract of sale, in this Act called future goods."

The problem here is to decide into which category future goods fall. Are they specific or are they unascertained? Examples of future goods are:

• 275 tonnes of barley to be grown by the seller (see *Sainsbury v Street*[12]).

• Animal feedstuff to be made according to a specification supplied by the buyer (see *Ashington Piggeries v Hill*[13]).

• A ship to be built by the seller to a specification (*McDougall v Aeromarine of Emsworth*[14]).

[10] [1927] 1 K.B. 298.
[11] [1927] 1 Ch. 606.
[12] [1972] 1 W.L.R. 834.
[13] [1971] 2 W.L.R. 1051.
[14] [1958] 1 W.L.R. 1126.

Although these particular examples each contain a contract for the sale of unascertained goods, it is not true that all future goods automatically fall into that category. For example X may agree to sell Y "the Morris car, registration ABC 123, at present in the ownership of Q and to be acquired from him by X". This is a contract for the sale of specific goods. In *Varley v Whipp*[15] the contract was for the sale of a specified second-hand reaping machine which at the time of the contract the seller did not own but still had to acquire. The court nevertheless regarded the reaping machine as specific goods.

General Reading

- Battersby, "A reconsideration of 'property' and 'title' in the Sale of Goods Act" [2001] J.B.L. 1;   **3–007**

- Ho, "Some Reflections on 'Property' and 'Title' in the Sale of Goods Act" (1997) 56 C.L.J. 571.

THE TIME OF THE TRANSFER OF PROPERTY

The rules as to what time that property passes are contained in ss.16–19 and they differ   **3–008** according to whether the contract is for the sale of specific or unascertained goods.

Specific Goods

Section 17 says that property in specific goods passes to the buyer at such time as the parties   **3–009** intend it to be transferred.[16] It also says that the intention of the parties can be determined by reference to the terms of the contract, the conduct of the parties and the circumstances of the case.[17] If the contract expressly states when property is to pass then that is fine and the matter is one of contractual construction.[18] Often, however, it does not do so. The seller is concerned about being paid and the buyer about getting hold of the goods.[19] It is not unusual therefore for the contract expressly to deal with the time for payment and the time for delivery but to be silent about the time of the transfer of property. In such a case, one must still examine all the circumstances of the case in order to discern what was the parties' intention as to the passing of property. For example, a clue may be obtained from the time that the parties have stipulated for delivery and/or payment. In *Ward v Bignall*,[20] Diplock L.J. said " . . . in modern

[15] [1900] 1 Q.B. 513.
[16] s.17(1).
[17] s.17(2).
[18] As was the case in *Re Anchor Line Ltd* [1937] 1 Ch. 1 where the Court of Appeal held that property had not passed under s.18, r.1 as the written contract established an intention that property was not to pass until the full price had been paid.
[19] This is certainly accurate in the majority of consumer sales, although still reflects the state of mind of the contracting parties in sales generally. See the observations of Lord Wright in *Smyth & Co Ltd v Bailey Son & Co Ltd* [1940] 3 All E.R. 60 at 67.
[20] [1967] 1 Q.B. 534.

times very little is needed to give rise to the inference that property in specific goods is to pass only on delivery or payment".[21]

One is attempting to discover what was the intention of the parties at the time they made the contract. If their intention subsequently changes, that is irrelevant and the property will pass in accordance with their intention at the time of making the contract. In *Dennant v Skinner*[22] the buyer had a van knocked down to him at auction. Shortly after this he paid for it by cheque and on request signed a statement that property in the van was not to pass to him until the cheque cleared. The court in attempting to discover the intention of the parties ignored the signed statement because it had been made after the making of the contract.[23]

Often even the diligent searcher will fail to discover when the parties intended property to pass. In this case property passes according to whichever of the rules in s.18 is relevant (see below).[24]

Unascertained Goods

3–010   Section 16 says:

> "Subject to section 20A below where there is a contract for the sale of unascertained goods no property in the goods is transferred to the buyer unless and until the goods are ascertained."

This is no more than common sense. Until the parties have identified the goods which the buyer is to have, no property can pass from seller to the buyer for the simple reason that it is impossible to tell in which goods the property is passing. So, in a case where the seller was to build a yacht for the buyer and they agreed that on payment of the first instalment the vessel and all materials used in its construction should become the absolute property of the buyer, the court held that no property passed on payment of the first instalment because at that time the boat's construction had not commenced and the materials to be used had not yet been identified.[25] A similar contract was involved in *Re Blyth Shipbuilding and Dry Dock Co.*,[26] but in that case the vessel was already in course of construction when the first instalment was paid. It was held that property in the incomplete ship passed on payment of the first instalment but that no property passed at that time in some materials which were lying in the ship yard and might be used in the ship's construction. The reason was that it was not at that time ascertained that those materials were definitely to be used.

Suppose a seller, S, has contracted with A in Aylesbury to sell him 60kg of potatoes and with B in Bristol to sell him 25kg and with C in Cardiff to sell him 15kg. Suppose also that the seller dispatches a lorry carrying 100kg of potatoes to make delivery to A,B and C in that order. Until the lorry has unloaded both A's and B's deliveries, the potatoes are all mixed up

---

[21] [1967] 1 Q.B. 534 at 545.
[22] [1948] 2 K.B. 164.
[23] Note, however, that subsequent conduct may provide evidence of intention at the time of contracting. See *The Filiatra Legacy* [1991] 2 Lloyd's Rep. 337.
[24] This is what happened in *Dennant v Skinner* [1948] 2 K.B. 164.
[25] *McDougall v Aeromarine of Emsworth* [1958] 1 W.L.R. 1126.
[26] [1926] Ch. 494.

and C's 15kg are unascertained. As soon as A's and B's deliveries have both been made, C's 15kg become ascertained through exhaustion, since it is then possible to say that all the potatoes left on the lorry are destined for C. Now suppose that before the lorry is dispatched, C sells his 15kg to B and arranges with S that the lorry shall drop 40kg to B in Bristol. In that case B's 40kg become ascertained through exhaustion as soon as A's 60kg have been unloaded. That is so even though B's 40kg may not have been subdivided or allocated as between separate contracts by which he bought them: *Karlshamns Oliefabiker v Eastport Navigation Corp, The Elafi.*[27]

No property can pass in goods until they are ascertained. There is one exception to this.   **3–011** It is that there are special rules, introduced in 1995 and stated in s.20A, which apply to a contract to sell a specified quantity of unascertained goods out of a specified bulk and these rules provide for a special kind of proprietary interest to pass even before the goods have become ascertained. These special rules are dealt with later at paras 3–033–3–039. So now we leave that exception aside for the moment and consider the ordinary rules which govern the passing of property in both contracts for the sale of specific goods and contracts for the sale of unascertained goods.

Although, apart from the exception just mentioned, no property can pass until the goods have become ascertained, it does not follow that the property will necessarily pass as soon as the goods are ascertained. Property passes when the parties intend it to—s.17. Section 17 applies to ascertained goods in exactly the same way as it does to specific goods. If the intention of the parties is not apparent, then property passes according to the relevant rule in s.18, i.e. in the case of a contract for the sale of unascertained goods, usually r.5.

Rules in Section 18

Section 17 is the governing section and the rules in s.18 are to be consulted only if the parties   **3–012** have not evinced their intention as to when property is to pass. This is clear from the opening words of s.18:

> "Unless a different intention appears, the following are rules for ascertaining the intention of the parties as to the time at which the property in the goods is to pass to the buyer."

Rule 1

> "*Rule 1:* Where there is an unconditional contract for the sale of specific goods in a   **3–013** deliverable state the property in the goods passes to the buyer when the contract is made, and it is immaterial whether the time of payment or the time of delivery, or both, be postponed."

[27] [1982] 1 All E.R. 208.

The essence of this is that if the goods are identified and agreed upon and ready to be handed over, the parties are taken to have intended the buyer to become the owner immediately, i.e. at the very instant that the contract is made. In *Dennant v Skinner*[28] a van was auctioned and knocked down to a Mr King. Hallet J. quoted r.1 and continued[29]:

> "Accordingly, upon the fall of the hammer the property of this car passed to King unless that prima facie rule is excluded from applying because of a different intention appearing or because there was some condition in the contract which prevented the rule from applying".

He held that therefore the van became King's immediately.

It is not completely settled what is the meaning in r.1 of "an unconditional contract". This could refer to a contract without any conditions whatsoever. Such an interpretation, however, would be absurd, since any contract of sale must have a condition somewhere at its core. It is difficult to imagine one without at least two conditions, namely, that the buyer will pay the price and that the seller will deliver the goods. The words "unconditional contract" therefore do not mean a contract without conditions in the sense just referred to, i.e. important terms of the contract (see Chapter 7). It seems sensible therefore to assume that they mean a contract which contains no condition preventing r.1 from applying. An example of such a condition would be if, to the buyer's knowledge at the time the contract was made, the seller was not the owner of the goods. In that case ownership will not pass to the buyer before the seller has himself succeeded in acquiring that ownership. This was precisely the position in the case, referred to earlier, of *Varley v Whipp*, where at the time of the contract the seller still had to acquire the second-hand reaping machine which he was agreeing to sell. It was held that the contract was not "unconditional" and that therefore r.1 did not apply.

3–014   The words "deliverable state" are defined in s.61(5) as, goods "in such a state that the buyer would under the contract be bound to take delivery of them". Thus if the goods require anything to be done to them in order for them to be ready for delivery or in order to make them comply with the contract, they will not be in a deliverable state. In *Underwood v Burgh Castle Brick & Cement Syndicate*[30] the contract was to sell a 30-ton condensing machine which at the time of the contract was standing bolted to a concrete emplacement in which it had become embedded because of its weight. It was an expensive and time-consuming task to remove it. In the contract the sellers had agreed to do this and to deliver the machine f.o.r. (free on rail) which meant that they undertook to see that the machine was conveyed to and loaded upon the train. The Court of Appeal had two reasons for deciding that r.1 did not apply. First, the parties had, by making an f.o.r. agreement, indicated their intention that property should pass when the goods were loaded on to the rail. Secondly, the machine was not at the time of the contract in a deliverable state, since it still had to be removed from the concrete emplacement.

We now come to the closing words of r.1, "it is immaterial whether the time of payment or the time of delivery, or both, be postponed". From these, it is clear that a buyer can be the owner of the goods even though he has not paid for them and even though they remain in the seller's possession. As we shall see in Chapter 12, the seller usually has the right to retain

---

[28] [1948] 2 K.B. 164.
[29] [1948] 2 K.B. 164 at 171.
[30] [1922] 1 K.B. 343.

possession of the goods until the buyer pays. This does not alter the fact that if r.1 applies the buyer becomes the owner at the instant the contract is made. As Hallet J. explained in *Dennant v Skinner,*

> "the passing of property and the right to possession are two different things. Here, in my judgment, the property had passed on the fall of the hammer, but still the (seller) had a right to retain possession of the goods until payment was made."[31]

In other words, what occurs after the contract is made, in relation either to the possession of the goods or to the payment of the price, can have no bearing upon the operation of r.1. However, what might affect it is if at the time of the making of the contract the parties make an *agreement* about delivery and/or payment, i.e. that they be postponed. Such an agreement could easily give rise to the inference that they intended property to be similarly postponed (see *Underwood v Burgh Castle Brick & Cement Syndicate,* above). In that situation none of the rules in s.18 would apply since those rules are only relevant "unless a different intention appears".

Rule 2

> **3–015** "*Rule 2:* Where there is a contract for the sale of specific goods and the seller is bound to do something to the goods for the purpose of putting them into a deliverable state, the property does not pass until the thing is done and the buyer has notice that it has been done."

Rule 2 is therefore concerned with the situation where, unlike in r.1, there is a conditional contract—the condition relating to the seller[32] doing something to render the goods in a deliverable state. One example of an act which renders the goods in a deliverable state is that of topping up casks of turpentine (where the agreement between the parties required this topping up).[33] The key issue here is whether the goods meet the "state in which they are to be delivered by the terms of the contract".[34]

One unanswered question here is what "notice" means. Suppose the seller puts a letter in the post informing the buyer that the goods are in a deliverable state. Does property pass when the letter is posted or when it arrives? "Notice" probably means actual knowledge in which case the property passes when the letter arrives. So, if the letter is lost, property does not pass until the buyer actually discovers that the goods are in a deliverable state. The Act is also silent on the issue of whether it is the seller who should give notice to the buyer.[35]

---

[31] [1948] 2 K.B. 164 at 172.
[32] Similarly to r.3, only acts to be done by the seller.
[33] *Rugg v Minett* (1809) 11 East 210.
[34] *Underwood v Burgh Castle Brick & Cement Syndicate* [1922] 1 K.B. 343 at 345, per Bankes L.J.
[35] It would appear likely that provided the buyer has notice, it is not relevant who provided that notice. Consider the similar concept of "assent" for the purposes of r.5 which specifies buyer and seller.

Rule 3

3–016   "*Rule 3:* Where there is a contract for the sale of specific goods in a deliverable state but the seller is bound to weigh, measure, test, or do some other act or thing with reference to the goods for the purpose of ascertaining the price, the property does not pass until the act or thing is done and the buyer has notice that it has been done."

It is important here to note that r.3 applies only if it is the seller who is to do the weighing, measuring, testing, etc. In *Nanka-Bruce v Commonwealth Trust Ltd*,[36] it was agreed that the buyer would pay 59s. per 60lb. The buyer was going to resell the goods and it was recognised that the buyer's sub-purchaser would test the weight and thus ascertain the precise sum to be paid to the seller. The Privy Council held that property passed from the seller before the sub-purchaser had tested the goods for weight. Thus, where specific goods are to be weighed or tested, etc., by some person other than the seller, property will pass under r.1 or r.2 unless the parties have agreed otherwise.

Rule 4

3–017   "*Rule 4:* When goods are delivered to the buyer on approval or on sale or return or other similar terms the property in the goods passes to the buyer:

   (a) when he signifies his approval or acceptance to the seller or does any other act adopting the transaction;
   (b) if he does not signify his approval or acceptance to the seller but retains the goods without giving notice of rejection, then, if a time has been fixed for the return of the goods, on the expiration of that time, and, if no time has been fixed, on the expiration of a reasonable time."

It is sometimes difficult to know whether the purchaser has done an act adopting the transaction. He will have done such an act if he does something which substantially impedes his ability to return the goods at the end of the period (whether that be a stipulated period or a reasonable length of time). Thus he "adopts" the transaction when he resells the goods or when he pledges them with a pawnbroker (*Kirkham v Attenborough*[37]). What is the position, though, where the buyer resells the goods on sale or return terms? Passages from the judgments from *Genn v Winkel*[38] are particularly helpful here. Fletcher Moulton L.J. said:

   " . . . a person who receives goods on sale or return and at once passes them on to someone else under a like contract is entitled to demand them from that third person just as soon as the original owner of the goods has the right to demand them from him, and, therefore, I do not see that he has lessened or impeded his power of returning the goods when the owner of the goods has a right to demand them back, but I am clear that, if

---

[36] [1926] A.C. 77.
[37] [1897] 1 Q.B. 201.
[38] (1911) 28 T.L.R. 483.

he allows a period to elapse before he hands them to a third person on sale or return, he has done an act which limits and impedes his power of returning the goods as soon as the owner of the goods demands them. For instance, if fourteen days be a reasonable time in such a contract in this particular trade, and if he waits seven days before entrusting the goods to a third person on sale or return, that third person has a right to keep them as against him for fourteen days, whereas the original owner of the goods has a right to the return of them within seven days from that date, and I think that that is clearly an act inconsistent with anything but his having adopted the transaction."

Buckley L.J. said:

"If A delivers goods to B on sale or return and B having received them immediately delivers them to C on sale or return, the reasonable time in the one case must, I think, be co-extensive with that in the other case, and if that reasonable time elapses and C brings back the goods to B and B takes them back to A, everybody is acting within his rights, and it appears to me that the property never passes. That is not the point for decision in this case, and those are not the facts here, but that is a first step towards explaining the reason why I arrive at my conclusion. If under like circumstances A delivers goods to B and B delivers them to C, in each case on sale or return, and the reasonable time be, let us say, fourteen days, and C after four days sells the goods or elects to buy the goods, the result will be, I think, that the property will have passed, because C will have done an act which renders it impossible for B to return the goods to A."

Two further points need to be made about r.4. First, if the cause of the purchaser being unable to return the goods within the approval period is something which occurs entirely without his fault and beyond his control (e.g. if the goods are stolen or accidentally destroyed) he can offer that as an excuse and property will not pass: *Re Ferrier.*[39]

Secondly, as with all the rules in s.18, r.4 is irrelevant if the parties when making the contract express their intentions as to when property should pass. Thus in *Weiner v Gill*[40] although jewellery sold on approval was subsequently resold by the buyer, the Court held that property had not passed because of an express statement in the original contract that property was not to pass until the seller was paid.

Rule 5

"(1) Where there is a contract for the sale of unascertained or future goods by   **3–018**
description, and goods of that description and in a deliverable state are unconditionally appropriated to the contract, either by the seller with the assent of the
buyer or by the buyer with the assent of the seller, the property in the goods then
passes to the buyer; and the assent may be express or implied, and may be given
either before or after the appropriation is made.

[39] [1944] Ch. 295.
[40] [1906] 2 K.B. 574.

(2) Where, in pursuance of the contract, the seller delivers the goods to the buyer or to a carrier or other bailee or custodier (whether named by the buyer or not) for the purpose of transmission to the buyer, and does not reserve the right of disposal, he is to be taken to have unconditionally appropriated the goods to the contract."

There are many contracts for the sale of unascertained goods where the parties do not express their intention as to when property shall pass. Rule 5(1) applies to these contracts. It contains two basic requirements for property to pass. First, goods complying with the contract must be unconditionally appropriated to the contract by one of the parties. Secondly, the other party must give his assent.

Take an example: Mrs Jones telephones her coal merchant asking him to deliver six bags of coal. He agrees. Next day the merchant, his lorry loaded with 200 bags of coal, sets out to make deliveries. He arrives at Mrs Jones's door with 150 bags left on the lorry. He knocks at the door. She unlocks the coal house door for him. He goes to his lorry where he drags six bags to the edge of the lorry's platform. He takes one of them, brings it to the coal house and empties it there. He repeats this with each of the other five bags. At what time does the property in the coal pass to Mrs Jones? It is not when the merchant set out on his round because at that time Mrs Jones' coal was as yet unascertained—*McDougall v Aeromarine of Emsworth* (above). For the same reason, it did not pass when the merchant drew up outside her house.

3–019   Rule 5(1) tells us that property passes when it is unconditionally appropriated by one party with the other's assent. In *Carlos Federspiel & Co v Charles Twigg & Co.*[41] Pearson J. had to consider what amounted to an "unconditional appropriation". He said[42]:

> "A mere setting apart or selection of the seller of the goods which he expects to use in performance of the contract is not enough. If that is all, he can change his mind and use those goods in performance of some other contract and use some other goods in performance of this contract."

Thus, in our example, property did not pass when the merchant moved the six bags towards the edge of the lorry's platform. Pearson J. went on[43]:

> "To constitute an appropriation of the goods to the contract, the parties must have had, or be reasonably supposed to have had, an intention to attach the contract irrevocably to those goods."

It would seem then that in our example there was an unconditional appropriation of the contents of each bag as it was emptied into Mrs Jones' coal house. Pearson J. was considering a contract where the seller had agreed to dispatch goods f.o.b. (free on board) a ship, i.e. the seller undertook to convey the goods to the ship and to load them.

He had got as far as packaging and labelling them at his premises prior to taking them to the ship. Pearson J. held that property had not passed under r.5(1) for two reasons. First, s.18

[41] [1957] 1 Lloyd's Rep. 240.
[42] [1957] 1 Lloyd's Rep. 240 at 255.
[43] [1957] 1 Lloyd's Rep. 240 at 255.

was irrelevant since the parties by making an f.o.b. contract had indicated their intention that property was to pass as and when the goods were loaded on to the ship (see *Underwood v Burgh Castle Brick & Cement Syndicate*, above). Secondly, the goods had been merely set aside and not unconditionally appropriated.

The approach of Pearson J. in *Carlos Federspiel & Co v Charles Twigg & Co* may be **3–020** contrasted with that in *Aldridge v Johnson*.[44] Here there was a contract for the sale of a specified quantity of barley from a bulk held by the seller. It was agreed that the buyer was to provide sacks, into which the seller would load the barley. Having filled some of the sacks, the seller then stopped and emptied all of the sacks, i.e. returning the barley to the general bulk. Shortly after this, the seller became bankrupt. The court held that the buyer was entitled to that quantity of barley which had been placed into the sacks by the seller prior to bankruptcy. The act of filling the sacks constituted the act of appropriation necessary for property to pass. It is difficult to reconcile the decisions in the *Federspiel* case and *Aldridge v Johnson*. Certainly, in a physical sense, the act of placing the barley into the sacks was not the "final and decisive" act as required under Pearson J.'s approach.

Re London Wine Co (Shippers)[45] also illustrates the principle that for an appropriation there has to be an apparent intention to attach the goods irrevocably to the contract. The selling company dealt in wine and maintained considerable stocks. It contracted to sell wine on terms that after the contract the wine would be stored for the purchaser by the vendor. The company issued each purchaser with a document confirming that the purchaser was the sole owner of the wine he had purchased. In one instance a contract was made to sell to one purchaser a quantity of a given type of wine which exactly equalled the seller's stock of it. In another instance several contracts with different purchasers exhausted the seller's stock of another type of wine. Each purchaser was given a document stating him to be the owner of the quantity he had purchased of the wine in question. It was held, nevertheless, that in neither instance was there an appropriation. Where there were several purchasers of the same type of wine, it was impossible to say who owned which of the bottles of wine in the seller's stock. Even where there was only one purchaser, there was nothing to identify the particular cases of wine in stock as the subject-matter of the purchaser's contract. It was quite open to the selling company, if it wished, to obtain more wine of the same description for delivery to the purchaser. Thus no property passed in any of the wine remaining in the seller's stock.

The decision in *Re London Wine Co (Shippers)* was distinguished in *Re Ellis Son & Vidler*,[46] where again wine was sold on terms that after the sale it would be stored for the purchasers by the vendor. In this case, however, there was to be, and was, a segregation of the wine within the seller's warehouse, so that upon a contract being made, wine of the appropriate year and description was segregated from the general trading stock of the seller and kept together with other wine bought by customers and stored for them by the seller. Within the segregated part of the warehouse, wine of any particular year and description was kept together but was not further allocated to the different customers who had bought wine of that year and description. When later (perhaps years later) a customer asked for delivery of, say, a case of his Chateau Plonk 1976, that request would be fulfilled by the seller taking and delivering any case from the quantity of the Chateau Plonk 1976 stored in the segregated

[44] [1857] 26 L.J.Q.B. 296.
[45] [1986] P.C.C. 121.
[46] [1994] 1 W.L.R. 1181.

part of the warehouse. The judge dealt with this situation in a combination of two novel ways. Firstly, he held that since the contract contemplated no immediate delivery of the goods but merely a segregation in the hands of the seller for retention purposes, the wine became sufficiently ascertained when that segregation occurred. That was so, even though the cases of wine were not at that stage allocated to each individual customer. Secondly, he held that property passed when the parties intended it to, namely when the wine was set aside for storage. Since at that time the cases of wine in storage were not allocated as between different purchasers, the nature of the property right which passed to the buyer was unusual. Thus each set of cases of identical wine which was held by the seller, not mingled with the trading stock, but segregated and in store for a group of customers, was the property of that group of customers, each holding the wine as tenant in common. This means that each customer had an undivided share in the set of cases, a share proportionate to the number of cases he had bought. The key distinctions between this case and *Re London Wine* were, first, that in this case there was to be a segregation of the wine by the seller for storage purposes, and secondly, that the London Wine Company, unlike the seller in the present case, was free to sell its stock and satisfy its customers from any other available source. The ruling in the present case anticipated the rules relating to a specified quantity of unascertained goods out of an identified bulk which were shortly afterwards introduced by s.20A.[47]

3–021   When goods have to be dispatched by a carrier (e.g. the Post Office) r.5(2) is often helpful. Thus the goods will normally be unconditionally appropriated when handed over to the carrier.[48] However, there are two limitations to this. First, there is no unconditional appropriation where the seller reserves the right of disposal—see s.19 (below). The other limitation is that property cannot pass in unascertained goods—see s.16 (above). To put it another way, goods are not appropriated unless it is clear which goods are appropriated. This is neatly illustrated by *Healy v Howlett*.[49] The seller contracted to sell 20 boxes of mackerel f.o.r. (free on rail). He dispatched by rail all at the same time 190 boxes to go to various customers. He did not label the boxes to go to particular destinations but left it to the rail company to allot the appropriate number of boxes to the various destinations. Ridley J. held that putting the 190 boxes on the rail was not in this case an unconditional appropriation because it was impossible to say which of them was appropriated to any given buyer. They therefore were still unascertained goods. Property therefore could not pass until the railway company made the allotments.

The problem of when does an unconditional appropriation occur can arise in a very different situation: when the buyer has to collect the goods, not from the seller, but from a third person. There is an unconditional appropriation when the goods are identified and the third person acknowledges that he now holds them for the buyer: *Wardars (Import & Exports) v W. Norwood*.[50] This case concerned the sale of 600 cartons of frozen kidneys out of a bulk of 1,500 cartons stored for the seller at a cold store. The buyer's carrier went to the cold store with a delivery order. He found that 600 cartons had been set aside ready for him. He handed his delivery order to an official who thereupon gave instructions for loading to commence. The Court of Appeal held that there was an unconditional appropriation when the delivery order was accepted and loading allowed to commence.

---

[47] See paras 3–033–3–039, below.
[48] Delivery being a straight forward example of an appropriation to the contract.
[49] [1917] 86 L.J.K.B. 337.
[50] [1968] 2 Q.B. 663.

Under r.5(1) an unconditional appropriation will not pass property unless the other party assents. This assent could sometimes be difficult to establish but fortunately r.5 allows it to be implied and to be given in advance. Thus, in our earlier example, Mrs Jones' assent can be inferred from the fact that she unlocked the coal house door. Similarly, in *Aldridge v Johnson*[51] where the buyer supplied bags for the seller to put the goods (barley) into, it was held that property passed when the seller filled the bags. An easy and neat example of assent can also be found in the case of a purchase of petrol at a garage. If a petrol pump attendant puts the petrol into the customer's car, that is clearly an unconditional appropriation to which the buyer's assent is clearly implied: *Edwards v Ddin*.[52] At a self-service garage it is the motorist who unconditionally appropriates the petrol by pouring it into his tank, the assent of the seller being equally clearly implied. Thus at a self-serve station, as in the case of a non-self-service one, property in the petrol passes to the buyer when it is poured into his tank: *R. v McHugh*.[53]

On the other hand, assent is sometimes given only after the unconditional appropriation is **3–022** made. In that case the property passes not upon appropriation but when the other party's assent is subsequently given. This was the position in *Pignataro v Gilroy*[54] where the sale concerned some unascertained bags of rice which the buyer was to collect. The sellers got the rice for collection and were requested by the buyer for a delivery order enabling him to collect the rice. They sent him a delivery order but he failed to come and collect the rice. He did nothing. The buyer's assent to the appropriation made by the sellers was inferred from his failure to object after receiving the delivery order. Therefore property passed to him when, after a reasonable length of time, he had failed to object.

> "*Rule 5:* (3) Where there is a contract for the sale of a specified quantity of unascertained goods in a deliverable state forming part of a bulk which is identified either in the contract or by subsequent agreement between the parties and the bulk is reduced to (or to less than) that quantity, then, if the buyer under that contract is the only buyer to whom goods are then due out of the bulk,
>
> (a) the remaining goods are to be taken as appropriated to that contract at the time when the bulk is so reduced; and
>
> (b) the property in those goods then passes to that buyer.
>
> (4) Paragraph (3) above applies also (with the necessary modifications) where a bulk is reduced to (or to less than) the aggregate of the quantities due to a single buyer under separate contracts relating to that bulk and he is the only buyer to whom goods are then due out of that bulk."

Rule 5(3) and (4) were added to the section by the Sale of Goods (Amendment) Act 1995. They give statutory authority to the decision in *Karlshamns Oliefabiker v Eastport Navigation Corp, The Elafi*,[55] explained at para.3–010, above. The principle involved is one of ascertainment and appropriation by exhaustion. Where the buyer agrees to buy goods out

[51] [1857] 26 L.J.Q.B. 296.
[52] [1976] 1 W.L.R. 942.
[53] [1977] R.T.R. 1.
[54] [1919] 1 K.B. 459.
[55] [1982] 1 All E.R. 208.

of a specified bulk, e.g. "50 tonnes out of the 110 tonnes of potatoes currently in the seller's Bedford warehouse", the complete property in the remaining potatoes at the warehouse passes to the buyer at the moment that the 100 tonnes is reduced to 50 tonnes (or less). At least that is so provided that: (a) the goods are in a deliverable state, (b) the buyer is the only buyer remaining entitled to potatoes from that warehouse, (c) the buyer has assented to the appropriation, and (d) the parties have not made an agreement for property to pass at some later stage. In the absence of some particular evidence to the contrary, the buyer's assent is likely to be implied from the mere fact that he agreed to buy from the specific bulk, since he must have meant to leave the seller free to deal with the remaining 60 tonnes and that automatically must involve the buyer assenting to the remaining ones being thereby appropriated to him. It makes no difference if it is under more than one contract that the buyer is entitled to the whole of the remaining quantity of the outstanding bulk: r.5(4). Of course, if the 110 tonnes have become reduced to less than 50 tonnes, then, whilst property in whatever tonnage is left will at some stage pass to the buyer, the buyer may well have a claim against the seller for breach of contract for delivery of less than the contract quantity. Nor can the seller within the terms of the contract make up the shortfall from another source.

On the question of what proprietary interest the buyer gets in the bulk *before* property passes under r.5(3) and (4), see paras 3–033–3–039 below.

Section 19

3–023   Section 19 provides that, if the seller reserves a right of disposal of the goods until certain conditions are fulfilled, property does not pass until those conditions are fulfilled. Thus if a seller entrusts identified and appropriated goods to a carrier with instructions that they be conveyed to the buyer but not handed over until the buyer has paid, the goods will remain the seller's property until the buyer pays for them.

It is quite common in an import or export sale for the seller to arrange the carriage of the goods by ship to the buyer and also to arrange for their insurance *en route*. Such contracts are termed c.i.f. because the cost (i.e. the price paid by the buyer to the seller) includes the insurance and freight. In this case the bill of lading (i.e. the document given by the shipowner acknowledging that he has received the goods) will usually indicate that the goods are held according to the seller's instructions. The seller will normally send by air to the buyer some documents: one will be the bill of lading transferred to the buyer allowing him to collect the goods at their port of destination; another will be a bill of exchange which the buyer will normally sign and return thereby undertaking to pay for the goods on the date specified on the bill of exchange. If the buyer finds that the bill of lading is not in order, i.e. it indicates that the contract has not been complied with, he can refuse to accept it and will therefore refuse to sign the bill of exchange. In such a case no property passes to the buyer—s.19. Also, s.19 requires the buyer to return the bill of lading to the seller. If on the other hand the buyer finds the bill of lading in order he will retain it and will sign and return the bill of exchange. When he does this, property will pass. This, of course, does not preclude the buyer from refusing to accept the goods if when they arrive they do not comply with the contract. If he does that, then property will pass back to the seller: *Kwei Tek Chao v British Traders*.[56]

---

[56] [1954] 2 Q.B. 459.

TRANSFER OF RISK IN NON-CONSUMER CASES

Section 20

Unless the parties agree otherwise, risk passes with property—s.20(1). Thus if the goods are   **3–024**
damaged or stolen this loss falls on the seller if it occurs before property has passed;
otherwise it falls on the buyer. This is so irrespective of whose possession the goods were in
at the time. This is illustrated by *Pignataro v Gilroy* where we have seen that property passed
to the buyer under s.18, r.5. The buyer failed to collect them and they were stolen from the
seller's warehouse. It was held that the buyer must bear this loss because property had passed
to him before the goods were stolen.

The basic rule that risk passes with property is subject to three limitations; they are s.20(2)
and (3) and the fact that s.20(1) only applies unless otherwise agreed.

Section 20(2)

> "But where delivery has been delayed through the fault of either buyer or seller the   **3–025**
> goods are at the risk of the party at fault as regards any loss which might not have
> occurred but for such fault."

This was applied in *Demby Hamilton v Baden*[57] where the buyer was supposed to take
delivery of some apple juice in weekly loads. The buyer held up delivery and the juice went
bad as a result. It was held that the buyer must bear the loss.

Section 20(3)

> "Nothing in this section shall affect the duties or liabilities of either seller or buyer as   **3–026**
> a bailee or custodier of the goods of the goods of the other party."

This means that the person in possession must take reasonable care of the goods even if
the ownership is with the other party. Thus if the goods are damaged or stolen because of his
negligence he will have to bear the loss even though at the time he was not the owner. To put
it another way, the risk which under s.20 passes with property (i.e. which falls upon the
owner) does not include the risk of loss or damage due to the other party's negligence.

"Unless otherwise agreed"

The parties can agree when risk shall pass. They can select a time before or after the passing   **3–027**
of property. In order for their agreement to have any effect it must be part of the contract. It

---

[57] [1949] 1 All E.R. 435.

may be remembered that in *Healy v Howlett*[58] no property passed in the mackerel put by the sellers on to the rail because the consignment was not allotted as to the various destinations. After putting them on the rail the sellers sent the buyers an invoice stating "At sole risk of purchaser after putting fish on rail here". Ridley J. said, "I do not see how those words form part of the contract". He therefore ignored them. The mackerel went bad before the railway had allotted particular boxes to particular destinations. Therefore, since property had not passed, the loss fell on the seller.

An agreement that the passing of risk shall not be simultaneous with the passing of property can be inferred from the circumstances. An example of this is the difficult case of *Sterns v Vickers*.[59] The sellers owned 200,000 gallons of white spirit stored for them by an independent person, X, in his tanks. They sold to the buyers 120,000 out of the 200,000 gallons and gave the buyers the benefit of free storage at X's for a given period, i.e. down to January 31. It was agreed that the buyers would make their own arrangement for storage thereafter. The sellers gave the buyers a delivery note to enable them to collect the spirit from X. However, the buyers chose to keep it at X's and did not come to remove it for some months by which time it had deteriorated. Clearly, the property had not passed because, until collected, the 120,000 gallons out of the 200,000 tank remained unascertained. In spite of this, the Court of Appeal held that the parties intended risk to pass when the buyers accepted the delivery note. The buyers therefore had to bear the cost of the deterioration. There are three things to note about this case. First, the agreement that risk should pass independently from property was not express but inferred by the court from the circumstances of the case. Secondly, that agreement resulted in risk passing before property. Thirdly, it resulted in the risk passing in unascertained goods.

The last point is not without difficulty. Which goods were at the buyer's risk? Clearly no more than 120,000 gallons. If, say, 100,000 out of the 200,000 gallons had deteriorated, it would have been difficult to allocate the loss as between seller and buyer. Presumably it would be done pro rata, i.e. the buyer would bear:

$$\frac{120,000}{200,000} \ (= 3/5 \text{ of the loss})$$

3–028   This is possible where, as in *Sterns v Vickers*, the contract is for the sale of unascertained goods out of a specified bulk. One can identify the bulk, calculate the total loss and make the buyer bear a proportion according to his share of the bulk. This could not be done for the sale of purely generic goods. In that case until the goods are ascertained it is impossible for risk to pass. Not only would it be impossible to identify the goods which were at the buyer's risk but it would also be impossible to identify any goods which were pro rata at his risk.

There is now a fourth point which can be made about the case. It is that if the facts had arisen after 1995, there would have to be a qualification to the statement that property had not passed to the buyer. The qualification is that, under the law as it now is, the buyer (assuming that he had paid for the goods) would have acquired an undivided share of 60 per cent of the 200,000 gallons and thus when all of the gallons deteriorated, he would have had to bear the

---

[58] [1917] 86 L.J.K.B. 337.
[59] [1923] 1 K.B. 78.

loss in so far as it affected his 60 per cent. In other words the net result would still be the same if the facts of *Sterns v Vickers* occurred again today.[60]

Let us now turn to a less difficult decision where the rule in s.20 may be affected, i.e. where the seller undertakes to deliver the goods. The seller does not have to agree to this and if he does, that will not normally affect the operation of s.20. Thus the risk of loss or damage (other than that caused by late delivery or the seller's negligence) will pass at the same time as the passing of property. If on the other hand the seller agrees to deliver "at his own risk" this will alter the operation of s.20. Its effect will be that even if property passes earlier to the buyer, the goods will remain at the seller's risk until their arrival. However, even in this case, unless the parties agree otherwise, the buyer must bear the "risk of deterioration necessarily incident to the course of transit".[61] Thus where the seller agrees to deliver the goods "at his own risk" the buyer will bear the risk of any unavoidable deterioration in the goods in transit but the seller will have to bear the risk of them being stolen from his lorry *en route*.

Effect of Loss Falling on One Party

If because risk had passed to him the buyer has to bear some loss, it follows that he is not   **3–029** excused from carrying out the contract. Thus if he refuses to accept the goods or to pay because they have deteriorated, he is in breach of contract. The seller will have all the usual seller's remedies.[62] If, because risk had not passed to the buyer, the seller has to bear the loss, it does not necessarily excuse him from performing the contract. It will do so only if it frustrates the contract (renders it impossible to carry it out.[63] Unless the contract is frustrated, the seller will still have to carry out the contract and if he delivers goods which do not comply with it, he will be in breach of contract.

TRANSFER OF RISK IN CONSUMER CASES

The general rule of when risk is to pass under a contract for the sale of goods detailed above   **3–030** is no longer valid in consumer cases. The Sale and Supply of Goods to Consumers Regulations 2002[64] inserted s.20(4) into the Sale of Goods Act which reads:

> "In a case where the buyer deals as consumer or, in Scotland, where there is a consumer contract in which the buyer is a consumer, subsections (1) to (3) above must be ignored and the goods remain at the seller's risk until they are delivered to the consumer".[65]

Thus, where the buyer is purchasing goods as a consumer,[66] the question of whether property has passed from seller to buyer is now irrelevant to whether the goods are at the risk

[60] As to the buyer getting an undivided share in an identified bulk, see paras 3–033–3–039 below.
[61] s.33.
[62] See the discussion of remedies available to the seller in Ch.12.
[63] See Ch.4.
[64] Sale and Supply of Goods to Consumers Regulations 2002 (SI 2002/3045).
[65] Inserted by SI 2002/3045 reg.4(2).
[66] For an explanation of "dealing as a consumer" see para.10–018 below.

of the buyer. The question to be asked under the new rule is simply that of whether the goods have been delivered to the customer. Until such time, they are to remain at the risk of the seller, irrespective of whether property has passed under either s.17 (contractual intention) or s.18 (rules for ascertaining intention).

The abolition of the *res perit domino* (risk passes with property) rule for buyers who deal as consumers is a very sensible change in direction for the law and certainly constitutes a more accurate reflection of when consumers would themselves expect to be liable for any loss or deterioration of the goods. Take for example the situation where a consumer purchases groceries online and those groceries deteriorate in transit. Under the new rules it is clear that the risk of those goods deteriorating in transit will be borne by the seller. The new s.32(4) prevents any argument[67] that delivery of goods to a carrier is not delivery of goods to the buyer:

> "In a case where the buyer deals as consumer or, in Scotland, where there is a consumer contract in which the buyer is a consumer, subsections (1) to (3) above must be ignored, but if in pursuance of a contract of sale the seller is authorised or required to send the goods to the buyer, delivery of the goods to the carrier is not delivery of the goods to the buyer".[68]

3–031   In our example, the old position of s.20(1) would require the parties to ascertain exactly when property passed. This would likely be a sale of unascertained goods since they would not be identified and agreed upon at the time of making the contract and in the absence of any contractual intention, property would pass when the requirements of s.18, r.5 were met. This would hinge on the interpretation of the final and decisive act theory of appropriation and could, in practice, be anytime after contracting up to actual delivery depending on business practice and the nature of the goods in question.[69] That these uncertainties have been removed from consumer sales is to be commended.[70]

General Reading

3–032
- Sealey, " 'Risk' in the law of sale" (1972) 31 C.L.J. 225;

- Sasson, "Deterioration of Goods in Transit" [1962] J.B.L. 352;

- Sasson, "Damage resulting from natural decay under insurance, carriage and sale contracts" (1965) 28 M.L.R. 180.

---

[67] It should be noted, however, that many retailers in fact operated a similar policy prior to the new rules as to risk came into force.

[68] Inserted by SI 2002/3045 reg.4(3).

[69] Consider for example, the practice of many online supermarkets to bag purchased groceries and pack the filled bags into crates to be delivered to the customer. What would the act of unconditional appropriation be in such a case?

[70] Further support for the reform comes from the expectation that a seller can reasonably be expected to insure his interest in the goods, whereas a consumer can not.

UNASCERTAINED GOODS FROM AN IDENTIFIED BULK

Until 1995 there was no statutory provision dealing expressly with the situation where the **3–033** subject matter of the contract was a specified quantity from an identified source, e.g. "nine bottles of the seller's current stock of 1992 Chateau Plonk", or "400 of the 1,000 tonnes of wheat currently in the Wally's Warehouse at Woodford". Since such a contract is for the sale of unascertained goods, it followed (by virtue of the rule in s.16) that no property could pass to the buyer until his nine bottles or his 400 tonnes had become ascertained. This was less than ideal in a situation where the buyer had paid the price and the seller had become insolvent before the particular goods to be supplied to the buyer had become identified. This was because in that situation the goods remained the property of the seller and hence became the property of the seller's trustee in bankruptcy and the buyer became simply an unsecured creditor.

The injustice of this situation is well illustrated by the decision in *Re Wait*.[71] We have already seen that Lord Hanworth M.R. identified a contract to sell 500 tonnes of wheat out of the cargo of 1,000 tonnes in the ship *Challenger* as being a contract for the sale of unascertained goods. As the 500 tonnes had not been appropriated to the contract at the time of the seller's bankruptcy, property could not pass and the seller's trustee in bankruptcy was able to claim the entire cargo, irrespective of the fact that the buyer had paid the price for the goods. The buyer's claim of an equitable assignment over the 500 tonnes was rejected by the Court of Appeal.[72] Atkin L.J. said that:

> "It would have been futile in a Code intended for commercial men to have created an elaborate structure of rules dealing with rights at law, if at the same time it was intended to leave, subsisting with the legal rights equitable rights inconsistent with, more extensive, and coming into existence earlier than the rights so carefully set out in the various sections of the Code".[73]

If any equitable assignment could not have survived the enactment of the Sale of Goods Act 1893, as suggested by Atkin L.J., then where the rules as to the passing of property within the Act were not satisfied, the pre-paying buyer was left as an unsecured creditor. This argument was applied by the Privy Council in *Re Goldcorp Exchange Ltd* where gold bullion was purchased and stored on behalf of customers. The Privy Council held that where the gold bullion of each customer was pooled (i.e. stored in bulk and not segregated) there was a sale of generic goods, and thus no property had passed to the buyer under the Sale of Goods Act as the gold remained unascertained and unappropriated.[74] This approach led to the unfortunate situation where, in the case of a seller's insolvency, a certificate or document of title

---

[71] [1927] 1 Ch. 606.

[72] See *Tailby v Offical Receiver* (1888) 13 App. Cas. 523. For an alternative approach to the proper interpretation of *Re Wait*, see Eaton and Friel, "Protecting Prepaying Buyers of Unascertained Goods: Why 'Pay Before You Go' May be Bad for You" Common Law World Review 36 1 (50).

[73] Eaton and Friel, at 635–6.

[74] See also *Re Stapylton Fletcher* [1994] 1 W.L.R. 1181 where the approach of Atkin L.J. was approved. In many cases on similar facts the identification of a contractual bulk could not be established. This is obviously not merely an issue of physical identification, but requires the seller to be contractually obliged to supply goods from a specified bulk. Where no bulk can be identified, clearly no equitable interest could be recognised even if (contrary to the now accepted view) such an interest could survive the Sale of Goods Act 1893. See further, Worthington, "Sorting out ownership interests in a bulk: gifts, sales and trusts" [1999] J.B.L. 1–21.

purporting to establish ownership of goods forming part of a bulk was ineffective. The Sale of Goods Act did not allow property to pass in unascertained goods and no equitable interest could be established over the bulk following the enactment of the Sale of Goods Act 1893.[75] It was to remedy this defect in the law that the Sale of Goods (Amendment) Act 1995 was passed.[76]

3–034   This Act created a qualification to the rule in s.16 of the Sale of Goods Act. It did this by inserting into the Sale of Goods Act a new section, s.20A. Section 20A(1) states:

> "This section applies to a contract for the sale of a specified quantity of unascertained goods if the following conditions are met:
>
> (a) the goods or some of them form part of a bulk which is identified either in the contract or by subsequent agreement between the parties; and
> (b) the buyer has paid the price for some or all of the goods which are the subject of the contract and which form part of the bulk."

This section applies to any contract for the sale of a specified quantity of goods which is part of an identified bulk. Its effect is that as soon as the buyer pays the price (or part of it), the buyer immediately acquires property in an undivided share in the bulk, becoming thereby an owner in common of the bulk.[77] The buyer's share is "such share as the quantity of the goods paid for and due to the buyer out of the bulk bears to the quantity of goods in the bulk". So, if the buyer has agreed to buy "400 tonnes out of the 1,000 tonnes of wheat in Wally's Woodford Warehouse", and he has paid for his 400 tonnes, then provided that there are 1,000 tonnes of wheat in the warehouse, the buyer will own an undivided share of 40 per cent of the 1,000 tonnes. If the seller should subsequently remove 200 tonnes from the bulk (e.g. to supply a second buyer), then the bulk is reduced by that amount. In that case the first buyer's undivided share will automatically become a larger proportion of the reduced bulk, i.e. it will then amount to 50 per cent of the now remaining 800 tonnes. Thus, although no property in the buyer's particular 400 tonnes can be transferred to the buyer until his particular 400 tonnes have been identified, he does acquire a proprietary right in the form of this undivided share in the bulk.

This cannot occur before payment and in any case the effect of s.20A is subject to contrary agreement by the parties. The parties can by agreement decide that s.20A will not apply at all (i.e. that the buyer will not get an undivided share in the bulk) or that the property in the undivided share will pass at some point of time *after* payment. They cannot agree to it passing at any earlier stage.

Of course, in the example given above the seller could remove all of the rest of the bulk, i.e. so that only 400 tonnes were left. In that case the buyer would cease to have an undivided share, but would then have complete property in the bulk by virtue of s.18, r.5(3).[78]

---

[75] On the issue of documents of title and goods stored in a bulk, see Proctor, "Documents Of Title—Or Are They?" (1995) 8 J.I.F.B.L. 382.

[76] For an excellent account of the pre-1995 Act difficulties, see Davies, "Continuing dilemmas with passing of property in part of a bulk" [1991] J.B.L. 111.

[77] By virtue of s.20A(2).

[78] See para.3–016, above.

Insufficient Quantity in the Bulk

What is the position if the bulk becomes reduced to less than the quantity to which the buyer **3–035**
is entitled? This could happen in several different ways.

The Seller Makes Contracts Under Which the Total Quantity Contracted to be Sold Out of the Bulk is Greater Than the Total Quantity in the Specified Bulk

Suppose the seller has 1,000 tonnes of wheat in the warehouse. Suppose that he agrees to sell **3–036**
500 tonnes of the bulk to A, 400 tonnes of it to B and 300 tonnes of it to C. Suppose also
that each of A, B and C have paid the seller in full. Suppose also that the contracts are made
and the payments are made in that order, i.e. A first, B second and C third. In that situation,
while the bulk is still undivided, it is an obvious matter of common sense that A, B and C
cannot each have an undivided share in a bulk of 1,200 tonnes, since the bulk contains only
1,000 tonnes. The result therefore has to be one of the two following:

(i) the seller can and does give C only that which the seller has still got, namely an
undivided share in one tenth of the bulk of 1,000 tonnes;

(ii) C is introduced as an extra purchaser having an undivided share of three-twelfths
of the bulk, thereby diluting A's and B's undivided shares to five-twelfths and
four-twelfths respectively.

The second of those two solutions cannot apply because of the rule that the seller cannot
give that which he does not have; he can give only that which he has got. This rule is known
by its Latin: *nemo dat quod non habet* (no one can give that which he does not have) and is
fully explained in Chapter 5. Since, immediately prior to the sale to C, the seller has only an
undivided share in one-tenth of the bulk of 1,000 tonnes, that is all C can get. Thus A's and
B's shares remain undiluted and C gets an undivided share in one-tenth of the bulk of 1,000
tonnes. Suppose now, however, that the seller delivers to C, pursuant to the seller's contract
with C, 300 tonnes out of the bulk. If at the time of that delivery C takes in good faith,
unaware of A's and B's contracts, C will obtain complete property in the 300 tonnes
delivered. This is because of s.24 of the Sale of Goods Act, which creates an exception to the
rule that the seller cannot pass property (i.e. ownership) which he does not have. Section 24
applies where a person, having sold goods, continues in possession and then delivers the
goods under any sale or other disposition to another person who takes them in good faith and
without notice of the previous sale.[79] When in these circumstances C obtains property in the
300 tonnes that are delivered to him, A's and B's rights are reduced to undivided shares in
the reduced bulk of 700 tonnes, shares of five-ninths and four-ninths respectively. That is the
effect of s.20A(4) which provides that where the aggregate of the undivided shares of buyers
in a bulk would exceed the whole of the bulk, the undivided share of each buyer is reduced
proportionately so that the aggregate of the undivided shares is equal to the whole bulk. If the

[79] s.24 is dealt more fully at para.5–022 below.

next thing that happens is that the seller becomes bankrupt, A and B will be entitled to take the remaining 700 tonnes and divide it between themselves in proportions of five to four. This will of course leave each of them with a shortfall and to that extent they will become unsecured creditors of the seller.

Of course it could have happened that, shortly before becoming insolvent, the seller delivered out of the remaining bulk of 700 tonnes to one or other of A or B. Suppose then that, before becoming insolvent and bankrupt, the seller delivered to B 400 tonnes from the bulk pursuant to B's contract. In that case complete property in the 400 tonnes will have at that point passed to B, by virtue of s.18, r.5(1). At the moment of delivery to B, A will have become the only buyer entitled to the remaining bulk which at a mere 300 tonnes was less than he contracted to buy. Thus at that moment complete property in the remaining 300 tonnes will have passed to A. So far as his shortfall of 200 tonnes is concerned, his only claim is as an unsecured creditor against the seller. Thus the effect of delivery to B is to transfer to A the full effect of the shortfall. At least, this is so unless there was an express contractual agreement to the contrary between A and B. This is because s.20B provides that each owner in common of the bulk (here A, B and C) is deemed to have consented to delivery out of the bulk to any other owner in common of the bulk.

The Seller Delivers Goods Out of the Bulk to Another Buyer in Pursuance of a Contract Other Than One to Supply Goods from That Particular Bulk

3–037   Suppose that the bulk is 1,000 tonnes and that A is the only buyer to whom the seller has contracted to sell goods (500 tonnes) from that particular bulk and suppose that A has paid for them. In that case a delivery to another buyer (X) of 100 tonnes will simply reduce the bulk to 900 tonnes and A will then have an undivided share of five-ninths of the 900 tonnes remaining. Now, however, suppose that the quantity sold and delivered to X is 600 tonnes out of the bulk. The effect of this delivery is to reduce the remainder of the bulk to 400 tonnes. Obviously, complete property in the remaining 400 tonnes will pass to A. The sale and supply of 600 tonnes to X appears to have reduced A's rights by 100 tonnes. How can A's proprietary rights in 100 tonnes be given to X? The answer lies again in s.24 that, despite the fact that the seller does not have a right to any more than 500 of the 1,000 tonnes, he can nevertheless pass to X good title to goods already sold to A. This occurs, by virtue of s.24, provided that X takes in good faith and unaware of A's contract.

The Bulk is Destroyed, Reduced or Damaged by Accident or Act of God

3–038   Suppose that there are 1,000 tonnes in the bulk and that A has contracted to buy, but has not yet paid for, 500 tonnes of them. In that case A will have acquired no property, not even an undivided share in the goods. That being so, no risk will have passed to A, unless the parties have agreed otherwise or else the seller can establish that delivery has been delayed through A's own fault.[80] A's contract will become frustrated at common law if the contract has

---

[80] See Sale of Goods Act 1979 s.20 at para.3–024, above.

become impossible, e.g. if the bulk is totally lost in an act of God, such as an accidental fire.[81]

Now, suppose that A has paid for his 500 tonnes before the fire occurs and suppose that there is no other buyer with an interest in the 1,000 bulk. A and B each had an undivided share of 50 per cent in the 1,000 tonnes. Normally, risk passes with property. So, assuming that the whole of the 1,000 tonnes are lost, each of A and B loses his entire interest in the bulk. The position is different, however, if the fire destroys only part of the bulk. According to the Law Commission Report whose recommendations the Sale of Goods (Amendment) Act 1995 was passed to implement, "the risk of partial destruction of the goods rests with the seller (in the absence of agreement to the contrary) so long as the quantity destroyed is within the quantity retained by the seller". To put it another way, in any case of destruction of any of the bulk, it is assumed that the share in the goods retained by the seller is destroyed first. Only when that has all been destroyed, do the various buyers with undivided shares begin each to suffer a loss proportionate according to the size of their respective undivided shares. Of course it is possible that none of the damaged goods are destroyed but that some or all of them are damaged. In that case the same principle applies. The damage is taken to have occurred first to the share of the goods retained by the seller. Of course if the damage is to all of the bulk equally, then the seller and the buyer(s) will bear the loss in proportion of their respective shares. So if the buyer has agreed to buy (and has paid for) 120,000 gallons out of a bulk of 200,000 gallons and the whole bulk is damaged equally, the buyer will have to bear 60 per cent and the seller 40 per cent of that loss.[82]

Limits to the New Rules

For the rules in s.20A to apply, the agreement must be for a specified quantity of goods forming part of an identified bulk. This section, whereby the buyer may acquire an undivided share in the bulk, applies only where the parties agree that the goods are to come from that bulk. It is not enough that each of the parties had in mind this particular source for the goods, if they have not actually agreed it. If they have agreed simply that the seller will supply "500 tonnes of wheat", then the contract can be fulfilled by the seller supplying wheat from any other source, even though they may both have assumed that this particular source would be used. Section 20A applies only where the particular bulk is identified either by the contract or else by subsequent agreement between the parties. Even then, the section will not apply unless that identified source amounts to a "bulk" which means: **3–039**

> "a mass or collection of goods of the same kind which
>
> (a) is contained within a confined space or area, and
> (b) is such that any goods in the bulk are interchangeable with any other goods therein of the same number or quantity."[83]

---

[81] For more explanation of frustration see para.4–009, below.
[82] See *Sterns v Vickers* [1923] 1 K.B. 78, para.3–027, above, for a case where similar facts arose before the advent of the new law on undivided shares.
[83] Sale of Goods Act 1979 s.61.

Even then s.20A will still not apply unless the agreement is for a "specified quantity" (e.g. 500 tonnes, 40 cases, nine bottles) of goods from the bulk. Thus a contract for the sale of "500 tonnes of the 1,000 tonnes of wheat in the seller's warehouse at Woodford" is one for unascertained goods and s.20A will apply to it. On the other hand, a contract to purchase a percentage or a fraction (e.g. 10 per cent or one-half) of the bulk is an example of a contract for the purchase of specific goods and s.20A will not apply to it. Thus a contract for the sale of "half of the 1,000 tonnes of wheat currently in the seller's warehouse at Woodford" is a contract for the sale of specific goods. Although the Act still has no provision for such a contract (beyond stating that it is a contract for specific goods), it is nevertheless still presumably intended by the parties that the buyer will acquire an undivided share in the bulk. The property in that undivided share will pass when the parties intend it to. If it turns out that the bulk is greater than the 1,000 tonnes, then the buyer will either gain or lose in comparison with his expectations. If it turns out to be less, presumably he may have a claim for misrepresentation or breach of contract, since the seller had informed and/or promised him that the bulk comprised 1,000 tonnes. It may be that the example of "half of a bulk of 1,000 tonnes of wheat" is unrealistic because the parties would be much more likely to state "500 tonnes out of the bulk of 1,000 tonnes". The percentage or fraction approach is more likely to be adopted by parties who are selling and buying part of an item which is indivisible, e.g. a racehorse.

General Reading

3–040
- Burns, "Better Late than Never: The Reform of the Law on the Sale of Goods Forming Part of a Bulk" (1996) 59 M.L.R. 260;

- Davies, "Continuing Dilemmas with Passing of Property in Part of a Bulk" [1991] J.B.L. 111.

RETENTION OF TITLE CLAUSES

3–041   In business it is not uncommon for a seller (X) to sell large quantities of a commodity to a buyer (Y Ltd) in the knowledge that Y Ltd will be able to pay for them only out of the proceeds of reselling them. It may be that Y Ltd is only a buyer and reseller, i.e. only a link in the chain of distribution. Alternatively it could be that Y Ltd is a manufacturer and that the commodity he buys from X is part of his raw materials. In either case the problem for X is the same, namely what is X's position if Y Ltd having taken delivery then becomes insolvent and goes into liquidation before paying for the goods? Has X got property rights over the goods entitling him to recover the goods (or their value) in priority to any other creditors of Y Ltd, or, on the other hand, is he merely an unsecured creditor having only a right to sue for the price? The latter will be the case if property has passed to Y Ltd. In that situation X, being an unsecured creditor, is likely to obtain no more than a small percentage of the price he is owed. In the absence of a contrary statement in the contract between X and Y Ltd, property will normally have passed by virtue of ss.16–18 of the Sale of Goods Act.[84]

---

[84] See paras 3–008–3–022, above.

However, a provision in the contract to the effect that property does not pass until Y Ltd has paid the price, will not entirely meet X's needs. Y Ltd has got to be allowed to sell the goods; otherwise Y Ltd may never be able to pay X. How can X protect himself against the possibility that Y Ltd, having sold the goods, might then go into liquidation before paying X? The way to do so was demonstrated by the Dutch sellers in *Aluminium Industrie Vaasen BV v Romalpa Aluminium Ltd*.[85]

The *Romalpa* Case

The contract was for the sale by a Dutch company of aluminium foil some of which the **3–042** buyers (an English company) were to use in their manufacturing process. At the time of manufacture the foil would obviously become mixed with other materials. The buyers took delivery of the foil but never made full payment. Later they became insolvent and a receiver was appointed. At that time the buyers still had some of the foil which had not yet been taken into the manufacturing process (i.e. unmixed foil). They had also sold some of the foil, some unmixed and some mixed (manufactured). The Dutch sellers now relied upon a clause (cl.13) in their contract of sale with the buyers and claimed therefore to have proprietary rights entitling them to have priority over the buyer's other creditors. This claim, however, was limited to unmixed foil and the proceeds of the sale of unmixed foil. Clause 13 was in two parts. The first part dealt with unmixed foil and stated that ownership in the foil would transfer to the buyers only when they had paid all that was owing to the sellers. The second part dealt with mixed foil and stated that the ownership of the sellers would transfer from the foil used in the manufacture to the finished products and that these would remain the property of the sellers until full payment had been made to them. Furthermore the buyers were to keep the finished goods as "fiduciary" for the sellers. The second part of cl.13 also authorised the buyers to sell these goods, on condition that they would if requested transfer to the sellers the benefit of those sales.

Foil (mixed or unmixed) which had been sold by the buyers clearly now belonged to whoever had bought it, since the Dutch sellers had expressly authorised the buyers to sell it. Any unmixed foil unsold by the buyers clearly still belonged to the Dutch sellers by virtue of the first part of cl.13. Ownership passes when (and not before) the parties intend it to. In relation to the unmixed foil which the buyers had sold, the Court of Appeal held that the Dutch sellers were entitled to receive from the buyers the proceeds of the sales by the buyers. The Dutch sellers were entitled to those proceeds of sale in priority to the buyers' other creditors (secured and unsecured). This was because of the right of an owner (here, the Dutch sellers) to "trace". This is a right to follow, and take, the proceeds of a sale where the owner's goods are disposed of by someone in a fiduciary relationship with the owner. It was held that cl.13 clearly imposed that fiduciary relationship upon the buyers.

In relation to the unmixed goods the clause worked by a combination of two things. First, it reserved title to the sellers and secondly it imposed a fiduciary duty upon the buyers which enabled the sellers to trace into the proceeds of sale.

[85] [1976] 1 W.L.R. 676.

Mixed Goods

3–043   What would be the position with mixed goods?[86] The answer is that the clause would, because it said so, give the sellers property rights over the mixed (manufactured) goods. This, however, is not because title in the mixed goods is reserved to the sellers. It is possible to *reserve* title only in goods in which one has got title to start with, i.e. the unmixed goods. In *Re Peachdart*[87] the sellers of leather which the buyers then made into handbags could *reserve* title in the leather which they supplied but could not *reserve* title in the handbags which were newly-created goods. When made into handbags, the leather ceased to exist as separate goods and became absorbed into the handbags. The contract of sale of the leather stated that the ownership in any mixed goods (i.e. handbags) should also be and remain with the sellers. The ownership which the sellers were thus given in the handbags was not, however, *reserved* to the sellers but was granted to them by those who would otherwise have been the owners, namely the buyers of the leather. This property right was therefore a charge created by the buyers of the leather. It was void because any charge created by a company is void unless registered: Companies Act 1948 (now Companies Act 1985, s.365).[88] It seems then that a *Romalpa* clause will, if properly worded, work in the case of unmixed goods and the proceeds of sale of unmixed goods, but that in the case of mixed goods (and their proceeds of sale) will work only if it is registered as a charge created by the buying company.

Where the goods subject to a retention of title clause are used by the buyer in a manufacturing process, it is a question of fact whether or not, like the leather in *Re Peachdart*, they have lost their identity and therefore cease to be the property of the seller. Grapes made into wine, olives into oil, wheat into bread, all clearly do thereby lose their identity. The following have been held similarly to have lost their identity: resin used to make chipboard (*Re Bond Worth*[89]); and Acrilan made into yarn and then into carpet (*Borden U.K. v Scottish Timber Products Ltd*[90]). In *Hendy Lennox Ltd v Grahame Puttick Ltd*[91] a diesel engine in which the seller had reserved title was used by the buyer as a major component of a diesel generating set which the buyer made. The engine remained unchanged and readily identifiable by a serial number and could be disconnected relatively easily from the generator in a matter of hours by undoing bolts and other connections. Distinguishing *Re Peachdart* and the other cases above, the judge held that the engine's incorporation did not preclude the seller from being entitled to retake the engine upon the buyer's liquidation. The engine had remained an engine, albeit connected to other things.[92]

Unmixed Goods

3–044   In *Clough Mill Ltd v Martin*[93] the Court of Appeal confirmed that the seller can, by virtue of the terms of the contract, effectively retain title in unmixed goods which the buyer has not

[86] See Webb, "Title and Transformation: who owns manufactured goods?" [2000] J.B.L. 513.
[87] [1983] 3 All E.R. 204.
[88] See the new s.860, Companies Act 2006.
[89] [1980] Ch. 228.
[90] [1981] Ch. 25.
[91] [1984] 1 W.L.R. 485.
[92] See generally, Hicks, "When goods sold become a new species" [1993] J.B.L. 485.
[93] [1985] 1 W.L.R. 111.

resold. Such a clause does not require registration under the Companies Act because the buyer is not creating a charge over his (the buyer's) assets. Rather the goods do not become the buyer's assets until the buyer has paid. Thus if the buyer goes into liquidation before fully paying for the goods, any of the goods which have not been resold by the buyer and which remain unmixed will belong to the seller. The seller, not the buyer's other creditors, will be entitled to take those goods. Assuming that the seller can resell them elsewhere for the same price as the buyer had agreed to pay, the seller will suffer no loss. If the seller is able to sell the goods elsewhere for more than the buyer had agreed to buy, the seller will in fact make a profit (i.e. will be better off than if the buyer had fully paid the seller before going into liquidation).

It is possible that before going into liquidation the buyer had paid part of the price to the seller. Clearly if the seller has been able to sell the goods elsewhere for the same price as the buyer had agreed to pay (or a greater price) the seller must refund the buyer's part payment. That part payment will then be available for the buyer's other creditors. If, however, the seller has been able to resell the goods elsewhere only at a loss (i.e. for less than the buyer had agreed to pay) the seller is entitled to deduct that loss from the refund. The loss (i.e. the amount to be deducted) is the difference between the price the buyer had agreed to pay and the lower price which the seller is able to get on a resale elsewhere. Suppose the buyer had agreed to pay £2,000 and at the time of liquidation had paid only £1,000. Assuming that the seller had retained title to the goods, the seller must refund the £1,000 unless the seller is unable to resell the goods elsewhere for at least £2,000. If the seller was only able to sell the goods elsewhere for £1,800, then the seller must refund £800.

Now, suppose that the buyer had agreed to pay £2,000 (for the goods, a load of timber) and had actually paid the £2,000 but that the contract reserved title to the seller until the buyer had satisfied *all* his liabilities towards the seller (i.e. under not only this contract but also *other* contracts there might be between them). Suppose also that at the time the timber was delivered and through to the time of the buyer's liquidation the buyer owed £500 to the seller under another contract. In *Armour v Thyssen*[94] the House of Lords upheld the validity of "all liabilities" retention clauses. Thus the retention of title clause would entitle the seller to take and resell such of the timber he had supplied under this contract as remained unsold and unmixed in the buyer's possession. The seller would then be entitled to deduct from the £2,000 refund, not only any loss on reselling the timber but also the £500 just mentioned. If, on the other hand, the seller were able to sell the goods for more than £2,000, say £2,200, the extra value would belong to the seller (see obiter dicta in *Armour v Thyssen*). In this respect "all liabilities" clauses are no different from other retention of title clauses. Thus, in the example just given, if the seller resells the goods for £2,000 or for a higher sum, the seller will still be refunding the same net figure of £1,500.

Proceeds of Sale of Unmixed Goods

In the *Romalpa* case, not only was the seller entitled, as owner, to the unmixed goods which   **3–045**
the buyer had not sold, but the seller was also entitled to the proceeds of sale which the buyer had received from sub-sales of unmixed goods. This was because the terms of the contract

[94] [1991] A.C. 339.

between seller and buyer made it clear that the buyer in reselling the goods was doing so, not for his own account, but as agent for, and on account of, the seller. This is not, however, the normal effect of a clause authorising the buyer to sub-sell the goods. The normal effect of such an authorisation is that the buyer is sub-selling for his own account. In *Pfeiffer GmbH v Arbuthnot Factors*[95] there was a clause retaining title for the seller and nevertheless authorising the buyer to make sub-sales. The contract required the buyer to pass on to the seller all the buyer's rights under the sub-sales contracts. However, it required this to be done only up to the amount of the buyer's outstanding indebtedness to the seller. It was held that this did not entitle the seller to take from the buyer the proceeds of the sub-sales of his (the seller's) property; instead it merely created a charge in favour of the seller which was void because it was not registered under the Companies Act. In order, without being registered, to entitle the seller to take the proceeds of sale in priority to the buyer's other creditors, the contract should, it seems:

(1) reserve the seller's title to the goods themselves (i.e. until either the buyer has paid or else the goods are sold by the buyer or lose their identity in the buyer's manufacturing process); and

(2) expressly state one or more of the following things:

    (a) that the buyer is (until title passes) in possession of the goods as bailee of the seller;

    (b) that the buyer, in having possession of the goods and in selling them, is in a "fiduciary" relationship with the seller;

    (c) that the buyer in selling them, does so on account of, and as agent for, the seller;

(3) not provide that the buyer's duty to account to the seller for the proceeds of sub-sales is limited to the buyer's outstanding indebtedness to the seller.

These provisions would give the seller a kind of property right over, and thereby give the seller entitlement to, *all* the proceeds of the sub-sales of unmixed goods (except those sub-sales made after title has already passed to the buyer). To make commercial sense of this arrangement, the contract would also need to contain a provision placing a duty on the seller to account to the buyer for any amount by which the proceeds of sub-sales of unmixed goods exceed the amount of the buyer's indebtedness to the seller.[96]

General Reading

3–046

- Hicks, "When goods sold become a new species" [1993] J.B.L. 485;

- Morse, "Retention of title in English private international law" [1993] J.B.L. 168;

- Webb, "Title and Transformation: who owns manufactured goods?" [2000] J.B.L. 513.

[95] [1988] 1 W.L.R. 150.
[86] See generally, Morse, "Retention of title in English private international law" [1993] J.B.L. 168.

Chapter 4

PERISHING OF GOODS

In the last chapter we considered the problem of who is to bear the loss when the goods perish. We now face a different problem—namely, what effect does the perishing of the goods have upon the contract? In other words, must both parties still carry out the contract and, if not, to what extent is either party excused? **4–001**

GOODS PERISHING BEFORE THE CONTRACT IS MADE

Section 6 of the Sale of Goods Act 1979 provides: **4–002**

> "Where there is a contract for the sale of specific goods, and the goods without the knowledge of the seller have perished at the time when the contract is made, the contract is void."

If the parties have made an agreement about goods which do not exist, it is an agreement about nothing. Thus in *Couturier v Hastie*[1] a contract to sell a cargo of corn was held to be void because, unknown to the seller, the ship's master had already sold it in Tunisia, as it had begun to ferment *en route*. At the time of the contract the cargo no longer existed.

The words "void contract" are a contradiction in terms; a void contract is no contract at all. Thus neither party is under any obligation to carry it out. In *Couturier v Hastie*, where the seller was suing the buyer for the price, the action therefore failed. It follows that if the buyer had paid he could have recovered that money.

One must not be misled by the apparent simplicity of s.6 and *Couturier v Hastie*. There are in fact some considerable difficulties.

---

[1] (1856) 5 H.L.Cas. 673.

"Perish"

4–003   The meaning of this word as used in the Sale of Goods Act is in doubt. In *Horn v Minister of Food*,[2] Morris J. considered that potatoes which had become seriously rotten had not "perished" because they were still potatoes, albeit worthless ones. From this it appears that they would have to become unrecognisable as potatoes before they could have been said to have perished. This view seems a little extreme and in *Asfar v Blundell*[3] it was held that dates, which were under water for two days and became impregnated with sewage, had perished—i.e. in a commercial sense. They could no longer be bought and sold as dates. Whichever of these two cases correctly reflects the meaning of "perish", one thing seems clear—goods which have deteriorated to some slight extent but not sufficiently to change their commercial character, have not "perished".

It was held in *Barrow, Lane & Ballard v Phillips*[4] where goods had disappeared (presumably stolen) that they had perished within the meaning of s.6. The case involved the sale of a specific lot of 700 bags of nuts lying in the seller's warehouse. Unknown to the parties, 109 of the bags had already disappeared. Wright J. applied s.6 and held that the contract was void. Had it been severable, i.e. if it had been for the sale of separate lots to be separately paid for, then presumably the contract would have been void only as to those lots which were not complete at the time of the contract. In that case the seller would have had to deliver and the buyer to pay for the lots remaining complete. The decision in *Barrow, Lane & Ballard v Phillips* clearly indicates that if only some of the goods have perished that is sufficient to make the contract void.

There remains one further point about the word "perish". Goods that never existed cannot perish. It follows that if A agrees to sell specific goods to B which both A and B believe to exist but which never have existed, s.6 cannot apply. However, the contract would still be void, because at common law a contract is void if it is made on a false assumption that its subject-matter is in existence. Section 6, like many other sections of the Act, is no more than an attempt to put into an Act of Parliament a rule of the common law. It was not intended to oust or restrict any of the common law rules.[5] Thus in our example where no goods perished because none ever existed, the contract is void at common law. The reason is that right from the start the contract is impossible to carry out. It is an agreement built upon a non-existent foundation.

"Unascertained Goods"

4–004   Section 6 applies only to specific goods.[6] However, again the common law may declare void a contract which does not fall within s.6. A contract for the sale of unascertained goods may or may not be void because of the fact that certain goods have perished or do not exist at the time of the contract. It will be void if that fact makes it impossible right from the outset to

[2] [1948] 65 T.L.R. 1906.
[3] [1896] 1 Q.B. 123.
[4] [1929] 1 K.B. 574.
[5] Sale of Goods Act 1979 s.62(2).
[6] The definition of "specific goods" under s.61(1) of the Sale of Goods Act 1979 was considered in the previous chapter.

carry out the contract. It is important to remember the distinction explained in the last chapter between purely generic unascertained goods (e.g. "500 tonnes of wheat") and unascertained goods from an identified bulk (e.g. "500 tonnes of wheat out of the 1,000 tonnes in the vessel *Neptune*"). In the case of purely generic goods, if the particular goods which the seller had in mind to supply had in fact perished at the time of the contract, this would not make it impossible for him to perform the contract. He could fulfil the contract by supplying wheat from any source; the contract is therefore not void. On the other hand, if he has to supply goods from a particular source and at the time of the making of the contract that source has ceased to exist (e.g. the *Neptune* has sunk) the contract is void at common law.

Contrary Agreement

Both s.6 and the common law rule making contracts void apply only in the absence of any   **4–005** agreement of the parties to the contrary. It is a matter of examining the contract to see whether the parties intended it to remain valid even if the goods were not in existence or had perished. For example, the buyer may have agreed to buy a *spes* (i.e. a chance). He may have agreed that if the goods were in existence he would acquire the ownership of them and if they were not in existence he would get nothing, but that in either event he would pay the price. If that were the agreement made by the parties the contract would be valid, even if the goods were not in existence, and the buyer would be liable to pay the price. In *Couturier v Hastie*,[7] the House of Lords said that it was a matter of construing the contract and it was only after doing so that their Lordships held that the buyer had not agreed to buy a *spes* and that the contract was therefore void. It will be relatively seldom that a buyer will agree to buy a *spes*. He will certainly be most unlikely to agree a very high price if he is to run the risk of getting absolutely nothing for his money.

A different possible interpretation of a contract is that not the buyer but the seller has undertaken to accept the risk that the goods might not exist, i.e. he has undertaken as part of the contract that the goods do in fact exist. In this case, if it turns out that the goods do not exist at the time of the contract, the seller will be liable in damages to the buyer for breach of his contractual undertaking. This is exactly what happened in the Australian case of *McRae v Commonwealth Disposals Commission*.[8] The Disposals Commission agreed to sell a wreck on the Jourmand Reef off the coast of Papua. The buyer subsequently discovered hat the wreck had never existed and that, indeed, neither had the reef! The Australian court construed the agreement and concluded that the contract was not void, because the sellers had impliedly warranted that the wreck existed at the spot specified. The sellers were therefore liable in damages to the buyer.

To sum up: a contract is void if, at the time the contract is made and unknown to the parties, goods have perished or do not exist, thereby rendering it impossible for the contract to be performed; this, however, is subject to the qualification that the contract will not be void if the parties expressly or impliedly agreed otherwise.

---

[7] (1856) 5 H.L.Cas. 673.
[8] (1951) 84 C.L.R. 377.

GOODS PERISHING AFTER THE CONTRACT IS MADE

4–006   Section 7 provides:

> "Where there is an agreement to sell specific goods, and subsequently the goods, without any fault on the part of the seller or buyer, perish before the risk passes to the buyer, the agreement is avoided."

Like s.6, this section is only part of a wider principle of common law. The principle this time relates to frustration of contract. It applies when, through no fault of either party, events take an unexpected turn making it impossible to carry out the contract as originally conceived. In such circumstances the contract is frustrated or (in the terminology of s.7) avoided. This can occur not only if the goods subsequently perish but also, for example, if after the contract is made, it becomes illegal to carry it out. It happened in *Avery v Bowden*[9] where there was a contract to bring goods from Russia. Before the ship was due to be loaded, the Crimean War broke out, making it illegal to trade with Russia (the enemy). It was held that no claim could be brought against the defendant for failing to load because the contract had been frustrated by illegality before the time for loading.

It can be seen that in the event of specific goods perishing, the contract may be avoided by s.7 but if in any other case the contract becomes impossible or illegal to perform, it will be frustrated at common law.

Again, there are some difficulties:

The Time of Perishing

4–007   Both s.7 and the common law doctrine of frustration are concerned with events occurring after the contract was made. If the goods had already perished at the time the contract was made then s.6 is the appropriate section. If s.6 applies, the contract is void. Where the events occur after the contract was made and the contract is avoided or frustrated the effect is not the same (see below).

"Perish"

4–008   The word "perish" presumably means the same as in s.6. Indeed, one of the cases quoted above, *Horn v Minister of Food*,[10] was a case on s.7.

The point was made in relation to s.6 that goods cannot perish if they have never been in existence. Thus a contract for the sale of future goods (e.g. a crop to be grown on a specific farm) will not be avoided by s.7 if the goods do not materialise. Nevertheless such a contract may be frustrated at common law. In *Howell v Coupland*,[11] the seller agreed to sell 200 tonnes of the potato crop on a specific piece of land, which would normally have produced

[9] (1856) L.J.Q.B. 3.
[10] [1948] 65 T.L.R. 1906.
[11] (1876) 1 Q.B.D. 258, CA.

easily that amount. However, the crop failed due to blight. The court held that the seller was not liable for non-delivery of the goods because the contract had been made on the assumption that the crop would materialise. The crop failure was an unexpected turn of events rendering it impossible to perform the contract which was therefore frustrated.

"Unascertained Goods"

Again like s.6, s.7 applies only to specific goods. However, a contract for the sale of   **4–009** unascertained goods can be frustrated at common law if it subsequently becomes impossible to perform because of an unexpected turn of events, as in *Howell v Coupland*. As with s.6, it is important to remember the difference between unascertained goods out of a specific bulk (e.g. *Howell v Coupland*) and purely generic goods. In his judgment in *Howell v Coupland*, Blackburn J. said[12]:

> "Had the contract been simply for so many tons of potatoes of a particular quality then, although each party might have had in his mind when he made the contract this particular crop of potatoes, if they had all perished, the defendant would still have been bound to deliver the quantity contracted for."

Thus a great deal turns on the exact terms of the contract—whether it stipulates "200 tonnes of potatoes to be grown on Blackacre" or simply "200 tonnes of potatoes". The failure of the crop of Blackacre will only render it impossible to perform the contract in the first example, whereas in the latter case the contract can be fulfilled by supplying potatoes from any source.

The Passing of Risk and Property

Once risk has passed to the buyer the contract cannot be avoided by s.7. Equally, a contract   **4–010** for the sale of unascertained goods out of a specific bulk will not be frustrated by the perishing of the bulk if it occurs after risk has passed to the buyer. All of this should easily understood when it is realised that the effect of the contract being avoided or frustrated is generally that the parties are no longer required to carry out the contract; they are excused. So, for example, the buyer is under no obligation to pay. If this were to be the position when goods perish after the risk has passed to the buyer, it would be a contradiction in terms. In such a case the only way to make some sense of the rule that the buyer must bear the loss is still to make him pay whilst allowing him to take whatever remains of the goods. That is exactly the legal position. The contract in such a case is most certainly not frustrated or avoided.

Neither will the contract be avoided or frustrated if at the time the goods perish, property has already passed to the buyer. Section 7, on its wording, applies only to agreements to sell. An agreement to sell becomes a sale when property passes to the buyer. The common law

[12] (1873–74) 9 Q.B. 462 at 466.

doctrine of frustration applies only where the main purpose of the contract has become impossible to achieve: *Herne Bay Steam Boat Co v Hutton*.[13] The main purpose of a contract of sale of goods is that the buyer should become the owner of the goods: *Rowland v Divall*.[14] That purpose is achieved the instant that property passes to the buyer. The contract cannot be frustrated by the goods perishing after that moment.

Effect of the Contract Being Frustrated or Avoided

4–011   The main effect is that the parties are excused from further performance of the contract. The seller need not deliver the goods and the buyer need not pay for them. The law is putting into effect what it reasonably presumes to have been the intention of the parties. It presumes, although the parties did not anticipate the contract becoming impossible or illegal to perform, that nevertheless, if they had thought about it, they would have stated that further performance was to be excused.

Thus, if the parties did actually turn their minds to the possibility that such things might happen (e.g. that the goods might perish) and provided in the contract for that eventuality, then the effect of the event occurring will be whatever is stated in their contract. In this case it is not in fact accurate to say that the contract is avoided or frustrated; the contract remains and its provisions apply. Indeed, s.7 applies only in the absence of contrary agreement.

Usually it is reasonable to presume that (if the parties had considered the eventuality that the contract would become impossible or illegal to perform), they would have intended all further performance to be excused. However, the law will not excuse all further performance of the contract if that, on the facts of the particular case, is an unreasonable presumption of what the parties would have intended. *Sainsbury v Street*[15] is a more recent case with facts similar to those in *Howell v Coupland*.[16] The contract was an agreement to sell 275 tonnes of barley to be grown by the seller on his farm. In the event the crop was an unexpectedly poor one and amounted to only 140 tonnes. Clearly, following the decision in *Howell v Coupland*, the seller was excused his obligation to deliver 275 tonnes. The question was whether he was entirely excused from performance for he had not offered to supply the reduced amount of 140 tonnes but instead sold it to someone else. MacKenna J. held that there was an implied term that in such a case the seller was not completely excused from all performance but that the buyer had the option of accepting delivery of the reduced quantity, at a pro rata price. Therefore the seller was liable in damages for non-delivery of 140 tonnes. So it can be seen that the parties will usually be excused further performance of the contract, either partly or entirely, according to what is a reasonable presumption of what the parties would have intended.

4–012   A problem can arise for the buyer if, before the contract is frustrated or avoided, he has paid all or part of the price. Can he recover his money? The answer differs according to whether the contract was avoided by s.7 or frustrated at common law. In the former case there is an "all or nothing" rule. The buyer is entitled to the return of his money in full provided he has suffered a total failure of consideration, i.e. has received no benefit under the contract:

---

[13] [1903] 2 K.B. 683.
[14] [1923] 2 K.B. 500. See further, para.7–010, below.
[15] [1972] 1 W.L.R. 834.
[16] (1876) 1 Q.B.D. 258.

Fibrosa Spolka Akcyjna v Fairbairn Lawson Combe Barbour Ltd.[17] This will be the position provided the goods perished before any had been delivered to the buyer. If, however, he had any benefit under the contract, i.e. some use of the goods, before the goods perished, then he will be unable to recover any of the money he has paid. It will, of course, seldom happen that after the buyer has had some benefit, the contract is avoided by s.7 because usually by the time goods are delivered to the buyer risk will have passed to him; s.7 applies only where the goods perish before the risk passes to the buyer.

On the other hand, if the contract is frustrated at common law (as occurred in *Howell v Coupland*) the position as to the return of the price to the buyer is now regulated by the Law Reform (Frustrated Contracts) Act 1943 (which does not apply to contracts avoided by s.7). The position under this Act is that the buyer can recover his money but the court can deduct, from that, a sum towards expenses incurred by the seller in performing the contact. Furthermore the 1943 Act empowers the court to order the buyer to pay a reasonable sum for any benefit he has received under the contract. This will occur if, for example, the buyer has had some use of the goods and subsequently they perished, thereby frustrating the contract. It should be emphasised again that this last situation will occur only very seldom, because usually by the time the buyer gets possession of the goods, risk will have passed to him and, if the goods perish after risk has passed to the buyer, that will not frustrate the contract. If the contract is not frustrated, the buyer will not be entitled to the return of any money and will have to pay any money outstanding.

Effect of Section 20A

Section 20A was introduced into the Sale of Goods Act in 1995. As was explained in the last chapter, it gives a proprietary interest to someone who buys and pays for goods which are agreed to be part of an identified bulk. Such a buyer has an undivided share in the bulk. We saw that, as between the seller and buyer, this has the effect that any destruction of the goods is taken to destroy the seller's share of the bulk first. What, however, is the position where more than the seller's share of the goods is destroyed? In that case some of the buyer's share of the goods is then taken to be destroyed and thus, if the whole bulk is destroyed, the whole of the buyer's as well as the whole of the seller's shares are destroyed. Section 20A imposes on the buyer the risk of any loss which would prevent the seller being able to carry out the contract. Let us return to the example where the contract is for the sale of "400 tonnes out of the 1,000 tonnes of wheat stored in Wally's Woodford Warehouse". Let us also assume that the buyer has paid for his 400 tonnes and that the seller has not contracted to sell any of the 1,000 tonnes to anyone else. In those circumstances, if, say, 700 tonnes of the bulk are destroyed by lightening, then it is assumed that 600 of those tonnes were the seller's and that the buyer has thus lost only 100 tonnes. That does of course render it impossible for the seller to fulfil his contract to supply the buyer with 400 tonnes from the stock in the warehouse. Nevertheless, the contract is not frustrated because, if it were, that would make nonsense of providing that the buyer must bear the loss of the 100 tonnes. Thus the buyer is not entitled to the return of any of the price though he is of course entitled to take delivery of the remaining 300 tonnes.

4–013

---

[17] [1943] A.C. 32.

Chapter 5

Seller not the Owner

Introduction

Someone not having the authority to do so sells or otherwise disposes of goods which do not **5–001** belong to him. This may involve an element of roguery but the knotty question which often comes before the courts is "who is the owner?" Is it the original owner or is it the innocent purchaser? Whichever of these two is the loser usually suffers a considerable loss. If it is the buyer he will have to give up the goods (or their value) for which he has already paid good money. It is true that whichever is the loser will have a remedy against the unauthorised seller. However, if the latter is a rogue he is likely to have disappeared and if he can be found will probably be penniless.

There is, then, a problem of ownership and remember, the law uses three words all meaning the same thing, "ownership", "property" and "title". In choosing between the original owner and the innocent purchaser, the law is having to choose between upholding the sanctity of property and giving effect to a commercial transaction. There is no obvious answer. The law's solution is to have a general principle in favour of the original owner with a number of exceptions in favour of the innocent purchaser. The goods will therefore be regarded as belonging to the original owner unless one of the exceptions applies.

The General Principle: *Nemo Dat Non Quod Habet*

Nemo Dat

The general principle is in s.21(1): **5–002**

"Subject to this Act, where goods are sold by a person who is not their owner, and who does not sell them under the authority or with the consent of the owner, the buyer acquires no better title to the goods than the seller had, unless the owner of the goods is by his conduct precluded from denying the seller's authority to sell."

This rule that someone without title cannot without authority transfer title is illustrated by the decision in *Greenwood v Bennett*.[1] Bennett, the original owner of a Jaguar car, entrusted it to one Searle for some repairs to be carried out. Searle was a rogue and used it for his own purposes. He had a crash and damaged it extensively. Entirely without authority he sold it for £75 to Harper, a garage proprietor who was unaware that Searle was not the owner. Harper spent some £226 on repairing it and sold it to a finance company. The court held that the car still belonged to Bennett. Searle did not have title and therefore could not transfer it to Harper. For the same reason Harper did not transfer title to the finance company. There was one further point: Harper carried out work in good faith believing the car to be his; because of this Bennett recovered a car worth more than it would otherwise have been. It was held that Bennett must compensate Harper for the work by paying him £226.

A Claim for Conversion

5–003   An owner who wishes to bring a claim to recover possession of his goods from someone who has refused to return them can bring a claim for conversion.[2] If the owner wishes to bring a claim against someone who has wrongfully sold the owner's goods, his claim will again be for conversion. Suppose the goods are sold by X to Y who in turn sells them to Z. Suppose the goods belong to O and that X sold them wrongfully and without authority. We have just seen that the general rule is that since X is not the owner he cannot confer ownership on Y, who similarly cannot confer ownership on Z. If Z refuses to return the goods to O, O has a claim against Z for conversion of the goods. Alternatively, O may choose to bring his claim for conversion against X or Y. Where O brings his claim against Z, Z will naturally wish to claim against Y who sold to him. He can do this. He can claim the return of the price he paid to Y. This claim is based upon a breach of contract by Y in that Y did not have any right to sell the goods and failed to confer any ownership upon his buyer, Z.[3] The fact that Y may have been quite innocent and genuinely believed at the time that the goods were his to sell gives him no defence either to a claim by Z for breach of contract or to a claim by O for conversion. Y can also reclaim from X the price Y paid to X.

Now suppose that Y had improved the goods (just as Harper did in *Greenwood v Bennett*). The Torts (Interference With Goods) Act 1977, passed after the decision in *Greenwood v Bennett*, provides a mechanism by which the innocent improver is to be reimbursed. If O sues Y for conversion (i.e. for selling O's goods to Z), then O will obtain judgment against Y for damages equal to the value of the goods on the date of the sale to Z, less the deduction of an improvement allowance. That allowance is the proportion of the value of the goods which is attributable to the improvement by Y. If O does not sue Y but instead sues Z for conversion, then Z gets the benefit of the improvement allowance. The judgment obtained by O against Z will not normally be an order to Z to return the goods. Such an order will be granted only

---

[1] [1972] 3 W.L.R. 691.
[2] Torts (Interference with Goods) Act 1977.
[3] See para.7–010, below.

where damages would not be an adequate remedy (e.g. if the goods were unique, or virtually so). O may, however, obtain judgment against Z in the alternative, i.e. judgment ordering Z either to return the goods or to pay damages equal to their value. Z is thereby given the option. In either case Z gets the benefit of the improvement allowance. In the latter case it is deducted from the damages he has to pay O. Where he returns the goods to O, O must pay Z the improvement allowance. In our example, this allowance relates to improvements performed by Y. Thus in a claim by Z against Y, Y is entitled to deduct the improvement allowance when returning Z the price paid by Z.

In all of this it has been assumed that the general rule applies and that X, not being the owner, could not confer ownership on Y who in turn could not confer ownership on Z. It now remains to examine those exceptional circumstances where the original owner may lose his ownership, i.e. where title may be conferred by someone who himself has no title.

EXCEPTIONS TO THE *NEMO DAT* PRINCIPLE

Sale by Agent

Section 21(1) begins by stating that: 5–004

> "where goods are sold by a person who is not their owner, and who does not sell them under the authority or with the consent of the owner"

good title is not passed. The common law rules of agency are preserved by s.62(2).[4] Thus where an agent sells goods on behalf of the owner (his principal) and that sale is within the common law rules of an agent's authority, good title will pass to the buyer, even where the agent's actual authority has been exceeded. The law of agency will be covered in Pt III of this book.[5] However, in summary, an agent may pass good title even though he has exceeded his actual authority in the following ways: apparent authority,[6] usual authority[7] or necessity.[8]

There are obviously similarities between the common law agency exception under s.21(1) and the mercantile agency exception under s.2 of the Factors Act 1889. As will be seen shortly, a mercantile agent will always be an agent under the common law. The reverse however is not necessarily true.[9]

---

[4] Unless the common law rules are inconsistent with the provisions of the Sale of Goods Act.

[5] See para.28–001 onwards, below.

[6] Where the principal clothes the agent with the appearance of authority to sell the goods. This must, similarly to a representation in estoppel, generally, go beyond merely allowing an agent to have possession of the goods or documents of title.

[7] Thus, where the sale is in the ordinary course of the agent's business, good title can pass to the innocent third-party purchaser even though there is no actual or apparent authority: *Watteau v Fenwick* [1893] 1 Q.B. 346, see para.28–010, below.

[8] This is still possible in the context of sale of goods, where, for example, the goods are perishable and sold by a carrier acting as agent: *Springer v Great Western Railway Co* [1921] 1 K.B. 257, see para.28–012, below.

[9] A common law agent may for example not be acting in the course of a business or indeed receive any payment or consideration for their service. This will take the sale or disposition outside the Factors Act 1889, but such an agent may still pass good title to the buyer under the common law rules of agency (though not, obviously, via the concept of usual authority).

Estoppel

5–005   When an estoppel is raised, the original owner is estopped (precluded) from asserting that the sale was unauthorised. Thus if an estoppel is raised the unauthorised sale takes effect as if it was authorised—i.e. it transfers ownership to the buyer in the ordinary way (see s.21(1) above).

An estoppel is raised when the original owner by his statements or conduct leads the innocent purchaser to believe that the unauthorised seller in fact has the right to sell the goods. More accurately, for the innocent purchaser to obtain a good title by estoppel, all the following requirements must be fulfilled:

  (i) The original owner must have made a representation (by statement or conduct) that the seller was entitled to sell the goods.

  (ii) The representation must have been made intentionally or negligently.

  (iii) The representation must have misled the innocent purchaser.

  (iv) The innocent purchaser must have bought (and not merely agreed to buy) the goods.

One problem with the first requirement is what conduct by the original owner will amount to a representation that the seller has the right to sell the goods. A case where a plea of estoppel succeeded and the innocent purchaser therefore obtained a good title was *Eastern Distributors v Goldring*.[10] The facts, however, can be appreciated only with knowledge of the role of the finance company in a modern hire-purchase transaction.[11] Briefly, the customer sees at a trader's premises the item he wishes to acquire. He asks for credit and, at the trader's suggestion, he fills in a finance company's hire-purchase proposal form, which is in fact an offer made by the customer and addressed to the finance company to acquire the item from the finance company on hire-purchase terms. The customer will leave the completed form with the trader. The trader himself will then fill in another form offering to sell the same item to the finance company. He will then send both forms to the finance company which will either accept or reject both offers. If it accepts, it thereby agrees to purchase the item for cash from the trader and at the same time agrees to transfer it on hire-purchase terms to the customer.

5–006   In *Eastern Distributors v Goldring*, the customer wished to raise a loan on his van. He and the motor trader got together to deceive the finance company. They each filled in their respective forms as if the van belonged to the trader and as if the customer wished to acquire the van on hire-purchase terms. Everything appeared in order to the finance company, which accepted the forms believing the trader to be the owner to be the owner of the van. Thus it bought the van from the trader and transferred it on hire-purchase to the customer. The customer did not pay his instalments under the hire-purchase agreement and sold the van to X, an innocent purchaser. The finance company discovered the fraud and the question arose as to who was the owner. The customer was the original owner and, provided he had not in the interim lost his ownership, he transferred that ownership to X. However, the court upheld

[10] [1957] 2 Q.B. 600.
[11] For a full explanation, see para.18–005, below.

the finance company's claim that the customer had by the doctrine of estoppel lost his ownership to the finance company. He had submitted through the trader a form offering to acquire the van on hire-purchase terms. Thereby he had represented to the finance company that the van was not his but that it belonged to the trader. This was an intentional deception. Since the customer was therefore stopped from asserting his ownership, the finance company obtained good title when it bought the van from the dealer. It still had that ownership because under a hire-purchase agreement property does not pass until the customer has paid all of his instalments.[12] Thus the car did not belong to the customer who therefore could not transfer ownership to X.

In *Goldring*'s case, the customer had done something clearly conveying to the finance company that he did not own the van and that so far as he was concerned the seller (the trader) had every right to sell it. An act which does not clearly convey that fact is not sufficient to raise an estoppel. So, if the owner of goods merely allows another person to have possession of them, (e.g. at a left luggage office) that act will not raise an estoppel for it does not convey to others that he considers the person in possession to have the right to dispose of them. If O lends his car to Q who then unauthorisedly sells it to P, O is still the owner and he can assert that ownership. In *Central Newbury Car Auctions v Unity Finance*[13] a customer wished to acquire a car on hire-purchase. He and the motor trader filled in the usual forms. Before the finance company's reply was received, the trader allowed the customer to take delivery of the car (together with its registration document). The customer sold the car to X. The finance company rejected the offers. It was held that the car still belonged to the trader. His allowing the customer to have possession of the car did not amount to a representation that the customer had the right to sell it. His giving him possession also of the registration document made no difference since a registration document is not in the eyes of the law a document of title.[14]

The same principle has been developed in respect of possession, not of the goods, but of a document of title. In *Mercantile Bank of India Ltd v Central Bank of India Ltd*[15] railway receipts were pledged with the Central Bank of India (i.e. used to raise finance). The receipts were then released in order for the pledgor to secure the goods. Instead of doing this however, he used the receipts to raise a further loan, this time with the Mercantile Bank of India. The argument of estoppel against the Central Bank failed with the Privy Council stating that possession of the railway receipts:

"no more conveyed a representation that the merchants were entitled to dispose of the property than the actual possession of the goods themselves would have done".[16]

This line of authority[17] restricts the possibility of successfully raising estoppel as a defence against conversion but does demonstrate a pragmatic approach to protecting the original

[12] See para.1–012, above and Ch.18, below.
[13] [1957] 1 Q.B. 371.
[14] In his dissenting judgment, Denning L.J. suggested that the log book was best evidence of title and adopted the dictum of Ashurst J. in *Lickbarrow v Mason* (1787) 2 Term. Rep. 63 whereby wherever the owner enables the rogue to dispose of the goods with the appearance of ownership (and occasion the loss) the original owner should be estopped.
[15] [1938] A.C. 287.
[16] [1938] A.C. 287 at 303, per Lord Wright.
[17] *Johnson v Credit Lyonnais Co* (1877) 3 C.P.D. 32; *Mercantile Bank of India Ltd v Central Bank of India Ltd* [1938] A.C. 287; *Jerome v Bentley* [1952] 2 All E.R. 114 and *Central Newbury Car Auctions v Unity Finance* [1957] 1 Q.B. 371.

owner's title to the goods. This must be correct: were the courts to allow a defence of estoppel purely through the act of (carelessly) allowing another person to have possession of the goods, the impact upon the *nemo dat* principle would be substantial and would be applicable in a broad range of cases.

5–007   An estoppel will not be raised unless the representation was intentional or negligent. In *Eastern Distributors v Goldring*[18] the original owner (the customer) clearly intended to make the deception. In *Mercantile Credit Co v Hamblin*[19] the customer had no such intention. Like the customer in the former case, Mrs Hamblin wished to raise a loan on her vehicle. She went to a motor trader who told her this could be done. He agreed that he would enquire as to what terms could be obtained from a finance company and would then telephone Mrs Hamblin to see if they were acceptable. He got her to sign a proposal form of a particular finance company. She believed this to be an application to the finance company for a loan on the security of her car. In fact it was the usual proposal form to acquire the car on hire-purchase terms. Placing her confidence and trust in him she was guided by the trader and signed the form in blank and agreed with the trader that, if he succeeded in obtaining terms acceptable to her, he would then be able to fill in the details on the form and send it to the finance company. However, the trader subsequently filled in the form without having reported back to her and thereby without her authority. He also filled in the usual trader's form offering to sell the car to the finance company and sent both forms off to the finance company. The finance company accepted the proposals. Who now owned the car? Mrs Hamblin had not intended to make it appear that the car belonged to the trader. The court held that neither was she negligent. She knew nothing of financial matters and had acted quite reasonably in placing her trust and confidence in a motor trader who had a good reputation in the area. In the absence of intention or negligence, no estoppel could be raised against her. The car was therefore still hers.

The question of negligence was discussed in *Moorgate Mercantile v Twitchings*.[20] Moorgate Mercantile were a finance company which owned a car. They let it on hire-purchase terms to a customer. Before completing his instalments, the customer without authority sold the car to Twitchings, a car dealer. Moorgate Mercantile and Twitchings were both members of H.P. Information Ltd (HPI). HPI was an organisation which operated a register where finance companies could register their hire-purchase agreements so that any other member (e.g. a car dealer) could, before buying a second-hand car, check with HPI to see if the car was the subject of a registered hire-purchase agreement. On this occasion Moorgate Mercantile had carelessly failed to register their hire-purchase agreement with the result that Twitchings was told by HPI that there was no hire-purchase agreement registered in connection with this particular car. Twitchings claimed that Moorgate Mercantile were estopped from denying that their hire-purchase customer was the owner of the car. This claim failed. Moorgate Mercantile had not made any representation to Twitchings. The only statement to Twitchings had been made by HPI, namely that there was no registered hire-purchase agreement relating to the car in question. That statement had been true and had in any case not been made by Moorgate Mercantile, since HPI was not an agent of Moorgate Mercantile for the purpose of making such a statement. As to negligence it was true that Moorgate Mercantile had been careless in failing to register their hire-purchase agreement.

[18] [1957] 2 Q.B. 600.
[19] [1965] 2 Q.B. 242.
[20] [1976] 3 W.L.R. 66.

However, carelessness did not amount to negligence unless the carelessness was a breach of a legal duty to take care. Moorgate Mercantile were under no legal duty to join HPI and, having joined, were under no legal duty to take care to register their hire-purchase agreements. Thus in the absence of either a deliberate misleading by Moorgate Mercantile or negligence on their part, no estoppel could be raised against them. Moorgate Mercantile therefore succeeded in their claim against Twitchings for conversion of the car.[21]

An estoppel can be raised only if the representation misled the innocent purchaser. In *Farquharson Bros. v King*[22] a timber firm owned some timber which was in the possession of a dock company. The firm told the dock company to deal with the timber according to the the instructions of a clerk of the firm. The clerk, a rogue, instructed the dock company to hold the timber to the order of "Brown" (which was the clerk under an assumed name). In his assumed name of Brown he sold the timber to an innocent purchaser. To whom did the timber belong? The House of Lords held that it still belonged to the timber firm. The statement made by the timber firm to the dock company had not come to the attention of the innocent purchaser; it therefore could not have misled him. The only thing which misled the purchaser was Brown's roguery. No estoppel could be raised against the timber firm.

Where an innocent purchaser is able to rely upon an estoppel, property in the goods passes **5–008** to him in the normal way, i.e. as if his seller himself has good title to give. Thus he will obtain good title if, and when, according to the terms of the contract of purchase, property in the goods is to pass to him. To put it another way, someone who has "bought" goods (i.e. to whom property has passed under his contract of purchase) can rely upon an estoppel. Someone who has only agreed to buy (i.e. to whom property has not yet passed) cannot do so: *Shaw v Commissioner of Police for the Metropolis*.[23] In this case the innocent purchaser had agreed to buy a car from, as he later discovered, someone who did not own it, on terms that property in the car would pass to him upon payment of the price. It was held that since he had not paid the price, no property in the goods could have passed to him. Therefore he could not claim a good title by raising an estoppel against the true owner.

It will be evident from the above discussion that instances where there has been a successful plea of estoppel in an action for conversion are few and far between. The clear requirement of a representation beyond simply allowing a non-owner to have possession of the goods (or documents of title)[24] and the very restrictive requirements of estoppel through negligence severely limit the ability of the doctrine to pass good title to the third party.[25]

Owner's Signature on Document Intended to Have Legal Effect

Quite apart from the doctrine of estoppel, there may be another alternative basis on which the **5–009** owner may be precluded from denying the seller's authority to sell, namely where the owner

[21] Since 1995 HPI, now run by Equifax, has offered a service to traders and to ordinary members of the public enabling them, on payment of a small fee, to have a search of the HPI register carried out and also to be given a guarantee of compensation if the information is incorrect or incomplete. The HPI report will cover not just existing finance agreements relating to the vehicle but also whether it has ever been: stolen, an insurance "write-off", or the subject of a number plate change. For an account of the interrelated provisions of the law in this area, see Dobson, "Risks in Buying a Used Car" (1996) 140 S.J. 1180. See also para.5–031 and *Barber v NWS Bank* at para.7–011, below.
[22] [1902] A.C. 325.
[23] [1987] 1 W.L.R. 1332.
[24] i.e. a representation which misleads the third party as to the actual ownership of the goods.
[25] See the comments of Lord Wright in *Mercantile Bank of India Ltd v Central Bank of India Ltd* [1938] A.C. 287 at 302.

has signed a document clearly conveying the implication that the seller is entitled or authorised to sell the goods. There is a rule that normally a person is bound by his signature: *Saunders v Anglia Building Society*.[26] This rule is not confined to someone signing a fully completed document. It applies also to someone signing a document with blanks for the particular transaction not filled in but agreeing to, or authorising, another to fill in those blanks later: *United Dominions Trust v Western*.[27] Thus in *Mercantile Credit v Hamblin*,[28] if Mrs Hamblin had authorised or agreed to the trader filling in the proposal form, the result of the case would have been different. Mrs Hamblin would have been precluded from denying the trader's authority to sell the car. This would have been not because of the doctrine of estoppel (which would have required either a deliberate misleading or negligence by her), but because of her signature on a document which, as was apparent on its face, was intended to have legal effect and which she had authorised the trader to complete.

There are two particular exceptions to this rule, i.e. where the signer will not be bound by his signature. The first is where he can plead *non est factum*. This plea will succeed where he can show two things: (i) that he was *radically* mistaken about the nature or effect of the document; and (ii) that he was not careless in signing it (*Saunders v Anglian Building Society*[29]). The mistake in *Mercantile Credit v Hamblin*[30] would not have been sufficiently radical to justify a plea of *non est factum*. The hire-purchase proposal (i.e. involving the sale of the car by Mrs Hamblin on hire-purchase terms) was not radically different in substance from a loan on the security of the car.

The second exception could arise in a *Mercantile Credit v Hamblin* type of situation. It would arise if the motor trader were the agent of the finance company in dealing with the customer. At common law the dealer is not normally the agent either of the finance company or of the customer. However, s.56 of the Consumer Credit Act 1974 now makes him in most cases the statutory agent of the finance company.[31] The customer cannot be bound to the finance company by his signature on a document which the finance company's agent knows does not reflect the customer's intention.

Mercantile Agents

5–010   The Factors Act 1889, s. 2(1) provides:

"Where a mercantile agent is, with the consent of the owner, in possession of goods or of documents of title to goods, any sale, pledge or other disposition of the goods, made by him when acting in the ordinary course of business of a mercantile agent, shall, subject to the provisions of this Act be as valid as if he were expressly authorised by the owner of the goods to make the same; provided that the person taking under the disposition acts in good faith, and has not at the time of the disposition notice that the person making the disposition has not authority to make the same."

[26] [1971] A.C. 1004.
[27] [1976] Q.B. 513.
[28] [1965] 2 Q.B. 242, see para.5–005, above.
[29] [1971] A.C. 1004.
[30] [1965] 2 Q.B. 242.
[31] See para.22–006, below.

There are six requirements to be fulfilled in order for an unauthorised sale by a mercantile agent to confer good title upon an innocent purchaser.

The Seller Must be a Mercantile Agent, i.e. a Factor

Broadly, a mercantile agent is an independent agent acting in a way of business to whom   **5–011** someone else entrusts his goods and upon whom is conferred authority of a type referred to in the Factors Act 1889, s.1(1). That section provides:

> "The expression 'mercantile agent' shall mean a mercantile agent having in the customary course of his business as such agent authority either to sell goods, or to consign goods for the purposes of sale, or to buy goods, or to raise money on the security of goods."

This statutory definition is not complete. In order to be a mercantile agent, an agent must have not merely the customary authority referred to in the statute but also three further characteristics. First, he must be independent from the person (his principal) for whom he is agent. A "mere servant or shopman" or "caretaker" is therefore not a mercantile agent.[32] Secondly, he must be acting as agent in a way of business. This "business" characteristic does not require that he should regularly carry on business as agent but simply that on the occasion in question he was acting as a business proposition. In *Lowther v Harris*[33] an agent was entrusted with a tapestry with a view to selling it. He was instructed not actually to conclude a sale without having first referred back to his principal; he was to receive commission if a sale was concluded. In fact, he sold the tapestry to an innocent purchaser without having first referring back to his principal. Wright J. held that the agent who had no general occupation as agent, who normally bought and sold goods on his own account and who was the agent for only the one principal, was nevertheless a mercantile agent. Therefore, since all the requirements in s.2 of the Factors Act were fulfilled, the innocent purchaser had good title to the tapestry.

The third characteristic referred to above is that the agent must be authorised to deal with the goods in his own name without disclosing his agency. In *Rolls Razor Co v Cox*[34] the court had to consider the status of some travelling salesmen. Lord Denning M.R. said[35]:

> "The usual characteristics of a factor are these. He is an agent entrusted with the possession of goods of several principals, or sometimes only one principal, for the purpose of sale in his own name without disclosing the name of his principal and he is remunerated by a commission. These salesmen lacked one of those characteristics. They did not sell in their own names but in the name and on behalf of their principals, the Company. They are agents pure and simple and not factors."

---

[32] Nor does the Act apply where the mercantile agent is selling goods in his own right, i.e. is the legal owner.
[33] [1927] 1 K.B. 393.
[34] [1967] 1 Q.B. 552.
[35] [1967] 1 Q.B. 552 at 568.

Before leaving the question of who is a mercantile agent, it should be said that someone who is not an agent cannot be a mercantile agent.[36] It can be difficult sometimes when someone takes goods on "sale or return" terms to decide whether he was acting as an agent or as principal.[37]

The Mercantile Agent Must be in Possession of the Goods or Documents of Title; and He Must Have the Possession at the Time He Sells, Pledges or Otherwise Disposes of the Goods

5–012   An example of a document of title is a bill of lading (i.e. the document given by a shipowner acknowledging that he has received goods which have been shipped). A motor vehicle's registration document is not, however, a document of title.[38] Thus, a mercantile agent in possession of the registration book but not of the vehicle itself can not confer good title under s.2 of the Factors Act: *Beverley Acceptances v Oakley*.[39]

A mercantile agent in possession of the vehicle itself might well be able to confer good title on an innocent purchaser, but the sale to the latter must occur whilst the mercantile agent is still in possession. Imagine a mercantile agent who obtains possession of the goods (perhaps by borrowing them from the owner) and who shows them to X, an innocent prospective purchaser. The mercantile agent then will not confer good title on X under s.2 of the Factors Act if he does not make the contract of sale with X until after he has returned the goods to their true owner.[40]

The Mercantile Agent Must be in Possession of the Goods or Documents of Title in His Capacity as a Mercantile Agent

5–013   The car owner who leaves his car with a garage for repairs to be carried out does not consent to the garage having possession in its capacity as a mercantile agent (i.e. as a dealer). Therefore the garage cannot confer good title under s.2 of the Factors Act. A case which illustrates this point neatly is *Staffs Motor Guarantee Ltd v British Wagon Ltd*[41] where a lorry was sold to the defendant finance company for the purposes of letting the vehicle back to the dealer under a hire-purchase agreement. During this time possession of the lorry remained with the dealer who then sold the lorry on to a third party. When the dealer failed to make the payments due under the hire-purchase agreement, the finance company sought to recover the vehicle. The third party sought to rely upon, inter alia, s.2(1) of the Factors Act. The court rejected this argument stating that at the time of the disposition to the third party, the dealer

---

[36] Equally, it is not necessarily true that someone who is an agent will be a mercantile agent under the definition of the Factors Act 1889 s.1(1) and the common law.

[37] See Ch.1, above.

[38] *Central Newbury Car Auctions v Unity Finance* [1957] 1 Q.B. 371. On the role of the vehicle registration document, see, Davies "Registration Documents and Certification of Title of Motor Vehicles" [2001] J.B.L. 489.

[39] [1982] R.T.R. 417.

[40] *Beverley Acceptances v Oakley* [1982] R.T.R. 417.

[41] [1934] 2 K.B. 305.

was in possession of the lorry not as a mercantile agent, but as a hirer under the hire-purchase agreement. This was sufficient to reject the s.2 defence.[42]

The Mercantile Agent Must be in Possession of the Goods or Documents of Title with the Consent of the Owner

The consent is presumed in the absence of evidence to the contrary and withdrawal of   **5–014** consent is of no effect until that withdrawal is brought to the notice of the person taking the goods.[43] The fact that consent was obtained by a trick or by fraud is irrelevant so long as the consent was given to the agent in his capacity as a mercantile agent. For the consent to be operative it must be such as to clothe the agent with apparent authority to sell the goods. This would occur in the case of a second-hand car only if the owner consented to the dealer having possession of not only the car but also of the registration book and the ignition key. Two cases illustrate the point. In *Pearson v Rose and Young*[44] the owner left his car with a dealer with instructions for the latter not to sell it but to see what offers could be obtained for it. The owner did not intend to leave the registration document but showed it to the dealer who arranged a trick whereby the owner was called away on an imaginary emergency thereby forgetting the registration document. The dealer sold the car. The dealer was in possession of the car with consent and in his capacity as a mercantile agent, since the possession was with a view to an eventual sale, but he was not in possession of the registration document with the consent of the owner. As regards the registration document, it was not a case of obtaining consent by a trick; he had obtained the possession by a trick but he had obtained no consent at all to the possession.

This case was followed in *Stadium Finance v Robbins*[45] where the owner left his car with a dealer with instructions to see what offers could be obtained for it. He retained the ignition key though he accidentally left the registration document locked in the glove compartment. The dealer supplied his own key, found the registration document and sold the car. It was held that the owner had not clothed the dealer with apparent authority since he had retained the ignition key and not consented to the dealer having possession of the registration document. In each of these cases, therefore, the innocent purchaser acquired no title to the car which still belonged to the original owner. This was extremely harsh on the innocent purchaser who bought goods in good faith from a mercantile agent and who could not reasonably have suspected that anything was wrong.

Sometimes the ownership of goods is split. This occurs for example when goods are pledged as security for a loan. The pledgor gives the pledgee (the lender) some rights but does not part with all rights of ownership. The pledgor and pledgee together combine to constitute "the owner". Someone in possession with the consent of both can be said to be in possession "with consent of the owner". *Lloyds Bank v Bank of America*[46] involved dealings not with goods but with documents of title. The owner, a mercantile agent, pledged bills of lading with Lloyds Bank. Lloyds Bank released the bills back to him so that he could sell

---

[42] Contrast the approach under s.24 of the Sale of Goods Act 1979.
[43] Factors Act 1889, s.2(3) and (4).
[44] [1951] 1 K.B. 275.
[45] [1962] 2 Q.B. 664.
[46] [1938] 2 K.B. 147.

them and thereby obtain the money to pay off the loan from the bank. However, instead of selling them, he pledged them, without authority from Lloyds, with the Bank of America. It was held that all the requirements of s.2 of the Factors Act were complied with including the requirement that the mercantile agent be in possession of goods or of the documents of title with the consent of "the owner". Therefore the Bank of America took its title entirely free from the interest of Lloyds Bank. Thus Lloyds Bank lost its security.

The Mercantile Agent in Disposing of the Goods Must Have Been Acting in the Ordinary Course of Business of a Mercantile Agent

5–015   Arguably, selling a second-hand car without an ignition key or registration document would not be acting in the ordinary course of business.[47] This was taken one step further in *Stadium Finance v Robbins*[48] where it was held that this requirement was not complied with. Willmer L.J. said[49]:

> "A sale involving delivery to the hirer of the car without its registration book would not in my judgment be in the ordinary course of business. Following *Pearson's* case, I think the same applies to a sale involving delivery . . . of a registration book obtained by larceny or fraud or other unlawful means."

On the other hand, the agent does not have to have been acting within the ordinary course of his own particular business or even within the normal course of business of his particular type of trade. It is sufficient that he was acting within the ordinary course of business of mercantile agents generally. The mercantile agent in *Oppenheimer v Attenborough*[50] was a diamond broker. Without authority he pledged the diamonds entrusted to him. Although diamond brokers do not ordinarily have authority to pledge diamonds in their possession it was held that the broker had acted in the ordinary course of business of a mercantile agent. The test for the disposition therefore is objective, i.e. whether it is in the ordinary course of business for mercantile agents generally. The pledgee therefore obtained good title to the diamonds.

The principle, that the disposition of a car where its log book is obtained through a trick will be outside the usual course of business, is difficult to reconcile with the approach taken in *Oppenheimer v Attenborough*. The basis for the decision in *Oppenheimer* was the issue of how the disposition appeared to the third-party purchaser, hence the need for an objective approach to the ordinary course of business of mercantile agents generally. This seems to be in conflict with the approach of the court in *Pearson* and *Stadium Finance*, where the presence of the log book (obtained through a trick) was ignored for the purposes of ascertaining whether the disposition was in the ordinary course of business. This approach is

---

[47] This was the view adopted in both the *Pearson* case and the *Stadium Finance* case, although has been questioned by Chapman J. in *Astley Industrial Trust Ltd v Miller* [1968] 2 All E.R. 36. What if the car, minus the registration document, was sold at a price which reflected the absence of the document? Logically, this ought to be within the ordinary course of business, although such a disposition would presumably be strong evidence to suggest that the third-party purchaser was not bona fide and without notice.
[48] [1962] 2 Q.B. 664.
[49] [1962] 2 Q.B. 664 at 675.
[50] [1908] 1 K.B. 221.

perhaps difficult to support. In the case of a mercantile agent who obtains possession of the registration document to a vehicle through a trick or who supplies his own ignition key in order to sell the vehicle, it is difficult to see why such a sale would not be in the ordinary course of business for a mercantile agent. Certainly, from the third party's point of view there would not necessarily be anything out of the ordinary regarding the disposition. As noted above, the impact of these two decisions is extremely harsh on the innocent purchaser.

The Person Taking the Goods Must Have Taken Them in Good Faith Without Notice of the Agent's Lack of Authority

The burden of proof lies on him to prove that he was in good faith, etc.[51] He will find it difficult to do this in circumstances where he is "put upon notice". An example can be found in the judgment of Lord Alverstone C.J. in *Oppenheimer v Attenborough*[52]:   **5–016**

> "there may be particular agents, such for instance as auctioneers, by whom a pledge would be such a departure from the ordinary course of their business as to put the pledgee upon notice."

We have already seen the difficulties caused by the disposition of motor vehicles without, for example, a log book or registration key on the question of whether the disposition was in the ordinary course of business for a mercantile agent. It may be suggested that where such a disposition occurs a more logical approach would be to regard the lack of a registration book (or ignition key) as a matter which goes towards the bona fides, or lack thereof, of the third-party purchaser.

Market Overt

Until 1995 there was a statutory rule in s.22(1) of the Sale of Goods Act that a sale by a trader in a market overt (i.e. a shop in the City of London or an open market) passed good title to an innocent purchaser even if the trader did not have title to the goods. This in effect, allowed stolen goods to be sold to an innocent third-party purchaser who would gain good title to the goods to the detriment of the original owner.[53] The rule was abolished, quite rightly, by the Sale of Goods (Amendment) Act 1994 which repealed s.22(1) of the Sale of Goods Act.[54]   **5–017**

---

[51] *Heap v Motorists Advisory Agency* [1923] 1 K.B. 577.
[52] [1908] 1 K.B. 221 at 226.
[53] Interestingly, the *Twelfth Report of the Law Reform Committee* (1966) Cmnd.2958 recommended amending this exception so as to broaden the scope of the provision to all retail sales. This was, unsurprisingly given the ability of the exception to confer good title in stolen goods onto a bona fide third-party purchaser, never acted upon.
[54] See generally, the Consultation Paper, "Transfer of Title: ss.21–26 of the Sale of Goods Act 1979" (1994).

Sale Under a Voidable Title

5–018   Section 23 of the Sale of Goods Act provides:

> "Where the seller of goods has a voidable title to them, but his title has not been avoided at the time of the sale, the buyer acquires a good title to the goods, provided he buys them in good faith and without notice of the seller's defect of title."

A voidable title is less than perfect and yet s.23 allows a seller with a voidable title to confer a perfect title upon an innocent purchaser. A void title on the other hand is no title at all and an innocent purchaser who buys from someone with a void title can derive no benefit from s.23 (although, of course, he might acquire good title by virtue of some other exception to the *nemo dat* principle).

What is a voidable title and how it differs from a void title can best be shown by an example: A owns some goods which he sells to B who in turn sells them to C. If the first contract (i.e. between A and B) is valid then title passes from A to B. If it is void for any reason then it is no contract at all and no ownership passes to B. If it is voidable then it is initially valid but can be avoided (set aside) later. Under a voidable contract ownership passes to B in the normal way but will pass back to A if and when the contract is later avoided. The commonest example of a voidable contract is one where a party has by making a mis-representation induced the other party to enter the contract. This gives the latter (the innocent party) the right subsequently to avoid the contract.[55] In our example, if B has induced A to sell him the goods by making a misrepresentation, then B will acquire only a voidable title. A will have the right to set the contract aside and to demand the return of the goods. If however, B sells the goods to C before A finds out that he has been duped, then C (provided he was innocent) will get a perfect title by virtue of s.23 and A will therefore be unable to recover the goods.

5–019   Although a misrepresentation by B can render the contract between A and B voidable, there can be present some factors which renders that contract completely void. The difficulties have arisen mainly in cases where B has misrepresented to A his (B's) identity. In these cases, the contract between A and B is void if the two following characteristics are both present:

(i) The buyer's identity was a vital factor for the seller (A) in deciding to make the contract.

(ii) The seller when making the contract was intending to deal with someone other than B.

In *Cundy v Lindsay*[56] the seller, Lindsay, received a letter from a rogue called Blenkarn from an address at 37, Wood Street, Cheapside. The letter ordered some goods and was signed by Blenkarn in such a way that the signature looked like "Blenkiron & Co". Lindsay knew of a reputable firm Blenkiron & Co who traded from 123, Wood Street. Without checking Blenkiron's address, Lindsay despatched the goods to "Messrs.Blenkiron & Co, 37,

---

[55] See Ch.6, below.
[56] (1878) 3 App. Cas. 459.

Wood Street". Blenkarn received the goods but never paid for them and sold them to Cundy who knew nothing of his fraud. The House of Lords held that the contract between Lindsay and Blenkarn was void and that therefore the goods still belonged to Lindsay.

Cundy v Lindsay involved a transaction conducted through the post. In a contract made between parties face-to-face the seller will find it difficult to show that to him the identity of the buyer was a vital factor in deciding to make the contract. In the absence of strong evidence to the contrary, the law presumes that in face-to-face agreements the seller is prepared to deal with the person in front of him whoever that may be. This is particularly so in the case of a shopkeeper. In *Phillips v Brooks*[57] a rogue called North entered a jeweller's shop, selected some items including a ring and asked to pay by cheque and to take the ring with him. The shopkeeper agreed to this after the rogue told him that he (the rogue) was Sir George Bullough. The rogue took the ring to Brooks, a firm of pawnbrokers, and pledged it with them for £350. The cheque given to the jeweller proved worthless and he sued the pawnbroker to recover the ring. It was held that the contract between the jeweller and the rogue was not void but merely voidable. Since it had not been set aside before the pawnbroker took the ring, the pawnbroker acquired good title to the ring. Of course, he did not get complete ownership for he did not buy the ring but the limited title he got was perfectly valid and he could enforce that against the jeweller.

Phillips v Brooks was followed by the Court of Appeal in *Lewis v Averay*.[58] Lewis **5–020** advertised his car for sale. A rogue responded to the advertisement. He told Lewis that he was Richard Green, a well-known film actor (which was untrue). They agreed on a price of £450 and after seeing "proof" of the buyer's identity as Richard Green (a pass for Pinewood Studios), Lewis agreed to accept a cheque. The rogue took the car and registration documents. The cheque was worthless. The rogue posed as Mr Lewis in selling the car to Averay, an innocent purchaser. The Court held that there was a contract between Lewis and the rogue and that therefore Averay now had perfect title to the car. Lord Denning M.R. said[59]:

> "When a dealing is had between a seller like Mr Lewis and a person who is actually there present before him, then the presumption in law is that there is a contract, even though there is a fraudulent impersonation by the buyer representing himself as a different man than he is. There is a contract made with the very person there who is present in person. It is liable no doubt to be avoided for fraud but it is still a good contract . . . ".

In both the last cases, the innocent purchaser (the pawnbroker in *Phillips v Brooks*,[60] and Mr Averay in *Lewis v Averay*[61]) acquired the goods before the contract between the original owner and the rogue had been avoided. If, before the innocent purchaser bought the goods, the original owner had avoided his contract with the rogue, ownership in the goods would have reverted to the original owner. If this had happened the rogue could not have conferred title upon the innocent purchaser (unless under some other exception to the *nemo dat* principle) for the rogue would no longer have a voidable title.

[57] [1919] 2 K.B. 243.
[58] [1972] 1 Q.B. 198.
[59] [1972] 1 Q.B. 198 at 207.
[60] [1919] 2 K.B. 243.
[61] [1972] 1 Q.B. 198.

The normal method of the original owner to "avoid" the contract is for him to inform the rogue that he does so. However, it is often impossible to locate the rogue. In this case the contract is avoided as soon as the original owner has done all that he reasonably can. *Car and Universal Finance v Caldwell*[62] was another case where a rogue bought a car and by fraud induced the seller to accept a cheque which proved to be worthless. On discovering this the seller immediately informed the police and the Automobile Association. It was held that this operated to avoid the contract. After this, but before the car or rogue had been traced, the rogue sold the car to an innocent purchaser. Since, at the time the rogue sold the car, his title had been avoided, it was held that the purchaser acquired no title under s.23.[63]

5–021   Although entirely pragmatic, it may be questioned why, as a matter of principle, communication of the seller's intention to avoid the contract, communicated only to a third party, i.e. the police, should have the effect of avoiding a contract. This rule is obviously designed to assist the original owner who having been deceived by a rogue is desperate to avoid the contract and reclaim the goods. Nevertheless, it is rather harsh on an innocent third-party purchaser as their legal claim to goods bought in good faith depends upon: (i) the speed with which the rogue sells the car on; and (ii) the speed with which the original owner takes steps to avoid the contract. This is particularly true in the (common) case where the original owner accepts a cheque as payment for the goods.[64]

Seller in Possession

5–022   Two provisions in two different statutes are almost identical: s.24 of the Sale of Goods Act and s.8 of the Factors Act 1889. Section 8 provides:

> "Where a person, having sold goods, continues, or is, in possession of the goods or of the documents of title to the goods, the delivery or transfer by that person, or by a mercantile agent acting for him, of the goods or documents of title under any sale, pledge, or other disposition thereof, or under any agreement for sale, pledge or other disposition thereof, to any person receiving the same in good faith and without notice of the previous sale, shall have the same effect as if the person making the delivery or transfer were expressly authorised by the owner of the goods to make the same."

This relates to the situation where A sells or agrees to sell goods to B and then later sells them to C. To whom do the goods belong? If under the contract between A and B property had not yet passed to B (see Chapter 3), then A was still the owner when he sold to C. Still being the owner, A could pass that ownership to C. One has to examine the two contracts, B's and C's, and find out under which of them property was to pass first. If it is C's then C will be the owner.

Usually (i.e. in the case of a sale of specific goods in a deliverable state, see Chapter 3), property will have passed first to B (i.e. at the time that he made his contract). In this case,

[62] [1965] 1 Q.B. 535.
[63] It is for the innocent third-party purchaser to show that his purchase was made before the original owner avoided the contract: *Thomas v Heelas* [1988] C. & F.L.R. 211.
[64] The Twelfth Report of the Law Reform Committee (1966) Cmnd. 2958 called for actual communication to be required in order for the original owner to avoid the contract, see para.16.

following the *nemo dat* principle, B is now the owner; they were B's goods at the time A sold them to C and therefore A could not, without B's authority, confer title upon C. The result would be different, however, if C could show that C's contract with A fell within one of the exceptions to the *nemo dat* principle.

The statutory provisions in s.8 of the Factors Act and s.24 of the Sale of Goods Act constitute one of those exceptions and were designed specifically to help someone in C's position. In order for C to acquire good title under these provisions, a number of requirements must be fulfilled.

The Seller Must Have Been in Possession of the Goods or Documents of Title

The point here is that the first purchaser can safeguard himself by taking immediate delivery **5–023** and not leaving the goods or documents of title with the seller. The seller's possession does not have to be a "personal possession". If they were in the possession of a warehouseman (or other agent) holding them on behalf of the seller, that is sufficient. In *City Fur Manufacturing Co v Fureenbond*[65] A owned some skins which were stored for him at an independent warehouse. A sold them to B who did not collect them. Later, A pledged them to C. On A's instructions the warehouseman handed them over to C who therefore acquired good title to the goods under s.25(1) of the Sale of Goods Act 1893 (now s.24 of the Sale of Goods Act 1979).

The nature of the seller's possession is immaterial. So if A sells to B who then decides to leave them for A to repair, A is a person who "having sold goods continues or is in possession of the goods": *Pacific Motor Auctions v Motor Credits*.[66] If A sells and delivers them to an innocent purchaser, the latter will acquire good title. It does not matter that A was at the time in possession in his capacity, not as a seller, but as a repairer. The decision of the Privy Council in *Pacific Motor Auctions v Motor Credits* necessitated the rejection of the previously accepted approach. Under the principle in *Staffs Motor Guarantee Ltd v British Wagon Ltd*[67] it had been generally accepted that the question of capacity was vital to a successful defence based on s.24, i.e. that mere physical possession was in itself, insufficient and that it must be established that the seller was in possession as a seller.[68] The decision in *Pacific Motor Auctions* removed such considerations and was followed by the Court of Appeal in *Worcester Works Finance v Cooden Engineering*.[69]

The Subsequent Purchaser Must Be "In Good Faith and Without Notice of the Previous Sale"

In *Worcester Works Finance v Cooden Engineering*[70] all the requirements of the section were **5–024** fulfilled. X sold a car to Y (a car dealer) who in turn sold it to Z (a finance company). The

---

[65] [1937] 1 All E.R. 799.
[66] [1965] A.C. 867.
[67] [1934] 2 K.B. 305.
[68] This was approved by the Court of Appeal in *Eastern Distributors v Goldring* [1957] 2 Q.B. 600.
[69] [1972] 1 Q.B. 210.
[70] [1972] 1 Q.B. 210.

reason for the sale by Y to Z was that Z at the same time accepted a hire-purchase proposal relating to the same car from M, a customer of Y's. Y (the car dealer) was fraudulent and two things occurred which ought not to have done. First, the cheque which Y had given X when Y took delivery of the car from X was dishonoured. Secondly, Y never gave possession of the car to his customer (M) as he should have done after the finance company (Z) had accepted the hire-purchase proposal. After Y's cheque to X was dishonoured, X (with Y's acquiescence) repossessed the car from Y's premises. At the time of this repossession by X the car clearly belonged to Z. This was because X had sold it to Y who had sold it to Z. It was held, however, that Y, in allowing X to repossess the car, was within the section. Having sold the car to Z, Y was a seller in possession of it. Since he had not delivered it to his customer (M) he had "continued" in possession (albeit wrongfully). His allowing X to repossess the car amounted to a "delivery or transfer" of it under a "disposition". This was because it amounted to a transfer back to X of *property* in the car (because Y's cheque had not been met) in return for X waiving any right to enforce payment from Y. At the time of the repossession, X was unaware of Y's sale to Z and thus, by repossessing the car with Y's acquiescence, X obtained ownership of it by virtue of s.25(1) of the 1893 Act (i.e. s.24 of the Sale of Goods Act 1979).

Buyer in Possession

5–025   There is normally no problem because a buyer in possession of goods will usually in fact be the owner of them, i.e. property will have passed to him (see Chapter 3). Being the owner, if he sells the goods he will be able to pass on that ownership to his purchaser. If he himself has not paid for them then the person who sold him the goods will be able to sue him for the price but will have lost any chance of recovering the goods.

However, it is possible in some circumstances for the buyer to take delivery of the goods before property has passed to him. This is most likely where he agrees with the seller that property shall not pass to him until he has paid for them. This occurred in *Weiner v Gill*.[71] In this situation he cannot confer good title on the sub-purchaser unless that sale falls under an exception to the *nemo dat* principle.

The most likely exception is that contained in two almost identical statutory provisions, s.25 of the Sale of Goods Act and s.9 of the Factors Act 1889. The latter reads:

> "Where a person, having bought or agreed to buy goods, obtains with the consent of the seller, possession of the goods or the documents of title to the goods, the delivery or transfer, by that person, or by a mercantile agent acting for him, of the goods or documents of title, under any sale, pledge, or other disposition thereof, to any person receiving the same in good faith and without notice of any lien or other right of the original seller in respect of the goods, shall have the same effect as if the person making the delivery or transfer were a mercantile agent in possession of the goods or documents of title with the consent of the owner".

---

[71] [1906] 2 K.B. 574, see para.3–017, above.

The requirements for the operation of this exception to the *nemo dat* principle are as follows:

The Person Selling (Pledging, etc.) Must Be Someone Who Has "Bought or Agreed to Buy"

Someone who has taken only an option to buy has not "bought or agreed to buy". This **5–026** excludes someone who has taken the goods on "sale or return" terms: *Edwards v Vaughan*.[72] For the same reason, someone hiring goods under a hire-purchase agreement is also excluded. Therefore if the hirer sells the goods, s.25 of the Sale of Goods Act and s.9 of the Factors Act will not operate to give his purchaser a good title. This is apparent from *Helby v Matthews*,[73] where someone who was hiring a piano on hire-purchase terms sold it to an innocent purchaser. The House of Lords held that the hirer had not "bought or agreed to buy" the piano which therefore still belonged to the person from whom it had been hired. In the light of this decision it is easy to understand why hire-purchase has become popular with traders and finance companies as a means of supplying goods on credit.[74]

It has been held that a buyer under a conditional sale agreement is someone who "bought or agreed to buy": *Lee v Butler*.[75] However, that position has been radically altered by the Consumer Credit Act 1974. A buyer under a conditional sale agreement which is a consumer credit agreement within the meaning of the Act is for the purposes of s.25 of the Sale of Goods Act and s.9 of the Factors Act, not someone who has "bought or agreed to buy".[76]

We have already seen that someone with a voidable title can nevertheless transfer to an innocent purchaser a perfect title, provided he does so before his title is avoided. However, if the transaction falls within s.25 (or s.9 of the Factors Act), he can pass on a good title even after his voidable title has been avoided: *Newtons of Wembley v Williams*.[77] The reason is that, even though his title has been avoided, he is still someone who has "bought or agreed to buy" the goods. In *Newtons of Wembley v Williams* a rogue bought a car and persuaded the seller to accept a cheque. When the cheque was dishonoured the seller did all he could to trace the rogue and car and he informed the police. After this but before the rogue was traced, the rogue took the car along to a market in Warren Street (where dealers commonly sold cars) and he sold it to an innocent purchaser. The Court of Appeal held that the innocent purchaser acquired good title under s.9 of the Factors Act.

The Person Selling the Goods Must Have Been a Buyer "In Possession", i.e. He Must Have Obtained "With the Consent of the Seller, Possession of the Goods or Documents of Title to the Goods"

Two principles derive from *Cahn v Pockett's Bristol Channel Steam Packet Co*.[78] First, it is **5–027** sufficient that he *obtains* possession with the seller's consent and it is immaterial whether that

---

[72] [1910] 26 T.L.R. 545.
[73] [1895] A.C. 471.
[74] For full discussion of the distinction between hire-purchase and sale, see para.18–002, below.
[75] [1893] 2 Q.B. 318, see Ch.18, below.
[76] Consumer Credit Act 1974, Sch.4 and s.25(2) of the Sale of Goods Act.
[77] [1965] 1 Q.B. 560.
[78] [1899] 1 Q.B. 643.

consent is later withdrawn. Secondly, it is immaterial whether or not he had obtained possession before he made the contract with the innocent purchaser; it is sufficient that the possession was obtained before he transferred or delivered the goods or documents of title to the innocent purchaser. The facts were that B agreed to buy goods from S. S sent to B a bill of lading together with a bill of exchange.[79] B did not, as he should have done, sign and return the bill of exchange. This meant that property did not pass to B.[80] However, B had already agreed to sell the goods to Cahn and, on receiving the documents from S, he transferred the bill of lading (the document of title to the goods) to Cahn. It was held that Cahn acquired good title to the goods by operation of s.25 of the Sale of Goods Act.

The question of whether the person selling had been a buyer "in possession" arose in *Four Point Garages Ltd v Carter*.[81] An innocent purchaser, Mr Carter, agreed to buy a new Ford Escort XR3i from X, a car dealer. X, who did not have one in stock, contracted to buy one from Four Point Garage. Under the terms of the contract, property in the car was not to transfer to X until he had paid Four Point Garage. Mr Carter paid X for the car. At X's request Four Point Garage delivered the car direct to Mr Carter, who believed himself to be taking delivery from X. X became insolvent without ever paying Four Point Garage. The latter claimed that the car was still theirs since X had never paid and property had therefore never passed to X. It was held, however, that Mr Carter had obtained good title under s.25. When Four Point Garage, at X's request, delivered direct to Mr Carter, it was exactly the same as if X had taken delivery from Four Point Garage and himself delivered the car to Mr Carter. In other words, X was deemed to have been a buyer "in possession" and deemed to have delivered the car to the innocent purchaser.

There Must Be a Delivery or Transfer of the Goods or Documents of Title to the Innocent Sub-Purchaser

5–028   Where documents of title are involved it will usually turn out that the buyer transfers to his sub-purchaser the same document of title which he received from his seller. This occurred in *Cahn v Pockett's*. The requirement is equally complied with if he receives a document of title from his seller and then transfers to the innocent sub-purchaser a different document of title relating to the same goods: *Mount v Jay*.[82]

The Buyer in Possession Must Have Acted in the Normal Course of Business of a Mercantile Agent

5–029   This may seem a little absurd since the buyer in possession may well not be a mercantile agent. It is, however, implicit in the closing words of both s.9 of the Factors Act and s.25 of the Sale of Goods Act. This was held to be so by the Court of Appeal in *Newtons of Wembley v Williams*.[83] The sale in that case (see above) was in fact in the ordinary course of business of a mercantile agent, since car dealers did commonly sell cars in Warren Street.

---

[79] See Ch.3, para.3–023, above.
[80] See Sale of Goods Act 1979 s.19, considered at para.3–023, above.
[81] *The Times*, November 19, 1984.
[82] [1960] 1 Q.B. 159.
[83] [1965] 1 Q.B. 560.

The Sub-Purchaser Must Be Bona Fide and Unaware that the Original Seller has any Rights in Respect of the Goods

The seller's lien and other rights will be explained in Chapter 12.   **5–030**

If any one of the above requirements is not fulfilled, the sub-purchaser will not acquire good title by virtue of the two sections under consideration. However, it is always possible that the person who sold him the goods later acquires the title to them. This can happen if, for example, the sub-purchaser bought the goods from someone who was hiring them on hire-purchase terms. Normally under a hire-purchase agreement as soon as the hirer pays off all moneys due under the agreement, the goods become the hirer's property. Thus if the hirer subsequently pays off all the remaining instalments, ownership will pass to the hirer and straight on to the purchaser from the hirer. This process is known as "feeding the title". It means that the purchaser from the hirer does eventually acquire good title, albeit somewhat delayed: *Butterworth v Kingsway Motors*.[84]

We have seen that s.25 of the Sale of Goods Act and s.9 of the Factors Act typically apply where a seller lets his buyer take possession but retains property (title to the goods) until the buyer pays the price. There is then a risk that the buyer, before he has paid and therefore before he has acquired title, sells and delivers the goods to a sub-purchaser who is unaware that he is buying from someone who has no title. The theory behind the sections is that, if an owner of goods agrees to sell them to someone and retains title but nevertheless lets the buyer have possession, that owner must bear the consequences (i.e. loss of title) if the buyer then sells and delivers the goods to the innocent sub-purchaser. Thus the sections give good title to the innocent sub-purchaser. Typically then they operate to defeat the title of the unpaid seller (let us call him C) who has entrusted his goods to a buyer who, without paying C, has in turn sold them to an innocent purchaser. In *National Mutual General Insurance Association Ltd v Jones*[85] the issue was whether the sections could operate to defeat the title of someone much earlier in the chain of events than C. Thieves had stolen a car and sold it to A who sold it to C (a car dealer) who sold it to D (another car dealer) who sold it to Jones. Jones claimed to have good title by virtue of the two sections, thereby defeating the title of the owner from whom the thieves had stolen the car. The House of Lords rejected this argument and held that the two sections could defeat the title only of an owner who entrusted possession of his goods to a buyer. Therefore the two sections could not take title away from the original owner from whom the goods had been stolen.

Disposition of Motor Vehicles under the Hire Purchase Act 1964, Pt III

Part III is all that remains of the 1964 Act, the rest having been repealed.[86] Section 27(1) of   **5–031**
the Hire Purchase Act 1964 lays down the scope of the exception and provides as follows:

---

[84] [1954] 1 W.L.R. 1286, see para.7–011, below.
[85] [1988] 2 W.L.R. 952.
[86] See generally, Davies, "Wrongful Dispositions of Motor Vehicles—a legal quagmire" [1995] J.B.L. 36.

"This section applies where a motor vehicle has been bailed or (in Scotland) hired under a hire-purchase agreement, or has been agreed to be sold under a conditional sale agreement, and, before the property in the vehicle has become vested in the debtor, he disposes of the vehicle to another person."

The section continues:

"(2) Where the disposition referred to in subsection (1) above is to a private purchaser, and he is a purchaser of the motor vehicle in good faith, without notice of the hire-purchase or conditional sale agreement (the 'relevant agreement') that disposition shall have effect as if the creditor's title to the vehicle has been vested in the debtor immediately before that disposition.

(3) Where the person to whom the disposition referred to in subsection (1) above is made (the 'original purchaser') is a trade or finance purchaser, then if the person who is the first private purchaser of the motor vehicle after that disposition (the 'first private purchaser') is a purchaser of the vehicle in good faith without notice of the relevant agreement, the disposition of the vehicle to the first private purchaser shall have effect as if the title of the creditor to the vehicle had been vested in the debtor immediately before he disposed of it to the original purchaser."

This provision is drafted in complex (and extensive) language, despite the fact that it is of application only in very limited circumstances. Nevertheless, the intent behind the exception is relatively straightforward. We have just seen that a hirer under a hire-purchase agreement is not someone who has "bought or agreed to buy" for the purposes of s.25 of the Sale of Goods Act. This meant that an innocent purchaser could buy a car from such a hirer only to discover at some later date that the car did not after all belong to him. The owner could reclaim the car and was entitled to come along and seize it. Part III of the 1964 Act was designed to protect the innocent purchaser in this situation.[87] The purchaser acquires good title providing the following requirements are fulfilled:

The Seller Must Be Someone Who is Hiring the Vehicle Under a Hire-Purchase Agreement or Buying It Under a Conditional Sale Agreement

5–032   The nature of these two types of agreement has already been explained in Chapter 1.

In *Shogun Finance v Hudson*[88] a rogue took possession of a Mitsubishi Shogun under hire-purchase terms using a stolen driving licence as proof of identity and address. The rogue then sold the vehicle on to an innocent third-party purchaser, Mr Hudson, and then disappeared. The finance company, as legal owner of the vehicle, sued Mr Hudson in conversion. The House of Lords, upholding the decision of the Court of Appeal held that the contract was void

---

[87] In *Eastern Distributors v Goldring*, Devlin J. summed up the problem in saying: "It is very hard on the defendant . . . his fate is a common one when hire purchase agreements are concerned and is now one of the regular ways in which unsuspecting buyers are deceived by what they take to be ownership": [1957] 2 Q.B. 600 at 614.

[88] [2003] 3 W.L.R. 1371.

for mistake as the finance company intended to deal with the person named on the hire-purchase documents, and not with the rogue. As the rogue was therefore not "someone who is hiring the goods under a hire-purchase agreement" the s.27 of the Hire Purchase Act did not apply. In order for a subsequent purchaser without notice to gain title under this provision that purchaser must be dealing with the individual named on the hire-purchase documents. This would appear to represent a significant restriction on the ambit of the section as it removes from the scope of s.27 any situation where a rogue impersonates another in order to gain possession of a vehicle on either hire-purchase or conditional sale terms.[89]

The Purchaser Must Be a Private Purchaser

Section 29(2) creates a statutory definition of a trade purchaser in the following terms: **5–033**

"In this Part of this Act, 'trade or finance purchaser' means a purchaser who, at the time of the disposition made to him, carries on a business which consists, wholly or partly—

(a) of purchasing motor vehicles for the purpose of offering or exposing them for sale, or

(b) of providing finance by purchasing motor vehicles for the purpose of bailing or (in Scotland) hiring them under hire-purchase agreements or agreeing to sell them under conditional sale agreements

and 'private purchaser' means a purchaser who, at the time of the disposition made to him, does not carry on any such business."

Put simply, a private purchaser is someone who is not a dealer (or finance house) carrying on a business in the motor trade. Dealers do not need the same protection since they know the importance of checking to see whether the seller is the owner of the car.[90] Thus a car dealer does not obtain the protection and that is so even if he is buying the vehicle for his own private purposes and not for his business purposes: *Stevenson v Beverley Bentinck*.[91]

The operation of this distinction can be seen in the recent decision of the Court of Appeal in *GE Capital Bank Ltd v Rushton*.[92] GE Capital Bank lent money to a car dealer, T&T Motors, for the purposes of purchasing stock. The title in the cars was to remain vested in GE Capital until the loan was repaid in full. T&T Motors ultimately sold the cars purchased under this stocking plan to Rushton, who was not a car dealer but admitted to buying the cars with a view to re-sale and profit. Rushton then sold one of the vehicles, a VW Golf, to Jenkins. Upon discovering the sale of the vehicles GE Capital, who had not been repaid the

---

[89] For commentary on the injustice of this decision upon the subsequent purchaser, see Elliot, "No Justice for Innocent Purchasers of Dishonestly obtained Goods: *Shogun Finance v Hudson*" [2004] J.B.L. 381.

[90] See previous discussion of HPI Ltd. This is accurate despite the availability of such a service to members of the general public.

[91] [1976] 1 W.L.R. 483.

[92] [2006] 1 W.L.R. 899. For commentary, see Chuah, "Definition of private purchaser under section 27 Hire Purchase Act 1964" (2006) F. & C.L. Feb, 6–7.

loan, sued Rushton and Jenkins in conversion. The Court of Appeal held that Rushton was a trade purchaser under s.27(2) on the basis that[93]:

> " . . . he clearly had decided to purchase them as a business venture with a view to selling them at a profit. In those circumstances purchasing the vehicles from T&T was no less a step in carrying on a business of purchasing motor vehicles for the purpose of offering or exposing them for sale than it would have been if he had already prepared a showroom or forecourt to receive them."

5–034   Accordingly Rushton was liable in conversion to the true owner, GE Capital Bank. Jenkins was not liable in respect of the VW Golf as s.27 had conferred good title upon him.[94]

Thus, it is possible for Pt III of the 1964 Act to operate even though the hirer sells the car to a dealer. Although the Act gives no protection to a dealer, it will give protection to the first private purchaser providing that he was bona fide, etc.[95] So if the dealer sells the car to an innocent private purchaser, the latter will acquire good title, as indeed did Jenkins in *GE Capital Bank Ltd v Rushton*.

The Goods Involved Must Be a Motor Vehicle

5–035   Thus the decision would be the same today, if the facts of *Helby v Matthews*[96] (a piano) were again to come before the courts.

The Private Purchaser Must Be Bona Fide and Unaware of Any Relevant Hire-Purchase or Conditional Sale Agreement

5–036   In *Barker v Bell*[97] the private purchaser of a motor car believed what he was told by the vendor, namely that the latter had bought the car under a hire-purchase agreement from B finance company. The vendor showed him a receipt from B finance company across which was written "final payment". In fact, unknown to the purchaser, the vendor was hiring the car under a hire-purchase agreement with A finance company. It was held that the purchaser was unaware of any relevant hire-purchase agreement. Lord Denning M.R. said[98]:

> " . . . a purchaser is only affected by notice if he has actual notice that the car is on hire purchase. He is not affected merely by being told that it was previously on hire purchase which has now been paid off."

---

[93] [2006] 1 W.L.R. 899 at [40], per Moore-Bick L.J. Curiously, the earlier decision in *Beverley Bentinck* appears not to have been considered, although authorities under equivalent provisions in the Money Lenders Act 1927 (ss.2 and 6); the Trade Descriptions Act 1968 (s.1(1)); the Unfair Contract Terms Act 1977 (s.12(1)) and the Sale of Goods Act 1979 (s.14(2)) were considered.

[94] Although he was liable for conversion of the other vehicles under the stocking plan by virtue of him having assisted Rushton in the removal and storage of the vehicles.

[95] By virtue of s.27(3).

[96] [1895] A.C. 471.

[97] [1971] 1 W.L.R. 983.

[98] [1971] 1 W.L.R. 983 at 986.

The purchaser therefore obtained good title to the car.

The test of the private purchaser's bona fides and unawareness of the hire-purchase agreement is a subjective one. It is not one of whether the private purchaser ought to have been suspicious or less gullible. It is purely a subjective question of honesty. Good faith is equated with honesty and bad faith with dishonesty. Also, the relevant time to apply the test is when the private purchaser makes his purchase. Thus a private purchaser who had suspicions that the motor vehicle was the subject of a hire-purchase agreement, but whose suspicions had at the time of the purchase been laid to rest, was a purchaser in good faith without notice of the hire-purchase agreement, who therefore obtained good title: *Dodds v Yorkshire Bank Finance Ltd*.[99]

The Transaction Under Which the Private Purchaser Buys the Goods Must Be an Ordinary Sale, or Hire-Purchase or Conditional Sale Agreement

Thus the 1964 Act gives no protection in the event of a pledge.   **5–037**

Having looked at the requirements, it remains to point out that there are no financial limits on the operation of the 1964 Act. It is immaterial for how much the car was being hired or bought, or how much credit was involved, and equally it is immaterial whether the hirer or buyer was a body corporate.[100]

The 1964 Act, then, gives protection to a bona fide private purchaser who buys a motor vehicle unaware that the seller is hiring or buying it under a hire-purchase or conditional sale agreement. For example, O supplies a car to P on hire-purchase terms and P, before he has finished paying off his instalments, sells the car to a bona fide purchaser, Q, who is unaware of the hire-purchase agreement. The Act gives good title to Q, *but only as against* O. Thus, if O were not the owner but had, for example stolen the car (or bought it from someone who had stolen it) then the true owner (i.e. from whom the car was stolen) will still have good title (i.e. unless one of the other exceptions to the *nemo dat* principle applies).

Finally, it is now possible for a buyer (whether a trade purchaser or a private purchaser) to have a check carried out to discover whether a motor vehicle is subject to an existing finance agreement, has ever been an insurance "write-off" or has been stolen.[101]

Sale under a Common Law or Statutory Power

Certain persons are given the right by common law or statute in certain circumstances to sell   **5–038** the goods of another. Examples are a pawnbroker selling the pledgor's goods when the loan is not repaid and an innkeeper selling the guest's property when the bill is not paid. When a sale is made under a common law or statutory power the purchaser acquires good title to the goods.[102]

---

[99] [1992] C.C.L.R. 92.
[100] Contrast the approach of the Consumer Credit Act 1974 (which regulates both hire-purchase and conditional sale agreements) prior to the amendments introduced by the Consumer Credit Act 2006.
[101] See para.5–007, above.
[102] Sale of Goods Act, s.21(2)(a).

It is also to be noted that under the Torts (Interference with Goods) Act 1977 a person such as a repairer, improver, valuer or storer has the right to sell uncollected goods. He must first serve upon the bailor (i.e. the person who left the goods for repair, treatment or valuation, etc.) a notice containing certain details of the intended sale. If after expiry of the notice the goods remain uncollected and the right of sale is duly exercised, the purchaser will obtain good title as against the bailor. However, if the bailor was not the owner but had, for example, stolen them before leaving them for repair or treatment, etc., then the true owner will still have good title (i.e. unless one of the other exceptions to the *nemo dat* principle applies).

Sale under a Court Order

5–039   The High Court has power in certain circumstances to order the sale of goods. If it exercises this power, the purchaser acquires good title, notwithstanding any claim by the original owner.[103]

Effect of Writ of Execution

5–040   When judgment is given in court for a sum of damages, the defendant usually pays up. If he does not, the successful claimant can enforce the judgment by causing a writ of execution to be issued. It is then the sheriff's duty to carry it out. He has the legal right to seize enough of the defendant's goods to satisfy the judgment. He has this right in relation to goods which the defendant owns at the time the sheriff receives the writ. Anyone who after that time purchases goods from the defendant therefore runs the risk of having them seized by the sheriff. However, s.138 of the Supreme Court Act 1981 protects the purchaser from this provided that when he bought the goods he was bona fide and unaware of any writ of execution relating to the defendant.

General Reading

5–041
- Davies, "Registration Documents and Certification of Title of Motor Vehicles" [2001] J.B.L. 489;

- Davies, "Wrongful Dispositions of Motor Vehicles—a legal quagmire" [1995] J.B.L. 36;

- Davies, "Transferability and Sale of Goods" (1987) 7 Legal Studies 1;

- Elliot, "No Justice for Innocent Purchasers of Dishonestly obtained Goods: Shogun Finance v Hudson" [2004] J.B.L. 381;

- QC, "Sale of a Motor Vehicle by Hire-Purchaser" (1954) 17 M.L.R. 238;

- Rutherford and Todd, "Section 25(1) of the Sale of Goods Act 1893: The reluctance to create a mercantile agency" [1979] C.L.J. 346;

- Schofield, "The notionally absent registration book" [1963] J.B.L. 344.

---

[103] Sale of Goods Act, s.21(2)(b).

Chapter 6

MISREPRESENTATION

GENERAL INTRODUCTION

The seller who makes a false statement in connection with the supply of goods can find   **6–001**
himself liable in one or more of a number of ways. There are three principal ways. First, he
may be liable to a conviction under the Consumer Protection from Unfair Trading Regulations 2008 which implement the Unfair Commercial Practices Directive 2005 (and replace,
inter alia, the Trade Descriptions Act 1968). This will be considered in Chapter 17. Secondly,
he may be liable to his purchaser for a breach of a term of his contract—a matter to be
considered in the next chapter. Thirdly, the purchaser may have a remedy for
misrepresentation.

WHAT AMOUNTS TO AN ACTIONABLE MISREPRESENTATION?

A misrepresentation is a false statement of fact made by one party (or his agent) which is   **6–002**
intended to and does induce the other party to enter the contract. A statement may be made
in writing, orally or even by conduct, for example, by making the goods tell a lie about
themselves, as in the case where the seller patched up a crack in the barrel of a cannon so as
to make it appear unfractured: *Horsfall v Thomas*.[1]

A mere statement of opinion, provided the opinion is genuinely held, is not a statement of
fact: *Bisset v Wilkinson*.[2] However, a statement of opinion by someone in a position to know
the facts will be regarded as a statement of fact. In *Smith v Land & House Property Corp*[3]
the seller of some premises described them as "let to Mr Frederick Fleck (a

---

[1] (1862) 1 H. & C. 90.
[2] [1927] A.C. 177.
[3] (1884) 28 Ch. D. 7.

most desirable tenant)". In fact it had been only with difficulty that the seller had managed to get rent from Mr Fleck, who was still in arrears. It was held that the seller made a misrepresentation.

A mere trader's puff is not a statement of fact. Thus the car dealer who describes a second-hand car as "a beautiful looking car" makes no misrepresentation. However, the distinction between a trader's puff and a statement having legal significance is a fine one. The car dealer who tells his purchaser "It's a good little bus. I would stake my life on it", will not be able to claim either that it was a mere trader's puff or that it was a mere statement of opinion. After all, the dealer is in a position to know whether the car has any serious defects.

6–003   The statement need not be made fraudulently. Although the remedies available may be less extensive, a statement made innocently can nevertheless amount to a misrepresentation, as in *Leaf v International Galleries*[4] where the sellers innocently stated that a painting was by Constable, a statement which they genuinely believed.

A statement is not an actionable misrepresentation unless it induces the other party to enter the contract. It does not have to be the only thing which persuaded him to do so but it does have to have been a factor in influencing him. If he placed no reliance at all upon it, he cannot complain of a misrepresentation. Thus in *Horsfall v Thomas*,[5] above, the purchaser lost his case because he had not bothered to examine the canon before purchasing it and therefore was unaware of the misrepresentation.[6] Equally, if the purchaser, though aware of the statement, chooses to place no reliance upon it, he cannot subsequently complain of it. This would be the position if a potential purchaser, on being told that a car was mechanically sound, nevertheless insisted, before buying, on having his own mechanic examine it. Where, however, the buyer does not insist upon having an independent examination of the goods, the fact that he had the opportunity to discover the truth (i.e. discover the misrepresentation) will not necessarily prevent a remedy for misrepresentation where it would be unreasonable to expect such an individual to make such an inspection.[7]

It is also clear that where a buyer places reliance on a misrepresentation, the fact that he had been given information casting doubt over the validity of the representation made by the seller will not necessarily prevent the buyer's action from succeeding. In *Flack v Pattinson and another*[8] the claimant (Flack) brought an action for misrepresentation arguing that Pattinson, acting as agent for Queensgate Industries Ltd, had made a material misrepresentation which induced him to purchase a vintage racing car. Pattinson had told the claimant that the car in question was "Innes Ireland's 2.5 Grand Prix car". This was, in fact, not true as, although the car had been owned by Innes Ireland, it had only been raced by Innes Ireland with a 1.5 litre engine. A motor engineer with knowledge of the car had informed Flack that the car "had always been a Formula 2 car, and not a Formula 1 car, i.e. it was a 1.5 litre car". Despite this warning, Flack nevertheless purchased the car for £180,000. At first instance, the court held that Flack was entitled to recover damages for misrepresentation since Pattinson had either known his statement to be untrue, or should have known it to be untrue. The

---

[4] [1950] 2 K.B. 86.
[5] (1862) 1 H. & C. 90.
[6] See also, *Ex p. Biggs* (1859) 28 L.J.Ch. 50. Consider the approach of s.14(2) (implied term as to satisfactory quality) in respect of pre-contractual examinations discussed in Ch.7 below.
[7] See *Smith v Eric S Bush* [1990] 1 A.C. 831 where the House of Lords held that it was unreasonable to expect the purchasers of a private property to commission an independent survey of the property (having relied upon a valuation commissioned by the lender (mortgage company).
[8] [2002] EWCA Civ 1762, affirming [2001] All E.R. (D) 301 (Dec).

defendant appealed, arguing that given the warning made to Flack, the misrepresentation made by Pattinson could not have been relied upon. The Court of Appeal rejected this argument, citing Lord Blackburn in *Smith v Chadwick*[9]:

> "I think that if it is proved that the defendants with a view to induce the plaintiff to enter into a contract made a statement to the plaintiff of such a nature as would be likely to induce a person to enter into a contract, and it is proved that the plaintiff did enter into the contract, it is a fair inference of fact that he was induced to do so by the statement."

Since the claimant could raise evidence that he wished to purchase a 2.5 litre (formula 1) car and not a 1.5 (formula 2) car,[10] the fact that a warning had been given by a third party was not sufficient to dissuade the court from finding that he had relied upon Pattinson's misrepresentation.

REMEDIES

There are two possible remedies: 6–004

Rescission

A misrepresentation by one party makes the contract voidable at the option of the other. This means that the latter can rescind the contract. This involves the parties being returned to their positions as they were before the contract, i.e. the return of the price to the buyer and the goods to the seller. If the innocent party is the buyer and he has not yet paid then he may simply refuse to do so and return the goods if he has already received them.

Rescission is an equitable remedy which means that it is not available if that would be unfair. Thus it is not available in the following situations:

(i) Where it is impossible to restore the parties to their pre-contract positions, e.g. if the purchaser had consumed the goods. In *Clarke v Dickinson*[11] Crompton J. gave the grisly example of a butcher purchasing livestock being prevented from rescinding where he has already slaughtered the animal.

(ii) Where it would involve upsetting the rights of an innocent third party, e.g. if the purchaser has sold the goods to an innocent sub-purchaser.[12]

(iii) Where there has been a lapse of more than a reasonable length of time from the time the contract was made. Thus in *Leaf v International Galleries*, above, the purchaser was unable to rescind the contract some five years after it was made. (In

[9] (1884) 9 App. Cas. 187 at 196.
[10] Flack already owned a formula 2 racing car.
[11] (1858) 120 E.R. 463.
[12] See Ch.5, above.

the case of a fraudulent misrepresentation, the purchaser is allowed a reasonable length of time from when he discovers it to be untrue.)

(iv) Where the innocent party has affirmed the contract, i.e. indicated his intention of continuing with it in spite of the misrepresentation. In *Long v Lloyd*[13] the seller had claimed that the lorry was capable of 40 m.p.h. and 11 m.p.g. On the first run the purchaser discovered a number of faults; the dynamo did not work and the lorry consumed petrol at the rate of 5 m.p.g. He telephoned the seller and complained. The seller offered to meet half the cost of repairing the dynamo. The buyer accepted that offer. When the lorry broke down again, the purchaser indicated that he was rescinding the contract. It was held that he could not, since by accepting the seller's offer on the telephone he had accepted the goods and thereby affirmed the contract.

Affirmation, which defeats the buyer's right to rescission for misrepresentation, is similar to "acceptance", which defeats the buyer's right to reject the goods and regard the contract as repudiated for breach of condition.[14]

Damages

6–005   Damages may be claimed on their own or in addition to rescission. Unlike rescission, damages are not available for all misrepresentations and the state of mind of the person who made the misrepresentation is important.[15]

(i) A fraudulent misrepresentation is one made (a) without belief in its truth, or (b) with such a degree of recklessness as amounts to dishonesty (careless whether it be true or false). For a fraudulent misrepresentation, damages are available in deceit: *Derry v Peek*.[16]

(ii) A negligent misrepresentation is one made by someone who believes it to be true but has no reasonable grounds for so believing, e.g. a car dealer who claims as having been made in 1989, a car of a type not manufactured before 1990. Damages are available for a negligent misrepresentation.[17]

(iii) A completely innocent misrepresentation is one made by someone who genuinely and on reasonable grounds believes it to be true. Damages are not normally available for this sort of misrepresentation, although the court does have a discretion to award damages instead of (but not in addition to) rescission.[18]

---

[13] [1958] 1 W.L.R. 753.
[14] See para.13–005, below.
[15] For a critique of damages available for misrepresentation see Poole and Devenney, "Reforming Damages for Misrepresentation: the Case for Coherent Aims and Principles" [2007] J.B.L. 269.
[16] [1889] 14 App. Cas. 337.
[17] Misrepresentation Act 1967 s.2(1).
[18] Misrepresentation Act 1967 s.2(2).

The burden of proof is upon the defendant to prove that he had reasonable grounds for believing his statement. Otherwise it will be presumed to have been a negligent one.[19]

In *Howard Marine & Dredging Co Ltd v Ogden*[20] the owner of a vessel which a customer was considering hiring told the customer that its payload was 1,600 tonnes, whereas its payload was in fact only 1,055 tonnes (so stated in the ship's documents). After the contract was made, the hirer brought a claim for damages for misrepresentation. The owner claimed to have had reasonable grounds to believe the truth of his misrepresentation because the Lloyd's Register had (in a rare mistake) wrongly stated the payload as 1,800 tonnes. It was held that in showing that he relied upon the figures in Lloyd's Register and had disregarded the figure in the ship's documents, he had failed to prove that he had reasonable grounds to believe the truth of his representation. The hirer therefore won his claim for damages.

EXCLUSION

Any provision in a contract which would have the effect of excluding, or restricting liability for a misrepresentation is ineffective, except to the extent that the clause is shown to satisfy the requirement of reasonableness.[21] The requirement of reasonableness is set out in s.11 of the Unfair Contract Terms Act.[22]   **6–006**

ADDITIONAL OR ALTERNATIVE DEFENDANT

We are in this chapter considering misrepresentations made to the buyer by his seller (or the seller's agent). It follows that the remedies we have discussed are those which the buyer has against the seller. Normally the seller will be the only person against whom the buyer will be entitled to make a claim. However, there is an exception, created by s.75 of the Consumer Credit Act 1974. So, where the buyer bought the goods under a credit agreement of a certain type, he will be able to bring against the creditor a claim similar to that which he can bring against the seller. The most common type of situation where this will occur is where the buyer uses his credit card to buy an item costing over £100. The credit card company is the person who provides the credit (i.e. is the creditor) and therefore the buyer may be able to bring a claim against the credit card company for a misrepresentation by the seller. The circumstances in which s.75 of the Consumer Credit Act applies will be more fully considered in Chapter 23.   **6–007**

Section 56 of the Consumer Credit Act also can operate to entitle a buyer in some cases to sue the creditor (e.g. a credit card company) in respect of a misrepresentation by the seller. Section 56 is more fully considered in Chapter 22.

---

[19] Misrepresentation Act 1967 s.2(1).
[20] [1978] Q.B. 574.
[21] Misrepresentation Act 1967 s.3, as amended by the Unfair Contract Terms Act 1977.
[22] See paras 10–021–10–024 below.

General Reading

6–008   • Halson, "Rescission for misrepresentation" (1997) 5 R.L.R 89;

• Poole and Devenney, "Reforming damages for misrepresentation: the case for coherent aims and principles" [2007] J.B.L. 269.

Chapter 7

TERMS OF THE CONTRACT

INTRODUCTION

Contracts of sale vary enormously. At one extreme one may find a written contract containing **7–001** many detailed clauses setting out the terms of the contract. At the other extreme, the parties may have expressly agreed only as to which goods were being sold and how much the price was. In the latter case the parties have left much unsaid, e.g. as to delivery, payment, the transfer of ownership, the quality of the goods, etc. Many provisions of the Sale of Goods Act were designed to remedy such deficiencies in the contract.

Freedom of Contract

The original Sale of Goods Act of 1893 was intended not to dictate to the parties what the **7–002** terms of their bargain should be, but only to provide solutions to problems and questions unforeseen and unconsidered by the parties. Thus most of the sections of the Act originally applied only in the absence of contrary agreement by the parties. The Act was based upon the notion of freedom of contract, i.e. that the parties were free to make their contract upon whatever terms they pleased. In relation to exemption clauses, however, the Unfair Contract Terms Act 1977 has made a large inroad into this notion and s.55(1) of the Sale of Goods Act 1979 now reads as follows:

> "Where a right, duty or liability would arise under a contract of sale of goods by implication of law, it may (subject to the Unfair Contract Terms Act 1977) be negatived or varied by express agreement, or by the course of dealing between the parties, or by such usage as binds both parties to the contract."

The provisions of the Unfair Contract Terms Act 1977 will be considered in Chapter 10. In the present chapter we shall consider terms other than exemption clauses. The Unfair

Terms in Consumer Contracts Regulations 1999 represent a further inroad into the doctrine of freedom of contract. These Regulations, which are capable of applying to other terms as well as to exemption clauses, will also be considered in Chapter 10.

Rights of Third Parties

7–003   As a general rule only the buyer and the seller can sue or be sued on a contract of sale. This results from two aspects of the privity of contract doctrine. First, the contract can be enforced only against someone who is party to it. Secondly, only someone who is a party to the contract can enforce it. The Contracts (Rights of Third Parties) Act 1999, however, created an exception to the latter.[1] Section 1 provides:

> "(1) Subject to the provisions of this Act, a person who is not a party to a contract (a 'third party') may in his own right enforce a term of the contract if—
>
>   (a) the contract expressly provides that he may, or
>   (b) subject to subsection (2), the term purports to confer a benefit on him.
>
> (2) Subsection (1)(b) does not apply if on a proper construction of the contract it appears that the parties did not intend the term to be enforceable by the third party.
> (3) The third party must be expressly identified in the contract by name, as a member of a class or as answering a particular description but need not be in existence when the contract is entered into.
> (4) . . . "

Suppose X buys an item, informing the retailer that it is a gift for Y (whom he names) and arranging that the retailer will send it to Y at her address. If the item proves to be defective can Y rely on this provision to enable her to claim against the retailer under the terms in the contract governing the quality of the goods? The answer is not easy. The effect of the 1999 Act is to enable Y to enforce a *term* which purports to confer a benefit upon her. Arguably the only term which purports to confer a benefit on Y is the term as to delivery, thereby giving her a right to sue the retailer if the item is not delivered. Much depends on the circumstances presented. Will the courts read the situation as one where there was a term of the contract that Y was to have the benefit of *all* the terms in the contract which give rights to the buyer? A similar situation arises where M buys a wedding present for P and Q from the shop where P and Q have informed M that they have arranged their wedding present list.

7–004   Where the 1999 Act gives a third party a right to enforce a contract term, that right is subject to any other relevant terms of the contract such as a clause expressly limiting such a claim—although no term will be effective to exclude or limit a right to sue for death or personal injury caused by negligence. Where the third party's right exists, the judicial remedies available to the third party for breach of contractual term are the same as if the third party had been a party to the contract, e.g. damages and/or rejection of the goods and return

---

[1] For a discussion of the effect of the 1999 Act, see M. Dean, "Removing a Blot on the Landscape" [2000] J.B.L. 143.

of the price (see Chapter 13). Also, the Act limits the ability of the parties to the contract subsequently to remove or alter the third party's right, e.g. by varying the contract. Unless the contract otherwise provides, they cannot (s.2) do so without the third party's consent, if:

"(a) the third party has communicated his assent to the term to the promisor, [i.e. to the party who was contracted to perform the term in question], or

(b) the promisor is aware that the third party has relied on the term, or

(c) the promisor can reasonably be expected to have foreseen that the third party would rely on the term and the third party has in fact relied on it."

When the third party seeks to enforce his right under the Act, the defendant is entitled to rely upon any defence (or set-off) which would have been available to the defendant if either (a) the other party to the contract had brought the claim, or (b) the third party had been a party to the contract.[2]

EXPRESS TERMS

Although the parties are free to agree what terms they choose, they will not be bound by any term which is not properly incorporated in the contract. In the case of terms in a written contract signed by both parties, there will be no doubt that the terms have been properly incorporated. Often, however, the terms will not be in a signed contract. It is perfectly possible for the parties to incorporate terms by agreeing to them either orally or in writing whether or not signed. Chapter 10 deals with the position where one of the terms is an exclusion clause. In that case, the party whom the clause favours (usually the seller) will not be found to have incorporated it in the contract unless either it was in a contractual document signed by the other party or else reasonable steps had been taken to bring it to the attention of the other party. This rule applies not only to exclusion clauses but also to any clause which is particularly onerous or unusual and unlikely to be known to the other party: *Interfoto Picture Library v Stiletto Visual Programmes*.[3] In that case an advertising agency telephoned a transparency library with whom the agency had never previously dealt. The agency asked to hire some transparencies of the 1950s. Accordingly the library sent 47 transparencies with a delivery note clearly requiring that they be returned by March 19. The delivery note included nine conditions, printed in four columns, which the agency never read. Condition 2 stated that a charge of £5 plus VAT per transparency was payable for each day that they were late being returned. After the agency returned the transparencies 14 days late, the library claimed over £3,500 under this condition. The court refused to allow the claim, holding that the clause (imposing an exorbitant charge) was particularly onerous and unusual and the library had not taken all reasonable steps to bring it to the attention of the agency. Presumably the library should have at least highlighted it in some way such as printing it in red, on the *front* of the delivery note, perhaps with a large red hand pointing to it. As Bingham L.J. put

7–005

---

[2] For a third party's right to rely on an exemption clause, see para.10–011 below.
[3] [1988] 2 W.L.R. 615.

it, " . . . the more outlandish the clause, the greater the notice which the other party, if he is to be bound, must in all fairness be given".[4]

As a general rule, if sufficient notice is given and the clause is therefore incorporated, the court will enforce it. That is unless it is: (i) an exclusion clause made unenforceable by the Unfair Contract Terms Act 1977 (see Chapter 10); (ii) a clause made unenforceable by the Unfair Terms in Consumer Contracts Regulations 1999 (also see Chapter 10); or (iii) a penalty clause.[5]

Terms which are not expressly agreed between the parties but are inserted by law into the contract are called implied terms. Any term, express or implied, may be a condition or a warranty.

Warranties and Conditions

7–006   The law classifies breaches of contract into two categories; first, breaches of a less serious nature which entitle the innocent party only to damages, and secondly, more serious breaches which also give them the option to regard the contract as repudiated. The difference is that with the first type, the innocent party, though entitled to damages, must still perform their part of the bargain, whereas with a repudiatory breach they may, in addition to claiming damages, regard themselves as discharged from their obligations under the contract. The former and less serious type is a breach of warranty and the latter is a breach of condition.

It is therefore important to know which terms are conditions and which merely warranties. With the terms implied by ss.12–15 of the Sale of Goods Act it is easy because the Act makes it clear. With terms expressly agreed by the parties it is not always so easy. It is a matter of construing (interpreting) the contract—conditions being those terms which "go to the root" of the contract or are "of the essence" of it. In *Wallis & Wells v Pratt and Haynes*,[6] Fletcher Moulton L.J. said that conditions "go so directly to the very substance of the contract or, in other words, are so essential to its very nature that their non-performance may fairly be considered by the other party as a substantial failure to perform the contract at all". Warranties "are other obligations which, though they must be performed, are not so vital that a failure to perform them goes to the substance of the contract". Section 61(1) of the Sale of Goods Act defines a warranty as:

> " . . . an agreement with reference to goods which are the subject of a contract of sale, but collateral to the main purpose of such contract, the breach of which gives rise to a claim for damages, but not to a right to reject the goods and treat the contract as repudiated."

7–007   The neat classification, just explained, of contract terms into two categories, conditions and warranties, has begun to crumble in recent years. So far as the effect of the breach of condition is concerned, the position, with one exception, remains unaltered. If the seller commits any breach (even a minor one) of a term which is clearly a condition, the buyer will

---

[4] [1988] 2 W.L.R. 615 at 624.
[5] Curiously, the clause in *Interfoto Picture Library v Stiletto Visual Programmes* was almost certainly a penalty clause and unenforceable even if it had been properly incorporated (see para.14–018 below).
[6] [1911] A.C. 394.

be entitled not only to damages but also to reject the goods and treat himself as discharged from his obligations. The exception was created by the Sale and Supply of Goods Act 1994 and applies where the following three circumstances are all present:

> (i) the buyer is not dealing as a consumer[7];
>
> (ii) the condition broken is one relating to description, quality or sample implied by ss.13, 14 or 15 of the Sale of Goods Act;
>
> (iii) the breach is so slight that it would be unreasonable for the buyer to reject the goods.

This limitation on the right to reject is further explained in Chapter 13.

Where there is a breach of any term which is not a condition, that breach could be either repudiatory (i.e. equivalent in effect to a breach of condition) or a mere breach of warranty (i.e. giving rise only to a claim to damages). It is a matter of looking at the extent of the actual breach which has occurred. If that breach "goes to the root of the contract" or deprives the other party of "substantially the whole benefit of the contract", then it entitles the latter to treat the contract as repudiated and himself as discharged from it. This approach was clearly adopted by the Court of Appeal in *Cehave v Bremner (The Hansa Nord)*[8] and approved by the House of Lords in *Reardon Smith Line v Hansen-Tangen*.[9] In *Cehave*, a written contract for the sale of fruit pellets contained the express term "Shipment to be in good condition". On shipment some (about a third) of the pellets were not in "good" condition. However, although they were worth less on the open market than if they had been in "good" condition, they were still fit for the purpose for which the buyer wanted them (making into cattle food) and were still so upon arrival. It was held that there was no breach of the condition implied by the Sale of Goods Act as to merchantable quality, because the pellets were still saleable, albeit at a reduced price. Also the express term was not a "condition" in the contract. Therefore, since the sellers' breach had not been serious enough to go to the root of the contract, the buyers were entitled only to damages. It seems that an express stipulation will not easily be construed by the court as a "condition". It will be a condition only if either there is an earlier case establishing that such a clause is a condition (i.e. "of the essence") or else it was clearly intended by the parties when they made the contract that *any* breach of that term would entitle the other party to repudiate the contract and reject the goods.

Stipulations As To Time

There is a presumption that the time of the payment is not "of the essence" (s.10), although **7–008** the parties could expressly agree otherwise. However, a stipulated time for delivery is likely to be more important and therefore in an ordinary commercial transaction a delivery date is normally "of the essence": *Hartley v Hymans*.[10] Similarly, if a date is specified for shipment by the seller, that will be "of the essence". So, if a delivery or shipment date is not met, the

---

[7] See Ch.10 below for an explanation of "dealing as a consumer".
[8] [1976] Q.B. 44.
[9] [1976] W.L.R. 989.
[10] [1920] 3 K.B. 479.

buyer, as well as claiming damages, can if he wishes regard the contract as repudiated, i.e. reject the goods and reclaim any money paid. Of course, if delivery is late the buyer may accept late delivery, thereby waiving his right to treat the contract as repudiated. If he does, he loses his right to reject the goods but still has a right to damages—s.11(4).

In *Rickards v Oppenheim*[11] the seller contracted to build a car for the buyer, the car to be built by March 20. It was not ready by that date. The buyer did not repudiate the contract but pressed for early delivery. When at the end of June it still was not finished, the buyer informed the seller that if it was not ready in another four weeks he would then regard the contract as repudiated. It was held that the buyer had acted within his rights. By his waiver he had lost the right to regard the contract as repudiated on March 20, but in the circumstances it was a condition of his waiver that delivery should take place as soon as possible. He could therefore revive his right by giving reasonable notice. At the end of four weeks, the car was still not ready. Therefore the buyer was under no obligation to buy it.

Suppose that under a contract, the seller is to deliver the goods to a ship and that the buyer is to nominate the ship so that delivery can be made. Then, if there is a stipulation as to the time by which the buyer must make his nomination, that stipulation as to time relates to delivery and will be "of the essence": *Bunge Corp v Tradax*.[12] Thus, if the buyer is late in making his nomination, the seller is entitled, if he wishes, to regard the contract as repudiated (i.e. entitled to refuse to supply the goods).

IMPLIED TERMS—SECTIONS 12–15

7–009 The expression "buyer beware" is not entirely reflected in the law. It is true that in the law relating to misrepresentation, the seller cannot be laible for failing to disclose defects in the goods but only for any actual statements made by him or his agents. However, the terms implied by ss.12–15 are designed to see that the buyer receives certain basic benefits from the transaction. They relate to title, description, quality and sample. In spite of this the words "buyer beware" still carry a very real warning in one type of purchase and that is what is colloquially called a private sale. The reason, as will be seen, is that the implied terms as to quality (in s.14) apply only where the goods are sold in the course of a business.

Before turning to the detail of ss.12–15 it must be noted that under the original Sale of Goods Act 1893 the wording of some of these sections was different. The Supply of Goods (Implied Terms) Act made some slight changes and, in relation to the implied condition as to merchantable (now satisfactory) quality, the Sale and Supply of Goods Act 1994 made more significant changes. Thus some of the cases which will be discussed in the next few pages were decided on sections which were not absolutely identical with the current provisions. However, because the changes were not substantial, this does not not significantly diminish the authority of those cases, except (and it will be indicated) in relation to some cases on merchantable quality. The current wording of the sections will be used in this book.

[11] [1950] 1 K.B. 616.
[12] [1981] 1 W.L.R. 711.

Title—Section 12

Section 12(1) and (2) reads: **7–010**

> "(1) In a contract of sale, other than one to which subsection (3) below applies, there is an implied term on the part of the seller that in the case of a sale he has a right to sell the goods, and in the case of an agreement to sell he will have such a right at the time when the property is to pass.
>
> (2) In a contract of sale, other than one to which subsection (3) below applies, there is also an implied term that:
>
> > (a) the goods are free, and will remain free until the time when the property is to pass, from any charge or encumbrance not disclosed or known to the buyer before the contract is made, and
> >
> > (b) the buyer will enjoy quiet possession of the goods except so far as it may be disturbed by the owner or other person entitled to the benefit of any charge or encumbrance so disclosed or known."

Section 12(5A) makes it clear that the term in s.12(1) is a condition and that the term in s.12(2) is a warranty. Most important is the implied condition that the seller has a right to sell the goods. This condition is commonly broken by someone selling goods which are not his. Chapter 5 was devoted to the question of who then owns the goods, the purchaser or the original owner. If the purchaser does so, then he has no quarrel with his seller. If, however, the original owner still owns them, the purchaser has an action against his seller for breach of the implied condition; he can claim for damages and/or return of the price.

Rowland v Divall[13] has attracted considerable criticism. Three months after buying and taking delivery of a car, the purchaser discovered that it had not belonged to the seller and still belonged to its original owner. It was returned to the latter and the purchaser brought an action against the seller under s.12. It was held that he was entitled to the return of the price, on the ground that he had suffered a "total failure of consideration". The whole object for a buyer in making a purchase is to obtain legal ownership of the goods. If he does not obtain that, then he suffers a total failure of consideration and is entitled to the return of the price. Thus, in effect, the buyer had over three months free use of the car.

If the buyer does obtain ownership, then he does not suffer a total failure of consideration. **7–011**
It can happen that at the time of the sale the seller is not the owner (and thus in breach of the condition in s.12) but that he subsequently obtains that ownership, e.g. by buying the goods from their owner. This "feeds" the purchaser's title.[14] Thus good title is conferred upon the purchaser but at a date later than it should have been. If this occurs, the buyer can no longer claim to have suffered a total failure of consideration. The goods will be his, he will not be able to reject them[15] and his only claim will be for damages. However, at any time before the purchaser's title is fed (i.e. before the seller obtains ownership). The buyer is entitled by virtue of the seller's breach of condition to regard the contract as repudiated, to reject the goods and thus to reclaim the price on a total failure of consideration. These principles were

[13] [1923] 2 K.B. 500.
[14] See para.5–030, above.
[15] This is because he will have "accepted" them, s.35, see para.13–005 below.

applied in *Butterworth v Kingsway Motors*.[16] Miss A acquired a car on hire-purchase terms. Before completing her payments and therefore before the car was hers, she sold it to B. B sold it to C, who sold it to Kingsway Motors, who in turn sold it to Butterworth. In all this time Miss A still had not completed her payments. It followed that each seller was liable to his buyer for breach of the condition in s.12. After using the car for 11 months, Butterworth discovered that he was not the owner. He thereupon immediately wrote to Kingsway Motors informing them of the situation and claiming the return of his purchase price. A week later Miss A completed her payments under her hire-purchase agreement and in doing so fed title down the line of purchasers. The process of feeding stopped at Kingsway Motors who thus became owners of the car. Ownership did not pass to Butterworth who by his letter had already indicated that he regarded his contract as repudiated. It was held that Butterworth had suffered a total failure of consideration and was entitled therefore to the return from Kingsway Motors of his purchase price. However, neither Kingsway Motors nor C nor B had suffered a total failure of consideration because their title had been fed. Once they had "accepted" the goods (see para.13–005 below) and their title had been fed, they lost the right to reject the goods for breach of condition. Kingsway Motors, C and B obtained only damages from their respective sellers. Kingsway Motors' damages were assessed as the difference between the value of the car when ownership should have passed to them (i.e. when they bought it) and its lower value when ownership actually passed to them (i.e. when title was fed). C obtained the same sum from B and B from Miss A.

Butterworth v Kingsway Motors involved a motor vehicle and was decided before the enactment of the Hire Purchase Act 1964, Pt III. We have seen (para.5–031 above) that by virtue of s.27 of the 1964 Act where someone, who has possession of a motor vehicle under a hire-purchase or conditional sale agreement, sells the vehicle before making all the payments under the agreement (i.e. before acquiring property in the vehicle), the first private purchaser (provided he was innocent and bona fide) will become the owner. Thus, if the facts of *Butterworth v Kingsway Motors* were to arise again today, Butterworth would acquire title to the car provided that the first private purchaser (either B, C or Butterworth himself) was innocent and bona fide. Would that prevent Butterworth being entitled to reject the car? The answer depends upon whether on the one hand B or C was the innocent bona fide first private purchaser or whether on the other hand B and C were trade purchasers and Mr Butterworth was himself the first private purchaser. If it were the former, then Kingsway Motors would have good title (acquired from C) and therefore Kingsway Motors would not be in breach of the term that they had the right to sell the car. If it were Mr Butterworth who was the first private purchaser, then Kingsway Motors would still be in breach of the term as to title and Mr Butterworth's right to reject the car for breach of condition would be unaffected by the 1964 Act. This was held in *Barber v NWS Bank*,[17] relying upon s.27(6) of the 1964 Act which provides that " . . . nothing in this section shall exonerate [the] trade or finance purchaser who becomes a purchaser of the vehicle and is not a person claiming under the first private purchaser, from any liability (whether civil or criminal) to which he would be subject apart from this section".

It can happen that the ownership of one person is subject to certain rights which someone else has over the goods. This could occur where someone has a lien over the goods, i.e. a

---

[16] [1954] 1 W.L.R. 1286.
[17] [1996] C.C.L.R. 30.

right to retain possession of them until a debt is paid. For example, when goods are entrusted to a repairer for repair, he has a lien over them to compel payment of his repair bill. The owner can still sell the goods even though they are in the possession of the repairer who is exercising his lien. In this case the seller will not be in breach of the terms implied by s.12, provided that before the contract was made he disclosed to the buyer the existence of the lien.

It can happen that there is some doubt about someone's title to goods, e.g. a finder's title. **7–012** A finder does have title to the goods (a "possessory" title) but it is subject to the title of the original owner. The latter, if he ever turns up, can therefore reclaim the goods. A finder who sells goods without first disclosing that he only has a finder's title is in breach of the condition in s.12. However, if he has disclosed that fact so as to indicate that he is transferring to the purchaser only his own possessory title, then he will not be in breach of the condition—s.12(3).

Section 12(3) applies to a contract where it appears from the contract or is to be inferred from the circumstances that the parties intended that the seller should transfer only a limited title (whether it be the limited title of the seller himself or of some third person from whom the seller would obtain it). In such a contract there is no implied condition that the seller has or will have a right to sell the goods. There are, however, implied warranties of quiet possession, etc. The seller will be in breach of these if all charges and encumbrances (e.g. liens) known to him were not made known to the buyer before the contract was made.

So far it may have appeared that the condition in s.12 will be broken only if the seller turns out not to be the owner, anything less serious being merely a breach of one of the warranties. There is, however, some overlap between the warranties and the condition in s.12. The condition is broken if for any reason (undisclosed to the buyer) the seller does not have the right to sell the goods. The sellers in *Niblett Ltd v Confectioners' Materials Co*[18] agreed to sell tins of condensed milk. They supplied tins labelled "Nissly Brand". This infringed the Nestlé trade mark. Nestlé Co could have obtained an injunction restraining the sale of those tins and they required the buyers not to resell them without first removing the labels. The buyers claimed damages from the sellers. It was held that the sellers were in breach of both the condition that they had the right to sell the goods and also of the warranty of quiet possession.

Niblett's case was considered in *Microbeads v Vinhurst Road Markings*.[19] Shortly after the sale of some road marking machines, a company unconnected with the contract of sale obtained a patent relating to road marking machines. This entitled them to bring a patent action against the buyers to enforce the patent. The buyers sued the sellers under s.12 claiming a breach of the condition as to title and a breach of the warranty of quiet possession. It was held that there had been no breach of the condition as to title because that condition related to the time of the sale. At that time no patent had been obtained; the buyers could use the machines undisturbed; and the sellers thus had the right to pass the ownership in the machines and to confer undisturbed possession upon the buyers. The warranty as to quiet possession, however, relates to the future. It states that the buyer "*will* enjoy quiet possession". The sellers were liable to the buyer in damages for breach of warranty.

[18] [1921] 3 K.B. 387.
[19] [1975] 1 W.L.R. 218.

Description—Section 13

7–013　Section 13[20] reads:

> "(1) Where there is a contract for the sale of goods by description, there is an implied term that the goods will correspond with the description.
> (1A) As regards England and Wales and Northern Ireland, the term implied by subsection (1) above is a condition.
> (2) If the sale is by sample as well as by description it is not sufficient that the bulk of the goods corresponds with the sample if the goods do not also correspond with the description.
> (3) A sale of goods is not prevented from being a sale by description by reason only that, being exposed for sale or hire, they are selected by the buyer."

The condition is implied only where there is a sale by description. Clearly, goods are sold by description where the purchaser has not seen the goods but is relying on the description alone. Equally, in the words of Lord Wright in *Grant v Australian Knitting Mills*[21]:

> "there is a sale by description even though the buyer is buying something displayed before him on the counter; a thing is sold by description, though it is specific, so long as it is sold not merely as the specific thing but as a thing corresponding to a description."

In that case the sale of woollen underwear across the counter was held to be a sale by description. The essence of a sale by description is that in deciding to buy the buyer placed some (but not necessarily exclusive) reliance upon the description. In *Beale v Taylor*[22] the buyer saw an advertisement for a "Herald, convertible, white, 1961". He answered the advertisement, inspected the car and bought it. Although the buyer had inspected the car, he had relied not purely on his own assessment of its value, but to some extent on the description. The seller was held liable under s.13, since the car consisted of the rear half of a 1961 car and the front half of an earlier model.

7–014　In most cases the mere fact that a description was given (e.g. "good condition" or "1996 model") will be sufficient and convincing evidence that the sale was by description. It will be obvious that the buyer has relied, at least to some extent, upon the description. If in fact, however, it is clear that there was no reliance at all upon the description, the sale will not be a sale by description. In *Harlingdon & Leinster Enterprises Ltd v Christopher Hull Fine Art*,[23] an art dealer contacted another art dealer informing him that he had two painings by Gabriele Munter (an artist of the German expressionist school). The latter visited the former (the seller) and inspected the paintings. The seller, as the buyer knew, had no expertise in, or knowledge of, the German expressionist school. Hence, the buyer placed no reliance upon the seller's attribution but relied solely upon his own judgment and assessment. It was held that,

---

[20] See generally, Feltham, "The Sale by Description of Specific Goods" [1969] J.B.L. 16.
[21] [1936] A.C. 85.
[22] [1967] 1 W.L.R. 1193.
[23] [1991] 1 Q.B. 564. For case commentary, see Robson and Adams, "Consumer Sales" [1990] J.B.L. 433.

since it was not within the reasonable contemplation of the parties that the buyer was relying upon the seller's attribution, there was no sale by description.

A sale in a supermarket is usually a sale by description. The reason that the buyer selects a packet labelled, say, "cocoa" from the shelf is that she wants cocoa and is relying on the description "cocoa" to accurately identify the packet and its contents. It is a sale by description even though it is the customer who decides which particular goods to select from the display—s.13(3).[24] Occasionally, goods, e.g. vegetables, are displayed without any label or notice describing them. It would seem that such goods are not sold by description.

A sale by sample will often be a sale also by description. Section 13(2) embodies a principle illustrated by *Nichol v Godts*.[25] The buyer bought by sample "foreign refined rape oil". It was held that the goods must correspond not only with the sample but must also be "foreign refined rape oil".

In order to determine whether the goods correspond with the contractual description it may **7–015** be necessary to determine the exact scope and meaning of the description. Obviously, the more detailed it is, the more stringent is the seller's obligation to supply goods corresponding with it. A contract to supply "staves" is one thing, but a contract to supply "staves, half an inch thick" is altogether more onerous. If in the latter case the seller supplies staves between half an inch and nine-sixteenths of an inch thick, he is in breach of the condition as to description: *Arcos v Ronaasen*.[26] If the seller wants a margin, he must stipulate for it in the contractual description.

The fact that the goods are of defective quality is usually irrelevant in deciding whether they correspond with their description. *Pinnock Bros v Lewis & Peat*[27] involved a contract for the sale of "copra cake" which was to be used to feed cattle. The goods actually supplied consisted of copra cake combined with a quantity of castor oil, the latter being poisonous to cattle. The sellers were in breach of the condition as to description. However, this was not because the goods were unfit for use but rather because they included goods of a different description. *Ashington Piggeries v Hill*[28] involved a contract for the sale of "Norwegian herring meal fair average quality for the season, expected to analyse . . . " which was to be used to feed mink. The sellers supplied Norwegian herring meal, i.e. Norwegian herrings plus preservative. The herrings and preservative had reacted together and produced a chemical which was poisonous to mink. Here, the sellers were not in breach of the condition as to description since, unlike *Pinnock's* case, there was no addition of goods outside the contractual description. The key to s.13 was said to be "identification" not "quality". Hence the expression "fair average quality for the season" was not held to be part of the contractual description, since it did not "identify" the goods sold. Goods which are useless or unsuitable for any normal purpose will still correspond with their description (here "Norwegian herring meal") if it accurately identified them. A balloon, though punctured, is nevertheless accurately identified and descibed as a "balloon".

Re Moore and Landauer[29] is now a controversial decision. The sellers had agreed to sell a quanitity of tinned pears which were to be packed in cases containing 30 tins each. They

---

[24] Traditionally, whether such a sale constituted a "sale by description", i.e. where the buyer had inspected (and/or selected the goods prior to the sale) had been doubted. See *Morelli v Fitch & Gibbons* [1928] 2 K.B. 636 and *Grant v Australian Knitting Mills* [1936] A.C. 85.
[25] (1854) 10 Exch. 191.
[26] [1933] A.C. 470.
[27] [1923] 1 K.B. 690.
[28] [1971] 2 W.L.R. 1051.
[29] [1921] 2 K.B. 519.

had delivered the correct total quantity of tins but half of them were packed in cases of 24 tins each. It was held that the contract requirement that they be packed in cases of 30 was part of the contract description. Therefore the buyers were entitled to refuse to accept delivery because the sellers had committed a breach of condition (i.e. of s.13) and the buyers were entitled to do so even if they would have suffered no loss by having the tins packed in cases of 24 instead of cases of 30. The correctness of the decision in *Re Moore and Landauer* has, however, been doubted by Lord Wilberforce in *Reardon Smith Line v Hansen Tangen*.[30] Because s.13 is an implied *condition*, anything which is regarded by the court as part of the contract description automatically becomes "of the essence" and, if not complied with, has until recently automatically given the buyer the right to reject the goods for breach of condition, no matter how slight the breach was. The modern trend has therefore been to regard as part of the contract description only those contract words which help in "identifying" the goods. Other expressions in the contract (such as "fair average quality for the season" or "packed in cases of 30") can then be regarded not as part of the contract description, but as express terms of the contract in their own right. Unless the contract clearly indicates otherwise, these express terms (not being stipulations as to the time of delivery) will then normally be warranties and not conditions. Thus if the seller is in breach of one of them, the buyer will not be entitled to reject the goods unless the seller's breach is such so as to deprive the buyer of substantially the whole benefit of the contract: *Cehave v Bremer*.[31] Of course, if there is a defect of quality, a buyer who wishes to reject the goods may still be able to do so, i.e. if he can show that there has been a breach of one of the conditions implied by s.14. Even then, however, a buyer who is a non-consumer will not be entitled to reject the goods if the breach was so slight as to make rejection unreasonable (see para.13–004 below).

It is clear from the wording of s.13(1) that the implied term as to description is of application to all sales, and not restricted to those which are "in the course of business". Thus in *Varley v Whipp*[32] a non-trade seller was liable under s.13 where a second-hand reaping machine was described, wholly inaccurately, as being little used. The implied term as to quality was inapplicable, due to the status of the seller, but the court held that the misdescription breached s.13. Thus the relationship between s.13 and s.14 will frequently be of great practical importance.[33]

QUALITY—SECTION 14

7–016 There are two conditions which may be implied by s.14—as to satisfactory quality (s.14(2)) and as to fitness for purpose (s.14(3)). Before considering in what circumstances these conditions will be implied, note should be made of s.14(1) which reads:

> "Except as provided by this section and section 15 below and subject to any other enactment, there is no implied term about the quality or fitness for any particular purpose of goods supplied under a contract of sale."

---

[30] [1976] W.L.R. 989.
[31] [1976] Q.B. 44, para.7–007 above.
[32] [1900] 1 Q.B. 513.
[33] See generally, the discussion above and *Ashington Piggeries v Hill* [1971] 2 W.L.R. 1051.

The two conditions implied by s.14 extend, not only to the goods actually bought, but also to goods "supplied under" the contract, e.g. a returnable bottle: *Geddling v Marsh*.[34] They also extend to the instructions. It would, for example, be no defence for the seller to say that his farm fertiliser was perfectly safe and effective when applied in the right concentration (at the right time of year) if the instructions supplied with the fertiliser stated in error the wrong concentration, whether too weak to be effective or so strong as to kill the crops. The law does not consider just the goods. It asks whether the goods with their instructions were of satisfactory quality and reasonably fit for their purpose: *Wormell v R.H.M. Agriculture (East)*.[35] In the case of a book, video cassette, or computer disk containing a software program, the two conditions extend, apparently, not just to the physical book, disk or video, but also to the contents.[36]

Satisfactory Quality—Section 14(2)

Section 14(2), (2A), (2B) and (2C) read: **7–017**

"(2)   Where the seller sells goods in the course of a business, there is an implied term that the goods supplied under the contract are of satisfactory quality.

(2A)   For the purposes of this Act, goods are of satisfactory quality if they meet the standard that a reasonable person would regard as satisfactory, taking account of any description of the goods, the price (if relevant) and all the other relevant circumstances.

(2B)   For the purposes of this Act, the quality of goods includes their state and condition and the following (among others) are in appropriate cases aspects of the quality of goods—

(a)   fitness for all the purposes for which goods of the kind in question are commonly supplied,

(b)   appearance and finish,

(c)   freedom from minor defects,

(d)   safety, and

(e)   durability.

(2C)   The term implied by subsection (2) above does not extend to any matter making the quality of goods unsatisfactory—

(a)   which is specifically drawn to the buyer's attention before the contract is made,

(b)   where the buyer examines the goods before the contract is made, which that examination ought to reveal, or

(c)   in the case of a contract for sale by sample, which would have been apparent on a reasonable examination of the sample."

---

[34] [1920] 1 K.B. 668.
[35] [1987] 1 W.L.R. 1091.
[36] See *St Albans DC v ICL* [1994] T.L.R. 579, discussed at para.1–011, above.

The implied term as to satisfactory quality is a condition. It is implied only if the goods are sold "in the course of a business". These words were new in s.14 by virtue of the Supply of Goods (Implied Terms) Act 1973. Someone can sell "in the course of business" without being a dealer in, or a regular seller of, goods of the description sold. The phrase is simply there to distinguish between a sale made in the course of a seller's business and a purely private sale outside the confines of any business. Of course a butcher selling meat or a baker selling bread are each selling in the course of their business. Equally, the baker sells his bread van in the course of a business when he part-exchanges it for a new one. The solicitor who sells off old office furniture or a computer no longer wanted for the practice, similarly is selling in the course of a business. This meaning of the phrase was established in *Stevenson v Rogers*,[37] in which a sale of his fishing boat by a fisherman was held to be a sale in the course of a business. This case casts doubt upon an earlier decision, *R & B Customs Brokers v UDT*,[38] giving the phrase a much narrower meaning in the Unfair Contract Terms Act 1977. It seems clear, however, that a similar phrase in the (now repealed) Trade Descriptions Act 1968 does indeed have a narrower meaning.[39] Section 61(1) of the Sale of Goods Act states that:

> " 'business' includes a profesion and the activities of any government department (including a Northern Ireland department), or local or public authority."

Thus someone buying goods from the local council does have the benefit of the implied condition that they shall be of satisfactory quality. Suppose that the seller is a private seller not selling in the course of a business, but that he gets an agent to make the sale for him. Suppose also that the agent is acting in the course of a business. In that case the seller is treated as if he were selling in the course of a business, unless either the buyer knew that he was not doing so or else reasonable steps had been taken to bring that fact to the buyer's attention before the contract was made: s.14(5) and *Boyter v Thomson*.[40]

7–018   There are three exceptions in s.14(2). First, the buyer cannot complain of defects which had been specifically drawn to his attention, although naturally the condition will still apply in relation to other defects rendering the goods of unsatisfactory quality. The second exception applies "where the buyer examines the goods before the contract is made". So, if the buyer does, he cannot complain of defects which he ought thereby to have discerned. In *Thornett & Fehr v Beers*[41] the buyers of some barrels of glue had examined only the outside. It was held that a normal examination would have involved looking inside and that they could not complain of defects in the glue which an inspection would have revealed. This decision may not be the same today, because the wording of s.14(2C)(b) now refers to defects "*that examination ought to reveal*" and not to any examination which ought to have been made. One could not say (it is arguable) that the examination actually made in *Thornett* (i.e. of the outside of the barrel) ought to have revealed defects apparent only on an examination which was not made (i.e. of the inside). Nevertheless, the buyer's legal position may be better if he

---

[37] [1999] 1 All E.R. 613.
[38] [1988] 1 W.L.R. 321. *R & B Customs Brokers* was nevertheless followed and applied by the Court of Appeal in *Feldaroll v Hermes Leasing (London) Ltd* [2004] EWCA Civ. 747, [2004] C.C.L.R. 8. See further, para.10–020, below.
[39] See para.17–016, below.
[40] [1995] 2 A.C. 628.
[41] [1919] 1 K.B. 486.

made no examination than if he made merely a superficial examination. This is not the case, however, where there is a sale by sample. The third exception prevents any liability under s.14(2) in respect of any defect which would have been apparent on a reasonable examination of the sample, i.e. even if no such examination was carried out.

Returning to the second exception, suppose the buyer examines the goods, discovers a defect but decides nevertheless to buy, taking the view that the defect is one that can be easily remedied. If it is easily remedied, then clearly the buyer cannot complain of the defect in question. If it turns out to be incapable of being remedied, the result may well be different. If at the time of making the contract, the buyer was unaware, and could not reasonably have been aware, of the gravity of the defect, then the court would probably hold that the condition as to satisfactory quality was implied. In *R & B Customs Co Ltd v United Dominions Trust Ltd*[42] the buyer had discovered that the car had a leak but did not discover until after the contract the gravity of the leak or that it was incurable. Neill L.J. said[43]:

> "I am not at present pesuaded, however, that the condition in section 14(2) is excluded if at the time the contract is made the buyer is reasonably of the opinion that the defect can be, and will be, rectied at no cost to himself."

The Court of Appeal side-stepped having to decide that issue, by holding that the buyer was entitled anyway to rely on s.14(3) (para.7–024 below); the car was not reasonably fit for the particular purposes (driving upon the roads in England, in English weather) for which the buyer had informed the seller that he wanted it.

Beyond these exceptions, it is clear that liability under s.14(2) is strict, i.e. it is not relevant **7–019** whether at the time of the contract the defect was such that it could have been detected or prevented.[44]

Prior to 1994 the implied term in s.14(2) was an implied condition that the goods would be of *merchantable* quality. The Sale and Supply of Goods Act 1994 amended s.14(2). It replaced the word merchantable with the word *satisfactory* and introduced a new definition set out in ss.14(2A) and (2B). According to that definition it is important to assess the quality of the goods against the description applied to them. Clearly, goods sold as "mink food" will not be of satisfactory quality if it is poisonous to mink. That is so even if it is perfectly wholesome for other animals. What, however, is the position if it sold as "animal food"? Under the previous law, there was clear authority that the goods did not have to be fit for all the purposes for which goods of that kind were commonly bought; it was sufficient if they were fit for one or more of those purposes: *Aswan Engineering Establishment v Lupdine*.[45] Now, however, s.14(2B)(a) seems to require the goods to be fit for all the purposes for which goods of that kind are commonly bought. Thus if the goods are sold as "animal food" and animal food is commonly bought to feed mink, then if the food is poisonous to mink, it would appear that it is not of satisfactory quality.

The definition also states that the price can be relevant. This appears to be no change from the previous law relating to merchantable quality. The relevance of the price was discussed

---

[42] [1988] 1 W.L.R. 321.
[43] [1988] 1 W.L.R. 321 at 333.
[44] See for example, the decision of the Court of Appeal in *Randall v Newson* (or *Newsom*) (1877) 2 Q.B.D. 102.
[45] [1987] 1 W.L.R. 1.

in *Brown v Craiks*[46] which involved the sale of industrial fabric. The buyer found it unsuitable for making into dresses. It was, however, perfectly suitable for other industrial purposes and could be sold for such, albeit at a slightly lower price. The House of Lords held that it was of merchantable quality because it was saleable without any substantial reduction of the price. Their Lordships said that if it had been saleable only at a "throw away" price, that would indicate that it was not of merchantable quality.

7–020   The word satisfactory in the definition indicates that the goods are not necessarily required to be of the very best quality but that the level of quality demanded depends upon the circumstances of the case, including the price. In this respect the law has not changed. For example, second-hand goods can hardly be expected to be in perfect condition. In *Bartlett v Sydney Marcus*[47] the seller, a car dealer, told the buyer that the car had a defective clutch and that if he bought it as it was he could have it for £550 but that if the seller were to repair it first, the price would be £575. The buyer opted to take the car as it was. About a month later the buyer had the clutch repaired at a cost of £45 and claimed this sum from the seller, alleging that the car was not of merchantable quality and not reasonably fit for the purposes of being driven on the road. The claim failed. "A buyer should realise that, when he buys a second-hand car, defects may appear sooner rather than later." The car came up to the standard required. On the other hand, major defects in a second-hand car might well mean that it is not of satisfactory quality.[48] A second-hand car which is not safe to be driven on the road (for example because the brakes are in such a state that they would fail if the driver had to carry out an emergency stop) is clearly not of satisfactory quality: *Lee v York Coach and Marine*[49] (unless of course the car was only sold for scrap).

In *Clegg v Andersson (t/a Nordic Marine)*[50] Clegg agreed to buy a yacht with a keel "in accordance with the manufacturer's standard specification" at a price of £236,000. Following delivery of the yacht in August 2000, the seller informed Clegg that the keel was substantially heavier than detailed within the manufacturer's specification. During August 2000 and March 2001 Clegg and Andersson corresponded on issues arising from the overweight keel before Clegg sought to reject the yacht for breach of s.14(2).[51] The Court of Appeal held that the yacht was not of satisfactory quality "because of the overweight keel, the adverse effect it had on rig safety and the need for more than minimal remedial work".[52] Hale L.J. emphasised the manner in which the objective test of s.14(2) should be implemented in stating that[53]:

> "The test is whether a reasonable person would think the goods satisfactory, taking into account their description, the price (if relevant) and all other relevant circumstances: see s 14(2A). The question, as the joint Report of the Law Commission and the Scottish Law Commission explained, is "not whether the reasonable person would find *the goods*

---

[46] [1970] 1 W.L.R. 752.
[47] [1965] 1 W.L.R. 1013.
[48] See *Crowther v Shannon* [1975] 1 W.L.R. 30, discussed at para.7–026 below.
[49] [1977] R.T.R. 35.
[50] [2003] EWCA Civ. 320.
[51] At first instance it was also contended that the yacht was in breach of s.13(1), though this matter was not pursued in the Court of Appeal.
[52] [2003] EWCA Civ. 320 [49].
[53] [2003] EWCA Civ. 320 [72], citing *Sale and Supply of Goods* (1987, Law Com. No. 160) at para.3.25.

acceptable; it is an objective comparison of the state of the goods with the *standard* which a reasonable person would find acceptable".

The application of that test to the facts of *Clegg* is relatively straightforward. As her Ladyship said[54]:

"If a reasonable person had been told in September 2000 that the seller himself had realised that a very large quantity of lead would have to be removed in some as yet unspecified way from the keel of a brand new boat costing nearly a quarter of a million pounds with as yet unspecified consequences for its safety and performance he or she would have had little difficulty in concluding that the boat could not be of satisfactory quality."

In *Rogers v Parish (Scarborough) Ltd*[55] the Court of Appeal gave an authoritative ruling on how the old definition of merchantable quality applied in the case of a motor vehicle. It seems very likely that this ruling will be held to be equally applicable to the new definition of satisfactory quality. The old definition referred, as the new one does in s.14(2B), to the purposes for which goods of that kind are commonly bought. In *Rogers v Parish* it was held that in the case of motor vehicles those purposes include not merely the purpose of driving it from place to place but of doing so with the appropriate degree of comfort, ease of handling and pride in the vehicle's outward and interior appearance. The appropriate degree varies with the price, the description and other relevant factors. The relative weight to be attached to the different characteristics of the vehicle depends upon which market it is to be aimed at. On a vehicle sold as new, the performance and finish to be expected are those of a model of average standard with no mileage. No less is to be expected of a vehicle sold with a manufacturer's warranty. This authoritative ruling made it clear that defects in appearance, if of sufficient degree, could render a vehicle unmerchantable. That is true also of the new definition of satisfactory quality (see s.14(2B)(b)). The merest blemish on a Rolls Royce might render it unsatisfactory whereas it might not on a humbler car (see s.14(2B)(c)). The concept of satisfactory quality is one of degree; deficiencies which are unacceptable on a car sold as new might be acceptable on a second-hand car. Nevertheless the general approach laid down in *Rogers v Parish (Scarborough) Ltd* applies equally to second-hand vehicles (*Business Applications Specialists Ltd v Nationwide Credit Corpn. Ltd*[56]) and, as noted earlier, sufficiently serious defects can render even a second-hand car of unsatisfactory quality. Thus in *Shine v General Guarantee Finance Co Ltd*[57] a 20-month-old Fiat was held to be unmerchantable because, unknown to the buyer, it had eight months earlier been totally submerged in water for over 24 hours and had consequently been treated as a "write-off" by its insurer. The car would equally be of unsatisfactory quality under the new definition.

The issue of minor defects and motor vehicles was recently litigated in *Egan v Motor Services (Bath) Ltd*[58] where an Audi TT displayed "a tendency to 'veer', 'deviate' or 'drift'

7–021

---

[54] [2003] EWCA Civ. 320 at para.73.
[55] [1987] Q.B. 933.
[56] [1988] C.C.L.R. 135.
[57] [1988] C.C.L.R. 14.
[58] [2007] EWCA Civ 1002.

to the nearside".[59] This was put down to camber sensitivity rather than an inherent abnormality. Nevertheless, tests on the rear wheels of the vehicle showed that the wheel alignment was outside the manufacturer's specifications. This, it was argued, was sufficient to constitute a breach of satisfactory quality, under s.14(2B)(c)—freedom from minor defects. This argument was rejected by the Court of Appeal. Smith L.J. stated:

> "However, it seems to me unlikely that a buyer will be entitled to reject goods simply because he can point to a minor defect. He must also persuade the judge that a reasonable person would think that the minor defect was of sufficient consequence to make the goods unsatisfactory. Of course, if a car is not handling correctly, one would expect any reasonable person to say that it is not of satisfactory quality. That the judge recognised. But, the mere fact that a setting is outside the manufacturer's specification will not necessarily render the vehicle objectively unsatisfactory".

This decision reinforces the point that the factors listed within s.14(2C) are merely indicative of issues which will raise the question of whether goods are of satisfactory quality. The test for whether goods are of satisfactory quality, however, is that laid down in s.14(2A): whether the defect is such that a reasonable person would conclude that the goods were not of satisfactory quality. Nevertheless, it is perhaps surprising that the goods, operating outside the manufacturer's specifications, were held to be of satisfactory quality. This is particularly so if one considers the general approach laid down in *Rogers v Parish*. The car in *Egan* was brand new, relatively expensive and a prestige model. Moreover, the closing words of Smith L.J. are telling: "This case was about abnormal handling. The judge held that the handling was not abnormal and that was fatal to the appellant's case". It may be suggested that where a car is found to have *abnormal* steering rather than merely "camber sensitivity" the car would obviously be of unsatisfactory quality, but not due to a minor defect. Abnormal steering would most likely constitute unsatisfactory quality with reference to fitness for purpose[60] safety[61] and durability.[62]

7–022   It is of interest to speculate whether the decision in *Aswan Engineering Establishment v Lupdine*[63] would be the same under the new definition of satisfactory quality. In that case some heavy-duty buckets (which were suitable for most purposes for which such buckets were normally bought or used) collapsed when left by the buyer for several days stacked in extreme heat such that the contents reached 70°C (156° Fahrenheit). It was held that they were of merchantable quality because the definition did not require the goods to be suitable for all the purposes for which such goods were commonly bought. It seems highly likely that the same result would be achieved under the new definition but by a slightly different line of reasoning, namely that the definition of satisfactory quality does not require that the goods be fit for extreme or outlandish purposes but just for such uses as such goods are commonly supplied, i.e. normally, used. Leaving the buckets stacked in such extreme temperatures could well be held to be an extreme, abnormal use.

[59] Such was the finding of fact at first instance, discussed in the Court of Appeal.
[60] The Sale of Goods Act 1979 s.14(2B)(a).
[61] The Sale of Goods Act 1979 s.14(2B)(d).
[62] The Sale of Goods Act 1979 s.14(2B)(e)—such abnormality would likely cause excessive tire wear.
[63] [1987] 1 W.L.R. 1.

Where goods are to be despatched to the buyer by carrier, it is reasonable to expect the goods to be of such a quality as to be able to withstand a normal journey—*Mash & Murrell v Joseph Emmanuel*.[64] More generally, it is now clear that durability is part of the definition of satisfactory quality—s.14(2B)(e). It may be accurate to say that the goods must be of satisfactory quality for a reasonable period after delivery so long as they remain in the same apparent state as that in which they were delivered, apart from normal wear and tear. That would bring s.14(2) into line with the implied condition as to fitness for purpose (see para.7–024 below).

The Sale and Supply of Goods to Consumer Regulations 2002[65] inserted s.14(2D) into the Sale of Goods Act.[66] This is designed to ensure that any public statements made by the manufacturer (or representative) are to be taken into account when assessing whether the goods are of satisfactory quality.[67] The new provision states that:

"If the buyer deals as consumer or, in Scotland, if a contract of sale is a consumer contract, the relevant circumstances mentioned in subsection (2A) above include any public statements on the specific characteristics of the goods made about them by the seller, the producer or his representative, particularly in advertising or on labelling."

Thus, where the buyer is a consumer, the objective assessment of the quality of the goods **7–023** undertaken in s.14(2) will be made through recourse to any applicable public statements concerning the goods, in addition to the factors within s.14(2B). This then allows for a breach of the condition as to satisfactory quality where the goods do not match up to, for example, promotional material released by the manufacturer. Therefore, if a manufacturer of LCD televisions advertises a new model with specific qualities (such as the quality of the screen or colour reproduction) these advertising statements will be considered as part of what the reasonable man is entitled to expect in the purchased product. This is so irrespective of the mode of advertising used by the manufacturer, i.e. whether through television or the internet etc. It is also now irrelevant whether the statement is made (or repeated) by the retailer to the consumer, i.e. the consumer will be entitled to pursue remedies for breach of the implied condition as to quality against the retailer using public statements made only by the manufacturer (e.g. on the manufacturer's internet site).

Given the possible impact of this amendment, it is not surprising that certain statutory limitations have also been incorporated into s.14. Section 14(2E) prevents public statements from being considered under s.14(2) in three separate circumstances and provides that:

"A public statement is not by virtue of subsection (2D) above a relevant circumstance for the purposes of subsection (2A) above in the case of a contract of sale, if the seller shows that—

(a) at the time the contract was made, he was not, and could not reasonably have been, aware of the statement,

---

[64] [1961] 1 W.L.R. 862.
[65] SI 2002/3045.
[66] The new provisions apply to contracts of sale of goods made after March 31, 2003.
[67] See generally, Willet, Morgan-Taylor and Naidoo, "The Sale and Supply of Goods to Consumers Regulations" [2004] J.B.L. 94.

(b) before the contract was made, the statement had been withdrawn in public or, to the extent that it contained anything which was incorrect or misleading, it had been corrected in public, or

(c) the decision to buy the goods could not have been influenced by the statement."

Thus where a seller is not (and could not reasonably have been) aware of a public statement made by the manufacturer, the statement will not be considered under s.14(2). The question of when a seller could reasonably be expected to be aware of the statement could raise some interesting disputes in the future, though the seller would presumably be expected to be aware of statements made through the manufacturer's official internet site and official literature relating to the product etc. Paragraph (c) will presumably prevent liability for trade puffs as well as in situations where the buyer was unaware of the public statement. The latter provides no difficulty, though the former once again raises the fine distinction on occasion between trade puffs and statements intended to convey factual information to the end-user.[68]

Fitness for Purpose—Section 14(3)

7–024   Section 14(3) reads[69]:

"(3) Where the seller sells goods in the course of a business and the buyer, expressly or by implication, makes known (a) to the seller or (b) . . . any particular purpose for which the goods are being bought, there is an implied term that the goods supplied under the contract are reasonably fit for that purpose, whether or not that is a purpose for which goods are commonly supplied, except where the circumstances show that the buyer does not rely, or that it is unreasonable for him to rely, on the skill or judgment of the seller . . . "

This is a condition and, like the one in s.14(2), is implied only where the goods are sold in the course of a business. Further, the buyer must have made known to the seller the particular purpose for which he was buying the goods. With goods having only one normal use the mere fact of purchase will, by implication, make it known that this is what the buyer wants them for, e.g. a hot-water bottle, as in *Priest v Last*.[70]

Someone who buys goods having more than one common use or someone who wants goods for an abnormal purpose will not benefit from s.14(3) unless the seller was expressly informed of the particular purpose for which they were required. In *Griffiths v Peter Conway*[71] the purchaser of a tweed coat contracted dermatitis from wearing it. Someone with normally sensitive skin would not have been affected but the purchaser had abnormally

---

[68] See, for example, the discussion of this point in relation to trade puffs, representations and contractual terms in Ch.6. See also, Willet, Morgan-Taylor and Naidoo, "The Sale and Supply of Goods to Consumers Regulations" [2004] J.B.L. 94, 97–98.
[69] For an explanation of the omitted words see para.23–020 below.
[70] [1903] 2 K.B. 148.
[71] [1939] 1 All E.R. 685.

sensitive skin. Not having made that fact known to the seller, she lost the case. This decision was approved in *Slater v Finning*,[72] where a boat owner had bought and had installed in his boat engine a new part, a camshaft. It failed while at sea as did two further replacement camshafts. The expert evidence was that the cause of the failures was excessive torsional resonance excited by some cause external to the engine and the camshaft. It was held that the camshaft was fit for the purpose for which the seller had been informed that it was required, namely use as a component part of the engine in the buyer's boat, i.e. an ordinary boat, the sellers not having been informed of any special characteristic of the boat. There is no breach of the implied condition where the failure of the goods arises from some idiosyncrasy, not made known to the seller, in the buyer or in the circumstances of the planned use of the goods. That is so even if the buyer is himself unaware of that abnormal feature or idiosyncrasy.

If the buyer does not rely, or it is unreasonable for him to rely, on the seller's skill or judgment, he will have no claim under s.14(3). However, the courts seem quite ready to infer the necessary reliance. Lord Wright, in *Grant v Australian Knitting Mills* said[73]:   **7–025**

> " . . . thus to take a case like that in question of a purchase from a retailer the reliance will be in general inferred from the fact that a buyer goes to the shop in confidence that the tradesman has selected his stock with skill and judgment."

On the other hand, if the buyer asks for an article by its trade or brand name and does so in such a way as to exclude any discussion of its suitability, then he is not relying on the seller's skill or judgment: *Baldry v Marshall*.[74]

Sometimes there will be partial reliance, the buyer relying in some respects upon the seller's skill and judgment, and in others upon his own. Should the goods prove unfit for their purpose, the buyer will have a claim only if their unfitness relates to the sphere of reliance placed upon the seller. In *Cammell Laird v Manganese Bronze & Brass*[75] the sellers were to supply a particular ship's propellers which they were to make according to a specification supplied by the buyer. The seller's skill and judgment were relied upon as to matters not within the buyer's specification. This included ensuring that adequate materials were used and that the specification was embodied in the propellers. It also included other matters not provided for in the specification. In fact the propellers were unfit for their purpose because they were not thick enough, a matter not included in the buyer's specification. The sellers were liable.

In *Teheran-Europe v S T Belton*[76] tractors were purchased for the purpose of exporting and   **7–026** reslling in Persia. They in fact infringed Persian regulations and the buyer was fined by a Persian criminal court. He sued the seller. It was held that since the buyer knew much more about Persia than the seller, he must have been relying on his own judgment as to whether the tractors were suitable for the Persian market. The buyer lost.

The words "reasonably fit" do not require the goods to be of the very best quality. The quality to be expected will depend upon all the circumstances of the sale. Second-hand goods

---

[72] [1997] A.C. 473.
[73] [1936] A.C. 85 at 99.
[74] [1925] 1 K.B. 260.
[75] [1934] A.C. 402.
[76] [1968] 2 Q.B. 545.

cannot be expected to be perfect. Minor defects must, for example, be expected to materialise in a second-hand car.[77] However, major defects existing at the time of the sale are another matter. In *Crowther v Shannon*[78] a car dealer sold for £390 an eight-year old Jaguar car with 82,000 miles on the milometer. Three weeks and 2,300 miles later, the engine seized up and needed replacing. It was held that the fact the engine seized up after only three weeks was evidence that at the time of the sale the car was not reasonably fit for the purpose of being driven on the road. The seller was liable for breach of the condition of fitness for purpose.

Although the words "reasonably fit" do not require the goods to be of the very best quality, they do impose upon the seller an absolute obligation. It is of no defence that he acted reasonably if in fact the goods are not reasonably fit for their purpose. In *Frost v Aylesbury Dairy*[79] milk was sold containing typhoid germs. It was no defence that the sellers had taken all reasonable precautions as to hygiene.[80]

It is at the time of delivery that the goods must be of reasonable fitness for the purpose for which the buyer indicated he wanted them. They must also continue to be so for a reasonable time after delivery. In *Lambert v Lewis*[81] Lord Diplock said that the condition of fitness for purpose was a continuing obligation:

> "that the goods will continue to be fit for that purpose for a reasonable time after delivery, so long as they remain in the same apparent state as that in which they were delivered, apart from normal wear and tear."

In that case a farmer had bought from a dealer a towing coupling for his Land Rover. He continued to use the coupling after it had become apparent to him that the locking mechanism of the coupling was broken. Subsequently, due to defective design (i.e. not the broken locking mechanism), the coupling failed while in use and a road accident occurred as a result of the trailer becoming detached from the Land Rover. Clearly, the farmer had been supplied with a coupling which was not reasonably fit for the purpose for which he had indicated he wanted it. Nevertheless, he was unable, on the the basis of that breach of condition, to claim from the seller any of the damage and losses which the farmer suffered in the accident. Once it had become apparent to the farmer that the locking mechanism was broken, that brought to an end the seller's obligation that the coupling continue to be reasonably fit for its purpose.

Relationship Between Sections 14(2) and 14(3)

7–027   The relationship between the implied terms as to quality and fitness for purpose has recently been considered by the Court of Appeal. In *Jewson Ltd v Boyhan (as Personal Representative*

---

[77] See *Bartlett v Sydney Marcus* above.
[78] [1975] 1 W.L.R. 30.
[79] [1905] 1 K.B. 608.
[80] Similarly, it is no defence to show that levels of a prohibited additive were (i) undetectable at the time of the contract, and (ii) were not hazardous to health: *Hazlewood Grocery Ltd v Lion Foods Ltd* [2007] All E.R. (D) 433 (Jul) (sale of chilli-powder with a banned food dye. The court was also prepared to find that the chilli-powder was not of satisfactory quality).
[81] [1982] A.C. 225.

of Thomas Michael Kelly)[82] Kelly purchased twelve electric boilers from Jewson, a builders' merchant, to be installed in a property Kelly was developing. Prior to the sale, Kelly met with the sellers and also representatives from Amptec, the manufacturers of the boiler in question. At the meeting, the Amptec representative produced promotional literature, detailing the nature and performance of the boiler, including, inter alia, its efficiency and its ability to provide "affordable warmth". Following the installation of the boilers, all of which worked satisfactorily, Kelly refused to pay, arguing that the sellers had breached ss.14(2) and 14(3) as the energy efficiency rating of the boilers was such that the flats were unsaleable. At first instance, the court held that the boilers were not of satisfactory quality[83]:

> "The fact that the boilers intrinsically worked satisfactorily was not sufficient for them to be of satisfactory quality since a reasonable person would have said that a new form of electric boiler claiming to provide efficient low-cost heating in residential dwellings ought to be capable of being shown to meet such a claim within the tests or procedures then prevailing or if not why not."

The Court of Appeal reversed this decision, however, finding that since an objective assessment of the quality of the goods would lead to the conclusion that the boilers were of satisfactory quality, there was no breach of s.14(2). Furthermore, since Kelly had not communicated any requirement to Jewson Ltd of boilers which would receive high energy efficiency rating, there was no breach of s.14(3). In fact neither Kelly, nor Jewson Ltd were aware of the SAP tests (the government energy efficiency tests). Sedley L.J. explained that[84]:

> "Section 14(2) is directed principally to the sale of substandard goods. This means that the Court's principal concern is to look at their intrinsic quality, using the tests indicated in subss. (2A), (2B) and (2C). Of these, it can be seen that the tests postulated in pars. (a) and (d) of subs. (2B), and perhaps others too, may well require regard to be had to extrinsic factors. These will typically have to do with the predictable use of the goods. But the issue is still their quality".

Moreover, "factors peculiar to the purposes of the particular buyer", i.e. the need for a boiler with a high energy efficiency rating, was a matter for s.14(3), and therefore requires communication to the seller in order that the seller may exercise reasonable skill and judgment in assessing whether the proposed goods would be suitable for that specific purpose.

SAMPLE—SECTION 15

Section 15 provides: **7–028**

> "(1) A contract of sale is a contract for sale by sample where there is an express or implied term to that effect in the contract.

---

[82] [2004] 1 Lloyd's Rep. 505.
[83] *Jewson Ltd v Kelly* [2002] EWHC 2515 at [82]. For a commentary of the first instance decision, see "Sale of Goods—Satisfactory Quality and Fitness for Purpose" *Consumer Law Today* 26 1 (1).
[84] [2002] EWHC 2515 at [77].

(2) In the case of a contract for sale by sample there is an implied term—

    (a) that the bulk will correspond with the sample in quality;

    (b) ...

    (c) that the goods will be free from any defect, making their quality unsatisfactory, which would not be apparent on reasonable examination of the sample."

Section 15 applies only if there is a term of the contract that it is a contract of sale by sample. In the case of a written contract the sale will be by sample only if that is included in the writing. Merely exhibiting a sample during the negotiations will not make it a sale by sample unless the parties agree that it is a sale by sample. In *Drummond v Van Ingen*,[85] Lord Macnaghten explained the function of a sample[86]:

> "The office of a sample is to present to the eye the real meaning and intention of the parties with regard to the subject-matter of the contract which, owing to the imperfection of language, it may be difficult or impossible to express in words. The sample speaks for itself."

The term in s.15(2) is a condition. Under s.15(2)(a) it is no defence that the bulk can easily be made to correspond with the sample. In *E & S Ruben v Faire Bros.*[87] Linatex was sold which was crinkly, whereas the sample was soft. The seller was liable even though, by a simple process of warming, the bulk could have been made soft.

The buyer cannot complain under s.15(2)(c) of defects which he could have reasonably have discovered on an examination of the sample. This is similar to the position under s.14(2) above.

REMEDIES

7–029 For breach by the seller of any term of the contract, the buyer can sue for damages. In the case of a breach of condition the buyer normally has the additional right to reject the goods and recover the price. The buyer however may lose the right to reject the goods either by waiver of that right or by "acceptance" of the goods. "Acceptance" has a technical meaning. This, together with a buyer's remedies for breach of contract, will be explained in Chapter 13.

General Reading

7–030   • Bridge, "Sale of Goods in Scotland—a second tender: *J&H Ritchie Ltd v Lloyd Ltd*" [2007] J.B.L. 814;

---

[85] [1887] App. Cas. 284.
[86] [1887] App. Cas. 284 at 297.
[87] [1949] 1 K.B. 254.

- Bridge, "The Sale and Supply of Goods Act 1994" [1995] J.B.L. 398;

- Davenport, "United Kingdom: Changes in the Quality Terms Implied into Contracts for the Sale and Supply of Goods" (1995) 3 J.I.B.F.L. 140;

- Ervine, "Satisfactory Quality: what does it mean?" [2004] J.B.L. 684;

- Mitchell, "The Development of Quality Obligations in Sale of Goods" (2001) 117 L.Q.R. 645.

Chapter 8

SUPPLY OF GOODS AND SERVICES ACT 1982

This Act is mainly concerned with certain types of contract which are not contracts of sale of goods. Nevertheless, some of these contracts are closely related to sale of goods ones, and much of the law in the Act is modelled on parts of the Sale of Goods Act. Furthermore, some of the Act's provisions (ss.12–16) will apply to certain contracts of sale of goods, i.e. where these contracts involve also the provision of some service or services. For these reasons a full account of the 1982 Act is given here. In this chapter references to sections are to sections of the 1982 Act unless otherwise stated. The Act consists of three sets of implied terms. Each set is implied in a defined category of contracts. The extent to which the parties can contract out of these terms will be explained in Chapter 10.[1]

8–001

THE FIRST SET—CONTRACTS FOR THE TRANSFER OF GOODS

The first set of implied terms (ss.2–5) applies, with certain exceptions, to contracts which are not contracts of sale of goods[2] or hire-purchase[3] but where nevertheless one person transfers, or agrees to transfer, property (ownership) in the goods to another.[4] The main kinds of contracts affected are contracts of exchange or barter (which are not contracts of sale of goods because they lack a *money* consideration) and contracts (e.g. of repair) where, although some goods are supplied, the substance of contract is the provision of services. Customers under such contracts are given rights in relation to title, description, quality and sample which are identical to those conferred by the Sale of Goods Act upon a buyer under a sale of goods

8–002

---

[1] At para.10–031, below.
[2] s.1(2)(a).
[3] s.1(2)(b).
[4] s.1(1) lays down the broad ambit of the first set of implied terms by defining the concept of a "contract for the transfer of goods" as a "contract under which one person transfers or agrees to transfer to another the property in goods, other than an excepted contract".

contract. The first set of implied terms consists of terms as to: title, freedom from encumbrances and quiet possession (s.2); description (s.3); satisfactory quality and fitness for purpose (s.4)[5]; and sample (s.5). These terms relate to the goods supplied and are implied in identical circumstances and are identical in effect as the terms implied by ss.12–15 of the Sale of Goods Act.

Even though the implied terms in ss.2–5 of the 1982 Act are identical to those in ss.12–15 of the Sale of Goods Act[6], it still may be necessary to distinguish between on the one hand a contract governed by ss.2–5 of the 1982 Act and on the other a contract of sale of goods. Two particular reasons spring to mind. First, the doctrine of "acceptance" (see para.13–005 below) applies only to sale of goods contracts. The result is that a customer under, say, a contract of barter, may have longer in which to reject the goods for a breach of condition than does a buyer under a sale of goods contract. In this respect all non-sale of goods contracts are the same, i.e. the question whether the customer has lost his right to reject the goods for breach of condition is determined not by whether he has "accepted" the goods but by whether he has affirmed the contract.[7] The second reason for distinguishing between sale of goods contracts and others is that the Sale of Goods Act applies only to contracts of sale of goods and the Supply of Goods and Services Act 1982 does not contain provisions corresponding to any other than ss.12–15 of the Sale of Goods Act. So, for example, there are no statutory rules relating to the passing of property and risk under a contract of barter. It is therefore a matter of common law and there is not much English case law on the matter. Consider now some different types of contract.

Collateral Contracts which are not Contracts of Sale of Goods

8–003   It will be remembered that if there is no money consideration, a contract will not be a sale of goods contract. Hence, in *Esso v Commissioners of Customs and Excise*,[8] although there was a contract of sale of goods in relation to the petrol, the collateral contract relating to the World Cup coin was not a contract of sale of goods. It is difficult, perhaps, to imagine a dispute about title, description, quality or sample arising in relation to a World Cup coin. Consider, however, the situation where an electrical retailer advertises that with every refrigerator sold in November a free electric toaster will be supplied. According to the reasoning in the *Esso* case, the advertisement is an offer (i.e. to supply a toaster). A member of the public can accept that offer during November by entering a contract to buy a refrigerator from the retailer. The consideration given by the customer for the toaster is not money but is the entering of the contract to buy the refrigerator. The result is that if the *toaster* is not of satisfactory quality the customer's claim is under s.4 of the Supply of Goods and Services Act, but if the *refrigerator* is not of satisfactory quality then his claim is under s.14 of the Sale of Goods Act. In the latter case the buyer could exercise his right to reject

---

[5] See generally, Davenport, "United Kingdom: Changes in the Quality Terms Implied into Contracts for the Sale and Supply of Goods" (1995) 3 J.I.B.F.L. 140.

[6] Note also, that the new s.5A, inserted by the Sale and Supply of Goods Act 1994, duplicates the modification of remedies in non-consumer cases (minor breach of condition to be treated as a breach of warranty) as found in the Sale of Goods Act, s.15A.

[7] For a discussion of the doctrine of affirmation in relation to hire-purchase agreements, see para.23–016, below.

[8] [1976] 1 W.L.R. 1. See para.1–008, above.

the refrigerator for breach of condition and then recover the price on a total failure of consideration. He would still presumably be entitled to retain the toaster which he obtained under a separate collateral contract. If, however, the toaster and not the refrigerator had been of less than satisfactory quality, then there would be no point in rejecting the toaster for breach of condition, since under the contract (i.e. the one relating to the toaster) no price was payable by the customer and therefore none would be recoverable. Nevertheless, the customer could of course sue for damages.

Contracts of Barter or Exchange

Where goods are swapped for other goods, then there is no contract of sale of goods, since there is no *money* consideration. What, however, about the situation where goods are swapped for a combination of money and other goods? This problem typically occurs where goods are part-exchanged or "traded in". For example, a customer buying a new car with a cash price of £5,000 might get the garage to allow him £500 part-exchange allowance on his old car. In this case there is still a contract of sale of the new car because there is for it a money consideration (of £4,500): *Dawson v Dutfield.*[9] The position is still the same even if the part-exchange allowance is for most or nearly all of the price—say, in our example, £4,800—because there is still a money consideration, albeit a small one.[10] Thus, if the new car proves not to match the description by which it was sold or not to be of satisfactory quality the customer's claim is founded on ss.13 or 14 of the Sale of Goods Act. **8–004**

Consider now the traded-in car. At first sight it appears that there is no money consideration given by the garage for the traded-in car. However, it is usual in the car trade for a value to be agreed for the traded-in car as well as for the new car, i.e. the trade-in allowance is a precise stated figure (e.g. £500). In this case it may be correct to regard the traded-in car, not as being exchanged or bartered towards the new car, but as sold for £500, which sum the customer uses towards payment for his new car. Looked at in this way, the whole transaction between the garage and the customer is not a sale of a new car and a part-exchange (or barter) of the old but represents a sale of each. In *Aldridge v Johnson*[11] barley valued at £215 was sold in return for £23 and bullocks valued at £192. The court considered that, each set of goods having been allocated a price, there were mutual sales. It seems to follow that if X agrees to swap his coat for Y's jacket, there is a contract of barter, but if in making the contract they allocate a value or price of say, £20 to each item, there would be mutual sales.

Contracts where Payment for Goods is Made by Cheque, Trading Check, Credit Card, or other Voucher

Are these contracts of sale of goods or are they contracts under which the customer gives no money consideration? Clearly, where the payment is by cheque, the contract is one of sale of **8–005**

[9] [1936] 2 All E.R. 232. See para.1–007, above.
[10] *Aldridge v Johnson* [1857] 26 L.J.Q.B. 296.
[11] [1857] 26 L.J.Q.B. 296.

goods. Indeed, s.38 of the Sale of Goods Act expressly contemplates this possibility. If the cheque bounces (i.e. is dishonoured), the seller will be able to sue for the price because acceptance of payment by cheque will have been conditional (i.e. upon the cheque being honoured).

Where a trading check is used to pay for goods, the contract is also one of sale of goods: *Davies v Commissioners of Customs and Excise.*[12] With a trading check, although the buyer does not actually hand over any cash, he does hand over something having an agreed cash value (i.e. agreed between himself and the seller). Just as it is sale of goods when a customer trades in a car in part exchange for another, so it is a sale of goods when a retailer supplies goods in return for a trading check. In each case the seller (i.e. the customer trading in his car and the retailer providing the goods in return for the trading check) receives no actual cash, but he receives something having an agreed cash value. The same can be said where payment is made by means of a credit (or charge) card. The seller, in accepting payment by the card, is taking something having an agreed cash value. Therefore, provided that the commodity being bought is goods (as opposed to services) the contract between seller and buyer is one of sale of goods. This is so despite the fact that the contract is in one respect different from that where payment is made by cheque. Where payment is made by means of a credit (or charge) card, that is an absolute, not a conditional, payment: *Re Charge Card Services Ltd.*[13] Thus if the card company fails to pay the seller, e.g. because the card company is insolvent, the seller is not entitled to recover payment from the card holder.[14]

Where a voucher, other than a trading check or credit card, is used (e.g. a book-token) there is no case law telling us into which category the contract falls. Where the voucher is used together with cash to buy goods, clearly there is a sale of goods contract. Where the voucher alone is used, presumably the same reasoning used in the last paragraph will apply. Thus, where, as in the case of a book-token, the voucher is used as having an agreed cash value (i.e. as a cash equivalent), the contract is one of sale of goods. Record-tokens and shop gift vouchers would come into this category also. Imagine, however, an offer on top of a soap powder packet, "Send three coupons for a free teddy bear", there being a coupon printed on the side of each soap powder packet. The customer who sends his coupons and obtains the teddy bear, obtains it, not under a sale of goods contract, but under a contract of barter or exchange, because the coupons are not used as representing any particular cash value. If the teddy bear infringes one of the implied conditions, e.g. is not of satisfactory quality, then the customer's claim lies under ss.2–5 of the 1982 Act.

Contracts for Work with Materials Supplied

8–006   Where the main purpose or "substance" of the contract is the provision of services, then it is not a sale of goods contract even though there is to be a transfer of ownership in some goods. Two examples are construction contracts (where the customer will become the owner of the bricks and tiles etc. used) and repair contracts (where the customer will become owner of any spare parts used). In these cases the first set of implied terms in the 1982 Act will apply

[12] [1975] 1 W.L.R. 204.
[13] [1988] 3 W.L.R. 723.
[14] Accounts of how trading checks and credit cards work are given at paras 18–025 and 18–026 below.

in relation to the *goods* supplied under the contract. Suppose an electrician is called in to repair the television and suppose that shortly afterwards the television breaks down again. This could be due to (i) faulty replacement parts fitted by the electrician, or (ii) failure to exercise due care and skill by the electrician, or (iii) some other reason, such as failure of some other part in the television. Only if it is the first of these will the customer have a claim under the first set of implied terms in the 1982 Act. If his claim relates not to the goods but to the quality of service provided, then the relevant law is that contained in the third set of implied terms in the 1982 Act.[15]

Sometimes goods are used (i.e. consumed) by someone in the course of providing a service. An example is the use of shampoo or hair-dye by a hairdresser. In cases such as this, there is no transfer to the customer of property (ownership) in the goods. Thus the contract is not governed either by the Sale of Goods Act or by the first set of implied terms in the 1982 Act. In these cases, although there are no *statutory* implied terms relating to the goods, it seems that similar terms are implied at common law: *Ingham v Emes*.[16] So, if for example the hair-dye is not of merchantable (i.e. satisfactory) quality and makes the customer's hair fall out, she will have a common law claim.

Excepted Contracts

The first set of terms in the 1982 Act is implied in any contract where one person transfers   **8–007** or agrees to transfer property (ownership) in goods to another.[17] There are, however, four categories of contract which are excepted from that.[18] The first two are contracts of sale of goods and hire-purchase contracts. The reason for these exceptions is that both categories are governed by its own set of statutory implied terms. The relevant statutory provisions are as follows: in the case of sale of goods contracts, ss.12–15 of the Sale of Goods Act 1979 and in the case of hire-purchase agreements, ss.8–11 of the Supply of Goods (Implied Terms) Act 1973.[19] The two other excepted contracts are, first, where the property is transferred under a deed (covenant) gratuitously made and, secondly, any contract intended to operate by way of mortgage, pledge, charge or any other security.[20]

THE SECOND SET—CONTRACTS OF HIRE

A contract of hire is a contract of bailment. Under it, the hirer (the bailee) obtains possession   **8–008** but not property (i.e. not ownership). Since there is no transfer, or agreement to transfer, property (ownership) to the hirer, the first set of implied terms in the 1982 Act is not implied in a hire contract. Sections 6–10 of the Supply of Goods and Services Act 1982 apply to

[15] See para.8–009, below.
[16] [1955] 2 Q.B. 366.
[17] s.1(1).
[18] s.1(2).
[19] See para.23–008, below.
[20] Until April 6, 2005 there was a further category of excepted contracts, namely where property in goods was obtained in exchange for trading stamps. This was repealed by the Regulatory Reform (Trading Stamps) Order (SI 2005/871) and such contracts are now governed by the 1982 Act. Where, however, a combination of cash and trading stamps are used the Sale of Goods Act 1979 will apply.

contracts of hire, other than hire-purchase agreements. The intention behind them is to imply in hire contracts, terms similar to those implied in sale of goods contracts by ss.12–15 of the Sale of Goods Act. In fact the implied terms as to description,[21] satisfactory quality and fitness for purpose[22] and sample[23] are identical in effect to the corresponding Sale of Goods Act provisions. Section 7 of the 1982 Act contains: (i) a condition as to title, namely that the bailor has (or, in the case of an agreement to bail in the future, will have) a right to transfer possession to the bailee (hirer) for the period of the hire; and (ii) a warranty of quiet possession during the period of hire, except in so far as the bailee's (hirer's) possession may be disturbed by someone entitled to the benefit of any charge or encumbrance disclosed or known to the bailee (hirer) before the contract.

THE THIRD SET—CONTRACTS FOR SERVICES

8–009 The third set of terms is implied into any contract where one party (the supplier) has agreed to carry out any service (whether or not he has also agreed to supply goods). By way of exception, however, these terms are not implied in any contract of employment or apprenticeship. It is clear that these terms are implied not only in contracts where the supply of service is the substance of the contract but also in contracts of hire and sale of goods where, although the substance of the contract is the hire or transfer of ownership of goods, there is nevertheless an undertaking by the seller that he will provide a service (e.g. of installing the goods). These terms are implied by the Supply of Goods and Services Act 1982, ss.13–15:

> "13 In a contract for the supply of a service where the supplier is acting in the course of a business, there is an implied term that the supplier will carry out the service with reasonable care and skill.
> 14(1) Where, under a contract for the supply of a service by a supplier acting in the course of a business, the time for the service to be carried out is not fixed by the contract, left to be fixed in a manner agreed by the contract or determined by the course of dealing between the parties, there is an implied term that the supplier will carry out the service within a reasonable time.
> (2) What is a reasonable time is a question of fact.
> 15(1) Where, under a contract for the supply of a service, the consideration for the service is not determined by the contract, left to be determined in a manner agreed by the contract or determined by the course of dealing between the parties, there is an implied term that the party contracting with the supplier will pay a reasonable charge.
> (2) What is a reasonable charge is a question of fact."

The Secretary of State has power by statutory instrument to exclude one or more of the terms in the third set from applying to specified services. One such exclusion order has so far been made, excluding s.13 from applying to:

[21] s.8.
[22] s.9.
[23] s.10.

"(i) the services of an advocate in court or before any tribunal, inquiry or arbitrator and in carrying out preliminary work directly affecting the conduct of the hearing; and

(ii) the services rendered to a company by a director of a company in his capacity as such."

The first of these was to prevent s.13 sweeping away the immunity from an action in negligence conferred upon advocates (notably solicitors) by the decision in *Rondel v Worsley*.[24] The exclusion order was not necessary in order to preserve the immunity of barristers because a barrister does not have a contractual relationship with his client and therefore s.13 would not apply to him anyway. The immunity for advocates has since been removed by the decision in *Arthur JS Hall & Co v Simons*.[25]

The third set of terms does not apply to contracts of employment. The exclusion of s.13 from applying to the services of a director is thus necessary in order to prevent it discriminating unfairly against non-employed directors. If s.13 had applied to directors it would have imposed on them an objective standard of care. That would have been a rather higher standard of care than the law in fact imposes upon directors.

[24] [1969] 1 A.C. 191.
[25] *The Times*, July 2, 2000.

Chapter 9

PRODUCT LIABILITY

A manufacturer of a defective product may find himself liable on any one of a number of grounds. There are five principal grounds which this chapter shall consider. It is important to realise that each ground has both advantages and disadvantages and moreover, multiple grounds may be applicable on the facts. For example, broadly speaking, in a case of a defective product that injures the consumer purchaser, both the implied terms of the Sale of Goods Act and the provisions of Pt I of the Consumer Protection Act 1987 may well apply. In such a situation the buyer will be able to pursue either the manufacturer (under the Consumer Protection Act) or the retailer (under the Sale of Goods Act).[1]

9–001

THE CONTRACT OF SALE

Like any other seller of goods, a manufacturer can be liable for a breach of a term of his contract of sale. This liability benefits only the immediate purchaser from the manufacturer, because liability for breach of contract exists only between parties to the same contract. In the case of direct marketing, the immediate purchaser may be the actual consumer. Where goods are marketed via wholesaler and retailer the person who buys the goods from the retailer cannot complain that the manufacturer was in breach of his contract of sale with the wholesaler. He can of course sue upon his own contract of sale, i.e. sue the retailer. The implied terms in ss.12–15 of the Sale of Goods Act are often seen, and correctly so, as important safeguards for the consumer. Nevertheless one must remember that, although they enhance the purchaser's contractual rights against his seller, they do not confer upon him any rights against other persons. Indeed, if X buys goods and passes them as a gift to Y, those implied terms are of no benefit at all to Y, unless the contract purports to confer that benefit

9–002

[1] See, for example, *Ide v ATB Sales Ltd* [2007] EWHC 1667, where the Consumer Protection Act was used rather than the seemingly more straightforward claim under s.14(2) of the Sale of Goods Act. See para.7–016, above.

upon him thereby enabling him to rely on the Contracts (Rights of Third Parties) Act 1999.[2]

There is another way, assignment, by which Y can be given the benefit of the purchaser's (X's) rights against the seller. The most effective way of doing this is for X to comply with the provisions of s.136 of the Law of Property Act 1925, i.e. to give Y a written notice, signed by X, unconditionally assigning to Y all X's rights as buyer under the contract of sale.[3] X can do this at the time of giving goods to Y or at any later stage. Of course in transferring his rights to Y, X is losing them himself. The consent of the seller is not needed for such an assignment. However, X cannot, without the seller's consent, assign his burdens under the contract (i.e. the obligation to pay).

COLLATERAL CONTRACT OR GUARANTEE

9–003   Where goods are marketed indirectly and the manufacturer therefore does not sell directly to the consumer, it can nevertheless happen that the manufacturer makes a collateral contract with the consumer. The classic case of this was *Carlill v Carbolic Smoke Ball Co*[4] where the defendants published an advertisement claiming that their product was a cure and pre-ventative of any number of illnesses. In particular, the company promised in the advertise-ment to pay £100 to anyone who contracted influenza after using a carbolic smoke ball as instructed for a specified period. Mrs Carlill saw the advertisement, purchased a smoke ball, used it as instructed for the specified period and nevertheless caught 'flu. Although she had not bought the smoke ball from the company, it was held that there was a contract between her and the company, albeit not a contract of sale. A contract is a bargain and the bargain was that the company made her the promise in the advertisement and she in return bought one of their smoke balls from a retailer. The company made her an offer in the advertisement which she accepted by buying a smoke ball from the retailer.

It can be seen then that manufacturers' "guarantees" (or "warranties") often form the basis of a contract between manufacturer and customer similar to that in *Carlill v Carbolic Smoke Ball Co*.[5] It is true that often they do not specify a sum of money and sometimes may contain many qualifications. Nevertheless, if a guarantee promise (e.g. "The goods are warranted to be in perfect condition on leaving the factory") is broken, then the manufacturer is liable, subject to the qualifications in the guarantee. An example of such a qualification might occur where a manufacturer promises to refund the purchase price "provided the goods are first returned carriage paid to manufacturer".

Sometimes a guarantee does more than qualify the benefits which it gives. It may take away or qualify other rights of the consumer which are quite independent of the guarantee. In particular it may claim to restrict or remove the consumer's ability to bring an action for negligence.[6] This may be achieved by some clause in the guarantee such as "Apart from his obligations under the terms of this guarantee, the manufacturer shall not be liable for any loss

---

[2] See para.7–003 above.
[3] See, for example, Curwen, "The problems of transferring carriage rights: an equitable solution" [1992] J.B.L. 245.
[4] [1893] 1 Q.B. 256.
[5] [1893] 1 Q.B. 256.
[6] See para.9–005, below.

however arising". This type of guarantee was in the past commonly created by the manufacturer supplying with the goods a reply paid postcard which the purchaser was asked to fill
in and post, thereby accepting the terms. Now, by virtue of s.5 of the Unfair Contract Terms
Act 1977, a clause in the manufacturer's or distributor's guarantee cannot operate to exclude
or restrict the manufacturer's or distributor's liability to the consumer.[7] This is so provided
three conditions are all satisfied:

   (i) the goods are of a type ordinarily supplied for private use or consumption;

   (ii) they prove defective whilst "in consumer use" (i.e. not used exclusively for the
        purposes of a business);

   (iii) the manufacturer or distributor in question is not also the person who sold the
         goods to the consumer.

This last point seems to suggest that where the consumer buys the goods direct from the
manufacturer, the manufacturer is free to exclude his liability. However, this is not necessarily so. In that case, although s.5 of the Unfair Contract Terms Act will not apply, other
sections of the same Act are most likely to apply and to prevent the seller from excluding his
liability. These other sections will be considered in Chapter 10.

Any question mark as to the validity of such guarantees at common law has now been   **9–004**
removed by the Sale and Supply of Goods to Consumers Regulations 2002[8] which implemented the European Directive on Consumer Guarantees.[9] Consequently any guarantee
offered by, for example, the manufacturer, will be legally enforceable.[10] Regulation 2 defines
"consumer guarantee" in the following terms:

   "any undertaking to a consumer by a person acting in the course of his business, given
   without extra charge, to reimburse the price paid or to replace, repair or handle
   consumer goods in any way if they do not meet the specifications set out in the
   guarantee statement or in the relevant advertising".

Two key points must be noted here. First, the scope of the Regulations is limited to
consumer contracts as defined in reg.2 as "any natural person who . . . is acting for purposes
which are outside his trade, business or profession".[11] Secondly, the application of the
Regulations to consumer guarantees extends only to guarantees freely given. So it is of no
application to extended warranties where consideration will be provided.[12]

NEGLIGENCE

Donoghue v Stevenson[13] was a landmark in legal development. The House of Lords estab-   **9–005**
lished the principle that a consumer who suffers damage because of a manufacturer's

---

[7] See, however, the proposed Unfair Contract Terms Bill which, if enacted, will remove s.5 of UCTA. See the
discussion at para.10–040 onwards, below.
[8] SI 2002/3045.
[9] Directive 1999/44.
[10] reg.15(1).
[11] This definition is discussed below at para.10–018.
[12] See Willett, Morgan-Taylor and Naidoo, "The Sale and Supply of Goods to Consumers Regulations" [2004]
J.B.L. 94, 115–116.
[13] [1932] A.C. 562.

negligence can sue the latter for damages and can do so irrespective of whether the consumer bought the goods. Mrs Donoghue and a friend went into a café where the friend bought for Mrs Donoghue a bottle of ginger beer, manufactured by Stevenson, and Mrs Donoghue drank some. When the remainder was poured out, she noticed that the bottle contained two half-decomposing snails. She suffered some shock as well as some gastro-enteritis.

From the consumer's point of view, there is a considerable drawback to an action in negligence; they have to prove that the manufacturer (or one or more of their employees) was negligent. This involves showing that reasonable care was not taken in the manufacture. This can be difficult because the consumer has no means of knowing what goes on (or went on) in the factory. Sometimes it may seem obvious that there must have been negligence, as in the case of the purchaser of a bath bun who found a stone in the middle of it.[14] In such a case, the facts may be said to speak for themselves—res ipsa loquitur. Then it is up to the manufacturer to prove that there was no negligence, i.e. that all reasonable care was taken. In *Chaproniere v Mason*[15] the manufacturer brought evidence to show that he had a safe system of operations such as to prevent alien matter entering the food. The court held that this did not show an absence of negligence since someone must have been careless in not following the proper system. The manufacturer was therefore liable.

A similar situation arose in *Daniels v White*[16] where some carbolic acid got into a bottle of lemonade. The manufacturer brought evidence that he had a safe system of operating and adequate supervision to ensure that the system was followed. Here it was held that this showed that all reasonable care had been taken. The manufacturer was therefore not liable. However, the reasoning behind the decision in *Daniels v White* seems questionable. If there was in operation a good system to prevent alien matter entering the lemonade then someone who worked there must have been very negligent if the alien matter got in despite the system. An employer is answerable for the negligence of their employees. Therefore in *Daniels v White*[17] it would seem that the employer (the defendant) ought to have been held liable. The decision has been criticised and in *Hill v James Crowe*[18] MacKenna J. refused to follow it.

9-006   It should be pointed out that an action in negligence is not restricted to shock and personal injuries but may also include damage to property or even sometimes purely financial loss.

It should also be pointed out that *Donoghue v Stevenson*[19] established a principle of wider application than it may so far have appeared. Anyone (whether he is a manufacturer or not) who ought to appreciate that his acts or omissions may well cause harm to another may be liable to that other for any damage caused by his negligence in carrying on those activities.

Suppose a manufacturer of catapults sells some to a wholesaler, who sells some to a retailer who in turn sells one to a young boy. Suppose also that, because it has a latent defect, the catapult is not of satisfactory quality and that it breaks in use and injures the boy's eye as a result. The boy will no doubt succeed in his claim for breach of contract against the retailer,

---

[14] *Chaproniere v Mason* (1905) 21 T.L.R. 633.
[15] (1905) 21 T.L.R. 633.
[16] [1938] 160 L.T. 128.
[17] [1938] 160 L.T. 128.
[18] [1978] I.C.R. 298.
[19] [1932] A.C. 562.

as will the retailer succeed against the wholesaler and the wholesaler against the manufacturer: *Godley v Perry*.[20] The retailer's claim against the wholesaler is a claim for indemnity. This simply means that retailer is entitled to claim from the wholesaler (as damages for breach of contract) the whole amount which the retailer is himself liable to pay his buyer. That is the amount of the retailer's loss arising from the wholesaler's breach of contract. On the same reasoning the wholesaler is entitled to indemnity from the manufacturer. In this way, liability is passed back up the chain of distribution. What if there is a blockage in the process? This could happen if, for example, the wholesaler has gone out of business or if in the contract between the wholesaler and the retailer there is a valid exemption clause which prevents the wholesaler being liable to the retailer. In this case, the retailer is liable to his buyer, the boy, but now has no contract under which he can recover indemnity. We have already seen that if the defect was due to the negligence of the manufacturer, the boy could himself have sued the manufacturer directly for negligence. That, however, is not much use to the retailer if the boy has chosen instead to sue the retailer for breach of contract. In *Lambert v Lewis*[21] Lord Diplock suggested that in that case someone down the chain of distribution who suffers economic loss (i.e. because he has to pay out damages for breach of contract), might well be able to claim indemnity direct from the negligent manufacturer under the principle in *Donoghue v Stevenson*.[22]

PRODUCT LIABILITY

From the customer's point of view, the drawback to the implied terms in the Sale of Goods **9–007**
Act is that only the buyer can sue the seller. If someone other than the buyer was injured by the goods, the Sale of Goods Act gives him no rights—other than in the exceptional case where the Contracts (Rights of Third Parties) Act 1999 applies.[23] A claim in negligence, on the other hand, can be brought by any consumer. The drawback to this claim is that the defendant (usually the manufacturer) must be shown to have been negligent. Part I of the Consumer Protection Act 1987 implemented the Product Liability Directive[24] and gives the consumer an additional right to make a claim which is free of both these drawbacks. Under this Act, anyone who is injured by a defective product can sue the manufacturer, irrespective of whether the manufacturer was negligent. Damage caused to non-business property can be claimed if it exceeds £275 in value. In giving this right, the Act does not remove or alter any other rights of the consumer, e.g. under the Sale of Goods Act or the law of negligence.

Basis of the Claim—Section 2

To succeed under Pt I of the Consumer Protection Act, the claimant must establish four **9–008**
things, namely that:

[20] [1960] 1 W.L.R. 9.
[21] [1982] A.C. 225.
[22] [1932] A.C. 562.
[23] See para.7–003, above.
[24] 85/374/EEC.

(a) a *product* contained a *defect*;

(b) the claimant suffered *damage*;

(c) the damage was caused by the defect;

(d) the defendant was *producer*, *own-brander* or *importer* into the European Community (or, sometimes, supplier of the product).

Meaning of "Defect"

9–009 A product is defective "if the safety of the product is not such as persons generally are entitled to expect".[25] Safety includes safety in the context of risks of damage to property as well as in the context of death or personal injury. Thus new furniture would be defective if it contained live woodworm, even though the presence of the woodworm posed no threat of personal injury. Safety is a relative, not an absolute, concept. A sharp kitchen knife cannot be made absolutely safe if it is to be any use as a kitchen knife. If, however, it were marketed as a child's toy or the blade were such that when used to peel potatoes it disintegrated into splinters, then it would not be as safe as people generally were entitled to expect. Thus s.3(2) provides that in determining whether a product is defective all the circumstances are to be taken into account, including:

"(a) the manner in which, and purposes for which, the product has been marketed, its get-up, the use of any mark in relation to the product and any instructions for, or warnings with respect to, doing or refraining from doing anything with or in relation to the product[26];

(b) what might reasonably be expected to be done with or in relation to the product; and

(c) the time when the product was supplied by its producer to another."

As in the knife example earlier, the marketing and/or labelling will affect the use as to which the product is likely to be put. Something advertised as a toy is likely to be used by children. If something is advertised and sold as a hover-mower, is it reasonable to expect it to be used as a hedge-trimmer? If not, then it is not defective just because it is dangerous when used in that way.

Public expectations as to safety are to be judged as at the time the *producer* supplied the product in question. A producer is not required to meet expectations of safety which arise after *they* have supplied the product. Suppose manufacturer A has for some years produced a razor which will not normally cut the user unless it is slid sideways across the skin. Suppose

---

[25] s.3(1). The fundamental distinction therefore, is that between dangerous goods and those which are merely shoddy. Pt I of the CPA operates only in respect to the former category.

[26] As to the relationship between "defect" and warnings supplied with the product, see *Worsley v Tambrands Ltd* [2000] P.I.Q.R. 95. In *Worsley* the court held that there was no liability (under either CPA or the common law) since the producer had done what the consumer was "entitled to expect: (1) they had a clearly legible warning on the outside of the box directing the user to the leaflet; (2) the leaflet was legible, literate, and unambiguous and contained all the material necessary to convey both the warning signs and the action required if any of them were present . . . ", at 103.

that in May 2001 manufacturer B markets a razor which is equally efficient but which will not normally cut the user, even when slid sideways. Imagine that a razor supplied by manufacturer A in February 2000 is bought from a retailer in June 2001 and when used in July 2001 cuts the user's face when slid sideways across it. The fact that manufacturer B produced a safer razor after the razor in question had been supplied by manufacturer A is not enough to enable us to say that manufacturer A's razor was defective. If, however, another user is cut by a razor which manufacturer A supplied after May 2001, this user can point to the safer design of manufacturer B's razor as evidence that the razor which cut him was not as safe as persons were (at the time manufacturer A supplied it) entitled to expect.

The courts have considered the definition of "defective". The leading case is that of *A v National Blood Authority (No.1)*[27] which concerned the claims of 114 claimants for recovery of damages arising out of their infection with Hepatitis C due to transfusions with contaminated blood. Leaving aside the issue of whether the state of the art defence applied to the facts, Burton J. had to determine whether the infected blood was defective under the Directive.[28] This issue was answered in the affirmative[29]:

"The blood products in this case were non-standard products, and were unsafe by virtue of the harmful characteristics which they had and which the standard products did not have".[30]

Therefore the presence of Hepatitis C within the blood constituted a defect since:

" . . . the public at large was entitled to expect that the blood transfused to them would be free from infection. There were no warnings and no material publicity, certainly none officially initiated by or for the benefit of the defendants, and the knowledge of the medical profession, not materially or at all shared with the consumer, is of no relevance. It is not material to consider whether any steps or any further steps could have been taken to avoid or palliate the risk that the blood would be infected."

This was so despite the facts: (i) that the defendant was unaware of the risk, and (ii) that **9–010** the medical profession was aware of the risk, since the issue was one of the legitimate expectations of the public.[31] In determining the meaning of "defect" in non-standard products, Burton J. suggested that the following issues were not relevant[32]:

(i) Avoidability of the harmful characteristic;

(ii) The impracticality, cost or difficulty of taking such measures;

[27] [2001] 3 All E.R. 289.
[28] Burton J. dealt with the issue of "defect" under art.6 of the Directive and not its equivalent, s.3 of the Act. See the comments at [2] of the judgment.
[29] [2001] 3 All E.R. 1289 at [79].
[30] "A *non-standard* product is one which is different, obviously because it is deficient or inferior in terms of safety, from the standard product: and where it is the harmful characteristic or characteristics present in the non-standard product, but not in the standard product, which has or have caused the material injury or damage", [2001] 3 All E.R. 289 at [36].
[31] As ascertained by the court. See *B (A Child) v McDonald's Restaurants Ltd* [2002] EWHC 490.
[32] [2001] 3 All E.R. 289 at [68].

(iii) The benefit to society or utility of the product.[33]

The approach of Burton J. on this issue has been subject to considerable criticism. One frequent criticism stems from the use of "consumer expectation" particularly where the product is particularly complicated since it is highly likely that the public at large will have no expectations whatsoever. A further criticism is in Burton J.'s failure to accept the relevance of the cost-benefit analysis. As Goldberg puts it[34]:

> "There is a strong argument in favour of such an approach, particularly in the context of medicinal products including whole blood and other blood products. It is arguable that all medicinal products carry a risk of adverse reactions, even in a minority of consumers, and that these consumers are not necessarily entitled to expect that the products will be risk-free. Despite the emphasis on consumer expectation in Burton J.'s judgment, there is an inherent logic in addressing the problems of defective medicinal products, including blood and blood products, by weighing the risks against the antici-pated benefits and against the 'costs' of not using the product, such as the risk of disease."

Recent decisions have, however, demonstrated the difficulties faced by claimants in establishing that the product concerned was defective under s.3. In *Foster v Biosil*[35] the claimant sought damages under the Act when a breast implant ruptured within seven months following a double mastectomy. The court held that in order to succeed the claimant had to be able to show that (i) the goods were defective and (ii) how the defect had occurred. Since there was scientific evidence showing that implants rarely ruptured, the claimant failed to show that the goods were defective under s.3(1). Similarly, in *Richardson v LRC Products Ltd*[36] the claimant, Mrs Richardson, became pregnant after a condom failed and sued the manufacturer under Pt 1 of the Consumer Protection Act. Despite considerable (conflicting) scientific evidence the judge was unable to identify any reason for the condom failing and thus the question was whether the condom failing, in itself, led to the conclusion that the product was defective under s.3. Kennedy J. held that the condom was not defective simply by reason of the fact that it had fractured and failed. In so finding, he was persuaded by evidence that condoms do suffer from "inexplicable failures" and that the condoms had been manufactured to standards in excess of the relevant British Standard.[37] Whilst this last point is, by itself, irrelevant to the meaning of defect, it is clear that the decision makes the distinctions between what people *actually* expect as to the safety of products and what persons generally are *entitled* to expect. In the case of the condom, Kennedy J. accepted that "the user's expectation is that a condom will not fail" but found that they were not *entitled* to this expectation. This was so, since, "there are no claims made by the defendants that one will never fail and no-one has ever supposed that any method of contraception intended to

---

[33] These points essentially form a cost-benefit analysis.
[34] Goldberg, "Paying for bad blood: strict product liability after the hepatitis C litigation" [2002] Med. Law Rev. 165, 174.
[35] (2001) 59 B.M.L.R. 178.
[36] [2000] P.I.Q.R. 164.
[37] [2000] P.I.Q.R. 164 at 170–171.

defeat nature will be 100 per cent effective".[38] Accordingly, Mrs Richardson's claim failed.

There are indications, albeit only tentative, that the courts are starting to alleviate some of the difficulties faced by claimants relying upon the Consumer Protection Act. In *Ide v ATB Sales Ltd*[39] the claimant sought damages for personal injury when the handlebar on his mountain bike fractured injuring his head and causing significant brain damage. The defendant importer argued that the claimant had somehow lost control of the bike and that the handlebar was fractured as a result of this, rather than any defect within the product itself. The court was, however, satisfied that on the balance of the evidence produced, the handlebar was defective within s.3(1). This was so despite the fact that the bicycle was manufactured to British standards.[40] Moreover, there is no requirement for the claimant to show *how* the defect occurred as was suggested in *Foster v Biosil*.[41] Given the criticism of the analysis of "defect" in *A v National Blood Authority (No.1)*[42] it is unfortunate that much of the case law under Pt I of the Consumer Protection Act, including *Foster* and *ATB Sales*, considered the precise meaning of "defect" under s.3.[43]

9–011

Meaning of "Product"

The definition of product is very wide. Thus there is liability for defects in virtually anything which might conceivably be considered a product, including goods,[44] electricity, gas and vapours. There is an exception in the case of land.

9–012

Liability is imposed for defective goods, not for defective land. "Goods" include "things comprised in land by virtue of being attached to it".[45] A building is land. A builder will therefore not be liable under the Act for damage caused by a defect in the building because it was badly built, e.g. because the foundations were inadequate, though he might be liable under some other legal provision.[46] A brick or tile used in the construction of a building is a thing comprised in land by virtue of being attached to it. Therefore, if a tile, because it is defective, breaks and falls on to a passer-by, the manufacturer of the tile will be liable under the Act.

Under the Act as originally enacted, agricultural produce and game were excluded from liability unless it had undergone an "industrial process" giving it "essential characteristics". These expressions were not defined in the Act. Presumably the freezing or canning of peas or the turning of meat into sausages would amount to such an industrial process. In that case,

---

[38] [2000] P.I.Q.R. 164 at 170.
[39] [2007] EWHC 1667, QB.
[40] This argument was advanced by the defendants as evidence that the bike met the test under s.3(1), i.e. that the bike was as safe as persons generally are entitled to expect. This submission was acknowledged (at [15]) but not considered in the judgment.
[41] [2007] EWHC 1667, QB, at [80].
[42] [2001] 3 All E.R. 289.
[43] The same criticism can be levelled at *Tesco Stores Ltd v Pollard* [2006] EWCA Civ 393. For an analysis of the earlier decisions under s.3, see Freeman, "Strict Product Liability Laws: Consumer Protection Act provisions fail to assist claimants in three recent cases" [2001] J.P.I.L. 26.
[44] s.1(2) provides that " 'product' means any goods or electricity and . . . includes a product which is comprised in another product, whether by virtue of being a component part or raw material or otherwise".
[45] s.45.
[46] e.g. negligence or the Defective Premises Act 1972.

the industrial processor was regarded as the producer and could be liable to anyone injured by a defect in the peas or sausages. That is so even if the defect (e.g. salmonella) was present in the produce before it reached the industrial processor. These provisions making the industrial processor liable as producer remain. However, in accordance with an amendment to the Product Liability Directive[47] and with effect from December 4, 2000, the immunity (i.e. of farmers) from liability in respect of primary agricultural produce and game has been removed. This was done by the Consumer Protection Act 1987 (Product Liability) (Modification) Order 2000.[48]

Damage—Section 5

9–013   Under Pt I of the 1987 Act damages can be claimed for death or personal injuries and also for the loss of, or damage to, property (including land) which is[49]:

(a) of a description of property ordinarily intended for private use, occupation or consumption; and

(b) intended by the person suffering the loss or damage mainly for his own private use, occupation or consumption.

Damage to business property cannot be claimed under the Act. Furthermore the claimant cannot claim even for his private (non-business) property loss or damage unless it exceeds £275. This is to prevent trivial claims for property damage.[50] If, however, the amount of the damage done to the claimant's private property exceeds £275, then the whole amount is recoverable, including the first £275.[51]

A claim under Pt I of the Consumer Protection Act cannot be made for any damage to the defective product itself.[52] Thus if a defective toaster catches fire damaging the house and contents, one adds up the value of the damage done (but not including either the toaster itself or any property used mainly for business purposes, e.g. a wordprocessor). If the value exceeds £275, then it can be claimed under the Act. If the defect had been a component of the toaster, say the heating element, the result would still be the same unless the heating element had not been supplied as part of the toaster (e.g. had been bought as a replacement later). If the defective element had not been supplied with the toaster, then the value of the damage done to the toaster (but not to the element) could be included in the claim.[53] The rule is that one cannot claim for damage to the defective product itself or to any product which was supplied with the defective product comprised within it.

[47] 1999/34/EC.
[48] SI 2000/2771.
[49] s.5(3).
[50] s.5(4).
[51] Someone suffering property damage not exceeding £275 may, of course, be able to claim for it in negligence or under the implied terms of the Sale of Goods Act.
[52] s.5(2).
[53] In this case, of course, the claim would not itself be against the toaster manufacturer but against the manufacturer of the heating element.

Where a defective product is used as a component by another manufacturer, there will be *two* defective products and *two* producers. Under the Act the claimant can sue either. Whichever he sues, he cannot include a claim for damage done to the component or to the larger item which was supplied with the component comprised in it.

The Defendant—Section 2

Under the 1987 Act a claim can be brought against the producer,[54] the own-brander[55] or the   **9–014** importer.[56] The producer is the manufacturer. In the case of products (like salt, oil or coal) which are won or abstracted, the person who wins or abstracts them is the producer. In the case of other products (e.g. agricultural produce) which are not manufactured, the producer is the farmer or the person who carries out an industrial process (e.g. freezing) which gives them essential characteristics.

An own-brander is liable if he has own-branded the goods in such a way as to hold himself out as being the producer. If Superstores own-brands the coffee it sells, it can avoid liability by labelling it with a statement such as "Made for Superstores by Coffee Fellers Inc".

The only importer liable under the Act is the person who imported the product into the European Community. If a product was made in France and brought to England, there is no importer to sue, but only a French producer. If the product was made in the United States and brought to France before being brought to England, then the person who imported it into France is liable. If judgment is obtained in this country against someone in France (and indeed, now in all Community states including Denmark[57]), that judgment can be enforced in the country concerned by virtue of the Regulation on Jurisdiction and the Recognition and Enforcement of Judgments in Civil and Commercial Matters.[58] The Regulation replaced the Brussels Convention[59] and came into force on March 1, 2002. The same is also true vice versa, i.e. regarding enforcement of a foreign (EU Member) judgment in a domestic court under Sch.1 of the Civil Jurisdiction and Judgments Order 2001[60] following the coming into force of the Regulation in 2002.[61]

Where there is a long chain of distribution, the claimant may find it difficult to identify   **9–015** who was the producer or importer into the European Community. He may ask anyone who has supplied the product in question, e.g. the retailer, wholesaler or distributor, to identify the producer, own-brander or importer into the European Community.[62] If the supplier fails to make the identification and also fails to identify the person who supplied the product to him, the supplier is liable as if he had himself been the producer.

---

[54] s.2(2)(a).
[55] s.2(2)(b).
[56] s.2(2)(c).
[57] This is only due to the special agreement negotiated by the European Commission and ratified by Denmark on January 18, 2007. Consequently, the Regulation came into force in Denmark on July 1, 2007. See further, [2005] OJ L299/62 and Ch.16 below.
[58] reg.44/2001/EC.
[59] Brussels Convention (on Jurisdiction and Enforcement of Judgments) 1968.
[60] SI 2001/3929. See "New rules on civil jurisdiction" [2002] S.L.T. 39.
[61] See generally, Ch.16 below.
[62] s.2(3).

Defences—Section 4

9–016   Section 4 provides the following defences:

1. The defect is due to compliance with any statutory requirement or rule of the European Community.

2. The defendant did not supply the product, e.g. it was stolen from his premises.

3. The defendant supplied the product otherwise than in the course of a business *and* the defendant did not produce it (or own-brand it or import it into the European Community) with a view to profit. This lets off grandad who makes grandson John a toy and gives it to him for Christmas. Similarly a tourist returning from Japan with a gift for a friend in Britain will not be liable either as supplier or as importer.

4. The defect did not exist in the product at the time it was supplied by the defendant (i.e. the producer, own-brander or importer). Thus the defendant would not be liable if chocolates he had made and supplied were poisoned by saboteurs at the retailer's premises.

5. A component manufacturer is not liable where the defect is attributable to instructions given by the manufacturer of the larger product. In such circumstances, the defence will not, of course, be available to the producer of the larger product.

6. The "developmental risks" defence is available where the defendant shows:

    "that the state of scientific and technical knowledge at the relevant time was not such that a producer of products of the same description as the product in question might be expected to have discovered the defect if it had existed in his products while they were under his control".[63]

    In short, a producer relying on this defence needs to show that the defect was not discoverable at the time he supplied the product. Suppose that in 2001 a pair of gloves supplied by the manufacturer in 1993 is proved to have caused arthritis to the wearer because the gloves were made with polyester. To succeed under the Consumer Protection Act, the claimant would have to establish that in 1993 people generally were entitled to expect the gloves not to carry the risk of causing arthritis.[64] If the claimant can establish that, then the manufacturer will have a defence if he can show that in 1993, given the then state of scientific and technical knowledge, the risk of the polyester causing arthritis was not discoverable. Establishing the defence might be very important to the manufacturer if over the years he has supplied a lot of such gloves and a lot of wearers have suffered arthritis because of them.

Whichever of these six defences in s.4 is raised, the burden of establishing it rests upon the defendant.

---

[63] This defence was rejected in *A v National Blood Authority (No.1)*, considered above, since the risk was known. It was immaterial that the contamination was undetectable by the producer. See also *Abouzaid v Mothercare UK (Ltd)* [2001] C.L.Y. 920.
[64] See para.9–009, above.

The same is true of the defence of contributory negligence.[65] With this defence the defendant is saying that the claimant has failed to take reasonable care and has thereby been partly responsible for his own injuries, loss or damage. This could apply where the claimant has made an unreasonable use of the product. In fact an unreasonable use of the product might allow the defendant three different arguments in his own defence. So suppose an adult sniffs glue, making himself very ill and subsequently sues the glue manufacturer. The latter could argue:

(i) That there was no defect in the glue, i.e. it was as safe as persons generally were entitled to expect. This argument would be especially strong if there were no commercially viable way of producing glue without the risk of toxic fumes and if the container had carried a clear warning of the risks.

(ii) That the claimant's illness was caused not by the alleged defects in the product but entirely by his own decision to sniff the glue.

(iii) That the claimant by his own failure to take reasonable care for his own safety contributed to his own illness.

In this example it is difficult to know which of these arguments would find favour with a court. If either of the first two did so, the defendant would not be liable. If only the third found favour, the damages awarded would be a reduced proportion of what would be awarded for such an illness in the absence of contributory negligence.

Exclusion of Liability and Limitation

No exclusion or limitation of liability clause can exclude or limit the liability imposed by Pt **9–017** I of the Consumer Protection Act.[66]

The rules on limitation are an entirely different matter. These are rules laid down by law which allow a claim to be brought only if legal proceedings are commenced before the expiry of a deadline. There are two such rules which apply to claims for product liability under the Consumer Protection Act[67]:

1. Proceedings must be commenced within three years of when the injury or damage occurred or, if the injury etc., was not discovered until later, within three years of when the claimant became aware of the injury or damage.

2. No proceedings may be commenced more than 10 years after the producer supplied the product. If the own-brander or importer is being sued, then the 10 years run from when *he* supplied the product.

The 10 years begin to run the moment that the particular product in question was supplied by its producer (own-brander or importer). If those 10 years have expired, it is immaterial

[65] s.6(1).
[66] s.7.
[67] See Sch.1 which amends the Limitation Act 1980.

that the defendant continued, or even is still continuing, to manufacture and supply identical goods.

PART II OF THE CONSUMER PROTECTION ACT 1987

9–018   Part II does four things. First, it empowers the Secretary of State to make safety regulations governing the making and supplying of goods, e.g. regulations designed to secure that goods are safe, that appropriate information is supplied with them and that inappropriate information is not supplied. Thus, for example, regulations may govern the composition or design of goods, may require goods to conform to a certain standard (e.g. a British Institute Standard) and may require a warning or instructions to be given with the goods. Some regulations made under earlier Acts continue to be effective under the 1987 Act. They relate to such things as children's nightdresses, carrycot stands, electric blankets, prams and pushchairs, cosmetics, colour coding of electrical appliances and upholstered furniture. The regulations will sometimes affect only a manufacturer (e.g. where they govern design or composition). Other regulations may affect any supplier, whether manufacturer, wholesaler or retailer (e.g. regulations requiring information to be supplied with the goods). It is a criminal offence to infringe the regulations.

The second thing Pt II does is enable quick action to be taken against the marketing of unsafe goods. Section 13 gives the Secretary of State powers to issue two types of instruction:

      (i) a "prohibition notice" can be issued to prevent the trader upon whom it is served from supplying any specified type of goods which the Secretary of State considers unsafe;

      (ii) a "notice to warn" can require the trader upon whom it is served to take specified steps to warn consumers about unsafe goods which that trader supplies or has already supplied.

A "notice to warn" might well be served, for example, upon a car manufacturer if it appears that a certain model had a dangerous design fault. The notice will specify what steps the manufacturer must take. It may require him to publish a warning in the newspaper or it could, for example, require him to write individually to all purchasers of that model. Failure by a trader to comply with a prohibition notice or notice to warn is a criminal offence.

A prohibition notice can, in practice, be made only when the fact that there are dangerous goods on the market has come to the attention of the Secretary of State. It has sometimes been the case, however, that unsafe imported goods have been in the shops and bought in considerable quantities before the Secretary of State has learnt of their presence in the country. Hence each enforcement authority (i.e. local trading standards department) now has power to serve a "suspension notice" upon a trader where it has reasonable grounds to think that legal safety requirements have been infringed.[68] The notice will prohibit the trader from supplying specified goods for up to six months. If it turns out that there had been no infringement of the law in relation to the goods in question, the trader may be entitled to

---

[68] s.14.

compensation from the enforcement authority.[69] In order to catch suspect goods at ports, customs officers have power to seize and detain goods for up to two working days in order to enable local trading standards officers to examine them to determine whether they infringe legal safety requirements.[70]

The third aspect of Pt II is that s.10 made it an offence for a trader to supply consumer   **9–019** goods which fail to comply with a general safety requirement. This offence was, however, rendered virtually redundant by the General Product Safety Regulations 1994 and repealed by the General Product Safety Regulations 2005.[71]

The fourth aspect of Pt II of the Consumer Protection Act relates to civil liability. The Act entitles a consumer to bring an action for damages against any trader in respect of damage or loss suffered by the consumer because of an infringement by the trader of safety regulations. Thus a child whose nightdress catches fire because when supplied it did not comply with the safety regulations will be able to claim compensation for her burns from the manufacturer. This is so even if she did not buy it direct from the manufacturer (or, indeed, even if she did not buy it). She does not have to prove any negligence on the part of the manufacturer and does not even have to rely on the product liability provisions of Pt I of the Act. Civil liability under the Act cannot be excluded or restricted by any exemption clause.

Criminal and civil liability under Pt II of the Consumer Protection Act attaches only to persons who are acting "in the course of carrying on a business". The defendant in *Southwark London Borough v Charlesworth*[72] was a shoe-repairer who also carried on a secondary business as a seller of second-hand goods. At his shop he sold an electric fire which infringed safety regulations.[73] The fire had come from his home and the money from the sale of the fire did not go through the books of the business. Nevertheless, there was no differentiation in the shop between the fire and other goods he was selling in his secondary line of business. That being so, the court held that the sale was in the course of a business. The result might have been different if there had been a notice attached to the goods making it clear that these goods had nothing to do with the defendant's business as a dealer in second-hand goods but had come from his home and that the sale of the goods was to be a private transaction.

THE GENERAL PRODUCT SAFETY REGULATIONS 2005

These Regulations[74] revoked and replaced the General Product Safety Regulations 1994   **9–020** which implemented the Directive on General Product Safety.[75] They create criminal offences which are concerned with the marketing of unsafe products. The Regulations potentially apply if a product:

---

[69] s.14(7).
[70] s.31.
[71] reg.46(2).
[72] (1983) 147 J.P. 470.
[73] In force under the Consumer Protection Act 1961.
[74] The General Product Safety Regulations 2005 (SI 2005/1803) implementing Directive 2001/95. The regulations came into force, for the most part, on October 1, 2005.
[75] 92/59/EC.

>   (i) is placed on the market by a producer; or
>
>   (ii) is supplied by a distributor.

For this purpose, placing on the market includes: offering or agreeing to place on the market, or exposing or possessing a product to place on the market. Supplying includes: offering or agreeing to supply, or exposing or possessing a product to be supplied.

Scope of the Regulations

9–021   The Regulations apply to the situation where a producer, in the course of a commercial activity, places on the market any product intended for consumers or likely to be used by consumers. They also impose requirements of care on a distributor of such a product.

- By reg.5 the producer commits an offence if he "places a product on the market" which is not a "safe" product.

- By reg.8 a distributor commits an offence if he does not act with due care in order to help ensure compliance with reg.5.

This latter requires, for example, that a distributor does not supply any products "which he knows, or should have presumed, on the basis of the information in his possession and as a professional, are dangerous".[76] The Regulations do not apply to any product which is used exclusively in the context of a commercial activity, e.g. a machine tool supplied to be used in a factory, or a computer to be used by a firm's secretary. Of course, if that same computer were instead sold direct to the secretary for her private use at home, then the Regulations would apply. " 'Commercial activity' includes a business and a trade". This expression does not expressly include a profession. Apparently, for example, if that same computer were supplied for use in the parish office of a church that would still be within the Regulations, since presumably the church could not be said to be a business or a trade.

There is only a very short list of products excluded from the Regulations. Second-hand goods, demonstration models and reconditioned goods are all included. The only products excluded are:

- Second-hand *antiques*;

- Products supplied *for* repair or reconditioning before use, provided the supplier clearly informs the customer to that effect;

- Any product where there are specific provisions in the rules of Community law governing *all* aspects of the safety of the product.

Meaning of "Safe"

9–022   Safety is defined in terms of risk to persons, not property. A safe product "means any product which, under normal or reasonably foreseeable conditions of use, including duration, does

---

[76] reg.8(1)(a).

not present any risk or only the minimum of risk compatible with the product's use, considered as acceptable and consistent with a high level of protection for the safety and health of persons".[77] Few products will be considered totally safe. It is enough, however, if three requirements are satisfied: (i) the risks presented are the minimum risk compatible with the product's use; (ii) those risks are "acceptable"; (iii) those risks are consistent with a high level of protection for the safety and health of persons. The following factors, in particular, are to be taken into account:

- The characteristics and composition of the product, its packaging and instructions for assembly and maintenance;

- Its effect on other products, where it is reasonably foreseeable that it will be used with other products;

- Its presentation, labelling, any instructions for use and disposal, and any other information provided by the producer;

- The categories of consumers at serious risk when using the product, especially children.

Obviously articles such as toys that are likely to be used by children will have to be safe for that group of consumers. The reference to instructions for disposal leaves open the possibility of a product being found to be unsafe because of the risks it poses when it is to be disposed of, i.e. after its useful life is over. This could well catch products which contain toxic chemicals. The reference to a product being used with other products might well apply, for example, to a shelf support bracket. Clearly such a bracket is only likely to be used together with other products, i.e. the shelf and the items to be placed on the shelf. The strength of the bracket will, in that situation, clearly be a feature of its safety.

The giving of information is a key feature. Thus reg.7 requires a producer to provide information to enable consumers to assess the risks inherent in it throughout the normal or reasonably foreseeable period of its use, where those risks are not immediately apparent without adequate warnings. It also requires producers to take measures, commensurate with the characteristics of the product, to enable consumers to be informed of the risks and to enable the producer, if necessary, to withdraw the product. In the case of many products, this in effect requires the producer to use a batch number system, so that different batches of the product can be identified from a mark or number on the product itself. It may also require sample testing of the marketed products, the investigation of complaints and keeping of distributors informed of risks which materialise after marketing.

In relation to many products there are published standards. Sometimes these are embodied in safety regulations, or they may be Community technical specifications, or they may be national voluntary standards, or contained in codes of good practice etc. There is no absolute defence in respect of a product which complies with safety regulations. There is in that case, however, a presumption, until the contrary is proved, that the product is safe.[78] So far as concerns other types of standards, these are things to be taken into account in determining the

[77] See the definition of "safe product" under reg.2.
[78] See reg.6.

safety which consumers may reasonably expect, and hence whether the risks presented by the product are acceptable.

Who is Liable?

9–023   Primarily, it is the "producer", as defined in reg.2, who is liable. There are, however, various people who may be regarded as the producer and thus liable. They are: the manufacturer provided that the manufacturer is established in the European Community; any own-brander in the Community[79]; anyone reconditioning the product; the importer of the product into the Community[80]; and the manufacturer's established representative in the Community. As seen above, a distributor also can be liable, e.g. for failing to act with due care to help ensure compliance.

Defences

9–024   The defence of due diligence is available to anyone charged with an offence under the Regulations.[81] The defence is commonly found in consumer protection legislation and was for example, also a defence to someone charged with an offence under s.10 of the Consumer Protection Act[82] or under safety regulations. It is that the defendant took all reasonable steps and exercised all due diligence to avoid committing the offence.[83] An importer or wholesaler will not be able to rely on this defence if he has taken no steps to require his supplier to supply goods which correspond with the relevant legal requirements. This may mean not only placing specific contractual obligations upon his supplier but also making tests on more than infrequent random samples of the goods supplied: *Riley v Webb*[84] and *Rotherham MBC v Raysun*.[85]

The amount of care required before the defendant can be said to have taken all reasonable steps and exercised all due diligence will be a question of fact in each case. In a situation where the defendant had imported goods from a source (e.g. the German wine industry) where there is known to be a thorough system of verification and testing to see the correct standard has been reached, he may not be expected to sample at all: *Hurley v Martinez*.[86] When considering whether he should sample, the degree of risk to be guarded against is an important factor. Thus, it is noticeable that in cases (such as *Rotherham MBC v Raysun*[87]) where the defendant is relying on the defence of due diligence to a consumer safety charge, the court is much more likely to demand a thorough sampling system than it is in cases (such

[79] Where, for example, someone who presents himself as the manufacturer by affixing to the product his name, trade mark or other distinctive mark.
[80] Where, for example, the manufacturer is not himself established, and has no representative established, in the Community.
[81] See reg.29.
[82] Now repealed by the General Product Safety Regulations 2005, see reg.46(2).
[83] See generally, Parry, "Judicial approaches to due diligence" [1995] Crim. Law Rev. 695.
[84] [1987] C.C.L.R. 65.
[85] [1989] C.C.L.R. 1.
[86] [1991] C.C.L.R. 1.
[87] [1989] C.C.L.R. 1.

as *Hurley v Martinez*[88]) where the defendant is relying on the same defence to a misleading statement charge. In *Hurley v Martinez*, the defendant was charged over a misstatement of the alcoholic strength (as 8 per cent instead of 7.2 per cent) on German wine.

Of course, taking steps to ensure that goods comply with a British Standards specification is not capable of being sufficient to satisfy the defence of due diligence, unless compliance with the British Standards specification will automatically involve compliance with the provisions (e.g. of the Toys (Safety) Regulations 1989) under which the proceedings are brought: *Balding v Lew Ways Ltd.*[89]

By way of exception, a distributor who is charged with an offence, under the Regulations,   **9–025** of failing to act with due care to help ensure compliance with the requirement that the product is safe, will not be able to rely upon the defence of due diligence unless, within the limits of his activities, he has participated in monitoring the safety of the products placed on the market, in particular by passing on information on product risks and co-operating in any action taken to avoid those risks. Thus, for example, a car dealer who failed to recall a model identified as being within a defective batch would not be able to rely upon the defence.

Prohibition Notices, Notices to Warn and Suspension Notices

Prohibition notices, notices to warn and suspension notices are all notices which can be   **9–026** issued under the terms of the General Product Safety Regulations 2005.[90] One available power is that of the requirement to mark and warn under regs 12 and 13. In order to comply with this the warning must be "suitable, clearly worded and easily comprehensible".[91]

The enforcement authorities also have the ability to serve a "suspension notice". This notice is available where the authority has "reasonable grounds for suspecting that a requirement of these Regulations has been contravened in relation to a product" and allows for a period of time as is necessary to "organise appropriate safety evaluations, checks and controls". During this time, the following actions are prohibited[92]:

(a) placing the product on the market, offering to place it on the market, agreeing to place it on the market or exposing it for placing on the market, or

(b) supplying the product, offering to supply it, agreeing to supply it or exposing it for supply.

Where the enforcement authority has reasonable grounds for believing that a product is a dangerous product (i.e. not a safe product)[93] they have the ability to issue a withdrawal notice which makes the same prohibition as the "suspension notice" previously discussed, but is

---

[88] [1991] C.C.L.R. 1.
[89] *The Times*, March 19, 1995.
[90] Unlike the 1994 version, the current General Product Safety Regulations contain built-in enforcement provisions in Pt 3.
[91] reg.12(2).
[92] reg.11(1). Under reg.11(2) the notice may also require that the authority be kept informed of the whereabouts of the product.
[93] See the definitions of both in reg.2.

permanent, rather than temporary.[94] This notice can be served in respect of a product already on the market, but where it is served in respect of such a product[95]:

> "a withdrawal notice may only be served by an enforcement authority where the action being undertaken by the producer or the distributor concerned in fulfilment of his obligations under these Regulations is unsatisfactory or insufficient to prevent the risks concerned to the health and safety of persons."

9–027   This notice is, therefore, designed to be employed only where the producer or distributor is either unwilling or unable to take the steps necessary to ensure compliance with the general safety requirement. This limitation on the availability of a "withdrawal notice" is not applicable, however, where the product poses a serious risk and requires (in the view of the enforcement authority) urgent action.[96]

In the event of a product being deemed unsafe which has already gone to market, the enforcement authorities have the power to issue a "recall notice" under reg.15. The content of this notice is governed by reg.15(2), which provides that the notice may require:

> "(a) the recall to be effected in accordance with a code of practice applicable to the product concerned, or
> (b) the recipient of the recall notice to—
>
>> (i) contact consumers who have purchased the product in order to inform them of the recall, where and to the extent it is practicable to do so,
>> (ii) publish a notice in such form and such manner as is likely to bring to the attention of purchasers of the product the risk the product poses and the fact of the recall, or
>> (iii) make arrangements for the collection or return of the product from consumers who have purchased it or for its disposal,
>
> and may impose such additional requirements on the recipient of the notice as are reasonable and practicable with a view to achieving the return of the product from consumers to the person specified in the notice or its disposal."

This list is therefore not exhaustive and is subject to reg.15(3) which provides that "the enforcement authority shall take into consideration the need to encourage distributors, users and consumers to contribute to its implementation" when deciding what the notice may contain.

9–028   Such a notice is available only where the product is dangerous and the requirements of reg.15(4) are satisfied. Regulation 15(4) requires that: (a) any other action possible under the regulations would be insufficient; (b) action taken by the producer or distributor is unsatisfactory or insufficient; and (c) a period of seven days notice has been given.[97]

---

[94] reg.14(1).
[95] reg.14(3).
[96] reg.14(4).
[97] Under reg.15(5), paras (b) and (c) are not necessary where the product poses serious risk and requires urgent action.

The sanctions for breach of these offences are stated in reg.20. Any person in breach of the general safety requirement under reg.5 is liable on conviction on indictment to imprisonment for a term not exceeding 12 months or to a fine not exceeding £20,000 (or to both). The same liability falls on any distributor in breach of reg.8(1)(a). A person in breach of reg.7(1) or reg.7(3) shall be guilty of an offence and liable on summary conviction to imprisonment for a term not exceeding three months or to a fine not exceeding level 5 on the standard scale (£5,000 at present) or to both. A person in breach of requirements relating to any of the safety notices (i.e. to mark; warn etc.) is guilty of an offence and liable on conviction on indictment to imprisonment for a term of up to 12 months or to a fine not exceeding £20,000 (or to both).[98]

General Reading

- Cartwright, "Total recall? the future of consumer product safety regulation" [2006] L.M.C.L.Q. 390;   **9–029**

- Fairgrieve and Howells, "General product safety—a revolution through reform?" (2006) 69 M.L.R. 59;

- Freeman, "Strict product liability laws—Consumer Protection Act provisions fail to assist claimants in three recent cases" [2001] J.P.I.L. 26;

- Goldberg, "Paying for bad blood: strict product liability after the hepatitis C litigation" [2002] Med. Law Rev. 165;

- Mildred and Howells, "Infected blood: defect and discoverability. A first exposition of the EC Product Liability Directive" (2002) 65 M.L.R. 95;

- Mildred, "Pitfalls in Product Liability" [2007] J.P.I.L. 141;

- Newell, "Product liability after the Consumer Protection Act 1987" [1988] Co Law 210;

- Parry, "Product safety: European style—an appraisal" [1995] J.B.L. 268;

- Shears, "The EU Product Liability Directive—twenty years on" [2007] J.B.L. 884;

- Tettenborn, "Components and product liability: damage to 'other property' " [2000] L.M.C.L.Q. 338.

---

[98] On summary conviction this is reduced to imprisonment for a term of up to three months or to a fine not exceeding the statutory maximum (or to both).

Chapter 10

EXEMPTION CLAUSES AND UNFAIR TERMS

INTRODUCTION

An exemption clause is a term of the contract intended to exclude or restrict the liability of **10–001** one of the parties, usually the seller. Sometimes a seller is so financially powerful that he can blatantly insist on such a clause being included in the contract; he can adopt a "take it or leave it" attitude. More common is the seller who, having inserted an exclusion clause into his conditions of sale, relies on his buyer not bothering to read (or not understanding) the small print; for example, the exclusion clause may be contained in the small print of a guarantee which he gives to the buyer.

An exemption clause may, contrary to appearances, have little or no effect. Such clauses are not looked upon with favour either by the courts or by Parliament. They are subject to several common law rules evolved by the courts as well as to certain pieces of legislation. In this respect the Unfair Contract Terms Act 1977 is particularly important. This Act will be considered later in the chapter. At the moment it is worth recording that s.55(1) of the Sale of Goods Act reads:

> "Where a right, duty or liability would arise under a contract of sale of goods by implication of law, it may (subject to the Unfair Contract Terms Act 1977) be negatived or varied by express agreement, or by the course of dealing between the parties, or by such usage as binds both parties to the contract."

As well as the 1977 Act there are the Unfair Terms in Consumer Contracts Regulations 1999. These Regulations render invalid certain exemption clauses and also other terms of the contract which are unfair. These Regulations will be considered at the end of this chapter. Before turning to the 1977 Act and the 1999 Regulations we shall first examine the common law rules relating to incorporation, misrepresentation, privity of contract and scope of the clause.

INCORPORATION

10–002 A clause is of no effect unless it is incorporated (included) as a term in the contract. It must be incorporated when the contract is made. Any attempt to incorporate it after the contract is made will be unsuccessful. Thus a document which is first brought to the purchaser's notice after the contract is made will not incorporate into the contract terms printed on the document. It is for this reason that a seller will usually be unable to rely on an exclusion clause printed on a receipt. Receipts are not usually handed over until the purchaser has paid (i.e. after the contract has been made). This rule, that a clause cannot subsequently be incorporated, was applied in *Olley v Marlborough Court*.[1] There the claimant had booked in at the reception desk of a hotel and only subsequently, on entering her room, did she discover behind the door a notice which claimed to exclude the hotel's liability for guests' property. The Court of Appeal held that the notice was not incorporated in the contract, since it was not displayed at a spot visible to the claimant before she made the contract. The defendant would have been better advised to display their notice in a prominent position near the reception desk.

We can now consider individually the different methods of incorporation.

Oral Agreement between Buyer and Seller

10–003 This method is not commonly used for two main reasons. First, it involves bringing the exclusion clause directly to the attention of the buyer. Secondly, there may be difficulty in proving that the buyer orally agreed to the exclusion.

Signed Contractual Document

10–004 The buyer will find it difficult to argue that the clause was not agreed upon if it is contained in a document signed by them. It will not help them to plead that they had not read the clause or were unaware of its existence. In *L'Estrange v Graucob*[2] a café proprietress bought a vending machine on the terms of a sales agreement which she signed without having read. Although she had been unaware that the small print contained a wide exclusion clause, the Court of Appeal held that the clause protected the seller from liability in respect of defects in the machine.

A clause will not be incorporated by a document which is not a contractual document. A document will be "contractual" if a reasonable person in the position of the prospective buyer would expect it to contain terms affecting their rights and liabilities. A buyer who has taken the formal step of signing a document will therefore find it difficult to show that it was not a contractual document.

[1] [1949] 1 K.B. 532.
[2] [1934] 2 K.B. 394.

Unsigned Contractual Document

There are two significant differences between signed and unsigned documents. First, an **10–005** exemption clause in an unsigned document is not incorporated unless at the time of making the contract either the buyer was aware of its existence or else reasonable steps had been taken to bring it to his attention. The harsher the clause, the greater the effort needed to bring it to the attention of the buyer.[3] In *AEG Ltd v Logic Resources Ltd*[4] the seller's confirmation of order form stated "Orders are subject to our conditions of sale—for extract see reverse". The term which excluded liability for breach of the implied terms in the Sale of Goods Act and left the buyer with no choice but to return defective goods was not included in the extract on the reverse. The Court of Appeal held that insufficient steps had been taken to bring the exclusion clause to the buyer's attention and therefore the clause was not incorporated into the contract. Secondly, in the case of an unsigned document, the buyer may find it easier to establish that it was not a contractual document. In *Chapelton v Barry UDC*.[5] Mr Chapelton wanted to hire a deckchair on the beach. He saw a pile of them and a notice nearby, "Hire of chairs 2d. per session of three hours". The notice continued by "respectfully requesting" the hirer to obtain a ticket from the attendant. This he did. He later brought an action claiming damages for injuries he received when his chair collapsed. As a defence, the Council pleaded an exemption clause printed on the back of the ticket. As Mr Chapelton had obtained his ticket from the attendant at the time of making the contract (i.e. when he collected his chair from the pile), the ticket had changed hands in sufficient time. The Court of Appeal rejected the Council's defence on the ground, not that the ticket changed hands too late, but that it was not a contractual document; for no reasonable person would expect to find contractual terms in a document which was no more than a receipt for him to prove that he had paid and which in many instances (i.e. in the absence of the attendant) would not change hands until long after the contract was made.

Displayed Notices

As with an unsigned contractual document, this method of incorporation will work only if at **10–006** the time of making the contract the buyer actually knew of the existence of the term or else reasonable steps had been taken to bring them to his attention. Thus the notice must be reasonably large and prominently displayed at a spot visible to the buyer when the contact is made. Exactly what amounts to "reasonable steps" is a question of fact in each case. The wider and more drastic the clause, the more care must be taken to bring it to the buyer's attention.

Even if reasonable steps have been taken to bring the exemption clause to the notice of the buyer, it will not be incorporated if it does not clearly cover the particular transaction in question. In *D & M Trailers (Halifax) Ltd v Stirling*[6] an extensive exemption clause was included in the conditions of sale posted up around an auction room. One of these conditions

[3] See *Interfoto Picture Library v Stiletto Visual Programmes*, para.7–005 above.
[4] (1995) unreported.
[5] [1940] 1 K.B. 532.
[6] [1978] R.T.R. 468.

stated, " 'Sale' used in these conditions shall include sale by private treaty as well as by auction". Mr Stirling attended the auction and bought some vehicles. On returning a day or two later to pay for them, he saw in the yard a Scania tractor which had been included but not sold at the auction which he had attended. He spoke privately with the auctioneers and agreed to buy the Scania (i.e. he agreed by private treaty and not in an auction). The Scania soon proved to be seriously defective and not of satisfactory quality. The buyer's claim for breach of condition succeeded. The Court held that the exemption clause, though it had been incorporated in the auction sales, had not been incorporated in the later sale by private treaty. This was a separate transaction from the auction and the auctioneers had not made it clear that the exemption clause was being incorporated into it.

Previous Course of Dealing

10–007   If, in the past, parties have regularly made contracts with each other upon the same terms (including exemption terms), then that course of dealing can incorporate those terms into a later contract between them. This later contract must be merely the latest in the established course of dealing. Thus three requirements must be satisfied before a course of dealing can incorporate an exemption clause into a later contract:

(i) The transactions between the parties must have been sufficiently numerous to constitute a "course of dealing".

(ii) The established course of dealing must have been consistent.

(iii) The established course of dealing must not have been deviated from on the occasion in question.

In *Hollier v Rambler Motors*[7] the first of these requirements was not satisfied. The Court of Appeal held that three or four transactions in the course of five years were not sufficient to establish a course of dealing.

In *Kendall v Lillico*[8] all the requirements were fulfilled. Just as he had done on over 100 occasions during the previous three years, the seller sold some animal food to the buyer. As had always previously happened, they made an oral agreement followed by the seller giving to the buyers a "sold note" which had on the back an exclusion clause. Plainly the clause was not on this occasion incorporated by virtue of the sold note, which had been handed over only after the bargain was struck. However, there had been a long and consistent course of dealing which was adhered to on this occasion. It was by virtue of this that the clause was incorporated. The House of Lords held this to be so, even though the buyers were unaware of the precise terms on the sold notes. Lord Pearce said[9]:

"The only reasonable inference from the regular course of dealing over so long a period is that the buyers were evincing an acceptance of, and a readiness to be bound by, the

[7] [1972] 2 Q.B. 71.
[8] [1969] 2 A.C. 31.
[9] *Kendall v Lillico* [1969] 2 A.C. 31 at 113.

printed conditions of whose existence they were well aware of although they had not troubled to read them."

Trade Usage

Whereas a course of dealing can incorporate a term that has in effect become customary between the two parties in question, trade usage can incorporate a term that has become a custom amongst all the buyers and sellers dealing in the environment in question. In the latter case there is no need for the particular seller and buyer to have dealt previously with each other, or, indeed, previously in the particular environment. It is sufficient that the custom was established in the market in which on this occasion the buyer bought from the seller. By dealing in this market, they are taken, unless they expressly agreed otherwise, to have been dealing in accordance with all the customs of the market. Thus in *Cointat v Myham*[10] where the claimant bought bad meat in the Central London Meat Market, it was held that any warranty as to the fitness or quality of the meat was excluded, because there was an established custom of the market to that effect.

10–008

Overriding Oral Warranty

An exclusion clause which would otherwise be incorporated by one of the methods referred to above may nevertheless be overridden by later statements made by the seller to the buyer. The claimant in *Harling v Eddy*[11] bought a heifer at a cattle auction. One of the printed conditions of sale in the auction catalogue was that no warranty was given in respect of any animal sold. However, when there had been some difficulty in getting the bidding started, the seller announced that there was nothing wrong with the heifer and he would absolutely guarantee her. After this the heifer was knocked down to the claimant. The Court of Appeal held that the oral statement overrode the exclusion clause which therefore did not form part of the contract.

10–009

MISREPRESENTATION

The seller cannot rely on any exclusion clause, no matter what liability it claims to exclude, to the extent that he or his agent has misrepresented the effect of the clause. In *Curtis v Chemical Dyeing Co*[12] the claimant took a wedding dress to the defendants for cleaning. The shop assistant asked her to sign a receipt, telling her that this was because the cleaners took no responsibility for damage to beads and sequins on the dress. In fact this was literally true but the clause on the receipt went further. It claimed to exempt the defendants from liability for "any damage howsoever caused". The claimant signed the receipt without reading it. The assistant had not deliberately or knowingly misled the claimant. Nevertheless she had, by

10–010

[10] (1914) 110 L.T. 749.
[11] [1951] 2 K.B. 739.
[12] [1951] 1 K.B. 805.

revealing part of the clause's effect, concealed its full effect. This amounted to a misrepresentation. The Court of Appeal held the defendants liable in negligence for damage caused to the dress. The misrepresentation, albeit an innocent one, "was a sufficient misrepresentation to disentitle the cleaner from relying on the exemption, except in regard to beads and sequins".

PRIVITY OF CONTRACT

10–011   The privity of contract principle is that someone who is not privy to (i.e. not a party to) a contract can neither rely upon the contract nor be bound by it. Generally, a contract can affect the rights and liabilities only as between the parties to it. Thus an exclusion clause in a contract is a defence available, generally, only to a contracted party and only against the other contracted party: *Scruttons v Midland Silicones.*[13] The Contracts (Rights of Third Parties) Act 1999, however, creates a limited exception whereby a third party, who is described or identified in the contract, can rely on an exclusion clause if either (a) the parties expressly provide that he may, or (b) the exclusion clause purports to enable the third party to rely on it.[14] Consider a common situation: a manufacturer sells a number of his products to a wholesaler, the wholesaler sells some of them to a retailer and the retailer sells one of them to a consumer. Here there are three separate contracts of sale. If the product proves to be defective, then this could give rise to three separate claims for damages for breach of contract—one by the consumer against the retailer, one by the retailer against the wholesaler and one by the wholesaler against the manufacturer. There is a chain of contracts and a breach of one may well cause a chain reaction, i.e. a breach of each of the others.[15] The law does not allow the consumer to ignore the intermediate links in the chain. He cannot sue the manufacturer for breach of the latter's contract of sale. However, in certain circumstances, the law of tort gives a consumer a right to sue a manufacturer with whom he has no contract.[16] In our example, if the manufacturer was careless in the manufacture of his product and this had injured the consumer, the latter will have a claim (in the law of tort) in negligence against the manufacturer even though he did not buy the goods from him. Whilst an exclusion clause in the manufacturer's contract of sale could provide the manufacturer with a good defence to a claim by the wholesaler, it would provide him with no defence to a claim in negligence by the consumer. Similarly, an exclusion clause in the contract between the retailer and the consumer could not be relied upon by the manufacturer—unless the clause purports to confer that right on the manufacturer. In the latter case the clause might nevertheless be rendered ineffective by the Unfair Contract Terms Act 1977.

Sometimes a manufacturer sells directly to a member of the public, e.g. by mail order or by door-to-door salesmen. In such a case an exclusion clause could, if appropriately worded, (and, again, subject to the provisions of the Unfair Contract Terms Act), provide the manufacturer with a good defence against a claim by the purchaser in negligence. However, someone other than the purchaser could be injured on account of the article's negligent manufacture and an exclusion clause would provide no defence in an action brought by them

---

[13] [1962] A.C. 446.
[14] See para.7–003, above.
[15] See para.9–006, above.
[16] See Ch.9, above.

against the manufacturer. Furthermore, a manufacturer can now be liable to their immediate purchaser or to anyone else who is caused injury (or private property damage) by a defective product. This liability, under Pt I of the Consumer Protection Act 1987, cannot be limited or excluded at all.[17]

Scope of the Clause

An exclusion clause is construed *contra proferentem*, i.e. narrowly against the interest of the person relying upon it. An exclusion clause is usually inserted for the sole benefit of one of the parties: in a contract of sale, the seller. The court, in interpreting the clause, leans against the seller. If the clause is ambiguous, the court will adopt the meaning less favourable to the seller and any ground of liability not clearly excluded will remain. In *Andrews v Singer*[18] the claimant made a written contract to buy a "new Singer car". The car delivered to him had in fact done a considerable mileage. It was held that a clause excluding all "implied conditions and warranties" did not exclude the seller's liability for breach of the *express* condition that he would supply a "new" car. A further illustration is to be found in *Wallis & Wells v Pratt and Haynes*[19] where the House of Lords held that the clause "Sellers give no warranty, express or implied" did not exclude conditions. A clause which does not expressly mention conditions will not normally exclude liability for breach of condition.

10–012

Old Approach to Interpretation

Until the 1970s there was no statutory control upon exemption clauses. So, if an exemption clause was part of the contract and if on its wording it excused one party from a given liability, then the court had to give effect to the clause, i.e. that party (usually the seller) had a valid defence. That is what happened in *L'Estrange v Graucob*.[20] The courts, however, did not very much like this sort of result and, when interpreting an exemption clause, used to adopt a hostile approach. There were two aspects to this. First the court would sometimes place a strained or tortured meaning on the words of the exemption clause in order to deprive it of effect. Secondly, the courts developed the doctrine of fundamental breach of contract. According to this doctrine, a party who had committed a fundamental breach of contract could not (at least, sometimes could not) rely for his defence upon an exemption clause. This doctrine was never, however, approved by the House of Lords.

10–013

New Approach to Interpretation

As will be explained later in this chapter, in the 1970s Parliament passed legislation which renders certain exemption clauses absolutely ineffective and imposes a test of reasonableness

10–014

---

[17] See paras 9–007–9–017, above.
[18] [1934] 1 K.B. 17.
[19] [1911] A.C. 394.
[20] [1934] 2 K.B. 394, see para.10–004, above.

on many others. This means that, even though an exemption clause on its wording apparently provides a defence, it may nevertheless be ineffective. This enabled the courts to adopt a less hostile approach to the interpretation of the wording of exemption clauses.

In *Photo Production Ltd v Securicor Transport Ltd*[21] the House of Lords swept away the doctrine that a fundamental breach of contract could prevent an exemption clause from providing a defence. Their Lordships overruled earlier decisions saying otherwise. After *Photo Production* there were two more decisions of the House of Lords, *Aisla Craig Fishing Co Ltd v Malvern Fishing Co Ltd*[22] and *George Mitchell Ltd v Finney Lock Seeds Ltd*.[23] From this trilogy of cases the modern approach to the interpretation of exemption clauses emerged.

Exemption clauses are still construed *contra proferentem*, i.e. if a clause is ambiguous the court will adopt the meaning which is less favourable to the party (usually the seller) wishing to rely upon the clause. The court will not, however, read an ambiguity into clear words by giving them a strained or tortured meaning. Clear and plain words will be given their clear meaning. One aspect of the *contra proferentem* rule is that, if there is more than one possible head of liability one of which is liability for negligence, then an exemption clause will not be interpreted as excluding liability for negligence unless it does so in clear terms. For example a manufacturer who sells his goods to a wholesaler may in the contract exclude liability in respect of defects in the goods. This clause might well be interpreted as excluding the manufacturer's liability to the wholesaler under the implied terms as to satisfactory quality and fitness for purpose. In the absence of clear words, however, it will not be interpreted as excluding the manufacturer's liability to the wholesaler for negligence, under the principle of *Donoghue v Stevenson*.[24] On the other hand the *Aisla Craig* case established that the *contra proferentem* rule is not applied quite as rigorously in interpreting clauses which merely *limit* the defendant's (usually the seller's) liability, as it is to clauses which claim to *exclude* his liability.

In *George Mitchell Ltd v Finney Lock Seeds Ltd*[25] some farmers contracted to buy from some seed merchants 30lb of Finney's "Late Dutch Special" cabbage seed. Unknown to the buyers, the sellers negligently delivered the wrong seed. The buyers planted the seed but only leaves came up and the crop proved worthless, causing the buyers a loss of £61,000. In defence to a claim for that loss, the sellers sought to rely on a contractual clause limiting the sellers' liability to the cost of replacement seeds, i.e. the clause excluded the sellers' liability for any consequential loss arising from "use or failure in performance of or any defect in any seeds or plants supplied or for any other loss or damage whatsoever", except for the cost of replacement of the seed. In interpreting the clause, their Lordships observed that this was a limitation of liability clause and not a complete exclusion clause. They unanimously held that on its wording it *limited* the sellers' liability to the cost of replacing the seed. That was so even though the breach of contract had been a negligent one. That, however, did not mean that the clause necessarily gave the sellers a valid defence because the clause still had to satisfy the legislation on exemption clauses.[26]

[21] [1980] A.C. 827.
[22] [1983] 1 W.L.R. 964.
[23] [1983] 3 W.L.R. 163.
[24] [1932] A.C. 562, see para.9–005, above.
[25] [1983] 3 W.L.R. 163.
[26] See further, para.10–023, below.

INTRODUCTION TO THE UNFAIR CONTRACT TERMS ACT 1977

The Unfair Contract Terms Act 1977 is a major landmark in the development of the law of   **10–015**
contract. It deals with exemption clauses and it replaced and greatly extended certain
provisions previously in the Supply of Goods (Implied Terms) Act 1973. The 1973 Act was
confined to exemption clauses which claimed to exclude or restrict the statutory implied
terms relating to title, description, quality and sample (implied by ss.12–15 of the Sale of
Goods Act). The 1977 Act places severe curbs upon the effectiveness of exemption clauses
of many sorts. The 1977 Act does not, however, deal with liability under the Consumer
Protection Act 1987.[27] The Consumer Protection Act itself provides, in ss.7 and 41(4), that
such liability cannot be excluded or limited.

Two preliminary matters must be explained. First, the 1977 Act applies to exemption
clauses and these include not only the clauses which claim to exclude liability for breach of
contract but also those which claim[28]:

(i) To prevent liability from arising in the first place (e.g. "Seller gives no warranty
as to fitness for purpose or satisfactory quality");

(ii) To restrict liability (e.g. to a maximum amount);

(iii) To restrict the buyer's remedies (e.g. to prevent him from rejecting the goods and
to confine him to damages for breach of condition);

(iv) To restrict the time within which a remedy may be claimed (e.g. "No claims to be
made more than six weeks after purchase"). The general rule is that a claim for
damages for breach of contract can be brought at any time up to six years after the
breach occurred. If the claim is for personal injuries the period is reduced to three
years. A clause claiming to shorten these periods is an exemption clause;

(v) To make the enforcement of any remedy subject to a restrictive condition (e.g.
"Seller accepts no liability unless the goods are first returned to him carriage
paid").

The other preliminary matter is that the Unfair Contract Terms Act 1977 does not tell you
whether the seller is liable. To put it another way, it does not alter the basis of liability. It
simply curbs the effectiveness of exemption clauses. Suppose a contract of sale contains an
exemption clause; suppose also that exemption clause is rendered ineffective by the Unfair
Contract Terms Act. There still remains the question "What, if any, is the liability of the
seller?" That question can be answered only by examining the express and implied terms of
the contract, including those implied by the Sale of Goods Act. Now let us turn to exemption
clauses and the effect upon them of the provisions of the Unfair Contract Terms Act.

Section 55(1) of the Sale of Goods Act was quoted at para.10–001 above. It allows an   **10–016**
exemption clause to take effect subject to the common law rules already outlined and subject
also to the provisions of the Unfair Contract Terms Act 1977. We shall examine first the
effect of the 1977 Act upon exemption clauses which claim to exempt from liability under

[27] Explained at paras 9–007–9–018, above.
[28] By s.13 of the 1977 Act.

the statutory implied terms as to title, description, quality and sample and then its effect upon other exemption clauses.

EXEMPTIONS FROM SECTIONS 12–15 OF THE SALE OF GOODS ACT: SECTION 6

10–017   Section 6 of the Unfair Contract Terms Act 1977 applies to any clause claiming to exempt the seller from any of the terms implied by ss.12–15 of the Sale of Goods Act, i.e. the terms as to title, description, satisfactory quality, fitness for purpose and sample. The effect of s.6 depends upon whether the buyer was "dealing as a consumer".

Consumer Deals

10–018   In any case where the buyer "deals as a consumer" it is impossible for the seller to exempt himself from any of his liability under ss.12–15 of the Sale of Goods Act. Section 12 of the Unfair Contract Terms Act 1977 tells us when a buyer "deals as a consumer":

> "(1) A party to a contract 'deals as consumer' in relation to another party if—
>
> > (a) he neither makes the contract in the course of a business nor holds himself out as doing so; and
> > (b) the other party does make the contract in the course of a business; and
> > (c) in the case of a contract governed by the law of sale of goods or hire-purchase, or by section 7 of this Act, the goods passing under or in pursuance of the contract are of a type ordinarily supplied for private use or consumption.
>
> (1A) But if the first party mentioned in subsection (1) is an individual paragraph (c) of that subsection must be ignored.
> (2) But the buyer is not in any circumstances to be regarded as dealing as consumer—
>
> > (a) if he is an individual and the goods are second hand goods sold at public auction at which individuals have the opportunity of attending the sale in person;
> > (b) if he is not an individual and the goods are sold by auction or by competitive tender.
>
> (3) Subject to this, it is for those claiming that a party does not deal as consumer to show that he does not."

Thus the following are not consumer deals:

> (i) The sale of goods for the purpose of resale by the purchaser to a wholesaler, retailer or distributor.

(ii) The sale of goods for use by the purchaser in an industrial process, e.g. manufacturing.

(iii) The sale of goods for use by the purchaser in the running of their business, e.g. a computer for use in a firm's office.

(iv) The sale of goods by a private individual.

(v) The sale of goods by competitive tender.

The Sale and Supply of Goods to Consumers Regulations 2002 have recently amended the wording of this section by inserting s.12(1A) and a new subs.(2) as above. The impact of the new s.12(1A) is to remove any difficulties where the goods supplied are goods *not* ordinarily supplied for private use where the buyer is an individual. Thus where the buyer is an individual, the status of the goods is now irrelevant. For example where an individual buys building materials, such as cement, timber, power-tools, etc., the fact that goods supplied are not ordinarily supplied for private use is irrelevant.[29]

The second change introduced by the 2002 Regulations continues the distinction between situations where the buyer is an individual and those where the buyer is not. Under s.12(2)(a) an auction sale can now be a consumer deal provided that:

(i) The buyer is an individual; and

(ii) The auction is for new goods (rather than second-hand goods); and

(iii) There was no opportunity of attending the auction in person.

Under s.12 as originally enacted, a buyer could never be regarded as dealing as a consumer **10–019** at an auction. This position has been retained for non-individual buyers under s.12(2)(a).

The question as to whether the contract was a consumer deal arose in *Rasbora Ltd v JCL Marine Ltd*.[30] A contract was made between Mr Atkinson and JCL Marine Ltd, a Norfolk boat builder, for JCL Marine to build a boat for Mr Atkinson. This contract included a clause claiming to exclude the sellers' (JCL Marine's) liability for breach of the statutory implied terms as to quality and fitness for purpose. Subsequently Rasbora Ltd, a company incorporated in Jersey, was substituted as buyer in place of Mr Atkinson. This was done by novation, i.e. by agreement between Mr Atkinson, JCL Marine Ltd and Rasbora Ltd. A novation is an extinguishing of rights under the earlier contract and the creation of a new contract. Rasbora Ltd was wholly owned by Mr Atkinson and, being a Jersey company, did not have to pay VAT (value added tax) on the boat. Shortly after it was purchased, the boat caught fire and sank off Dungeness. The buyers, Rasbora Ltd, sued the sellers for breach of the implied term as to merchantable (now satisfactory) quality. The sellers tried to rely upon the exemption clause. The judge held that the contract originally made between Mr Atkinson and JCL Marine was a consumer deal and that the new one made between Rasbora Ltd and JCL Marine was also a consumer deal, i.e. that the novation did not alter the consumer

---

[29] Unless, of course, the individual purports to be a trade purchaser in which case there will be a non-consumer deal. The Law Commission Report has recommended that this "holding-out" provision should be abolished, i.e. an individual's status as a consumer should not be lost by holding themselves out to be acting in the course of a business, see paras 3.25 and 3.26 of the Report, discussed at para.10–040, below.

[30] [1977] 1 Lloyd's Rep. 645.

nature of the contract. How was it that a limited company made a contract otherwise than in the course of its business? His Lordship pointed out that Rasbora had been formed by Mr Atkinson for the purpose of buying the boat and with the intention that the boat was to be used only by Mr Atkinson and his friends; there was no intention to hire it out. It being a consumer deal, the condition as to merchantable quality could not be excluded and the sellers were therefore liable.

In *R & B Customs Brokers v United Dominions Trust*[31] the Court of Appeal held that a company making a purchase (or sale) was not doing so "in the course of a business" unless it made that type of purchase (or sale) regularly. A company (whose business was shipping brokerage) had bought a car for the use of its directors. This was only the second or third time in its five years existence that the company had bought a car. It was held that the company had dealt as a consumer in buying the car, because it had not bought it "in the course of a business". The decision was almost certainly wrong. It was distinguished in *Stevenson v Rogers*[32] where the Court of Appeal held that a sale was a sale "in the course of a business" (for the purposes of the Sale of Goods Act, s.14) unless it was a purely private sale outside the confines of any business.[33] In *R & B Customs Brokers*,[34] the Court should have held the sale to be a non-consumer sale.

10–020   In *Feldarol Foundry Plc v Hermes Leasing (London) Ltd*[35] the Court of Appeal rejected the argument that the earlier decision in *R & B Customs Brokers* should not be followed in light of the decision in *Stevenson v Rogers*. In *Feldarol* a company (whose business was the operation of an aluminium foundry) had hired a car for its managing director under a hire-purchase agreement. The car was of unsatisfactory quality and the company sought to reject the vehicle despite an exclusion clause in the contract which purported to exclude all liability, e.g. under s.10(2) of the Supply of Goods (Implied Terms) Act 1973. The Court of Appeal held that the decision in *R & B Customs Brokers* was binding on the court and the exclusion clause was ineffective since Feldarol were not acting "in the course of a business". The decision of the courts in both *Feldarol* and *R & B Customs Brokers* may well be overturned in the near future if the Law Commission's draft Unfair Contract Terms Bill is enacted.[36] The proposed definition of a consumer contract is as follows[37]:

> "(1) 'Consumer contract' means a contract (other than one of employment) between—
>
>   (a) an individual ('the consumer') who enters into it wholly or mainly for purposes unrelated to a business of his, and
>   (b) a person ('the business') who enters into it wholly or mainly for purposes related to his business."

The reference to an "individual" within this definition removes the difficulty evident in *R & B Customs Brokers* and *Feldarol Foundry Plc* considered above and more closely follows

[31] [1988] 1 W.L.R. 321.
[32] [1999] 1 All E.R. 613.
[33] See para.7–017, above.
[34] [1988] 1 W.L.R. 321.
[35] [2004] EWCA Civ. 747; [2004] C.C.L.R. 8.
[36] See the discussion of the Bill and the Report of the Law Commission and Scottish Law Commission at para.10–040, below.
[37] cl.26 of the draft Contract Terms Bill.

the equivalent definition within the Unfair Terms in Consumer Contracts Regulations 1999.

Non-Consumer Deals

Where the buyer is not "dealing as consumer" the effect of s.6 of the Unfair Contract Terms   **10–021**
Act 1977 is as follows. It is impossible for the seller to exempt himself from liability under s.12 of the Sale of Goods Act. It is, however, possible for the seller to be exempted from liability under ss.13–15 of the Sale of Goods Act, but only in so far as the seller can show that the exemption clause satisfies the requirement of reasonableness, i.e. that it was a "fair and reasonable one to be included having regard to the circumstances which were, or ought reasonably to have been, known to or in the contemplation of the parties when the contract was made".[38]

Schedule 2 provides "guidelines" for the application of the reasonableness test:

> "(a) the strength of the bargaining positions of the parties relative to each other, taking into account (among other things) alternative means by which the customer's requirements could have been met;
>
> (b) whether the customer received an inducement to agree to the term, or in accepting it had an opportunity of entering into a similar contract with other persons, but without having to accept a similar term;
>
> (c) whether the customer knew or ought reasonably to have known of the existence and extent of the term (having regard, among other things, to any custom of the trade and any previous course of dealing between the parties);
>
> (d) where the term excludes or restricts any relevant liability if some condition is not complied with, whether it was reasonable at the time of the contract to expect that compliance with that condition would by practicable;
>
> (e) whether the goods were manufactured, processed or adapted to the special order of the customer."

It would appear from paragraph (a) that a seller who has a monopoly over the supply of the kind of goods in question is unlikely to convince the court of the reasonableness of a wide exemption clause, especially if it was a large demand for the product which enabled him to insist on the clause being in the contract. In the light of paragraph (b) the seller having a monopoly will be more likely to succeed if the buyer had been offered the chance of buying the goods, perhaps at a slightly higher price, on terms not including the exemption clause. Obviously, if the alternative offer had involved a considerably or prohibitively higher price, that would tell against the seller.

Paragraph (c) would appear not to affect decisions in cases such as *Kendall v Lillico*[39] and   **10–022**
Cointat v Myham,[40] where the purchaser chooses to buy goods for his business from a seller whose terms he has, in a consistent course of dealing, been apparently quite happy to accept,

---

[38] s.11.
[39] [1969] 2 A.C. 31, see para.10–007, above.
[40] (1914) 110 L.T. 749, see para.10–008, above.

or where the purchaser buys goods in a market in which a trade custom shows that merchants have found exclusion terms to be acceptable.

In light of paragraph (d), a clause excluding, for example, all liability "other than that in respect of defects and defaults notified to the seller within three days of purchase" would clearly not be reasonable.[41]

Paragraph (e) would be particularly relevant where the purchaser required the goods to be made or adapted from some use for which the seller did not normally supply goods. It would seem reasonable for the seller to stipulate that he will not guarantee the goods' suitability for that purpose.

10–023   Paragraphs (a) to (e) are only guidelines and all the circumstances of the case should be taken into account. So, for example, the scope and harshness (or otherwise) of the clause will also be relevant.

The leading case on the requirements of reasonableness arose, not under the Unfair Contract Terms Act 1977, but under the earlier provisions of the Supply of Goods (Implied Terms) Act 1973 which were replaced by the 1977 Act. The requirement of reasonableness under the earlier Act was different in two respects. First, the onus of proof was upon the buyer to show that the exemption clause did not pass the test, whereas under the 1977 Act the onus is on the seller to show that the clause passes the test. Secondly, under the 1973 Act the test was whether it was fair and reasonable to allow reliance upon the exemption clause, whereas under the 1977 Act the test is whether the clause is a fair and reasonable one to have been included in the contract. Nevertheless the former test and the current test are very similar and indeed the "guidelines" laid down by the two Acts are the same. The leading case is *George Mitchell v Finney Lock Seeds*.[42] There the exemption clause, according to its wording, limited the liability of some seed merchants (for supplying defective seed) to the cost of replacing the seed; it excluded liability for consequential loss of the buyers' crop. These limitation terms were incorporated in all contracts between seedsmen and farmers and had been for many years. They had not been negotiated by any representative body of farmers, such as the National Farmers' Union. They had been introduced by seed merchants putting them into their catalogues and invoices—and never objected to by farmers. It was held that the exemption clause did not in the circumstances pass the test of reasonableness and that therefore the sellers could not rely on it to limit their liability. The relevant circumstances were that: (i) the limitation terms had not been negotiated by any representative body; (ii) the buyers could not have discovered the error, (i.e. that the wrong seed had been delivered) until the crop was sown, whereas the sellers were in a position to have known; (iii) the buyers could not reasonably have been expected to cover such a risk (i.e. of crop failure) by insurance, whereas it was possible for seedsmen to cover their liability by insurance at a modest premium which would not have put up the cost of the seeds by very much; (iv) the error could not have occurred without some negligence on the part of the sellers.

George Mitchell v Finney Lock Seeds[43] was different from *Green v Cade*,[44] which had involved the sale of seed potatoes on the standard terms of the National Association of Seed Potato Merchants. In that case one clause, which on its wording excluded liability if the

[41] *Green v Cade* (1978) 1 Lloyd's Rep. 602, see para.10–023, below.
[42] [1983] 3 W.L.R. 163, for the facts see para.10–014, above.
[43] [1983] 3 W.L.R. 163.
[44] (1978) 1 Lloyd's Rep. 602.

buyers had not given notice of any defects within three days of purchase, was held to fail the reasonableness test. Another clause, restricting the sellers' liability for a consequential loss and limiting that liability to the amount of the contract price, was held to pass the reasonableness test. The latter clause, however, had had the approval of negotiating bodies representing both potato merchants and farmers; no blame for the infection of the seed potatoes was attributable to either side; and, further, the buyers, if they had so wished, could have bought at a small extra cost, seed potatoes certified by inspectors of the Ministry of Agriculture.[45]

In *St Albans City and District Council v International Computers Ltd*[46] the court had to apply the requirement of reasonableness to a limitation of liability clause in an international computer firm's standard conditions in a contract made with a local council to supply the council with a database for a large community charge register. At that time the community charge was a local tax. The clause limited the computer firm's liability to a maximum of £100,000. The database supplied was defective in that it overstated the local population by 2,966. This in turn had the effect that the rate of tax levied was lower than it would have been if the population had been accurately stated. This in turn caused a loss of tax revenue to the council of over £1.3 million. The relevant factors taken into account by the court were: (a) the parties were of unequal bargaining power; (b) the figure of £100,000 was small in relation to the potential and the actual risk; (c) the computer firm was insured for an aggregate sum of £50 million worldwide; (d) it was, in practical terms, easier for the computer firm to secure insurance and to pass the cost of that on to its customers and it was not unreasonable that the firm which made the profit by supplying the program should carry the risk. Thus the clause failed to satisfy the requirement of reasonableness and was unenforceable.[47]

10–024

EXEMPTIONS FROM OTHER TERMS OF THE CONTRACT: SECTION 3

We have just considered the extent to which the Unfair Contract Terms Act 1977 allows the seller to exclude his liability under ss.12–15 of the Sale of Goods Act. However, the contract will doubtless contain other terms, some of them expressly agreed between the parties (e.g. the date of delivery) and some of them implied (often by other sections of the Sale of Goods Act, e.g. as to the place of delivery, s.29(2)). The Unfair Contract Terms Act does not totally prohibit the seller from exempting himself from liability for breach of these other terms.[48] Section 3 of that Act, however, does, in certain circumstances, render such an exemption clause subject to the requirements of reasonableness. This section applies if two conditions are both satisfied:

10–025

　　(i) the seller's liability is "business liability",

---

[45] The Law Commission has recently rejected a suggestion that terms negotiated by trade bodies etc. should be exempted from the reasonableness test under the draft Unfair Contract Terms Bill, see the discussion of the Law Commission Report at para.10–040, below.

[46] [1996] 4 All E.R. 481.

[47] On the question of whether the contract in this case was a sale of goods contract see para.1–011, above.

[48] See *Kevin Berwick v Lloyds Bank TSB Bank Plc*; *Michael Haughton v Lloyds TSB Bank Plc* (2007) unreported, where s.3 (and s.4) was not applicable to an action seeking to recover various charges applied to a bank account since there had been neither a breach of contract (or negligence) on the part of the bank. For a discussion of this case, see White, "Banker's duties: bank charges" [2007] J.I.B.L.R. 100.

(ii) in buying the goods, the buyer "deals as consumer" or on the seller's written standard terms of business.

The first of these requirements will clearly be satisfied where the seller sells the goods in the course of his business. The meaning of "deals as consumer" has already been considered.[49] The Act does not define "written standard terms of business". This expression clearly covers the situation where a seller insists that all (or a considerable proportion of) his buyers buy on the terms of his written contract, there being no variation in the terms from one buyer to another. This would still seem to be so if most, though not all, the terms are standard—if, say, there are minor variations from one buyer to another (e.g. as to the commodity or the quantity bought or the price to be paid). Even where the only "standard" terms of the seller are those in the exemption clause itself, still a buyer whose contract includes that exemption clause could well be regarded as buying on the seller's "written standard terms of business".

Where the two conditions mentioned above are satisfied, s.3 applies and its effect is that the seller cannot[50]:

"(a) when himself in breach of contract, exclude or restrict any liability of his in respect of the breach; or

(b) claim to be entitled—

(i) to render a contractual performance substantially different from that which was reasonably expected of him, or

(ii) in respect of the whole or any part of his contractual obligation, to render no performance at all,

except in so far as the contract term [i.e. exemption clause] satisfies the requirement of reasonableness."

There is a great deal of room for the courts to interpret these words. Confining ourselves to the obvious, it is clear that for paragraph (a) to apply the seller must be in breach of contract. Clearly, therefore, a maximum damages clause would be caught by it.

10–026   Three important points must be made. First, s.3, where it applies, does not render a clause ineffective if the clause is shown to satisfy the requirement of reasonableness. This requirement has already been explained in relation to s.6 of the Unfair Contract Terms Act.[51] It is exactly the same here except that the Act does not say that the "guidelines" in Sch.2 should be referred to. Nevertheless, it seems likely that similar factors will in fact be taken into account by the courts. Secondly, an exemption clause may be partially effective if it is shown to be to some extent reasonable. A clause might, for example, claim (i) to exclude liability for certain fundamental breaches of contract, and (ii) to limit any damages to a maximum of £5,000. A court might well be persuaded that the clause is reasonable as to (ii) but not as to (i).

The third point is that where an exemption clause is not invalidated (or not completely so) by s.3 of the Unfair Contract Terms Act 1977, the buyer may still be able to defeat the exemption clause by relying on s.6, s.8 or s.2 of that Act. Section 6 has already been considered and applies where the buyer's claim is based upon a breach by the seller of the

[49] At para.10–018, above.
[50] s.3(2).
[51] See paras 10–021–10–024, above.

terms implied by ss.12–15 of the Sale of Goods Act. Section 8 applies where the claim is based upon misrepresentation and will be returned to later. Section 2 applies where the claim is based upon negligence.

EXEMPTIONS FROM LIABILITY FOR NEGLIGENCE: SECTION 2

In Chapter 9 we saw that a manufacturer can be liable to a consumer for any loss or damage **10–027** caused by the negligence of the manufacturer or any of his employees. This is so irrespective of whether the consumer bought the goods from the manufacturer. A distributor or seller who was not the manufacturer (e.g. a retailer) could also be liable under the same principle if he was negligent, e.g. if he negligently failed to pass on to the customer a warning label ("Not to be taken internally") which he had received with a bottle of medicine. We have also seen that a manufacturer or distributor who does not supply the goods directly to the consumer cannot (e.g. in a guarantee document) exclude any liability for negligence that he may have towards the consumer.[52] What about the trader who does sell directly to the consumer? This could be a manufacturer or, say, a retailer. Can he exclude his liability for negligence? Section 2 of the Unfair Contract Terms Act applies here. Its effect is twofold. First, it is impossible to exclude liability for death or personal injuries caused by negligence. Secondly, it is possible to exclude or restrict liability for other loss of damage (e.g. to property) caused by negligence, but only to the extent that the exemption clause is shown to satisfy the requirement of reasonableness. The requirement of reasonableness is exactly the same here as it is in relation to s.3.[53]

There are three final points about s.2. First, like ss.3 and 5, it applies only to "business liability". Secondly, where an exemption clause is not invalidated by s.2, the buyer may be able to sue the seller for breach of contract and defeat the exemption clause by virtue of ss.6 or 3 of the Unfair Contract Terms Act. Thirdly, he may be able to establish a claim for product liability under the Consumer Protection Act 1987 (such liability cannot be excluded).[54] Alternatively, he may be able to sue for misrepresentation.

EXEMPTIONS FROM LIABILITY FOR MISREPRESENTATION: SECTION 8

Section 8 of the Unfair Contract Terms Act 1977 amended s.3 of the Misrepresentation Act **10–028** 1967.[55] The latter section, as amended, renders any exemption clause ineffective except to the extent that the clause is shown to satisfy the requirement of reasonableness. This requirement is exactly the same here as it is in relation to s.3 of the Unfair Contract Terms Act.[56]

BUSINESS LIABILITY

Some sections (ss.2, 3 and 5) of the Unfair Contract Terms Act apply to exemption clauses **10–029** only where those clauses claim to exempt from "business liability". "Business" includes a

---

[52] See s.5 of the Unfair Contract Terms Act, para.9–003, above.
[53] See para.10–021, above.
[54] See para.9–007, above.
[55] See para.6–006, above.
[56] See para.10–021, above.

profession and the activities of any government department or local or public authority.[57]
Thus a private house-holder selling his old lawn mower or even his second-hand car is free
to insist on an exemption clause excluding his liability for, say, negligence. Such a clause will
be effective, subject only to the common law rules outlined earlier in this chapter. Two
sections of the Unfair Contract Terms Act apply to both business and to non-business
liability—ss.6 and 8. Thus, by s.8, the private seller cannot exempt himself from liability for
misrepresentation unless he can show that the exemption clause satisfies the requirement of
reasonableness. By s.6, the position is the same if he tries to exempt himself from ss.13–15
of the Sale of Goods Act. This is because it is not a consumer deal if the seller does not sell
in the course of a business. All of this does not, however, mean that if the goods prove
defective the private seller can easily be made liable for breach of the terms of ss.13–15 of
the Sale of Goods Act. He is unlikely to have sold by sample; that rules out s.15. By
definition the private seller did not sell in the course of a business; that rules out the
conditions in s.14 (i.e. as to satisfactory quality and fitness for purpose). Finally, provided the
goods correspond with the description, there will be no liability under s.13.

MIXED EXEMPTION CLAUSES

10–030   Suppose one exemption falls within more than one section of the Unfair Contract Terms Act
1977. Suppose, for example, it claims to exclude all the following liabilities of the seller; for
misrepresentation, for negligence and also for breach of the terms implied by ss.12–15 of the
Sale of Goods Act. Which section of the Unfair Contract Terms Act is relevant? The answer
depends upon what claim the buyer makes. Section 8 of the Unfair Contract Terms Act is
relevant to a claim for misrepresentation; s.2 to a claim for negligence; s.6 to a claim under
ss.12–15 of the Sale of Goods Act; and s.3 to a claim for any other breach of contract.
Following a consumer deal in which the consumer bought a hot water bottle direct from the
manufacturer, the consumer may claim for damage to his bed after the bottle burst. It is
possible here that his claims (if any) against the manufacturer for misrepresentation or
negligence will fail because of an exemption clause which satisfies the requirement of
reasonableness (imposed by ss.2 and 8 of the Unfair Contract Terms Act). A claim for
product liability under the Consumer Protection Act 1987 will also fail unless the damage to
the bed exceeds £275 in value.[58] A claim under s.14 of the Sale of Goods Act will, however,
succeed because s.6 of the Unfair Contract Terms Act totally prevents the exclusion from a
consumer deal of the terms implied by ss.12–15 of the Sale of Goods Act.

CONTRACTS OTHER THAN FOR THE SALE OF GOODS

10–031   The Unfair Contract Terms Act applies to hire-purchase contracts in exactly the same way as
it does to contracts of sale of goods. This will be explained in Chapter 25. There are certain
other contracts which are not contracts of sale of goods but which are analogous contracts
because the ownership of goods passes under them, e.g. contracts of exchange and barter and
contracts for labour and materials supplied.[59] The Unfair Contract Terms Act 1977 applies to

---

[57] s.14.
[58] See para.9–013, above.
[59] See Ch.8 above.

these analogous contracts in the same way as it applies to contracts of sale of goods. The statutory terms (as to title, description, quality and sample) implied by ss.2–5 of the Supply of Goods and Services Act 1982 are dealt with in the same way as the corresponding terms implied in contracts of sale of goods. There is the same distinction between "consumer deals" and others, the distinction having exactly the same effect.

Turning to hire contracts, it will be remembered that there are statutory implied terms as to title, description, quality and sample implied by ss.6–10 of the Supply of Goods and Services Act 1982.[60] The Unfair Contract Terms Act 1977 applies, with one small difference, to hire contracts as it does to contracts of sale of goods, hire-purchase, barter and exchange, etc. Thus, its effect is the same in relation to a clause claiming to exempt the supplier from liability under the terms relating to description, quality or sample. It is impossible to exclude such liability in a consumer deal, and in any non-consumer deal the clause is subject to the requirement of reasonableness. The one difference is that in a hire contract the terms as to title and quiet possession can be excluded or restricted by an exemption clause provided that exemption clause satisfies the requirement of reasonableness.

Finally, let us turn to the third set of terms implied by the Supply of Goods and Services Act 1982. These are the terms implied in a contract where the supplier has agreed to carry out a service.[61] These are terms that: the supplier acting in the course of a business will carry out the service with reasonable skill and care[62]; within a reasonable time[63]; and that the customer will pay a reasonable charge.[64] An exclusion clause, which purports to exclude or limit liability under these terms, is subject to the rules already outlined in this chapter, including the rules laid down in the Unfair Contract Terms Act 1977. In particular, s.3 of that Act will apply.[65] Thus a clause purporting to exclude or limit the supplier's liability will be subject to the requirement of reasonableness, provided the supplier's customer was either dealing as a consumer or else had contracted on the supplier's written standard terms of business. A further explanation is required in relation to the term as to reasonable care and skill implied by s.13 of the Supply of Goods and Services Act 1982. This is because a claim for breach of that term is treated by the Unfair Contract Terms Act, s.1, as a claim for negligence. Thus, liability for death or personal injury arising from such a breach of contract can not be excluded or restricted at all; liability for other loss or injury arising from such a breach can be excluded only in so far as the exclusion clause satisfies the requirement of reasonableness.[66]

THE UNFAIR TERMS IN CONSUMER CONTRACTS REGULATIONS 1999

The Unfair Terms in Consumer Contracts Regulations 1999[67] have a considerably broader ambit than the Unfair Contract Terms Act which is primarily concerned with exclusion   **10–032**

---

[60] See para.8–008, above.
[61] See para.8–009, above.
[62] s.13.
[63] s.14.
[64] s.15.
[65] See para.10–025, above.
[66] Unfair Contract Terms Act 1977, s.2, see para.10–027, above.
[67] SI 1999/2083

clauses and may apply to any contractual term. These Regulations are virtually identical in their effect on contracts as the Unfair Terms in Consumer Contracts Regulations 1994[68] which they replaced. They apply to a wide range of contracts as considered below. Where they apply they make any unfair term not binding on the consumer.

Contracts to which the Regulations Apply

10–033   The basic rule is that these Regulations apply to any contract where a trader is contracting to supply goods or services to a private consumer. Put more precisely, they apply to a contract between, on the one hand a seller or supplier (of goods or services)[69] who is acting for purposes relating to his business and, on the other hand, an individual consumer who is acting for purposes which are outside his business. The Regulations apply where goods or services are being sold or supplied. Certainly, therefore, they apply to a situation where goods are being hired because, though not a sale, such a contract does involve a supply of goods. It is possible, however, that for these purposes "goods" also includes land.[70]

These Regulations implement the Directive on Unfair Terms in Consumer Contracts.[71] The word "goods" is not defined in the directive or in the Regulations. In some countries' text of the Directive the word used is not a word confined in its meaning to what we would call chattels. Thus the French language version of the directive includes the word "biens", which includes both goods and land. If this is what is meant by "goods", then a contract between a house-builder/estate developer and the first-time private house purchaser is subject to these Regulations. On any view, a contract where a private house owner is engaging an estate agent to sell the house for him is subject to the Regulations, since clearly the estate agent is providing a "service" to the consumer. Equally, a residential mortgage contract is simply a contract for a loan on the security of a mortgage, and where the borrower (mortgagor) is a private house buyer the lender is providing the service of lending money to the borrower; thus such a contract is subject to the Regulations.

Turning to financial services, there is no doubt, for example, that a contract between a stockbroker and a private client is subject to the Regulations, since the former in the course of his business is providing a service to the consumer.

Clarity and Interpretation

10–034   Any written term must be expressed in plain, intelligible language. If there is any doubt about the meaning of a written term, the interpretation most favourable to the consumer prevails.[72]

---

[68] SI 1994/3159.
[69] The term "seller or supplier" is defined by reg.3(1) as "any natural or legal person who, in contracts covered by these Regulations, is acting for purposes relating to his trade, business or profession, whether publicly owned or privately owned".
[70] See, for example, Bright and Bright, (1995) 111 L.Q.R. 655.
[71] 93/13/EEC.
[72] See reg.7.

What is an Unfair Term?

This is any term "if, contrary to the requirement of good faith, it causes a significant **10–035** imbalance in the parties' rights and obligations under the contract to the detriment of the consumer".[73] The requirement of good faith is not defined within the Regulations. Recital 16 of the Directive does, however, offer a definition and was considered by Lord Bingham in *Director General of Fair Trading v First National Bank*[74]:

> "The requirement of good faith in this context is one of fair and open dealing. Openness requires that the terms should be expressed fully, clearly and legibly, containing no concealed pitfalls or traps. Appropriate prominence should be given to terms which might operate disadvantageously to the customer. Fair dealing requires that a supplier should not, whether deliberately or unconsciously, take advantage of the consumer's necessity, indigence, lack of experience, unfamiliarity with the subject matter of the contract, weak bargaining position or any other factor listed in or analogous to those listed in Schedule 2 to the Regulations".

Moreover, Lord Bingham stated[75]:

> "The member states have no common concept of fairness or good faith, and the Directive does not purport to state the law of any single member state. It lays down a test to be applied, whatever their pre-existing law, by all member states. If the meaning of the test were doubtful, or vulnerable to the possibility of differing interpretations in differing member states, it might be desirable or necessary to seek a ruling from the European Court of Justice on its interpretation. But the language used in expressing the test, so far as applicable in this case, is in my opinion clear and not reasonably capable of differing interpretations."

The Regulations do not state upon whom rests the burden of proof, i.e. to establish fairness or unfairness. The burden therefore falls upon the consumer as the party alleging unfairness.[76] In determining whether the term is unfair the court must take into account the nature of the goods or services and must refer to: all the circumstances attending the making of the contract; all the other terms of the contract and of any contract upon which it is dependant.[77]

   In Sch.2 of the Regulations there is an indicative list of the sorts of terms which *may* be regarded as unfair. The list, which is not exhaustive, includes exemption clauses, limitation of liability clauses, penalty clauses, and clauses:

---

[73] reg.5(1). Clearly, therefore, any term which creates an imbalance to the detriment of the seller or supplier is not unfair under reg.5.

[74] [2002] 1 A.C. 481 at [17]. Considered at para.24–008, below.

[75] [2002] 1 A.C. 481 at [17].

[76] The Law Commission Report, *Unfair Terms in Contracts* suggests that "where an issue has been raised as to whether a term is fair and reasonable, the burden of proving that it is fair and reasonable should rest on the business", (2005) Cmnd. 6464 at [3.130].

[77] See reg.6.

- which the consumer had no real opportunity to become acquainted with before the contract;

- giving the seller/supplier the discretion to terminate the contract without conferring the same right upon the consumer;

- giving the seller/supplier the power to terminate a contract of indefinite duration without giving reasonable notice (except where there are serious grounds to do so);

- automatically extending a contract of fixed duration unless the consumer indicates to the contrary within an unreasonably early deadline;

- enabling the seller/supplier to retain a deposit or part payment when the consumer cancels the contract, without also giving the consumer a similar right to compensation where it is the seller/supplier who cancels the contract;

- enabling the seller/supplier to retain a deposit or part payment for services not yet supplied when it is the supplier who cancels the contract;

- enabling the seller/supplier to vary the agreement unilaterally for an invalid reason or for a reason not specified in the contract;

- providing for the seller/supplier to raise the price without at the same time giving the consumer the right in such a case to cancel the contract if the price is then high as compared with the original contract price;

- providing for the price to be determined at the time of delivery but not allowing for the consumer to cancel the agreement if the price is then high as compared to the original contract price;

- giving the seller/supplier the exclusive right to interpret any term of the contract;

- giving the seller/supplier the right to determine whether goods or services are in conformity with the contract;

- giving the seller/supplier the possibility of transferring his obligations under the contract, where this may reduce the guarantees for the consumer, without the consumer's agreement;

- excluding or hindering the consumer's right to take legal action or take any other legal remedy, particularly by requiring the consumer to take disputes exclusively to arbitration not covered by legal provisions.

Two kinds of term are not subject to the requirement to be fair:

(i) a term which is individually negotiated;

(ii) core terms of the contract (in so far as they are in plain and intelligible language).

10–036   The burden to establish that a term was individually negotiated rests on the seller/supplier. A term will not be regarded as individually negotiated if it was drafted in advance and the consumer was therefore unable to influence its substance.

Core terms are those that:

    (i) define the main subject-matter of the contract;

    (ii) concern the adequacy of the price or remuneration for the goods or services supplied.

Thus the terms that are subject to the Regulations are those that are ancilliary, e.g. those relating to quality; time (of delivery/completion and of payment); arbitration; making complaints; giving (and forfeiting) deposits or down payments; cancellation; powers to vary the agreement, etc. *Oceano Grupo Editorial SA v Rocio Muriciano Quintero*[78] involved a number of contracts by a company which had its principal place of business in Barcelona, each such contract being a contract to sell, on instalment credit terms, an encyclopedia to a consumer domiciled in another part of Spain. Each contract contained a clause, not individually negotiated, giving exclusive jurisdiction to the Barcelona courts, which is where the seller commenced proceedings against consumers who had defaulted on their repayments. The European Court clearly considered the clause to be unfair (within the meaning of the Directive). It was held that the Barcelona court should of its own motion (a) determine whether the jurisdiction clause was unfair and, (b), it being unfair, should decline the jurisdiction it conferred.

Effect of a Term being Unfair

This matter is dealt with by reg.8:   **10–037**

    (1) An unfair term in a contract concluded with a consumer by a seller or supplier shall not be binding on the consumer.

    (2) The contract shall continue to bind the parties if it is capable of continuing in existence without the unfair term.

Thus the contract is treated as if the unfair term were not in it. Therefore, provided the contract is capable of subsisting without the unfair term, the rest of the contract survives.

Relationship with other Legislation

In making these Regulations the Government implemented a European directive. The   **10–038**
Regulations are clearly capable of applying to exclusion clauses. Any such clause held to fail the fairness requirement cannot be relied upon against the consumer. These Regulations have not repealed or amended any other legislation. In particular, the Unfair Contract Terms Act 1977 remains fully in force. Thus there are now two separate pieces of legislation which can potentially be used to render an exclusion clause ineffective; the consumer who is trying to

---

[78] June 27, 2000 C-240/98, ECJ.

prevent the trader relying on such a clause can rely on either the Regulations or the 1977 Act or both. The Regulations are wider in one respect than the Act, since the Regulations can apply to any term, whether or not it is an exclusion clause. As we have seen above, they could for example apply to a liquidated damages clause[79]; or to a penalties clause[80]; or indeed to something which, though not a penalty, is nevertheless very close to being one.[81] On the other hand, in a different respect the 1977 Act is wider than the Regulations, since the Act, though confined to exclusion clauses, is capable of applying to such a clause if it is a standard term used in a contract between two businesses.

So far, reported cases under the Regulations have involved, not exclusion clauses but clauses in credit agreements which, though not extortionate, could be regarded as somewhat oppressive. These cases, including *Director General of Fair Trading v First National Bank,*[82] are explained at paras 26–08 and 26–24 below.

Power of the Office of Fair Trading

10–039   One imagines the Regulations being of significance in contractual disputes between consumer and trader. However, the Regulations also give a power of enforcement to the Office of Fair Trading. The OFT, on receiving a complaint that a contract term is unfair, can bring proceedings for an injunction to stop a trader using an unfair term.[83] In addition, the OFT is given the power to accept undertakings from traders and will take these into account in determining whether to start proceedings for an injunction.[84] To facilitate this power, the OFT (or other qualifying body) may require any person to provide copies of any relevant documentation[85] (e.g. copies of their standard contracts) and information regarding their use.[86] The 1999 Regulations now give similar enforcement powers to other regulatory bodies (e.g. water and gas regulators) and to local Trading Standards Departments.[87] In addition, the power to seek an injunction has now been extended to a non-statutory body, the Consumers' Association.

REFORM

10–040   In 2002 the Law Commission and the Scottish Law Commission released a Consultation Paper assessing the following three issues[88]:

> (1) Replacing the Unfair Contract Terms Act 1977 and the Unfair Terms in Consumer Contracts Regulations 1999 with a unified regime.

---

[79] See para.14–018, below.
[80] See para.25–029, below.
[81] See for example *Associated Distributors v Hall* at para.25–030, below.
[82] [2000] All E.R. 759.
[83] See reg.12.
[84] See regs 10(3) and 11(2).
[85] See reg.13 generally and reg.13(3)(a).
[86] See reg.13(3)(b).
[87] See reg.3(1) and Sch.1.
[88] "*Unfair Terms in Contracts*", Law Commission Consultation Paper No. 166; Scottish Law Commission Paper 119. See the terms of reference at para.1.1.

(2) Extending the scope of the Unfair Terms in Consumer Contracts Regulations to protect businesses, in particular small enterprises.

(3) Making any replacement legislation clearer and more accessible to the reader, so far as is possible without making the law significantly less certain.

The need for a unified regime is well illustrated by the complications considered above by the dual regime surrounding unfair terms. The Unfair Contract Terms Act 1977 applies to exclusion clauses only, yet has a broader application in that it covers consumer and business contracts. The Unfair Terms in Consumer Contracts Regulations 1999 by contrast have a broader remit in applying to any contractual term, and not merely to exclusion clauses, yet has a narrower application in applying to consumer contracts. The difficulties caused by the dual regime were laid down by the Law Commissions' in the following terms[89]:

(1) the statutory controls over unfair terms are split between two pieces of legislation and must be located in each text;

(2) the UTCCR and UCTA contain inconsistent and overlapping provisions;

(3) the scope of application of each piece of legislation is different;

(4) UCTA and the UTCCR use different language and terminology;

(5) UCTA is drafted in a very dense and highly technical style; and

(6) the UTCCR are a fairly literal version of the text of the Directive whose language and, in some instances, concepts are not always easily understood by UK lawyers.

The consequence of these difficulties is that, as Beale and Goriely state[90]:

" . . . the law on unfair contract terms, which affects ordinary people in their everyday lives, is unnecessarily complicated and difficult to understand. It leads to widespread confusion among consumers, businesses and their advisers."

The consultation period was followed in 2005 by a final report and a draft Unfair Contract Terms Bill which addressed each of the three issues under the term of reference.[91] The proposals can be split into two broad categories, those relating to consumer contracts and those relating to business to business contracts.[92]

Consumer Contracts

The recommendations relating to consumer contracts focus upon the central aim of increasing clarity and accessibility to the law of unfair contract terms whilst retaining the level of **10–041**

[89] Law Commission Report No. 292, (2005) Cmnd. 6464, at para.2.4.
[90] "An unfairly complex law" (155) New Law Journal 318.
[91] Law Commission Report No. 292, (2005) Cmnd. 6464.
[92] The proposals have been accepted by the Government, subject to evaluation of the costs of implementation (i) generally; (ii) on the courts; and (iii) on small businesses.

protection currently afforded to consumers. The fundamental recommendations are as follows:

1. There should be a single piece of legislation for the whole of the UK[93];

2. As far as possible, the new, unified regime should be clearer and more accessible to the reader rather than being based on UCTA or the UTCCR;

3. With some minor exceptions, there should be no reduction of consumer protection[94];

4. Those terms that are of no effect under UCTA should remain of no effect; and

5. Other "non-core" terms (including terms that were individually negotiated) should be required to satisfy a "fair and reasonable" test.[95]

Business to Business Contracts

10–042   The most controversial proposal by the Law Commissions was that the protection afforded to consumer contracts by the Unfair Terms in Consumer Contracts Regulations should be extended so as to include contracts between one business and another.[96] This was removed from the final report which recommends that the controls within the Unfair Contract Terms Act should be replicated in the new legislation. Thus the fundamental recommendations are as follows:

1. The ineffectiveness of any exclusion of business liability for death or personal injury caused by negligence remains (s.2(1))[97];

2. The exclusion, where reasonable, of business liability for other damage caused by negligence remains (s.2(2))[98];

3. The ineffectiveness of any exclusion clause relating to title remains (ss.6(1) and 7(3A))[99];

4. Certain provisions within UCTA should not be replicated in the new legislation. These include: s.6(3), s.7(3) and s.7(4), so the implied terms (other than as to title) would be freely excludable;

---

[93] Consequently, the draft Bill contains no separate Parts for any single jurisdiction. See paras 3.6–3.9 of the final report.

[94] The minor exceptions are two-fold. First, the definition of "consumer" being limited to natural persons removes protections in *R & B Customs Brokers* situations. Secondly, certain provisions within UCTA would not be replicated within the new regime. These include s.5 (consumer guarantees); s.9 (effect of breach); and s.28 (sea-passengers). See paras 3.48 and 3.49 of the final report.

[95] See paras 3.50–3.55 of the final report. This measure allows terms which have been individually negotiated to be reviewed for fairness. Consequently, cl.4 of the draft Bill extends to both negotiated and non-negotiated terms. Core terms remain unaffected and are not subject to the fairness test, see paras 3.56–3.66 of the final report.

[96] See *"Unfair Terms in Contracts"*, Law Commission Consultation Paper No. 166; Scottish Law Commission Paper 119, Pt 5.

[97] See paras 4.18–4.21 of the final report and cl.1(1) of the draft Bill.

[98] See paras 4.36–4.40 of the final report and cl.1(2) of the draft Bill.

[99] See paras 4.18–4.21 of the final report and cl.5 of the draft Bill.

5. The protections in s.3 of UCTA should be replicated.[100]

Micro-Business Contracts

The most radical element to the Law Commissions recommendations concerns the extension   **10–043**
of protection to "micro-businesses". Whilst these businesses are protected by the general
business-to-business framework as discussed above, they are also afforded the ability "to
challenge any 'non-core' contract term under the 'fair and reasonable' test, provided it is a
standard term".[101] A "micro-business" is defined as a business that has employed an average
of nine or fewer full-time equivalent employees over the preceding year. This is subject to an
exemption whereby any contract with a value higher than £500,000 will not qualify as a
micro-business contract.

The "Fair and Reasonable" Test

In creating a unified Bill, combining the Unfair Contract Terms Act 1977 and the Unfair   **10–044**
Terms in Consumer Contracts Regulations 1999, one of the key issues was the reconciliation
between the "reasonableness" under the Unfair Contract Terms Act and "unfair" under the
Unfair Terms in Consumer Contracts Regulations. The proposed "fair and reasonable" test
is laid down in cl.14 of the Bill:

> "(1) Whether a contract term is fair and reasonable is to be determined by taking into
> account—
>
> (a) the extent to which the term is transparent, and
> (b) the substance and effect of the term, and all the circumstances existing at the
> time it was agreed.
>
> (2) Whether a notice is fair and reasonable is to be determined by taking into
> account—
>
> (a) the extent to which the notice is transparent, and
> (b) the substance and effect of the notice, and all the circumstances existing at the
> time when the liability arose (or, but for the notice, would have arisen).
>
> (3) 'Transparent' means—
>
> (a) expressed in reasonably plain language,
> (b) legible,
> (c) presented clearly, and
> (d) readily available to any person likely to be affected by the contract term or
> notice in question."

---

[100] See paras 4.45–4.57 of the final report and cl.9 of the draft Bill.
[101] See paras 5.27–5.30 of the final report.

In proposing this test the Law Commission have removed the reference within reg.5(1) to the requirement of "good faith". This was motivated primarily by the concept itself being "unfamiliar to English and Scottish lawyers in this area of law".[102]

At the time of writing, whilst the proposals have been accepted in principle, there has been no indication as to when there will be released an assessment of the impact of the proposed Bill.

General Reading

10–045

- Adams and Brownsword, "The Unfair Contract Terms Act: A Decade of Discretion" (1988) 104 L.Q.R. 94;

- Brown and Chandler, "Unreasonableness and the Unfair Contract Terms Act" (1993) 109 L.Q.R. 41;

- Hedley, "Defective Software in the Court of Appeal" (1997) 56 C.L.J. 21;

- Law Commission Consultation Paper, *Unfair Terms in Contracts*, No. 166, (2002);

- Law Commission Report, *Unfair Terms in Contracts*, No. 292 (2005) Cmnd. 6464;

- Macdonald, "Mapping the Unfair Contract Terms Act 1977 and the Directive on Unfair Terms in Consumer Contracts" [1994] J.B.L. 441;

- Macdonald, "Unifying Unfair Terms Legislation" (2004) 67 M.L.R. 69;

- Macmillan, "Evolution or Revolution? Unfair Terms in Consumer Contracts" [2002] C.L.J. 22;

- Palmer, "Limiting Liability for Negligence" (1982) 45 M.L.R. 763;

- Peel, "Reasonable Exemption Clauses" (2001) 117 L.Q.R. 545;

- Reynolds, "Unfair Contract Terms" (1994) 110 L.Q.R. 1.

---

[102] Law Commission Report at para.3.86.

Chapter 11

DELIVERY AND PAYMENT

INTRODUCTION

The parties can make what agreement they wish about the time, place and manner of delivery   **11–001**
and payment. What follows is an explanation of the rights and duties between the seller and
buyer when they have not agreed anything different in their contract.

Concurrent Conditions

Section 28 provides: **11–002**

> "Unless otherwise agreed, delivery of the goods and payment of the price are concurrent
> conditions . . . "

Thus, although s.49 states that the seller can sue for the price in certain circumstances,[1] he
will nevertheless not be able to do so unless he is also ready and willing to deliver the goods.
Equally, the buyer will not be able to sue for non-delivery unless he was ready and willing
to pay, or else it had been agreed that he could have credit. The rule that delivery and payment
are concurrent conditions ties in with the unpaid seller's lien[2] which entitles him, in the
absence of a contrary agreement, to retain the goods until payment.

---

[1] See Ch.12.
[2] See Ch.12.

DELIVERY

11–003   Delivery is the voluntary transfer of possession from one person to another.[3] Delivery may be achieved in one of several ways. The seller may physically hand over the goods, i.e. actual delivery. He may hand over the means of control of the goods, e.g. the key to the premises where they are housed which may amount to constructive delivery (where actual delivery does not occur, but *control* of the goods is transferred from seller to buyer). Alternatively, the seller may, where the goods are at the time of the sale in the possession of a third party (e.g. at a warehouse), instruct the third party to hold the goods to the order of the buyer. In that case, delivery occurs when the third party attorns, i.e. acknowledges to the buyer that he holds the goods on his behalf.[4] Delivery can be made in an appropriate case by the transfer of a document, or documents, of title, as in c.i.f. contracts.[5] Sometimes there could be confusion between the last two methods of delivery. For example, X could own a cargo in course of transit which is therefore in the hands of a third party, the carrier. If X sells it by dealing with the documents of title, then delivery occurs when he transfers the bill of lading to the buyer, irrespective of whether the carrier attorns.[6]

Place of Delivery

11–004   Section 29 provides:

> "(1) Whether it is for the buyer to take possession of the goods or for the seller to send them to the buyer is a question depending in each case on the contract, express or implied, between the parties.
>
> (2) Apart from any such contract, express or implied, the place of delivery is the seller's place of business, if he has one, and if not, his residence: except that, if the contract is for the sale of specific goods, which to the knowledge of the parties when the contract is made are in some other place, then that place is the place of delivery."

Thus, unless otherwise agreed, it is not for the seller to convey the goods to the buyer but for the latter to collect them. If the seller does agree to convey them, he must do so within a reasonable length of time—s.29(3). If on arrival he hands them over to someone whom he reasonably assumes to be authorised to receive them, then he has carried out his duty of delivery: *Galbraith and Grant v Block*.[7] One possible consequence of this is exemplified in the recent decision of the Court of Appeal in *Computer 2000 Distribution Ltd v ICM Computer Solutions Plc*[8] where a rogue convinced the buyer to arrange delivery to an address where they were received by a security guard and subsequently handed over to the rogue. The

---

[3] Defined in s.61(1).
[4] s.29(4).
[5] See para.3–023, above.
[6] s.29(4).
[7] [1922] 2 K.B. 155.
[8] *The Times*, November 17, 2004.

Court held that the (legitimate) buyer must pay for the goods since they had been delivered.

Time of Delivery

We have already seen[9] that, in a commercial contract, the time of delivery is normally "of the essence". Thus, if a delivery date is stipulated and the seller cannot make delivery by that date, that is a breach of condition and the buyer is entitled to repudiate the contract and sue for non-delivery.   **11–005**

When no time is stipulated and it is for the buyer to collect, the seller must be ready to hand over the goods (against payment) to the buyer on demand at any time after the making of the contract.[10] If he fails to do so, he is in breach of condition; the buyer can treat the contract as repudiated and sue for non-delivery.

Expenses

Unless otherwise agreed, the seller must bear the expenses, if any, connected with putting the goods into a deliverable state.[11]   **11–006**

Delivery of Wrong Quantity

Section 30 provides: **11–007**

"(1) Where the seller delivers to the buyer a quantity of goods less than he contracted to sell, the buyer may reject them, but if the buyer accepts the goods so delivered he must pay for them at the contract rate.

 (2) Where the seller delivers to the buyer a quantity of goods larger than he contracted to sell, the buyer may accept the goods included in the contract and reject the rest, or he may reject the whole.

(2A) A buyer who does not deal as consumer may not—

  (a) where the seller delivers a quantity of goods less than he contracted to sell, reject the goods under subsection (1) above, or
  (b) where the seller delivers a quantity of goods larger than he contracted to sell, reject the whole under subsection (2) above,

  if the shortfall or, as the case may be, excess is so slight that it would be unreasonable for him to do so.

(2B) It is for the seller to show that a shortfall or excess fell within subsection (2A) above.

[9] At para.7–008, above.
[10] Provided made at a reasonable hour, s.29(5).
[11] s.29(6).

(2C) Subsections (2A) and (2B) above do not apply to Scotland.

(2D) Where the seller delivers a quantity of goods—

   (a) less than he contracted to sell, the buyer shall not be entitled to reject the goods under subsection (1) above,

   (b) larger than he contracted to sell, the buyer shall not be entitled to reject the whole under subsection (2) above,

   unless the shortfall or excess is material.

(2E) Subsection (2D) above applies to Scotland only.

(3) Where the seller delivers to the buyer a quantity of goods larger than he contracted to sell and the buyer accepts the whole of the goods so delivered he must pay for them at the contract rate.

(4) *(Subsection (4) was repealed in 1995).*

(5) This section is subject to any usage of trade, special agreement or course of dealing between the parties."

The law ignores trifling breaches of contract. In *Shipton, Anderson v Weil Bros*[12] the sellers were entitled to deliver 4,950 tonnes. They in fact delivered 4,950 tonnes 55lb. It was held that this did not entitle the buyers to reject the whole consignment.

A breach of the obligations to deliver the contract quantity will be a breach of the condition implied by s.13.[13] This leads to the observation that s.30(5) must presumably be read subject to the provisions of the Unfair Contract Terms Act 1977 which has drastically reduced the ability of the parties to exclude or restrict the seller's liability.[14]

11–008   Sections 30(1) and 30(2) allows the buyer to reject the goods (all of them) if too many or too few are delivered. In the case of a buyer who is not dealing as a consumer, this is now subject to the rule in s.30(2A) that the buyer does not have this right of rejection if the shortfall or excess is so slight as to make rejection unreasonable.[15] Section 30(1) entitles the buyer to reject all the goods if less than the contract quantity is delivered. Section 30(1) does not, however, apply where a contract is severable, i.e. where the parties have agreed that delivery can be made in instalments and, on a true construction of the contract, the parties did not intend that a breach of one consignment was to justify rejection of them all: *Regent v Francesco*.[16] In that case a shortfall in one instalment will normally only justify a rejection of that one instalment. It would not entitle the buyer to reject all other instalments unless the seller's breach was so serious as to amount to a repudiation of the contract.[17]

Delivery by Instalments

11–009   There are three possible situations:

   (i) The parties did not agree that delivery could be by instalments. In this case the buyer is not bound to accept delivery by instalments. In *Behrend v Produce*

---

[12] [1912] 1 K.B. 574.
[13] See para.7–013, above.
[14] See para.10–015 onwards, above.
[15] For an explanation of who "deals as a consumer", see paras 10–018–10–020, above.
[16] [1981] Com. L.R. 78.
[17] See para.11–009, below.

Brokers[18] part of the goods were delivered which the buyers accepted. It was held, applying s.30, that the buyers were entitled to refuse to accept later delivery of the rest of the goods and that they should pay pro rata for those they had accepted.

(ii) The parties agreed that delivery could be by instalments but the contract is not severable. A breach of condition (e.g. as to quality) in relation to the first instalment will entitle the buyer to repudiate the whole contract. If, however, he has accepted one or more instalments (or any part thereof), he will not be able to reject later instalments if there is a breach of condition in relation to them— s.11(4).[19] This appears to remain the position even after the introduction in 1995 of the right of partial rejection.[20]

(iii) The parties agreed that delivery could be made by instalments (either on specified dates or "as required") and the contract is severable (divisible). The contract is severable if, on its true construction, the parties did not intend that a breach as to one consignment would justify rejection of all the consignments. If the parties had agreed that each consignment was to be separately paid for, the court will normally construe the contract as severable. That, however, is not an essential requirement of a severable contract. In the case of a severable contract, acceptance of one or more instalments does not preclude rejection of later instalments for breach of condition—s.11(4). In *Jackson v Rotax Motor and Cycle Co*[21] the buyer accepted as satisfactory the first delivery of motor horns but claimed to reject the later deliveries because they were not of merchantable quality. It was held that he was entitled to do this.

A more difficult question in relation to severable contracts is whether a breach of condition in relation to one or more instalments entitles the innocent party to regard the whole contract as repudiated or whether it is a severable breach confined to the instalments in question. It is a question of fact in each case depending upon the circumstances.[22] *Maple Flock Co v Universal Furniture Products (Wembley)*[23] concerned a severable contract for the sale of 100 tonnes of flock by instalments. The first 15 instalments were satisfactory, the 16th was defective, and there were four more satisfactory deliveries. The buyers claimed to regard the whole contract as repudiated. It was held that they could not. The court said that whether the breach was a repudiatory one depended on two factors:

(a) the ratio the breach bore quantitatively to the whole contract; and

(b) the likelihood of the breach being repeated in later instalments.

On neither factor did the breach appear serious in this case. Sometimes the contract includes a clause such as "each instalment to be considered as a separate contract". This has little effect and the courts will still regard the contract as one contract (albeit a severable one)

---

[18] [1920] 3 K.B. 530.
[19] Unless he can bring himself within s.30 above.
[20] See para.13–008, below.
[21] [1910] 2 K.B. 937.
[22] s.31(2).
[23] [1934] 1 K.B. 148.

and therefore it is possible for a sufficiently serious breach to be a repudiation of the whole contract: *Smyth (Ross) v Bailey.*[24]

11–010   The problem of classifying the contract as either non-severable (i.e. (ii) above) or severable (i.e. (iii) above) arose in *Rosenthal v Esmail.*[25] Under a c.i.f. contract which provided "each shipment to be regarded as a separate contract", the sellers had an option whether to send separate shipments or to send all the goods by one shipment. They chose the latter course but they sent to the buyer separate shipping documents in respect of two different lots in the one ship. The buyer claimed that the contract was severable, accepted one lot and rejected the other for breach of condition. The House of Lords held that since the sellers had opted for the one shipment, albeit with separate documents, the contract was not severable. Therefore, the buyers having accepted part of the goods, could not reject the rest.[26] This decision must now, however, be read in the light of the right of partial rejection introduced in 1994.[27]

Delivery to a Carrier

11–011   Where the seller is authorised or required to send the goods to the buyer, delivery to a carrier for that purpose will normally constitute complete performance of the seller's duty of delivery.[28]

The seller must, unless otherwise authorised, make the best reasonably possible contract with the carrier on behalf of the buyer.[29] In *Thomas Young v Hobson*[30] the seller made a contract for the goods to be carried at the "owner's risk". The carrier would have agreed to carry them for the same price at the carrier's risk. The goods were damaged in transit and it was held that the seller was in breach of his duty under s.32(2) and the buyer was entitled to reject the goods.[31]

Where customary, the seller must give sufficient information to the buyer to enable him to insure the goods whilst in transit by sea.[32]

11–012   Where the buyer deals as consumer, s.32 is of no application and must be ignored under s.32(4).[33] Therefore, where the buyer is a consumer and the seller is authorised or required to send the goods to the buyer, delivery of the goods to the carrier is not delivery of the goods to the buyer.[34]

PAYMENT

11–013   Normally, in the absence of contrary agreement, the buyer need not make payment until delivery is made—s.28. However, where the goods have been destroyed or stolen at a time

---

[24] [1940] 3 All E.R. 60.
[25] [1965] 1 W.L.R. 1117.
[26] s.11.
[27] See para.13–008, below.
[28] s.32(1).
[29] s.32(2).
[30] (1949) 65 T.L.R. 365.
[31] As to risk generally during transit, see paras 3–028 and 7–027, above.
[32] s.32(3).
[33] Inserted by the Sale and Supply of Goods to Consumers Regulations (SI 2002/3045), reg.4(3).
[34] For the definition of "dealing as consumer" see para.10–018, above.

when they were at the buyer's risk,[35] then of course he is under a duty to pay, even though delivery is impossible.

Apart from that situation, if the buyer has paid and the goods are not delivered, he is entitled to recover the price because he has received no consideration for it.[36] Two matters are dealt with elsewhere, the amount of the price[37] and when the seller can sue for the price.[38]

---

[35] See para.3–029, above.
[36] s.54.
[37] See paras 2–010–2–012, above.
[38] See para.12–003, below.

Chapter 12

SELLER'S REMEDIES

A seller has two sets of remedies available: personal remedies enforceable by taking action **12–001** in the courts against the buyer and remedies exercisable against the goods (referred to as "real remedies").

PERSONAL REMEDIES

The seller has two possible actions: for the price or for damages for non-acceptance. **12–002**

The Price

Section 49 of the Sale of Goods Act 1979 allows the seller to maintain an action for the price **12–003** where both the following conditions are fulfilled:

> (i) The buyer has wrongfully refused or neglected to pay according to the terms of the contract.
>
> (ii) Either property has passed to the buyer or "the price is payable on a day certain irrespective of delivery".

The buyer's refusal or failure to pay must have been wrongful. It is not wrongful if he has rightfully rejected the goods for breach of condition. Similarly, he is entitled (subject to contrary agreement) to refuse to pay except in exchange for taking delivery of the goods— s.28. Therefore the seller will be unable to sue for the price unless, at the time of the neglect or refusal to pay, he was ready and willing to deliver. Again, if the seller has granted the buyer credit, he cannot sue for the price before the end of the agreed credit period; until then the buyer's failure to pay is not wrongful.

In relation to the second requirement, if a particular date has been stipulated for payment then an action can be maintained after that date irrespective of whether property has passed to the buyer. When no "day certain" has been agreed, the seller will succeed only if property has passed to the buyer. A "day certain" may be a fixed date or could be fixed by reference to the seller's performance of his part of the contract. Different days certain may be agreed for the payment of different instalments of the price. In *Workman Clark v Lloyd Brazileno*[1] the seller was building a vessel for the buyer and the price was to be paid by instalments on dates to be determined by reference to the stage of construction. It was held that at the relevant stages the seller could sue for the instalments then due.

12–004 In addition to an action for the price, the seller may have a claim under s.37 which provides:

> "(1) When the seller is ready and willing to deliver the goods, and requests the buyer to take delivery, and the buyer does not within a reasonable time after such request take delivery of the goods, he is liable to the seller for any loss occasioned by his neglect or refusal to take delivery, and also for a reasonable charge for the care and custody of the goods.
>
> (2) Nothing in this section affects the rights of the seller where the neglect or refusal of the buyer to take delivery amounts to a repudiation of the contract."

This might apply, if, for example, the goods had perished or contaminated others.

Where a buyer has paid with a cheque which has been dishonoured, he is still liable to pay and can be sued for the price. Where, however, he has paid with a credit or charge card and then the card issuing company fails to pay, the seller is not able to sue the buyer for the price.[2]

Damages for Non-Acceptance

12–005 If the seller cannot maintain an action under s.49, he may still have a claim for damages which he can bring under s.50 "where the buyer wrongfully neglects or refuses to accept and pay for the goods". The measure of damages is considered in Chapter 14. Usually damages will be much less than the price and the seller also has the inconvenience of having to find another buyer.

REMEDIES AGAINST THE GOODS

12–006 There are three possible remedies against the goods—lien, stoppage in transit and resale. They are available to an "unpaid seller". By s.38 a seller is an "unpaid seller",

> "(a) when the whole of the price has not been paid or tendered;

---

[1] [1908] 1 K.B. 968.
[2] See generally para.8–005, above and also para.12–006, below.

(b)   when a bill of exchange or other negotiable instrument has been received as
       conditional payment, and the condition on which it was received has not been
       fulfilled by reason of the dishonour of the instrument or otherwise."

A cheque is a bill of exchange. Thus a seller who in the normal way has accepted a cheque
which is later dishonoured, is an unpaid seller.

Lien

The unpaid seller has a right in the circumstances provided by s.41(1) to retain possession of   **12–007**
the goods until he is paid or payment is tendered to him. As a matter of strict terminology,
this right is called a "lien" if property has passed to the buyer and a "right of retention" if
property is still with the seller.[3] This right complements the rule in s.28 that, in the absence
of contrary agreement, payment and delivery are concurrent conditions. By s.41(1) the right
exists in each of the following circumstances:

"(a)   where the goods have been sold without any stipulation as to credit;
 (b)   where the goods have been sold on credit, but the term of credit has expired;
 (c)   where the buyer becomes insolvent."

Obviously, agreement by the seller to allow credit is agreement contrary to the rule in s.28.
In such circumstances the seller is not entitled to refuse delivery unless the agreed period of
credit has already expired. Usually by that time, delivery will already have been made, thus
depriving the seller of his lien. Section 41(1)(c) represents an exception to the rule that the
seller has no lien during an agreed period of credit. In spite of having agreed to grant credit,
the seller does have a lien if, before the seller relinquishes possession, the buyer becomes
insolvent. A person is insolvent (whether or not he is bankrupt) "if he has either ceased to
pay his debts in the ordinary course of business or he cannot pay his debts as they become
due".[4]
    The seller's lien relates only to the price. He is not entitled to withhold the goods until
other debts owed to him by the buyer are paid. Thus there is no lien for damages due by the
buyer under s.37.[5]
    Where delivery is made in instalments, the extent of the unpaid seller's lien depends upon   **12–008**
whether the contract is severable. If it is not severable, the seller can retain any part of the
goods to compel payment of any part or all of the price. Section 42 provides:

"Where an unpaid seller has made part delivery of the goods, he may exercise his lien
or right of retention on the remainder, unless such part delivery has been made under
such circumstances as to show an agreement to waive the lien or right of retention."

A severable contract is generally one where goods are to be delivered in instalments which
are to be separately paid for.[6] In this case the seller has no lien over one instalment of goods

[3] s.39(2).
[4] s.61(4).
[5] See para.12–004, above.
[6] See para.11–009, above.

to compel payment for a different (earlier) instalment. However, if the buyer's failure to pay amounts to a repudiatory breach of contract,[7] the seller can refuse to make further deliveries, not by virtue of any lien, but because the buyer's repudiatory breach excuses the seller from further performance of his contractual obligations. If the reason for the buyer's failure to pay is his insolvency then the breach is a repudiatory one, although in this case the seller must deliver those instalments which have actually been paid for.

The seller's lien is lost if any of the following situations arises:

    (i) The seller ceases to be unpaid, i.e. if the whole of the price is paid or tendered to him.

    (ii) One of the terminating events in s.43 occurs.

    (iii) An innocent third party acquires title free from the lien, under one of the exceptions to the *nemo dat* principle.

12–009   The last two of these require explanation. Section 43 states:

"(1) The unpaid seller of goods loses his lien or right of retention in respect of them

    (a) when he delivers the goods to a carrier or other bailee or custodier for the purpose of transmission to the buyer without reserving the right of disposal of the goods;

    (b) when the buyer or his agent lawfully obtains possession of the goods;

    (c) by waiver of the lien or right of retention."

Although delivery to a carrier without the reservation of a right of disposal terminates the unpaid seller's lien, he may still be able to recover the goods by exercising his right of stoppage in transit. Lawful acquisition of possession by the buyer will deprive the seller of his rights of lien and stoppage and those rights will not revive even if the buyer later returns the goods to the possession of the seller. Allowing the buyer to have access to the goods, e.g. to paint or repair, will not amount to giving him possession provided the seller retains control over the goods. If the buyer without authority from the seller seizes possession of the goods that is unlawful and does not destroy the seller's lien.

Waiver of his lien by the seller may take the form of first an express agreement to forego the lien, or secondly an act clearly indicating an intention to forego it, or thirdly a wrongful act inconsistent with delivery to the buyer. Examples of the last of these are consumption of the goods by the seller or a resale of them by the seller when he has no right to resell. In these cases the buyer can lawfully bring an action for damages against the seller but the damages will be awarded only after deducting the price still owed by the buyer. An example of the second form of waiver is assent by the seller to a sub-sale by the buyer. To amount to a waiver it must be such an assent as to show that the seller intends to renounce his rights against the goods. In *Mordaunt v British Oil & Cake Mills Ltd*[8] the seller was told of the sub-sale by the buyer only after it had been made. It was held that the seller's acknowledgment of the

---

[7] See para.11–009, above.
[8] [1910] 2 K.B. 502.

existence of the sub-sale was not assent such as to defeat his lien. In spite of the sub-sale the seller was entitled to retain possession of the goods until they were paid for.

If the buyer disposes of the goods within one of the exceptions to the *nemo dat* principle,[9] **12–010** the innocent sub-purchaser obtains title free from the seller's lien. In this case the seller must surrender the goods to the sub-purchaser and will be reduced to pursuing his personal remedies against the buyer. Most of the exceptions to the *nemo dat* principle apply only if the goods are disposed of by someone in possession of them and if the buyer is lawfully in possession of the goods the seller's lien is lost anyway.[10] The exceptions may, however, be relevant where the buyer has unlawfully obtained possession. Further, certain exceptions can apply where the buyer has possession only of documents of title. The seller can lose his lien by virtue of one of these. The provisions of s.25 of the Sale of Goods Act 1979 and s.9 of the Factors Act 1889 have already been considered.[11] However, there is a further provision by virtue of which an innocent sub-purchaser may acquire title free from the seller's lien, s.47. It reads:

"(1) Subject to this Act, the unpaid seller's right of lien or retention or stoppage in transit is not affected by any sale, or other disposition of the goods which the buyer may have made, unless the seller has assented to it.

(2) Where a document of title to goods has been lawfully transferred to any person as buyer or owner of the goods, and that person transfers the document to a person who takes it in good faith and for valuable consideration, then—

(a) if the last-mentioned transfer was by way of sale the unpaid seller's right of lien or retention or stoppage in transit is defeated; and

(b) if the last-mentioned transfer was made by way of pledge or other disposition for value, the unpaid seller's right of lien or retention or stoppage in transit can only be exercised subject to the rights of the transferee."

Subsection (2) was applied in *Ant. Jurgens Margarinefabrieken v Louis Dreyfus & Co.*[12] Some mowra seed was sold. The buyers paid by cheque and the sellers gave the buyers a delivery order which the buyers endorsed and transferred to a sub-purchaser. The cheque was dishonoured and the sellers claimed to have a lien over the mowra seed which was still in their possession. It was held that since all the requirements of subs.(2) were fulfilled, the seller's lien was defeated. Subsection (2) is clearly an exception to the *nemo dat* principle, since the buyers were able to confer upon the sub-purchaser a title better than that which the buyers had themselves, namely, a title free from the sellers' lien and which therefore gave to the sub-purchaser the right to immediate possession.

In the last mentioned case the delivery order transferred by the buyers to the sub-purchaser was the same document as that which has been transferred to the buyers by the sellers. If, instead of transferring the same document, the buyers had transferred a different one, then s.47(2) would not have applied. This was held by Salmon J. in *Mount v Jay & Jay Ltd*[13] where the buyers wrote their own delivery order which they sent off to the sub-purchaser. His

[9] See Ch.5.
[10] s.43(1)(b).
[11] See para.5–025, above.
[12] [1914] 3 K.B. 40.
[13] [1960] 1 Q.B. 159.

Lordship thought, however, that s.25 applied to defeat the sellers' lien.[14] Nevertheless, he did not base his decision upon s.25, but held that the sellers' lien was defeated because the sellers, who knew in advance of the sub-sale, had assented to it in a way that indicated their intention to forego the lien.

Stoppage in Transit

12–011   Section 44 provides that the seller can resume possession of the goods and retain them until payment or tender of the price to him, if two conditions are both fulfilled:

> (i) The buyer has become insolvent.
>
> (ii) The goods are "in course of transit".

The meaning of "insolvent" has already been considered when dealing with the seller's lien.

Section 45 is a long section dealing with the "course of transit". Broadly, goods are in course of transit from the time that they are delivered to an independent middleman for the purpose of transmission to the buyer, until the time that the buyer actually obtains or is entitled to obtain possession. The carrier will of course be paid for his service by the buyer or seller. Apart from that, however, he must be independent. If, for example, the buyer sends his own lorry driven by one of his own employees to collect the goods, then the goods, once loaded on to the lorry, are not in the course of transit but are in the buyer's possession.

12–012   The course of transit ends:

> (i) when the buyer obtains delivery, or
>
> (ii) when the carrier acknowledges that he holds for and on behalf of the buyer, e.g. by accepting and acting upon the buyer's instructions not to convey the goods as far as their original destination or to convey them to a further destination, or
>
> (iii) when the carrier wrongfully refuses to deliver the goods to the buyer.

Part delivery to the buyer does not prevent the remainder being stopped in transit unless the part delivery is made under such circumstances as to show an agreement to give up possession of the whole of the goods.

Section 46 deals with how stoppage in transit may be effected, by the seller either taking actual possession of the goods or giving notice of his claim to the carrier. The carrier is under a duty to comply with the seller's instructions as to redelivery, although the seller must bear the expenses involved. The seller can give his instructions to the person in actual possession of the goods, but it may be difficult for him to discover who that is, if, for example, the goods are on the railways. If, as is more likely, the seller gives his instruction to that person's employer or principal, he must allow reasonable time for the instructions to be communicated to the person in actual possession before delivery is made to the buyer.

---

[14] See para.5–028, above.

With one exception, the right of stoppage in transit is lost in the same circumstances as is the seller's lien. It can therefore be lost by waiver or the operation of s.47(2), etc. The exception is of course that delivery to a carrier without the reservation of a right of disposal will terminate the seller's lien whereas it marks the commencement of the "course of transit".

Resale

Section 48 governs the right of the unpaid seller to resell the goods. Section 48(1) reads: **12–013**

> "(1) Subject to this section, a contract of sale is not rescinded by the mere exercise by an unpaid seller of his right of lien or retention or stoppage in transit."

Since the contract is not rescinded by the seller exercising his rights of lien or stoppage, the seller's obligations under the contract remain, including his obligation to deliver the goods against payment of the price. Thus he has no right to resell the goods other than that allowed him by later subsections of s.48. In fact s.48(3) and (4) allow him quite generous rights of resale:

> "(3) Where the goods are of a perishable nature, or where the unpaid seller gives notice to the buyer of his intention to resell, and the buyer does not within a reasonable time pay or tender the price, the unpaid seller may resell the goods and recover from the original buyer damages for any loss occasioned by his breach of contract.
> (4) Where the seller expressly reserves the right of resale in case the buyer should make default, and on the buyer making default, resells the goods, the original contract of sale is rescinded, but without prejudice to any claim the seller may have for damages."

When the seller exercises his right of resale—whether under subs.(3) or under subs.(4)—the contract with the first buyer is thereby rescinded. The effect of rescission is that property (title), if it had passed to the buyer, reverts to the seller. Thus, on exercising his right of resale, the seller resells as owner. Since he resells as owner it follows that he can keep any profit he makes by reselling at a higher price than the original buyer had agreed to pay. That is in addition to keeping any deposit he obtained from the original buyer.[15] In the more likely event that the seller makes a loss on the resale, he can claim that loss from the original buyer as damages together with any other damage caused to him by the buyer's failure to pay.

Ward v Bignall[16] concerned a contract for the sale of two cars for £850. After paying a   **12–014** deposit of £25 the buyer refused to pay the rest. The seller informed the buyer in writing that, if he did not pay the balance by a given date, the seller would try to resell the cars. The buyer still did not pay. The seller sold one car for £350 but failed to find a purchaser for the other. He brought a claim against the original buyer for the balance of the purchase price (£475) and

---

[15] See para.2–012, above.
[16] [1967] 1 Q.B. 534.

advertising expenses (£22.10s). It was held that the seller could not recover any of the price since the buyer was no longer the owner of either of the cars, the ownership having reverted to the seller on the resale. The seller was entitled to damages. The remaining car being worth £450, the seller's loss on the resale was £850 minus (£450 plus £350) equals £50. From that figure was deducted the amount (£25) of the deposit paid by the original buyer. The seller was also entitled to his reasonable advertising expenses for the resale, i.e. £22.10s. Therefore the damages awarded to him totalled £47.10s.

It is, of course possible for the unpaid seller to resell the goods in circumstances where he has no right to do so. If he does, he will confer good title on the new purchaser provided the resale falls within one of the exceptions to the *nemo dat* principle. One particular exception which may well apply is that contained in s.8 of the Factors Act and s.24 of the Sale of Goods Act. This exception applies where the seller continues or is in possession of the goods or documents of title and subsequently delivers them to a new innocent purchaser.[17] A further exception is to be found in s.48(2) of the Sale of Goods Act:

> "(2) Where an unpaid seller who has exercised his right of lien or retention or stoppage in transit resells the goods, the buyer acquires a good title to them as against the original buyer."

This provision can apply in much the same circumstances as s.24, namely where someone who has sold goods to one person then later resells them to another. However, for the subsequent purchaser to acquire good title under this provision there are different requirements to be fulfilled:

(i) The seller must have been "unpaid" by the first buyer.

(ii) He must also have exercised his right of lien or retention or stoppage in transit.

(iii) He must "sell" the goods. Thus someone taking only a pledge cannot acquire good title by virtue of this provision.

12–015   Unlike s.24, s.48(2) has no requirement that there be a delivery to the second purchaser and no requirement that the latter should be bona fide.

Finally it should be noted that if the seller does resell the goods and confer good title upon the new purchaser, the original buyer will be able to bring an action against the seller for non-delivery, provided the seller did not have the right to resell.

General Reading

12–016   ● Adams, "Damages in sale of goods: a critique of the provisions of the Sale of Goods Act and Article 2 of the Uniform Commercial Code" [2002] J.B.L. 553;

   ● Mak, "The seller's right to cure defective performance—a reappraisal" [2007] J.M.C.L.Q. 409.

---

[17] It was considered in para.5–022, above.

Chapter 13

BUYER'S REMEDIES

INTRODUCTION

This chapter considers the remedies available to a buyer when faced with a seller in breach **13–001** of contract. Traditionally this was a relatively straightforward issue with the available remedies being:

- Specific performance of the contract.

- Rejection of the goods.

- Damages.

This has now been modified where the buyer deals as consumer following the implementation of the Sale and Supply of Goods to Consumers Regulations 2002. Under the Regulations a consumer buyer now has the ability to elect for either repair of the goods or a replacement. Where such a remedy is not forthcoming the consumer may elect to receive a reduction in the purchase price of the goods or rescind the contract. Since these new remedies are available only to consumers and are an addition to a consumer's remedies, there is now in force a patch-work of remedies, the availability of which is primarily dependent upon the status of the buyer. The remedies available only to a consumer will be dealt with later and this chapter will begin by considering the remedies available to all buyers under a contract of sale of goods.

SPECIFIC PERFORMANCE

Section 52 of the Sale of Goods Act 1979 allows the court to make an order of specific **13–002** performance against the seller in the case of a contract to deliver specific or ascertained goods. Thus the order cannot be made in the case of a contract for the sale of unascertained goods which have not been appropriated to the contract—*Re Wait.*[1]

An order for specific performance is one which requires the seller actually to deliver the goods and does not give him the option of paying damages instead. Even in the case of specific or ascertained goods the court will not make such an order unless damages for non-delivery would not be an adequate remedy. This is likely to be the case only where similar goods are unobtainable elsewhere, e.g. if the goods are unique or virtually so, as in *Behnke v Bede Shipping Co.*[2] A German shipowner had agreed to buy for immediate use a specific ship, *The City,* which had engines and boilers which were practically new and satisfied German regulations. There was only one other such ship afloat. An order for specific performance was granted since damages would not have been an adequate remedy. Since the situations where damages would be an inadequate remedy are rare, it should not be surprising that the courts have been reluctant to make an order of specific performance against a seller. As we shall see later in this chapter, however, something akin to specific performance (to, for example, repair or replace the goods) is available to a consumer buyer under s.48E(2).[3]

REJECTION OF THE GOODS

13–003   A breach of condition by the seller gives the buyer, as well as a claim to damages, the right to reject the goods (and therefore not to have to pay for them). The buyer can exercise this right by refusing to take delivery or informing the seller that he rejects the goods. He need not return them to the seller, who if he wants them must come and collect them.[4] If the seller fails to collect goods which the buyer has rightly rejected and as a result the buyer reasonably incurs storage expenses, the buyer is entitled to claim those expenses from the seller as damages for breach of contract: *Kolfor Plant Ltd v Tilbury Plant Ltd.*[5] The buyer has no lien over rejected goods and therefore must hand them over on request even though he has not received the return of his purchase money: *Lyons v May & Baker.*[6] He can bring an action to recover his price on the ground of a total failure of consideration.

The right of rejection is not given for an ordinary breach of warranty. Unless the seller commits a breach of condition or commits a breach of warranty which is so serious as to deprive the buyer of substantially the whole benefit of the contract, the buyer has no right to reject the goods or recover the price.[7] If he unjustifiably rejects them, the seller may sue him for damages for non-acceptance or, possibly, will have an action for the price.[8]

---

[1] [1927] 1 Ch. 606, see para.3–005, above.
[2] [1927] 1 K.B. 649.
[3] See the discussion, in respect to remedies available in consumer contracts, below at para.13–013. See also the analysis of Harris on this point, "Specific Performance—A Regular Remedy for Consumers?" (2003) 119 L.Q.R. 541.
[4] Sale of Goods Act 1979 s.36.
[5] (1977) 121 S.J. 390.
[6] [1923] 1 K.B. 695.
[7] See para.7–007, above.
[8] See para.14–003, below and Ch.12, above.

Trivial Breaches of Implied Condition

The normal rule is that any breach of condition by the seller, however small or trivial, entitles   **13–004**
the buyer to reject the goods. Section 15A creates an exception where there is a minor breach
of one of the implied conditions as to description, quality and sample contained in ss.13, 14
and 15.[9] Section 15A provides that if the breach:

> "is so slight that it would be unreasonable for him to reject them . . . the breach is not
> to be treated as a breach of condition but may be treated as a breach of warranty".

This is the position "unless a contrary intention appears in, or is to be implied from, the
contract". It would seem extremely likely that if this provision had been in force at the time,
the decision in *Re Moore and Landauer*[10] would have been different.[11] In that case the only
breach by the seller was that, although he had delivered the correct quantity of tins of pears,
he had delivered them packed in cases of 24 tins instead of in cases of 30 tins. In a situation
where this breach would cause the buyer no loss or inconvenience, this breach would seem
to be so slight that it would be unreasonable for the buyer to reject the goods. Section 15A,
which denies the buyer the right to reject for a slight breach of condition, applies only to
breaches of the conditions in ss.13–15. Even in relation to those conditions, it does not apply
to a buyer who "deals as a consumer", the definition of this latter expression being the same
as that used in the Unfair Contract Terms Act 1977.[12]

Acceptance

Faced with a breach of condition, the buyer's choice is either to reject or to accept the goods.   **13–005**
Acceptance of any part of the goods will preclude the buyer from later rejecting the goods
accepted and may cause him to lose the right to reject other goods under the contract.
   Simply taking delivery does not amount to acceptance. Acceptance may take one of three
forms[13]:

(i) If the buyer informs the seller that he has accepted the goods.

(ii) If the buyer takes delivery and he does some act inconsistent with the seller being
     the owner of them (e.g. by selling them).

(iii) If the buyer retains the goods for more than a reasonable length of time without
      informing the seller that he rejects them.

   Neither of the first two of these, however, will amount to acceptance unless either the
buyer examined the goods before the contract was made or, alternatively, has had a reasonable opportunity after delivery of the goods to examine the goods for the purpose of

[9] See Ch.7, below.
[10] [1921] 2 K.B. 519.
[11] See para.7–015, above.
[12] See paras 10–018–10–020, above.
[13] s.35.

ascertaining whether they are in conformity with the contract.[14] Thus, reselling the goods does not constitute acceptance unless the buyer has had a reasonable opportunity of examining them. For example, where a manufacturer sells goods in sealed containers to a distributor who resells them, that distributor does not thereby lose his right of rejection. If the distributor's buyer opens them up and finds them not to comply with a condition in the contract between himself and the distributor, he may reject them. If they also do not comply with a condition in the contract between the manufacturer and distributor, the latter may also reject them.

13–006   In *Lee v York Coach and Marine*,[15] the buyer had been supplied in March with a second-hand car which was not of merchantable quality because its brakes were defective. Because the buyer did not claim to reject the car until September, it was held that she had accepted it and that therefore she was entitled only to damages. This is an example of the third form of acceptance, which occurs if the buyer retains the goods for more than a reasonable length of time without intimating to the seller that he is rejecting them. It used to be thought that this meant a reasonable length of time to try the goods out (i.e. a relatively short period) and not a reasonable length of time in which to discover any defects there might be in the goods: *Bernstein v Pamsons Motors (Golders Green) Ltd*.[16] In that case the buyer of a new Nissan car had had it for less than three weeks and had made two or three short journeys in it for the purpose of trying it out, before the engine seized up because of a latent manufacturing fault. Rougier J. held that, before the seizure the buyer had already had the car a reasonable length of time for trying it out generally. Therefore the buyer had accepted the car and was entitled only to damages. Since then, however, s.35 has been amended by the Sale and Supply of Goods Act 1994. Thus we now know that in measuring whether a reasonable length of time has elapsed, the court has to take into account whether the buyer has had a reasonable opportunity of examining the goods for the purpose of ascertaining whether they are in conformity with the contract.

In *Fiat Auto Financial Services v Connolly*[17] the buyer purchased (with a loan provided by a finance company) a new car which quickly manifested a wide range of problems, including a fault with the engine management system which led to poor engine performance generally and also caused the car to break down 10 days after delivery. This fault was investigated by the dealer but never diagnosed and the fault persisted throughout the time the buyer had the car. After nine months (and over 40,000 miles) use of the car the buyer sought to reject the car since the engine management system had not been satisfactorily repaired. The finance company sought to enforce the loan agreement and maintained that the buyer had accepted the car under s.35, thereby losing the right to reject. This claim was made on two alternative bases. First, it was argued that the buyer's use of the car amounted to an act inconsistent with the ownership of the seller. Secondly, that the period of nine months from delivery to rejection was more than a reasonable length of time without intimating rejection.

The court held that neither argument could succeed since throughout the nine month period the buyer was in regular contact with the seller regarding the faults with the car and his continued use of the car did not constitute an act inconsistent with the reversionary interest of the seller. Furthermore, the period where the buyer is waiting for information to make an

---

[14] s.35(2).
[15] [1977] R.T.R. 35.
[16] [1987] 2 All E.R. 220.
[17] [2007] S.L.T. (Sh. Ct.) 111.

informed decision as to whether to accept or reject does not count towards an unreasonable length of time. This decision does, it seems, leave the seller vulnerable to a buyer rejecting the goods at *any point* in the future where the goods are subject to a continuous period of failed repairs such as that which occurred in *Connolly*.

The 1994 amendments to s.35 introduced two further new provisions which clarify what **13–007** is not acceptance. First, the buyer will not be deemed to have accepted the goods merely because he asks for, or agrees to, their repair by or under an arrangement with the seller. Secondly, he will not be deemed to have accepted the goods merely because they are delivered to another under a sub-sale or other disposition. Suppose, however, that the sub-purchaser retains the goods for more than a reasonable length of time so that, vis-à-vis the buyer, the sub-purchaser has accepted them. In that case the buyer will then be deemed to have accepted the goods vis-à-vis his seller. These provisions were considered in *Truk (UK) Ltd v Tokmakidis GmbH*.[18] It involved a contract between two businesses for the sale and fitting of some lifting equipment to be paid for six months after delivery. The equipment was to be fitted to, and form part of, a towing vehicle which the buyer was then going to re-sell. Approximately six months after delivery the buyer was informed by a potential purchaser of the towing vehicle that the equipment was defective. The buyer immediately informed the seller and refused to pay the price pending investigation (by an appropriate company). About three months later, promptly upon receipt of the result of the investigation which confirmed the allegation, the buyer unequivocally rejected the goods. The judge held as follows. Where goods are sold for resale, a reasonable time in which to give notice of rejection should normally be the time actually taken to resell the goods, together with an additional period in which they can be inspected and tried out (by the sub-purchaser). Where the price is payable at a date after delivery, that reasonable period of time should normally last at least until the date for payment. The reasonable time had not expired when about six months after delivery, the buyer first questioned compliance. The buyer was entitled to a further period in which to investigate that issue. Accordingly the buyer had not accepted the goods when he (validly) rejected them nine months after delivery.

The impact of an agreement to have the contract goods inspected and, if possible repaired, upon acceptance and the right to reject goods under s.35 was considered by the House of Lords in *J&H Ritchie Ltd v Lloyd Ltd*.[19] In that case the buyer carried on a farming business and bought some equipment from the seller, a supplier of agricultural machinery. The equipment (which was sold as a single item) consisted of a seed drill and a power harrow and was delivered in early March 1999. The buyer first used the harrow in late April 1999 and discovered that the harrow appeared to have a fault causing it to vibrate. The buyer contacted the seller who sent a member of staff who, with the agreement of the buyer, removed the harrow for inspection and, if possible, for repair. A few weeks later the seller informed the buyer that the harrow had been repaired and was ready for collection. The buyer asked the seller to explain what the problem had been but this request was refused and the seller would only say that the harrow had been repaired to "factory gate specification". The buyer was not satisfied and was concerned, inter alia, that the fault (missing bearings) could have caused other damage to the harrow and that it would not be clear until the next sowing season (i.e. spring the following year) whether the harrow had been satisfactorily repaired. Therefore the

[18] [2000] 1 Lloyd's Rep. 543.
[19] [2007] 1 W.L.R. 670.

buyer sought to reject the goods (both harrow and seed drill) and reclaim the purchase price.

The House of Lords held that the agreement to have the harrow inspected and, if possible, repaired, did not amount to an acceptance of the goods which would take away the buyer's right of rejection under the sale of goods contract. The agreement of inspection and repair was subject to an implied term that, if asked, the seller would tell the buyer the nature of the defect and what repairs had been made in order to rectify that defect. This was necessary in order that the buyer can, where the nature of the defect is not readily apparent, make an informed choice as to whether or not to accept the re-tendered goods. The seller's refusal to provide that information was a breach of the inspection and repair agreement. Thus the buyer was entitled to treat that agreement as repudiated and exercise his right under the sale of goods contract to reject the goods. Accordingly the buyer was entitled to recover the purchase price.[20]

Partial Rejection

13–008   Until s.35 was amended by the 1994 Act, there was a rule that acceptance by the buyer of all or any part of the goods precluded the buyer from being able to reject any of the goods. There were exceptions to that rule: (a) in the case of a severable contract, where acceptance of goods under one severable part of the contract did not preclude the possibility of rejecting the goods under another part; (b) where goods more than the contract quantity were delivered, in which case the buyer had the option of accepting the contract quantity and rejecting the rest. These two exceptions remain. However, there is also now a general exception to that rule. Section 35A was inserted into the Sale of Goods Act and it states:

> "(1) If the buyer—
>
>   (a) has the right to reject the goods by reason of a breach on the part of the seller that affects some or all of them, but
>   (b) accepts some of the goods, including, where there are any goods unaffected by the breach, all such goods, he does not by accepting them lose his right to reject the rest.
>
> (2) In the case of a buyer having the right to reject an instalment of goods, subsection (1) above applies as if references to the goods were references to the goods comprised in the instalment.
> (3) For the purposes of subsection (1) above, goods are affected by a breach if by reason of the breach they are not in conformity with the contract.
> (4) This section applies unless a contrary intention appears in, or is to be implied from, the contract."

Thus, in order to exercise a right of partial rejection under this provision, the buyer must first have a right to reject the goods, e.g. because of a breach of condition, and must secondly

---

[20] For a critique of this decision, see Loi, "Sale of Goods in Scotland—Repairing Defects in the Law: *J&H Ritchie Ltd v Lloyd Ltd*" [2007] J.B.L. 807.

accept all the goods which comply with the contract. Providing he accepts all the goods which comply with the contract, he is not precluded from rejecting some, or all, of those which do not. It should be observed that although s.35(A)(4) states that this section applies only if a contrary intention does not appear, nevertheless, a clause in a contract which purported to deprive the buyer of his right of partial rejection would be an exclusion clause and therefore could well be rendered ineffective by the Unfair Contract Terms Act 1977.

There is one qualification to the right of partial rejection just mentioned. This lies in the concept of a "commercial unit". A commercial unit is a unit of goods, "division of which would materially impair the value of the goods or the character of the unit". An example might be a two-volume dictionary, the first volume dealing with, say, A to K and the second with L to Z. Suppose that one of the volumes is, and the other is not, of satisfactory quality. By virtue of s.35(7), a buyer accepting any goods in the commercial unit is deemed to have accepted all the goods in that unit. Thus the buyer could not accept one of the volumes and reject the other.

Waiver

The buyer may lose his right to reject by waiver of that right.[21] This may be particularly relevant where the seller is, to the buyer's knowledge, in breach of condition before the goods are delivered. If the buyer indicates that he will nevertheless accept delivery in spite of the breach of condition, that may well amount to waiver.[22] **13–009**

Treatment of Contract as Repudiated

The buyer's right to treat the contract as repudiated arises in the same circumstances as his right to reject the goods, i.e. if the seller commits a breach of condition or a breach of warranty which deprives the buyer of substantially the whole benefit of the contract.[23] Often the buyer will exercise both remedies at once, i.e. will reject the goods and will also indicate that he is not going on with the contract, e.g. by demanding his money back. He can, however, reject the goods without treating the contract as repudiated. If he does, then the seller is at liberty, if he can do so, to re-tender the goods which comply with the contract. If the seller does so, he will be entitled to the price. It can of course also occur that the buyer treats the contract as repudiated by the seller and yet does not reject any goods. This could occur if the breach by the seller is a failure to deliver the goods by the contractual delivery date, or if the seller commits an anticipatory repudiation, e.g. informs the buyer that he will not be delivering or will not be delivering by the contractual delivery date. In the circumstances where the buyer accepts the seller's breach as a repudiation of the contract, the buyer will be entitled to damages assessed as for non-delivery of the goods.[24] To exercise his right **13–010**

---

[21] s.11(2).
[22] See *Rickards v Oppenheim* [1950] 1 K.B. 616 discussed at para.7–008, above.
[23] See paras 7–006–7–007, above.
[24] See Ch.14.

to treat the contract as repudiated by the seller's repudiatory breach, the buyer must inform the seller that he regards the contract as at an end.

Suppose the seller commits a wrongful anticipatory repudiation which the buyer does not accept as a repudiation. This latter point would be clear if, for example, the buyer responded to the anticipatory breach by indicating that due delivery was still expected. If then the seller duly makes delivery in accordance with the contract, the buyer must accept it. This is because an anticipatory repudiation terminates a contract only if it is accepted by the innocent party: *Fercometal S.a.r.l. v Mediterranean Shipping Co.*[25] If after having failed to accept the seller's breach as a repudiation, the buyer himself subsequently repudiates the contract, e.g. by rejecting goods which conform to the contract, he will himself be liable to the seller for damages assessed as for non-acceptance (see Chapter 14). These principles work exactly the same vice versa. Thus where the buyer commits an anticipatory repudiation which the seller fails to accept as terminating the contract, the seller will be liable if he himself subsequently fails to perform the contract.

Where one of the parties, say the buyer, treats the contract as repudiated giving a bad reason (e.g. simply that he has changed his mind about buying) or even giving no reason at all, that repudiation will not be wrongful if at the time of the repudiation he in fact had a valid reason for it. A party who gives a bad reason for his refusal to perform the contract, does not thereby deprive himself of a justification which in fact existed, whether or not he was aware of it: *Glencore Grain Rotterdam BV v Lebanese Organisation for International Commerce.*[26] The only exceptions to this are: (i) where that party is estopped from relying on the valid reason by virtue of an earlier representation of his, or (ii) where the valid reason later relied upon is one which if given at the time, could have been put right by the other party. In this regard, however, note that in the case of a c.i.f. contract, the fact that goods were not shipped in conformity with the contract, does not justify the buyer in rejecting documents which conform to the contract.

Action for Damages

13–011 The buyer can claim damages for non-delivery or for breach of any other condition or warranty. This right is an addition to any right to reject the goods or to recover the purchase price. The measure of damages will be considered in Chapter 14.

Recovery of Purchase Price

13–012 Where the consideration has totally failed, the buyer can recover any payments he has already paid. This rule clearly applies in the case of a non-delivery. It also applies where the buyer exercises his right to reject the goods and treat the contract as repudiated because of a breach of condition. We have also seen a surprising application of it in the case of *Rowland v Divall.*[27]

---

[25] [1988] 3 W.L.R. 200.
[26] [1997] 4 All E.R. 514.
[27] [1923] 2 K.B. 500, discussed at para.7–010, above.

Of course, in the situation where the buyer can and does accept part and reject part of the goods,[28] he is entitled to recover any part of the price that he has paid in respect of the rejected part of the goods and remains liable to pay, if he has not done so already, pro rata for the goods he has accepted.

ADDITIONAL REMEDIES AVAILABLE IN CONSUMER SALES

The remedies considered above apply, broadly speaking, to all sale of goods transactions (that is irrespective of the status of the buyer). The Sale and Supply of Goods to Consumer Regulations[29] has improved the position of a consumer purchaser[30] where, at the time of delivery, goods do not conform with the contract[31] by introducing the additional remedies of repair, replacement, replacement or rescission. The new remedies are incorporated into domestic law by the insertion of new ss.48A–48F into the Sale of Goods Act and came into force on March 31, 2003. It must be emphasised that these new remedies co-exist with the traditional remedies considered above. Thus a consumer can elect to reject the goods and rescind the contract under s.15A without first giving the retailer the opportunity to repair or replace the goods.[32]   **13–013**

In order to rely on the new remedies available under Pt 5A of the Sale of Goods Act, two requirements must be satisfied under s.48A. First, the buyer must be dealing as consumer, and secondly, the goods do not conform to the contract. The definition of a "consumer" is defined by reg.2 as meaning, "any natural person who . . . is acting for purposes which are outside his trade, business or profession". We have already considered the definition of dealing as consumer in the context of the Unfair Contract Terms Act 1977 and the definition is now the same across both the Sale of Goods Act and the Unfair Contract Terms Act.[33]

The issue of non-conformity is dealt with by s.48F which states:

> "For the purposes of this Part, goods do not conform to a contract of sale if there is, in relation to the goods, a breach of an express term of the contract or a term implied by section 13, 14 or 15 above."

Thus the new hierarchy of remedies is applicable only where there has been either a breach of the implied terms as to description, quality, fitness for purpose and sample, or breach of an express term. Consequently, where there is a breach of a different implied undertaking, e.g. as to title, the remedies in Pt 5A are not applicable.   **13–014**

The difficulty of establishing non-conformity at the time of delivery has, however, been removed where Pt 5A applies. Under s.48A(3) there is now a rebuttable presumption that where goods develop a fault within six months of delivery, those goods were not in conformity with the contract at the time of delivery. This presumption is removed in two situations:

[28] See para.13–008, above.
[29] Sale and Supply of Goods to Consumer Regulations 2002 (SI 2002/3045), implementing Directive 1999/44.
[30] s.48A(1)(a).
[31] s.48A(1)(b).
[32] Under s.48B(1). For a justification of this position, see Willett, Morgan-Tailor and Naidoo, "The Sale and Supply of Goods to Consumers Regulations" [2004] J.B.L. 94 at 108–109.
[33] See reg.14 which amends the definition within the UCTA 1977, see para.10–018, above.

1. Where it is established that the goods did so conform at that date[34];

2. Where its application is incompatible with the nature of the goods or the nature of the lack of conformity.[35]

An obvious example of the second situation would be where the goods have a life span of less than six months such as cut flowers. We can now turn to the substance of the new remedies available under Pt 5A of the Sale of Goods Act.

Repair or Replacement

13–015 Prior to March 31, 2003, there was no legal right to demand either a replacement or a repair where goods did not conform to the contract. This was so irrespective of the fact that: (i) this is generally the remedy consumers will seek; and (ii) this is generally the remedy retailers will offer. The right of a consumer to require either a repair[36] or a replacement[37] therefore more accurately reflects current business practice in most cases.[38]

The right to request either a repair or replacement of the goods is expanded by s.48B(2) which states:

"If the buyer requires the seller to repair or replace the goods, the seller must:

(a) repair or, as the case may be, replace the goods within a reasonable time but without causing significant inconvenience to the buyer;

(b) bear any necessary costs incurred in doing so (including in particular the cost of any labour, materials or postage)."

Thus it is clear that the initial decision as to whether to elect repair or replacement is down to the consumer and not to the seller. Equally, the cost of such repair or replacement must be borne by the seller, including, for example, the costs of returning the defective goods to the manufacturer for the repair to be carried out.

13–016 It is likely that there will be judicial consideration of what exactly is meant by "reasonable time" and "significant inconvenience". As a starting point, s.48B(5) is of relevance, stating that:

"Any question as to what is a reasonable time or significant inconvenience is to be determined by reference to:

(a) the nature of the goods, and

(b) the purpose for which the goods were acquired."

---

[34] s.48A(4)(a).
[35] s.48A(4)(b).
[36] Under s.48B(2)(b). "Repair" is defined by s.61(1) as bringing the goods into conformity with the contract.
[37] Under s.48B(2)(b).
[38] In situations where business practice is reluctant to replace goods (such as in the sale of motor vehicles) s.48B(1)(b) clearly represents an important right for the consumer.

Where, for example, the non-conforming goods are required for a specific purpose, such as a wedding dress, the time reasonably necessary to effect either a repair or a replacement may be taken into account in determining what is a "reasonable time".[39] This may therefore trigger the second set of additional remedies, reduction in purchase price or, more likely in the wedding scenario, the rescission of the contract.[40] The definition of "significant inconvenience" raises similar issues. Would, for example, the seller of a motor vehicle need to offer a courtesy car whilst a faulty car is being repaired in pursuance to a request under s.48B(1)(a)? There is a cross-over here between the concepts of "reasonable time" and "significant inconvenience" since a minor fault would presumably be repaired in very little time whereas a more substantial one might reasonably take longer to repair, therefore necessitating the provision of a courtesy car in order to avoid "significant inconvenience". Whilst the exact meaning and scope remains to be determined, it is clear that these provisions give considerable power to the consumer.

It is, however, not entirely bad news for retailers. Under s.48B(3) the buyer may not require the seller to repair or replace the goods where that remedy is either:

(a) impossible, or

(b) disproportionate in comparison to the other of those remedies, or

(c) disproportionate in comparison to an appropriate reduction in the purchase price, or rescission.

The issue of proportionality is expanded within s.48B(4) which provides:

"One remedy is disproportionate in comparison to the other if the one imposes costs on the seller which, in comparison to those imposed on him by the other, are unreasonable, taking into account:

(a) the value which the goods would have if they conformed to the contract of sale,
(b) the significance of the lack of conformity, and
(c) whether the other remedy could be effected without significant inconvenience to the buyer."

The impact of these subsections is such that a seller will be entitled to refuse a request for **13–017** a repair of the goods where, for example, a repair would cost considerably more to effect than a replacement. Where both repair and replacement options would be considerably more expensive than the value of the goods once repaired or replaced, the seller is entitled to refuse both options. Under s.48B(4)(b) it would appear that a buyer cannot insist on a replacement where there is, for example, a very minor defect with the goods.

Where the seller fails to comply with a request for either repair or replacement of the goods, the buyer may either ask the court to compel the seller to comply under s.48E or move on to pursue one of the other additional remedies within s.48C.

---

[39] See the examples raised in the DTI Guidance, *The Law Relating to the Supply of Goods and Services* (2005), p.12, available online through the BERR website.
[40] Considered at para.13–018, below.

Reduction in Price or Rescission

13–018   Under s.48C a consumer may require the seller either to reduce the purchase price in order to appropriately reflect the non-conformity in question or alternatively, to rescind the contract. Section 48C(2) makes it clear that these remedies are only available where either the repair or replacement of the goods is not possible under s.48B(3) or the seller has not complied with the request for repair or replacement within a reasonable time and/or without causing significant inconvenience. The ability of a consumer to pursue either a reduction or rescission is therefore secondary to the first set of additional remedies within s.48B.

The ability to elect to receive a reduction in purchase price certainly offers flexibility to the consumer, but will be relevant (presumably) only to certain goods. It will be of little use or interest, for example, to a consumer who discovers that a board game has pieces missing, or that a set of nine golf clubs contains only six clubs. In such a case, assuming that s.48B(3) applies, the consumer would seek to rescind the contract and reclaim the purchase price. The issue of whether the buyer would be entitled to receive a full or partial refund is laid down by s.48C(3) which provides:

> "For the purposes of this Part, if the buyer rescinds the contract, any reimbursement to the buyer may be reduced to take account of the use he has had of the goods since they were delivered to him."

It follows that there is no automatic right to a full refund within s.48C. Where the goods have already been used, a partial refund may be the more appropriate remedy. However, the consumer may, subject to not having accepted the goods under s.35, instead rely on the established provisions of the Act (e.g. s.14(2) as to satisfactory quality) and reclaim the whole price.[41]

ADDITIONAL OR ALTERNATIVE DEFENDANT

13–019   Of course, the seller will be liable for his own breach of contract. However, as an exception to the general rule, s.75 of the Consumer Credit Act 1974 allows the buyer in certain circumstances to bring against someone else (the creditor) a claim for the seller's breach of contract or misrepresentation. Section 75 has already been noted in connection with mis-representation.[42] It applies in exactly the same way in the case of a breach of contract by the seller. The claim that the buyer can bring against the creditor (e.g. the credit card company when the buyer has used his credit card to buy an item for more than £100) is the same as that which he can bring against the seller. The section only enhances the buyer's rights and therefore does not in any way reduce his right to sue the seller. The circumstances in which s.75 applies are set out in Chapter 25.

[41] See para.7–017, above.
[42] See para.6–007, above.

General Reading

- Adams, "Damages in sale of goods: a critique of the provisions of the Sale of Goods **13–020** Act and Article 2 of the Uniform Commercial Code" [2002] J.B.L. 553;

- Ervine, "The Sale and Supply of Goods to Consumers Regulations 2002" Scots Law Times [2003] 67;

- Hacker, "Rescission of contract and revesting of title: a reply to Mr Swadling" (2006) 14 R.L.R. 106;

- Harris, "Specific performance—a regular remedy for consumers?" (2003) 119 L.Q.R. 541;

- Low, "Repair, rejection & rescission: an uneasy resolution" (2007) 123 L.Q.R. 536;

- O'Sullivan, "Rescission as a self-help remedy: a critical analysis" [2000] C.L.J. 509;

- Swadling, "Rescission, property, and the common law" (2005) 121 L.Q.R. 123;

- Willett, Morgan-Taylor and Naidoo, "The Sale and Supply of Goods to Consumers Regulations" [2004] J.B.L. 94.

Chapter 14

THE MEASURE OF DAMAGES

GENERAL CONTRACTUAL PRINCIPLES

According to the rules in *Hadley v Baxendale*[1] damages for breach of contract can be **14–001** obtained for two kinds of loss:

(i) any loss naturally arising from the breach;

(ii) any loss which at the time of making the contract the defendant could have predicted as likely (or not unlikely) to result from the breach of it.

These principles were applied in *Victoria Laundry v Newman Industries*[2] where the laundry had agreed to buy a new (larger) boiler. In breach of contract the boiler was delivered five months late. For that period the buyers were therefore without its larger capacity and therefore unable to cater for a larger volume of business. They were awarded damages for this loss of ordinary business which arose naturally from the late delivery. They received no damages for the loss of some exceptionally lucrative government dyeing contracts which they would have secured if the boiler had been delivered on time. This loss did not arise naturally—in the usual course of business. Neither was it within the second type of loss above, because the sellers were unaware of the buyers' chance of obtaining those lucrative contracts.

PRIMA FACIE RULES

The general principles just outlined apply in sale of goods, for although there are sections of **14–002** the Sale of Goods Act 1979 governing the assessment of damages, those sections do little more than embody the general principles.

[1] (1854) 9 Exch. 341.
[2] [1949] 2 K.B. 529.

Non-Acceptance

14–003   Section 50 provides:

> "(1) Where the buyer wrongfully neglects or refuses to accept and pay for the goods, the seller may maintain an action against him for damages for non-acceptance.
>
> (2) The measure of damages is the estimated loss directly and naturally resulting, in the ordinary course of events, from the buyer's breach of contract.
>
> (3) Where there is an available market for the goods in question the measure of damages is prima facie to be ascertained by the difference between the contract price and market or current price at the time or times when the goods ought to have been accepted, or (if no time was fixed for acceptance) at the time of the refusal to accept."

Subsection 3 lays down the prima facie measure of damages. The idea is that if the seller can sell the goods elsewhere at the same or a higher price than the buyer had agreed to pay, the seller has lost nothing, in which case he will receive only nominal damages. However, if the market price is less than the contract price, the difference between the two represents the seller's loss. The market price for these purposes is the price which in normal business dealings those goods would have fetched on the date when the buyer should have accepted the goods. If the market price subsequently rose or fell, that is irrelevant, even if the seller actually sold at that subsequent greater or lower price. This is clear from some words of Salmon L.J. in *Pagnan v Corbisa*[3] which are quoted below.

The measure of damages in subs.3, being prima facie, does not apply where it does not represent the seller's loss. In *Thompson v Robinson*[4] the purchaser ordered from a motor trader a Vanguard car and later refused to accept it. The price of Vanguard cars did not fluctuate and the contract price and market price at the date of the buyer's breach were the same. However, the trader's loss was not merely nominal because he had lost a sale. It was held that the prima facie rule was displaced and the seller received as damages his loss of profit on one transaction. This was his loss "directly and naturally resulting".

14–004   That case was distinguished in *Charter v Sullivan*[5] where the buyer refused to accept a Hillman Minx which he had ordered from a trader. The difference was that in *Charter v Sullivan* there was a shortage of Hillman Minx cars. The number of sales the trader could make was limited to the number of cars he could get. Demand exceeded supply. Thus when one purchaser backed out, the trader did not lose a sale. He received only nominal damages.

Thompson v Robinson was distinguished also in *Lazenby Garages v Wright*[6] where Mr Wright refused to accept a second-hand car which he had previously agreed to buy for £1,670 from a car dealer. The dealer sold it a little later to another buyer for £1,770. The dealer claimed from Mr Wright the loss of profit on one sale. However, it could not be said with any certainty that because Mr Wright had backed out, the dealer had sold one car less. This was

---

[3] [1970] 1 W.L.R. 1306.
[4] [1955] Ch. 177.
[5] [1957] 2 Q.B. 117.
[6] [1976] 2 All E.R. 770.

because second-hand cars are all unique. It was held that since the dealer had sold the car for more than the price Mr Wright had agreed to pay, he had suffered no damages at all.

Even when it is not displaced, the prima facie rule does not exclude any further loss which was reasonably foreseeable as a result of the buyer's breach. So, for example, the seller will also be able to recover any reasonable extra storage expenses he has had to incur.[7]

Non-Delivery

Section 51 provides: **14–005**

> "(1) Where the seller wrongfully neglects or refuses to deliver the goods to the buyer, the buyer may maintain an action against the seller for damages for non-delivery.
> (2) The measure of damages is the estimated loss directly and naturally resulting, in the ordinary course of events, from the seller's breach of contract.
> (3) Where there is an available market for the goods in question the measure of damages is prima facie to be ascertained by the difference between the contract price and market or current price of the goods at the time or times when they ought to have been delivered, or (if no time was fixed) at the time of the refusal to deliver."

This section is converse of s.50. If on the date the seller fails or refuses to deliver, the buyer can buy similar goods from elsewhere at the same or a cheaper price, then prima facie the buyer's damages are only nominal. If the market price is higher, then the prima facie measure of damages is the extra, i.e. the difference between the contract price and the market price on the date of the seller's breach. Again, it is the market price on the date of the breach which is important. In *Pagnan v Corbisa*[8] Salmon L.J. explained the prima facie rule:

> " . . . the innocent party is not bound to go on the market and buy or sell at the date of the breach. Nor is he bound to gamble on the market changing in his favour. He may wait if he chooses; and if the market turns against him this cannot increase the liability of the party in default; similarly, if the market turns in his favour, the liability of the party in default is not diminished."

Thus, if the buyer does not immediately buy replacement goods but does so subsequently and at a different price from the market price at the date of the breach, that is normally irrelevant. His subsequent purchase is an "independent and disconnected" transaction.

The prima facie rule would be displaced by a subsequent transaction which was not "independent and disconnected", as illustrated by the facts in *Pagnan v Corbisa*. The sellers delivered goods which did not comply with the conditions of the contract. The buyers rejected them but, before doing so, obtained from an Italian court a sequestration order which gave them the right to detain the goods against payment of damages. They then negotiated

---

[7] Sale of Goods Act 1979 s.37.
[8] [1970] 1 W.L.R. 1306.

a new contract with the sellers whereby they bought the goods at a price considerably less than the market price—the price being depressed because of the sequestration order. The buyers nevertheless claimed under the first contract damages based on the difference between the contract price and market price on the date of the breach. The claim failed. The second contract could not be ignored since it was not an "independent and disconnected" transaction; the same buyer bought the same goods from the same seller. On the facts, the benefit of the second contract price being depressed was greater than the loss caused by the breach of the first contract. Therefore the buyers obtained no damages.

Anticipatory Breach

14–006   Often a contract is to be performed in the future, i.e. delivery of the goods is to be in the future, either at a fixed date or within a reasonable length of time. In such a case it is possible for either the seller or the buyer to commit an anticipatory breach of contract, i.e. to repudiate the contract before the time for performance. This can be done by the seller informing the buyer that he will not deliver the goods or the buyer informing the seller that he will not accept them. When one side commits an anticipatory breach, the other party (the innocent party) is given an option. Either he can at once accept the anticipatory breach as a repudiation and immediately claim damages or else he can refuse to accept it as a repudiation and wait until there has been actual failure to perform the contract (as opposed to an anticipatory one).

If the innocent party adopts the latter alternative then he can claim damages if and when the actual breach (non-delivery or non-acceptance) occurs. In that case his damages are assessed on the principles already given (ss.50 and 51 above).[9] Thus the measure of damages is the difference between the contract price and the market price on the date for *actual* performance. *Tai Hing Cotton Mill Ltd v Kamsing Knitting Factory*[10] established that the same principle applies where the innocent party immediately accepts the anticipatory breach as a repudiation of the contract. The measure of damages is still the difference between the contract and the market price. The relevant market price is still that prevailing on the date for *actual* performance and not that prevailing on the earlier date of the anticipatory breach. This is so irrespective of whether the contract had a fixed future date for delivery or whether delivery was to be within a reasonable length of time.

Consider an example. On May 1, B agrees to buy from S 50 tonnes of cob nuts at £100 per tonne, delivery to be on December 1. On June 1, when the market price of cob nuts is £101 per tonne S informs B that S will not supply the nuts. B may refuse to accept that as a repudiation by S. In that case B will be able to sue for damages for non-delivery if on December 1 S does not deliver. The market price of cob nuts on December 1 is £110 per tonne. Thus B is entitled to the market price (£110 × 50) less the contract price (£100 × 50) = £500. Suppose that B had in June accepted S's repudiation of the contract. Then the assessment of B's damages would be on the same basis and B would similarly be entitled to £500.

---

[9] See paras14–003–14–005, above.
[10] [1978] 2 W.L.R. 62.

There are just two qualifications to this last point, i.e. which apply where the innocent party   **14–007**
immediately accepts the repudiation. First, if B's claim for damages comes to trial before
December 1 (i.e. before the actual date of delivery), the court must determine the market
price on that future date as best it can: *Melachrino v Nickoll and Knight*.[11] This will often be
little more than guesswork. The second qualification is that an innocent party who accepts an
anticipatory breach becomes under a duty to mitigate (minimise) his loss. Thus if B accepts
S's repudiation in June and he sees the market price begin to rise, he has a reasonable
opportunity to minimise his loss by buying replacement nuts immediately at less than £100
per tonne. In that case the court may well reduce his damages from the £500. It will do so
irrespective of whether the buyer actually used the opportunity to buy replacement nuts.

Suppose now, however, that B, having accepted S's repudiation in June, sees the market
beginning to rise rapidly in July and, in an attempt to minimise his loss before the market
rises further, buys replacement goods on July 15 at £115 per tonne—only to discover that by
the delivery date under the original contract (December 1) the market price has fallen back
to £110 per tonne. In that case the court has a discretion (in order to avoid injustice) to award
damages at the higher level of £750 (i.e. by reference to the market price at July 15 instead
of the later contract delivery date of December 1): *Johnson v Agnew*.[12]

The duty to mitigate does not apply where the innocent party refuses to accept the
anticipatory breach as a repudiation. Because he is waiting to see if the anticipatory breach
turns into non-performance in fact, he is not expected to buy any replacement goods until the
date of actual non-performance.

Now suppose that the buyer commits a wrongful anticipatory repudiation of the contract   **14–008**
and the seller immediately accepts that repudiation as terminating the contract and sues for
damages. Clearly the seller does not have to remain ready and willing to deliver. The buyer
is the only party to have broken the contract and the seller will be entitled to damages from
him according to the principles just outlined. What, however, is the position if, at the time of
the buyer's wrongful anticipatory repudiation, the seller had already been disabled from
completing the essential terms of the contract (e.g. the seller's factory making the goods was
already so far behind in production that the seller could not possibly have delivered the goods
by the contractual delivery date)? In that case the seller's damages would be reduced from
the prima facie level in s.50: *British & Benningtons v North West Cachar Tea Co*.[13] To
achieve a reduction, however, the burden of proof rests upon the buyer to show that the seller
would have been unable to comply with the essential terms of the contract if it had not been
terminated: *Gill & Duffus v Berger & Co*.[14] Even if the buyer were able to do that, the
greatest reduction the buyer could achieve would still leave the seller entitled to nominal
damages.

Late Delivery

Late delivery by the seller will normally be a breach of condition.[15] If the buyer rejects the   **14–009**
goods for breach of condition, his damages are assessed as in the case of non-delivery. If it

[11] [1920] 1 K.B. 693.
[12] [1970] A.C. 367.
[13] [1923] A.C. 48.
[14] [1984] 2 W.L.R. 95.
[15] See para.7–008, above.

is only a breach of warranty or if the buyer accepts the goods, the damages are prima facie assessed according to the difference between the value of the goods on the date they should have been delivered and their value (if lower) when actually delivered.

As always, the prima facie method of assessment may be displaced and damages awarded for any loss which falls within the rules in *Hadley v Baxendale*.[16] *Victoria Laundry v Newman Industries*[17] (above) is an example of this.

Breach of Condition

14–010   If the buyer rejects the goods, damages are assessed as in the case of non-delivery. If he accepts the goods, the damages are assessed as if it were a breach of warranty under s.53.

Breach of Warranty

14–011   Section 53(2) and (3) provide:

> "(2) The measure of damages for breach of warranty is the estimated loss directly and naturally resulting, in the ordinary course of events, from the breach of warranty.
>
> (3) In the case of breach of warranty of quality such loss is prima facie the difference between the value of the goods at the time of delivery to the buyer and the value they would have had if they had fulfilled the warranty."

The prima facie rule in subs.(3) can be termed a "capital value" assessment. In fact the buyer has a choice. He can claim either his capital loss or his loss of profit. He cannot claim both: *Cullinane v British Rema*.[18] In that case the sellers had warranted that a clay-pulverising machine would process clay at six tonnes per hour. In fact it could not do so. The purchaser claimed under two heads, first for the capital loss and secondly for his loss of profits—the latter head being based on the difference over three years between the profits made at the machine's actual rate of output and the higher profits which would have been made at the warranted rate of output. The Court of Appeal held that both claims could not succeed and disallowed the first (that being the smaller claim). It was also pointed out that the buyers could have claimed loss of profits for the whole of the estimated useful life of the machine (10 years in this particular case).

In addition to a claim for capital loss or loss of profits, a claim can be made for any consequential loss which falls within the rules in *Hadley v Baxendale*, i.e. loss of a type which at the time of the contract could reasonably have been predicted by both parties as liable (i.e. not unlikely) to occur in the event of the breach. Indeed this is sometimes the only claim made, as in *Frost v Aylesbury Dairy Co.*[19] It does not matter that the extent of the

[16] (1854) 9 Exch. 341.
[17] [1949] 2 K.B. 529.
[18] [1954] 1 Q.B. 292.
[19] [1905] 1 K.B. 608, see para.7–027, above.

damage could not have been foreseen. Damage is recoverable provided the type of damage and the way it occurred were predictable. In *Vacwell Engineering v B.D.H. Chemicals*[20] the sellers supplied (in glass ampoules) a chemical for use in the buyer's factory. The chemical was liable to explode on contact with water. No warning was given of this. Indeed, the sellers were unaware of it. The sellers were in breach of the implied condition that the goods should be reasonably fit for their purpose. Had the sellers known, they could have predicted that perhaps water would come into contact with the contents of an ampoule and cause an explosion. This is what occurred in the buyer's factory but, because a number of ampoules were being washed together, the explosion was much greater than might have been predicted and the damage much more extensive. Rees J. held that nevertheless the sellers were liable for all the damage.

It should be apparent from this case that in assessing what damages are recoverable (i.e. **14–012** within the rules in *Hadley v Baxendale*) for breach of a term as to quality, one does not ask simply "What type of damage could the seller at the time of the contract have predicted?" Rather one asks, "Had he known of the defect, what type of damage could the seller at the time of the contract reasonably have predicted?" A similar point arose in *Parsons v Uttley Ingham*.[21] The buyers, who were pig farmers, bought a 28 ft-high hopper which, as the sellers knew, the buyers intended to use for the storage of pig nuts. On delivery the ventilator on top of the hopper was shut and nobody noticed. As a result nuts stored in the hopper became mouldy. A large number of the buyers' pigs died from an infection, E. Coli, triggered by eating the mouldy pig nuts. The sellers were in breach of the implied condition that the hopper would be reasonably fit for the purpose for which the buyers required it. Was the resulting loss of the pigs recoverable under the rules in *Hadley v Baxendale*? E. Coli was a hitherto unknown disease and also, apparently, it could not reasonably have been expected that pigs would become ill from eating mouldy pig nuts. However, the breach of contract by the sellers consisted not of feeding mouldy pig nuts to the buyers' pigs, but of supplying an unventilated hopper. If the sellers had known they were supplying an unventilated hopper, could they reasonably have regarded illness in pigs as a not unlikely consequence of that breach? It was held that they could and were therefore liable for the loss of the pigs. It was immaterial that the seller could not have predicted either the particular illness that resulted nor the severity of it.

Section 53(1) allows the buyer to set off damages due to him for breach of warranty against the price he owes the seller. He can of course sue for any excess under s.53(4).

SUB-SALES

Non-Delivery

Suppose that on December 1, X agreed to buy from Y for £100 one tonne of corn to be **14–013** delivered on January 1. Y does not deliver the corn and market price on January 1 is £105. Prima facie X is entitled to £5 damages. Suppose further that on December 15, X had agreed

---

[20] [1971] 1 Q.B. 88.
[21] [1978] Q.B. 791.

to sell a tonne of corn to Q, delivery to be on January 1. That sub-sale can affect X's loss. His loss could be less than £5 if, for example, in his contract with Q the price was £104. Alternatively, it might be greater if for example the price in Q's contract was £106 or if he himself is liable to Q for breach of contract. Does the law take sub-sales into account?

Generally, the effect of a sub-sale is ignored and the prima facie rule prevails. In *Williams v Agius*,[22] Williams agreed to buy from Agius a cargo of coal at 16s. 3d. per ton. Later he agreed with a sub-purchaser to sell him a similar cargo at 19s. per ton. Agius failed to deliver. Williams' damages were assessed at the difference between the contract price (16s. 3d.) and the market price on the date when delivery should have been made (23s. 6d.).

In *Re Hall & Pim's Arbitration*[23] the House of Lords established an exception. The prima facie rule will be displaced and a sub-sale taken into account when the following circumstances all exist:

(i) The first contract contemplated the creation of sub-sales—so that the seller could predict from the outset that in the event of non-delivery the buyer might suffer loss in connection with sub-sales.

(ii) The sub-contract was for the sale, not merely of similar goods, but of the very same goods as were to be supplied under the first contract.

(iii) The sub-contract was not an extravagant or unusual bargain.

(iv) The sub-contract was created before the delivery date under the first contract.

If these circumstances all exist then the loss connected with the sub-sale(s) falls within the second rule in *Hadley v Baxendale*.[24] This was the position in *Re Hall & Pim's Arbitration*. On November 3 the buyers agreed to buy a cargo of wheat at 51s. 9d. per quarter. The contract clearly referred to the possibility of sub-sales. On November 21 the buyers made a sub-sale of the same cargo at 56s. 9d. per quarter. On March 22, when the seller refused to deliver, the market price was 53s. 9d. per quarter. The buyers were awarded damages assessed at 5s. per quarter and also damages which the buyers had to pay to their sub-buyer.

Late Delivery

14–014 From *Wertheim v Chicoutimi Pulp Co*[25] it appears that sub-sales are taken into account more readily in the case of a late delivery. The contract price was 25s. per ton. Before the delivery date, the buyer made a sub-contract to sell similar goods at 65s. per ton. On the date when delivery should have been made under the first contract, the market price was 70s. When delivery was actually made, the market price had dropped to 42s. 6d. The buyer used the goods to fulfil his sub-contract. The Privy Council took the buyer's sub-sale into account and awarded damages assessed at only 5s. per ton.

---

[22] [1914] A.C. 510.
[23] (1928) 139 L.T. 50.
[24] (1854) 9 Exch. 341.
[25] [1911] A.C. 301.

Breach of Term as to Quality

Here also sub-sales are taken into account more readily than in the case of non-delivery. The   **14–015**
buyer can include in his claim for damages the amount of the damages he has had to pay out
to his sub-purchaser for breach of contract, see *Godley v Perry*.[26] For this, it is sufficient that
the seller knew or ought to have known that the buyer bought the goods for resale.

Sub-sales which are within the reasonable contemplation of the parties, can result in the
seller's damages being either more or less than the prima facie measure laid down in s.53(3).
Bence Graphics v Fasson UK[27] involved the sale of vinyl film. The sellers knew that the
buyer was going to make it into decals (identification labels for bulk containers) and sell them
to companies involved in the international container business. Over a period of years the
sellers supplied the buyer with vinyl film which, in breach of an express contract term, was
not such that it would survive in good legible condition for at least five years. This was
discovered only much later. The value of the film supplied with this latent defect was in fact
zero and thus the prima facie measure of damages laid down in s.53(3) (i.e. difference
between the value the goods should have had on delivery and the lower value of the goods
actually supplied) was the whole of the contract price. The breach meant, however, that the
buyer was exposed to the risk of claims by their sub-buyers, which would have greatly
exceeded that prima facie amount. Nevertheless no such claims were made. The Court of
Appeal held that the prima facie measure of damages was displaced. Just as the buyer could
have claimed a greater figure if he had had to meet claims in excess of the prima facie
amount, equally the sellers did not have to pay the prima facie amount where it exceeded the
buyer's actual loss.

MITIGATION

The innocent party is under a duty to take reasonable steps to mitigate (minimise) his loss.   **14–016**
Any loss which he could reasonably have avoided will be deducted from his damages.

His duty is to act reasonably. So, in the case of non-delivery, the buyer is not expected to
hunt the globe to find similar goods: *Lesters Leather & Skin Co v Home & Oversees
Brokers*.[28] Similarly, a purchaser need not force defective goods upon his sub-purchaser
(even if contractually entitled to do so) if that would involve damaging his own commercial
reputation: *Finlay v Kwik Hoo Tong*.[29]

Sometimes the party in default makes an offer to put things right, e.g. the seller offers to
buy back defective goods. If the offer is a reasonable one then it is likely to be reasonable
to accept it. An unreasonable refusal will be a breach of the duty to mitigate: *Payzu v
Saunders*.[30]

Occasionally, albeit rarely, steps taken by the claimant in an attempt to minimise his loss   **14–017**
result in fact in increasing it. In that case the extra loss is recoverable in a claim for damages.

---

[26] [1960] 1 W.L.R. 9, see para.9–006, above.
[27] [1997] 3 W.L.R. 205.
[28] [1848] W.N. 437.
[29] [1929] 1 K.B. 400.
[30] [1919] 2 K.B. 581.

The defendants in *Hoffberger v Ascot International Bloodstock Bureau*[31] had contracted to buy a mare from Mr Hoffberger for £6,000 in October 1973 provided that on that date the mare was in foal. When the time came the mare was in foal but they failed to buy her and finally refused to do so in December 1973. Mr Hoffberger was unable to sell the mare at the December 1973 sales because she was ill. In an attempt to obtain a good price, he paid a stud fee of over £1,400 to have her covered again so that he would be able to sell her in foal at the December 1974 sales. In fact the market fell and the mare in foal fetched only £1,085 at those sales. Mr Hoffberger was awarded damages of over £7,000. This sum included all the loss and expenses he had incurred in attempting to mitigate his damages. This was because those steps had been reasonable ones to take even though they had in the event aggravated the losses.

PENALTIES

14–018 Sometimes the contract stipulates how much is to be paid by the party in breach, e.g. "£100 per day for each day delivery is delayed". Such a clause is a liquidated damages clause and is binding upon the parties provided it is not a penalty. If it binds the parties, the stipulated amount is the amount payable and that is the case, whether the loss actually caused is greater or smaller.

It is a penalty if it was not a genuine attempt by the parties to pre-estimate the likely damages but was intended to hang in terror over one party to ensure that he carried out the contract. Some sentences of Lord Dunedin's in *Dunlop Pneumatic Tyre Co v New Garage Motor Co* are particularly instructive[32]:

> "Though the parties to a contract who use the words 'penalty' or 'liquidated damages' may prima facie be supposed to mean what they say, yet the expression used is not conclusive. The court must find out whether the payment stipulated is in truth a penalty or liquidated damages . . .
>
> It will be held to be a penalty if the sum stipulated for is extravagant and unconscionable in amount in comparison with the greatest loss that could conceivably be proved to have followed from the breach . . .
>
> There is a presumption (but no more) that it is a penalty when 'a single lump is made payable by way of compensation, on the occurrence of one or more or all of several events, some of which may occasion serious and others but trifling damage . . . '
>
> On the other hand: it is no obstacle to the sum stipulated being a genuine pre-estimate of damage, that the consequences of the breach are such as to make precise pre-estimation almost an impossibility. On the contrary, that is just the situation when it is probable that pre-estimated damage was the true bargain between parties."

If it is a penalty, the clause is void and the innocent party can sue in the usual way for whatever is his actual loss. That loss will be calculated according to the principles outlined in the earlier parts of this chapter. Finally, a penalty within a consumer contract might well

---

[31] (1976) 120 S.J. 130.
[32] [1915] A.C. 79.

be rendered ineffective by the Unfair Terms in Consumer Contracts Regulations even if it were not struck down by the doctrine of penalties.[33]

General Reading

- Bridge, "Mitigation of damages in contract and the meaning of avoidable loss" (1989) L.Q.R. 398; **14–019**

- Coote, "Contract damages, Ruxley, and the performance interest" 1997 (56) C.L.J. 537;

- Lawson, "Contract law: incorporation of terms—rejection of goods and the measure of damages" Tr. Law 1995, 14(5), 418;

- McInnes, "Breach of contract and compound interest as damages" (2002) 118 L.Q.R. 516;

- McMeel, "Contract damages: the interplay of remoteness and loss of a chance" [2004] L.M.C.L.Q. (1) 10;

- Opeskin, "Damages for breach of contract terminated under express terms" (1990) 106 L.Q.R. 293;

- Watterson, "The law of damages in the 21st century" [2004] L.M.C.L.Q. 513;

- Webb, "Performance and compensation: an analysis of contract damages and contractual obligation" [2006] O.J.L.S. 41.

[33] See paras 10–032–10–039, above.

Chapter 15

AUCTION SALES

In most respects a purchase made at an auction constitutes an ordinary contract for the sale **15–001**
of goods. Except in so far as the parties agree otherwise, the provisions of the Sale of Goods
Act 1979 apply.

ADVERTISEMENTS BEFORE THE AUCTION SALE

An advertisement that an auction is to be held is not an offer or a promise that the auction **15–002**
will be held. There is no liability if the auction is not in fact held. In *Harris v Nickerson*[1] the
claimant travelled to the advertised place for the auction sale which he then found to be
cancelled. It was held that he was not entitled to claim his travelling expenses from the
advertiser.

It seems, however, that if the auction is in fact held, then anything advertised to be
"without reserve" must be sold to the highest bidder. If it is withdrawn, then the advertiser
is in breach of contract with any bidder who had come in response to the advertisement:
Warlow v Harrison.[2]

SECTION 57 OF THE SALE OF GOODS ACT 1979

Section 57 states: **15–003**

> "In the case of a sale by auction—
>
> (1) Where goods are put up for sale by auction in lots, each lot is prima facie deemed
> to be the subject of a separate contract of sale.

[1] (1873) L.R. 8 Q.B. 286.
[2] (1859) 1 E. & E. 309, confirmed in *Barry v Heathcote Ball & Co* [2000] 1 W.L.R. 1962, CA.

(2)   A sale by auction is complete when the auctioneer announces its completion by the fall of the hammer, or in other customary manner; and until such announcement is made any bidder may retract his bid.

(3)   A sale by auction may be notified to be subject to a reserve or upset price, and a right to bid may also be reserved expressly by or on behalf of the seller.

(4)   Where a sale by auction is not notified to be subject to a right to bid on behalf of the seller, it is not lawful for the seller to bid himself or to employ any person to bid at such a sale, or for the auctioneer knowingly to take any bid from the seller or any such person.

(5)   A sale contravening subsection (4) above may be treated as fraudulent by the buyer.

(6)   Where, in respect of a sale by auction, a right to bid is expressly reserved (but not otherwise) the seller or any one person on his behalf may bid at the auction."

RESERVE PRICE

15–004   A problem arises if the seller (i.e. the person who puts the goods into the sale) imposes a reserve price and the auctioneer nevertheless accepts a bid for less than the reserve price. If the reserve price had been notified as allowed by s.57(3), then the bidder has no claim against the seller or auctioneer who will not be liable for refusing to deliver the goods: *McManus v Fortescue*.[3] If the reserve price had not been notified and the bidder had no reason to know of it, then the bidder will have an action against the auctioneer for breach of the auctioneer's warranty of authority. That is the implied warranty given by any agent (whether auctioneer or not) that he is acting within his principal's (in this case the seller's) authority.[4]

EXEMPTION CLAUSES

15–005   The principles that apply are those applicable to sale of goods contracts generally. An illustration is provided by *Dennant v Skinner*[5] where, after the goods had been knocked down to him, the buyer was persuaded to sign a statement that property was not to pass until his cheque was paid. The signed statement was held to be ineffective since it was given after the contract was made and therefore could not incorporate terms into the contract.

The usual method of incorporation is for the exemption terms to be set out in printed conditions which are commonly attached to or referred to in the auction catalogue and copies of which are usually displayed on the premises.

A sale by auction will not be a consumer deal for the purposes of the Unfair Contract Terms Act 1977. Therefore any contractual clause exempting from the provisions of ss.13–15 of the Sale of Goods Act will normally be effective provided it is shown to satisfy the requirement of reasonableness in the Unfair Contract Terms Act.[6]

[3] [1907] 2 K.B. 1.
[4] On breach of warrant of authority, see Ch.31, above.
[5] [1948] 2 K.B. 164, see para.3–009, above.
[6] See para.10–021 onwards, above.

The Unfair Terms in Consumer Contracts Regulations 1999 apply to any auction sale where the seller is a trader and the buyer is buying for a purpose outside any business. They render ineffective any term which is unfair.[7]

POSITION OF THE AUCTIONEER

In selling goods, an auctioneer is an agent of the owner. In *Chelmsford Auctions v Poole*[8] **15–006**
Lord Denning M.R. explained that on a sale by auction there are three contracts. They are:

   (i) Between the owner (vendor) and the highest bidder (purchaser).

   (ii) Between the owner (vendor) and the auctioneer.

   (iii) Between the auctioneer and the highest bidder (purchaser).

The first of these is a simple contract of sale to which the auctioneer is no party. The auctioneer's rights and obligations arise under the other two contracts.

Contract between Auctioneer and Owner (Vendor)

Of this contract Lord Denning said[9]:   **15–007**

> "The understanding is that the auctioneer should not part with possession of them [the goods] to the purchaser except against payment of the price; or if the auctioneer should part with them without receiving payment, he is responsible to the vendor for the price . . . The auctioneer is given as against the vendor, a lien on the proceeds for his commission and charges."

This last means that the auctioneer when he receives payment from the purchaser can deduct his commission charges before passing on the money to the vendor. *Chelmsford Auctions v Poole* involved the sale of a car which the auctioneers knocked down to the purchaser for £57. The purchaser paid an immediate deposit of £7. The auctioneers retained possession of the car. The auctioneers, without waiting for further payment from the purchaser, paid to the vendor the full amount of the price less their commission charges (£3.50). This deduction was quite proper. Subsequently the auctioneers, as they were entitled to, sued the purchaser for the outstanding balance of the price.

The terms of the contract between the auctioneer and the vendor can of course be varied by contrary agreement (i.e. usually by the printed auction conditions).

---

[7] See paras 10–032–10–039, above.
[8] [1973] Q.B. 542.
[9] [1973] Q.B. 542 at 548.

Contract between Auctioneer and Highest Bidder (Purchaser)

15–008   In the absence of contrary agreement, the common law implies the following terms into the contract:

  (i) a warranty by the auctioneer that he has authority to sell;

 (ii) a warranty by the auctioneer that he will give the purchaser possession of the goods against the price paid into his hands;

(iii) a warranty by the auctioneer that the possession given to the purchaser will be undisturbed by the vendor or by himself;

 (iv) a warranty that he knows of no defect in the vendor's title.

The auctioneer, however, does not warrant the vendor's title in the case of a sale of specific goods (or unascertained goods out of a specific bulk) which the purchaser knows do not belong to the auctioneer. In *Benton v Campbell, Parker Co.*[10] the auctioneer knocked down the car to the highest bidder. It turned out that the person who put the car into the auction (the vendor) was not the owner. It was held that the auctioneer was not liable to the purchaser. (The purchaser could, of course, have brought an action against the vendor under s.12 of the Sale of Goods Act 1979.)

As well as giving the implied warranties listed above, the auctioneer has certain rights at common law. He has a special property in the goods, which gives him a lien over the goods until the whole of the price is paid or tendered. In *Chelmsford Auctions v Poole*[11] it was held that he also had the right personally to sue the purchaser for the price. Lord Denning further pointed out:

" . . . the purchaser cannot avoid his liability to the auctioneer by paying the vendor direct without telling the auctioneer. If he does so, the auctioneer can make the purchaser pay the full price again, even though it means that the purchaser pays twice over."

These rights and obligations can be varied by the auction conditions.

AUCTIONS (BIDDING AGREEMENTS) ACTS 1927–69

15–009   These Acts are aimed at preventing auction rings. A ring is an arrangement whereby several dealers all of whom are interested in a given item agree not to compete in outbidding each other at the public auction but instead to allow one of their number to buy it as cheaply as possible.[12] The idea is that they subsequently hold their own private auction amongst themselves. Under the Acts it is a criminal offence for a dealer to offer or agree to give an inducement or reward to another for abstaining or having abstained from bidding. If goods

---

[10] [1925] 2 K.B. 410.
[11] [1973] Q.B. 542 at 549.
[12] See, for example, s.1(1) of the Auctions (Bidding Agreements) Act 1969.

are sold at an auction to someone who has been a party to such an agreement to abstain from bidding, then the seller can rescind the contract.[13]

It should be noted that these rules relate only to agreements where at least one dealer is involved and also that they do not apply in the case of an agreement to purchase the goods bona fide on a joint account, e.g. where two dealers in partnership together wish to purchase goods for their business and agree that only one of them will bid. For the purpose of the Acts a dealer is "a person who in the normal course of his business attends sales by auction for the purpose of purchasing goods with a view to reselling them".

Apart from cases where the Auctions (Bidding Agreements) Acts apply, there is nothing illegal in two potential bidders agreeing that one of them will not bid with the result that the one who does bid obtains the property more cheaply than he otherwise would. The auction sale to the one who does bid remains perfectly valid: *Harrop v Thompson*.[14]

MOCK AUCTIONS

Mock auctions are sham auctions designed to entice unsuspecting members of the public to buy shoddy goods at over-inflated prices by creating the appearance that the auctioneer is offering goods at a fraction of their normal retail price. The Mock Auctions Act 1961, now repealed (see below), defined a mock auction as an auction where persons were invited to buy goods by way of competitive bidding and: **15–010**

(i) any goods of a type listed in the Act were sold to a bidder for less than his highest bid or part of the price is repaid or credited to him (or stated to be so); or

(ii) the right to bid for any such goods was (or was stated to be) restricted to persons who had bought or agreed to buy one or more articles; or

(iii) any articles were given away or offered as gifts.

One form of mock auction was exemplified by the facts of *Allen v Simmons*[15] where the defendant offered just one set of glasses and asked his audience who would pay him 30 pence for the set. A number of hands went up. The defendant then selected one of them and then sold the set to the person for one penny. It was held that the defendant was guilty, since in raising their hands the members of the audience were engaging in competitive bidding— namely in competing against one another for the chance of getting in first by raising a hand before anyone else or for the chance of attracting the defendant's favour in selecting the lucky buyer.

The Mock Auctions Act 1961 has now been repealed by the Consumer Protection from Unfair Trading Regulations 2008[16] which easily apply to mock auctions which are therefore prohibited as an unfair commercial practice. The operation of a mock auction may well fall under the activities automatically deemed unfair through the "Black List" in Sch.1. The

---

[13] See s.3 of the Auctions (Bidding Agreements) Act 1969.
[14] [1975] 1 W.L.R. 545.
[15] [1978] 1 W.L.R. 879.
[16] Consumer Protection from Unfair Trading Regulations 2008 (SI 2008/1277). The Regulations came into effect on May 26, 2008.

majority of mock auctions will no doubt fall foul of one or more of the following activities:

- Making an invitation to purchase products at a specified price and then refusing to show the advertised item to consumers (bait and switch)[17];

- Falsely stating that a product will only be available for a very limited time, or that it will only be available on particular terms for a very limited time, in order to elicit an immediate decision[18];

- Claiming that the trader is about to cease trading or move premises when he is not[19];

- Creating the impression that the consumer cannot leave the premises until a contract is formed.[20]

Where the auction does not fall under the practices detailed in Sch.1, it is likely, nevertheless, that the auction will be deemed unfair either as a "misleading commercial practice"[21] or alternatively, as an "aggressive practice".[22] The Regulations are explained in more detail in Chapter 17 below.

General Reading

15–011
- Breward and Miller, "Online Auctions—when the virtual hammer falls, who does it hit?" (2000) 2 Electronic Business Law 3, 11;

- Downey, "Mock Auctions" (1962) 25 M.L.R. 224;

- Groote and Vulder, "European framework for unfair commercial practices: analysis of Directive 2005/29" [2007] J.B.L. 16;

- Hörnle, "Is an online auction an 'auction' in law?" (2007) 8 Electronic Business Law 12, 7;

- Reifa, "Consumer protection on online auction sites: just an illusion?" (2005) Computers & Law 16(3) 34.

---

[17] Sch.1 para.6.
[18] Sch.1 para.7.
[19] Sch.1 para.15.
[20] Sch.1 para.24.
[21] Under reg.3(3).
[22] Under reg.7.

Chapter 16

E-COMMERCE AND DISTANCE SELLING

INTRODUCTION

This chapter concentrates on legislation relevant to the increasing trend towards the buying **16–001** and selling of goods and services at a distance—including cross-border transactions— whether by mail, telephone, the internet or any other means. This chapter deals with a number of recent European Directives before concluding with an outline of the law's approach to questions, relevant to cross-border contracts, of which countries have jurisdiction, and which country's law applies.[1]

E-COMMERCE

Electronic Communications Act 2000 and the Electronic Signatures Regulations 2002

The Electronic Signatures Directive[2] is implemented in the United Kingdom by the Elec- **16–002** tronic Communications Act 2000[3] and the Electronic Signatures Regulations 2002.[4] The

---

[1] For the principles of offer and acceptance applied to sales via the internet, see para.2–005, above.
[2] Electronic Signatures Directive 1999/93.
[3] Note that only Pt 2 of the Electronic Communications Act 2000 has survived repeal. It deals primarily with the admissibility of electronic signatures and related certificates.
[4] Electronic Signatures Regulations 2002 (SI 2002/318).

implementation of the Directive achieves two objectives. First, it creates a statutory approvals scheme for businesses and other organisations providing cryptography services.[5] Cryptography services are essential for ensuring that electronic signatures fulfil their purposes. The statutory approvals scheme is no more than a scheme for giving a mark of quality, i.e. approval. It is not a licensing system and there is no legal requirement for anyone to have the statutory approval. Secondly, the Electronic Communications Act 2000 provides for the legal recognition of electronic signatures. An electronic signature is defined by s.7 of the 2000 Act as something in electronic form which:

"(a) is incorporated into or otherwise logically associated with any electronic communication or electronic data; and

(b) purports to be so incorporated or associated for the purpose of being used in establishing the authenticity of the communication or data, the integrity of the communication, or both."

The purposes served by an electronic signature are thus twofold: to confirm both authenticity (that the communication comes from the person it purports to come from, and is accurately timed and dated and intended to have legal effect) and also integrity (that it and the communication have not been tampered with).

The effect of the Electronic Communications Act 2000 (and subsequent regulations) on electronic signatures is as follows. First, electronic signatures are admissible as evidence of authenticity and integrity.[6] Secondly the Electronic Communications Act 2000, s.8, gives relevant government ministers the power to amend any legislation for the purpose of authorising or facilitating the use of electronic communications and storage. This presents a formidable task, given the multitudinous examples of legislation requiring something to be done "in writing". It should come as no surprise, therefore, that there is a substantial (and growing) number of s.8 orders, spanning areas far beyond the scope of this book (such as the electronic provision of carer's allowance within the social security framework).[7] The impact of s.8 of the Electronic Communications Act 2000 is particularly pronounced in the area of consumer credit law. In particular, the Consumer Credit Act 1974 (Electronic Communications) Order 2004[8] which came into effect on December 31, 2004 allows for the use of electronic communication in, inter alia, the following areas:

- termination of consumer credit licenses[9];
- formation of regulated agreements[10];
- guarantees and indemnities[11];
- cancellation notices and copies of documents.[12]

[5] See reg.3 of the Electronic Signatures Regulations 2002.
[6] Electronic Communications Act 2000, s.7.
[7] Social Security (Electronic Communications) (Carer's Allowance) Order (SI 2003/2800).
[8] Consumer Credit Act 1974 (Electronic Communications) Order 2004 (SI 2004/3236).
[9] reg.3, amending the Consumer Credit (Termination of Licences) Regulations 1976 (SI 1976/1002).
[10] reg.4, amending the Consumer Credit (Agreements) Regulations 1983 (SI 1983/1553).
[11] reg.5, amending the Consumer Credit (Guarantees and Indemnities) Regulations 1983 (SI 1983/1556).
[12] reg.6, amending the Consumer Credit (Cancellation Notices and Copies of Documents) Regulations 1983 (SI 1983/1557).

Electronic Commerce Directive 2000

In 1999 the European Commission issued a draft (proposed) directive which then formed the **16–003** basis for the Electronic Commerce Directive 2000.[13] The Directive is implemented in the United Kingdom by the Electronic Commerce (EC Directive) Regulations 2002.[14]

The key features of the regulations are:

    (i) provision of information to the recipient of online services;

    (ii) clear marking of unsolicited commercial communications as being unsolicited[15];

    (iii) clear identification of commercial communications as commercial communications[16];

    (iv) clarification of the legal liability for online service providers.[17]

The regulations are, broadly speaking, designed to facilitate electronic commerce across the internal market whilst ensuring basic measures designed to clarify the position of both businesses and consumers thus facilitating greater use of electronic commerce. The regulations apply to what the Directive terms, a "service provider", which is defined as "any person providing an information society service".[18] This cumbersome term,[19] is defined by reg.2(1) as[20]:

> " ... any service normally provided for remuneration, at a distance, by means of electronic equipment for the processing (including digital compression) and storage of data, and at the individual request of a recipient of a service".

Despite the exclusions detailed in reg.3,[21] this is a very broadly defined term and therefore covers an extremely wide range of economic activities[22] including the following:

- selling goods or services through electronic means (e.g. via the internet);

- providing commercial communications by email[23];

- advertising on the internet;

---

[13] Electronic Commerce Directive 2000/31.
[14] Electronic Commerce (EC Directive) Regulations 2002 (SI 2002/2013).
[15] reg.8.
[16] reg.7.
[17] See reg.17 onwards.
[18] reg.2(1).
[19] For a convincing critique of the scope of "information society service" see Harrington, "Information Society services: what are they and how relevant is the definition?" [2001] J.B.L. 190.
[20] See also, art.2(a) of the Electronic Commerce Directive 2000/31.
[21] For example, betting and gaming activities.
[22] Note that consideration is not, at least in the traditional sense, required. Thus where an information society service is not directly paid for by the recipient, the regulations still apply, e.g. a search engine provided by an internet service provider where that service is funded by advertising revenue.
[23] See reg.7 (solicited commercial communications) and reg.8 (unsolicited commercial communications).

- providing access to a communication network;
- web-hosting.[24]

The term "service provider" therefore encapsulates a variety of commercial activities and catches, inter alia: (i) online traders/suppliers; (ii) those advertising goods or services online; and (iii) those who operate online databases. The specific obligations upon the service provider will vary according to the nature of the service provider's activities and are detailed within the regulations, which will now be considered.

16–004   A convenient starting point is the general requirement for information to be provided to the recipient of online services and the specific (additional) requirements relating to online ordering. The general information to be provided in a "form and manner which is easily, directly and permanently accessible" includes[25]:

- the name of the service provider;
- the geographic address at which the service provider is established;
- the details of the service provider, including his electronic mail address, which make it possible to contact him rapidly and communicate with him in a direct and effective manner;
- where the service provider is registered in a trade or similar register available to the public, details of the register in which the service provider is entered and his registration number, or equivalent means of identification in that register; and
- where the provision of the service is subject to an authorisation scheme, the particulars of the relevant supervisory authority.

Moreover, under reg.6(2):

"Where a person providing an information society service refers to prices, these shall be indicated clearly and unambiguously and, in particular, shall indicate whether they are inclusive of tax and delivery costs."

Where this obligation is not complied with the recipient can maintain an action for damages against the service provider, e.g. the trader, under reg.13.

In addition to the requirements of reg.6, where an order[26] has been placed through electronic means, the trader is under a duty to[27]:

"(a)   acknowledge receipt of the order to the recipient of the service without undue delay and by electronic means; and
(b)   make available to the recipient of the service appropriate, effective and accessible technical means allowing him to identify and correct input errors prior to the placing of the order."

---

[24] See reg.19.
[25] See reg.6(1).
[26] For the meaning of "order" in this context, see reg.12.
[27] See reg.11. Note, however, that this requirement does not apply where the contract is concluded solely through electronic mail, see reg.11(3).

This is a powerful provision: where a trader does not comply with reg.11(1)(a) the trader faces liability for breach of a statutory duty as is made clear in reg.13. Where the requirement under reg.11(1)(b) is not complied with, the contract may be rescinded at the option of the consumer unless the service provider can satisfy the court that this is inappropriate.[28]

The regulations also provide for additional information to be provided where a contract is concluded by electronic means. Under reg.9(1) where a contract is concluded by electronic means the following information must, in a clear, comprehensible and unambiguous manner, be provided[29]:

(a) the different technical steps to follow to conclude the contract;

(b) whether or not the concluded contract will be filed by the service provider and whether it will be accessible;

(c) the technical means for identifying and correcting input errors prior to the placing of the order; and

(d) the languages offered for the conclusion of the contract.

This information, however, need not be provided where the contract is concluded solely by electronic mail (or equivalent).[30]

Distance Selling

Distance Selling Regulations

The Distance Selling Directive[31] is aimed at providing a common degree of consumer protection throughout the European Union where a consumer makes a contract without any face-to-face communication with the supplier. The consumer protection includes both ensuring that the consumer gets good information prior to the contact being made and also giving the consumer a right to cancel the contract during a subsequent cooling-off period. Further protection extends to prevention of inertia selling, exempting the consumer from having to pay for unsolicited supplies and protection in the event of fraudulent use of a payment card. The Directive has been implemented by the Consumer Protection (Distance Selling) Regulations 2000.[32]

16–005

---

[28] reg.15. This statutory remedy no doubt goes some way to explaining the various "confirmation" pages when placing an order online.
[29] Unless the parties are not consumers and have agreed otherwise.
[30] reg.9(4).
[31] Distance Selling Directive 97/7.
[32] Consumer Protection (Distance Selling) Regulations 2000 (SI 2000/2334). As amended by the Consumer Protection (Distance Selling) Regulations 2005 (SI 2005/689).

Contracting Out

16–006   It is not possible to contract out of the regulations. Under reg.25(1) any contract term is void to the extent that it is inconsistent with any provision of the regulations for the protection of the consumer.

Distance Contracts

16–007   The regulations apply only to distance contracts. A contract is a "distance contract" if[33]:

    1. it concerns goods or services,

    2. it is between a supplier (acting for commercial or professional purposes) and a consumer (a natural person acting for purposes outside his business),

    3. it is concluded under an organised distance sales or service provision scheme run by the supplier, and

    4. the supplier makes exclusive use of distance communication up to, and at the moment, when the contract is made.

Distance communication is any means of communication not involving the simultaneous presence of the consumer and the supplier (or the supplier's representative)—e.g. telephone, mail order, letter, fax, email, television. A transaction where initial contact is made by distance communication but where the contract is made face-to-face is not subject to the regulations. There is thus no chance of a contract being cancellable both under these regulations and also under either the Consumer Protection (Cancellation of Contracts Concluded away from Business Premises) Regulations 1987 or the Consumer Credit Act 1974, since the latter two sets of provisions in practice cannot apply where there has been no face-to-face contact between the parties.[34]

The expression "an organised distance sales or service provision scheme" is obscure. What about a telephone enquiry by a consumer as a result of consulting Yellow Pages which leads to a contract being made during that telephone conversation? The fact that the supplier, e.g. a department store, has placed an advertisement in such a telephone directory does not in itself show that the supplier has a "distance sales scheme". On the other hand if it advertises its telephone number and runs a "home delivery service" then it does run such a scheme. The requirement for an "organised distance sales . . . scheme" will certainly exclude the regulations from applying to a supplier who does not normally indulge in distance sales but who does, for example, on a one-off occasion agree to take an order from a customer by telephone.

---

[33] As defined in reg.3(1).
[34] For these two sets of provisions, see paras 2–013, above and 24–040, below.

Excepted Contracts

Even if a contract apparently falls within the definition of "distance contract", the regulations   **16–008**
do not apply to it at all if it is an excepted contract. Excepted contracts are listed in reg.5 and
include the following:

- for the sale or disposition of an interest in land (except for rental)[35];

- for the construction of a building where the contract also provides for the sale of an
  interest in the land upon which the building is constructed[36];

- relating to financial services[37];

- concluded by means of an automated vending machine or automated commercial
  premises[38];

- concluded with a telecommunications operator through the use of a public pay-
  phone[39];

- concluded at an auction.[40]

There are two further groups of contracts to which the main provisions of the regulations
(i.e. the requirements on prior information and the cancellation provisions) do not apply. The
first of these are contracts for the supply of food, beverages or other goods intended for
everyday consumption supplied to the consumer's residence or workplace by regular rounds-
men.[41] This group includes, for example, doorstep deliveries by the milkman. The second
such group comprises contracts for the provision of accommodation, transport, catering or
leisure services, where the supplier undertakes, at the time the contract is made, to provide
those services on a specific date or within a specific period.[42] This group includes, for
example, the following when ordered or booked over the telephone or internet: hotel rooms;
mini-cabs; theatre tickets; home delivery of a pizza; railway tickets (unless they are open-
dated). Whether this group also includes a hair "wash and cut" booked over the telephone,
depends upon whether that is a "leisure" service. A contract to hire a marquee and have it
erected in the consumer's garden for a party on a specific date might well be made over the
telephone. Presumably this is not "accommodation". Very likely, however, it is a "leisure"
service. If it is not, then the contract would seem to be fully subject to the regulations.

In addition, two further categories of contracts which are partially exempted from the
regulations are timeshare agreements and package holidays which are exempted from regs
7–20 and 7–19(1) respectively (in particular, the requirements on prior information and the
cancellation provisions).

---

[35] reg.5(1)(a).
[36] reg.5(1)(b).
[37] reg.5(1)(c).
[38] reg.5(1)(d).
[39] reg.5(1)(e).
[40] reg.5(1)(f).
[41] reg.6(2)(a).
[42] reg.6(2)(b).

Information to Consumer

Pre-Contract Information

16–009   The pre-contract information[43] required is:

1. The supplier's identity and, where payment in advance is required, the supplier's address.

2. A description of the main characteristics of the goods or services.

3. The price, including all taxes.

4. Any delivery costs.

5. The arrangements for payment, delivery or performance.

6. The existence of a right of cancellation (except where there is no such right).

7. The cost of using the means of distance communication.

8. The period for which the offer, or the price, remains valid.

9. The minimum duration (where appropriate) in the case of contracts for the supply of products or services to be performed permanently or recurrently.

This information must be provided:

> " . . . in a clear and comprehensible manner appropriate to the means of distance communication used, with due regard, in particular, to the principles of good faith in commercial transactions and the principles governing the protection of those who are unable to give their consent."

The burden of proof rests on the supplier to show that he provided the required information in accordance with these requirements. Failure to do so renders the contract unenforceable against the consumer. It may be appropriate to provide the information other than in writing (e.g. in the case of a contract made by telephone). If it is provided in writing, the required information must be easily legible and be at least as prominent as any other information in the document (except the heading, the names of the parties to the contract and any information in handwriting). However it is provided, the supplier must when providing it makes clear his commercial purpose.[44] In the case of a contract made during a telephone conversation, the supplier must, at the beginning of the conversation, have made clear his identity and the commercial purpose of the telephone call.[45] If he did not, the contract is unenforceable against the consumer.

---

[43] reg.7.
[44] reg.7(3).
[45] reg.7(4).

Information in Durable Form

The requirement to give pre-contract information can be satisfied by provision of the required **16–010** information in a non-permanent form (provided it is a form appropriate to the means of communication used). However, under reg.8, there is a requirement to give that same information to the consumer either in writing or in another durable medium which is available and accessible to the consumer. This must be provided either:

(a) prior to the making of the contract, or

(b) in good time before or during performance of the contract.

Where the contract concerns goods (not for delivery to third parties) this information in durable form must be provided at the latest at the time of delivery of the goods. It seems likely that where the contract is made over the internet, provision of the information in writing in an email would satisfy the requirement that it be in a "durable medium available and accessible to the consumer". If the information is not provided as required, the contract is unenforceable against the consumer.

Notice of Cancellation Rights and Where to Complain, etc.

Further information also has to be provided to the consumer. Again, if it is not, the contract **16–011** is unenforceable against the consumer. This information is:

(i) the supplier's geographical business address to which complaints may be addressed;

(ii) information on any after-sales service and guarantees;

(iii) the conditions for cancelling the agreement, where its duration exceeds a year or is unspecified;

(iv) the supplier's name;

(v) the supplier's reference number or code or other details (i.e. to enable the contract to be identified);

(vi) a notice of the consumer's cancellation right and where and how it may be exercised.

The consumer may be given a cancellation form which the consumer can use to cancel the contract.

There is an exemption from the requirement to give the further information in the case of a distance contract where services are supplied on one occasion only and are invoiced by the operator of the means of distance communication.[46] This would apply, for example, in the

---

[46] reg.9.

case of information provided over the telephone via a premium rate call. Even in this exceptional case, however, the supplier must, when requested, provide the consumer with a geographical address of the supplier's place of business to which complaints can be addressed. Failure to do so renders the contract unenforceable against the consumer.

Cancellation

Cancellable Agreements

16–012   The regulations give the consumer a right to cancel a "distance contract" agreement during a short period after the contract has been made. As has been seen, however, some distance contracts are excepted from the application of the regulations or the main part of the regulations.[47] The regulations deny the right of cancellation in certain other cases as well:

    (a) a contract for the provision of services, if performance of the contract has begun with the consumer's consent before the end of the cancellation period[48];

    (b) a contract where the price of the goods or services is dependent on fluctuations in the financial market which cannot be controlled by the supplier[49];

    (c) a contract for the supply of goods made to the consumer's specifications or clearly personalised or which by their nature cannot be returned or are liable to deteriorate or expire rapidly (e.g. flowers)[50];

    (d) a contract for the supply of audio or video recordings or computer software which have been unsealed by the consumer[51];

    (e) a contract for the supply of newspapers, periodicals or magazines[52];

    (f) a contract for gaming or lottery services.[53]

In any case where the regulations do not confer a right of cancellation, it is, of course, possible for the contract expressly to do so.[54]

Cancellation Notice

16–013   The consumer can exercise the right of cancellation by serving, within the cancellation period, a written notice of cancellation (whether or not by using a cancellation form provided

[47] See paras 16–008–16–009, above.
[48] reg.13(1)(a).
[49] reg.13(1)(b).
[50] reg.13(1)(c).
[51] reg.13(1)(d).
[52] reg.13(1)(e).
[53] reg.13(1)(f).
[54] Something made clear by reg.13(1).

by the supplier) indicating the intention to cancel the agreement.[55] The notice of cancellation must be served on the supplier or on the person specified in the information given to the consumer as being a person to whom such a notice may be sent.

Cancellation Period

Normally, the cancellation period expires: **16–014**

- in the case of goods, at the end of a period of seven working days after the goods are delivered[56]; and
- in the case of services, at the end of a period of seven working days after the contract is made.[57]

The cancellation period is extended where, at the time of delivery (in the case of goods) or the making of the contract (in the case of services), the supplier has failed to comply with the requirement to supply certain information in writing or in another durable medium. In that case the cancellation period will expire at the *earlier* of the following two times:

(i) the end of a period of seven working days after the supplier complies with the requirement to provide the required information in a durable medium[58];

(ii) the end of a period of three months and seven working days after delivery (in the case of goods) or after the making of the contract (in the case of services).[59]

Effect of Cancellation

Broadly the position after cancellation is that the consumer is entitled to recover any   **16–015**
payments already made[60] and any goods given in part-exchange (or their part-exchange allowance)[61] and is under a duty to allow the supplier to recover possession of any goods supplied.[62] In fact the legal position is virtually identical to the position following cancellation under the Cancellation of Contracts made in a Consumer's Home or Place of Work etc. Regulations 2008.[63] The main difference between the two sets of regulations is that whereas under the 2008 regulations the consumer does not have to return perishable goods or goods which have been consumed before cancellation but remains under a duty to pay for them,

[55] reg.10.
[56] reg.11.
[57] reg.12.
[58] See reg.11(3) for goods and reg.12(3) for services.
[59] See reg.11(4) for goods and reg.12(4) for services.
[60] See reg.14.
[61] See reg.18.
[62] See reg.17.
[63] For details see para.2–013, above.

under the 2000 regulations contracts for those two types of goods are, as we have seen at para.16–14 above, not cancellable at all. The net result, however, is the same.

Cancellation (under the 2000 regulations) of a distance contract, also results in the automatic cancellation of any related credit agreement, i.e. any agreement whereby the supplier or a third party (acting under arrangements with the supplier) provided (or was to provide) credit to the consumer. Presumably this means that the related credit agreement is cancelled to the extent that it was to provide credit to finance the consumer's duty to pay the price under the distance contract. In such a case, if the credit provider is a different person from the supplier, the latter is under a duty to inform the credit provider as soon as the supplier receives the consumer's notice of cancellation. The consequences of cancellation of the related credit agreement (or that aspect of it involving credit to finance the distance contract) are virtually identical to those applicable when a cancellable debtor-creditor agreement is cancelled under the cancellation provisions of the Consumer Credit Act 1974. Those consequences are explained at para.24–55, below.

Performance

16–016   The regulations require that: unless the parties agree otherwise, the supplier shall perform the contract within a maximum of 30 days beginning with the day following that on which the consumer forwarded his order to the supplier.[64]

Where the supplier is unable to perform the contract, he must inform the consumer and repay any sum paid by the consumer as soon as possible and in any event within 30 days of his informing the consumer of his inability to perform. In the case of outdoor leisure events which by their nature cannot be rescheduled, however, the requirement to make a refund does not apply if the parties have so agreed.[65] The requirement to give notice of inability to perform (and to make a refund) is subject to the possibility of the supplier being allowed to provide substituted performance in the form of goods or services of equivalent quality and price. This is allowed, however, only if three conditions are all satisfied[66]:

  (i) The possibility (of the substituted performance) was provided for, either in the contract or prior to its making.

  (ii) The consumer was informed of this possibility in a clear and comprehensible manner.

  (iii) The cost of returning the goods in the event of the consumer exercising her right of cancellation is to be borne by the seller and the consumer is informed of this.

Presumably failure to comply with the requirement to perform within the 30-day period renders the seller/supplier liable to pay damages.

[64] reg.19(1).
[65] See reg.19(8).
[66] See reg.19(7).

Fraudulent Use of Payment Cards

The regulations entitle the consumer to "cancel a payment"[67] where "fraudulent use" has **16–017** been made of her payment card in connection with a contract to which the regulations apply.[68] This provision applies not just to regulated credit cards but also, for example, to current account debit cards (e.g. Delta or Swift) and to charge cards (e.g. American Express and Diners Club), which are exempt from being regulated by the Consumer Credit Act 1974. The regulations do not explain what is meant by "fraudulent" use of the card. Presumably it covers, not only use by someone who has stolen the card from the cardholder (e.g. by taking the cardholder's handbag), but also by someone who has simply noted the card number and then, without any authority from the cardholder, used that number to make a payment over the telephone. The regulations do not, however, apply where a rogue uses the card to withdraw some money from the cardholder's bank account via an automated teller machine (ATM), since the rogue is not in that instance using the card to make a "payment". Nor do the regulations apply where the rogue uses someone else's card to make a payment when buying goods or services over the counter, since they apply only to distance contracts. In these cases the cardholder would have to rely on the cardholder's rights under the Banking Code of Practice or, in the case of a card regulated by the Consumer Credit Act 1974, that Act.[69]

Enforcement

Certain bodies may consider complaints[70] about alleged contraventions of the regulations, **16–018** including the Office of Fair Trading (OFT) and all Weights and Measures Authorities (i.e. local Trading Standards Departments). There are provisions for such a body to notify the OFT that it is considering a complaint. In the absence of such a notification, the OFT is under a duty to consider any such complaint it receives. The enforcement authorities have the power to ask the court for an injunction against an offending trader under reg.27.

CROSS-BORDER CONTRACTS

We are dealing with the situation where someone in England buys goods (or services) from **16–019** or sells them to, someone in another country, principally where the other country is an EU country. There are three important issues: (i) jurisdiction, (ii) applicable law, (iii) enforcement of judgments. The rules on the first two vary according to whether the buyer is a consumer, i.e. someone buying for a purpose outside her trade or profession. In the EU, the law on the first and third of these issues used to be dealt with in the Brussels Convention 1968[71] (as amended) which was incorporated in United Kingdom law by the Civil Jurisdiction and Judgments Act 1982.

---

[67] reg.21(2) entitles the consumer to have any sums involved recredited to their card.
[68] See reg.21.
[69] See para.19–017, below.
[70] Under reg.26.
[71] Brussels Convention (on Jurisdiction and Enforcement of Judgments) 1968.

As a result of the Treaty of Amsterdam, the matters covered by these conventions have moved into the mainstream of EU business. Consequently, Council Regulation 44/2001 of December 22, 2000 on jurisdiction and the recognition and enforcement of judgments in civil and commercial matters (the "Brussels Regulation") replaced the Brussels Convention with effect from March 1, 2002.[72] Until July 1, 2007 the Brussels Regulation did not apply to Denmark which therefore remained subject to the Brussels Convention 1968. This dichotomy was removed following the special agreement negotiated by the European Commission and ratified by Denmark on January 18, 2007.[73] Consequently, the Regulation came into force in Denmark on July 1, 2007 and the Brussells Regulation now applies to all the Member States of the European Union.[74] Accordingly, all references to articles below are references to the relevant article of the Brussels Regulation unless indicated otherwise.

By virtue of the Lugano Convention 1988, the law on these issues is virtually identical in the case of a contract between someone in an EU state and someone in an EFTA state which is not part of the EU. This presently includes Iceland, Norway and Switzerland. On October 30, 2007 a new Lugano Convention was signed by the EC,[75] Denmark, Iceland, Norway and Switzerland. This Convention was required in order to ensure alignment between the new Lugano Convention and the Brussels Regulation (i.e. in the same way that the Lugano Convention 1988 essentially mirrored the Brussels Convention 1968, the new Lugano Convention now mirrors the Brussels Regulation).[76]

The rules as to the applicable law were established by the Rome Convention 1980 which was incorporated into United Kingdom law by the Contracts (Applicable Law) Act 1990. The Rome Convention is not confined, however, to EU countries.

Jurisdiction

16–020   The general rule is that jurisdiction for contract claims lies with the country where the defendant is domiciled.[77] Thus normally the defendant must be sued in his own country. An individual is domiciled in a country if he resides there and has a substantial connection with it. A company or other corporate body is domiciled in the country where it has its seat, i.e. if either: (i) it was incorporated there and has its registered office or some other office address there; or (ii) its central management or control is exercised there. There are exceptions or variations to the general rule. The main ones applicable in the context of contracts to supply goods or services are as follows.

---

[72] The Regulation came into effect on March 1, 2002.

[73] See further, [2005] O.J. L299/62.

[74] The Brussels Regulation was incorporated into domestic law by the Civil Jurisdiction and Judgments Order 2001 (SI 2001/3929), amending the Civil Jurisdiction and Judgments Act 1982.

[75] On the institutional competence of the EC to sign the new Lugano Convention see, "ECJ confirms Community's competence to sign Lugano Convention" [2006] EU Focus 5.

[76] The new Convention is likely to come into force in 2009. Until such time, the Lugano Convention 1988 remains, as also does therefore, the divergence between the Brussels Regulation and the earlier Brussels Convention 1968 (upon which the Lugano Convention 1988 is based).

[77] art.1.

Branch or Agency

Where a defendant company is domiciled in an EU country and the proceedings arise out of the operations in another EU country of a branch, agency or other establishment of the defendant company, the defendant company can be sued in the country where the branch, agency or other establishment is situated.[78] Even where the defendant company is not domiciled in the EU, a consumer can bring a contract action in an EU country if the proceedings arise out of the operation in that EU country of a branch, agency or other establishment of the defendant company.   **16–021**

Country of Performance

A contract claim can be brought either in the country where the defendant is domiciled or in the country where the obligation in question was to be performed.[79] This would seem to allow, for example, proceedings to be brought in England against a German seller who has contracted to deliver the goods in England. The position is more doubtful, however, where all that the German seller has agreed to do is to package them up and send them to England.   **16–022**

Claim by Consumer

Article 15 gives a consumer the option[80] of suing in the country where the consumer is domiciled. Thus a consumer who buys goods or services from a seller/supplier in another EU country, can bring proceedings in the consumer's own country.[81] This applies to contracts for the sale of goods on instalment credit terms[82] and to contracts for loans repayable by instalments or for any other form of credit made to finance the sale of goods.[83] These provisions are identical to their counterparts under art.13 of the Brussels Convention and present no significant difficulties. A third provision, however, has been significantly amended. Article 15(1)(c) provides that a consumer has the option of suing in his country of domicile: **16–023**

> "in all other cases, the contract has been concluded with a person who pursues commercial or professional activities in the Member State of the consumer's domicile or, by any means, directs such activities to that Member State or to several States including that Member State, and the contract falls within the scope of such activities".

[78] art.5(5).
[79] art.5(1)(a).
[80] Note that the other contracting party, i.e. the trader, can only bring proceedings against the consumer (e.g. an action for the price) in the courts of the Member State of the consumer, art.16(2).
[81] See art.16 and art.17 (restrictions on departing from the consumer's choice of jurisdiction).
[82] art.15(1)(a).
[83] art.15(1)(b).

The equivalent provision under the Brussels Convention required the consumer contract to be for the supply of goods or services and that the following two conditions were satisfied:

(a) in the State of the consumer's domicile the conclusion of the contract was preceded by a specific invitation addressed to him or by advertising, and

(b) the consumer took in that State the steps necessary for the conclusion of the contract.

This revision no doubt reflects the development of electronic commerce. Thus, the requirement under the Brussels Convention that the consumer took in his own state, the steps necessary for the conclusion of the contract has been removed. Therefore, where an English consumer travels to France and purchases goods from a French company through that company's website, provided that the company's website is available in England, the consumer will be able to rely on art.15(1)(c). It is important to note, however, that art.15(1)(c) is not limited to contracts made through electronic means. Thus, in the example above, the outcome would be the same if instead of visiting the company's website, the consumer responded to a newspaper advertisement (subject to that advertisement being similarly directed to England).[84]

In any situation where art.15 does not apply, it may nevertheless still be possible for the consumer to bring a claim in England (for the seller/supplier's breach of contract) against the bank or finance company whose credit the consumer used to make the overseas purchase in question. An example is where the consumer has used her English credit card to pay for an item (costing over £100) in another country.[85]

Claim Relating to Land

16–024 In the case of a claim relating to immovable property, the general rule (giving jurisdiction to the country of the defendant's domicile) is displaced. Instead, the country where the property is situated, has exclusive jurisdiction.[86] This applies to tenancies and also even to short term lets or licences to occupy premises—the only exception being where the object of the claim is a let for temporary private use for a maximum period of six months and where the parties are both natural persons who are domiciled in the same country.[87] Timeshare agreements are almost always made by *companies* supplying the timeshares to consumers and thus in such cases the country where the timeshare property is situated has exclusive jurisdiction. The English purchaser of a timeshare in Portugal will therefore not be able to sue the timeshare supplier other than by bringing proceedings in Portugal. That is so even if the timeshare supplier was domiciled in England. If, however, the timeshare purchase was financed by a regulated consumer credit agreement made in England between the purchaser and, say, a bank, the purchaser may well be able to bring a "like" claim against the bank (instead of

---

[84] For a detailed analysis of art.15(1) and art.13 of the Brussels Convention, see Oren, "International jurisdiction over consumer contracts in e-Europe" [2003] I.C.L.Q. 667.

[85] See *Jarrett v Barclays Bank* considered in the next para. See also, *Office of Fair Trading v Lloyds TSB Bank Plc* [2008] 1 All E.R. 205 (HL).

[86] art.22, replacing art.16 of the Brussels Convention.

[87] See art.22(1).

against the Portuguese timeshare supplier) under s.75 of the Consumer Credit Act 1974. In that case the proceedings against the bank could be brought in England: *Jarrett v Barclays Bank and Royal Bank of Scotland*.[88]

Non-European Connection

The Brussels Regulation does not apply where the overseas country of the buyer or seller is   **16–025** a non-European one. In this case the English courts will take jurisdiction in the following cases:

(i) The defendant is present in person when served with the claim form. A company is present if it has a place of business in England or if it has filed with the registrar of companies the name of a person authorised to accept service on behalf of the company.

(ii) The defendant submits to the jurisdiction by accepting service of the claim form.

(iii) The court gives permission for service of the claim form outside the jurisdiction.

The court will not grant such permission unless England is a convenient forum for the dispute to be litigated (taking into account such matters as whether the witnesses are present in England, the place of residence of the parties, whether the law applicable to the agreement is English law). In any case, permission can be granted only if it falls within one of the following four categories:

(a) The contract was made in England.

(b) The contract was made through an agent trading or residing in England on behalf of the defendant who was trading or residing elsewhere.

(c) The law applicable to the contract is English law.

(d) The contract states that the High Court shall have jurisdiction.

Applicable Law

The law which will be applied to the contract is not necessarily the law of the country which   **16–026** has jurisdiction and where the proceedings take place. Thus if proceedings are brought in England for breach of a contract to which French law applies, the English court will apply French law. Under the Rome Convention, the applicable law is the law chosen by the parties and, failing any choice having been made by the parties, it is the law of the country with

---

[88] For the ability (under s.75) to be able to sue a "connected lender" for beaches of contract by the supplier, see para.23–003 below.

which the contract is most closely connected. There is a presumption that this is the law of the party who has to effect "the performance which is characteristic of the contract". In effect therefore, unless the parties have expressly chosen a different law, the applicable law will usually be that of the seller rather than that of the buyer.

Where the parties have themselves chosen a law, that law may or may not be the law of an EU country. It is not possible, however, by choosing a different law to avoid the "mandatory provisions" of the law of the country where the litigation takes place. Where the litigation takes place in England, those mandatory provisions include the Unfair Contract Terms Act 1977, the Unfair Terms in Consumer Contracts Regulations 1999 and the Consumer Protection (Distance Selling) Regulations 2000. These mandatory provisions will apply to the contract, even if the law of another country is chosen by the parties as the applicable law.

Where an English buyer or seller deals with a seller or buyer in an overseas country to which the Rome Convention does not apply (i.e. country which has not become a signatory to the Convention, usually a country outside Europe), the rules as to which law applies to the contract are common law rules but are roughly similar in effect to the rules applicable under the Rome Convention.

Enforcement of a Foreign Judgment

16–027   The Brussels Regulation, implemented by Civil Jurisdiction and Judgments Order 2001,[89] applies in the case of a judgment in an EU country which relates to a civil or commercial matter (e.g. a breach of contract). Such judgments are enforceable in England by a simple process of registration in the High Court. An application to enforce in England a judgment from another EU state is made "without notice" to the defendant, i.e. so as not to give him notice and thus enable him to avoid enforcement. There is a variety of procedures for enforcing judgments obtained in non-European countries.

General Reading

16–028
- Butler and Darnley, "Consumer Acquis—Proposed Reform of B2C Regulation to Promote Cross-Border Trading" [2007] Computer and Telecommunications Law Review 109;

- Hall, "Cancellation rights in distance-selling contracts for services: exemptions and consumer protection" [2007] J.B.L. 683;

- Harrington, "Information Society services: what are they and how relevant is the definition?" [2001] J.B.L. 190;

- Harris, "Sale of Goods and the Relentless March of the Brussels I Regulation" (2007) 123 L.Q.R. 522;

---

[89] SI 2001/3929, amending the Civil Jurisdiction and Judgments Act 1982.

- Hellwege, "Consumer protection in Britain in need of reform" [2004] C.L.J. 712;

- Meads, "E-consumer protection—distance selling" [2002] I.C.C.L.R. 179;

- Oren, "International jurisdiction over consumer contracts in e-Europe" [2003] I.C.L.Q. 667;

- Rawson, "Mobility and Liability: The Hazards of Handhelds" (2002) 18 *Computer Law and Security Report* 164;

- Takahashi, "Jurisdiction in matters relating to contract: Article 5(1) of the Brussels Convention and Regulation" [2002] E.L.Rev. 530;

- Warner, "The new E.C. Regulations" [2002] Co. Law 313.

Chapter 17

UNFAIR TRADING PRACTICES

INTRODUCTION

This chapter deals with the law relating to unfair trading practices and in so doing introduces **17–001** an area of law which has undergone significant (and substantial) reform in recent months. In particular the chapter considers the Unfair Commercial Practices Directive 2005 and its implementation into domestic law through the Consumer Protection from Unfair Trading Regulations 2008. These regulations have, as shall be discussed shortly, radically affected much of the previous legislation designed to protect the consumer in ways other than conferring rights upon individual consumers, including, for example the Trade Descriptions Act 1968 and Pt III of the Consumer Protection Act 1987. This chapter will only offer a brief account of these pieces of legislation since the regulation of such activities has now been subsumed within the Consumer Protection from Unfair Trading Regulations 2008. Where the reader requires a detailed account of previous legislation such as the criminal offences under ss.1 and 14 of the Trade Descriptions Act 1968 the previous edition of this text will prove useful. The chapter will also introduce the Enterprise Act 2002 which confers powers on enforcement authorities to secure court orders against traders guilty of malpractices. Such enforcement action is vital to the consumer protection movement and has also undergone considerable reform in recent years.

It was noted above that many of the old criminal offences have now been subsumed by those in the Consumer Protection from Unfair Trading Regulations 2008. It is important to understand that the fact a criminal offence is committed by a trader or creditor does not confer upon the consumer any right to bring an action or obtain redress in the civil courts. Someone who commits an offence can be prosecuted in a criminal court and fined (or, sometimes, imprisoned). However, the Powers of Criminal Courts Act 1973 enables the criminal court to give redress to the victim of the offence.[1] After the offender has been

---

[1] s.35.

convicted, it can order the offender to pay compensation to the victim. This can be done irrespective of whether it was the victim who brought the prosecution and, if the court fails to make a compensation order in a case where it is empowered to do so, it must give reasons. In the case of magistrates' courts the amount is subject to a maximum of £5,000 per conviction.[2]

THE UNFAIR COMMERCIAL PRACTICES DIRECTIVE 2005

17–002   The Unfair Commercial Practices Directive 2005[3] was incorporated into domestic law on May 26, 2008 by the Consumer Protection from Unfair Trading Regulations 2008.[4] This section will briefly outline the purpose of the Directive before focusing upon its implementation into domestic law through the regulations. The purpose of the Directive is deceptively simple and is stated in art.1 in the following terms:

> " . . . to contribute to the proper functioning of the internal market and achieve a high level of consumer protection by approximating the laws, regulations and administrative provisions of the Member States on unfair commercial practices harming consumers' economic interests."

The Directive therefore imposes a legal framework designed to govern unfair commercial practices in business-to-consumer dealings. Moreover, it does so uniformly in that the Directive is one of full (or maximum) harmonisation, i.e. it lays down the standard which must be transposed into domestic law by the Member States, which cannot provide a lesser or greater level of protection to consumers than that required by the Directive.[5]

Scope of the Consumer Protection from Unfair Trading Regulations 2008

17–003   The regulations create a broad system of prohibitions upon unfair commercial practices; they do not alter or enhance the consumer's contractual rights. As reg.29 states, "[An] agreement shall not be void or unenforceable only by breach of these Regulations". Before analysing the approach of the regulations in prohibiting unfair practices, it is necessary to define certain key concepts which run throughout the regulations. Fundamental is the definition of "commercial practice" laid down in reg.2(1) as meaning:

> "any act, omission, course of conduct, representation or commercial communication (including advertising and marketing) by a trader, which is directly connected with the

---

[2] See, for example, the approach of the court in *R. v Thomson Holidays* [1974] Q.B. 592 (a decision on s.14 of the old Trade Descriptions Act 1968).
[3] Directive 2005/29 EC.
[4] SI 2008/1277. The regulations came into effect on May 26, 2008.
[5] The significance of maximum harmonisation is clearly demonstrated through Sch.2, which lists 115 amendments to previous legislation required in order to comply with the Directive.

promotion, sale or supply of a product to or from consumers, whether occurring before, during or after a commercial transaction (if any) in relation to a product".

When understood in conjunction with the definition of "product"[6] which includes both goods[7] and services and also "immovable property, rights and obligations", this is clearly extensive in scope and extends well beyond simply the supply of goods (or offer thereof) by a trader to a consumer. Indeed, as the definition above makes clear, there need not actually be any commercial transaction, thus the advertising of a product to consumers will constitute a commercial practice under the regulations. The reference to trader and consumer within the definition is instructive and ensures that the regulations comply with the Unfair Commercial Practices Directive which employs the term "business-to-consumer commercial practices".[8] The definition of "consumer" under the regulations adopts the standard European meaning, focusing upon the idea of a natural person (i.e. not a company or other corporate body) acting for purposes outside his trade, business or profession.[9] The definition of "trader" also has the meaning expected and includes any person (whether natural or legal) "acting for purposes relating to his trade, business, craft or profession".[10] The regulations do not apply to consumer-to-consumer dealings (in the same way, for example, that the old Trade Descriptions Act 1968 did not) nor do the regulations apply to business-to-business dealings.[11] This particular issue will be returned to in para.17–xx below in relation to the Business Protection from Misleading Marketing Regulations 2008.[12]

Now that the concepts of "commercial practice", "consumer" and "trader" have been considered, the key issue is that of defining what is meant by unfair.

Unfair Commercial Practices

Under the Consumer Protection from Unfair Trading Regulations there are five categories of **17–004** "unfair commercial practice".[13] Accordingly, a commercial practice is unfair if:

- it is contrary to the general prohibition against unfair commercial practices under reg.3(3); or

- it is a misleading action under reg.5; or

- it is a misleading omission under reg.6; or

- it is aggressive under reg.7; or

---

[6] reg.2(1).
[7] Defined in reg.2(1) as including "ships, aircraft, animals, things attached to land and growing crops".
[8] See art.2(d).
[9] reg.2(1).
[10] reg.2(1). In adopting this definition, the difficulties evident through *Havering London Borough v Stevenson* [1970] 3 All E.R. 609 and *Davies v Sumner* [1984] 1 W.L.R. 1301 should be avoided, with the broader definition under *Havering* being preferred under the regulations.
[11] At least not directly, there may well be some advantages flowing from the Directive to legitimate businesses, see further, Griffiths, "Unfair commercial practices—a new regime" [2007] Comms. Law 196, 196.
[12] SI 2008/1276.
[13] reg.3(2) referring to regs 3(3) and 3(4).

- it is listed in Sch.1 (in which case it is considered unfair in all circumstances).[14]

Practices Deemed Unfair as being Contrary to the General Prohibition of Unfair Commercial Practices

17–005 The general prohibition under reg.3(3) has two requirements. First, the practice must be contrary to the requirements of professional diligence and secondly it must materially distort (or be likely to materially distort) the economic behaviour of the average consumer with regard the product. Furthermore, where the practice is directed to a specific group of consumers, the test is that of whether the practice materially distorts (or is likely to materially distort) the economic behaviour of the average member of that group, rather than consumers generally.[15]

The meaning of "professional diligence" here is crucial, and is defined in Sch.2 in the following terms:

> "the standard of special skill and care which a trader may reasonably be expected to exercise towards consumers, commensurate with either:
>
> (a) honest market practice in the trader's field of activity; or
> (b) the general principle of good faith in the trader's field of activity".

Compliance with industry standards and market practice may not satisfy this requirement, where for example, the industry standard is not what may be reasonably expected.[16] The material distortion test is defined with reference to the ability of a consumer to make an informed decision. Therefore, where the commercial practice "appreciably" impairs the ability of the average consumer to make an informed decision, and consequently, consumers make or are likely to make transactional decisions that they would not have taken otherwise, this element of the test will be satisfied.

17–006 Where a trader knowingly or recklessly engages in a commercial practice which contravenes the requirements of professional diligence and materially distorts (or is likely to do so) the economic behaviour of an average consumer, he is guilty of an offence under reg.8. Regulation 8(2) explains that a trader cannot avoid committing this offence by not considering whether the commercial practice contravenes the requirements of due diligence. This is so even where the failure is an innocent one. Such a trader is deemed to have recklessly engaged in the commercial practice and therefore satisfies the test laid down in reg.8(1)(a).[17] Where guilty of an offence under reg.8 the trader is liable, on conviction on indictment, to either a fine or imprisonment for up to two years, or both.[18]

---

[14] See Annex 1 of the 2005 Directive.
[15] See also, art.5(3) which creates a similar provision in respect of vulnerable consumers (those with mental or physical infirmity and age etc.).
[16] For parallels with the similar attitude towards industry standards in product liability under the Consumer Protection Act 1987, see Ch.9.
[17] For judicial consideration of recklessness under the old s.14 of the Trade Descriptions Act 1968, see *MFI Warehouses v Nattrass* [1973] Crim. L.R. 196.
[18] reg.13(b). See also, reg.13(a) (summary conviction).

Misleading Actions

Under reg.5 of the Consumer Protection from Unfair Trading Regulations 2008 there are two **17–007** ways in which a commercial practice may be deemed misleading. First, under reg.5(2) a commercial practice is misleading if it contains false information and is therefore untruthful in relation to one or more of the specified matters (see below) or if the practice (or its overall presentation) deceives, or is likely to deceive, an average consumer in relation to any of the specified matters. In addition, the practice must also cause (or be likely to cause) an average consumer to take a transactional decision he would not have otherwise taken. The second category of misleading commercial practices is laid down in reg.5(3) and relates to marketing practices which either (i) create confusion with any products of a competitor,[19] or (ii) relates to a breach of any code of conduct which the trader has signed up to, and cause (or be likely to cause) an average consumer to take a transactional decision he would not have otherwise taken.

The matters to be considered in determining whether the practice is misleading under the first subcategory of misleading actions are detailed in reg.3(4) and include:

- the existence or nature of the product;
- the main characteristics of the product[20];
- the extent of the trader's commitments[21];
- the price or the manner in which the price is calculated[22];
- the need for a service, part, replacement or repair;
- the nature, attributes and rights of the trader or his agent[23];
- the consumer's rights.[24]

The fundamental test to be applied here is therefore twofold. First, the practice must contain false information or be such that it deceives (or is likely to deceive) the average consumer. Secondly, that falsity or deception must be such that it "causes or is likely to cause him to take a transactional decision that he would not have taken otherwise". The definition of "transactional decision" is laid down in reg.2(1) in the following terms:

"any decision taken by a consumer, whether it is to act or to refrain from acting, concerning:

(a) whether, how and on what terms to purchase, make a payment in whole or in part for, retain or dispose of a product; or
(b) whether, how and on what terms to exercise a contractual right in relation to a product".

---

[19] Including, though obviously not limited to, comparative advertising.
[20] e.g., fitness for purpose, availability, quantity etc. See the list laid down by reg.5(5).
[21] Including any statement as to approval of either the trader or product (whether direct or indirect), reg.5(4)(c).
[22] Including the existence of any price advantage, reg.5(4)(g).
[23] Including his identity, qualifications or status, reg.5(4)(j).
[24] e.g., as to a repair or replacement etc. under the Sale and Supply of Goods to Consumers Regulations 2002.

The concept of a "transactional decision" is a recurring feature within the regulations and is arguably "not dissimilar to a test considering whether the trader's actions would cause a reasonable person to act in reliance on these to his detriment".[25]

This does represent a departure from the traditional approach of, for example, the Trade Descriptions Act 1968. Under the 1968 Act there was no need to establish any transactional impact whatsoever once it had been found that the trade description was false (or literally true, yet still misleading). It remains to be seen whether this additional requirement under the Directive causes any loss to domestic consumer protection.

17–008   Where a trader engages in a commercial practice which is a misleading omission under reg.5,[26] he is guilty of an offence under reg.9 and is thereby liable, on conviction on indictment, to either a fine or imprisonment for up to two years, or both.[27]

Misleading Omissions

17–009   There is a similar provision to that of misleading actions in respect of misleading omissions which cause the consumer to make a transactional decision that he would not have taken otherwise.[28] Under reg.6(1) a commercial practice will constitute a misleading omission where it (i) causes, or is likely to cause, the consumer to make a transactional decision as considered above, and (ii) the practice either:

- omits material information; or

- hides material information; or

- provides material information in an unclear, unintelligible, ambiguous or untimely manner; or

- fails to identify its commercial intent (unless this is clear from the context of the practice).

In making this assessment reg.6 provides that the following matters must be taken into account. First, all of the features and circumstances of the commercial practice. Secondly, the limitations, if any, of the medium used to communicate the commercial practice (e.g. advertising through text messaging services). Thirdly, where there are limitations imposed by the nature of the communication medium, any measures taken by the trader to make the information available through other means (such as, for example, using the trader's internet site to provide all material information where the text message advertisement does not allow for this information to be included).[29]

Unsurprisingly, the definition of "material information" has been drafted in broad terms and has two elements (which will no doubt overlap). The first is any information which the

---

[25] Twigg-Flesner, "Deep impact? The EC Directive on unfair commercial practices and domestic consumer law" (2005) 121 L.Q.R. 386, 387.
[26] Other than the offence under reg.5(3)(b) (failure by trader to comply with code to which he has agreed to comply with).
[27] reg.13(b). See also, reg.13(a) (summary conviction).
[28] art.7.
[29] Similarly contrast, for example, a sales brochure with an advertising poster.

average consumer needs to make an informed transactional decision. The second element of the definition is any information which must be included within commercial communications as a result of Community law, e.g. the information requirements under the Electronic Commerce Directive 2000[30] as implemented by the Electronic Commerce (EC Directive) Regulations 2002.[31]

Where the commercial practice is an invitation to purchase, reg.6(4) expands the definition of "material information" to include the following[32]:

(a) the main characteristics of the product, to the extent appropriate to the medium by which the invitation to purchase is communicated and the product;

(b) the identity of the trader, such as his trading name, and the identity of any other trader on whose behalf the trader is acting;

(c) the geographical address of the trader and the geographical address of any other trader on whose behalf the trader is acting;

(d) either—

   (i) the price, including any taxes; or
   (ii) where the nature of the product is such that the price cannot reasonably be calculated in advance, the manner in which the price is calculated;

(e) where appropriate, either—

   (i) all additional freight, delivery or postal charges; or
   (ii) where such charges cannot reasonably be calculated in advance, the fact that such charges may be payable;

(f) the following matters where they depart from the requirements of professional diligence—

   (i) arrangements for payment,
   (ii) arrangements for delivery,
   (iii) arrangements for performance,
   (iv) complaint handling policy;

(g) for products and transactions involving a right of withdrawal or cancellation, the existence of such a right.

Where a trader engages in a commercial practice which is a misleading omission under reg.6, he is guilty of an offence under reg.10 and is thereby liable, on conviction on indictment, to either a fine or imprisonment for up to two years, or both.[33]

---

[30] Directive 2000/31/EC.
[31] SI 2002/2013, e.g. reg.6 (general information relating to the service provider). See Ch.16 above.
[32] Unless, of course, context of the practice is such that the information would be required in any event for the average consumer to make an informed transactional decision under reg.6(3).
[33] reg.13(b). See also, reg.13(a) (summary conviction).

Aggressive Practices

17–010   An aggressive commercial practice is defined by reg.7(1) as any commercial practice that:

(i) significantly impairs or is likely to significantly impair the average consumer's freedom of choice or conduct in relation to a product through either harassment, coercion[34] or undue influence[35]; and

(ii) causes, or is likely to cause, the consumer to make a transactional decision he would not have taken otherwise.

Under reg.7(2), harassment, coercion and undue influence are to be assessed in light of various factors including:

- its timing, location or persistence;
- threatening or abusive language or behaviour;
- exploitation by the trader of any specific misfortune, thereby impairing the consumer's judgment and influencing the consumer's decision regarding the product;
- onerous or disproportionate non-contractual barrier in relation to the consumer's rights under the contract;
- the threat of legal action where none can legally be taken.

Where a trader engages in an aggressive commercial practice under reg.7, he is guilty of an offence under reg.11 and is thereby liable, on conviction on indictment, to either a fine or imprisonment for up to two years, or both.[36]

Unfair in All Circumstances

17–011   Schedule 1 of the Consumer Protection from Unfair Trading Regulations 2008 implements the "blacklist" prescribed by art.5(5) and Annex 1 of the Directive. Where a practice is included on the list (which can only be amended through revision of the Directive itself) it will be regarded as unfair in all circumstances. The blacklist is as follows:

1. Claiming to be a signatory to a code of conduct when the trader is not.
2. Displaying a trust mark, quality mark or equivalent without having obtained the necessary authorisation.
3. Claiming that a code of conduct has an endorsement from a public or other body which it does not have.

---

[34] Including the use of physical force, reg.7(3)(a).
[35] See reg.7(3)(b).
[36] reg.13(b). See also, reg.13(a) (summary conviction).

4. Claiming that a trader (including his commercial practices) or a product has been approved, endorsed or authorised by a public or private body when he/it has not or making such a claim without complying with the terms of the approval, endorsement or authorisation.

5. Making an invitation to purchase products at a specified price without disclosing the existence of any reasonable grounds the trader may have for believing that he will not be able to offer for supply or to procure another trader to supply, those products or equivalent products at that price for a period that is, and in quantities that are, reasonable, having regard to the product, the scale of advertising of the product and the price offered (bait advertising).

6. Making an invitation to purchase products at a specified price and then:
   (a) refusing to show the advertised item to consumers; or
   (b) refusing to take orders for it or deliver it within a reasonable time; or
   (c) demonstrating a defective sample of it, with the intention of promoting a different product (bait and switch).

7. Falsely stating that a product will only be available for a very limited time, or that it will only be available on particular terms for a very limited time, in order to elicit an immediate decision and deprive consumers of sufficient opportunity or time to make an informed choice.

8. Undertaking to provide after-sales service to consumers with whom the trader has communicated prior to a transaction in a language which is not an official language of the Member State where the trader is located and then making such service available only in another language without clearly disclosing this to the consumer before the consumer is committed to the transaction.

9. Stating or otherwise creating the impression that a product can legally be sold when it cannot.

10. Presenting rights given to consumers in law as a distinctive feature of the trader's offer.

11. Using editorial content in the media to promote a product where a trader has paid for the promotion without making that clear in the content or by images or sounds clearly identifiable by the consumer (advertorial).

12. Making a materially inaccurate claim concerning the nature and extent of the risk to the personal security of the consumer or his family if the consumer does not purchase the product.

13. Promoting a product similar to a product made by a particular manufacturer in such a manner as deliberately to mislead the consumer into believing that the product is made by that same manufacturer when it is not.

14. Establishing, operating or promoting a pyramid promotional scheme where a consumer gives consideration for the opportunity to receive compensation that is derived primarily from the introduction of other consumers into the scheme rather than from the sale or consumption of products.

15. Claiming that the trader is about to cease trading or move premises when he is not.

16. Claiming that products are able to facilitate winning in games of chance.

17. Falsely claiming that a product is able to cure illnesses, dysfunction or malformations.

18. Passing on materially inaccurate information on market conditions or on the possibility of finding the product with the intention of inducing the consumer to acquire the product at conditions less favourable than normal market conditions.

19. Claiming in a commercial practice to offer a competition or prize promotion without awarding the prizes described or a reasonable equivalent.

20. Describing a product as "gratis", "free", "without charge" or similar if the consumer has to pay anything other than the unavoidable cost of responding to the commercial practice and collecting or paying for delivery of the item.

21. Including in marketing material an invoice or similar document seeking payment which gives the consumer the impression that he has already ordered the marketed product when he has not.

22. Falsely claiming or creating the impression that the trader is not acting for purposes relating to his trade, business, craft or profession, or falsely representing oneself as a consumer.

23. Creating the false impression that after-sales service in relation to a product is available in a Member State other than the one in which the product is sold.

24. Creating the impression that the consumer cannot leave the premises until a contract is formed.

25. Conducting personal visits to the consumer's home ignoring the consumer's request to leave or not to return except in circumstances and to the extent justified, under national law, to enforce a contractual obligation.

26. Making persistent and unwanted solicitations by telephone, fax, email or other remote media except in circumstances and to the extent justified under national law to enforce a contractual obligation.

27. Requiring a consumer who wishes to claim on an insurance policy to produce documents which could not reasonably be considered relevant as to whether the claim was valid, or failing systematically to respond to pertinent correspondence, in order to dissuade a consumer from exercising his contractual rights.

28. Including in an advertisement a direct exhortation to children to buy advertised products or persuade their parents or other adults to buy advertised products for them.

29. Demanding immediate or deferred payment for or the return or safekeeping of products supplied by the trader, but not solicited by the consumer except where the product is a substitute supplied in conformity with art.7(3) of Directive 97/7/EC (inertia selling).

30. Explicitly informing a consumer that if he does not buy the product or service, the trader's job or livelihood will be in jeopardy.

31. Creating the false impression that the consumer has already won, will win, or will, on doing a particular act, win, a prize or other equivalent benefit, when in fact either:—there is no prize or other equivalent benefit, or—taking any action in relation to claiming the prize or other equivalent benefit is subject to the consumer paying money or incurring a cost.

Where a trader engages in an activity listed within Sch.1[37] he is guilty of an offence under reg.12 and is thereby liable, on conviction on indictment, to either a fine or imprisonment for up to two years, or both.[38]

Defences

If the defendant can establish any of the defences under regs 17 and 18 he has a good defence to the offences laid down in regs 9–12. Under reg.17 the trader must prove that: **17–012**

1. The commission of the offence was due to:

   * a mistake;
   * reliance on information supplied to him by another person;
   * the act or default of another person[39];
   * an accident; or
   * another cause beyond his control; and

2. That he took all reasonable precautions and exercised all due diligence to avoid the commission of the offence.

This is a recasting of the old defences laid down in s.24(1) of the Trade Descriptions Act 1968.[40] The old case law under s.24 is therefore instructive in considering the nature of the defences laid down by reg.17 and what follows is an overview of such case law.

In *Simmons v Potter*[41] the defendants, second-hand car dealers, succeeded in proving that the commission of the offence was due to "reliance upon information supplied to him" but failed to prove that they themselves had taken "all reasonable precautions", etc. They had sold a car with the wrong mileage recorded on the odometer. Before doing this they had first made enquiries about the car's history from its previous owner and learnt nothing suggesting that the odometer reading was false. It was held that the defendants had no defence under s.24 because they had, in failing to display a disclaimer, failed to take *all* reasonable precautions. They had failed to adopt an obvious and easy method of avoiding commission of the offence. If they had displayed a disclaimer (sufficiently bold, precise and compelling) they would

[37] With the exception of Sch.1 paras 11 and 28.
[38] reg.13(b). See also, reg.13(a) (summary conviction).
[39] See also reg.16.
[40] See also s.39 Consumer Protection Act 1987.
[41] [1975] R.T.R. 347.

have avoided commission of the offence even without having to rely upon s.24. There is, however, no absolute rule that a failure to display an effective disclaimer will rule out the defences in s.24. There can be exceptional cases where, despite a failure to display an effective disclaimer, the defendant might be held to have taken all reasonable precautions. Thus in *Ealing LBC v Taylor*[42] the Divisional Court declined to overturn the magistrates' finding that the defendant car dealer had taken all reasonable precautions (in relation to the mileage reading) in checking the consistency of the condition of the car with the recorded mileage and in obtaining from the person who sold him the car a signed warranty guaranteeing the accuracy of the mileage reading.

In *Hurley v Martinez*[43] the defendant had supplied bottles of German wine on which the labels indicated the alcoholic strength as 8 per cent instead of 7.2 per cent, the bottles having come to him from Germany thus labelled. It was held that the defendant could rely upon the defence in s.24, it not being necessary for him to have indulged in sample testing the accuracy of the statement on the labels.[44]

17–013   When the defence relied upon is "act of default of another person" or "reliance on information supplied by another person" the defendant will have a good defence only if he has also made available to the prosecution such information as he has identifying that other person.[45] This is to enable the prosecution to find and charge the other person. The other person will often be the employee of the defendant, as he was in *Tesco Supermarkets Ltd v Nattrass*.[46] There, the defendant company, which operated a large number of supermarkets, had instituted in their stores an effective system to prevent the commission of an offence. One of their employees, a store manager, failed properly to carry out the system with the result that Radiant washing powder was advertised in the window at 2s. 11d. when in fact the only packets available in the shop were 3s. 11d. The House of Lords held that the defendant company was not guilty; the commission of the offence was due to the default of "another person" (the store manager) and the defendant company had, by instituting an effective system, taken all reasonable precautions, etc., in the circumstances.

Thus where, for example, the defendant owns a chain of stores he can rely upon the acts of a store manager provided that the defendant can show that he (the defendant) took all reasonable precautions to avoid the commission of the offence. These precautions will usually consist of instructions sent out to managers. The defendant must show that he sent out *adequate* instructions. He will have no defence if the instructions were such that even if they were followed the offence was still likely to be committed.[47]

Regulation 18 allows a defence where an offence under regs 9–12 has been committed by the (innocent) publication of an advertisement. The defendant will have a good defence where he can prove that:

(a) he is a person whose business it is to publish (or to arrange for the publication of advertisements); and

---

[42] [1995] Crim. L.R. 156.
[43] [1991] C.C.L.R. 1.
[44] For a comparison with the defence of due diligence when used by someone charged with a consumer safety offence, see para.9–024, above.
[45] See reg.17(2).
[46] [1973] Crim. L.R. 196.
[47] See *Haringey London Borough v Piro Shoes Ltd*, [1976] Crim. L.R. 462 (instruction that goods were not to leave the shop without label having first been removed was insufficient).

(b) he received the advertisement for publication in the ordinary course of business; and

(c) he did not know, and had no reason to suspect, that its publication would amount to an offence.

Like that in reg.17, this is a recasting of the "innocent publication" defence found in previous consumer protection measures, including s.25 of the Trade Descriptions Act 1968 and s.24 of the Consumer Protection Act 1987. So, for example, a newspaper which innocently publishes an advertisement which contravenes one or more of the offences in regs 9–12 will have a good defence provided the advertisement was received in the ordinary course of business and they did not know, and had no reason to suspect, that its publication constituted an offence.

Enforcement

The duty to enforce the Consumer Protection from Unfair Trading Regulations 2008 falls on the OFT and every local weights and measures authority. Enforcers are aided by various powers laid down in Pt 4 of the regulations, including powers to make test purchases and powers of entry and investigation. In addition, the Unfair Commercial Practices Directive 2005 has been added to the list of "Community infringements" under the Enterprise Act 2002 and therefore the framework of Pt 8 powers (in that Act) now extends to breaches of the Directive. This framework is explained at para.17–021 below.   **17–014**

Impact on Previous Consumer Protection Measures

The implementation of the Unfair Commercial Practices Directive 2005 into domestic law through the regulations considered above has necessitated considerable amendments to a wide range of legislation previously in force. This section will outline some of these changes and summarise the law replaced by the Consumer Protection from Unfair Trading Regulations 2008.[48] It will also introduce a second set of regulations, the Business Protection from Misleading Marketing Regulations 2008 which have come into force in parallel with the Consumer Protection from Unfair Trading Regulations 2008.   **17–015**

Trade Descriptions Act 1968

This Act created criminal offences to protect the consumer, although, similar to the Consumer Protection from Unfair Trading Regulations 2008, it in no way enhanced his contractual rights.[49] The Act had three main sets of provisions. First, the Department of Trade   **17–016**

---

[48] For a more detailed account of these historical laws, the reader may be directed to the 6th edition of this book.
[49] As the Act made clear through s.35.

and Industry was empowered to make certain orders. These could specify and require information to be included in advertisements or descriptions of goods and they could specify and require instructions to be supplied with the goods. Secondly, the Act laid down offences intended to prevent anyone wrongly claiming to have supplied goods to the Queen (or to anyone else) or wrongly claiming royal approval, e.g. by displaying an emblem resembling that of the Queen's Award to Industry. Thirdly, and most significantly, the Act created two offences relating to misdescriptions of goods, and misleading statements about services. The majority of the Trade Descriptions Act 1968, including the various criminal offences dealing with misdescriptions of goods and services, has been repealed by the Consumer Protection from Unfair Trading Regulations 2008.[50]

Part III of the Consumer Protection Act 1987

17–017   Part III of the Consumer Protection Act 1987 replaced earlier provisions dealing with misleading price indications. These were the Trade Descriptions Act 1968 s.11 and the Price Marking (Bargain Offers) Order 1979. These provisions had loopholes and proved technical and obscure with the result that enforcement was difficult. Part III of the 1987 Act adopted a different approach to the problem of defining the mischief which it sought to stamp out, i.e. the giving of misleading price information. It contained a statement of the offence[51] and a generally worded definition of "misleading"[52] and provided for a code of practice to be approved by the Secretary of State which gives practical guidance.[53] Part III has been repealed by the Consumer Protection from Unfair Trading Regulations 2008.[54]

Control of Misleading Advertisements Regulations 1988

17–018   These regulations implemented the Misleading Advertisements Directive.[55] They required the Office of Fair Trading (or OFCOM where the advertisement was broadcast) to consider complaints (other than vexatious or frivolous ones) about misleading advertisements.[56] The OFT could bring proceedings for a High Court injunction to stop the publication of a misleading advertisement.[57] The OFT, before considering a complaint, could require the complainant to satisfy him that alternative methods of dealing with the matter have been tried and found inadequate. Thus, where the advertisement constituted a criminal offence, it was pointless to complain to the OFT. It was more sensible to complain to the local trading standards department. Even where the advertisement did not amount to an offence, the OFT could consider that an approach to the Advertising Standards Authority (a non-statutory body

[50] Sch.2 para.8.
[51] s.20.
[52] s.21.
[53] s.25.
[54] Sch.2 para.34.
[55] 84/450/EEC replaced by Directive 2006/114/EC.
[56] See reg.4. Regulation 4A details various conditions which must be satisfied in respect of comparative advertisements.
[57] See regs 5 and 6. Where the court grants an injunction (other than an interlocutory injunction) it must be satisfied that the advertisement is either misleading or a type of prohibited comparative advertising under reg.4A.

with no legal powers) would be an adequate way of dealing with the complaint. The regulations were clearly useful as a last resort, where the advertisement was not caught by any other legal provision and there was no other effective way of dealing with it, e.g. an advertisement falsely stating "closing down sale". Before the OFT could take action under the regulations, the advertisement had to be such that it *both* deceived or was likely to deceive *and* was likely to affect the economic behaviour of those whom it reached or to injure a competitor of the trader (usually the advertiser) whose interests the advertisement was promoting.

The Control of Misleading Advertisements Regulations 1988 have been revoked and replaced by the Consumer Practice from Unfair Trading Regulations 2008.[58]

Business Protection from Misleading Marketing Regulations 2008

The Unfair Commercial Practices Directive was directed solely at protecting *consumers* from unfair business practices. In implementing the Directive the approach adopted was, as set out above, to repeal, either in whole or in part, various pieces of legislation which had performed similar roles in domestic law. The difficulty was that many of those pieces of legislation were not aimed specifically at consumers. For example, the offences within the Trade Descriptions Act 1968 were general provisions of the criminal law. In repealing the offences in ss.1 and 14 of the 1968 Act the Consumer Protection from Unfair Trading Regulations 2008 risked creating a distinct gap. Where there had traditionally been protection in a business context there would, if the problem was left unaddressed, be no protection following the implementation of the Directive. Moreover, the repeal of the Control of Misleading Advertising Regulations 1988 by the Consumer Protection from Unfair Trading Regulations 2008 also required action in order to implement the EU Directive on misleading and comparative advertising.[59] These issues led to the introduction of a second set of regulations, the Business Protection from Misleading Marketing Regulations 2008.[60]

The key feature of these regulations is the prohibition on advertising which misleads traders.[61] The concept of advertising which is misleading is set out in reg.3(2) and is explained as requiring one of the following two elements. It is misleading if it:

"(a) in any way, including its presentation, deceives or is likely to deceive the traders to whom it is addressed or whom it reaches; and by reason of its deceptive nature, is likely to affect their economic behaviour; or

(b) for those reasons, injures or is likely to injure a competitor."

In assessing whether an advertisement is misleading, reg.3 requires account to be taken of all its features, although the following are of particular relevance:

(i) the characteristics of the product;

17–019

---

[58] Sch.2 para.81.
[59] Directive 2006/114/EC which replaced Directive 84/450/EEC. See the discussion of the Control of Misleading Advertising Regulations 1988 at para.17–018, above.
[60] SI 2008/1276. The Regulations came into effect on May 26, 2008.
[61] reg.3(1).

(ii) the price or manner in which the price is calculated;

(iii) the conditions on which the product is supplied or provided; and

(iv) the nature, attributes and rights of the advertiser.

The first feature, that of the characteristics of the product, includes therefore characteristics such as availability; composition; method, place and date of manufacture; fitness for purpose; and quantity.[62]

Where a trader engages in advertising which is contrary to reg.3, he is guilty of an offence as is liable to either a fine on summary conviction, or to a fine and/or imprisonment for up to two years on indictment.[63]

17–020   The regulations also contain a framework for the use of comparative advertising under reg.4. Broadly speaking, comparative advertising will be permitted under the new regulations only where certain conditions are satisfied. Those conditions are that:

(i) it is not misleading under reg.3;

(ii) it is not a misleading action under reg.5 of the Consumer Protection from Unfair Trading Regulations 2008(a) or a misleading omission under reg.6 of those regulations[64];

(iii) it compares products meeting the same needs or intended for the same purpose;

(iv) it objectively compares one or more material, relevant, verifiable and representative features of those products, which may include price;

(v) it does not create confusion among traders;

(vi) it does not discredit or denigrate the trade marks, trade names, other distinguishing marks, products, activities, or circumstances of a competitor;

(vii) for products with designation of origin, it relates in each case to products with the same designation;

(viii) it does not take unfair advantage of the reputation of a trade mark, trade name or other distinguishing marks of a competitor or of the designation of origin of competing products;

(ix) it does not present products as imitations or replicas of products bearing a protected trade mark or trade name.

As in the equivalent pieces of legislation which preceded the regulations the two core defences are replicated, namely: due diligence and innocent publication. These have already been considered.[65]

---

[62] See reg.3(4). These characteristics are broadly similar to the list previously to be found in s.2 of the Trade Descriptions Act 1968.
[63] See regs 6 and 7.
[64] See the discussion at para.17–004, above.
[65] See para.17–012, above.

Like the Consumer Protection from Unfair Trading Regulations 2008, the Business Protection from Misleading Marketing Regulations 2008 are to be enforced by both the OFT and all local weights and measures authorities. Moreover, the powers of investigation are also replicated in Pt 4 and so the OFT, for example, has the power to make test purchases etc. in order to ascertain whether the regulations are being breached.[66]

FAIR TRADING ACT 1973 AND THE ENTERPRISE ACT 2002

The Fair Trading Act created the office of Director General of Fair Trading, giving that **17–021** official certain functions in relation to consumer affairs. This was amended by the Enterprise Act which abolished the office of Director General and transferred his powers to the Office of Fair Trading.[67] In its new guise, the OFT is a statute corporate body with a Chairman, a Chief Executive and a minimum of four other members who cumulatively form the OFT Board.

The Enterprise Act 2002 details the statutory duties of the OFT:

- the duty to produce an annual plan and report (s.4)[68];

- the acquisition of information regarding commercial activity impacting upon consumers (ss.5 and 6)[69];

- the duty to provide information and advice to Ministers (s.7)[70];

- the duty to promote good practice (s.8).[71]

Neither the Fair Trading Act nor the Enterprise Act were designed to enhance consumers' individual rights: Pt II of the Fair Trading Act 1973 established a mechanism for creating new criminal offences to combat, as they arise, trading malpractices adverse to consumers. Part III gives the Director General powers of enforcement against traders guilty of malpractices. In addition the opportunity was taken to deal with pyramid selling, a particular malpractice which had become a nuisance at the time the Act was being passed. This will now be considered first, before we turn to Pts II and III.

In their heyday, before 1973, pyramid selling schemes worked something like this. The typical scheme was ostensibly concerned with marketing goods or services through a chain of private distributors. An individual was persuaded to join the scheme as a "distributor" (or "agent" or "representative" or whatever). He may have been persuaded to pay a large sum

---

[66] See the discussion of the equivalent provision within the Consumer Protection from Unfair Trading Regulations 2008 at para.17–004, above.

[67] See ss.2 and 273.

[68] The obligation under s.4 of the Enterprise Act 2002 replaces the previous duty to produce annual reports under legislation where so required under s.125 Fair Trading Act 1973.

[69] The OFT is also required to provide "information or advice in respect of matters relating to any of its functions to the public" under s.6(1)(b).

[70] This replaces the old duty under the Fair Trading Act 1973 to provide recommendations for action under s.2 to the Secretary of State.

[71] s.8 is a considerable extension of role in this regard from the previous general obligation to encourage trade associations to develop codes of practice safeguarding and promoting the interests of consumers under s.124(3) of the Fair Trading Act 1973.

of money (perhaps hundreds or thousands of pounds) for the privilege of joining. Whether he could recover this sum would depend upon whether he could introduce further people into the scheme, for he would receive a payment for each new participant whom he introduced. Sometimes the fee he paid for joining was expressed to be payment for a consignment of the goods which the scheme was supposed to be marketing. However, he could still find it difficult to recoup his joining fee if he could not find new members for the scheme, because he would find it difficult to sell the goods. It was not always easy for a private householder to find buyers for a large number of packets of soap!

17–022   Sections 118–123 deal with pyramid selling.[72] Section 120(3) makes it an offence for a promoter or participant to receive any payment (or the benefit of any payments) which some other participant is induced to make by reason that the prospect is held out to him of receiving payments or other benefits for introducing other persons into the scheme. Further, s.119 empowers the Secretary of State to make regulations for the purpose of preventing participants being unfairly treated. These powers have been used thereby effectively banning pyramid selling as it was previously practised.[73]

Creation of Criminal Offences—An Outdated Mechanism

17–023   The aim of Pt II of the Fair Trading Act was to discover, and by ministerial order prevent, consumer trade practices which adversely affected the economic interests of consumers. It established a legislative mechanism for the creation of criminal offences to combat malpractices. The intention was to have a fast legislative response to malpractices as and when they arose in the market place. In the event the legislative mechanism proved cumbersome and slow, including a requirement for a committee report before any regulations could be made. In fact only three Orders were ever made under this mechanism, which soon fell into disuse until it was eventually repealed by s.10 of the Enterprise Act 2002. None of these Orders is any longer of any effect. The only legal consequence of infringing one of the Orders was that a criminal offence was committed contrary to s.23 of the Fair Trading Act 1973—and that section was repealed by the Consumer Protection from Unfair Trading Regulations 2008. The fact is that the mechanism in Pt II of the Fair Trading Act had become outmoded in the modern legislative climate. Now we have the Consumer Protection from Unfair Trading Practices Regulations 2008 which are a widely drafted set of Regulations controlling unfair trading practices. There is no longer any need for additional legislation targeted at specific narrowly defined malpractices, since such practices will be banned by the 2008 Regulations anyway. This is surely true, for example, of the following malpractices which were previously banned under Orders made under Pt II of the Fair Trading Act 1973:

> (i) The misleading use of void or unenforceable exemption clauses (e.g. signs displayed in shops stating that goods will in no circumstances be returnable), leading to the impression that defective goods can not be rejected.[74]

---

[72] Part VI of the Act which deals with pyramid selling survived the repeals made by the Enterprise Act 2002.
[73] See the Trading Schemes Regulations 1997 (SI 1997/30).
[74] Previously banned by the Consumer Transactions (Restrictions on Statements) Order 1976.

(ii) The advertising of goods for sale by a trader in circumstances where the reader would not realise that the advertisement was placed by a trader and not by a private seller.[75]

Power to Enforce the General Law on Protection of Consumers

Part III of the old Act (ss.34–43) gave the Director power to act against someone who in the **17–024** course of business persistently breaks the law (civil or criminal) in a way detrimental to the interests of consumers. These provisions, unlike those just outlined, are concerned not only with the economic interests of consumers but also their "interests in respect of health, safety or other matters".[76] Sections 34 to 43 were repealed by the Enterprise Act and a new system introduced which operates not through "consumer detriment" but through listed infringements. These infringements are listed in two parts: First, domestic infringements under s.212 and secondly, Community infringements under s.213. Whether the infringement is classified as "domestic" or "Community" the requirements of s.210 must be satisfied. Namely:

1. goods or services are (or are sought to be) supplied to the individual (whether by way of sale or otherwise) in the course of a business; and

2. the individual receives or seeks to receive the goods or services otherwise than in the course of a business.

The ambit of Pt 8 is therefore very broadly defined. In principle there must be an infringement which harms the collective interests of consumers. Under the Enterprise Act (Pt 8 Domestic Infringements) Order 2003 the following Acts, amongst a very long list, were all specified as "domestic infringements":

- Administration of Justice Act 1970;

- Consumer Credit Act 1974;

- Misrepresentation Act 1967;

- Sale of Goods Act;

- Supply of Goods (Implied Terms) Act 1973;

- Supply of Goods and Services Act 1982;

- Trade Descriptions Act 1968;

- Unfair Contract Terms Act 1977.

A similar list is laid down in Sch.13 for the purposes of detailing a "Community infringement". It includes the Sale of Consumer Goods and Associated Guarantees Directive[77]; The

[75] Previously banned by the Business Advertisements (Disclosure) Order 1977 (SI 1977/1918).
[76] s.34.
[77] Directive 1999/44/EC.

Directive on Electronic Commerce[78]; and The Misleading Advertising Directive[79] amongst others.

Where a trader is committing a listed infringement (under either s.212 or s.213) the OFT is the lead-enforcer of Pt 8[80] and must engage in "appropriate consultation" with the trader before applying for an enforcement order. "Appropriate consultation" is defined in s.214(2) as being consultation for the purpose of:

"(a) achieving the cessation of the infringement in a case where an infringement is occurring;

(b) ensuring that there will be no repetition of the infringement in a case where the infringement has occurred;

(c) ensuring that there will be no repetition of the infringement in a case where the cessation of the infringement is achieved under paragraph (a);

(d) ensuring that the infringement does not take place in the case of a Community infringement which the enforcer believes is likely to take place."

There is no need for such a consultation where the OFT thinks that enforcement should be made without delay.[81]

During this consultation, the enforcer may accept from the trader in question an undertaking that he[82]:

"(a) does not continue or repeat the conduct;

(b) does not engage in such conduct in the course of his business or another business;

(c) does not consent to or connive in the carrying out of such conduct by a body corporate with which he has a special relationship."

17–025   Where such an undertaking is not forthcoming (or breached), the OFT[83] can apply for an enforcement order under s.215. This order must detail both the trader and the conduct which constitutes an infringement and will be drafted in the same terms as the s.219 undertaking considered above.

General Reading

17–026
• Cartwright, "Trade descriptions, corporations and mens rea" [1997] J.B.L. 465;

• Cartwright, "Reckless statements, trade descriptions and law reform" (1996) N.I.L.Q. 47 171;

---

[78] Directive 2000/31/EC.
[79] Directive 97/55/EC.
[80] See s.213 which also lists every local weights and measures authority and also any person or body designated as an enforcer under Pt 8, e.g. the Information Commissioner.
[81] s.214(3).
[82] s.219(4).
[83] As for the OFT and others, see s.217.

- Cartwright, "Servicing and supplying: a judicial muddle" [2000] Crim. L.R. 356;

- Griffiths, "Unfair commercial practices—a new regime" [2007] Comms. Law 196;

- Groote and De Vulder, "European framework for unfair commercial practices: analysis of Directive 2005/29" [2007] J.B.L. 16;

- Johnson, "Advertisers beware! The impact of the Unfair Commercial Practices Directive" [2005] Comms. Law 164;

- Milne, "The Trade Descriptions Act and breach of contract" (1997) 113 L.Q.R. 382;

- Shears, "Overviewing the EU Unfair Commercial Practices Directive: concentric circles" (2007) E.B.L.Rev. 18. 781;

- Stuyck, Terryn and Van Dyck, "Confidence through fairness? The new Directive on unfair business to consumer commercial practices in the internal market" (2006) C.M.L.Rev. 43, 107;

- Twigg-Flesner, "Deep impact? The EC Directive on unfair commercial practices and domestic consumer law" (2005) 121 L.Q.R. 386;

- Twigg-Flesner et al, "An Analysis of the Application and Scope of the Unfair Commercial Practices Directive" DTI Report 2005.

Part II

CONSUMER CREDIT

Chapter 18

INTRODUCTION AND DEFINITION OF HIRE-PURCHASE AND OTHER FORMS OF NEVER-NEVER

A contract of hire-purchase, as its name suggests, contains two elements. It is a contract of **18–001** hire which also gives the hirer an option to purchase the goods. Hire is a form of bailment which is a word used to describe the situation where one person is put in possession of goods belonging to another. The hirer is a bailee. Thus a hire-purchase agreement is an agreement for the bailment of goods whereby the bailee has an option to purchase them.

Two particular contracts relating to goods have long been recognised by the law, one of bailment and one of sale. Of which type then, is a hire-purchase agreement? Is it bailment or is it sale? To put it another way, is it hire or is it purchase? The emphatic answer is that it is not a contract of sale. Thus the parties to a hire-purchase agreement are termed, not "seller" and "buyer", but "owner" and "hirer". Under the Consumer Credit Act 1974 they are termed "creditor" and "debtor".

DISTINCTION BETWEEN HIRE-PURCHASE AND SALE

It is the hallmark of a contract of sale of goods that the parties enter into a mutual **18–002** commitment that the buyer thereby acquires or will acquire ownership of the goods. A "buyer" is described in s.61 of the Sale of Goods Act as "a person who buys or agrees to buy goods". If the buyer does not commit himself to acquire ownership of the goods there is no contract of sale and indeed it is inaccurate to describe him as "buyer". This was made clear by the House of Lords in the leading case of *Helby v Matthews*.[1] The agreement in that case was between the owner of a piano (a dealer) and his customer. The latter agreed to hire the piano for 36 months at a rent of 10s. 6d. per month. The agreement provided that the

---

[1] [1895] A.C. 471.

piano would become the property of the customer on payment of all the instalments of rent but that he could, at any time before then, terminate the hiring by returning the piano to the dealer. In the event of the hiring being terminated, the hirer would be liable only for arrears of rent in respect of the period prior to the termination. The House of Lords held that this agreement was not a contract of sale and that the customer was not a "buyer". The fact that he could terminate the hiring meant that he was under no commitment to acquire ownership of the goods. He had in effect an option to purchase, which he could exercise by not terminating the agreement and by paying all 36 monthly instalments. An option is not a commitment. Their Lordships said that the option was an irrevocable offer by the owner to sell. That offer could be accepted only when the option was exercised. Until then there was no purchase and no contract of sale. Therefore the hire-purchase agreement was not a contract of sale within the meaning of the Sale of Goods Act. Thus a hire-purchase contract is a contract of bailment, albeit one with a difference—namely an option to purchase.

In deciding *Helby v Matthews* their Lordships distinguished the case of *Lee v Butler*.[2] In that case the agreement provided that the customer should have immediate possession of the goods (furniture) and should pay £1 on May 6 and £96 on August 1. These sums were termed "rent". The agreement further provided that the furniture would become the customer's property when the instalments had both been paid and not before. There was no clause in the agreement giving the customer the right to terminate it, although there were provisions entitling the dealer to do so (and to repossess the goods) if the customer defaulted. The Court of Appeal held that this agreement was a contract of sale. The difference between this and *Helby v Matthews* is that here the customer was committed to making all the payments and therefore to acquiring ownership of the goods.

It will be observed that in *Lee v Butler* the goods were not to become the buyer's property until he had paid all the money. This, however, did not prevent the agreement from being a contract of sale. Indeed, as we saw in Chapter 3, ss.17 and 18 of the Sale of Goods Act expressly recognise that property passes to the buyer at the time the parties intend it to.

18–003   In each of the cases mentioned above, the customer disposed of the goods (in return for money) to an innocent third person and he did so before completing his payments. The importance of the distinction between hire-purchase and sale becomes apparent when it is realised that different legal results followed. In neither case was the customer owner of the goods at the time he disposed of them. In *Helby v Matthews* he was merely hiring them and in *Lee v Butler* it had been expressly agreed that the furniture was not to become his property until the payments had been completed. However, in *Lee v Butler* he was a "buyer" in possession of the goods and thus, although he was not the owner, he could pass good title to an innocent purchaser.[3] So in *Lee v Butler* the dealer could not recover the goods from the innocent purchaser to whom his customer has sold them. In *Helby v Matthews*, on the other hand, the dealer was held entitled to recover the goods. Someone hiring goods under a hire-purchase agreement is not a "buyer" and therefore cannot pass good title under either the Factors Act s.9, or the Sale of Goods Act s.25. Therefore, from the dealer's point of view, the hire-purchase transaction has the advantage that he will not be prevented by either of those sections from recovering the goods after they have been passed on by the hirer to an innocent third party. It should be remembered that there are other provisions which could in certain

---

[2] [1893] 2 Q.B. 318.
[3] Factors Act s.9, see Ch.12 above.

circumstances prevent him from doing so.[4] In particular the Hire Purchase Act 1964, Pt III can have this effect in the case of a motor vehicle. Also note that, since *Lee v Butler*, s.9 of the Factors Act and s.25 of the Sale of Goods Act have been amended. The result is that the rule in *Lee v Butler* (that under those sections a buyer under a conditional sale agreement can pass good title to an innocent purchaser) applies only if the conditional sale agreement is not regulated by the Consumer Credit Act 1974.[5]

Since the House of Lords decision in *Helby v Matthews*, the hire-purchase agreement has become very common indeed. The usual form it has come to take is an agreement whereby the customer (a) agrees to hire the goods for a fixed period (e.g. 48 months) in return for a monthly payment, and (b) is given an option to purchase the goods for a nominal amount (e.g. £1) which option is exercisable only after the customer has first completed payment of all the monthly instalments. In economic terms the customer has paid for the goods by means of the monthly instalments. Having paid all the monthly instalments, he would be mad not to exercise his option to buy for the nominal amount. Nevertheless he is not legally bound to do so and thus the agreement is still only a hire-purchase agreement and is not a contract of sale unless and until the customer exercises his option to buy: *Close Asset Finance v Care Graphics Machinery Ltd.*[6] Suppose, on the other hand, that the customer is contractually bound to pay all the monthly instalments, is not required to pay anything at all for exercising his "option to buy" and is deemed to have exercised that option simply by completing his instalment payments without informing the owner that he wishes not to exercise it. In that unusual case, the agreement is a sale of goods contract (a conditional sale agreement) and not a hire-purchase agreement: *Forthright Finance Ltd v Carlyle Finance Ltd.*[7] Following the decision of the Court of Appeal in *Forthright Finance Ltd* it is clear that the distinction between contracts of conditional sale and hire-purchase is one of substance, and the language used by the parties is not conclusive. Phillips L.J. observed that "this contract has all the ingredients of a conditional sale agreement" and that the option not to take title did "not affect the true nature of the agreement". Consequently the fact that the contract referred to the agreement as one of hire-purchase was irrelevant.

Consider the emergence in modern times of a new species of hire purchase agreement: the "Lease Purchase" or "Personal Contract Purchase" commonly used within the motor industry to finance sales of new motor vehicles. Rent is payable throughout the agreement period and is calculated on the amount of depreciation likely on the vehicle. At the end of that period, the leasee has the option to purchase the vehicle for a sum calculated to be the capital/ residual value of the vehicle. What is the economic objective of such a contract? Clearly it is distinct from that of a hire-purchase agreement, which is in effect a secured sale.[8] That much is self evident from the nature of the instalment payments being calculated on the estimated depreciation of the vehicle (or goods) over the contract period. This however, may be contrasted with the payment structure of a typical modern hire-purchase agreement, where the option to buy the goods at the end of the contract period is frequently only a nominal fee, and certainly not representative of the estimated value of the goods at the end of the contract

---

[4] See Ch.12, above.
[5] See para.5–026, above.
[6] [2000] C.C.L.R. 43.
[7] [1997] 4 All E.R. 90.
[8] Indeed, this fact is responsible for the number of cases examining the sale of goods by a non-owner. In many instances, a hirer under a hire-purchase agreement sells the goods on due to the (mistaken) belief that he or she is entitled to do so.

period. The courts have not yet had the opportunity to determine whether this new form of instalment contract should be regarded as a simple hiring or as a hire-purchase agreement.

CONDITIONAL SALE AND CREDIT SALE AGREEMENTS

18–004   Each of these is a type of contract of sale of goods and each has the characteristic that the buyer is committed to acquiring ownership of the goods. "Conditional" and "Credit" are commonly used to describe contracts of sale of goods where the price is payable in instalments. In that respect they therefore have some similarity with hire-purchase agreements.

At common law there is only one difference between a credit and a conditional sale agreement. It is that in a conditional sale agreement the passing of property to the buyer is expressly postponed until some condition (usually all the instalments being paid) is fulfilled. So, the agreement in *Lee v Butler*[9] can be described as a conditional sale agreement. In a credit sale agreement there is no such condition to the passing of property and the goods therefore normally become the buyer's immediately the contract is made.[10] Thus under a credit sale agreement, the buyer will, as soon as he takes delivery, be in possession of goods of which he is the owner. Under a conditional sale agreement the buyer will be in possession of goods which will continue to belong to the seller until all the instalments have been paid. Apart from this, there is, at common law, no difference between credit sale and conditional sale agreements.

Although this is the position at common law, we shall see that the Consumer Credit Act 1974 radically alters the position with respect to conditional sale agreements regulated by its provisions, thus making them significantly different in effect from credit sale agreements.

THE FINANCE COMPANY

18–005   In both *Helby v Matthews*[11] and *Lee v Butler*,[12] the customer took the goods under an agreement between himself and the dealer. There was no intermediate party. No doubt some dealers still do business in that way. Today, however, it is common for the dealer to sell goods for cash to a finance company which then parts with them on instalment terms to the customer. Thus today's customer often finds that he is hiring or buying the goods, not from the dealer, but from a remote and powerful finance company. This is a classic example of a weak party (the customer) contracting with a strong one (the finance company). Finance companies, by adopting a "take it or leave it" attitude, used to insist on inserting terms that were very onerous for the customer—terms to the effect that all implied conditions and warranties were excluded; that in the event of the customer's payments falling into arrears the finance company could repossess the goods; that in order to repossess the goods the company's agents could trespass upon the customer's premises; that in the event of the customer terminating the agreement he should pay a large sum of money to the finance

[9] [1893] 2 Q.B. 318.
[10] SGA 1979 s.18 r.1.
[11] [1895] A.C. 471.
[12] [1893] 2 Q.B. 318.

company, etc. The Consumer Credit Act 1974 and the Unfair Contract Terms Act 1977 largely prevent these abuses, but it is true that, in so far as those Acts allow them to, finance companies still insist on the terms being as beneficial to themselves as possible. Finance companies have now also to take account of the Unfair Terms in Consumer Contracts Regulations 1999.

The usual process by which the contract is made is as follows. The customer selects the goods from the dealer's stock. He asks for instalment terms. At the dealer's request (and sometimes with his assistance) he fills in a form. This form will have been supplied to the dealer by a finance company with whom the dealer maintains regular contact. When completed and signed by the customer, it will constitute an offer to the finance company by the customer to take the goods either on hire-purchase or on credit sale or conditional sale terms. The customer will leave that form with the dealer. The dealer will himself complete another form which will constitute an offer by him to the finance company to sell it the goods. The dealer will send both forms to the finance company which will either accept or reject both offers. It will accept offers only if made on its own forms and thus incorporating the terms that it wishes to include. If it accepts the offers, the finance company will have agreed with the dealer to buy the goods from him and with the customer to supply the goods to him on hire-purchase (or credit sale or conditional sale) terms.

THE DEALER

Much of the following chapter is devoted to the contractual relationship between the customer and the person (often a finance company) from whom he hires or buys the goods. However, a little time should be spent considering the position of the dealer who sells his goods to the finance company.   **18–006**

Dealer and Customer

The relationship between these two is not that of seller and buyer, because the dealer has sold the goods, not to the customer, but to the finance company. It follows that, if the goods prove defective, the customer has no action against the dealer under s.14 of the Sale of Goods Act.[13] Nevertheless he may well still have a remedy against the dealer. In *Andrews v Hopkinson*[14] the dealer told the customer "It's a good little bus. I would stake my life on it". After this the customer made a hire-purchase contract, in the usual way, with a finance company. Soon after taking delivery of the car, he had a crash in it, due to its defective steering mechanism. McNair J. held that the dealer was liable in damages to the customer for two reasons.   **18–007**

    (i) There was a contract, albeit not one of sale, between the dealer and the customer. The contract consisted of the dealer promising that the car was a "good little bus" in return of the customer applying to the finance company to acquire it on hire-

---

[13] *Drury v Victor Buckland* [1941] 1 All E.R. 269.
[14] [1957] 1 Q.B. 229.

        purchase terms. The dealer was therefore liable for breach of his warranty (i.e. his promise).

(ii) The defect in the steering mechanism was due to negligent lack of inspection and servicing by the dealer who was therefore liable—irrespective of whether there was a contract—to anyone foreseeably injured by his negligence. This was an application of the general principle in *Donoghue v Stevenson*.[15]

Dealer and Finance Company

18–008   The relationship of dealer and finance company is primarily that of seller and buyer. Their contract will therefore, in the absence of contrary agreement, be subject to the provisions of the Sale of Goods Act. However, the finance company will often require the dealer to take on further obligations and to enter into a recourse agreement. The extent of the dealer's liability under one of these will depend upon the terms of his particular agreement. Often it will be worded so as to constitute a contract of indemnity under which the dealer must make good any loss suffered by the finance company in the event of the customer defaulting on his payments or terminating his agreement.

    The question of to what extent the dealer is the agent of the finance company in dealing with the customer will be discussed in Chapter 29.

Guarantors and Indemnifiers

18–009   There are risks involved in credit trading. Apart from the chance that the customer may default on his payments (perhaps even go bankrupt), there is the risk that he may also sell, damage or even destroy the goods. In the typical transaction, it is the finance company which runs these risks. The finance company can to some extent safeguard itself by including certain terms in the contract it makes with the customer. For example, in the case of a motor vehicle the contract may require the hirer/buyer to have comprehensive insurance. However, this does not provide any safeguard against the irresponsible customer who does not comply with such terms of the agreement or against the out and out rogue who, having paid his initial deposit, disappears with the goods without trace.

    Thus it is quite possible for a finance company to insist that some third person acts as a safeguard against the finance company making a loss on the transaction. The contract made between the third person and the finance company will, depending upon its terms, be a contract either of guarantee or of indemnity. The difference between these two types of contract has already been considered.[16] From the finance company's point of view a contract of guarantee is the less satisfactory, for two reasons. First, it is enforceable only if there is sufficient written evidence of its existence,[17] though this is perhaps not very important since the agreement will usually be in writing anyway. Secondly, a contract of guarantee is enforceable only if the principal contract is valid (i.e. the one between the finance company

---

[15] [1932] A.C. 562. See para.9–005, above.
[16] See Ch.9, above.
[17] See the Statute of Frauds 1677.

and the customer). To put this another way, if the customer has a defence to a claim against him under the hire-purchase agreement, then any guarantor will also be able to use the same defence. An indemnifier, however, can be liable when the customer has a valid defence and can sometimes be liable to a greater extent than the customer.[18]

It is useful at this stage to indicate that guarantors and indemnifiers are of two types, those who act as such at the request of the customer and those who were not requested by the customer to do so. An example of the latter is the dealer who has a recourse agreement with the finance company.

OTHER FORMS OF NEVER-NEVER

With the coming of the affluent society the consumer credit business has boomed. In earlier days, having goods on hire-purchase or similar terms came to be known colloquially as having them on the "never-never"—because the repayment periods were so long it sometimes seemed as though they would never be paid for. Hire-purchase is today only one of the ways in which the consumer can obtain credit. The rest of this chapter is a "whistle-stop tour" of the rest of the never-never land, a quick passing look at a number of different ways in which credit is provided and security taken. It is concerned not so much with the law, as with the way business is carried on.   **18–010**

Hire-purchase, conditional sale and credit sale have in common that the goods and the credit are provided in the same agreement. The same agreement regulates both the supply of the goods and also the indebtedness of the hirer or buyer. However there is no legal or practical reason why this should be the case with every credit agreement. Take the typical situation where a finance company lets goods on hire-purchase terms to a customer. From a practical view (though not a legal one) the finance company is not really the supplier of the goods. The dealer is the real supplier of the goods. Indeed, when the agreement has been made, it is from the dealer that the customer will collect the goods which he is hiring on hire-purchase terms from the finance company. Practically speaking, the finance company is in business, not really to sell or hire out goods, but to give loans. It supplies goods (i.e. purchases them from the dealer and lets them to the borrower on hire-purchase terms) in order to make the loan and at the same time to retain some collateral for the loan. The collateral is the finance company's right to recover possession of the goods in the event of the hirer defaulting on his payments or disposing of the goods.

Why does the finance company not achieve the same result (i.e. the giving of a loan on the collateral of the goods) by granting a loan to the purchaser and taking a mortgage of the goods? This is how house purchases are financed and it would have the advantage that the borrower buys the goods directly from the person who is actually the supplier of them, i.e. the dealer. The finance company would not then be cast in the role of a seller or owner (i.e. supplier) of the goods. The reason that finance companies do not commonly take mortgages of goods lies in the Bills of Sale Acts 1878–1882.[19]

However, there are various methods in use today by which credit is quite commonly granted under an agreement which is separate from that which regulates the selling or hiring   **18–011**

---

[18] See *Coulston Discount Co Ltd v Clark*, para.25–027, below.
[19] See "Mortgage of Goods" below.

of the goods, e.g. the customer borrows the money from X and uses it to buy the goods from Y. We are about to examine some of these methods but two preliminary points need to be made. First, the credit (i.e. the loan) does not necessarily have to be for the supply of goods. It could be for the purchase of services (e.g. a holiday or the erection of a garage) or for the purchase of a plot of land or for any other use to which the borrower wants to put it. Secondly, the two agreements (i.e. loan and purchase) could be with the same person, e.g. the borrower borrows money from X and uses it to buy goods also from X. Now let us examine first some general categories and then some more particular examples.

Unsecured Loan

18–012   The notion of an unsecured loan is very simple. It consists of the lender giving money to the borrower in return for a promise by the borrower to repay it. The only means for the creditor to enforce the agreement is for him to sue the borrower in the courts. If the borrower becomes insolvent or bankrupt, the creditor has no other remedy open to him and therefore runs a considerable risk of losing part or all of his money. Since the lender runs high risks, the cost of the loan (i.e. the interest) will usually be high. Unsecured loans can be obtained from various sources, mainly banks and finance companies.

It is worthwhile comparing an unsecured loan with a credit sale agreement. The effect of both is that the creditor provides unsecured credit. Under a credit sale agreement the credit is, by the nature of the transaction, directly related to the purchase of the goods in the credit sale agreement, i.e. the credit is for the purchase of particular goods. (Incidentally, this last statement is true also of hire-purchase and conditional sale agreements.) A direct loan, on the other hand, need not be associated with the purchase of a specific item or items. The vast majority of hire-purchase, conditional sale and credit sale agreements involve the giving of credit by a finance company which has business connections with the dealer. These agreements often arise out of a regular relationship between a dealer and a finance company to whom the dealer regularly introduces potential purchasers who require credit terms. A direct loan may also be given by such a connected lender but, equally, may be given by a lender completely unconnected with the dealer (i.e. a lender contacted by the borrower for himself, whether it be a bank, a finance company or even a friend).

Unsecured Credit

18–013   An unsecured loan is only one type of unsecured credit and is in reality no different from any other form. The word "loan" conjures up a picture of money passing physically from the lender to the borrower who then uses it as desired and makes repayments later. A loan is but one way of creating a debt and a credit. (It must of course create both, since one person's debt is another person's credit.) However, a debt can be created in other ways. Whenever there is an agreement that a debt may be paid later there is something which can be called a credit agreement. A credit sale agreement provides an excellent example. Others (e.g. credit card and trading check agreements) will be given shortly.

Secured Credit

The purpose of security for the creditor is to reduce the risk for him that he will not recoup   **18–014**
the debt that is owing to him—the main risks being either that the debtor does not have the
means to pay (i.e. becomes insolvent) or that he disappears without trace. The main
advantage to the debtor of giving security is that the creditor, because the risks are reduced,
may offer better terms (i.e. charge less interest).

    Generally, the fact that a credit agreement is secured does not in any other way alter its
nature. Generally, even if for some reason the security fails, the creditor will still be able to
sue the debtor on his promise to repay.

Guarantee or Indemnity

The notion of someone acting as guarantor or indemnifier has already been considered in   **18–015**
relation to hire-purchase agreements. His position and function are exactly the same in
relation to any other credit agreement. He does, in a very real sense, provide security. He is
someone to whom the creditor can look if the debtor defaults. He may be the only security
that the creditor has or, equally, may be additional to security in one of the following
forms.

Mortgage of Goods (Chattel Mortgage)

A mortgage of goods is created when the owner of goods (the borrower) transfers ownership   **18–016**
to the lender (e.g. a finance company) on condition that the lender will retransfer the
ownership when the loan is duly repaid. The borrower retains possession throughout. The
borrower could create a mortgage over goods he has owned for some time or could do it at
the time he purchases them. Mortgages of goods are seldom used, because any document
creating one must comply with the very technical and obscure requirements of the Bills of
Sale Acts 1878–1882 and must be registered. Failure to comply with these requirements is
likely to render the security void.

Pledge

A pledge is created when the owner of goods transfers possession of them (or of the   **18–017**
documents of title) to a lender as security for a loan. A pledge differs from a mortgage in that
with a pledge the borrower retains his ownership throughout and parts with possession,
whereas with a mortgage of goods the borrower parts with ownership and retains possession
throughout.

Mortgage of Land

This is a particularly sound form of security—more so than any security over goods, which   **18–018**
can be lost, stolen or destroyed or can simply depreciate in value. Land on the other hand

tends to increase in value and cannot be moved. It is this last fact which has made land mortgages increasingly widely used in the consumer credit field. It is well known that someone who buys a house is able to mortgage the house as security for the loan of the money to buy it. After he has occupied it for a while it may have increased in value and would be good security for a further loan. Thus there exists what might be termed second mortgage companies which will give the house owner a loan and take a second mortgage as security for the loan. The agreement will usually allow the borrower to use the loan for whatever he likes.

Assignment of Life Assurance Policy

18–019   A policy of this type presents, for the assured person, a means of saving combined with seeing that in the event of his premature death his dependents are not left without money. The policy is an agreement whereby he agrees to pay for, say, 20 years, a regular premium to the insurance company. In return, the company agrees to pay him a fixed sum (perhaps plus bonuses) at the end of the period; it further agrees that if he dies earlier it will immediately pay the fixed sum (perhaps plus any bonuses already accumulated). That is a typical agreement. Now, suppose the agreement has been running for 10 years. It has by then got some value and could, for example be sold (i.e. surrendered) back to the insurance company for an immediate cash payment.

Instead of doing that, the insured could obtain a loan and assign (i.e. transfer the benefit of) the policy to the lender until the loan is repaid. A bank will sometimes accept an assignment of such an insurance policy as security for a loan and may then charge a lower rate of interest.

Methods of Providing Credit

18–020   Arrangements vary. There are three different roles which may or may not be combined in one person:

(i) That of creditor, i.e. the lender, the person who provides the credit for the debtor.

(ii) That of seller/supplier, i.e. the person who makes a contract with the debtor to supply him with goods or services.

(iii) That of dealer, i.e. the retailer of the goods (or services).

There are three common combinations:

(a) All three roles are combined in the same person, e.g. when a dealer makes a credit sale or hire-purchase agreement directly with the customer, as occurred in *Helby v Matthews*.[20]

[20] [1895] A.C. 471.

(b)   The first two roles are combined in one person but the dealer is someone else, e.g. in the typical hire-purchase or credit sale agreement where a finance company is involved.

(c)   The last two roles are combined in one person, the creditor being someone else, e.g. when a bank makes a personal loan to a customer who uses it to buy goods directly from the dealer.

It is useful to bear this analysis in mind when considering the following methods that are used to provide credit.

Bank Loan

This term is usually used to describe an arrangement whereby the customer borrows a fixed   **18–021** sum at a fixed rate of interest and agrees to pay it off by fixed regular (usually monthly) instalments. The repayments will often be made by automatic deductions from the customer's current account at the bank. The loan will usually be unsecured but may be secured, e.g. by the assignment of a life policy. A bank loan will invariably be an example of the third possibility (c) above.

Bank Overdraft

This is an arrangement whereby the customer is allowed to overdraw (i.e. borrow) on his   **18–022** current account. Like a bank loan, it will fall within the third possibility (c) above. Unlike a bank loan, it will be flexible in a number of ways. First, the interest rate is liable to fluctuate over the period of the loan. Secondly, the debtor may not be required to pay it off at any particular rate but may be trusted to pay it off as and when he can. Thirdly, it may not be for a fixed sum but may simply allow the customer to overdraw up to a maximum amount. Lastly, it may not be restricted to one occasion. The customer is usually allowed, as he pays it off, to overdraw again and again—always subject to a maximum amount.

Bank's Revolving Credit

This is simply a version of a bank loan but has one feature of an overdraft—namely that the   **18–023** debtor, as his debt becomes reduced by his regular repayments, is automatically allowed to borrow again up to the original or an agreed figure. He can do this again and again.

Shop's Revolving Credit

Some large shops and chain stores, e.g. men's tailors, operate a system whereby the customer   **18–024** agrees to pay so much a month (say, £30) and at the same time the customer can buy goods on credit up to a certain value (e.g. 12 times his monthly payments). Thus, in this example the customer could immediately buy £360 worth of clothes and will take about 12 months to pay for them. If that was all that the arrangement was, it would be no more than an ordinary credit sale agreement. However the customer is normally allowed to "top up" his debt, i.e. as his repayments reduce his outstanding debt, he can then purchase more clothes so as to bring his debt back up to £360. This sort of arrangement is often termed by the shop a "budget account". It is an example of the first possibility (a) above. The credit is usually unsecured.

Check Trading

18–025   A trading check is a piece of paper or token or voucher. It is a device for providing a fixed amount of credit which is (usually) unsecured. The customer will acquire the check first and then use it to buy goods or services. Suppose the check has a face value of £90. Then the customer can buy goods up to that value at any shop prepared to accept the check. The value of the goods he has bought, say £45, will be marked on the back of the check thus leaving the customer free to spend the rest of the check elsewhere. The shops will actually get payment from the check trading company from which the customer acquired the check. The customer will pay off the check trading company in instalments over a period of weeks, e.g. 36 weekly instalments of £3. The total of his instalments will of course be more than the face value of the check, the extra representing the interest. Check trading is an example of the third possibility (c) above. The creditor is one person (i.e. the check trading company). The seller and supplier of the goods is another person (i.e. the shop which accepts the trading check in payment). The contract between the customer and the shop which accepts the trading check in payment is a contract of sale of goods: *Davies v Customs and Excise*.[21] A trading check can be used only at those shops which are prepared to accept them. There will be an arrangement between the check trading company and a large number of stores whereby the latter agree to accept the checks.

Check trading is more common in the north of England than in the south and has traditionally involved quite small sums (i.e. up to about £100) and weekly repayments. Trading checks are often acquired from a door-to-door representative of the check trading company, who also will collect the weekly repayments. However, checks are in some instances being used for much larger sums in which case the repayments are usually monthly. Sometimes the check is restricted to the purchase of a specified item from a specified shop. Such checks are usually termed trading vouchers.

A trading check or voucher is not a revolving credit. Once the debtor has spent the value of his check he cannot, as his repayments are made, automatically have more credit. He must apply again to the check trading company (or, rather, to its representative) for another check.

Credit Cards

18–026   The credit card system[22] has much in common with that of trading checks. It is a further example of the third possibility (c) above. Again three parties are involved, the customer, the

---

[21] [1975] 1 All E.R. 309. See para.8–005 above.
[22] See generally, Jones, "Credit Cards, Card Users and Account Holders" [1988] J.B.L. 457.

creditor (in this case the credit card company) and the seller/supplier. A credit card is used in much the same way as a trading check. The buyer (i.e. the credit card holder), having decided what to purchase, buys it but does not pay either cash or by cheque; instead he uses his credit card. The seller is then paid by the credit card company and the latter, within about two to seven weeks, sends an account to the customer for payment. The normal arrangement between a credit card company and a retailer is that the retailer gives the card company a discount. Thus if a card holder uses his card to pay for an item costing £100, the card company will pay only about £95 or £96 to the retailer. This discount is part of the card company's profit. The card holder will of course still be required to pay the card company the full amount. Now, those card companies which require the customer to pay the whole amount at once are providing no more than a sophisticated form of general trade debt—debt deferred for a short time to be repaid in one instalment (e.g. Diner's Club and traditional American Express cards). Such cards are often termed charge cards to differentiate them from credit cards properly so-called. Some companies, e.g. American Express, offer charge card agreements and credit card agreements. With the latter the card holder is allowed to pay the account off in monthly instalments. The best known of these are "Visa" and "Mastercard".

The legal nature of a typical credit card or charge card arrangement was considered in *Re Charge Card Services Ltd.*[23] There were two underlying agreements. One was between the card company and card holder and regulated the basis on which credit could be obtained and was to be paid off. The other was between the card company and retailer; under it the retailer agreed to accept payment by means of the card and was to receive payment, less a discount, from the card company. In the case, a number of card holders had used their cards to pay for petrol at various garages before the card company became insolvent. This left a number of the garages owed money by the card company. Being unable to get it from the insolvent company, the garages claimed it from the individual card holders. The garages claimed that payment by credit or charge card was like payment by cheque. If a customer's cheque had been dishonoured by the bank, the garage would be entitled to claim the price direct from the customer. This is because payment by cheque is conditional upon the cheque being honoured. A number of the card holders had, however, already paid the card company for the petrol in question. So if they now had to pay the garage, they would end up having to pay twice for the same petrol. The Court of Appeal held that payment by means of a credit or charge card is not conditional, but absolute. It is a complete payment by the card holder who is not liable to pay the garage if the card is not honoured. Thus it is the retailer who runs the risk that the card company may become insolvent. It was also held, interpreting the agreement between the card company and the card holder, that the company had the right to claim payment from the card holder irrespective of whether the card company had paid the garages. Thus the neat result was that those card holders who had not yet paid the card company in respect of petrol purchased using their card remained liable to do so, but no card holder was liable to pay the garage for such petrol. It should be added that a card might be dishonoured for a reason other than the card company becoming insolvent, i.e. because the person using the card was doing so in excess of his credit limit, or had stolen the card. It might be, under the terms of the agreement between the card company and the retailer, that in those circumstances the card company is not liable to pay the retailer. If so, there is no doubt that the retailer in those

[23] [1989] Ch. 497.

circumstances would be entitled to claim payment from the person who had used the card, though probably not the full cash price but only the lesser amount that the retailer had expected to be paid by the card company. This is the only amount the retailer has lost because of the customer's representation (implied by his action of using the card) that he was authorised by the card company to use the card on that transaction.

There are two significant differences between the credit card system and the trading check system. First, the credit card holder does not actually draw upon any credit (i.e. owe any money) until he uses his credit card to purchase something. Thus when the credit card holder obtains his credit card he does not agree to any fixed amount of credit. The amount of the credit he obtains will depend upon the value of what he chooses to buy with the card. However, there will be a credit limit which he must not exceed at any one time. Secondly, a credit card provides a type of revolving credit. Thus the card holder can use the card again and again to obtain more credit, subject to the promise that his total credit does not at any one time exceed the credit limit stipulated in his credit card agreement. The credit card will normally be valid for two years but on expiry a replacement card will usually be sent automatically to the card holder.

18–027 A credit card provides an extremely useful and flexible form of credit. Even if the card is not used, the card holder has the sure knowledge that he can obtain instant credit. He can use it (or not) as and when he chooses. Although he can use it only at shops and other establishments which have an arrangement with the credit card company, it is true to say that a great many places at home and abroad have made such arrangements to accept both Visa and Mastercard. Further, the debtor can make repayments more or less as he pleases. He can pay it all off when the first account is sent to him or he can pay off some (not necessarily the same amount) each month. The only restriction is that there is normally a minimum amount which he must repay each month. Naturally, the longer he takes to make repayment, the more he will have to pay in interest.

A further point needs to be made. A credit card can usually be used not only to buy goods or services but also to obtain a cash loan from a bank. The bank will then obtain immediate repayment from the credit card company. The latter can be repaid by the card holder in the flexible way described above.

Visa and Mastercard are cards which can be used by the card holder at any shop which has an agreement with the relevant credit card company enabling the shop to accept that company's cards. However, some large stores or chains of stores have their own credit card schemes under which the card holder is limited to being able to use the card in that company's own stores. Some of these "in-house" credit cards are operated by the company which owns the store. These are therefore sometimes termed in the trade "two party" credit cards. There are only two persons involved in the transaction, the card holder and the company owning the store. This arrangement is an example of the first possibility (a) mentioned at para.18–020 above. The roles of creditor, seller and dealer are all combined in one person. Sometimes one of these "in-house" credit card schemes (e.g. the John Lewis Partnership Card) will be operated, not by the store itself, but by a subsidiary company or by a bank or finance company in arrangement with the store. The main difference between this "three party" type of "in-house" credit card and the more common Visa and Mastercard cards is that the in-house card can be used only in the store (or chain of stores) with which it is connected. Many stores operating in-house schemes also have arrangements with the major operators (e.g. Visa and Mastercard) enabling them to accept payment via the major credit cards. Some stores are more exclusive and recognise only their own in-house cards.

Besides stores, other large-scale retail operators, e.g. hotel chains and petrol companies, also operate in-house credit card schemes.

Rental Agreements

Where goods are hired but the hirer is given no option to purchase, the agreement is not a hire-purchase agreement but is simply an ordinary bailment. There is in a sense no element of credit, since the hirer pays each week for what he gets each week (i.e. one week's use of the goods). There is no element of "have now, pay later". However, it is becoming quite common with certain types of goods (e.g. televisions) for the goods to be hired by the same person for virtually the whole of the useful life of the goods. It is true that the hirer never becomes owner of the goods but he does have them (to keep indefinitely) and pay later. This is in a very real sense never-never, even though it is not a "credit" agreement.   **18–028**

Credit-Hire Agreements

The "credit-hire" agreement, a modern phenomenon, is a hire agreement which does involve the provision of credit.[24] The hirer is typically a motorist whose car has been put off the road in an accident caused entirely by the other's driver's fault. The agreement provides for the motorist to hire a replacement car for so long as her own is off the road, and also provides that the hire charges will become payable, not at the end of the hire period but only when the motorist's damages are recovered from the other motorist whose negligence caused the accident. Commonly the credit-hire company (or its chosen solicitor) will pursue that claim on her behalf, recover her damages and deduct the credit-hire charges before handing those damages over to her. A credit-hire agreement undoubtedly involves an element of "have now" (i.e. the hire of the car) and "pay later". Unsurprisingly, hire charges under credit-hire agreements are much higher than under conventional hire agreements (known as "spot hire"). The higher charges reflect the fact that, under a typical credit-hire agreement, the hirer receives the following benefits not provided under a spot hire agreement: **18–029**

    (i) she is relieved of having to lay out money for the car hire;

    (ii) she is relieved of having to pursue a claim against the other motorist, i.e. because normally the credit-hire company does that for her;

    (iii) she is thus also relieved of having to bear the costs of pursuing litigation against the other motorist.

The majority of the House of Lords in *Dimond v Lovell*[25] considered, obiter, that the cost of these extra benefits was not compensatable in damages obtainable from the other motorist. This, if correct, means that the hirer can recover, in damages from the other motorist, hire charges only at the equivalent spot hire rate. Thus the difference between the credit-hire

[24] Macleod, "Credit hire in the House of Lords" [2001] J.B.L. 14.
[25] [2000] 2 All E.R. 897.

charges and the lower spot hire rate will have to be borne either by the hirer or by the credit-hire company (i.e. if it chooses not to, or cannot, enforce the credit-hire agreement fully against the hirer).

The extent to which credit-hire agreements are regulated by the Consumer Credit Act is explained later in Chapter 19.[26]

General Reading

18–030

- Curwen, "Hire-Purchase Agreements: the unfortunate triumph of form over function" (2007) 11 *Mountbatten Journal of Legal Studies* 21;

- Johnson, "Problems with Hire-Purchase" [1993] J.B.F.L. 39;

- Jones, "Credit Cards, Card Users and Account Holders" [1988] J.B.L. 457;

- Macleod, "Credit hire in the House of Lords" [2001] J.B.L. 14;

- McCormack, "Hire-Purchase, Reservation of Title and Fixtures" [1990] Conv. 275.

---

[26] For a detailed and comprehensive account see Dobson, "Recovery of Credit Hire Charges" [1888] C.I.C.C. 25.

Chapter 19

THE CONSUMER CREDIT ACT 1974

INTRODUCTION

This chapter introduces the Consumer Credit Act 1974 and outlines the recent developments **19–001** in this area of law introduced by the Consumer Credit Act 2006. The 1974 Act followed the Crowther Committee's Report on Consumer Credit[1] and in large part implemented its recommendations. The basis of the Report was that consumer credit, although it might take many different forms, was always basically the same thing. Thus the Act, which is concerned with providing reasonable protection for those consumers who obtain credit, brings under one umbrella consumer credit agreements generally—whatever form they take. The Act repealed previous Acts which applied only to particular forms of consumer credit, i.e. the Pawnbrokers Acts 1872 and 1960, the Moneylenders Acts 1900–1927, the Hire Purchase Act 1965 and the Advertisements (Hire Purchase) Act 1967. Two sets of provisions, however, remain in force—the Bills of Sale Acts and the Hire Purchase Act 1964, Pt III. The former means that chattel mortgages are likely to remain uncommon.[2] The latter was dealt with at para.5–031 above.

The repeal of the Hire Purchase Act 1965 did not mean that the whole of the law relating to hire-purchase was recast—rather the reverse. Before 1974 the law of hire-purchase was generally thought to be satisfactory. Thus, in the Consumer Credit Act 1974, it was largely re-enacted with little alteration except that much of it applies to other consumer credit agreements as well. In the 1974 Act the terms "creditor" and "debtor" are used. The creditor means the person who provides the credit, i.e. in the case of a hire-purchase agreement, the owner; in the case of a direct loan, the lender; and in the case of a credit sale agreement, the seller. The debtor means the person who receives the credit, i.e. in the above examples, the hirer, borrower or buyer.

---

[1] (1971) Cmnd. 4596.
[2] See para.18–016, above.

There are three aspects to the way the Act operates.

(i) It regulates virtually the whole range of consumer credit agreements. That is to say, it controls the contractual position, the rights and duties existing between the creditor and debtor.

(ii) It creates a number of criminal offences designed to prevent unfair and undesirable practices by those engaged in the business of providing or advertising credit and by those engaged in connected businesses such as credit brokerage. These offences are principally concerned with the advertising of credit and the canvassing of customers.

(iii) It gives additional duties to the Office of Fair Trading. They are to keep under review the whole of the consumer credit business, to superintend the working and enforcing of the Act and to operate the licensing system. This system was created by the Act and generally requires anyone carrying on a business of providing consumer credit to have a licence.

19–002   The following two chapters will deal with licensing and with criminal offences relating to advertising and seeking business. After that the remaining chapters will be primarily concerned with the first of these three aspects of the Act—namely, those provisions which deal with the rights and liabilities between the creditor and debtor, i.e. which deal with the formation, validity and enforcement of a consumer credit agreement.

These provisions of the Act cannot be circumvented. Two sections see to that. First, s.173 prevents the parties from contracting out of the effect of the Act's provisions. A term of an agreement regulated by the Act is void to the extent that it is inconsistent with any provision in the Act (or any regulations made under the Act) for the protection of the debtor.[3] Where the Act imposes upon the debtor a duty or liability, that duty or liability cannot be increased by any term of the agreement.[4]

The second section referred to is s.113, which prevents the Act being evaded by the use of security. Thus where an agreement is regulated by the Act, the creditor cannot enforce any security so as to benefit himself to an extent greater than if the debtor carried out his obligations to the full extent that they would be enforced under the Act. The effect of this is that the creditor can take security as an added safeguard to ensure that the debtor carries out all his obligations to the full extent that they would be enforced against him under the Act, but where an obligation would not be enforced under the Act, the creditor cannot use the security to enforce that obligation.

19–003   Many regulations have been made under the Act. A number of them contain a lot of detailed requirements. This is true, for example, of those which deal with credit advertisements and those which deal with the form and contents of regulated agreements. Others of the regulations exclude specified persons or specified agreements from certain of the provisions of the Act. In this book it is not possible to give all the detail of all these various regulations. Thus although all the more important regulations are referred to, often only a summary of their provisions is given.

---

[3] s.173(1).
[4] s.173(2).

The rest of this chapter will deal with the definitions (mainly of different types of agreement which fall within the Act) in ss.8 to 20.

DEFINITIONS

Those agreements that are regulated agreements under the Act are of two types—consumer credit agreements and consumer hire agreements.　　**19–004**

Consumer Credit Agreements

The definition of a consumer credit agreement is to be found in s.8(1) which reads:　　**19–005**

> "A consumer credit agreement is an agreement between an individual ('the debtor') and any other person ('the creditor') by which the creditor provides the debtor with credit of any amount."

This was supported by s.8(2) which restricted the definition of a personal credit agreement to those agreements providing credit not exceeding £25,000.[5] This credit ceiling was abolished by s.1 of the Consumer Credit Act 2006[6] which repealed s.8(2) and thus for agreements made on or after April 6, 2008 the amount of credit provided under the agreement is no longer relevant to whether or not the Act applies.[7] The role and operation of s.8(2) will be considered shortly since it still plays an important role in relation to agreements entered into before its repeal came into effect.

Section 9(1) completes the picture:

> "(1) In this Act 'credit includes a cash loan, and any other form of financial accommodation."

Because of the word "individual" in s.8(1), any agreement where the debtor is a company　　**19–006**
(or any other corporate body) is outside the definition of a consumer credit agreement. On the other hand small partnerships and other unincorporated associations are treated as individuals.[8]

The definition of a consumer credit agreement does not include rental agreements which are dealt with under the definition of consumer hire agreement but it does include the other types of agreement considered in the last two chapters. Thus it includes credit sale and

---

[5] For agreements made before May 20, 1985 the figure of £25,000 was £5,000. For agreements made on or after that date and before May 1, 1998, the figure was £15,000.

[6] For an account of the policy considerations behind the 2006 Act, see Patient, "The Consumer Credit Act 2006" [2006] J.I.B.L.R. 309. See also, Lomnicka, "The reform of consumer credit in the UK" [2004] J.B.L. 129.

[7] Where the new business purposes exception does not apply, see para.19–021, below.

[8] s.189(1) as amended by the CCA 2006, s.1, which limits the application of the 1974 Act to partnerships consisting of two or three partners only (one of those partners must not be a body corporate).

conditional sale agreements, bank loans, check trading and credit card agreements. Section 9(3) specifically states that it includes hire-purchase agreements.[9]

No agreement falls within the definition unless it provides "credit". The explanation of "credit" in s.9(1) is less than complete. An element of "have now, pay later" is a fairly good indication of credit. Sometimes it is said that credit involves the "deferment of a debt" or the "deferment of an obligation to pay". Professor Goode, in his Consumer Credit Legislation, suggested that credit is provided "whenever the contract provides for the debtor to pay, or gives him the option to pay, later than the time at which payment would otherwise have been earned". *Dimond v Lovell*[10] involved a "credit-hire" agreement.[11] As explained at para. 18–029 above, this did not require the hirer to pay the car hire charges at the end of the hire period, but allowed her to postpone paying them until the conclusion of her claim against another motorist whose negligence had damaged the hirer's own car. In holding that the agreement thus provided credit to the hirer, the House of Lords applied Professor Goode's test, although Lord Hobhouse thought that it would not always be a satisfactory one to apply. The result is that a credit-hire agreement can be regulated under the Act as being both a consumer credit agreement and, if the hire period is capable of lasting over three months, also a consumer hire agreement.[12]

Former Financial Ceiling

19–007   No agreement made prior to the repeal of s.8(2) (i.e. before April 6, 2008) is a consumer credit agreement unless it is within the financial limit of £25,000. For the purpose of applying the financial limit, a distinction is made between fixed-sum credit and running-account credit. The idea of fixed-sum credit is easy. It is a once-only credit, e.g. a single loan. It is still fixed-sum credit even if later the creditor agrees to make a further loan to the debtor and even if he does so before the first loan is repaid. There will then be two fixed-sum credit agreements. Hire-purchase agreements, credit sale agreements, conditional sale agreements, ordinary bank loans and trading checks are all examples of fixed-sum credit. Running account credit is what is often termed in the credit trade revolving credit, where the debtor does not have to re-apply for a further credit but automatically as part of his original credit agreement has the right to further credit (usually subject to a credit limit). Examples of running-account credit are bank overdrafts, revolving credit from a bank or a shop and credit card agreements.

If a credit agreement provides fixed-sum credit of £25,000 or less then it is within the definition. The relevant figure is not the total amount which the debtor is to pay but the amount of the *credit*. That is, roughly speaking, the capital amount which the debtor is borrowing and it therefore does not include the interest payable by the debtor. To be precise, the amount of the credit does not include any item in the "total charge for credit". What is meant by the "total charge for credit" is considered a little further on.[13] All that can be said

---

[9] Necessary since a hire-purchase agreement would not otherwise be regarded as extending credit to the hirer during the period of hire.

[10] [2000] 2 W.L.R. 1121.

[11] See Macleod, "Credit hire in the House of Lords" [2001] J.B.L. 14.

[12] For the definition of consumer hire agreement, see para.19–011, below.

[13] At para.19–027, below.

now is that the total charge for credit will reflect the cost to the debtor of having the credit. Thus the biggest item in the total charge for credit will be the interest charged to the debtor, which will therefore not be part of the "credit". Thus an agreement would fall within the definition of a consumer credit agreement if it gave the debtor a cash loan of £25,000 to be repaid by him in 50 monthly instalments of £560. The amount of the credit would be £25,000 even though the repayments would total £28,000. The extra £3,000 is interest, falls within the "total charge for credit" and therefore is not part of the "credit". For the definition of a consumer credit agreement, the relevant figure is the credit (the amount borrowed), not what it costs the debtor to borrow it.

With a hire-purchase agreement the calculation is not quite so easy but the principle is the same. Suppose Sam wishes to buy a yacht for which the retail cash price is £33,000. Sam has only £8,000 saved up. So he acquires the yacht under a hire-purchase agreement under which he makes an immediate deposit of £8,000 and agrees to pay 50 monthly instalments of £560 each. The agreement gives him an option to buy the yacht for £2 provided he has first paid the deposit and all the instalments. This hire-purchase agreement would fall within the definition of a consumer credit agreement because the amount of the credit is £25,000.

Suppose, however, that the retailer had offered to insure (or buy insurance for) the yacht for two years at an additional price of £100. To buy the yacht thus insured would cost £33,100 in cash. However, since Sam still only has £8,000 saved up, he takes it on hire-purchase terms whereby he pays an immediate deposit of £8,000 and agrees to pay 50 monthly instalments of £562 each (the option money still being £2). Now, in this case the agreement would seem to fall outside the definition since the amount of the credit is £25,100. Thus where the credit would otherwise be at or just under £25,000 it is possible to get the agreement outside the definition by persuading the prospective debtor to borrow just a little bit more. This could be done by offering some optional extra item which is sufficiently tempting to persuade the debtor to have it. In the case of a yacht a particularly tempting extra might be the provision of a mooring for a certain number of years. A similar service is sometimes provided in the "mobile home" (i.e. caravan) business where one can buy a caravan and sometimes with it also the right to have it on a given site for a given number of years.

A warning must be given; a point made earlier must be repeated. It is that a distinction must be made in every case between (a) the amount of the credit and (b) the total charge for credit. These terms are mutually exclusive. The amount of the credit does not include any sum which is within the total charge for credit. In the example just given about Sam and his yacht the £100 for the insurance was not within the total charge for credit. In *Humberclyde Finance Ltd v Thompson*[14] the Court of Appeal considered the status of a payment waiver insurance premium. Thompson acquired a car on finance supplied by Humberclyde Finance Ltd. The amount of credit was £14,497 but the agreement also included a payment of £796 as an insurance premium in the event of the debtor being unable to make the necessary repayments. At first instance the court held that the insurance payment was part of the credit supplied under the agreement and that the agreement was therefore not regulated since the credit ceiling at the time was £15,000. The Court of Appeal held that the insurance premium was properly regarded as part of the total charge for credit and was not part of the credit. Consequently the agreement was regulated under the Act since the amount of credit fell under the s.8(2) limit. It would seem therefore that the courts are prepared to extend the

19–008

[14] [1997] C.C.L.R. 23.

natural meaning of what is part of the total charge for credit so as to ensure that where a debtor has been tempted to take an "extra" which would take the agreement over the credit ceiling he is still protected by the provisions of the Act. This approach does leave the question of what extras will be regarded as part of the credit and which will not, rather unpredictable.[15]

This distinction has in recent years been given attention by the courts not least because of the consequences for an agreement falling within the old definition of a regulated agreement but also because of the consequences if a regulated agreement wrongly identified a fee which was part of the total charge for credit, as being within the credit itself. In *Wilson v Robertsons (London) Ltd*[16] a pawnbroking agreement for a six month loan of £400 was struck. From that loan an £8 documentation fee was deducted, although the agreement referred to the amount of credit as £400. At trial on preliminary issues Laddie J. held that the documentation fee was properly to be regarded as part of the total charge for credit and therefore not, as part of the credit itself. Thus the loan was in fact for £392 since the £8 fee was to be ignored under s.9(4). Consequently the agreement was not properly documented and was unenforceable.[17]

19–009   The £25,000 financial limit applies also in relation to running-account credit agreements. Here the governing figure is the credit limit, i.e. the maximum debt which the debtor is allowed to run up. If the debtor's credit limit is £25,000 or less, the agreement is within the financial limit and, providing the debtor is an individual (not a company), it is a consumer credit agreement. The agreement will still be a consumer credit agreement even if the debtor is allowed *temporarily* to exceed this credit limit. However, even where the agreement has no credit limit or has one in excess of £25,000, there are three situations when it will still be within the financial limit. These three situations are where:

(i) The debtor is unable on any one occasion to draw credit in excess of £25,000.

(ii) The terms of the agreement are such that if the debt (the debit balance) exceeds a certain figure (of £25,000 or less) the terms (e.g. the rate of interest) become more onerous for the debtor.

(iii) It is probable, at the time the agreement is made, that the debt will not at any time rise above £25,000.

Thus most running-account credit agreements will be within the definition. A clear example of one which would not would be one restricted to large credits of over £25,000 and which could not be used (even on one occasion) to acquire a credit of £25,000 or less.

Abolition of Financial Ceiling

19–010   The removal of the financial limit for agreements made on or after April 6, 2008 has for the most part removed such difficulties and it is now clear that the amended Consumer Credit Act

---

[15] See, for example, *London North Securities Ltd v Meadows* [2005] EWCA Civ 956 where the Court of Appeal held that the insurance premium was part of the total charge for credit whereas payments against the arrears of previous mortgages were part of the credit.
[16] [2005] 3 All E.R. 873.
[17] On the issue of unenforceable agreements see Ch.22.

regulates all consumer credit agreements and all consumer hire agreements, unless exempt, with no distinction based on the amount of credit provided. It is, however, still very important to understand the approach of the courts to the old s.8(2) issue of calculating the amount of credit provided. First, as mentioned above, agreements entered into before April 2008 will only be regulated agreements where the financial limit is satisfied. Secondly, the issue of distinguishing between "credit" and the "total cost for credit" is still vitally important for other sections of the Act. Thirdly, the new business purpose exemption in s.16B of the 1974 Act retains a financial limit of £25,000 and for the purposes of that section, the same calculations must be made.[18]

Consumer Hire Agreements

A consumer hire agreement is any agreement for the bailment (hiring) of goods which fulfils three conditions[19]:   **19–011**

    (a) It is not a hire-purchase agreement.

    (b) It is capable of lasting more than three months.

    (c) The hirer is not a body corporate.

    The first condition does not, of course, mean that a hire-purchase agreement is not regulated. We have just seen that hire-purchase agreements fall within the definition of a consumer credit agreement. The second condition means that, for example, an agreement to hire a car for two months would fall outside the Act. Like s.8 previously discussed, s.15 in its original form also included a financial limit. The agreement was not regulated if it required the hirer to make payments exceeding a specified figure. For agreements made before May 20, 1985 the specified figure was £5,000. For agreements made on or after that date and before May 1, 1998, the figure was £15,000. For agreements made on or after May 1, 1998 and before April 6, 2008, the figure was £25,000. This financial limit has also been removed following the implementation of the Consumer Credit Act 2006. Thus for agreements made on or after April 6, 2008, a consumer hire agreement, unless exempt, will be regulated irrespective of the amount of the hire payments. The former financial limit coupled with the requirement that the agreement is "capable of subsisting for longer than three months" is best understood through an example. Consider a hire agreement made in March 2008 which is not a hire-purchase agreement and which provides:

    (i) That the hirer (an individual) shall pay a deposit of £15,000.

    (ii) That the hirer shall pay a monthly rental of £10,000.

    (iii) That the hiring shall continue for a maximum of one year but that the hirer shall be able to terminate it at or at any time after the end of the first month.

[18] See para.19–021, below.
[19] s.15.

This agreement falls within the definition since it might last longer than three months and the payments might not exceed £25,000. If the same agreement had been made in May 2008 (i.e. after the removal of the financial limit) the outcome would be exactly the same (i.e. it would be regulated under s.15) but the amount of the deposit and monthly rental would be irrelevant in arriving at this conclusion. Consider another example—a hire agreement which is not a hire-purchase agreement and which provides:

(i) That the hirer (an individual) shall not pay any deposit but shall pay a rental of £100 per month.

(ii) That the hiring shall last three months.

(iii) That the hirer shall have the right to renew the agreement for a further three months.

This agreement is *capable* of lasting more than three months and is also within the definition.

19–012   It was necessary for the Act to have a separate definition of a consumer hire agreement since, as explained in the last chapter, a hire agreement does not normally involve any element of credit and thus does not fall within the definition of consumer credit agreement. A "credit-hire" agreement is an unusual type of agreement which involves both hire and credit and thus can fall within both definitions, consumer credit agreement and consumer hire agreement.

It will be found that a great many sections of the Act refer to the "creditor or owner" and the "debtor or hirer". The words "owner" and "hirer" refer to the parties to a consumer hire agreement and not to the parties to a hire-purchase agreement. The words "creditor" and "debtor" include (and refer to) the owner and hirer respectively under a hire-purchase agreement. This is because, as we have just seen, a hire-purchase agreement falls within the definition of a consumer credit agreement under s.8.

Regulated Agreements

19–013   A regulated agreement is any consumer credit agreement or consumer hire agreement other than an exempt agreement.

Most of the provisions of the Act apply, not to all consumer credit agreements, but only to regulated agreements. This is true in particular of those sections which relate to the formation, validity and enforcement of agreements. The position is similar in relation to the licensing provisions so that someone who carries on a consumer credit business which is confined to giving credit under exempt agreements does not require a licence.

The question of which agreements are exempt agreements will be examined a little later. First, it is necessary to consider certain sub-categories of consumer credit agreement.

Restricted Use and Unrestricted-Use Agreements

19–014   Credit will be either restricted-use credit or unrestricted-use credit as explained by s.11. It is unrestricted-use credit if it is in fact provided in such a way as to leave the debtor free to use it as he chooses. Thus hire-purchase agreements, credit sale and conditional sale agreements, check trading agreements, credit-hire agreements and a shop's revolving credit are all examples of restricted-use credit agreements. A bank loan or overdraft will almost always be unrestricted-use credit, since the money is usually paid directly to the borrower who is therefore free to use it as he chooses. In this case it is still unrestricted-use credit even if the borrower had agreed to use it only for one particular purpose, e.g. to repay a debt to X. It would of course be a restricted-use credit agreement if the bank stipulates that the money is to be paid directly by the bank to X.

A credit card agreement is an example of a multiple agreement, i.e. it can be used to buy goods or services at a restricted number (albeit a large number) of shops, etc. and it can be used to obtain a cash loan. This is an unrestricted-use credit agreement with respect to the provision of cash, and a restricted-use credit agreement with respect to the provision of goods or services.

Debtor-Creditor and Debtor-Creditor-Supplier Agreements

Every regulated consumer credit agreement must be either a debtor-creditor-supplier agree-   **19–015** ment or a debtor-creditor agreement under ss.12 and 13 respectively. The former describes the type of agreement where either there is a business connection between the creditor and the supplier of the goods (as occurs in check trading) or the creditor is also the supplier of the goods (as in every credit sale, conditional sale, hire-purchase and credit-hire agreement). In order to determine whether there is a business connection between the creditor and supplier (i.e. whether the credit agreement is a debtor-creditor-supplier agreement) it must first be decided whether the credit agreement is for restricted-use or for unrestricted-use credit.

The rule can be formulated as follows. The following agreements are debtor-creditor-supplier agreements:

(a) An agreement for restricted-use credit where the creditor and supplier are one and the same person.

(b) A restricted-use credit agreement "made by the creditor under pre-existing arrangements, or in contemplation of future arrangements, between himself and the supplier".

(c) An unrestricted-use credit agreement made by the creditor under pre-existing arrangements between himself and the supplier, in the knowledge that the credit is to be used to finance a transaction between the debtor and the supplier.

Any agreement not in one of these three categories is merely a debtor-creditor agreement.

In many cases a restricted-use credit agreement will be a debtor-creditor-supplier agreement and an unrestricted-use credit agreement will be a debtor-creditor agreement. These are the common combinations. Thus hire-purchase, conditional sale, credit sale, trading check agreements and credit-hire are all restricted-use debtor-creditor-supplier agreements. Further illustrations are provided by a typical credit card agreement which is, as has been seen, a multiple agreement. In so far as it relates to a cash loan, it is an unrestricted-use credit agreement and is a debtor-creditor agreement. In so far as it relates to goods or services it is a restricted-use credit agreement and is also a debtor-credit-supplier agreement. It is the latter because the supplier of goods or services who accepts payment by means of a credit card does so under an arrangement between himself and the credit card company—an arrangement which either pre-existed, or was contemplated by, the credit agreement.

19–016   It is, however, possible for the combination to be different. For example a bank loan may be granted to the debtor to pay off a pre-existing debt of his and it may be payable directly by the bank to the person to be paid off. This would be an agreement for restricted-use credit but would merely be a debtor-creditor agreement. Exactly the same result occurs where a bank agrees to enable its customer to buy a new car by making him a loan, but at the same time stipulates that the money is to be payable directly by the bank to the supplier (i.e. the car dealer). The agreement between the bank (creditor) and its customer (debtor) is clearly for restricted-use credit but it is still merely a debtor-creditor agreement because it is not made under pre-existing arrangements or in contemplation of future arrangements between the bank and the car dealer.

Take one further example, this time of an agreement in the third category (above) of debtor-creditor-supplier agreements—namely, an agreement where the creditor furnishes the credit in such a way as to leave the debtor free to use the credit as he likes but where the creditor makes the agreement under pre-existing arrangements between himself and the supplier in the knowledge that the credit is to be used to finance a transaction between the debtor and the supplier. This situation could arise on facts like these: Shiver wants central heating installed in his house. He approaches Warmitup Ltd who indicate that they will deal only on a cash payment basis and suggest that Shiver gets in touch with Hotmoney Ltd who have an arrangement with Warmitup Ltd whereby Hotmoney Ltd will make loans to potential customers of Warmitup Ltd. After some negotiations, Hotmoney Ltd make a loan to Shiver which is paid directly into Shiver's hands. This is a debtor-creditor-supplier agreement even though it is an unrestricted-use credit agreement.

The Act nowhere uses the words "business connection". Nevertheless the policy behind the classification into debtor-creditor-supplier agreements and debtor-creditor agreements it to identify the former as credit agreements where there is some business connection between the creditor and supplier. The policy is that where there is that business connection between the creditor and the supplier, both of them (and not just the supplier) should be answerable to the customer if the goods or services supplied do not correspond with representations made to him before he bought them or if the supplier is in breach of contract with the customer. This point will be returned to later.[20]

Electronic Funds Transfer and Debit Cards

19–017   In the light of the foregoing, consider one particular development in banking services, namely Electronic Funds Transfer (EFT). This is a modern means of payment in supermarkets, department stores and other places. In the shop at the point of sale there will be a terminal which will have a direct electronic link with the major clearing banks. A bank customer who holds a "debit" card is able to hand his debit card to the shop's checkout

---

[20] See paras 22–017 and 25–003.

assistant who will run it through the terminal. That terminal via its electronic link automatically transfers the money (more or less immediately) from the customer's own bank account to the shop's bank account. There is no need for the customer to write a cheque. Unlike a cheque guarantee card, a "debit" card does not enable the customer to obtain an unauthorised overdraft. That being so, the Consumer Credit Act does not apply at all to a "debit" card unless the customer has from his bank an agreed overdraft authority. In the absence of an overdraft (or an agreement of the bank authorising one), there will be no credit agreement.

One piece of plastic may serve several purposes. It may be a "debit" card, a cheque guarantee card, a cash withdrawal token and a credit card. In that case, how can the agreement be classified for the purposes of the Consumer Credit Act? The answer is to regard each aspect of the card as a separate agreement and to classify that. Thus when used as a debit card by a holder who has an agreed overdraft authority it is a debtor-creditor agreement. When used as a regulated credit card to purchase goods or services, it is a debtor-creditor-supplier agreement. When used as a regulated credit card to draw cash it is a debtor-creditor agreement. In short, the agreement is a multiple one and some aspects of it may be regulated and others not; some aspects of it may be within one category of regulated agreement and others within another.[21]

Exempt Agreements

Subject to one important exception, exempt agreements are not regulated by the Act. The **19–018** exception is that the court has power to reopen an exempt consumer credit agreement if it gives rise to an unfair relationship between creditor and debtor.[22] The principal exempt agreements are:

(i) Consumer credit agreements secured on land (i.e. a mortgage) and made by a local authority.

(ii) Certain land mortgage agreements granted by a building society, bank (or wholly-owned subsidiary of a bank) or (providing the body is specified for this purpose in an Order made by the Secretary of State) any of the following bodies— insurance company, friendly society, trade union, employers' association, charity, land improvement company or body corporate named in a public general Act of Parliament, or named in an Order under the Housing Act 1965 or the Home Purchase and Assistance and Housing Corporation Guarantee Act 1978. Not all land mortgage agreements are exempt when made by these bodies, only debtor-creditor agreements financing land purchases or the provision or alteration of dwellings or business premises. Thus, if a bank or building society grants a mortgage loan to an individual for some other purpose, e.g. to buy a car, the credit agreement is likely to be regulated.

[21] On credit cards and multiple agreements see paras 19–014 and 19–015, above.
[22] Under ss.140A–140C, see para.24–006, below.

(iii) A "fixed-sum" "debtor-creditor-supplier" agreement under which the debtor is to repay the credit in no more than four instalments and within a period of 12 months. The following is an exempt agreement. Footsore buys a luxury armchair under a credit sale agreement, agreeing to pay 35 per cent immediately and the rest by four equal monthly instalments. The 12-month period begins with, and includes, the date the agreement is made. Thus an agreement requiring the repayments to be made within 12 months *after* the date of the agreement will not qualify for this exemption.[23] Some credit-hire agreements stipulate that the hire charges must be paid before the first of the following events: (i) conclusion, settlement or abandonment of the hirer's claim against the other motorist; (ii) expiry of a period of 365 days *beginning* with the date the agreement is made. Such an agreement appears to satisfy the requirements for this exemption and the House of Lords, obiter, said as much in *Dimond v Lovell*.[24]

By way of exception, hire-purchase agreements, conditional sale agreements, agreements financing the purchase of land and agreements secured by pledge (i.e. pawn) cannot fall within this exemption.

(iv) A "debtor-creditor-supplier" agreement financing the purchase of land where the number of payments to be made by the debtor does not exceed four.

19–019

(v) A "running-account" "debtor-creditor-supplier" agreement where the debtor is required to pay the whole of each periodical account by a single payment. This exemption means that the milk, newspaper and grocery accounts of many households will be exempt. So also are those charge card agreements (e.g. Diners Club and American Express) which require the card holder to settle each account by a single repayment. If, however, such an agreement allowed the card holder to draw a cash loan (of £25,000 or less) to use as he wished then the exemption would be lost. The agreement would be a multiple one (see para.19–017 above). In so far as it related to the cash loan it would be a debtor-creditor agreement and thus not exempt. In determining whether an agreement falls within this exemption, some caution is needed because some card issuers (e.g. American Express) operate two different kinds of agreement; one which allows extended credit and is a regulated agreement; and another which is exempt because it requires each periodical account to be settled with a single payment.

(vi) A "debtor-creditor" agreement which is of a type offered only to a certain class or classes of individuals and not offered to the public generally, where there can be no increase in the charge for credit and where the cost of the credit is low, i.e. where the true annual rate of the total charge for credit does not exceed a rate one per cent higher than the highest of the base rates operated by the main English and Scottish banks at the close of business 28 days before the making of the credit agreement.

Few businesses will wish to grant loans at a rate low enough to gain this exemption, since the business would probably then become unprofitable. However, those companies which grant cheap loans to their employees as fringe

---

[23] *Zoan v Rouamba* [2000] 2 All E.R. 620; cf. *Ketley v Gilbert* [2001] 1 W.L.R. 986; *Clark v Tull (t/a Ardington Electrical Services)* [2003] Q.B. 36; *Thew v Cole, King v Daltry* [2003] C.C.L.R. 2.
[24] [2000] 2 All E.R. 897. On credit-hire agreements generally, see paras 18–029 and 19–006 above.

benefits may well set their rates sufficiently low to gain exemption. A company loan agreement of this sort might well contain a clause providing that if the employee leaves that employment, the rate will rise (i.e. above the limits just mentioned). Such a clause will not cause the agreement to lose its exemption.

(vii) A "debtor-creditor" agreement which is of a type offered only to a certain class or classes of individuals and not offered to the public generally, where there is no charge for credit other than interest and where the rate of that interest, though possibly variable, is low, i.e. cannot at any time exceed a rate of one per cent higher than the highest of the base rates operated by the main English and Scottish banks 28 days earlier.

(viii) A consumer credit agreement providing credit to be used by the debtor in connection with overseas trade.

(ix) Consumer hire agreements for the hire of metering equipment (for metering gas, water or electricity) hired from a corporate body (e.g. British Gas Plc) authorised to supply gas, water or electricity.

The above agreements are exempt by virtue of s.16 and the Consumer Credit (Exempt Agreements) Order 1989.[25]

The Consumer Credit Act 2006 has introduced two further categories of exempt agreement under the new ss.16A and 16B. The first of the new exceptions relates to high net worth debtors (and hirers)[26] and allows a debtor or hirer to exempt themselves from all provisions of the Act barring those provisions relating to unfair agreements. In order for this exemption to apply, four requirements must be satisfied[27]:   **19–020**

(a) the debtor or hirer is a natural person;

(b) the agreement includes a declaration made by him to the effect that he agrees to forgo the protection and remedies that would be available to him under this Act if the agreement were a regulated agreement;

(c) a statement of high net worth has been made in relation to him; and

(d) that statement is current in relation to the agreement and a copy of it was provided to the creditor or owner before the agreement was made.

Thus, for an agreement to be exempted under s.16A, the debtor or hirer must be a natural person and the agreement must include a declaration, in the specified form, that the debtor or hirer agrees to forgo the protection which would be available under the 1974 Act if the agreement were a regulated agreement. In addition a statement of high net worth must be made in relation to the debtor or hirer. The form and content of such a statement is laid down by the Consumer Credit (Exempt Agreements) Order 2007 which came into force on April 6, 2008. Article 4(1) provides that the statement must be made by either the creditor or

---

[25] SI 1989/869 (as amended).
[26] Introduced by s.3 of the CCA 2006.
[27] s.16A(1) and the Consumer Credit (Exempt Agreements) Order 2007 (SI 2007/1168).

owner[28] or an accountant.[29] In order to be deemed a "high net worth" individual the debtor or hirer must satisfy at least one of the two threshold tests. The first threshold is that the debtor received a net income of at least £150,000 during the previous financial year. Alternatively, the debtor may nevertheless obtain the required statement where, throughout the previous financial year, he held net assets with a total value of £500,000 or more.

The impact of this exemption is to allow greater freedom of contract between such high net worth individuals and the credit industry. Moreover, it is a natural consequence of the financial limits being removed coupled with the general prohibition on contracting out. Without the new s.16A every consumer credit agreement would be regulated under the Consumer Credit Act, including for example, credit cards with no credit limit or a hire-purchase agreement for an extravagant item such as a bespoke sports car or yacht.

19–021   The second new category of exempt agreement introduced by the 2006 Act is where the agreement is entered into for business purposes. It has already been seen that the definition of "individual" under the Act extends protection to agreements entered into for business purposes. This may occur in a number of situations. First, for example, an unincorporated business (e.g. a sole trader) may enter into a regulated agreement. Secondly, a partnership (of up to three partners) may similarly enter into a regulated agreement. The new s.16B exemption removes such agreements from the scope of the revised Act where the amount of credit provided is greater than £25,000 and where "the agreement is entered into by the debtor or hirer wholly or predominantly for the purposes of a business carried on, or intended to be carried on, by him".[30] The test for whether an agreement has been entered into solely or predominantly for business purposes is one of fact for the court to decide on a case-by-case basis. This represents a significant change in approach since, in relation to agreements made prior to the introduction of the 2006 Act, the purpose behind the agreement was irrelevant to the question of whether it was regulated. Now, under s.16B, the courts must enquire as to the purpose of the agreement and, where that purpose is exclusively or predominantly business it is once again the amount of credit provided that will determine whether or not the agreement is regulated.

For example, if a solicitor leases a new car on hire-purchase terms for £30,000, (subject to any impact of s.16A detailed above) the agreement will be regulated where the car is intended primarily for private use (notwithstanding the fact that the agreement is on the books of the partnership). Where the car is predominantly intended for business use, the agreement will be unregulated. Perhaps the greatest challenge for the courts here will be to ascertain where the division lies between predominantly business use and predominantly private use.

To alleviate this difficulty the prospective debtor or hirer can, under s.16B(2) make a declaration. If he makes a declaration:

> "to the effect that the agreement is entered into by him wholly or predominantly for the purposes of a business carried on, or intended to be carried on, by him, the agreement

---

[28] Though only where the creditor or owner is authorised to accept deposits under Pt IV of the Financial Services and Market Act 2000.
[29] Who is a member of one of the professional organisations listed in art.4(2) for example, the Institute of Chartered Accountants in England and Wales.
[30] s.16B(1).

shall be presumed to have been entered into by him wholly or predominantly for such purposes."

In order to prevent abuse of this exemption, the new s.16B(3) provides that any such presumption does not apply if, when the agreement is entered into the creditor (or owner), or: **19–022**

"any person who has acted on his behalf in connection with the entering into of the agreement, knows, or has reasonable cause to suspect, that the agreement is not entered into by the debtor or hirer wholly or predominantly for the purposes of a business carried on, or intended to be carried on, by him".

Small Agreements

A regulated agreement which does not exceed a specified financial limit (£50) is a small agreement—s.17. A fixed-sum credit agreement is a small agreement provided the "credit" does not exceed £50 (the credit is the capital amount, i.e. excluding the total charge for credit). A running-account credit agreement is a small agreement if it has a credit limit of £50 or less.   **19–023**

There are exceptions to all of this. First, no hire-purchase or conditional sale agreement falls within the definition of a small agreement. Secondly, neither does any agreement which is secured by anything other than a guarantee or indemnity. Thirdly, it is not possible artificially to contrive to make several small agreements in place of one larger one. If, where one agreement would exceed the £50 limit, two or more agreements are made so as to bring each agreement below the limit, the agreements will be regarded together as one agreement which exceeds the limit.

The object of defining small agreements is so that it is easy for later sections to exclude such agreements (i.e. where small sums are involved) from some of the technical requirements of the Act (e.g. from the formality and cancellation provisions).

Non-Commercial Agreements

Section 189(1) defines a non-commercial agreement as "a consumer credit agreement or a consumer hire agreement not made by the creditor or owner in the course of a business carried on by him". Thus an agreement for a loan between friends or from a father to his son would be a non-commercial agreement. It will be seen that non-commercial agreements are excluded from many provisions of the Act (e.g. the formality and cancellation provisions).[31]   **19–024**

In *Hare v Schurek*[32] the claimant carried on business as a car dealer and did not normally extend credit to his customers. On one occasion, however, he agreed to supply a car to a friend of his on hire-purchase terms. The Court of Appeal held that the word "business" in

---

[31] For an explanation of "carrying on a business" see para.20–003, below
[32] [1993] C.C.L.R. 47.

the definition of non-commercial agreement meant a consumer credit or consumer hire business. It was held that, since the claimant did not carry on a consumer credit business or consumer hire business, this agreement was not made in the course of a business and was therefore a non-commercial agreement; thus the creditor did not need a consumer credit licence. This reasoning was probably wrong, since there is, in the definition of non-commercial agreement, no qualification to the word "business" and the claimant did not need a licence in any event.[33]

Linked Transactions

19–025 The object of the definition in s.19 is to enable later sections to provide for what will be the effect on linked transactions in the event of the debtor or hirer withdrawing an offer to enter a regulated agreement or exercising his right of cancellation of a regulated agreement. The effect will be that any linked transaction is similarly (and automatically) withdrawn from or cancelled—ss.19(3) and 69. It is therefore not possible for a creditor or owner to get around the cancellation provisions of the Act by persuading the debtor or hirer to enter a linked transaction.

The following are linked transactions:

(a) A transaction which the debtor or hirer has to enter as a condition of the principal agreement, e.g. if his credit agreement requires him to take out an insurance policy to ensure that the debt will be repaid if he dies.

(b) A transaction financed or to be financed by the credit agreement where the credit agreement is a debtor-creditor-supplier agreement. Thus an agreement to buy goods by using one's credit card is a linked transaction in relation to the credit card agreement.

(c) A transaction which has all the three following characteristics:

(i) It was suggested to the debtor by someone who knew that the principal agreement had been or might well be made, e.g. the creditor or owner himself, the credit broker, or, depending upon the circumstances, the dealer.

(ii) It was a transaction between the debtor or hirer and a person who knew that the principal agreement had been (or might well be) made or for whom the dealer acted as credit broker in negotiating the transaction.

(iii) The debtor entered the transaction to induce the creditor or owner to enter the principal agreement or for another purpose related to the principal agreement or for a purpose related to the transaction to be financed by the principal agreement (provided in the last case that the principal agreement was a restricted-use credit agreement).

There are three further points in the definition. First, no agreement will be a linked one except in relation to a regulated agreement. Secondly, no security agreement (e.g. one of guarantee

---

[33] See para.20–003, below.

or indemnity) can be a linked agreement. Thirdly, a transaction which would be a linked agreement if the debtor were a party to it will still be a linked agreement even though it is a relative who, instead of the debtor or hirer, is a party to it.

It will be appreciated that the definition is indeed a complex one. It may become easier if it is remembered that the definition is intended to embrace those transactions which, if the debtor or hirer is allowed to cancel his regulated agreement, ought also to be automatically cancelled. Assistance may also be gained from a few examples:

(i) X agrees to buy on credit sale terms a deep freezer from Y, a dealer. X also enters a separate agreement with Y whereby Y agrees to install the freezer. X enters a further agreement with Y that Y shall restock the freezer six months after delivery. The credit sale agreement is the principal agreement and the other two agreements are linked transactions.

(ii) The situation is exactly the same as in (i) except that the principal agreement is made by X not with the dealer Y but with a finance company. The other two agreements with Y, the dealer, are still linked agreements.

(iii) The situation is the same as in (i) or (ii) except that X's wife is the person who makes the installation or stocking agreement with Y, the dealer. The installation and stocking agreements are still linked transactions.

(iv) An agreement by a supplier, Z, to sell goods to X for which X pays by using a trading check is a linked transaction.

(v) In the example at para.19–016 (above) the agreement between Shiver and Warmitup Ltd is a linked transaction—the principal agreement being that between Shiver and Hotmoney Ltd.

There are three provisions of the Act which apply directly to linked transactions. Their effect is as follows. First, a linked transaction made before the regulated agreement is made is of no effect unless and until the regulated agreement is made.[34] Secondly, if the regulated agreement is withdrawn from or cancelled, then any linked transaction is similarly withdrawn from or cancelled under s.69(1). Thirdly, if for any reason the debtor's indebtedness is discharged early, the debtor is discharged from any further liability under any linked transaction under s.96(1). To see what all of this means, suppose that the credit sale agreement in example (i) above is one which X has the right to cancel.[35] Then if X were to cancel the agreement before the freezer was installed, he would not be obliged to have it installed and thus would not be obliged to pay for the installation. That is all very sensible since if X has cancelled the credit sale agreement then he is not going to have the freezer. If X did not cancel the credit sale agreement but paid off the whole of his credit within six months of delivery he would not be obliged to have Y restock the freezer. As we shall see later, a debtor has a right to pay off the credit early at any time he wishes.

Three types of linked transaction are exempted from the three provisions (mentioned above) which would otherwise have applied to them.[36] These three types of transaction will

19–026

---

[34] s.19(3).
[35] See para.22–040, below.
[36] Consumer Credit (Linked Transactions) (Exemptions) Regulations 1983 (SI 1983/1560).

therefore be unaffected by the debtor withdrawing from or cancelling his regulated agreement or discharging his debt under that agreement ahead of time. These three exempted transactions are:

(i) contracts of insurance;

(ii) written guarantees of goods;

(iii) any transaction which is (or is made under) an agreement for the operation of a savings, deposit or current account.

The first of these exemptions means that if the debtor cancels the regulated agreement (i.e. assuming that it is cancellable), any connected insurance contract will not also automatically be cancelled. There is nevertheless a possibility that the insurance contract, e.g. of life insurance, may be cancellable under the cooling-off provisions of other legislation, e.g. the Financial Services (Distance Marketing) Regulations 2004.[37] The second and third of the exemptions require an explanation. The second deals with written guarantees of goods. It seems peculiar and can lead to absurdity. To show this, let us return to the example, given earlier, of X making a credit sale agreement to buy a freezer. Suppose that at the time of the making of the agreement, X makes a written contract with the dealer whereby X undertakes to pay £25 and in return the dealer guarantees to rectify any defects or breakdowns occurring within five years of delivery of the freezer. Now suppose also that the credit sale agreement is one which X has the right to cancel within a few days of making it. If he exercises that right of cancellation he would of course not have the freezer (or, if it had already been delivered to him, he would have to let the dealer recover it from him). Nevertheless, he would still have the guarantee and would still have to pay for it—a guarantee for a freezer he has not got! That is the absurd result of exempting the written guarantee from the rule which would otherwise have meant that the guarantee was cancelled when the regulated agreement was cancelled. The Regulations clearly need to be amended.

The third exemption is more sensible. It would not be unusual for a bank manager, before agreeing to grant a bank loan to a new customer, to get that customer first to open a current account at the bank. If the customer did so, then that current account would then become effective immediately and would remain so even if the customer then withdrew from the prospective bank loan agreement or if he took the bank loan and then paid it off earlier than the loan agreement required. That is the sensible result of the third exemption.

The Total Charge For Credit

19–027   The Act makes a basic distinction between the credit and the cost to the debtor of having it. The idea behind having a definition of the "total charge for credit" is that the definition should produce a figure which, if stated to the debtor, will accurately tell him the cost of having the credit. The "credit" and the "total charge for credit" are mutually exclusive. Any sum which is part of the total charge for credit cannot be part of the credit. A simple agreement to borrow £25,000 and to repay it at the end of a year with £25,000 + £3,000

---

[37] SI 2004/2095.

interest involves credit of £25,000 and a total charge for credit of £3,000. A creditor may, however, try to conceal his charges. He may require a repayment of only £25,000 whilst at the same time requiring the debtor, as a precondition to getting the loan, to buy a peanut for £3,000. More subtly, he may, as condition of the loan, require the debtor to take out an insurance policy with a particular insurance company—a company which, perhaps, has agreed to pay the creditor a handsome commission on such new business. There are numerous ways in which a debtor may find that he has to pay for having credit. The definition of the total charge for credit is designed to include such costs so that when the total charge for credit is stated, it represents the true cost of the credit.[38]

The amount of the total charge for credit may have to be calculated for any one of a number of reasons, including the following:

(i) It is a necessary first step towards the calculation of the annual percentage rate of charge.

(ii) It may in some cases have to be included in the agreement in accordance with the formality requirements.[39]

(iii) It will be relevant in determining the debtor's liability under a debtor-creditor agreement after cancellation.[40]

(iv) In conjunction with the annual percentage rate of charge, it will be relevant in determining whether an agreement creates an unfair creditor/debtor relationship.[41]

The calculation of the total charge for credit is to be made at the time the credit agreement is made. It is done simply by adding up all the items which fall within the definition. The definition is a two-stage one. First, there is a general rule. Secondly, there are exceptions. An item is within the definition if it is within the general rule and is not excluded by the exceptions. This is all set out in the Consumer Credit (Total Charge for Credit) Regulations 1980, made under s.20 of the Act.

The General Rule

By this rule, the total charge for credit includes any interest which is payable under the credit agreement and also any charges payable under the five following kinds of transactions: **19–028**

(i) the credit agreement itself;

(ii) transactions entered into in compliance with the credit agreement;

(iii) transactions required to be made or maintained as a condition of the making of the credit agreement;

---

[38] See generally, Devenney and Ryder, "The cartography of the concept of 'total charge for credit' under the Consumer Credit Act 1974" [2006] Conv. 475.
[39] See para.22–028, below.
[40] See para.22–048, below.
[41] See para.24–006, below.

(iv) transactions for the provision of security;

(v) any credit brokerage contract relating to the credit agreement.

Charges under these five different types of transaction are within the general rule even if some other benefit is derived from them (e.g. the peanut or the benefit of the insurance policy referred to earlier). The charges are still included even though they are payable, not by the debtor, but by a relative of his (e.g. if his wife had agreed to buy the peanut as a precondition of the debtor being granted a loan). Furthermore the whole of the charge is included, e.g. in the case of the insurance policy, the whole of the premiums. Until the Regulations were amended in 1989, credit brokerage fees were not included in the definition. It is sensible that they are now included (see item (v) above), since a fee that the customer has to pay in order to be introduced to the source of finance is truly part of the cost of getting the credit.

It may occur that an item within the general rule is something upon which the debtor will be entitled to income tax relief. Nevertheless the whole of that item must be included within the total charge for credit. To put it another way, the calculation must be made on the assumption that the debtor will obtain no tax relief; the fact that he will obtain tax relief is to be ignored.

The Exceptions

19–029 Certain charges are excluded by these exceptions from the total charge for credit. They are:

(a) default charges;

(b) charges that would also be payable by a customer buying the same goods or services for cash instead of on credit terms;

(c) certain charges for the care, maintenance or protection of goods or land;

(d) variable bank charges on current accounts;

(e) certain other charges for transfer of funds and for keeping an account open;

(f) certain club membership and similar charges;

(g) most charges for guarantees;

(h) most insurance premiums.

Default charges are excluded because they are not payable if the debtor honours his agreement. Charges which would be payable by a cash customer (e.g. delivery charges payable on a new car) are excluded because, as a matter of common sense, they are not part of the cost of the credit. This rule also means that if a discount is given to cash customers, and not to credit customers, then the discount is part of the total charge for credit.[42] As to care or maintenance charges, it may be (e.g. in a hire-purchase agreement relating to a colour

---

[42] *R. v Baldwin's Garage* [1988] Crim. L.R. 438.

television) that the credit agreement requires the debtor to enter a maintenance contract covering the goods. In that case, the charges payable under this maintenance agreement are excluded from the total charge for credit, provided the debtor is allowed by the terms of this credit agreement (and in practice has) a free choice as to with whom he makes the maintenance agreement. Also excluded are any maintenance charges which are payable only if something goes wrong; these are excluded even if the debtor is not allowed a free choice as to who is to do the maintaining. The exclusion of variable bank charges (other than interest) on current accounts covers the case where a bank manager agrees to grant a bank loan requiring as a condition that the debtor maintains a current account at his branch. Bank charges on the current account which vary according to the use made of the current account are not part of the total charge for credit under the loan agreement. Also excluded are other charges for the transfer of funds and charges for keeping open an account intended to receive payments towards the repayment of the credit (and payment of charges). This exclusion does not apply, however, if the charges are abnormally high and the debtor does not have reasonable freedom of choice in the matter. The exclusion of club membership fees deals with the situation where, for example, a motoring organisation or a trade union has arrangements whereby a member can obtain credit (perhaps on preferential terms) from a particular finance company. It may well be a term of any resulting credit agreement that the debtor remains a member of the club or trade union. However, his membership fee will still not be part of the total charge for credit provided it entitles the debtor to other benefits besides the credit facilities and provided he was a member before applying for the credit.

With one exception, all charges for guarantees and all insurance premiums are excluded. The exception relates to any guarantee or policy which the creditor requires to be made (or maintained) in order to ensure that the creditor is repaid (fully or partially) in the event of the death, invalidity, illness or unemployment of the debtor.

General Reading

- Bamforth, "Human rights and consumer credit" (2002) 118 L.Q.R. 203;   **19–030**

- Devenney and Ryder, "The cartography of the concept of 'total charge for credit' under the Consumer Credit Act 1974" [2006] Conv. 475;

- Lomnicka, "The reform of consumer credit in the UK" [2004] J.B.L. 129;

- Macleod, "Credit hire in the House of Lords" [2001] J.B.L. 14;

- Macleod, "Credit Hire" [1999] J.B.L. 452;

- Patient, "The Consumer Credit Act 2006" [2006] J.I.B.L.R. 309;

- Philpott, "E-Commerce and Consumer Credit" [2001] J.I.F.M. 131.

Chapter 20

LICENSING

The licensing system created by the Consumer Credit Act is intended to secure consumer protection. The consequences of unlicensed trading are severe for the trader and in the case of malpractices the Office of Fair Trading (operating through the Consumer Credit Licensing Bureau) has wide powers, including that of taking away the trader's licence. The licensing system is not a means of restricting competition and the Consumer Credit Licensing Bureau cannot, for example, refuse a licence or withdraw one on the ground that there are already enough credit traders. The Office of Fair Trading, whose duty it is to administer the licensing system, has the duty of maintaining a public register of licences. Any member of the public can on payment of a fee inspect the register. **20–001**

There are two kinds of licence, a group licence[1] and a standard licence.[2] The vast majority of traders will have to obtain a standard licence. Group licences are not intended for groups of companies. Rather, a group licence is likely to be granted to cover a group of people when it seems unnecessary to ask each of them to apply for a standard licence. This can occur where there is some other means of control over the business practices of members of the group. Thus, for example, the Law Society has obtained a group licence covering all solicitors who hold a practising certificate. The licence is limited to activities arising in the course of the solicitor's practice and does not cover a solicitor carrying on a consumer hire business or operating as a credit reference agency. A solicitor wishing to carry on one of these latter businesses should apply for a standard licence covering those categories (B and I, see below). The rest of this chapter will be concerned with standard licences, which are generally now effective indefinitely as a measure to streamline the licensing regime.[3]

The licensing system is intended to be particularly instrumental in controlling malpractices in the door-to-door peddling of credit, described in the Act as "canvassing off trade

---

[1] s.22(1)(b).
[2] s.22(1)(a).
[3] By virtue of the Consumer Credit Act 2006 which introduced the new s.22(1A). The licence period had previously been five years.

premises". An attempt orally to induce a consumer to enter into a regulated agreement amounts to canvassing off trade premises if[4]:

(a)   it is made during a visit by the canvasser carried out for the purpose of making those oral representations; and

(b)   the visit is to somewhere other than where a business is carried on by the canvasser, the creditor or owner, the supplier or the consumer; and

(c)   the visit is not made in response to an earlier request.

20–002   The canvassing off trade premises of debtor-creditor agreements (e.g. ordinary cash loans) is a criminal offence.[5] There is no such absolute prohibition of the canvassing off trade premises of other regulated agreements. Thus the doorstep promotion of the sale of goods or services (e.g. the installation of double glazing) on credit terms is permitted. However, for it to be lawful to canvass off trade premises these other regulated agreements (i.e. debtor-creditor-supplier agreements and consumer hire agreements), the canvasser must be operating under a licence which specifically and expressly covers such activity. If the Office of Fair Trading finds that a trader is using unfair doorstep methods it may well either withdraw the licence or else vary it so as to remove the authority to canvass off trade premises.

BUSINESS NEEDING A LICENCE

20–003   Broadly, someone needs a licence if he carries on a business in the course of which regulated agreements are made with customers (debtors and hirers) or if he carries on an ancillary credit business. There are now nine categories of standard licence[6]:

Category	Business
A	Consumer credit
B	Consumer hire
C	Credit brokerage
D	Debt adjusting
E	Debt counselling
F	Debt collecting
G	Debt administration
H	Credit information services
I	Credit referencing agencies

In each category it is only if a business (which includes profession or trade) is carried on that a licence is required. Thus if someone on one occasion lends money to a friend—even if the friend is to pay interest—the lender would not be regarded as thereby carrying on a

---

[4] s.48.
[5] See Ch.23.
[6] Under s.24A(4) of the Consumer Credit Act debt adjusting and counselling now require separate licences, and there are new categories for debt administration and credit information services.

business. "A person is not to be treated as carrying on a particular type of business merely because occasionally he enters into transactions belonging to a business of that type".[7] A garage proprietor who (more than occasionally) hired out cars under consumer hire agreements would be carrying on a consumer hire business even if the main part of his business consisted of selling cars and petrol for cash. Though a trader's business may fall predominantly outside the six categories, he still needs a licence if a part of it falls within any of the six categories—unless that part amounts to only "occasional" transactions. *In R. v Marshall*[8] a double glazing firm had, over a period of 16 months, introduced six customers (or told them that they could be introduced) to a source of credit finance. In determining whether the proprietor was carrying on a business of credit brokerage (i.e. whether these six transactions were more than "occasional"), it was immaterial whether the introductions were initiated by the firm (in order to induce customers to buy the firm's products) or by customers simply wanting help. The court declined to say that the transactions were definitely more than occasional. Similarly, a car dealer who never normally provides credit but who on one occasion agrees to supply a car to a friend on hire-purchase terms will not be carrying on a consumer credit business.[9]

If a creditor lends money in order to make a profit, it does not necessarily follow that he is carrying on a business. This is because there is a distinction between carrying on a business and being an investor: *Wills v Wood*.[10] In that case a hotelier had retired, sold his hotel for £26,000 and been advised by his solicitors to invest part of it in buying shares and the remainder in loans secured by mortgage. Thus he gave £11,000 to his solicitors to lend to clients of theirs at about 12 per cent interest. As one loan was paid off it was replaced by another or the money was retained by the solicitors as cash, presumably on deposit with a bank. Taking into account the very small number of loans involved, the lack of advertisement, the restriction of potential borrowers to the clients of one solicitor, the restriction to loans secured on real property and the fact that the interest rate was more comparable to a building society rate than to a money lender's rate, it was held that the retired hotelier was not carrying on a business of money lending but was merely an investor. Although this case was decided under the Moneylenders Acts, the finding that he was not carrying on a business would presumably be the same under the Consumer Credit Act and could mean not only that the creditor need not be licensed, but also that the mortgage loan agreement in question (a £2,000 loan to an individual) would be a "non-commercial agreement".[11]

Someone carrying on a business in more than one category needs a licence covering all the **20–004** categories of his business. A separate licence is not required for each address at which a business is carried on. A bank which has many branches need have only one licence. Where a business is carried on under more than one name, all the names used must be specified on the application and also on the licence. Trading under a name not specified on the licence is unlicensed trading and is a criminal offence.

There are two specific exclusions from the whole of the licensing requirements laid down in s.21. Thus a local authority does not need a licence[12] and neither does a corporate body

---

[7] s.189(2).
[8] (1989) 90 Cr. App. Rep. 73.
[9] See *Hare v Schurek*, para.19–024, above.
[10] [1984] C.C.L.R. 7, (1984) Sol. Jo. 222.
[11] An agreement not made by the creditor or owner in the course of a business carried on by him, s.189(1).
[12] s.21(2).

named in a public general Act of Parliament empowering the body to carry on a business.[13] The latter exception does not excuse companies incorporated under the Companies Act, since that Act does not name companies incorporated under it. The exception does excuse, for example, the Post Office. The fact that these bodies are excused from having to be licensed does not mean that their agreements (i.e. which they make with their customers) are thereby rendered exempt from regulation by the Act. Thus a regulated agreement made by a local authority would have to comply with the documentation requirements of the Act. It is only if a consumer credit or consumer hire agreement falls within the definition of exempt agreement that the agreement itself is not regulated. Subject to the two exceptions just mentioned, someone carrying on a business in one of the nine categories needs to be licensed.

Under s.34 of the Consumer Credit Act 2006 a standard licence shall have effect indefinitely unless either (i) the application requests a licence of specified duration or (ii) the Office of Fair Trading has good reason not to issue an indefinite licence, e.g. due to the applicant's previous dealings etc.[14] This represents a fundamental shift from the licensing system as originally envisaged which allowed for licences of specified duration only.[15] In contrast, a group licence is normally issued only for a limited (five year) duration, unless the Office of Fair Trading thinks there is good reason to the contrary.

Partial Exclusions

20–005   The definitions of the various types of ancillary credit business (categories C through to I) are given in s.145. Section 146 has the effect of excluding from some or all of these definitions certain people who might otherwise have fallen within them. It follows that if someone is excluded from any definition, he need not be licensed under that category. None of these exclusions applies to categories A and B (consumer credit and consumer hire businesses).

Barristers acting as such and solicitors engaged in contentious business are excluded from all categories of ancillary credit business. Although a solicitor not engaged in contentious business is not excluded, he will be covered (except as regards categories B and I) by the group licence in respect of any activity arising in the course of his practice. The creditor or owner is excluded from the definitions of debt counselling, debt adjusting and debt collecting. If this were not so, every time he collected a payment or gave advice to his debtor or hirer, he would need to be licensed in category D, E or F in addition to his category A or B licence. Also excluded from the same definitions is someone who on purchasing the creditor's or owner's business takes over (i.e. by assignment) the debts owed to the business. Of course, in order to carry on the business he has bought, he does need himself to have a category A or B licence. Furthermore, the creditor selling the business can not transfer his licence. The purchaser must apply for his own. He would be wise not to complete the purchase before obtaining it.

Finally there is an exclusion designed to cover a particular type of person. This is the person (typically a housewife) who has what is sometimes called a "home catalogue"

---

[13] s.21(3).
[14] s.22(1C).
[15] Prior to the implementation of the 2006 Act the licence period had settled at five years.

belonging to a mail order company and who acts as the company's agent in selling goods from the catalogue to her friends and acquaintances. The goods are usually sold on credit sale terms and the housewife is not an employee of the company but receives a commission on each sale. She *should* be effectively excluded from the definitions of credit broker (category C), debt adjuster and debt counsellor (categories D and E) and debt collector (category F). This exclusion applies to anyone who is not acting in the capacity of an employee and who[16]:

(a) asks someone to enter either a regulated consumer hire agreement or a debtor-creditor-supplier agreement where the creditor is to be the supplier, and

(b) effects the introduction after canvassing off trade premises.

The difficulty arises when the home catalogue housewife concludes the bargain not during a visit by her to a friend's house but during a visit by a friend (the debtor) to hers. This is because an activity is not within the definition of canvassing off trade premises unless the *canvasser* is making a visit when he or she orally asks the customer to enter the regulated agreement. The housewife could hardly be said to be "visiting" her own house. Thus in this case she is not excluded and falls within the definition of credit broker (and, if she collects payments under the agreements, of debt collector as well). It seems she ought to be licensed if she proposes to conclude bargains when her friends visit her.[17]

UNLICENSED TRADING

A licence covers all lawful activities done in the course of the business whether by the **20–006** licensee or by other persons on his behalf.[18] Under the (now repealed) s.23(2) the Office of Fair Trading had power in granting the licence to expressly limit the activities it covers.[19] Under s.24A in applying for a licence the trader is required to state whether he is applying for a licence with no limit or alternatively for a licence "to cover the carrying on of that type of business only so far as it falls within one or more descriptions of business".[20] The various types of business referred to have already been considered at para.20–003 above. Subject to additional requirements in satisfying the fitness test (considered shortly) there seems to be little reason to limit the licence to specific types of business, particularly when considering the criminal and civil sanctions for unlicensed trading.

Irrespective of whether a licence with no limitation has been applied for, however, a licence does not cover canvassing off trade premises unless it expressly says so. In any case it is the canvassing off trade premises only of debtor-creditor-supplier agreements and regulated consumer hire agreements that can be licensed, it being an offence to canvass off trade premises debtor-creditor agreements.[21] It is unlicensed trading and a criminal offence for anyone to indulge in an activity for which a licence is required, if he is not licensed for

---

[16] s.146(5).
[17] For a fuller explanation, see Dobson, "Do Housewives Need a Licence?" [1980] New L.J. 528.
[18] s.23(1).
[19] Repealed by the Consumer Credit Act 2006, Sch.4 para.1.
[20] s.24A(1)(b).
[21] By virtue of s.49. Thus cash loans cannot be canvassed door-to-door.

that activity.[22] Thus someone who indulges in canvassing off trade premises when that is not expressly covered by his licence will be guilty of unlicensed trading. It is an offence, and it is also unlicensed trading, to trade under a name not specified in the licence.[23] Unlicensed trading, besides being a criminal offence, can also result in agreements being unenforceable.

AGREEMENTS RENDERED UNENFORCEABLE

20–007 There are three ways in which unlicensed trading can render agreements unenforceable.

Regulated Agreements Made by Unlicensed Creditor or Owner

20–008 Section 40(1) creates a general rule that a regulated agreement made when the creditor or owner was unlicensed is not enforceable against the debtor or hirer. It is the time at which the agreement is made that is the relevant time. If at that time the creditor or owner is not licensed to make that particular agreement, then he cannot enforce it. If for example the agreement was made by the creditor canvassing off trade premises and the creditor's licence did not expressly authorise that activity, the agreement will not be enforceable. Section 40 applies only to regulated agreements. Thus other agreements (e.g. exempt agreements) made by an unlicensed trader are fully enforceable. Also the section affects enforcement only by the creditor or owner. It does not prevent the debtor or hirer enforcing the agreement.

There are two exceptions to the general rule in s.40:

(i) It does not apply to non-commercial agreements.[24]

(ii) It does not apply where the Office of Fair Trading makes a validating order, i.e. an order that regulated agreements made by a particular trader during a period when he was unlicensed are to be treated as if he had been licensed.

The second exception enables the Office of Fair Trading in effect to excuse the trader (except for any criminal charge) for not having obtained a licence, if it thinks no harm has been done. In considering any application[25] for a validating order, the following circumstances will be taken into account[26]:

(a) how far customers were prejudiced by the trader's conduct;

(b) whether the trader would have been likely to be granted a licence if he had applied for one;

(c) the degree of culpability on the trader's part for being unlicensed.

[22] s.39(1).
[23] s.39(2).
[24] Made clear by the wording of s.40(1).
[25] It is for the unlicensed trader to apply to the OFT for an order, see s.40(2).
[26] s.40(4).

Where the Office of Fair Trading makes an order the agreements are to be treated as if the   **20–009**
trader did have the necessary licence.[27] The Office of Fair Trading may, however[28]:

(a)   limit the order to specified agreements, or agreements of a specified description or
      agreements made at a specified time; or

(b)   make the order conditional on the doing of specified acts by the applicant.

Agreements for the Services of Unlicensed Ancillary Credit Trader

Any agreement for the services of any unlicensed person carrying on an ancillary business   **20–010**
is generally unenforceable by the party who should have been licensed.[29] The relevant time
is when the agreement is made. Thus an unlicensed credit broker who makes an agreement
to effect an introduction in return for the promise of a fee or commission will be unable to
sue for that fee or commission. It may well be the customer looking for credit who agreed
to pay the fee and who will therefore benefit. Sometimes, however, the credit grantor has
agreed to pay a commission to a broker introducing customers. If the broker was unlicensed
when making the agreement with the credit grantor, the latter will benefit from the agreement
being unenforceable. The rule applies in the same way to all ancillary credit traders (credit
brokers, debt counsellors etc.). The trader must have a licence covering the relevant category.
If someone licensed only as a credit broker makes an agreement to act as debt adjuster, he
will be unable to enforce that agreement. As under s.40, the trader can apply for an order
validating his agreements and the same factors will be taken into account by the Office of Fair
Trading in considering the application.[30]

Regulated Agreements Made After Introduction by Unlicensed Credit Broker

Section 149, in effect, makes the creditor or owner bear the consequences of his credit broker   **20–011**
being unlicensed. A regulated agreement made by a debtor or hirer who was introduced for
the purpose of making that agreement by an unlicensed credit broker is unenforceable against
the debtor or hirer. There are three differences between the position here and that under s.40
(i.e. where the creditor or owner was unlicensed). First, it is the time of the introduction by
the credit broker that is relevant and not the time when the regulated agreement is made.
Secondly, non-commercial regulated agreements are affected. Thirdly, there are two people
entitled to apply for a validating order. Thus the Office of Fair Trading can grant to the credit
broker an order[31] validating agreements for the services of the credit broker, in which case
that validating order, unless the Office of Fair Trading states otherwise, will automatically

---

[27] s.40(2).
[28] s.40(5).
[29] s.148.
[30] s.148(4) provides a non-exhaustive list of factors to be considered by the OFT and replicates the equivalent list
in s.40(4).
[31] Under s.148.

also validate regulated agreements made after introductions by the credit broker. Alternatively the Office of Fair Trading can grant to the creditor or owner an order validating regulated agreements made by that particular creditor or owner after introductions by the unlicensed credit broker.

The moral of s.149 for creditors and owners is to take all reasonable precautions to see that the credit brokers who introduce customers to them are licensed and are licensed to conduct business in the way that they do (e.g. by canvassing off trade premises). If no such steps have been taken, the Office of Fair Trading may well refuse a validating order. Thus, for example the finance company which is creditor in the typical hire-purchase transaction may find that all its agreements made through a particular unlicensed dealer are unenforceable.

OFFICE OF FAIR TRADING'S LICENSING POWERS

20–012   Besides the power to grant or refuse validating orders, the Office of Fair Trading has powers to refuse, to refuse to renew, to vary, to suspend and to withdraw licences. It does not have a free hand in the exercise of these powers. Thus on receipt of a valid application, it *must*[32] grant a standard licence if two criteria are both satisfied:

(i) The applicant is a fit person to engage in the activities to be covered by the licence.[33]

(ii) The name or names under which he applies to be licensed are not misleading or undesirable.[34]

The sorts of thing likely to make an applicant not a fit person are if he or any of his employees, associates, agents or directors has been guilty of violence, fraud or dishonesty, or otherwise persistently broken the law, practised racial or sexual discrimination or indulged in unfair or improper practices. Exactly the same criteria apply in relation to renewals (where for some reason the licence is not of indefinite duration), variations, suspensions, and withdrawals as they do on an initial application. Section 25(2) offers the following non-exhaustive list of factors which shall be considered by the Office of Fair Trading when assessing whether the applicant is a fit person:

(a) the applicant's skills, knowledge and experience in relation to consumer credit businesses, consumer hire businesses or ancillary credit businesses;

(b) such skills, knowledge and experience of other persons who the applicant proposes will participate in any business that would be carried on by him under the licence;

---

[32] This is the result of the word "entitled" in s.25(1) and limits the discretion of the OFT in determining applications to the two factors in s.25(1). This gives rise to two interesting issues. First, the discretion afforded to the OFT is still very wide and secondly, the wording of s.25(1) offers no indication as to whether the OFT *may* grant a licence despite the fitness requirement not being satisfied.
[33] Where an application for a licence with no limitation is made, see s.25(1)(a). Where the application is for a licence limited to certain categories of business, see s.25(1AA)(a).
[34] s.25(1AD).

(c) practices and procedures that the applicant proposes to implement in connection with any such business;

(d) evidence of the kind mentioned in subs.(2A).

Under s.25(2A) any evidence of the following practices by the applicant,[35] shall also be considered:

- Any offence involving fraud or other dishonesty or violence;

- The contravention of any provision made by the Consumer Credit Act 1974 (or a corresponding provision in force in an EEA[36] State);

- The contravention of any provision made by Pt 16 of the Financial Services and Markets Act 2000 relating to consumer credit (or a corresponding provision in force in an EEA State);

- The contravention of any other enactment regulating the provision of credit to individuals or other transactions with individuals (or a corresponding provision in force in an EEA State);

- Any discrimination on grounds of sex, colour, race or ethnic or national origins in, or in connection with, the carrying on of any business;

- Engagement in business practices appearing to the OFT to be deceitful or oppressive or otherwise unfair or improper (whether unlawful or not).

Section 25(2B) expressly includes within the definition of deceitful etc. practices the carrying on of a consumer credit business which appears to the OFT to involve irresponsible lending. This latter provision was inserted by s.29 of the Consumer Credit Act 2006 and ought to be a sufficient deterrent to any lender engaging in irresponsible lending. The practical impact of this addition, however, is uncertain, not least because there is no statutory definition of "irresponsible lending" and so this will remain at the discretion of the Office of Fair Trading. Unsurprisingly, given the vast powers afforded to the Office of Fair Trading under the consumer credit licensing regime, s.25A requires the OFT to publish guidance on how it determines whether an applicant meets the fitness requirement under s.25.[37]   **20–013**

The powers of the Office of Fair Trading in relation to unenforceable agreements under s.40 have already been considered. The Consumer Credit Act 2006, however, introduced an entirely new system of civil penalties which are designed to offer the Office of Fair Trading greater flexibility in ensuring compliance with the licensing requirements. Under the new s.33A the OFT may by notice require the licensee to either do, not do, or to cease doing anything which dissatisfies the Office of Fair Trading. The matters in connection with which such a notice may be given reinforce this wide breadth. Under s.33A(1) a notice may be issued in respect of any of the following[38]:

---

[35] Or any of the applicant's employees, agents or associates (whether past or present), s.25(2A).

[36] European Economic Area.

[37] The current version (January 2008) of the guidance is available from the OFT website *http://www.oft.gov.uk* [Accessed July 17, 2008].

[38] Similar requirements are imposed on any supervisory body in relation to a group licence, see s.33B.

(a) a business being carried on, or which has been carried on, by a licensee or by an associate or a former associate of a licensee;

(b) a proposal to carry on a business which has been made by a licensee or by an associate or a former associate of a licensee; or

(c) any conduct not covered by paragraph (a) or (b) of a licensee or of an associate or a former associate of a licensee.

Where the trader fails to meet the requirements imposed by such a notice, the Office of Fair Trading can impose a civil penalty of not more than £50,000[39] in accordance with s.39A. The Office of Fair Trading has discretion over the actual sum prescribed under the penalty notice, but such notice must[40]:

(a) specify the amount of the penalty that is being imposed;

(b) set out the OFT's reasons for imposing a penalty and for specifying that amount;

(c) specify how the payment of the penalty may be made to the OFT; and

(d) specify the period within which the penalty is required to be paid.

---

[39] s.39A(3).
[40] s.39A(2).

Chapter 21

ADVERTISING AND SEEKING BUSINESS

The Consumer Credit Act places controls and restrictions upon canvassing off trade prem- **21–001** ises. It totally prohibits certain kinds of promotion of credit facilities and it regulates the content of advertisements and quotations.

CANVASSING OFF TRADE PREMISES

The Act has a two-pronged method of protecting the consumer from what can loosely be **21–002** termed "doorstep selling" of credit. By one prong, it makes certain agreements cancellable, i.e. it gives the consumer a short "cooling-off period" in which he can cancel the agreement after he has made it. This prong does not, however, place any restriction or control upon the way in which a customer may be persuaded to make an agreement. The second prong places restrictions and controls upon canvassing off trade premises. The two prongs are entirely independent of each other and it by no means follows that because an agreement is made as a result of canvassing off trade premises, it is cancellable. Similarly, an agreement could be cancellable even though no canvassing off trade premises was involved. The first prong, which deals with cancellation, will be considered in Chapter 24 and will not figure any more in the present chapter.

There are two different kinds of canvassing off trade premises. One is concerned with persuading a member of the public (a consumer) to make a regulated agreement and the other with persuading someone to agree to engage the services of an ancillary credit trader. We shall consider them separately.

Canvassing a Consumer to Make a Regulated Agreement

The definition in s.48 of "canvassing off trade premises" is technical. It deals with oral **21–003** persuasion aimed at getting a customer to make a regulated agreement. Making oral representations in an attempt to induce a consumer to enter into a regulated agreement amounts to canvassing off trade premises if:

(a)   the oral representations are made during a visit by the canvasser carried out for the purpose of making them, and

(b)   the visit is to somewhere other than where a business is carried on by any of the following—namely the canvasser, the creditor or owner, the supplier or the consumer, and

(c)   the visit is not made in response to a request made on a previous occasion.

It is only if the canvassing falls within this definition that it is controlled in the ways shortly to be explained. Thus, there is no control upon visits made to the consumer at the consumer's business premises. A visit made, for example to a shop in order to persuade the shopkeeper to take a loan is not canvassing off trade premises. Nor would it be canvassing off trade premises if the canvasser, having visited some premises (e.g. his golf club) for just one purpose (e.g. to play golf), fell, whilst there, into conversation (e.g with another member) during which he found himself suggesting that the other should consider taking credit (perhaps to buy a new set of golf clubs). It is only if the canvasser made the visit for the purpose of making such a suggestion that he will be canvassing off trade premises.

There are two controls upon activity which does fall within the definition. First, there is a total ban on the canvassing off trade premises of debtor-creditor agreements (e.g. ordinary cash loans). It is a criminal offence under s.49. Even if the visit is made in response to an earlier request, it will still be an offence unless that request was in writing and signed. The second control relates to other regulated agreements. These are not totally prohibited. However, for it to be lawful to canvass off trade premises these other regulated agreements, the canvasser must be operating under a licence which specifically authorises canvassing off trade premises.[1] Thus, whilst doorstep attempts to persuade the consumer to take an ordinary loan are totally banned, the doorstep sale of trading checks and the doorstep promotion of goods or services (e.g. double glazing) on credit terms is allowed, provided the canvasser has a licence specifically authorising it.

21–004   There is one very limited exception to what has been said so far. It arises from a determination by the Office of Fair Trading under s.49(3). It applies only in the case of an ordinary current account (a cheque book account), only where the canvasser is trying to persuade an account holder to take an overdraft on a current account, and only where the canvasser is the creditor or an employee of the creditor. In this case, there is no ban on canvassing off trade premises and no need for specific authorisation in the licence. Thus, a bank manager can visit an existing customer in the customer's home to try to persuade that customer to take an overdraft on a current account.

Canvassing the Services of an Ancillary Credit Trader

21–005   An ancillary credit trader is anyone who carries on a business as a credit broker, debt collector, debt counsellor, debt adjuster, debt administrator, credit information service or

[1] s.23(3).

credit reference agency.[2] The definition here (in s.153) is the same as the definition of the first kind of canvassing off trade premises, except that here the object of the canvassing is to persuade the person who is the target of it to enter into an agreement to engage the services of an ancillary credit trader.

Thus, making oral representations for that purpose amounts to canvassing off trade premises if:

(a) the oral representations are made during a visit by the canvasser carried out for the purpose of making them, and

(b) the visit is to somewhere other than where a business is carried on by any of the following—namely, the canvasser, the canvasser's employer or principal or the person to whom the representations are made, and

(c) the visit is not made in response to a request made on an earlier occasion.

There is just one very strict control upon this second kind of canvassing off trade premises. It is a criminal offence to canvass off trade premises the services of a credit broker, debt adjuster, debt counsellor or a provider of credit information services.[3] This is a total ban, but there is no ban whatsoever upon the canvassing off trade premises of the services of a debt collector, debt administrator or credit reference agency.

CRIMINAL OFFENCES

Circulars to Minors

It is an offence, with a view to financial gain, to send to a minor (someone under 18) a **21–006** circular inviting him to obtain credit (or goods on hire) or to seek further information about it—s.50. If, however, a circular is sent to a minor which includes a statement that loans are not available to anyone under 18, then the offence is not committed because the circular does not amount to an invitation to the minor to obtain credit.[4] The same case decided that if the advertiser had a policy and system to ensure that applications from minors were refused, then also the offence would not be committed, since the advertiser would then clearly not have sent the circular to the minor "with a view to financial gain".

Unsolicited Credit Tokens

It is an offence to issue a credit token to someone who has not asked for it in writing signed **21–007** by himself.[5] This is intended to prevent the unsolicited sending out of credit cards.[6] There is

---

[2] s.145(1). The new categories of debt administration and credit information services were added to the list of ancillary credit traders by the Consumer Credit Act 2006.

[3] s.154.

[4] *Alliance & Leicester Building Society v Babbs* [1993] C.C.L.R. 77.

[5] s.51.

[6] As occurred, for example, when, before the Consumer Credit Act was passed, the Access credit card scheme was launched.

an exception where the credit token is issued as a renewal or replacement for a previous one.[7]

ADVERTISING

Advertisements Controlled by the Act

21–008   There are three sorts of advertisements controlled by the Act (under ss.43 and 151):

(i) Advertisements issued by anyone carrying on a consumer credit or consumer hire business or by anyone carrying on a business providing credit on the security of land. The advertisements which are controlled are those which indicate that the advertiser is willing to provide credit or goods on hire. *Jenkins v Lombard North Central*[8] concerned an advertisement for a car which bore not only the price of the car but also the words "Lombard North Central Limited" together with that company's logo. This was held not to be a controlled advertisement because, although it suggested that the company might provide credit, it did not state as a fact that the company was willing to provide credit. The Consumer Credit (Exempt Advertisements) Order 1985[9] creates a number of exceptions[10] so that an advertisement is not controlled by the Act if it relates to any of the following exempt agreements—namely agreements (other than agreements financing the purchase of land) which are exempt by virtue of them involving (a) trade with a country outside the United Kingdom, or (b) the hire of metering equipment from bodies such as British Gas Plc or water or electricity companies, or (c) repayments not exceeding a specified number.[11] The last of these means that advertisements for exempt charge cards (e.g. American Express) are not controlled by the Act, although advertisements for regulated credit cards are.[12]

(ii) Advertisements issued by any credit brokerage business. Here the advertisements which are controlled are those which advertise the credit brokerage services and those which advertise the services of the credit or hire business to which the credit brokerage business introduces customers.

(iii) Advertisements issued by a debt adjusting or debt counselling business, indicating that it is willing to advise on debts or engage in transactions concerned with the liquidation of debts.

---

[7] For an example of a conviction under this section, see *Elliott v Director-General of Fair Trading* [1980] 1 W.L.R. 977.
[8] [1984] 1 All E.R. 828.
[9] SI 1985/621.
[10] See art.2 for a complete list.
[11] For details of which agreements are within these three categories of exemption, see para.19–018 above.
[12] See also, s.43(2).

The Control

The control over these advertisements is exercised by a number of criminal offences which   **21–009**
it is possible for the advertiser to commit. He commits an offence if the advertisement:

(a) indicates a willingness to supply goods or services on credit terms at a time when
the supplier is not also prepared to supply the goods or services for cash,[13] or

(b) infringes the advertising regulations.[14]

The Consumer Credit Act 1974 also laid down an offence where the advertisement conveys
information which in a material respect is false or misleading.[15] This offence has now fallen
and been subsumed by the general framework of unfair trading practices as laid down by the
Consumer Protection form Unfair Trading Regulations 2008.[16] An illustration of the operation of the old s.46 offence is apparent from the facts of *Rover Group Ltd and Rover Finance
Ltd v Sumner*[17] where the advertiser was convicted since the advertisement was misleading
in that it indicated the cash price of £5,995 and only in very small print in a footnote indicated
that this excluded the cost of delivery and number plates.

Advertising Regulations

The Consumer Credit (Advertisements) Regulations 2004[18] apply to advertisements which   **21–010**
are controlled by the Act and which indicate that the advertiser is willing to provide credit.[19]
The Regulations do not, however, apply to advertisements which on their wording are aimed
solely at business, e.g. "Hire your office photocopier from us" or "Business loans, £500 to
£50,000".[20]
The detail of the Regulations is too great to be given here. Their broad thrust can be
outlined. Their aims are to see that the consumer is given sufficient information[21] in such a
way that he gains a fair impression of what is being advertised and also can make a
meaningful comparison between different sources of credit. The 2004 Regulations[22] remove
the former three-tier approach to credit advertising laid down under Consumer Credit
(Advertisements) Regulations 1989 and create a general duty to comply with "all applicable
requirements".[23] Under reg.3 every advertisement must:

[13] s.45.
[14] See para.21–010, below.
[15] Under s.46.
[16] Sch.4(1) of the 2008 Regulations.
[17] [1995] C.C.L.R. 1.
[18] SI 2004/1484 (as amended). These Regulations replaced the Consumer Credit (Advertisements) Regulations 1989
and came into effect on October 31, 2004.
[19] The regulations no longer apply to advertisements which indicate that the advertiser is willing to provide goods
on hire. Sch.3 (which detailed information to be provided in such advertisements) has been repealed by the
Consumer Protection from Unfair Trading Regulations 2008, sch.4(2), with effect from May 26, 2008. See Ch.17
for an account of the regulations.
[20] reg.10(1).
[21] See, for example, reg.4 which controls the content of such advertisements.
[22] See generally Griffiths, "Consumer credit advertising—transparent at last?" [2006] *Communications Law* 75.
[23] reg.2.

(a) use plain and intelligible language;

(b) be easily legible (or, in the case of any information given orally, clearly audible); and

(c) specify the name of the advertiser.

In order to ensure that a consumer is not misled by the terminology of a credit advertisement the regulations also dictate certain restrictions. These include banning (i) the use of the term "overdraft" for a general running account credit arrangement (i.e. where the facility is not drawing on a current account) and (ii) the use of the term "gift" or similar unless there are no conditions requiring the debtor to return either the credit or the free item.[24]

Quotations, Advertisements and Health Warnings

21–011   There is a rather complicated combination of regulations governing the form and content of written quotations given in response to requests from prospective customers. This includes the Consumer Credit (Content of Quotations) and Consumer Credit (Advertisements) (Amendment) Regulations 1999[25] (as amended in 2000)[26] and the Consumer Credit (Advertisements) Regulations 2004. These do not, however, lay down a comprehensive code for credit and hire quotations; nor do they require a trader to respond to a request for a quotation. They simply require health warnings to be included in advertisements and also in any written quotation given in relation to particular types of agreement. For example, where there is a chance that the customer will be asked to provide his home as security, the quotation must make that fact clear and must include the following warning: "YOUR HOME IS AT RISK IF YOU DO NOT KEEP UP REPAYMENTS ON A MORTGAGE OR OTHER DEBT SECURED ON IT."[27] A further example is where the agreement might be secured on land and the repayments would be made in a currency other than sterling, in which case the quotation must include the warning: "CHANGES IN THE EXCHANGE RATE MAY INCREASE THE STERLING EQUIVALENT OF YOUR DEBT."[28]

A third, and common, example is a mortgage of the debtor's home, typically taken out by an elderly householder in order to realise part of the value of his or her house whilst being allowed still to live in it for the rest of his or her life. Thus the quotations must include a prescribed statement where:

(i) the mortgage does not require repayment of credit or interest while the debtor continues to occupy the home as his main place of residence; or

(ii) the mortgage does not require repayment of the credit (though it may require payment of interest) while the debtor continues to occupy the home as his main

---

[24] See reg.9 for a complete list.
[25] SI 1999/2725.
[26] SI 2000/1797.
[27] See reg.7(2) of the Consumer Credit (Advertisements) Regulations 2004.
[28] reg.7(4).

residence *and* the creditor cannot resell the home to enforce the agreement whilst the debtor continues to occupy the home as his main residence.

The statement which must be included in quotations for such agreements is "CHECK THAT THIS MORTGAGE WILL MEET YOUR NEEDS IF YOU WANT TO MOVE OR SELL YOUR HOME OR YOU WANT YOUR FAMILY TO INHERIT IT. IF YOU ARE IN DOUBT, SEEK INDEPENDENT ADVICE".[29]

General Reading

- Azim-Khan, "Those Winter Sales Offers—Festive Cheer or New Year Gloom?" (2004) 66 *Commercial Law* 54.   **21–012**

- Besemer, "New Rules on Misleading and Comparative Advertising" [2008] *Entertainment Law Review* 115;

- Johnson, "Advertisers Beware! The Impact of the Unfair Commercial Practices Directive" [2005] *Communications Law* 164.

---

[29] reg.7(2).

Chapter 22

FORMATION OF A CONSUMER CREDIT AGREEMENT

Because different types of consumer credit agreements are made in different ways, it will be **22–001** necessary to deal with the different types to some extent separately. Many of the problems arising in connection with hire-purchase, conditional sale and credit sale agreements are due to the fact that the agreement between debtor and creditor (finance company) is often negotiated through the dealer. Thus these agreements will be considered first. Before embarking upon that, we should note that the formality and cancellation provisions of the Consumer Credit Act apply to regulated agreements of all types. These provisions and also provisions relating to credit brokers' fees and credit reference agencies will be considered later in this chapter.

HIRE-PURCHASE, CONDITIONAL SALE AND CREDIT SALE AGREEMENTS

Offer, Acceptance and Revocation

As we have seen, the customer usually makes an offer to the finance company by filling in **22–002** a form and leaving it with the dealer. That offer will usually be accepted by the finance company posting their acceptance to the customer. In that case the contract will be made when the acceptance is put in the post. It usually takes several days and sometimes much more. At any time before the letter of acceptance is posted (or the offeror is in some other way informed of the finance company's acceptance) the offeror can revoke his offer. Normally, in order for revocation to be effective, it must actually be notified to the other party before the contract is made. So, if the customer (i.e. the offeror) posts to the finance company a revocation of his offer, that revocation will be effective only if it actually arrives before the finance company posts its letter of acceptance. However, there is no need for the revocation to be in writing. Furthermore, the dealer is agent of the finance company for the purpose of receiving revocations. Thus, when the customer tells the dealer that he revokes his offer to the finance company, that has the same effect as if he had told the finance company. Provided he does so before the finance company posts its letter of acceptance, there will be no contract between the customer and the finance company.

In *Financings v Stimson*[1] the customer filled in at the dealer's premises a hire-purchase proposal form and he was allowed to drive the car away. The dealer sent the form off in the usual way to the finance company. After four days the customer returned the car to the dealer declaring that he did not want it. Shortly after that the car was stolen from the dealer's premises. It was recovered fairly quickly but in a badly damaged state. The following day the finance company purported to accept the customer's offer and sent him a copy of the "agreement". The Court of Appeal held that there was no agreement and therefore no contract for two reasons: (i) by returning the car to the dealer and declaring that he did not want it, the customer revoked his offer to the finance company. Communication of that revocation to the dealer was sufficient, as the latter was the finance company's agent for the purpose of receiving a revocation; (ii) the customer's offer to the finance company must be taken to have been conditional upon the goods being in substantially the same state at the time of acceptance as they were at the time the offer was first made. Thus for two reasons the customer's offer was, at the time in question, incapable for being accepted. There being no contract, the customer was under no liability to the finance company.

The position as so far stated is that at common law. The customer's position at common law is strengthened where s.57 of the Consumer Credit Act applies. That section applies to all regulated hire-purchase and conditional sale agreements other than non-commercial ones and it applies to all regulated credit sale agreements other than non-commercial agreements and small agreements. It has two important provisions. First, the dealer is agent of the creditor for the purpose of receiving notice (oral or written) that the debtor's offer is withdrawn.[2] This reinforces the rule in *Financings v Stimson*. Secondly, the withdrawal of either party from a prospective agreement takes effect as if the agreement[3]:

(i) had been actually made, and

(ii) had been a cancellable one, and

(iii) had been cancelled by the debtor under s.69.

22–003   Thus the debtor will be in the same position as he would be in after cancelling a cancellable agreement. As we shall see shortly the debtor is in a strong position after cancellation. Thus s.57 has the effect of strengthening his position after withdrawal from a prospective agreement.

A withdrawal from a prospective agreement means that there is no agreement and therefore no obligation under the agreement. If the debtor has taken delivery of any goods he will have to return them and if he has made any payments he will be entitled to recover them. However, where s.57 applies, the effect of treating it as a cancelled agreement is that the

---

[1] [1962] 3 All E.R. 386.
[2] s.57(2) and s.57(3).
[3] s.57(1) and s.57(4).

debtor has, in addition, a lien over the goods to compel the repayment. This entitles him to retain possession of the goods until he is repaid. This could be very useful where for example the dealer has allowed the customer to drive away the car as soon as the customer had signed the proposal form and paid the deposit. If the debtor then withdrew his offer to the finance company, he could retain possession of the car until his deposit was repaid.

Uncertainty

It is true of any agreement that it is not a contract unless the parties have agreed on the basic   **22–004**
terms. We saw in Chapter 2 that an agreement for the sale of goods will not normally constitute a contract if the parties have not agreed on something as basic as the price.

Similarly, a hire-purchase agreement may be void for uncertainty. In *Scammell v Ouston*,[4] Ouston had been negotiating to acquire a van from Scammell on hire-purchase terms. They reached an agreement "that the balance of purchase price can be had on hire-purchase terms over two years". Ouston sued Scammell for non-delivery. The House of Lords found Scammell not liable because there was no contract, the agreement being too vague. The parties had not reached any agreement as to what the hire-purchase terms were to be.

Mistake

It may happen that the parties, though believing themselves to have agreed the terms, have   **22–005**
not in fact done so. In *Campbell Discount v Gall*[5] the customer selected a car from the dealer's stock. They agreed that the customer would apply to a finance company to acquire it on hire-purchase terms—the cash price being £265. The customer signed the finance company's proposal form in the usual way and left it with the dealer for the latter to fill in the details and send it off to the finance company. The dealer filled in the cash price as £325. The finance company accepted this proposal. The Court of Appeal held that there was no contract between the finance company and the customer, because they were not agreed on the price. In law one is bound by an agreement made by one's agent.[6] However, the Court rejected any idea that the dealer was, for the purpose of completing the form, agent for either party. Thus, although the dealer is agent of the finance company for the purpose of receiving revocations, it was held that he is not, unless expressly authorised, their agent for the purpose of making a hire-purchase contract. This is the position at common law.

The rule that the dealer is not normally the agent of the finance company was confirmed in *Branwhite v Worcester Works*.[7] The facts were the same as in *Campbell Discount v Gall*. The customer signed the proposal form leaving the cash price still to be filled in. He paid to the dealer the initial deposit (£130) which would be due to the finance company if the proposal was accepted. The dealer filled in the wrong cash price on the proposal form, which he sent off, together with his own offer to sell the vehicle, to the finance company. The

---

[4] [1941] A.C. 251.
[5] [1961] 1 Q.B. 431.
[6] See generally Pt III, below.
[7] [1969] 1 A.C. 552.

finance company accepted both these proposals and sent to the dealer the cash price less the deposit (£130) which the dealer had already received from the customer. It was assumed and accepted that following *Gall's* case there was no valid contract between the finance company and the customer because they were not agreed on the price. The customer therefore claimed the return from the finance company of his deposit of £130, arguing that the dealer who had received it was agent of the finance company in doing so and that therefore the dealer receiving it was equivalent to the finance company itself receiving it. This argument was rejected. The dealer is not, unless expressly authorised, agent of the finance company for the purpose of receiving deposits. However, the customer was held entitled to the return of his money on a different ground—namely that the finance company had itself received the deposit. Although the dealer had not actually sent the £130 to the finance company, the latter had nevertheless obtained it by deducting it from the purchase money which it had sent to the dealer. There being no contract between the customer and the finance company, the customer was entitled to the return of his initial deposit on the ground of a total failure of consideration.

Branwhite's case (like *Gall's* case) was decided upon the assumption that there was no contract between the customer and the finance company. This assumption was wrong. It does not follow that there is no contract just because the dealer is nobody's agent and sends the finance company a form with figures different from those intended by the customer. This is because of the rule that normally someone who signs a document intended to have legal effect is bound by the terms of that document if the other party (here the finance company) relies upon that signature and is unaware that the document does not accord with the signer's intentions. In *United Dominions Trust Ltd v Western*[8] the customer and dealer agreed a price for a car and the dealer produced a finance company's proposal form for the customer to sign. This he did, leaving the dealer subsequently to fill in the agreed figures. He believed it to be a hire-purchase proposal form but it was in fact a proposal for a loan agreement. The dealer did not disillusion him and, unknown to the customer, filled in, not the agreed figures, but inflated figures. He then sent the form off to the finance company, which duly accepted the proposal as it then appeared. The Court of Appeal held that the customer was bound by the terms of the document he had signed, including the figures subsequently inserted by the dealer. Thus the position at common law can be summarised as follows. The dealer (unless expressly authorised by the finance company) is not the finance company's agent. The customer is bound by the terms of the document he signs unless the finance company knows that it does not accord with the customer's intentions. That is so, irrespective of whether he signs a completed document or he signs an uncompleted one leaving it to be completed by someone else. The position would be very different if the dealer were the agent of the finance company. In that case there would be no binding agreement because the finance company would be regarded as knowing what its agent knows, namely that the proposal form does not represent the customer's intended offer.

22–006   The common law rule, settled in *Branwhite's* case, is that the dealer, who typically has possession of the finance company's proposal forms and has knowledge of the finance company's charges and who may help the customer complete the form, is not normally agent of the finance company. It is possible, however, that exceptional facts could exist which in a particular case could establish the dealer as agent. That occurred *in Purnell Secretarial*

[8] [1976] Q.B. 513.

Services v Lease Management Services Ltd.[9] The dealer was Canon (South West) Ltd, from whom the customer had bought several photocopiers over a period of years. During a visit by the dealer's sales representative, the customer made it plain that it was essential that any new machine should be capable of making "paper plates" as indeed the demonstration model was. On this basis the customer signed an agreement to hire a new machine, only to discover after delivery that the machine was incapable of making "paper plates". It transpired that the customer had made the hire agreement not, as the customer had thought, with the dealer, but with a finance company, Lease Management Services Ltd. This was a surprise to the customer since the agreement was headed "Canon (South West) Finance" and below that in a large box beside the word "supplier" appeared "Canon (South West) Limited", the word "Canon" being printed in that company's distinctive logo. Much further down, in more tightly typed print, there appeared the words "Lessor/Owner: Leaser Management Services Limited trading as Canon (South West) Finance". It was held that the finance company, Lease Management Services, by customising its form, had chosen to identify itself with Canon (South West) Ltd and had thereby misled the customer into thinking the contract was with Canon (South West) Ltd. Therefore the finance company was estopped from denying the authority of Canon (South West) Ltd's staff to speak for the finance company. The dealer was agent (by estoppel) of the finance company which was thus liable for misrepresentations and breaches of promises made by the dealer. This case involved a hire agreement and not a hire-purchase agreement but the common law principles are the same in relation to each.

The common law rule that for most purposes the dealer is not the finance company's agent has in the case of regulated agreement, been overturned. Section 56(2) of the Consumer Credit Act provides that antecedent negotiations in relation to the goods shall be deemed to be conducted by the dealer "in the capacity of agent of the creditor as well as in his actual capacity".

The dealer is, by virtue of s.56, agent of the finance company in any antecedent negotiations with the customer—and negotiations include any dealings between customer and dealer. That means that any deposit received by the dealer from the customer is received by him as agent for the finance company. Thus if there is no binding agreement between the finance company and the debtor, the latter can reclaim the deposit from the finance company; and that is so even if the finance company never received it from the dealer.

Non Est Factum

Someone who signs a document in the mistaken belief that it is of a totally different type can   **22–007** evade liability on his signature provided he was not careless in signing. He can plead non est factum—that it was not his deed. If the plea succeeds, his signature is null and void. There are two requirements for the plea to succeed:

  (a) The document must be radically different from what the signer believed.

  (b) The signer must not have been careless in signing.

[9] [1994] C.C.L.R. 127.

A mistake merely as to the details, e.g. as to the number of instalments or the dates when due, will not be sufficient. Believing a personal loan agreement to be a hire-purchase agreement is not a sufficient mistake either.[10] However, if the signer believes himself to be witnessing a will or to be guaranteeing a friend's debt when he is in fact signing a hire-purchase agreement, that is a sufficient difference.[11]

Even if the signer can establish a sufficient mistake, he will usually fail because it will usually have been careless of him not first to have read what he signed. He will therefore find it easier for the plea to succeed if he is illiterate or blind or if, like the old lady in *Gallie v Lee*,[12] he had just lost his glasses.

Misrepresentation

22–008 If before the contract is made, one party makes an untrue statement of fact which induces the other party to make the contract, the latter may have a remedy for misrepresentation. The principles applicable and remedies available were set out in Chapter 6.

A particular problem arises where goods are selected from a dealer's stock and subsequently acquired on instalment terms from a finance company. The problem is that most of the statements made to the customer to persuade him to have the goods are made not by the other party to the instalment contract (the finance company) but by the dealer.

We have already seen that if such a statement proves to be untrue, the customer may have a claim for damages from the dealer for breach of collateral warranty.[13] Does the customer have a remedy also against the finance company for misrepresentation? This is an important question because if he does, not only may he be entitled to damages from the finance company, but he may also be able to rescind the contract in accordance with the principles set out in Chapter 6. However, the answer at common law is "no". There is a remedy for misrepresentation only in respect of statements made by one party or his agent to the other party. For most purposes (other than receiving revocation of an offer) the dealer is not agent of the finance company. Thus when a dealer makes statements about the goods, he is not, unless expressly authorised, doing so as agent of the finance company.

22–009 Although that is the common law position, it has in the case of regulated agreements been reversed by the Consumer Credit Act. By s.56 the dealer is a negotiator in antecedent negotiations and in conducting these negotiations the dealer is deemed to be an agent of the finance company. Antecedent negotiations begin when the dealer and the customer first get into communication and that includes communication by advertisement. The antecedent negotiations include any representations made by the dealer. Section 56 is important in that, in respect of misrepresentations about the goods by the dealer, it confers upon the customer the armoury of the law of misrepresentation with which to attack the finance company. In particular he will be entitled to rescind the regulated agreement. It is sufficient that he gives notice of rescission to the dealer, for by s.102 of the Consumer Credit Act the dealer is agent of the finance company for receiving notice of rescission.

[10] See *United Dominions Trust v Western* above.
[11] *Muskham Finance v Howard* [1963] 1 Q.B. 904.
[12] [1971] A.C. 649.
[13] See *Andrews v Hopkinson*, para.18–007, above.

By the terms of s.56(1)(b), the antecedent negotiations in which the dealer is deemed to be agent of the creditor are those conducted by him "in relation to goods sold or proposed to be sold" by the dealer to the creditor. Consider the following situation. A customer has a car on hire-purchase terms and is still paying off the instalments under her hire-purchase agreement with finance company X. She approaches a car dealer asking to trade in her existing car and to acquire a new one on hire-purchase. Enquiries made of finance company X reveal that the settlement figure needed to pay off the customer's existing debt is £1,000. The car dealer suggests that the customer acquires the new car under a hire-purchase agreement with finance company Z. The customer agrees and they come to an arrangement. It is that: the cash price of the new car is £6,000; the trade-in allowance for the existing one is £3,000; the customer completes a hire-purchase proposal form of finance company Z proposing to take the new car on hire-purchase terms, make a down payment of £2,000 and pay the balance of £4,000 (plus credit charges) in monthly instalments over three years. The car dealer undertakes to receive the trade-in car, to pay off the £1,000 owing to finance company X and to use the balance of the trade-in allowance as the customer's £2,000 down payment under the new hire-purchase agreement. Finance company Z accepts the customer's proposal and pays the car dealer £4,000 (i.e. the cash price of £6,000 less the £2,000 down payment received, as part of the value of the traded-in car, by the car dealer direct from the customer). The customer takes delivery of the new car and subsequently discovers that the car dealer has gone out of business, disappeared and has never kept his promise to pay the £1,000 to finance company X. Can the customer claim that finance company Z is liable for breach of the dealer's (its agent's?) promise to pay the settlement figure to finance company X? Yes. For the customer her buying of the new car and the trade-in arrangement and settlement of her debt on her traded-in car were all one transaction. Thus the dealer's promise to pay off the customer's existing debt was something done "in relation to" the car she was buying.[14]

Legality

A party who makes a contract knowing it to be illegal will be unable to sue the other party. **22–010** In *Snell v Unity Finance*[15] the customer made a hire-purchase contract in the usual way with a finance company. He had not enough money to pay the minimum deposit required by regulations then in force. The cash price of the car was £185. The minimum deposit required by the regulations was 20 per cent, but the customer had only £25. The dealer and the customer filled in the forms to show (wrongly) that the customer had paid a deposit of £50 and that the cash price was £210. The finance company accepted the proposals. Later the customer sued the finance company on the ground that the car was defective and not reasonably fit for its purpose. He lost because the court would not allow him to enforce an illegal contract. Incidentally, there have been no regulations requiring a minimum deposit, since the last regulations were revoked in 1982.

Suppose that in *Snell v Unity Finance* the customer had defaulted in his payments. In that case the finance company could have enforced the agreement against him and sued him for the arrears, because the finance company was not *in pari delicto*, i.e. as much to blame as the

---

[14] *Forthright Finance Ltd v Ingate* [1997] 4 All E.R. 99.
[15] [1964] 2 Q.B. 203.

customer. The finance company could also have exercised its right to recover possession of the goods on default by the customer, for the same reason. However, there is also an alternative reason. Under a hire-purchase agreement ownership does not pass until all the instalments have been paid and the option exercised. Until then, the finance company is owner and that ownership gives it the right to recover the goods (or their value) unless the customer can establish a right to retain them.[16] If, on the other hand, the customer pays off all the instalments and exercises his option, then ownership passes to him and this happens even under an illegal contract.[17] The right (if any) of the creditor (i.e. the owner) to recover possession of the goods on default by the debtor (i.e. the customer) will be considered further at paras 25–014 and 25–015.

OTHER REGULATED AGREEMENTS

22–011   The contracts we have considered so far in this chapter (i.e. hire-purchase, conditional sale and credit sale agreements) have one thing in common—namely that the credit agreement and the contract by which the customer agrees to have the goods are one and the same thing. That being so they are (i.e. it is) made at the same time. However, we come to consider a number of other kinds of credit agreement where often the seller and the creditor are two different people, where the customer therefore makes two agreements and where he will usually make one before the other. This fact can be crucial. Usually the credit agreement will be made first so that the debtor then has the funds or the credit facilities to make the purchase. Thus someone who has a credit card will have made his credit agreement (i.e. the credit card agreement) when he accepted his card by signing it or first using it.[18] When some time later he uses his card to purchase some goods he will not be making a new credit agreement but simply using the credit facilities available under the credit agreement made earlier. Thus although the dealer who sells him the goods is made by the Act agent of the creditor, he is not the agent of the creditor in the making of the credit agreement. This is because the debtor will not have made contact with the dealer until after the credit agreement was made.

There are two people who are to a greater or lesser extent deemed to be the agent of the creditor or owner—namely the debtor's or hirer's representative in negotiations and the negotiator in antecedent negotiations.

Customer's Representative

22–012   The Act uses the formula "any person who, in the course of a business carried on by him, acts (or acted) on behalf of the debtor or hirer in any negotiations for the agreement".[19] This formula clearly includes those persons who run businesses whereby they arrange loans or other forms of credit for the customer. They do not grant the credit themselves but will negotiate on behalf of the customer with a prospective creditor. They sometimes describe

---

[16] *Bowmakers v Barnet Instruments* [1945] K.B. 65.
[17] *Belvoir Finance v Stapelton* [1971] 1 Q.B. 210.
[18] s.66.
[19] s.57(3)(b).

themselves as finance brokers. It is also possible for a customer's own solicitor or accountant to fall within the formula—if for example the customer got him to negotiate a loan for the customer. Anyone falling within the formula is deemed for three limited purposes to be agent of the creditor or owner. Someone falling within the formula will in this book be described as the customer's representative. The customer's representative is of course primarily an agent of the customer and is not agent of the creditor or owner except where the Consumer Credit Act states that he is.

The three purposes for which he is made the agent of the creditor or owner are:

    (i) For receiving notice from the customer that the customer withdraws his offer to enter a regulated agreement.[20]

    (ii) For receiving notice of cancellation.[21]

    (iii) For receiving notice from the customer that the customer rescinds his regulated agreement.[22]

Section 102 should not be misunderstood. The customer's representative is not the agent of the creditor or owner for the purpose of making representations. Therefore s.102 does not mean that misrepresentations by the customer's representative will entitle the customer subsequently to rescind his agreement with the creditor. It means simply that if for some other reason (e.g. a misrepresentation made by the creditor himself) the customer is entitled to rescind a regulated agreement, it is sufficient that he gives notice of that rescission to the customer's representative. Whenever the Act makes someone the agent of the creditor or owner for the purpose of receiving a notice or payment, he is under a duty to the creditor or owner to transmit it to him forthwith.[23]

Negotiator in Antecedent Negotiations

A negotiator in antecedent negotiations is a deemed agent of the creditor or owner. The purpose for which he is deemed the creditor's or owner's agent include and are wider than those for which the customer's representative is a deemed agent. Thus if a customer's representative falls also within the definition of a negotiator in antecedent negotiations, he can be regarded simply in the latter capacity.   **22–013**

There are just three types of person who fall within the definition of a negotiator in antecedent negotiations[24]:

    (a) The creditor or owner. Plainly no question of agency arises here.

    (b) The dealer in the case of a hire-purchase, conditional sale or credit sale agreement. This was considered in the earlier part of this chapter.

    (c) The dealer (termed by the Act, the supplier) in the case of any other debtor-creditor-supplier agreement.

[20] s.57.
[21] s.69, see para.22–043, below.
[22] s.102.
[23] s.175.
[24] s.56.

Our concern here then is with who falls within category (c). Debtor-creditor-supplier agreements other than those mentioned in (b) include credit card agreements and trading check agreements.[25] Thus the trader who supplies goods under a credit card agreement (i.e. because the buyer uses his credit card instead of paying cash) is a negotiator within s.56.

22–014   Any person (except the creditor) falling within the definition of a negotiator in s.56 is deemed in conducting negotiations with the debtor (the customer) to be an agent of the creditor.[26] This does not however alter any other capacity he may have. Thus the supplier of goods under a credit card agreement is a seller of goods to the customer as well as being an agent of the creditor in negotiations with the customer. Section 56 gives a wide meaning to the "negotiations" during which the negotiator is agent of the creditor. These negotiations begin when the negotiator and the customer first get into communication (including communication by advertisement). The negotiations include any representations made by the negotiator to the customer and any other dealings between them. Thus statements (e.g. about the quality of the goods) made by the negotiator during the negotiations are made by him in two capacities. They are regarded as made not only by the dealer but also by the creditor (because made by his agent). The exact effect of them being so regarded will be considered a little later.

"Antecedent" needs to be explained. Section 56 talks of a negotiator in antecedent negotiations. Antecedent means previous or earlier—but previous to what, earlier than what? It is clear from category (c) above that it is possible for a supplier to be a negotiator in antecedent negotiations which occur after the relevant credit agreement has been made, e.g. the supplier of goods under a credit card agreement. Thus antecedent sometimes means previous to the making of a credit agreement (e.g. in categories (a) or (b) above) and sometimes means previous to the making of an agreement to be financed by an already existing credit agreement.

Let us put it another way. In the case of a hire-purchase agreement antecedent negotiations will occur before the credit agreement (i.e. the hire-purchase agreement) is made. In the case of a purchase of goods by use of a credit card, the antecedent negotiations will occur before the purchase but after the credit agreement was made. Although representations made by the dealer to the customer will in both cases be treated as if made also by the creditor, the effect of that will be much more significant when those statements were made before the credit agreement was made (i.e. in the hire-purchase case). In that case a misrepresentation by the creditor will entitle the debtor to rescind the whole credit agreement in accordance with the principles outlined in Chapter 6. However, a misrepresentation by the creditor after the credit agreement was made (e.g. in the credit card situation) will not entitle the debtor to rescind the whole credit agreement. It will, however, entitle him (as we shall shortly see) to rescind that aspect of the credit agreement relating to the purchase in question.

Offer and Acceptance

22–015   It is true of any contract that the contract is made at the time when both sides agree to be bound by the same terms, i.e. when one side makes an offer which the other accepts.

---

[25] See Ch.21, above.
[26] s.56(2).

To discover whether or when an acceptance occurred the communications between the parties must be examined. We have seen that in the case of a hire-purchase agreement the finance company will require the customer to make an offer by filling in its proposal form containing the terms of the prospective agreement. The agreement (i.e. the contract) will be made if and when the finance company communicate to the customer their acceptance of his offer. Other credit agreements are not always made in the same way. Thus a customer who wishes to have a credit card—i.e. to enter into a credit card agreement—will no doubt be asked to fill in an application form. He may find, however that the credit card company, although it is satisfied with the application, regards the application not as an offer but as only a request for the company to make an offer. Thus the customer is likely to receive an offer (together with the credit card) from the company.

The offer will state that the customer will accept the offer when he signs or uses the credit card. The agreement will be made therefore when the customer first signs or first uses the card. Arrangements vary from one creditor to another. Some will insist on the customer making the offer and others will insist on making the offer themselves and leaving the customer to accept it. Yet other creditors will not invariably be insistent one way or the other. Thus a bank manager may make an offer of an overdraft to one customer and from another customer receive an offer to take an overdraft. Whichever party makes an offer, the agreement will be made when the acceptance of it by the other party takes effect. In the case of regulated agreements the exact point of time when the agreement is made has added significance. Not only is it important because a withdrawal of an offer cannot be effective after acceptance of the offer but it also marks the beginning of the seven-day period within which a second copy of the agreement may have to be served upon the customer. This will be dealt with later under the formalities provision.

Withdrawal of Offer

An offer can be withdrawn at any time before the offer has been effectively accepted. The **22–016** time when acceptance takes effect was explained in Chapter 2—in particular, if the post was expected to be used, the acceptance takes effect upon posting. This is a general rule of the law of contract and applies therefore to regulated agreements. There is also a general rule that a withdrawal of an offer does not take effect upon posting but only upon its receipt or communication to the other party. Thus a withdrawal will have no effect unless it actually arrives before the acceptance is posted. If it does not, both sides are bound and neither can back out.[27]

Section 57 applies to prospective regulated agreements which are subject to the formalities requirements—and that includes most regulated agreements. Its effects are twofold as they are in relation to hire-purchase agreement. First, the customer's representative and the negotiator in antecedent negotiations are deemed to be agents of the creditor or owner for receiving notice of withdrawal by the customer. Secondly, where either party withdraws from a prospective agreement, the debtor or hirer will be in the same position as he would be in if the agreement had been made, had been a cancellable one and had been cancelled under s.69. That position will be explained later.

[27] i.e. unless it is a cancellable agreement, see para.22–040, below.

We will now consider some particular types of regulated agreement in the light of what has so far been said in this chapter.

CREDIT CARDS

22–017 By s.57 a negotiator in antecedent negotiations—i.e. the supplier of goods under the credit card agreement—is agent of the creditor for the purpose of receiving from the debtor notice withdrawing an offer to enter the credit agreement. However, this will be of little importance in practice because an offer cannot be withdrawn once it has been accepted and the debtor is unlikely to attempt to get credit by means of his credit card agreement until after the offer has been accepted (and after the credit card agreement has therefore been made). In any case a great many credit card agreements are made, not by an offer from the debtor which the creditor accepts, but by an offer by the creditor to the debtor (the card holder) which the latter accepts by signing or using his credit card.

It has already been seen that by virtue of s.56 representations by the supplier to the debtor are made by him also as agent of the creditor. It was also seen that this would not enable the debtor to rescind the whole credit card agreement. It would, however, entitle him to rescind that part of the credit card agreement relating to the transaction in relation to which the misrepresentation was made. This requires explanation. There is no doubt that a credit card agreement (unless it is exempt like certain American Express and Diners Club agreements) is itself a regulated running-account credit agreement.[28] As a matter of ordinary contract law, that agreement is a standing offer under which the credit card company is offering credit to the card holder. The card holder is not committed to take any particular amount of credit or indeed any credit at all. He may keep the card and never use it. When he uses it to pay, say, £40 for a pair of shoes he accepts the standing offer to provide him with credit and the accepts it to the extent of £40 worth of credit. In thus accepting the standing offer he creates a contract with the credit card company for the provision to him of £40 worth of credit. Each time he uses the card he makes a new contract with the credit card company. Suppose the supplier makes a misrepresentation (e.g. the shoe seller falsely states the shoes to be 100 per cent leather). If the credit card agreement is a regulated one, that is a misrepresentation by the credit card company, i.e. through their agent, a negotiator in antecedent negotiations. It has presumably induced not just the sale of the shoes but also the accompanying use of the credit card. The card holder therefore has the right to rescind the contract for the £40 worth of credit. This is because a misrepresentation by the other party to that contract (the credit card company) induced him to make it. He could exercise this right by informing the credit card company that he is rescinding the transaction. He would then be entitled to refuse to make any payments relating to that particular transaction. Of course, if he had made some repayment of the £40 to the credit card company, he might be regarded as having affirmed the contract and thereby having lost the right of rescission. In an appropriate case the card holder may even wish to claim damages from the credit company for the misrepresentation.[29]

As already observed, at common law a credit card agreement amounts to a standing offer and thus each new use of the card creates a new contract between the card holder and the

[28] See para.19–007, above.
[29] For an explanation of the remedies available for misrepresentation see Ch.6, above.

credit card company. It is therefore tempting to regard each such new contract as a new regulated agreement. Such an approach would be wrong, contrary to the scheme of the Act.[30] Every time a new regulated agreement is made, the formality and documentation provisions have to be complied with. The Act clearly contemplated that with a running-account credit agreement those formalities could be satisfied when the agreement was first made and would not apply each time the agreed credit facility was used.[31]

In practice it will be in only very rare cases that a card holder will need to rely upon s.56 **22–018** to make a claim against the credit card company. He has considerable rights against the supplier and will usually get satisfaction direct from him for any misrepresentation or breach of contract by the supplier.[32] Where the supplier agrees to take back the goods and give a refund, he will not usually hand money over to the card holder but will instead credit the card holder's credit card account with the credit card company. Even where he cannot obtain satisfaction from the supplier (perhaps because the latter has disappeared or become insolvent), the card holder will very often be able to make a claim under s.75 against the credit card company for the supplier's misrepresentation or breach of contract. It is only where s.75 does not apply (e.g. where the cash price of the item in question did not exceed £100) that the card holder will be forced to rely upon s.56.[33] So far it has been assumed that there is just one card holder. Sometimes, however someone with a credit card agreement has a second person (often the husband or wife) who also has a card which can be used on the same account. Where it is the latter who has used his card on the purchase in question, can he rely on s.56 in the same way as if he were the principal card holder? The answer depends upon the same arguments as apply to whether he may claim under s.75. A similar point is that s.56 probably cannot be relied upon by any card holder who made his credit card agreement before April 1, 1977—though there probably are not too many such credit card agreements which are still operating. Here again there is a similar issue in relation to s.75.[34] The debtor might not use his credit card as a means of paying the dealer, but might instead use his credit card to obtain a cash loan and then use the cash to make a purchase from the dealer. In this case the credit card agreement will, in relation to the loan and subsequent purchase, be for unrestricted-use credit and will be a debtor-creditor agreement.[35] If in this case the debtor were able to show a misrepresentation or breach of contract by the dealer, that would not give him any claim against the creditor. The dealer would not be an agent of the creditor because he would not in this case fall within the definition of a negotiator in antecedent negotiations. Also s.75 would not apply to give a remedy against the creditor. The debtor would thus be left to his remedies against the dealer.

CHECK TRADING

The supplier will always be a negotiator within the meaning of s.56 and will therefore be **22–019** agent of the creditor. Also the credit agreement will usually already have been made before the debtor approaches the supplier of the goods or services.

[30] See [1978] New L.J. 448.
[31] For a fuller analysis, see Dobson, "Credit Cards" [1979] J.B.L. 331.
[32] See Chs 6 and 7.
[33] s.75 is explained at para.23–003, below.
[34] See generally the treatment of s.75 at para.23–004, below.
[35] See para.19–015, above.

With check trading it can happen that the customer first sees the item in the supplier's showroom, indulges in antecedent negotiations with the salesman and then goes to the creditor to make the necessary credit agreement. This situation is likely to occur with more expensive items in which case the document he obtains from the creditor is likely to be termed a trading voucher and be specifically restricted to the purchase of the specified item. If this sequence of events has occurred, any misrepresentation made by the supplier to the customer before the latter made his trading voucher agreement will entitle the customer to rescind both his agreements, i.e. not only the agreement with the supplier but also the trading voucher agreement. Furthermore, in order to rescind the latter (as well as the former) it is sufficient that the customer gives notice of rescission to the supplier since by s.102 the supplier is agent of the creditor for the purpose of receiving notice of rescission.

Section 75 may enable the debtor to bring a claim against the creditor for a breach of contract or a misrepresentation by the supplier.

CASH LOAN

22–020   It is with a cash loan that there is more likely to be a customer's representative involved, who is agent of the creditor for certain purposes including the receiving of a withdrawal of the customer's offer to enter the regulated agreement. Also, even though the debtor borrows the cash from the creditor and uses it to buy goods or services from the dealer, it is nevertheless possible for the latter to be a negotiator in antecedent negotiations, i.e. agent of the creditor. It would happen where, for example, the dealer has a regular arrangement with the creditor whereby the latter is prepared to make loans to potential customers of the dealer, i.e. to put a potential customer in a financial position to make a purchase from the dealer. Such arrangements between dealers and lenders tend to occur where the dealer does not wish (or cannot afford) himself to give credit terms to this customer.

If in pursuance of such an arrangement between creditor and dealer, the creditor agrees to make a cash loan to the customer, the resulting regulated credit agreement will be a debtor-creditor-supplier agreement and the dealer will be a negotiator in antecedent negotiations. This is exactly the situation in the example given at para.19–016 above, where Warmitup Ltd is therefore agent of Hotmoney Ltd in conducting negotiations with Shiver.

However, most cash loans are not made in such circumstances but are mere debtor-creditor agreements. This is certainly the case with the vast majority of bank loans and overdrafts. In these cases the position is as with a cash loan obtained under a credit card agreement. Thus the dealer is not the bank's agent for the purpose of any representations about the goods or services he supplies, i.e. s.56 does not apply. That being so, the bank is free of any liability for any misrepresentation or breach of contract by the dealer.

CONSUMER HIRE AGREEMENTS

22–021   There is with this type of contract no question of the prospective hirer obtaining the goods from one person (the owner) and credit from another. There is after all no element of credit. Thus in the case of a consumer hire agreement there is only one person who falls within the definition of a negotiator in antecedent negotiations—namely the owner himself. There is therefore no negotiator in antecedent negotiations who is deemed to be the agent of the owner. However, if there is "any person who, in the course of a business carried on by him, acts on behalf of the hirer in any negotiations for the agreement" then that person (the customer's representative) is deemed to be agent of the owner for the purposes indicated earlier.[36]

Just as with hire-purchase agreements, so with consumer hire agreements, there is sometimes a triangular arrangement whereby the dealer sells the goods to a finance company which contracts with the customer to supply them to him. This process was explained at para.18–005 in relation to hire-purchase. The difference is that here the finance company supplies the goods to the customer on hire instead of hire-purchase terms. We saw that at common law the normal rule is that the dealer is not the agent of the finance company.[37] This is the position at common law in relation to hire-purchase and it is exactly the same where the agreement is a hire agreement.[38] This is so unless, as in *Purnell Secretarial Services v Lease Management Services Ltd*,[39] there is some very exceptional factual material which establishes an agency.

Although the common law position is the same as it is in the case of hire-purchase, the application of the Consumer Credit Act is not the same. This is because where it is a consumer hire agreement instead of a consumer credit agreement, the dealer is not made agent of the finance company.[40] As just stated, the owner is the only negotiator in antecedent negotiations, (i.e. the finance company).

CREDIT BROKER'S FEES AND CREDIT REFERENCE AGENCIES

There are two types of ancillary credit trader who may have a role to play in connection with the making of a regulated agreement, a credit broker and a credit reference agency.   22–022

Credit Broker's Fees

An individual consumer will sometimes go to a credit broker for an introduction to a source   22–023
of credit. Section 155 establishes a rule designed to prevent the credit broker from charging the consumer more than £5 for any introduction which does not result in the consumer obtaining credit. The rule applies where the consumer wants to make a consumer credit agreement, a consumer hire agreement, a credit agreement (e.g. for £30,000) to finance the purchase of a house or flat or a credit agreement secured by a mortgage of land (e.g. a second mortgage). The rule is that if the credit broker's introduction of the consumer does not result in an agreement (of one of the types just indicated) within six months of the introduction, the consumer cannot be liable to pay the credit broker any fee or commission in excess of £5. If he has already paid such a fee or commission, he is entitled to recover it all back (except the £5). He is of course not entitled to recover it until the six months have elapsed.

---

[36] See para.22–012, above.
[37] At para.22–005, above.
[38] *Woodchester Equipment (Leasing) Ltd v BACFID* [1995] C.C.L.R. 51.
[39] [1994] C.C.L.R. 127.
[40] *Moorgate Mercantile Leasing Ltd v Gell and Ugolini* [1988] C.C.L.R. 1.

Credit Reference Agencies

22–024   The general function and definition of a credit reference agency has already been explained in para.20–003. The bank of knowledge that an agency has about any one person can be formidable and, if it indicates that the person is uncreditworthy, can mean that it is very difficult for that person to obtain credit—except perhaps from the most speculative of creditors who lend without reference to the borrower's creditworthiness and who also charge correspondingly high interest rates.

Concern has been felt at the secrecy with which credit reference agencies have in the past operated. Very often their information has been available only to the trade (i.e. finance companies, etc.) so that an individual has been unable to discover the accuracy of reports about his creditworthiness, or indeed whether any such reports have in fact been obtained. The aim of ss.157–159 is to rectify the situation.

Section 157 entitles the debtor or hirer to discover from the creditor, owner or negotiator in any antecedent negotiations, the name and address of any credit reference agency which has been consulted as to the creditworthiness of the debtor or hirer. If the creditor, owner or negotiator does not supply that information after receiving a written request for it, he commits an offence. Once that information has been obtained, the debtor or hirer is then in a position to take advantage of s.7 of the Data Protection Act 1998 (or, in the case of a partnership or other unincorporated body, s.158 of the Consumer Credit Act). This entitles an individual (or unincorporated body) to make a written request (plus payment of a small fee for expenses)[41] for details of information relating to the individual (or body) which is kept at the agency. Such a request can be made, irrespective of whether the person making it has obtained credit or has merely tried to obtain it or has not even tried to do so. The agency must comply with the request and failure to comply is an offence.[42]

By s.159, a consumer who considers an entry in the file relating to him to be incorrect and likely to prejudice him if not corrected, can require the agency either to remove the entry or to amend it. Then the agency must within 28 days either do that and notify the consumer that it has done so or else notify him that it has not.[43] If the latter course is taken the consumer can require the agency to add to his file an accompanying notice of correction of not more than 200 words drawn up by the consumer.[44] If the agency refuses to do so, either the consumer or the agency can refer the matter to the relevant authority, who may make such order as he or she thinks fit.[45] Failure to obey the order is a criminal offence. The relevant authority is the Information Commissioner unless the consumer is an unincorporated body, in which case it is the Office of Fair Trading.

FORMALITIES

22–025   Sections 60–65 deal with formalities which must be complied with in the making of a regulated agreement. The aim is to ensure:

[41] Currently £2, s.158(1)(c).
[42] s.158(4).
[43] s.159(2)
[44] s.159(3).
[45] s.159(4).

(i) That the debtor is fully aware of the nature and cost of the transaction he is about to enter (including the cost of the credit).

(ii) That his written agreement gives him a clear account of his rights and obligations.

Agreements Subject to the Formalities Requirements

These provisions apply only to regulated agreements. However, they do not apply to any non-commercial agreement or to any agreement which fulfils all the following conditions[46]: **22–026**

(a) It is a small agreement.

(b) It is a restricted-use agreement.

(c) It is a debtor-creditor-supplier agreement.

An example of an agreement which fulfils these conditions is a trading check agreement for £50 or less. Another example is a credit sale agreement under which the credit does not exceed £50. A regulated hire-purchase or conditional sale agreement will always be subject to the formalities requirements unless it is a non-commercial agreement. This is because hire-purchase and conditional sale agreements are excluded from the definition of "small agreements" in s.17. The exception, just mentioned, whereby certain small agreements are not subject to the formalities requirements, does not apply to any agreement which both falls within the Consumer Protection (Cancellation of Contracts Concluded away from Business Premises) Regulations 1987 and also either provides credit exceeding £35 or is a consumer hire agreement requiring payments totalling over £35.[47]

The reason that non-commercial agreements are not subject to the formalities requirements is that those requirements are intended to protect the consumer against the financially powerful creditor (whether that be the dealer or, say, a finance company). It is however quite possible for two private individuals to enter into what is in fact a regulated consumer credit agreement. For example, the man who sells his car privately (perhaps following a small advertisement in the local paper) may agree to his buyer paying him later—perhaps in instalments.

A similar example would be where a private individual lends money to a friend to be repaid over a period of time. In these cases the law would be unreasonable and unrealistic to insist that the agreement be put into writing and copies of it served on the debtor, etc. **22–027**

Section 74 also enables the OFT to except from having to comply with the formality requirements two further types of agreement which sometimes have to be made hastily. They are certain agreements to overdraw on a current account and certain agreements to finance payments arising out of a death. The latter might be an agreement to finance the paying of inheritance tax or court fees payable in order to get probate of a will. This exception the OFT has limited to agreements where the creditor is a bank and the debtor is someone acting in the course of his trade or profession. As to the former, imagine the situation where the bank

---

[46] s.74(2). Such agreements are still subject to the requirements of ss.55 and 56.
[47] For an account of those Regulations, see para.2–013, above.

manager is presented with a cheque which, if he pays it, will put the customer's account into the red. If the manager pays out on the cheque—as often happens in practice—he is in effect agreeing to the customer having an overdraft. It would be plainly unrealistic to require every such agreement to be in writing, etc. The overdraft exception applies to all debtor-creditor agreements for overdrafts on current accounts.

Form and Content

22–028   The regulated agreement must comply with the Consumer Credit (Agreements) Regulations 1983,[48] made under ss.60 and 61. These Regulations lay down detailed requirements as to the form, legibility and contents of agreements. In particular an agreement must have whichever is the appropriate one of the following headings: Hire-Purchase Agreement regulated by the Consumer Credit Act 1974; Conditional Sale Agreement regulated by the Consumer Credit Act 1974; Credit Agreement regulated by the Consumer Credit Act 1974; Hire Agreement regulated by the Consumer Credit Act 1974. As to the contents of an agreement the Regulations require the inclusion of such things as:

(i) names and addresses of the parties;

(ii) the cash price (though not in the case of hire agreements or of unrestricted-use credit or debtor-creditor agreements);

(iii) the amount of any deposit or advance payment required of the customer;

(iv) the amount of the credit (or the credit limit);

(v) the APR;

(vi) the total amount payable;

(vii) the amount of each payment and when payable;

(viii) details of default charges;

(ix) details of any security provided by the debtor or hirer.

In addition the agreement will have to contain notices, in a precise form laid down in the Regulations, informing the debtor or hirer of certain of his statutory rights and protections. These include: his right of cancellation of a cancellable agreement; his right of early termination if it is a hire-purchase or conditional sale agreement; his statutory protection if he loses a credit-token; his right of early settlement. These rights and protections are explained in later chapters of this book.

Apart from complying with the Regulations, the agreement must embody all the terms of the agreement (other than implied terms).[49]

---

[48] SI 1983/1553 as amended by the Consumer Credit (Agreements) (Amendment) Regulations (SI 2004/1482).
[49] s.61(1)(b).

Signatures

By s.61 the agreement must be contained in a document which is signed: **22–029**

> (i) by the debtor or hirer, and

> (ii) by or on behalf of the creditor.

Thus the debtor must sign it in person, unless the debtor or hirer is a partnership or other unincorporated body in which case it can be signed by one person on behalf of the debtor or hirer. It is not sufficient that the debtor or hirer signs it when it is still blank. When it is presented or sent to him for signature, it must include all the terms of the agreement (other than implied terms) and it must be readily legible. This means that deals ought not to follow the practice whereby the dealer persuades the customer to sign the form (say a hire-purchase proposal form) in blank and then the dealer fills in the spaces later—see, for example, *Campbell Discount Co v Gall.*[50]

The Consumer Credit (Agreements) Regulations 1983 require the agreement to include a signature box in a particular form. The debtor or hirer must sign within that box. Other signatures, e.g. of the creditor or of a witness, must be made outside the box. Normally the date of each signature must be inserted, although this is not necessary if the agreement is not a cancellable one and the date when the agreement becomes an executed agreement is inserted. The agreement becomes executed when the completed document is signed by (or on behalf of) both sides.

Copies

Sections 62 and 63 provide for the debtor or hirer to receive a copy or copies of the   **22–030** agreement. Depending upon the circumstances, the debtor or hirer must be given either one or two copies of the agreement. Whatever the circumstances, he should always receive one copy when he signs the agreement. If the agreement is sent to him for his signature then the copy should be sent at the same time. If the agreement is presented personally to him for his signature, then the copy should be given to him there and then.

A further (i.e. second) copy must be given to the debtor or hirer if the agreement was not actually made on the occasion when he signed it.[51] This situation commonly arises. An agreement is not made until both sides accept it—or to be more accurate until one side makes an offer which the other side accepts. Now, often, when a customer signs a finance company's form (e.g. for hire-purchase) that is no more than a proposal (i.e. an offer) by the customer. There is no agreement and therefore no contract until the finance company accepts the proposal. The finance company will seldom agree immediately. It (or rather one of its officials) will probably sign the form a few days later and post it or a copy of it back to the customer. That will constitute acceptance of the customer's offer and that will therefore be when the agreement is made (i.e. when the fully signed, executed, agreement is posted or

---

[50] At para.22–005, above.
[51] s.63.

given back to the debtor). That being so, the agreement will not have been made when the debtor signed the agreement. This will normally be the situation where, as explained at para.18–005 above, the customer signs a finance company's hire-purchase proposal form at the dealer's place of business.

When a second copy is required it must in the case of a cancellable agreement be sent by post. In any case the second copy, when required, must be received by the debtor or hirer within seven days following the making of the agreement. Note that the seven days begin to run when the agreement is made, which will not be when the customer signs the agreement, because in that case a second copy would not be necessary. Thus when a second copy is required, the agreement will usually be made when the customer's proposal is accepted. If, as is usual, the means of acceptance is the posting of a duly signed copy back to the customer, that copy (i.e. the second) must necessarily reach the customer within the required time (seven days) of the making of the agreement (the posting of the acceptance)![52]

22–031   The rule as to the time limit for delivery of the second copy (if required) is more lenient in the case of a credit token agreement (e.g. a credit card or trading check agreement). In that case the creditor need not comply with the time limit set out above provided the second copy is given to the debtor before or at the time when the credit token itself is given to him.[53]

When an agreement is signed by or on behalf of both parties it is an "executed" agreement. Until then it is "unexecuted". We have just considered those situations where a second copy is required. These situations arise when the agreement was still unexecuted at the time the first copy was given, and when therefore the first copy will necessarily have been a copy of an unexecuted agreement. The second copy, of course, must be a copy of the executed agreement.

In addition to those copies which must be given to the customer at or about the time of making the agreement, the customer is entitled at any time during the currency of the agreement to request, inter alia, a further copy of the executed agreement under ss.77–79. Section 77 is reinforced by the new s.77A[54] which requires creditors in the case of regulated fixed sum agreements to provide debtors with annual statements. Where an annual statement is not provided there are three consequences, none of which are favourable to the creditor[55]:

(i) the creditor is unable to enforce the agreement during the period of non-compliance;

(ii) the debtor is not liable to pay any interest during the period of non-compliance; and

(iii) the debtor will not be liable to pay any default sum which is incurred during the period of non-compliance.

22–032   One further point must be made in relation to all copies. Whenever the Consumer Credit Act requires a copy of a regulated agreement to be given or posted, it is part of that

---

[52] s.63(2).
[53] s.63(4).
[54] Inserted by the Consumer Credit Act 2006, s.6 with effect from October 1, 2008.
[55] s.77A(6)

requirement that the copy is given or posted together with a copy of any document referred to in the agreement.

Each copy must, in its form and contents, comply with the Consumer Credit (Cancellation Notices and Copies of Documents) Regulations 1983.[56] Those Regulations also contain certain stated exemptions from the requirement that each copy must be accompanied by a copy of any document referred to in the agreement. Otherwise, every copy would have to be accompanied by a copy of the Consumer Credit Act!

Special Formalities for Cancellable Agreements

The question of which agreements are cancellable will be dealt with presently. Section 64 **22–033** lays down additional formalities for them. Every copy of the agreement given to the debtor or hirer under s.62 or s.63 must contain a notice telling him of his right to cancel the agreement and giving the name and address of a person to whom notice of cancellation may be given. That notice of cancellation must be in the form laid down in the Regulations mentioned in the last paragraph.

Also, in the case of an agreement where a second copy need not be sent under s.63 (i.e. where the agreement is made on the occasion when the customer signs it), a notice must generally be sent by post to him. The time limit for sending it is the same as applies for the sending of a second copy under s.63. That notice must give the debtor or hirer details of his right of cancellation and the name and address of a person to whom notice of cancellation may be given. This notice too must be in the form prescribed by the Regulations.

Special Formalities for Second Mortgages

Sections 58 and 61(2) are intended to protect the debtor against high pressure sales methods **22–034** of what are loosely termed second mortgage companies, i.e. finance companies who will lend money usually for unrestricted-use to any houseowner provided he gives to the finance company security in the form of a mortgage on his land (i.e. his house). This need not in fact be a "second" mortgage but in practice usually will be, because the houseowner will probably have created a first mortgage in order to raise the money to purchase the house. Sections 58 and 61(2) do not apply to any mortgage created specifically to finance the purchase of the land which is in fact mortgaged or to any bridging loan connected with the purchase of land.

The effect of s.58 is that the customer must receive a copy of the prospective agreement in advance of receiving the actual agreement to sign. The copy is for his information for him to think about and is not for him to sign. By s.61(2) the agreement (i.e. for his signature) must be sent to him by post but must not be sent until a lapse of at least seven days after the earlier copy was given to him. During that lapse of time the prospective creditor or owner must leave the customer alone to make up his own mind. The creditor must not in any way approach the customer during the interval between delivery of the copy and of the agreement for signature.

---

[56] SI 1983/1557, as amended.

He must continue to stay away until either a further seven days have elapsed after delivery of the agreement for signature or the customer has signed and returned the agreement.

The aim and effect of these arrangements is that there may be a reasonable period during which the prospective customer is relieved of the "sales" pressure of the prospective creditor or owner. The length of this consideration period will depend upon whether and when the customer signs and returns the agreement. He will have in any case a minimum of seven days and, if he does not sign and return the agreement, he will have at least a further seven days. During the consideration period, the only circumstance in which the prospective creditor or owner will be entitled to approach the customer will be if the customer has during the consideration period specifically requested him to do so. Furthermore, the advance copy must clearly indicate to the customer his right to withdraw from the prospective agreement. It must contain a notice to this effect in the form laid down in the Consumer Credit (Cancellation Notices and Copies of Documents) Regulations 1983.

The advance copy required to be given by s.58 is in addition to those required by ss.62 and 63.[57]

Effect of Non-Compliance with the Requirements

22–035 Any agreement which does not comply with all the formality requirements is "improperly executed". The debtor or hirer will not in any way be penalised for this. Thus he can if he wishes enforce the agreement even if it was never signed or never even put into writing. For example he may wish to claim damages under a hire-purchase agreement for breach of an implied condition that the goods will be of satisfactory quality.[58]

It is the creditor or owner who may find it either impossible or difficult to enforce an improperly executed agreement. Where the agreement was made before April 6, 2007 the creditor is entirely unable to enforce it (or any security) if the formality requirements were infringed in any of the following three respects[59]:

    (i) If the debtor or hirer did not sign the agreement or a document containing certain minimum basic terms of the agreement (set out in Sch.6 of the Consumer Credit (Agreements) Regulations 1983).

    (ii) If, in the case of a cancellable agreement, the requirements of s.64 were not complied with, i.e. if any copy given to the debtor did not contain the required details of the right of cancellation or if a notice of those rights should have been served separately and was not.

    (iii) If, in the case of a cancellable agreement, the creditor has failed to serve the copy (or copies) required by ss.62 and 63 and has also not served, at some time before commencing proceedings, a copy of the fully-signed agreement.

Only in these very restricted situations will it be entirely impossible for the creditor or owner to enforce the agreement. In relation to the first of them, the minimum basic terms

[57] See para.22–030, above.
[58] See para.23–007, below.
[59] s.127.

required are laid down in Sch.6 to the Consumer Credit (Agreements) Regulations 1983. These are: a term stating how the debtor or hirer is to discharge his obligations to make payments under the agreement; a term stating any power of the creditor or owner to vary the amount payable; plus (in the case of a credit agreement) the amount of the credit (or the credit limit) and the rate of any interest on the credit. Unless the debtor or hirer signed a document containing at least these minimum basic terms, the creditor or owner cannot enforce the agreement against him. It follows that the creditor or owner will not be able to enforce a purely oral agreement unless that agreement was not subject to the formality requirements. The third situation above was easily avoided by the simple expedient of the creditor or owner serving a copy of the fully signed agreement on the debtor or hirer immediately before commencing proceedings against him.

These three situations could cause hardship to the creditor. In *Wilson v First County Trust Ltd (No.2)*[60] the agreement was properly documented except that a documentation fee of £250 was included as part of the credit provided under the agreement rather than as part of the total charge for credit. The Court of Appeal held that this misstatement rendered the agreement permanently unenforceable under s.127(3) and that therefore the loan was unrecoverable. This view was confirmed by the House of Lords and resulted in the £5,000 loan being unrecoverable due to the inclusion of a £250 documentation fee being incorrectly assigned as part of the credit. This was certainly a windfall for the debtor under such an agreement! To rectify this injustice the Consumer Credit Act 2006 repealed ss.127(3)–127(5) which results in the enforceability of such improperly documented agreements being subject to judicial discretion as considered below.   **22–036**

Where an agreement is not subject to the (now repealed) provisions of s.127(3)–(5), the creditor can enforce it—but subject to five restrictions:

(i) He can enforce it only by action in court.[61]

(ii) He cannot, without an order of the court, retake possession of the goods or land associated with the agreement (even if otherwise he would be entitled to) because that would constitute enforcement of the agreement.[62]

(iii) He cannot enforce any security except to the extent that the court allows him to enforce the regulated agreement.[63] This is important where the security is provided otherwise than in the regulated agreement itself, e.g. in the case of a guarantor or indemnifier.

(iv) The court has power in granting any order enforcing the agreement:

(a) To reduce or extinguish any sum payable by the debtor or hirer (i.e. so as to compensate him for any prejudice caused to him by reason of the default).[64]

---

[60] [2001] 3 All E.R. 229, affirmed [2004] 1 A.C. 816 (HL). See, Seager, "*Wilson v First County Trust*: first declaration of incompatibility under the Human Rights Act 1998" [2001] J.I.B.L. 163.
[61] s.65.
[62] s.65.
[63] s.113.
[64] s.127(2) and 127(1)(i).

(b) To impose any conditions (e.g. the delivery of a further copy to the hirer).[65]

(c) To suspend the operation of an enforcement order or any part of it (e.g. until certain conditions have been fulfilled).[66]

(d) To amend the agreement as the court considers just.[67]

These powers, especially those given by ss.135 and 136 are very wide and will enable the court in many cases to wipe out or minimise any prejudice caused to the debtor by the non-compliance with the formalities requirements. For example, in *Rank Xerox Finance v Hepple and Fennymore*[68] the county court granted an enforcement order but in doing so significantly reduced the amount of money payable by the customer because the agreement had not fully indicated the charges payable upon default.

(v) Before the court will make any order enforcing the agreement, the creditor or owner will have to convince the court that in view of the non-compliance it is nevertheless just and fair that the order be made. The court must consider to what extent the debtor or hirer has been prejudiced by the non-compliance and to what extent the creditor or owner is to be blamed for it.[69]

Plainly the court has power to waive purely technical infringements of the requirements. Moreover, in view of the wide powers given to the court to minimise the prejudice caused to the debtor or hirer, it would seem unlikely that the court will often refuse to grant an enforcement order. It must of course refuse in the three situations mentioned earlier in para.22–035 where the agreement was entered into before April 6, 2007. One rare situation where the court would also be likely to refuse would be where the creditor or owner has knowingly not complied with the requirements with the deliberate intention of prejudicing the debtor or hirer. In the unlikely event that the court cannot minimise or remove the prejudice caused to the debtor by the creditor's non-compliance, no order will be granted and thus, the agreement will remain unenforceable by the creditor.

Security

22–037   Often the security (if any) will be given by the debtor or hirer. In that case the security should be described in the regulated agreement or in a document referred to in the regulated agreement—Consumer Credit (Agreements) Regulations 1983.

However, the position is not so simple where the security is given by another person—in the case of a contract of guarantee or indemnity. As we have seen finance companies quite often demand that someone acts as guarantor or indemnifier of a credit agreement—particularly when the prospective debtor is a young person under about 25.[70] Such a

---

[65] s.135(1)(a)
[66] s.135(1)(b).
[67] s.136.
[68] [1994] C.C.L.R. 1.
[69] s.127.
[70] See para.18–009, above.

guarantor or indemnifier is often a parent or friend and will normally agree to the arrange-ment at the request of the debtor or hirer—because otherwise the finance company will not agree to the credit transaction.

On the other hand someone may act as guarantor or indemnifier without any request to do so from the debtor or hirer. Recourse agreements made between finance companies and dealers are examples. The Consumer Credit Act applies to security only if given at the request (express or implied) of the debtor or hirer.[71] Thus a recourse agreement does not have to comply with formalities laid down in the Act and will still be enforceable even though the principal agreement between creditor and debtor did not comply with the formalities requirements.

A guarantor or indemnifier who acted as such at the request (express or implied) of the debtor or hirer is given a considerable measure of protection by the Act. First, where the court refuses or would, if asked, refuse to enforce a regulated credit agreement because it was improperly executed, any security (i.e. the guarantee or indemnity) will also be unenforceable.[72]   **22–038**

Secondly, certain formalities must be observed in relation to the security (guarantee or indemnity) itself.[73] The person providing the security (the guarantor or indemnifier) is termed the surety. Section 105 requires the security agreement to be in writing and signed by or on behalf of the surety. It authorises regulations to be made as to the form and contents of the written document and it requires copies of that document and of the principal agreement (the credit agreement) to be given to the surety. Those Regulations are the Consumer Credit (Guarantees and Indemnities) Regulations 1983.[74]

If any of the above formalities are not complied with, the security is "improperly executed" and is not enforceable against the surety except on an order of the court. In deciding whether to make an order to enforce the security, the court has to weigh similar considerations to those it must take into account in deciding whether to enforce an improp-erly executed regulated agreement. To put it another way, ss.127, 135 and 136 apply in both cases. Thus the court has wide powers to put right any prejudice suffered by the surety (e.g. by reduction of any sum payable by the surety or by amending the security document). There is one significant difference. Whereas a regulated agreement which, contrary to the formal-ities requirements is not in writing or not signed by the debtor, is never enforceable, there is no such rigid rule in the case of an unsigned or unwritten security agreement. There is simply the rule that the court must have regard to the prejudice caused to the surety and the degree of culpability of the creditor or owner.

At this stage three notes of warning must be sounded. First, the fact that a security document is improperly executed does not affect the validity or enforceability of the credit agreement to which it relates. The credit agreement is still valid even though the security may be unenforceable.[75]   **22–039**

Secondly, the formalities requirements in s.105 of the Consumer Credit Act apply only to security given in relation to a regulated agreement. The third warning is that those formalities (which apply to security whatever form it takes) are in addition to formalities laid down by

---

[71] s.189.
[72] s.113, see para.19–002, above.
[73] See s.105.
[74] SI 1983/1556.
[75] The same is not true vice versa, s.113, see para.19–002, above.

other Acts of Parliament in relation to particular form of security, e.g. the Bills of Sale Acts 1878–1882 (mortgages of goods), the Policies of Assurance Act 1867 and the Law of Property Act 1925, s.136 (assignment of life assurance policies), and the Statute of Frauds 1677 (guarantees).

CANCELLATION

22–040 The cancellation provisions (ss.67–73) represent an attempt to combat a particularly undesirable selling technique. Door-to-door salesmen used to persuade people to commit themselves to acquire on credit terms goods or services for which the payments might be crippling and the need for which would seem to recede in the cool light of reason after the salesman had left. At one time, certain encyclopaedia salesmen were guilty of this. Thus the cancellation provisions are aimed at what might be termed doorstep credit agreements. Where an agreement is cancellable, the debtor has a short period of a few days in which he may cancel the agreement, even after it has been made. These provisions, therefore, create an important exception to the principle that after a contract is made, neither party can back out of it. A contract not cancellable under these provisions (of the Consumer Credit Act) about to be discussed may be cancellable under either the Cancellation of Contracts made in a Consumer's Home or Place of Work etc. Regulations 2008 or the Consumer Protection (Distance Selling) Regulations 2000.[76] These two sets of regulations extended the principle of a cooling-off period, respectively to cash agreements made on the doorstep and to contracts made solely via distance selling (e.g. by mail or over the internet.[77]

Cancellable Agreements

22–041 Section 67 provides that certain regulated agreements can be cancelled by the debtor or hirer. A regulated agreement is cancellable if two conditions are fulfilled:

   (i) The antecedent negotiations included oral representation made when in the presence of the customer by or on behalf of the negotiator. It will be recalled that either the creditor or owner or the dealer may be a negotiator in antecedent negotiations—though in the case of a consumer hire agreement, the dealer will not be a negotiator in antecedent negotiations.[78]

   (ii) The customer signed the agreement elsewhere than at certain business premises— namely those of the creditor or owner, of the dealer and of any party to a linked transaction (other than the customer or his relative).

The first requirement will be fulfilled in almost any case where the agreement is made after the prospective customer has spoken face-to-face either with the dealer or with the creditor or owner. It would not of course be fulfilled where the agreement was negotiated by the

---

[76] See generally, Hellwege, "Consumer protection in Britain in need of reform" (2004) 63 C.L.J. 712.
[77] The former are discussed at para.2–013 and the latter at para.16–007, above.
[78] See *Lloyds Bowmaker Leasing Ltd v MacDonald* and para.22–021, above

customer entirely through the post. Suppose the only oral representations made to the customer by the dealer or the creditor or owner were made over the telephone. Here again the first requirement would not be fulfilled. Not every statement made during antecedent negotiations will amount to a "representation" for the purposes of s.67. For example a simple greeting, "Good day", or an inconsequential bit of small talk, "Nice day isn't it?" would not suffice. A statement will amount to a representation for the purposes of s.67 only if it is a statement of fact, or of opinion, or an undertaking as to the future, which is capable of inducing the proposed customer to enter into the regulated agreement: *Moorgate Services Ltd v Kabir.*[79] It is sufficient if there is at least one such statement made in the presence of the customer during the antecedent negotiations.

The second requirement is fulfilled if the customer signed the agreement away from the business premises mentioned, e.g. at his own business premises or at his home. Thus a hire-purchase agreement which the debtor signs at the dealer's premises is not cancellable. On the other hand if, after listening to the dealer's sales talk, the customer takes the agreement away and signs it at home, then the agreement will be cancellable. Thus although the cancellation provisions were aimed at what might loosely be termed "doorstep" credit agreements, their net is cast rather more widely than that.

Two categories of regulated agreement are, however, excluded altogether from the cancellation provision: **22–042**

(i) An agreement involving a land mortgage or credit restricted to being used to purchase land or a bridging loan in connection with the purchase of land—s.67. There is in these cases no need for a cooling-off period after the agreement is made because as we have seen the formalities provisions provide for a consideration period before the agreement is made. One reason for these special arrangements is no doubt that it can be difficult to unravel a transaction involving land after that transaction has been completed.

(ii) Any agreement not subject to the formalities requirements—namely, non-commercial agreements, small agreements which are debtor-creditor-supplier agreements for restricted-use credit, and debtor-creditor agreements for overdrafts on current accounts and certain agreements to finance payments arising out of a death.[80]

The exclusion of certain small agreements involves the exclusion of a great many credit sale agreements by which housewives buy small household items from mail order firms. However, a good many of these mail order firms expressly include in each credit agreement a term that the customer can cancel it and return the goods within so many days of delivery. In any case, the buyer will be entitled to reject the goods if they do not comply with the conditions as to description and quality, etc., implied by the Sale of Goods Act.[81]

This raises the important question of who is to bear the expense of returning the goods. If the customer rejects goods for breach of condition then he is under no obligation to pay for their carriage but is entitled to wait for them to be collected. This is also the position where

---

[79] [1995] C.C.L.R. 74.
[80] See s.74. These exclusions are more fully explained at para.22–025, above.
[81] See Ch.7 above.

he cancels the agreement under the cancellation provisions of the Consumer Credit Act (or under the Cancellation of Contracts Made in a Consumer's Home or Place of Work etc. Regulations 2008). However, if the agreement is outside those provisions and he cancels under an express term of his agreement, then he may well find that the agreement requires him to be responsible for the carriage of the goods back to the creditor or owner.

Notice of Cancellation

22–043   To exercise his right of cancellation the debtor or hirer must serve a written notice indicating his intention of withdrawing from the transaction. The notice of cancellation must be served upon one of the following persons[82]—the creditor or owner (or his agent), the person specified in the agreement as being a person to whom such notice may be sent, the dealer, any person who in the course of a business acted on behalf of the customer in negotiations for the agreement. The notice can be sent by post and must be sent or served within the time limit in s.68.

Time Limit

22–044   After the debtor or hirer has signed the agreement (or prospective agreement) the cooling-off period during which he can serve a notice of cancellation lasts for several days. By s.68 he can serve the notice any time after he signs and before the end of a period of five clear days. However, that period of five days does not begin until the day after he receives his second copy of the agreement (required by s.63).[83] The day after he receives his second copy is the first of the five days. He may serve his notice of cancellation at any time before that day or on that day or on any of the subsequent four days. If posted on the last of these days it will still be effective even though it does not arrive until later (or even if it never arrives at all).[84]

The exact cooling-off period available to the debtor or hirer will depend upon how long elapses between him signing the agreement (or prospective agreement) and his receipt of his second copy. It is wrong to refer to it as a five-day or a six-day period, because it will almost always be more than that. The second copy has to be sent to him by post after the making of the agreement and need not be sent until several (maximum seven) days later. Furthermore, the agreement may not have been made until some time after the debtor or hirer signed the prospective agreement (i.e. the proposal form).

In those cases where a second copy does not have to be sent under s.63, the five-day period begins on the day after the debtor or hirer receives the notice informing him of his rights of cancellation (required by s.64).[85] It can happen that a second copy is not required under s.63 and also that regulations have been made excusing the creditor or owner from serving a notice of cancellation rights under s.64. In that case the cooling-off period lasts until the end

---

[82] s.69.
[83] See para.22–030, above.
[84] s.69(7).
[85] See para.22–033, above.

of day 14 after the debtor or hirer signed the agreement—the first of the 14 days being the day after he signed.[86]

Effect of the Notice

A distinction is drawn between two categories—on the one hand consumer hire agreements and debtor-creditor-supplier agreements for restricted use credit and, on the other hand, other regulated agreements. Thus the following agreements fall within the first category—all hire-purchase, conditional sale and credit sale agreements and also all trading check agreements and consumer hire agreements. A typical credit card agreement is a multiple agreement and will fall within the first category as regards the provision of goods or services and within the second category as regards the provision of cash. The second category will include most ordinary cash loans. Agreements within the second category are postponed for later consideration and the effect of cancellation of agreements in the first category will now be considered.   **22–045**

Broadly the position is that the parties are freed from any further commitment in the agreement or in any linked transaction.[87] If the agreement or linked transaction has not been made, i.e. the offer to enter it has not been accepted—the notice of cancellation operates as a withdrawal of that offer. If the agreement has been made, it is cancelled. The debtor or hirer must return the goods (if any), can get his money back if he has paid any, and need pay no more money.[88] This broad picture will be qualified and expanded in the following paragraphs. One qualification is that the Consumer Credit (Linked Transactions) (Exemptions) Regulations 1983 exclude certain types of linked transactions from the cancellation provisions.[89] Apart from that, whenever a regulated agreement is withdrawn from or cancelled, so is any linked transaction. It is upon this latter basis that further details of the effect of cancellation will be given.

The debtor or hirer (and any relative of his) is under no obligation to make any payment under the agreement or under any linked agreement. Any sums he has already paid are with one exception repayable by the person(s) to whom they were paid. The exception is that any money paid as a fee or commission to a credit broker can be recovered only to the extent that it exceeds £5.[90] Although money which is repayable is always recoverable from the person to whom it was paid, in some situations the debtor will have a choice as to the person from whom he recovers it—either from the creditor or from the supplier. This choice is available in the case of a restricted-use debtor-creditor-supplier agreement where the supplier is not the same person as the creditor, e.g. trading voucher agreements. This choice is particularly valuable where either the creditor or supplier has become insolvent.

If the debtor or hirer has traded in other goods in part-exchange, he is entitled to their return in substantially the same condition within 10 days of serving his notice of cancellation. If they are not so returned, he is entitled to a sum equivalent to their part-exchange allowance. He is then entitled to that sum as if he had paid it as cash under the agreement. The choice   **22–046**

---

[86] s.68(1)(b).
[87] s.69(1).
[88] s.70(1).
[89] See para.19–025, above.
[90] s.70(6).

as to whether to return the part-exchanged goods or to repay the part-exchange allowance is that of the person who took the goods in part-exchange (i.e. usually the dealer).

The debtor or hirer can enforce his rights upon cancellation by taking action in the courts. In addition he is given a lien over any goods of which he (or a relative of his) is in possession under the terms of a cancelled agreement (or linked transaction).[91] This enables him to retain those goods until he receives the return of any money to which he is entitled and the return of his part-exchanged goods (or their part-exchange allowance).

Subject to that lien, s.72 requires the return of certain goods which has been obtained—namely goods of which the debtor or hirer (or his relative) is in possession, under:

(a) a cancelled restricted-use, debtor-creditor-supplier agreement relating to goods, or a consumer hire agreement, or

(b) a cancelled linked transaction relating to goods.

22–047   The duty imposed on the debtor or hirer (or his relative) by s.72 requires him to take reasonable care of the goods. Unless he is holding the goods to compel repayment of sums due to him, he must hand them over provided he is requested to do so in writing signed by or on behalf of the supplier or owner of them. He is not under any other duty to return them. In particular he need not transport them or arrange for their carriage and is entitled to wait until they are collected. If he does convey the goods (or send them at his own expense) to the dealer or owner, then that is quite satisfactory and he is discharged from any further obligation. If, 21 days after serving the notice of cancellation, he is still in possession of the goods and has received no written request to return them, he no longer has any obligation to take reasonable care of them.[92] Section 72 does not apply to perishable goods, goods supplied to meet an emergency or goods which before cancellation were consumed or incorporated in something else. One example would be materials (e.g. spare parts) used in repairs.[93] These exceptions are necessary because it would generally be unreasonable to expect the debtor to return such goods!

Pause and consider the effect of cancellation from the point of view of the person who has contracted to supply the goods or services. That person may be the creditor (e.g. in a credit sale agreement) or he may be the supplier under a linked transaction (e.g. the supplier under a trading voucher agreement). Often after cancellation he will be no worse off than if the agreement had never been made. This will be so where at the time of cancellation either he has not provided any goods or services or else he has provided only goods which must after cancellation be returned to him. He will not then be out of pocket because although he will have to refund any money received, he will not have to provide any goods or services and can recover the goods he has supplied.

However, as we have seen, there are certain special categories of goods which the debtor need not return. Add to that the fact that the debtor need not return any services he has received. It is then obvious that if before cancellation the supplier has already supplied goods in the special categories or any services, he may well be out of pocket. He will have to refund payments received but will not be able to recover anything (either goods or money) in respect

---

[91] s.70(2).
[92] s.72(8).
[93] s.72(9).

of the goods or services he has supplied. This unfortunate position can for example arise whenever an agreement to provide services on instalment credit (of over £50) is cancelled. Those services could be anything, e.g. chimney sweeping, repairing a house or car, landscaping a garden, felling trees, transporting persons or goods. If such an agreement is cancelled, the debtor is under no obligation either to pay any money or to return any goods incorporated in the house, car or garden (e.g. building materials, spare parts or plants). Furthermore he can recover payments already made. Obviously a supplier will try to prevent the situation arising where cancellation can occur after such goods or services have been supplied. He could do this by for example:

(i) Refusing to provide the services or goods on credit terms (and also refusing to allow the agreement under which the goods are supplied to be a linked transaction). This will ensure that the agreement is not a regulated agreement and not affected by the Consumer Credit Act—though it could be cancellable under other legislation.[94]

(ii) Allowing credit terms but insisting that the debtor signs the agreement at the supplier's trade premises. This will ensure that although it is a regulated agreement, it is not a cancellable one.

(iii) Allowing credit terms but making it a condition of the agreement that the goods or services will not be supplied until after the cancellation period has elapsed. In this case the agreement may well be a cancellable one but at the time when cancellation can occur no goods or services will have been provided.

These are entirely reasonable methods for a supplier to protect himself. Nevertheless they **22–048** are liable to result in the customer being forced either to do without credit or to wait for his goods or services. There are two situations where the supplier may understandably fail to adopt any of those methods to protect himself, namely:

(i) where goods or services are supplied to meet an emergency, or

(ii) where goods are supplied which, by the act of debtor (or his relative), have before cancellation become incorporated in something else.

By s.69(2) there is a special rule in these two cases to prevent the supplier being out of pocket. Thus although the agreement is cancelled and although no goods or services are returnable, nevertheless the debtor remains liable after cancellation to pay for the services or goods.

We come now to consider the effect of cancellation in the case of the second category of agreements referred to earlier, i.e. unrestricted-use credit agreements and debtor-creditor agreements. The obvious example is of an ordinary cash loan. The rules applicable are basically the same as those already set out in relation to agreements within the first category—but with one important difference created by s.71. Its effect is that although the agreement is cancelled, the debtor must repay (together with interest) any credit which he has already received. To that there are two slight qualifications. First, no interest is payable on

---

[94] See para.22–040, above.

any money which the debtor repays either within one month of cancellation or (if there were to be instalments) before the date of the first instalment. Secondly, in a case where the credit is to be repaid entirely in instalments the debtor is not liable to repay it unless he receives a written, signed request from the creditor which states the remaining instalments. That request must be in the form laid down in the Consumer Credit (Repayment of Credit on Cancellation) Regulations 1983. The debtor is under no duty to pay anything beyond what is specified in s.71. Any other payment, if already made, can be recovered (except the first £5 of any agreed credit broker's fee). The provisions of s.71 requiring repayment of credit already received are only fair since there are no goods obtained under an agreement in this second category which have to be returned—and without the rule in s.71 the debtor would be able to avoid repaying a loan by the simple expedient of cancelling the agreement.

Chapter 23

CREDITOR'S LIABILITY IN RESPECT OF GOODS OR SERVICES SUPPLIED

INTRODUCTION

A distinction can be drawn between two types of contractual terms—those relating to the credit and its repayment and those relating to the goods or services supplied. It is the latter with which this chapter is concerned. These include terms relating to the quality of the goods supplied, the time of delivery, the title of the seller, etc. Sometimes both types of terms (i.e. as to the credit and as to the goods or services supplied) are contained within the same agreement—i.e. in the case of hire-purchase, conditional sale and credit sale agreements. Most of this chapter will be devoted to dealing with these agreements. However, first we shall consider those situations where there are two agreements—one relating to the credit and a separate one relating to the supply of goods or services. This occurs for example in the case of a bank loan, a credit card purchase or a trade check purchase. The credit agreement is with one person (the bank or finance company) and the agreement to buy goods or services is with another (the supplier). In relation to the latter agreement two questions arise: **23–001**

(i) What are the terms of the agreement to buy goods or services?

(ii) To what extent is the creditor (as well as the supplier) liable for breaches of those terms by the supplier?

TERMS OF THE GOODS OR SERVICES AGREEMENT

The debtor may use his credit (be it a bank loan, credit card or whatever) to buy either goods or services. If he buys goods, then it will be a contract of sale of goods that he makes with the supplier. The terms of that contract will include those which were discussed in Chapter **23–002**

7. If he buys services then the terms of the agreement will be those that are expressly agreed between him and the supplier plus any terms that are implied. The terms of a contract for services will therefore vary a great deal according to the type of agreement made. He may buy a package holiday or a cruise, have central heating installed or an extension built, have his garden landscaped or his yacht repaired, etc. All these are contracts for services and the terms expressly agreed or implied will be different in each case. There is no room here to consider them all, but only to make some general observations.

In contracts for services the implied terms will include those implied by the Supply of Goods and Services Act 1982. These were explained in Chapter 8 and the circumstances in which they could be excluded were explained in Chapter 10. Without repeating the detail it might be useful to recall that the following terms are implied by the Supply of Goods and Services Act 1982:

   (i) Where the services are provided in the course of a business, there is an implied term that the work will be done with reasonable care and skill.[1]

  (ii) If no time is mentioned in the contract, then there will usually be an implied condition that the services will be provided and completed within a reasonable length of time.[2]

 (iii) Where the contract involves the supply of some goods, there are implied terms as to title, description, quality and sample which are similar to those in ss.12–15 of the Sale of Goods Act.[3]

CREDITOR'S LIABILITY FOR THE SUPPLIER'S BREACH

23–003   We are here concerned with the situation where the debtor has two contracts—a credit agreement with the creditor and a contract with the supplier to buy goods or services. It is a basic common law rule that only a party to a contract can be liable for breach of that contract. Therefore, at common law even if the seller who sells the goods or services is in breach of contract, the buyer will have no remedy against the creditor because the latter was not a party to the contract to sell the goods or services. The buyer will have a remedy only against the seller.

However, s.75 of the Consumer Credit Act 1974 has made a considerable inroad into this rule. This section, which applies to debtor-creditor-supplier agreements, has already been quoted in connection with misrepresentation.[4] Section 75 provides that if the debtor has:

> "any claim against the supplier in respect of a misrepresentation or breach of contract, he shall have a like claim against the creditor".

Thus the debtor can bring the claim against the seller or the creditor or both.[5] Take an example: X uses his credit card to buy an armchair (cash price £145) from a shop. The

[1] SGSA 1982 s.13.
[2] s.14.
[3] ss.1–5.
[4] See paras 22–017 and 22–019, above.
[5] For the general criticism of the policy behind s.75, see [1978] New L.J. 703.

armchair is not of satisfactory quality and collapses, causing X some injury. By virtue of s.75, X can sue the credit card company (as well as the shop) for damages for injury and damage caused. This right to sue the creditor could be very valuable in the situation where the shop has become insolvent. If X exercises his right to claim against the creditor, the creditor (the credit card company) can claim against the supplier under a right of indemnity. The effect of s.75 is therefore that it is the creditor who stands the risk of the supplier becoming insolvent.

Turning briefly to debit cards used in conjunction with Electronic Funds Transfer, these debit card agreements, unlike credit card agreements, are debtor-creditor agreements. Thus s.75 does not apply to them because it applies only to debtor-creditor-supplier agreements.

As just observed, s.75 applies only in the case of a debtor-creditor-supplier agreement, i.e. broadly, where there is some business connection between the creditor and supplier, as in the example of Shiver, Warmitup Ltd and Hotmoney Ltd given at para.19–016, above. However, there are two further restrictions upon the operation of the section. First, it does not apply to a non-commercial agreement. Secondly, it does not apply to a claim in respect of "any single item to which the supplier has attached a cash price not exceeding £100 or more than £30,000". So, if X, as well as buying an armchair, had used his credit card to buy a hot water bottle which had burst and ruined his bed, he could not make a claim for that damage against the credit card company because the hot water bottle will not have had a cash price in excess of £100. That is so even if the damage caused was in excess of £100. X would of course still have his remedies against the seller. Section 75 applies to items having a cash price of over £100 but not over £30,000. **23–004**

Section 75 probably can not be relied upon by any credit card holder who made his credit card agreement before July 1, 1977.[6] It seems unlikely, however, that many credit card agreements made so long ago are still active.[7]

Whenever a regulated credit card agreement was made, a complication arises where there is a second authorised user. This occurs where someone with a credit card agreement has as part of that agreement an arrangement whereby a second person (often husband or wife) has a card which can be used on the same account. The latter person, the authorised user, is not, however, made liable to pay the debts incurred. Thus there is one account and one person liable to make repayments on that account, but there are two card holders each able to draw on the account. Where it is the authorised user who has used his card on the purchase in question, can that authorised user rely on s.75 in the same way as if he were the principal card holder? Exactly the same question could be asked in relation to s.56 and the answer is exactly the same. At first sight the answer appears to be no, since the wording of both sections makes it clear that they operate only in favour of the *debtor*. Imagine a wife, Joan, who is authorised user of a card on her husband's, Darby's, account. Suppose she uses the card to pay £200 for a coat from Bill's shop. She is clearly the person who makes a contract with Bill's shop.[8] She is not acting as her husband's agent in making that contract but is clearly herself buying the coat. If the coat is not fit to wear, it is she who has a claim against Bill for the coat not being of satisfactory quality. Is she perhaps Darby's agent in using the credit card to debit his credit card account? If she is, then could he (instead of her) rely on the sections? The answer still

---

[6] Similarly, s.56 probably cannot be relied upon by a card holder who made his credit card agreement before April 1, 1977.
[7] Thus for a full explanation readers are referred to the 5th edition of this book and to [1978] New L.J. 448.
[8] It is a sale of goods contract, see para.8–005, above.

appears to be no. In relation to s.75, the debtor is given a right to bring against the creditor any claim which he could have brought against the supplier, but *Darby* has no claim against Bill. Joan's problem is that ss.56 and 75 confer rights only on the debtor and the debtor is Darby.

23–005   In order to succeed under either section, Joan needs to show that she too is a debtor. Perhaps she can. The word "debtor" in the Act does not have the simple meaning of someone who owes a debt. It means the "individual receiving credit under a consumer credit agreement"—s.189(1). Presumably Joan got her card (of which she is the authorised user) by agreement of the credit card company. In that case the card company in making the agreement with her provided her with a financial accommodation, credit upon which she can draw. If that is so, the credit card company has a credit agreement with Darby and also has one with Joan. The difficulty with that is that if the card company has provided a financial accommodation to Joan, then one would have expected Joan to have to be responsible for repaying any credit she draws. It is surely much more accurate to say that in letting Joan have a card on Darby's account, the card company has granted a further financial accommodation to Darby and that Joan when she uses her card is actually acting as Darby's agent to pledge *his* credit. The plain fact is that the legal position of the second authorised card holder needs clarifying, preferably by an amendment to s.75. Clearly, as matter of policy, the law *should* be that the second authorised card holder has exactly the same rights against the credit card company as if she had been the principal card holder.[9]

Leaving the problem of the second authorised card holder, we can turn to another situation in which the card companies have sought to avoid liability under s.75. This is where the card holder has used his card to make a purchase abroad. The contract of purchase abroad may be governed by the law of the country (e.g. Japan) in which that purchase occurs. Nevertheless the credit card agreement, if made in England between a card issuer in England and a card holder resident in England, will be governed by English law, including s.75. It should still be possible first to discover whether the card holder has a claim against the supplier (i.e. according to whatever law governs the supply contract) and secondly to hold the card issuing company jointly and severally liable for that claim. The credit card companies' attempts to avoid s.75 liability in respect of transactions when the card is used abroad were in each case a "try on". In *Office of Fair Trading v Lloyds TSB Bank plc and others*[10] the Court of Appeal held that s.75 applies where the transaction is conducted abroad. The decision was confirmed by the House of Lords and thus it is now settled that s.75 is capable of supporting an action by a card holder in respect of a transaction conducted abroad. Whilst this could be unfair on the card issuer (who may well struggle to impose liability on the foreign supplier in question) it reflects the consumer-protection orientation of s.75.[11]

In *Porter v General Guarantee Corporation Kilner*[12] Brown J. said in relation to a hire-purchase agreement that s.75 was relevant. He was plainly wrong. In fact s.75 does not apply to hire-purchase, conditional sale and credit sale agreements. This is, after all, only common sense, since in these cases there are in the credit agreement itself terms relating to the delivery, description and quality of the goods and if one of those terms is broken the creditor

---

[9] For a fuller discussion of the position of the second authorised card holder see [1994] Sol. Jo. 1212.
[10] [2006] EWCA Civ. 268, [2007] Q.B. 1 affirmed [2007] UKHL 48, [2007] 3 W.L.R. 733. See also *Jarrett v Barclays and Royal Bank of Scotland* [1999] Q.B. 1 (purchaser of timeshare in Portugal held entitled to succeed under s.75 against British banks which had financed the purchase).
[11] See further, Hare, "Your Flexible Friend?" (2005) 64 C.L.J. 287.
[12] [182] R.T.R. 384.

will in any case be liable for what is his own breach of contract. Where a finance company makes a hire-purchase, conditional sale or credit sale agreement with the debtor, the finance company buys the goods from the dealer and contracts with the debtor to supply the goods to the debtor. Thus the finance company supplies the goods on credit terms to the debtor.

The situation is different, however, where the finance company does not itself buy the goods and then supply them to the debtor, but instead lends the debtor the money to enable the debtor himself to buy the goods direct from the dealer. In this situation the agreement between the finance company and the debtor is not a hire-purchase, conditional sale or credit sale agreement. It is simply a loan contract. If the loan contract is a regulated debtor-creditor-supplier agreement (i.e. made as a result of business arrangements between the dealer and the finance company), s.75 will apply. That was the situation in the Scottish case, *United Dominions Trust v Taylor*[13] where a finance company lent money to Mr Taylor to enable him to buy a car from Parkaway Cars. The finance company brought proceedings against him to enforce the loan agreement. He based his defence on s.75. He said he had a claim against Parkaway Cars for breach of contract and for misrepresentation because the car had been misrepresented to be in a good condition when in fact it was unroadworthy. It was held that this, if proved, gave him a good defence under the loan agreement. Where the debtor had a right to rescind the supply contract (i.e. his contract of sale of goods with Parkaway Cars), he had under s.75 a "like claim" against the finance company; a "like claim" meant a claim to rescind the loan agreement.[14] In this situation, where the customer has obtained the loan to buy the car and then rescinds his two contracts, i.e. with the dealer and the creditor, then of course he must return the car to the dealer, but presumably the creditor and dealer are left to sort out between them the return by the dealer to the creditor of the loan which the customer had used to buy the car. Despite a certain amount of academic criticism, the decision in *UDT v Taylor* was followed in another Scottish case, *Forward Trust Ltd v Hornsby*.[15]

23–006

HIRE-PURCHASE

We now come to the terms as to title, description, quality, sample and delivery which are implied in hire-purchase agreements. First, a few words must be said about terminology. Traditionally the parties to a hire-purchase agreement have been called "hirer" and "owner". These are the words that have usually appeared in the agreement itself and they therefore have also tended to be used in the judgments of decided cases. However, the Consumer Credit Act has brought about a change. That Act and other Acts of Parliament now use the words "debtor" and "creditor" to describe the parties. This change of terminology has not changed the essential nature of a hire-purchase contract. The debtor under a hire-purchase agreement will still be the hirer of goods with an option to purchase them. Many finance companies continue to use the old terminology in their hire-purchase agreements. There is nothing wrong with that and it is not inaccurate. Indeed it serves to make it clear that the agreement is a hire-purchase agreement and not a credit sale agreement or some other kind of credit agreement. In this chapter, however, the new terminology will be used. The written

23–007

[13] [1980] C.C.L.R. 29.
[14] For an analysis of this case, see [1981] J.B.L. 179.
[15] [1996] C.C.L.R. 18.

hire-purchase agreement seldom contains many terms securing the debtor's interest. Indeed, in the past, such agreements have often included exemption clauses designed to prevent the debtor being able to make a claim for the creditor's breach of the agreement. Parliament has stepped in to protect the interests of debtors. The position is regulated by the Supply Goods (Implied Terms) Act 1973 and the Unfair Contract Terms Act 1977. The relevant sections of the 1973 Act are ss.8–11 and these apply to all hire-purchase agreements irrespective of whether they are regulated agreements. They imply terms relating to title, description, quality and sample. The Unfair Contract Terms Act 1977 severely restricts the creditor's ability to exclude his liability.

The Supply of Goods (Implied Terms) Act implies terms into hire-purchase agreements which are virtually identical to the corresponding terms implied in sale of goods contracts. The result is that, whether a customer buys goods or whether he takes them on hire-purchase terms, his rights as to title, description, quality and sample are the same. Apart from necessary changes of wording, ss.8, 9, 10 and 11 are identical to ss.12, 13, 14 and 15 of the Sale of Goods Act. Since the latter sections have been considered in detail in Chapter 7, ss.8–11 of the 1973 Act will be considered here only to the extent that there are matters specially relevant to hire-purchase contracts.

Terms implied in a hire-purchase contract at common law have in large measure been rendered redundant and superseded by the terms implied by the 1973 Act. Nevertheless in one or two instances they may be significant and this will be seen as the chapter proceeds—particularly in relation to delivery and acceptance.

Title

23–008   Section 8 of the Supply of Goods (Implied Terms) Act 1973 is virtually identical to s.12 of the Sale of Goods Act. Section 8(1) reads:

> "In every hire-purchase agreement, other than one to which subsection (2) below applies, there is—
>
> (a)   an implied condition on the part of the creditor that he will have a right to sell the goods at the time when the property is to pass."

In hire-purchase contracts, it is usually some time before property passes to the debtor. Property will not pass until the debtor exercises his option to buy and that option will not be exercisable until he has paid all his instalments. Provided the creditor has the right to sell the goods at the time the debtor exercises his option, the creditor is not in breach of the condition in s.8(1)(a).

However, there are three other grounds upon which the creditor may be liable unless he has the right to sell much earlier than the time at which the debtor exercises his option. The first ground is breach of the condition implied by the common law as to title—namely that the creditor will have good title to the goods at the time when the debtor takes delivery. In the situation where goods are handed over as soon as the agreement is made, the creditor must have good title right from the start. On the other hand, where the goods are not to be delivered until some time after the making of the agreement, the creditor will not be in breach of the condition provided he acquires good title to the goods before the debtor takes delivery of them. *Mercantile Guarantee v Wheatley*[16] concerned an agreement made by a finance company on February 7 to let out a lorry on hire-purchase terms. On that date the finance company did not own the lorry but subsequently purchased it on February 11. Thus the finance company had good title when, on March 8, the debtor took delivery of the lorry. Goddard J. held that the common law condition as to title was not broken since the relevant time was when the goods were delivered.

The second ground of possible liability of the creditor who does not have the right to sell **23–009** the goods is for breach of an express term of the agreement. *Barber v NWS Bank*[17] involved an agreement which included an express term that until full payment the property in the goods would remain vested in the creditor. It was conceded that this amounted to an express term that at the time of the contract the creditor had good title and it was held that this amounted to a condition of the contract. The case involved a conditional sale agreement but the law is the same in the case of hire-purchase.

The other ground of possible liability of the creditor who does not have the right to sell the goods is breach of the warranty implied by s.8(1)(b) of the Supply of Goods (Implied Terms) Act—the warranty of quiet possession and freedom from undisclosed charges or encumbrances. This warranty relates to the period of hire, i.e. the period before the debtor exercises his option to buy. The warranty of quiet possession (as in sale of goods) also relates to the future, i.e. after the debtor has exercised his option and acquired ownership in the goods.[18]

Breach of a condition as title—whether the one implied by s.8(1)(a) or the one implied by the common law or an express one—gives the debtor the right to treat the contract as repudiated and to reclaim all the payments he has made. The reason he can recover all his payments is that he can be said to have suffered a total failure of consideration. This is just a way of saying that the law regards him as having received no benefit from the contract. Because he has received no benefit, he can recover the whole amount that he has paid. We saw in Chapter 7 that this was the position in sale of goods when the seller is in breach of the condition as to title in s.12 of the Sale of Goods Act, i.e. the buyer can recover the whole price he has paid as was held in *Rowland v Divall*.[19] *Rowland v Divall* has been followed in a hire-purchase case, *Warman v Southern Counties Finance*.[20] The facts in the latter case were that the debtor had paid all instalments and had enjoyed the use of the goods for some months before having to surrender them to their true owner. Finnemore J. said that the true basis of a hire-purchase agreement was that the debtor should be able to acquire ownership of the goods. The debtor was unable to acquire ownership and his Lordship held that therefore the debtor had suffered a total failure of consideration and was entitled to the return of all his payments. The result, as in *Rowland v Divall*, was that the plaintiff enjoyed the use of the goods for some months at no cost to himself. The basis of these decisions—that the plaintiff derived no benefit from the contract—would appear questionable! Nevertheless these cases, both decisions at first instance, were approved and followed by the Court of Appeal in *Barber v NWS Bank*.[21]

---

[16] [1938] 1 K.B. 490.
[17] [1996] 1 All E.R. 906.
[18] See *Microbeads v Vinhurst Road Markings* [1975] 1 W.L.R. 218, para.7–012, above.
[19] [1923] 2 K.B. 500.
[20] [1949] 2 K.B. 576.
[21] [1996] 1 All E.R. 906.

23–010   The situation could come about that a creditor is in breach of a condition as to title but subsequently manages to cure his defect in title. He could do this, for example, by buying the goods from their true owner. If this occurs whilst the debtor is still enjoying the use of the goods, then the debtor will not subsequently be able to treat the contract as repudiated: *Butterworth v Kingsway Motors*.[22] Also he will not suffer a total failure of consideration, since the creditor will now be able to give him good title—even if a little belatedly. He will therefore not be able to reclaim all his payments. His claim will be simply for damages for the fact that he did not obtain good title as soon as he should have done. If the creditor cures his defect in title before property is to pass to the debtor, i.e. before payment of the final instalment—then the debtor will suffer no delay in obtaining good title. He will acquire it at exactly the time that he should do so, i.e. on exercising his option. In this case he will be entitled only to nominal damages. Thus the debtor who discovers that his creditor is in breach of a condition as to title would be well advised to treat the contract as repudiated immediately, i.e. before the creditor cures his defect in title. If the debtor does this, he will be able to recover all his payments. If, instead, he waits until after the defect is cured, he may be reduced to a claim for nominal damages. His method of treating the contract as repudiated is to inform the creditor that he rejects the goods and regards the contract as repudiated.

Description

23–011   Section 9 of the Supply of Goods (Implied Terms) Act is virtually identical to s.13 of the Sale of Goods Act. Section 9 reads:

> "(1) Where under a hire-purchase agreement goods are bailed or (in Scotland) hired by description, there is an implied term that the goods will correspond with the description, and if under the agreement the goods are bailed or hired by reference to a sample as well as a description, it is not sufficient that the bulk of the goods corresponds with the sample if the goods do not also correspond with the description.
> (1A) As regards England and Wales and Northern Ireland, the term implied by subsection (1) above is a condition.
> (2) Goods shall not be prevented from being bailed by description by reason only that, being exposed for sale, bailment or hire, they are selected by the person to whom they are bailed or hired."

Where the debtor has agreed to take the goods as a result of a previous inspection, the creditor's obligation may be greater than merely to see that the goods match the description in the written agreement. As Denning L.J. said in *Karsales v Wallis*[23]:

> "When the hirer has himself previously seen and examined the [item] and made application for hire-purchase on the basis of his inspection, there is an obligation on the lender to deliver the [item] in substantially the same condition as when it was seen. It

---

[22] [1954] 2 All E.R. 694, see para.7–011, above.
[23] [1956] 2 All E.R. 866.

makes no difference that the lender is a finance company which bought the [item] in the interval without seeing it."

The facts in that case were that the debtor had inspected at the dealer's premises a roadworthy Buick car which, after he had made the usual hire-purchase agreement with the finance company, was delivered to him in such a deplorable condition that it was incapable of self-propulsion without a major overhaul. The Court of Appeal held the creditor liable for what was in fact a fundamental breach of its obligation—so radically different was the car from that which the debtor had contracted to take.

Quality

Again, s.10 of the Supply of Goods (Implied Terms) Act is, apart from changes of working **23–012** necessary to make it apply to hire-purchase agreements, identical to s.14 of the Sale of Goods Act.

It may be remembered that the condition that the goods be reasonably fit for a particular purpose is not implied unless that particular purpose, for which the goods are required, is made known before the contract is made. By s.10 it is sufficient that the debtor makes it known either to the creditor or to the negotiator in antecedent negotiations. Thus it is sufficient that he tells the dealer for what purpose he requires the goods. The same is true of a sale of goods contract (e.g. a credit sale or conditional sale agreement) by virtue of s.14(3)(b) of the Sale of Goods Act. This rule does not, however, apply where the debtor is a corporate body, e.g. a limited company. Here the particular purpose for which the debtor requires the goods must be made known to the *creditor* before the contract is made. That is so in the case both of hire-purchase contracts and also of sale of goods contracts.[24]

The conditions as to satisfactory quality and fitness for purpose are exactly the same in hire-purchase contracts as they are in contracts of sale of goods.

Sample

The same can be said of the conditions relating to the hire-purchase of goods by reference **23–013** to a sample. There is no significant difference between s.11 of the Supply of Goods (Implied Terms) Act and s.15 of the Sale of Goods Act.

Delivery and Payment

There are no statutory implied terms relating to delivery and acceptance. That leaves us to **23–014** consider what terms are implied at common law. There is a lack of authority but there seems no reason to suppose that the terms are any different from those in sale of goods.

---

[24] For an explanation of all this see [1983] J.B.L. 312.

Thus, in the absence of any contrary agreement by the parties, it is the creditor's duty to hand over the goods upon demand, i.e. it is up to the debtor to collect them and it is not the creditor's obligation to arrange transport for the goods. If the goods are known to be at the premises of a third party, then those premises will be the place of delivery, i.e. it is from the dealer's premises that the debtor must collect them.

If the creditor refuses to deliver (i.e. to hand over) the goods, that is a breach of condition and the debtor can treat the contract as repudiated and reclaim any money paid and also claim damages (if he has suffered any).

23–015 Where the subject matter of the hire-purchase agreement is a second-hand motor vehicle, the creditor is under an obligation also to hand over the registration document. In *Bentworth Finance v Lubert*[25] Lord Denning M.R. said of the debtor[26]:

> "She was entitled to say 'Produce the log book. Until you do, there is no contract'. There may, of course, be circumstances in which the condition may be waived by taking delivery of the car and using it."

The debtor is under a duty to accept the goods, provided that those supplied fulfil the contract. When he fails to do so, the proper remedy for the creditor is not to claim arrears of instalments but to claim damages for the debtor's failure to take delivery: *NCR v Stanley*.[27] The measure of damages is the same as that in sale of goods—*Inter-Office Telephones v Freeman*,[28] i.e. the loss arising naturally from the breach of contract. Thus the creditor will be able to recover his loss of profit on the transaction. That loss will normally include:

(a) the difference between the creditor's purchasing price and the retail cash price of the goods, and

(b) the creditor's lost finance charges, i.e. the extra profit he would have made by disposing of the goods on instalment terms instead of by a cash sale.

However, if the debtor had gone through with the hire-purchase agreement, the creditor would have received his profit over a period of time. Thus, when awarding damages to the creditor for loss of profit the court will make a deduction to take account of the fact that the creditor is then receiving his profit immediately in one lump sum, i.e. earlier than he otherwise would have received it.

Remedies

23–016 Broadly speaking, the remedies are similar to those in sale of goods. Thus where the creditor is in breach of a warranty the only remedy normally available to the debtor is to sue for damages. Where the creditor is in breach of condition, the debtor has, in addition to a claim for damages, a right to treat the contract as repudiated and reclaim money that he has paid.

---

[25] [1968] 1 Q.B. 680.
[26] [1961] 1 Q.B. 680 at 687.
[27] [1921] 3 K.B. 292.
[28] [1958] 1 Q.B. 190.

As in sale of goods, the method of treating the contract as repudiated is either to refuse to take delivery of the goods or, if delivery has already been taken, to reject them. He can reject them simply by informing the creditor that he does so. Just as in sale of goods, a debtor who is not dealing as a consumer will not have a right to reject for a breach of an implied condition as to description, satisfactory quality, fitness for purpose or as to sample, if the breach is so slight that it would be unreasonable to reject the goods. For this purpose someone buying in the course of a business is not dealing as a consumer.[29]

We saw in Chapter 13 that in sale of goods the right to treat a breach of condition as having repudiated the contract is lost when the buyer "accepts" the goods (s.11(4) of the Sale of Goods Act). When that occurs, the buyer can treat the breach of condition only as if it were a breach of warranty and it follows that his only remedy is a claim for damages. In hire-purchase law there is no exact equivalent to s.11(4) of the Sale of Goods Act. However, there is a somewhat similar rule that, if after the breach of condition, the debtor affirms the contract, he will then be able to treat it only as a breach of warranty. In sale of goods, we saw that the buyer may be taken to have accepted goods if after a fairly short time he has not indicated that he is rejecting them.[30] It may be that in hire-purchase rather more time has to elapse before he will be taken to have affirmed the contract. In any case, if he returns the goods requiring them to be repaired that is quite likely to be interpreted as not being an affirmation. In *Farnworth Finance Facilities v Attryde*[31] the subject matter of the hire-purchase agreement was a new motor cycle. After taking delivery, Mr Attryde found that the motor cycle had a lot of defects and he repeatedly returned it to be put right. The repairs were never satisfactory and eventually, when the rear chain broke, he rejected the cycle. Up to this time he had had the cycle for four months and had driven it some 4,000 miles. Nevertheless the Court of Appeal held that he had not in fact affirmed the contract. His conduct indicated rather the reverse—namely that he was prepared to affirm the contract only if the defects were remedied. It followed that he was within his rights when he rejected the cycle, thereby treating the contract as repudiated. It was further held that he was entitled to recover all of the payments that he had made. No deduction was made for the use he had had of the cycle because that was offset by the inconvenience caused by the defects.

It used to be thought that in hire-purchase, if the debtor affirmed the contract and the goods remained unfit for their purpose (or otherwise in breach of condition) after the affirmation, the debtor's right to reject the goods revived. This, however, is not so: *UCB Leasing Ltd v Holtom*.[32] Once the debtor has affirmed the contract, he has lost for good his right to reject. If he subsequently rejects the goods or otherwise repudiates the contract, he will himself be in breach and liable to pay damages to the creditor. This may not be as disastrous for the debtor as it first appears. It is true that if the goods are not of satisfactory quality (or the creditor is in breach of some other condition) affirmation by the debtor removes the debtor's right to reject the goods. Nevertheless the debtor will still be able to claim damages for that breach of contract. So when the debtor is sued by the creditor for damages for wrongful rejection, the debtor has a counterclaim. The amount of that counterclaim will be assessed on the basis that the debtor is entitled to recover as damages all of his payments already made

---

[29] See paras 10–018–10–020, above.
[30] Though recent amendments to the Sale of Goods Act 1979 have to some extent relaxed this rule in favour of the buyer, see para.13–005, above.
[31] [1970] 1 W.L.R. 1053.
[32] [1987] C.C.L.R. 101.

and all his outstanding liabilities to the creditor. The only deduction that will be made will be in respect of such use as the debtor has had of the goods before they were rejected. In *Charterhouse Credit Co Ltd v Tolly*[33] he was awarded the total of his initial deposit, *the damages awarded to the hire-purchase company on its claim* and the cost of new tyres he had had fitted to the car, less a small deduction for the slight use he had had of the car. The same principles were applied in *UCB Leasing Ltd v Holtom*, where the sum awarded to the debtor included also an amount for inconvenience and distress. These were caused by the fact that, during the time the debtor had it, the car had persistent electrical problems, sometimes suffering a complete electrical failure, which on a couple of frightening occasions could have led the debtor to have an extremely serious accident.

Exclusion

23–017   The law relating to exemption clauses in hire-purchase contracts is the same as that relating to those in contracts of sale of goods. The common law rules are equally applicable. The Unfair Contract Terms Act 1977 applies to hire-purchase agreements in precisely the same way as it does to contracts of sale of goods. The statutory terms implied by ss.8–11 of the Supply of Goods (Implied Terms) Act are dealt with in exactly the same way as the terms implied in contracts of sale by ss.12–15 of the Sale of Goods Act. There is the same distinction between "consumer deals" and others—the distinction having exactly the same effect.

CREDIT SALE AND CONDITIONAL SALE

23–018   A credit sale agreement is a contract of sale of goods and the terms implied in it are those implied into any other contract of sale of goods. In particular ss.10–15 of the Sale of Goods Act apply equally to credit sale agreements as to other sales. So also do the provisions of the Unfair Contract Terms Act 1977.

One thing explained in relation to hire-purchase was that, in connection with the statutory implied condition as to fitness for purpose, it is sufficient that the debtor has told the dealer (i.e. the negotiator in antecedent negotiations) the particular purpose for which the goods were required. The same is true in relation to contracts of sale of goods. This is the effect of certain words in s.14(3) of the Sale of Goods Act—which words were omitted at para.7–024, above.

With one exception, ss.10–15 of the Sale of Goods Act also apply to conditional sale agreements as they do to credit sale agreements. The exception is that s.11(4) of the Sale of Goods Act does not apply to conditional sale agreements which are "consumer deals".[34] Thus in these types of agreement the right to reject the goods for breach of condition is not lost by the buyer "accepting" them. This is the effect of s.14 of the Supply of Goods (Implied Terms) Act. Instead, the position is as in hire-purchase agreements. Thus the right to treat the contract as repudiated may be lost not by "acceptance" but by affirmation.

[33] [1963] 2 Q.B. 683.
[34] See para.10–018, above.

General Reading

- Campbell, "Credit cards and section 75: time for a change in the law?" [1996]   **23–019**
  J.I.B.L. 527;

- Hare, "Your Flexible Friend?" (2005) 64 C.L.J. 287;

- Griffiths and Griffiths, "Joint Liability under the Consumer Credit Act 1974" [1995]
  I.B.F.L. 103.

Chapter 24

ENFORCEMENT BY THE CREDITOR OR OWNER

This chapter outlines the broad principles relating to the enforceability of the credit agreement. In particular, it will focus upon the recent developments whereby the old extortionate credit provisions have been replaced by the new law of unfair credit relationships and it will explain default notices and time orders.   **24–001**

BROAD PRINCIPLES OF ENFORCEMENT

This is the most important part of the chapter and deals with certain provisions of the Act which apply to all regulated agreements. Running through them all is Parliament's intention to protect the debtor from harsh terms in the agreement and generally to ensure that he receives fair treatment.   **24–002**

County Court

Any court action by the creditor or owner to enforce the agreement or any security for it must be brought in the county court.[1] Not only must the debtor or hirer be made a party to the proceedings but so also must any surety. While the action is still undecided the court can, on application by the creditor, make any order it thinks just for protecting any property of the creditor or owner, or any property which is subject to any security, from damage or depreciation.   **24–003**

---

[1] Consumer Credit Act 1974 s.141.

Payment Ahead of Time

24–004   The debtor under a regulated consumer credit agreement is entitled to discharge his debt ahead of time whenever he wishes by giving written notice to the creditor and making full payment of all his payments due under the agreement.[2] Early payment by the debtor of all sums payable under the agreement will mean that if the agreement is a hire-purchase or conditional sale agreement, the debtor will become the owner of the goods at an earlier date than he otherwise would.

The Consumer Credit (Early Settlement) Regulations 2004[3] provide for a rebate to a debtor who pays off his debt ahead of time. The rebate is calculated according to the Regulations or according to the terms of the agreement, whichever give the higher rebate.[4] The amount required to discharge the debt under s.94 is reduced by the amount of the rebate.

Payment Behind Time

24–005   It is not uncommon for a debtor to be late in paying off his debt or some instalments of it. In these circumstances the creditor does not receive his money as soon as he ought to. It is quite possible for the agreement to state that in that event the creditor shall be entitled to an additional payment as interest for the period of the delay. However, that interest must not be at a rate higher than that which the debtor was already paying under the agreement. If the agreement stipulates for a higher rate to be payable on default, the creditor will be able to recover only interest calculated at the rate payable under the contract as a whole—s.93.

Unfair Agreements

24–006   The Consumer Credit Act 2006 introduced a new concept of unfair relationships (between debtor and creditor). This was designed to remedy some of the difficulties evident with the previous provisions (ss.137–140) which permitted the court to "re-open" a credit agreement where that agreement was extortionate.[5] In particular the requirement that the agreement must be grossly exorbitant, under the old s.138(1), placed a high threshold which had to be reached before the court could intervene. This threshold led to reluctance on the part of the courts to intervene with any frequency.[6] This was accepted by the government in the White Paper, *Fair Clear and Competitive: The Consumer Credit Market in the 21st Century*[7] where

---

[2] Consumer Credit Act 1974 s.94.
[3] Consumer Credit (Early Settlement) Regulations 2004 (SI 2004/1483). The Regulations came into force on May 31, 2005 and revoked the Consumer Credit (Rebate on Early Settlement) Regulations 1983 (SI 1983/1562).
[4] See, inter alia, reg.3 and reg.4.
[5] The new provisions came into effect, for the most part, on 6 April, 2007. For a discussion of the previous law, see the 6th edition of this book.
[6] See, for example, the comments of Dyson L.J. in *Broadwick Financial Services Ltd v Spencer* [2002] 1 All E.R. (Comm) 446. See also, *Paragon Finance Plc (formerly National Home Loans Corp) v Pender* [2005] 1 W.L.R. 3412.
[7] Cm. 6040 (2003).

it was noted that only 30 extortionate credit cases had reached the courts![8] Accordingly, ss.137–140 were replaced by the new ss.140A–140D which allow the court to reopen agreements where there is an unfair credit relationship.

Under s.140A the court may make an order (under s.140B) where it determines that the relationship between debtor and creditor arising out of the agreement is unfair due to one of more of the following:

(i) any of the terms of the agreement or of any related agreement[9];

(ii) the way in which the creditor has exercised or enforced any of his rights under the agreement or any related agreement[10];

(iii) any other thing done (or not done) by, or on behalf of, the creditor (either before or after the making of the agreement or any related agreement).[11]

Section 140A(2) requires the court to take into account "all matters it thinks relevant". Furthermore, the court must, where appropriate, consider acts done (or not done) by, or on behalf of, an associate (or former associate) of the creditor.[12]

Where the court is satisfied that an unfair relationship has arisen under s.140A, s.140B(1) **24–007** allows the court to make an order for one, or more, of the following:

(a) require the creditor, or any associate or former associate of his, to repay (in whole or in part) any sum paid by the debtor or by a surety by virtue of the agreement or any related agreement (whether paid to the creditor, the associate or the former associate or to any other person);

(b) require the creditor, or any associate or former associate of his, to do or not to do (or to cease doing) anything specified in the order in connection with the agreement or any related agreement;

(c) reduce or discharge any sum payable by the debtor or by a surety by virtue of the agreement or any related agreement;

(d) direct the return to a surety of any property provided by him for the purposes of a security;

(e) otherwise set aside (in whole or in part) any duty imposed on the debtor or on a surety by virtue of the agreement or any related agreement;

(f) alter the terms of the agreement or of any related agreement;

(g) direct accounts to be taken, or (in Scotland) an accounting to be made, between any persons.

It is interesting to note that, nowhere in the amended Consumer Credit Act 1974 is the term "unfair" defined. It might have been expected that the approach of, for example, the Unfair

---

[8] Furthermore, few of those cases were actually proven.
[9] s.140A(1)(a).
[10] s.140A(1)(b).
[11] s.140A(1)(c).
[12] s.140A(3).

Commercial Practices Directive could have been adopted in drafting a list of factors for the court to consider when assessing whether there was an unfair relationship between the parties. No doubt similar considerations will be adopted by the courts but it seems clear that this absence is a response to the strict interpretation of "extortionate" and "grossly exorbitant" under the old provisions. The absence of any such list means that the courts now have considerable flexibility in assessing the relationship between debtor and creditor and will, it may be expected, be more proactive in their approach to unfair relationships. In any event, it is clear that the new law is considerably more generous to debtors as to both the threshold to be satisfied and the breadth of the court's powers under s.140B(1) once the threshold is satisfied.

Alternative Legislative Provisions

24–008   Where a debtor is unable to persuade a court to re-open an agreement under the unfair relationship provisions, he may nevertheless be able to challenge the agreement, or part of it, under other provisions. Firstly, where the court makes any order under the Act, it has a supplementary power under s.136 to amend the agreement "in consequence of a term of the order". This can, for example, involve reducing the rate of interest, when a time order is granted.[13]

Secondly a contract term can be challenged as being an unfair term under the Unfair Terms in Consumer Contracts Regulations 1999.[14] Under them the consumer cannot challenge the validity of a core term (e.g. one which sets the interest rate under the agreement) but can challenge other terms. In *Falco Finance Ltd v Gough*[15] a County Court had to consider three aspects of a £30,000 mortgage loan agreement:

    (i) a "dual rate" clause by which a "concessionary" rate of interest, lower than the normal contractual rate, was charged unless and until the debtor fell into arrears at any point, in which event the normal contractual rate would be payable for the rest of the term of the loan;

    (ii) a clause providing for a rebate of charges on early repayment to be calculated as if the repayment took place six months later than in reality;

    (iii) a clause providing for the interest payable under the agreement to be calculated on a "flat rate" basis.

Whereas only the first was found to be extortionate, all three clauses were found to be "unfair" within the Unfair Terms in Consumer Contract Regulations—despite the fact that the last of the three appears to be a core term.

Director General of Fair Trading v First National Bank[16] involved a clause in a standard form loan agreement. It provided that interest at the contractual rate was payable on outstanding arrears until the arrears were paid off. It provided that this obligation to pay

---

[13] See para.24–018, below.
[14] These regulations were explained at para.10–033, above.
[15] [1999] C.C.L.R. 16.
[16] [2000] All E.R. 759.

interest did not merge with any judgment and thus interest would continue to be payable even after judgment until the debt was paid. In the absence of the clause, the matter of interest on a judgment debt would be governed by the County Court (Interest on Judgments) Order 1991. Under that order, not only would the relevant rate of interest be lower than that payable under the defendant's loan agreements, but no interest at all would be payable on judgments for less than £5,000 or judgments for money due under regulated consumer credit agreements. Under powers in the Unfair Terms in Consumer Contracts Regulations[17] the Director General asked the court to declare the clause unfair and to grant an injunction to stop the defendant using it. His evidence was that often a debtor against whom the bank brought proceedings would agree to a "consent" order being made by the judge, such judgment being for the outstanding balance to be payable by instalments over an extended period. The consent order would then be made by the judge without any hearing of the merits of the case and, because of the clause, interest at the contractual rate would be payable on the judgment debt. The Court of Appeal held the clause to be unfair because its effect in practice was to impose post-judgment interest without the court considering whether to make a time order or, if it did, whether also to make an order under s.136 reducing the contractual interest rate.[18] This decision was reversed by the House of Lords which held that the clause was assessable for fairness under the Unfair Terms in Consumer Contracts Regulations[19] but that it met the requirements of the fairness test. The impact of this decision upon consumers has, to some extent, been alleviated by the changes introduced by the Consumer Credit Act 2006 which impose obligations on the creditor to inform a debtor of the difficulties stemming from falling into arrears.[20]

Default Notice

Section 87 operates where the debtor is in breach of the agreement. Its effect is to prevent the creditor from pursuing certain remedies unless and until a default notice has first been served upon the debtor giving him a chance to put right his default. The remedies which the creditor is thereby prevented from pursuing are, broadly, those which would involve the debtor in more than just being compelled to honour the agreement and put right his default, i.e. those remedies of the creditor which operate as a sort of threat to induce the debtor to honour the agreement.   **24–009**

Thus by s.87(1) a notice of default must be served before the creditor or owner is entitled:

"(a)   to terminate the agreement, or
 (b)   to demand earlier payment of any sum, or
 (c)   to recover possession of any goods or land, or
 (d)   to treat any right conferred on the debtor or hirer by the agreement as terminated, restricted or deferred, or
 (e)   to enforce any security."

[17] Explained at para.10–039, above.
[18] A clause which is unfair within the regulations is of no effect, see para.10–037, above.
[19] i.e. the clause was not a core term of the agreement but, rather, it was an incidental or ancillary provision.
[20] See for example, the information sheets prepared by the OFT under s.86A which contain information for debtors that have received a default notice. See also, s.130A, which deals with interest payable on judgment debts.

By way of exception to s.87(1), no default notice need be served before the creditor can become entitled to treat the debtor's right to draw upon any credit as restricted or deferred. Thus, for example, a credit card company which discovers that a card holder has exceeded his credit limit can take immediate steps to prevent him using the card to obtain still further credit. No default notice is required where the creditor seeks a remedy which would do no more than compel the debtor to honour the agreement in the normal way. Thus where the debtor is in arrears, no default notice is required before the creditor can sue for the arrears.

24–010   When the default notice is required, it must make certain things clear to the debtor[21]:

    (i) The nature of the alleged breach.

    (ii) What action is required to remedy it or, if it is not remediable, how much (if anything) is required to be paid in compensation.

    (iii) The exact date by which the breach must be remedied or the compensation paid.

    (iv) The consequences if the debtor does not comply with the notice.[22]

The time allowed must be at least 14 days[23] from the date the notice is served upon the debtor. If the default notice overstates the amount owing, it will be invalid, unless (possibly) the error was so small as to be insignificant: *Woodchester Lease Management Services Ltd v Swain.*[24] The default notice must also be in the form prescribed by the Consumer Credit (Enforcement, Default and Termination Notices) Regulations 1983.[25] If the debtor complies with the notice within the specified time by rectifying the breach or paying the stipulated compensation, the breach must be treated as if it had never occurred.[26]

If at the end of the specified time the breach has not been remedied or the compensation has not been paid, then the creditor is free to pursue any of the remedies in s.87(1), provided that under the terms of the agreement he is entitled to do so. If the default notice included no requirement for the breach to be remedied or for any compensation to be paid, then after 14 days the creditor is free to pursue any of the remedies in s.87(1), again, provided that he is entitled to do so under the terms of the agreement. Two points of explanation are required. First, s.87 does not confer any remedies or rights upon the creditor. It simply restrains him from pursuing certain remedies. Thus, when the restraint is lifted, he can pursue any given remedy only if, quite apart from s.87 (i.e. under the terms of the agreement), he is entitled to do so. Secondly, the creditor cannot avoid giving the debtor a chance to put things right by the simple expedient of failing to include in the default notice any requirement for the breach to be remedied or compensation paid. If the breach can be remedied then a requirement for that must be included. If it cannot, and compensation is required, then a requirement for payment of compensation must be included.

---

[21] s.88.
[22] There will soon be a further requirement, namely, that the default notice must also include a copy of the default information sheet under s.86A. This requirement is due to come into effect on October 1, 2008.
[23] Increased from seven days by the CCA 2006, s.14(1).
[24] [1999] C.C.L.R. 8.
[25] Consumer Credit (Enforcement, Default and Termination Notices) Regulations 1983 (SI 1983/1561), to be amended by the Consumer Credit (Information Requirements and Duration of Licences and Charges) Regulations (SI 2007/1167) from October 1, 2008.
[26] s.89.

Consider an example. Flotsam buys a boat under a credit sale agreement in which there is   **24–011**
a condition that Flotsam will not sell the boat until he has paid all the instalments. The
agreement states that if Flotsam breaks the agreement by selling the boat, all the remaining
instalments shall fall due immediately. Flotsam does sell the boat. Now, the breach cannot be
put right, since the boat now belongs to someone else, and the creditor will not require
compensation. In this situation the creditor can serve a default notice without any requirement for the breach to be remedied or for any compensation. After 14 days he can commence
an action against Flotsam for the whole of the remaining instalments.[27]

The default notice requirement is exactly the same where a hirer is in breach of a regulated
consumer hire agreement as it is where the debtor is in breach of a regulated consumer credit
agreement.

Death of the Debtor

Consumer credit agreements quite often include a clause which provides for what is to be the   **24–012**
position if the debtor dies. The agreement may, for example, provide that on the death of the
debtor, all remaining instalments shall immediately become payable in one lump sum. Hire-
purchase agreements sometimes provide that the hiring and the agreement shall terminate
upon the debtor's death.

Section 86 applies to any regulated agreement where the debtor dies. Its effect depends
upon whether the agreement was "fully secured" or not. Where the regulated agreement is
fully secured and the debtor or hirer dies, then by s.86(1) the creditor or owner cannot do any
of the acts specified in paras (a)–(e) of s.87(1).[28] There is a complete embargo. In short, this
means that, in spite of anything written in the agreement, the death of the debtor or hirer will
not affect the operation of the agreement. The debtor's or hirer's personal representatives will
simply take over his rights and duties under the agreement.

Where the agreement is not fully secured, s.86 does not place an absolute embargo upon
the operation of clauses in the agreement which would, upon the death of the debtor or hirer
either (for example) terminate the agreement or cause the remaining payments to fall due
immediately. Nevertheless it does severely restrict the operation of such clauses. The creditor
or owner can do one of the acts specified in paras (a)–(e) of s.87(1) only if two requirements
are both fulfilled:

   (i) the creditor or owner applies to the court, and

   (ii) the creditor or owner proves to the court that he has been unable to satisfy himself
        that the present and future obligations of the debtor or hirer under the agreement
        are likely to be carried out.

In practice this will involve showing that none of the personal representatives or relations   **24–013**
of the debtor or hirer is willing to take over the agreement.

There are three qualifications to s.86. First, the credit agreement may provide that on the
death of the debtor or hirer, the outstanding debt (or part of it) shall be paid out of the

---

[27] Less any rebate for early payment under s.95, see para.24–004, above.
[28] See para.24–009, above.

proceeds of a policy of life assurance taken out on the debtor's or hirer's life for that purpose. Such a provision in the agreement is enforceable and not affected by s.86. Secondly, s.86 does not prevent the creditor from treating the right to draw on any credit as terminated by the debtor's death. Thus, for example, the debtor's personal representatives would not be able to use his credit card or to draw money under his overdraft agreement. Section 86 is concerned only with debts which the debtor had before he died. Thirdly, s.86 does not apply in relation to the termination of an agreement which is of an unspecified duration or where the specified period of duration has expired.

Let us examine the effect of s.86 in some particular examples:

(i) The debtor dies owing money under an ordinary unguaranteed credit sale agreement. Unguaranteed is used here to mean that the debtor had no guarantor. In this case the agreement will be unsecured. The debtor's personal representatives will be entitled to continue the agreement (i.e. to pay the instalments as and when due from the debtor under the agreement). However, if they refuse to do so and the creditor is unable to make satisfactory arrangements with anyone else (e.g. the debtor's relatives) for the carrying out of the agreement, then the creditor could ask the court to enforce a term of the credit sale agreement (if it contained such a term) which stipulates that the whole outstanding balance becomes due on the death of the debtor.

(ii) The debtor died owing money borrowed on an unsecured bank loan. If the loan was for a specified period then the result would be exactly the same as with the credit sale agreement. If the loan was not for a specified period and included a term that the creditor (the bank) could terminate it and demand immediate repayment at any time, then there would be no restriction upon the bank doing just that.

(iii) The debtor died owing money under this credit card agreement, which is of unspecified duration and includes a term that on the death of the debtor the agreement shall terminate and the outstanding debt become repayable immediately. Because the agreement is of unspecified duration, s.86 will not apply and the effect of the debtor's death will be as stated in the agreement.

(iv) The debtor died owing money under an unexpired regulated agreement of specified duration (e.g. a credit sale agreement) under which the liability of the debtor and of his personal representatives was fully guaranteed by someone who acted as guarantor at the express or implied request of the debtor. Now, such a guarantee is within the definition of "security"[29] and therefore such an agreement would be "fully secured". That being so, the creditor (even if satisfactory arrangements could not be made for the carrying out of the debtor's obligations) could not do any act within paras (a)–(e) of s.87(1). Thus the creditor could not regard the agreement as terminated by the debtor's death, nor could he sue for any instalment earlier than it would have been due from the debtor had he lived.

[29] s.189.

(v) The hirer under an unguaranteed consumer hire agreement of specified duration dies while the agreement is still running. Under such agreements there is usually no security given for the payments due under the agreement. Nevertheless the owner will be able to regard the agreement as terminated and recover the goods only if he applies to the court and can show that he was unable to satisfy himself that the hirer's obligations under the agreement would be carried out.

(vi) The debtor dies leaving outstanding instalments to be paid under an unguaranteed hire-purchase agreement. A hire-purchase agreement will in practice always be of a specified duration. The debtor's personal representatives will have the right to continue the agreement just as if he had not died. The problem arises if such satisfactory arrangements cannot be made for the carrying out of the debtor's obligations. Is the agreement "fully secured"? If it is, the position is the same as in the case of a credit sale agreement with a guarantor of the liability of the debtor and of his personal representatives. If it is not "fully secured", then the creditor (in the absence of satisfactory arrangements) could ask the court to enforce any provisions in the agreement allowing the creditor to terminate it, to take possession of the goods, etc.

The Act nowhere defines "fully secured" which presumably describes an agreement where **24–014** the creditor or owner has taken security which, if realised at the time of the debtor's or hirer's death, would cover the whole of the outstanding payments under the agreement. Section 189 defines "security" as:

"... a mortgage, charge, pledge, bond, debenture, indemnity, guarantee, bill note or other right provided by the debtor or hirer, or at his request (express or implied) to secure the carrying out of the obligations of the debtor or hirer under the agreement."

Has the creditor under a hire-purchase agreement got any "security"? In any ordinary sense of the word he has, because he has the right to the return of his goods (subject to the provisions of the Consumer Credit Act) if the debtor defaults in circumstances entitling the creditor to terminate the agreement.[30] However, is this right "provided by the debtor"? The answer would appear to be that the agreement is "fully secured" if in the agreement itself the debtor gives the creditor the right to take possession of the goods upon termination of the agreement. If, however, the agreement does not give the creditor such a right then there is no "security" and it follows that the agreement cannot be "fully secured". This is so even though the creditor may still be entitled to recovery of the goods on termination of the agreement, because in this case the right to recovery of the goods is not "provided by the debtor" but derives from the basic property rights which belong to the owner of goods (the creditor under the hire-purchase agreement). Since most hire-purchase agreements do not today expressly provide for what is to happen to the goods upon termination of the agreement, it follows that in relation to the vast

[30] See paras 25–014 and 25–015, below.

majority of hire-purchase agreements there is no "security" and that they are therefore not "fully secured".

Non-Default Notice

24–015   In the event of the debtor or hirer being in a breach of a regulated agreement, there is a list of things (in s.87(1)) which the creditor or owner by reason of the breach become entitled to do without first serving a default notice. Sections 76 and 98 contain similar provisions which apply where the creditor or owner is entitled to do one of those things otherwise than by reason of a breach of the agreement by the debtor or hirer. For example, an agreement may provide that the creditor can terminate it at any time or that he can terminate it if the debtor is convicted of an offence of dishonesty or is sent to prison or changes his address, or becomes unemployed, etc.

Section 98 prevents the creditor or owner terminating a regulated agreement without first serving on the debtor or hirer a notice of his intention to do so. Section 76 requires the creditor or owner to serve a similar notice before enforcing a term of regulated agreement by:

"(a)   demanding earlier payment of any sum, or
 (b)   recovering possession of any goods or land, or
 (c)   treating any right conferred on the debtor or hirer by the agreement as terminated restricted or deferred."

The notice must give the debtor or hirer at least seven days' warning of the creditor's or owner's intention and must be in the form prescribed by the Consumer Credit (Enforcement, Default and Termination Notices) Regulations 1983. Like a default notice, the notice in this case does not prevent the creditor from treating the right to draw on any credit as restricted or deferred.

24–016   Unlike s.87 (default notice), ss.76 and 98 apply only to agreements which have a specified period of duration. Thus they apply to hire-purchase, conditional sale and credit sale agreements. They do not, however, apply for example to an agreement for a bank overdraft for an indefinite period. If such an agreement gives the bank the right at any time to demand immediate repayment of the whole debt then no notice need be served before the bank can do just that.

The Act does not give any name to the notice which ss.98 and 76 require to be served. In this book it is termed a non-default notice to distinguish it from a default notice. It will be appreciated that these two types of notice are very close cousins. In the case of an agreement of specified duration, before the creditor or owner can take certain kinds of action (e.g. terminating the agreement) he will have to serve one of these types of notice. Which one he must serve will depend upon whether the creditor's right to take that action derives from the debtor's breach of the agreement (default notice) or some other event (non-default notice). Whichever one it is, service of the notice will entitle the debtor to apply for a time order. With a default notice the debtor normally has an opportunity to put right his default, whereas plainly there is no question of that with a non-default notice.

Time Order

The debtor or hirer can ask the court for a time order in any court action brought by the   **24–017**
creditor or owner to enforce a regulated agreement. Alternatively when the debtor or hirer has
been served either with a default notice (under ss.87 and 88) or with a non-default notice
(under ss.76 or 98), then he can apply for a time order without waiting for the creditor or
owner to sue him.[31]

The power given by s.129 to the court to make a time order is twofold. It can allow time
(a specified period) for the debtor or hirer to remedy any breach of the agreement other than
non-payment. It can also give time for the payment of any sums owed by the debtor or hirer
under the agreement. Where the court does make a time order, it can make the payment(s)
"payable at such times, as the court having regard to the means of the debtor or hirer and any
surety, considers reasonable." The court's power is confined to sums which at the time the
order is made have already fallen due. It does not extend to future instalments. Thus the
debtor under a credit sale agreement cannot ask the court to alter the amount or dates of
future instalments but can ask it to give him time to pay instalments which have already
fallen due. There are three exceptions to the rule that the power to make a time order does
not extend to future instalments. First, if there has come into operation a term (an accelerated
payments clause) of the agreement which stipulates that all remaining instalments are due
immediately, the debtor can ask the court to give him time to pay those because they have
(owing to that term of the agreement) fallen due already. The second exception arises where
a mortgage of land has been granted as security for a loan and, after the debtor's default, the
creditor (no doubt after having served a default notice) commences repossession proceedings.
It has been held that commencing repossession proceedings amounts to a "calling-in" of the
loan, i.e. causes the creditor to be entitled to the whole of the outstanding balance: *Southern
District Finance Plc v Barnes*.[32] Thus it has the same effect as the operation of an accelerated
payments clause and thus the court is empowered to make a time order in respect of the
whole debt including future instalments. The third exception arises where the agreement in
question is a hire-purchase or conditional sale agreement. In that case the court has special
powers when asked for a time order.[33] In particular it can, even in the absence of an
accelerated payments clause, make a time order in respect of future instalments which have
not yet fallen due and thus is able (if it considers it just and reasonable to do so) to rewrite
the whole instalment pattern.

The court has power to vary or revoke any time order it makes. So, for example, the debtor
could come back to the court later and ask that he be given a further extension of time in
which to make the payments subject to the time order. Alternatively the creditor could ask
that the time order be revoked (e.g. if the debtor was not in fact making payments as required
under the time order). In that case the creditor might ask for immediate judgment in his
favour for the total amount then due or for any other remedy (e.g. enforcement of any
security).

---

[31] s.16 of the CCA 2006 allows the debtor or hirer to make an application under the new s.129(1)(ba) and s.129A
where he has been given a notice under ss.86B (notice of sums in arrears under fixed-sum credit agreements) or 86C
(notice of sums in arrears under running-account credit agreements) and 14 days have passed. This is due to come
into effect on October 1, 2008.
[32] [1995] C.C.L.R. 62. See Johnson, "Time Orders" [1995] J.B.F.L. 6.
[33] s.130(2).

Court's Supplementary Powers

Suspended and Conditional Court Orders

24–018   Section 135 gives the court certain extra powers in making any order in relation to a regulated agreement. It can make any order (or any term of the order) conditional upon the doing of specified acts. It can also suspend the operation of any order or term of an order.

The court's powers under s.135 can be particularly useful where the creditor or owner brings an action to recover possession of goods to which the agreement relates (e.g. in the case of a hire-purchase, conditional sale or consumer hire agreement). He will probably be bringing the action because the debtor or hirer is in arrears. In that case the court could make a time order (giving the debtor or hirer time to make up his arrears) and could also order the debtor to return the goods. The court could then suspend the operation of the return order so that it will not take effect unless the debtor or hirer fails to comply with the time order. Alternatively it could suspend the order indefinitely, requiring the creditor to return to the court again before being able to enforce it.

This is only an example and the court's power to impose conditions or to suspend the operation of an order apply in relation to any order relating to a regulated agreement.

Amendment of Agreement

24–019   Section 136 provides:

> "The court may in an order made by it under this Act include such provision as it considers just for amending any agreement or security in consequence of a term of the order."

Can the court vary the rate of interest when granting a time order? The court clearly has power to vary the rate of interest where it finds that an agreement gives rise to an unfair debtor/creditor relationship. Apart from that, however, the court when granting a time order can vary the interest rate (under s.136) only where that variation in the interest rate is "in consequence of a term of the time order": *Southern and District Finance plc v Barnes*.[34] This could come about as follows.

It could very well be, for example, that the effect of making a time order is to delay the receipt of payments by the creditor, e.g. by the court in the time order providing for a greater number of smaller payments over an extended repayment period. If no reduction were made in the contractual rate of interest, that rate would continue to apply to the monthly deficiency arising between the contractual monthly instalment and the monthly instalment directed by the court. This would result in the creditor on the one hand receiving overall a higher total amount of interest whilst on the other receiving a slower rate of repayment.

In the case of an agreement with a high, albeit not extortionate, rate of interest, it would then be appropriate for the court to reduce the rate of interest "in consequence of" the time

---

[34] [1995] C.C.L.R. 62.

order. The fact is that if the court is able to reduce the interest rate, that may well be a way of achieving justice. Suppose the court is dealing with a loan secured by a mortgage at a rate of interest which, though not extortionate, is nevertheless very high. The debtor has got into arrears. These are piling up at an alarming rate because interest is accumulating on the arrears. The creditor commences repossession proceedings. The court is then facing a choice of either granting an immediate repossession order or else giving the debtor a chance to catch up by making a time order, a time order being normally made for a stipulated period on account of temporary financial difficulty. The court cannot make a time order unless the debtor has some reasonable chance of keeping up with the payments required under the time order. If the court is able to find a reason to reduce the interest rate, i.e. "in consequence of a term of the time order", then that may make all the difference, thereby enabling the court to make a time order for payments which the debtor has some chance of maintaining.

Chapter 25

TERMINATION OF HIRE-PURCHASE CONTRACTS

At the outset the parties will no doubt expect that the contract will run its full course—that **25–001** the debtor will pay all his instalments and at the end will exercise his option to purchase the goods. Nevertheless, the hiring may be terminated before the debtor has paid all his instalments. This chapter is concerned with the causes and consequences of such premature termination. It is not, however, concerned with the right of cancellation which is given for the first few days to some debtors who sign the agreement elsewhere than at certain trade premises. That was considered in Chapter 22.

Unlike cancellation, termination is seldom in the debtor's best interest. The normal consequences of termination are that the debtor has no right to retain the goods and that he is unable to recover any payments he has already paid; he may even have to make a further payment. Thus it is rarely a positive decision on the debtor's part to terminate the agreement. The most common cause is in fact the debtor's inability or failure to keep up his payments. We shall see, however, that the debtor whose agreement is a regulated agreement has much less to fear from termination. The Consumer Credit Act gives him considerable protection. One set of provisions of the Consumer Credit Act will not, however, be mentioned further in this chapter; those relating to unfair creditor/debtor relationships.[1] It should nevertheless be borne in mind throughout that these provisions can be used if the court finds that the agreement creates an unfair debtor/creditor relationship and that they are not confined to regulated agreements but can be used in relation to any consumer credit agreement even if it is an exempt agreement.

We shall be dealing with the position at common law, i.e. where the agreement is not regulated by the Consumer Credit Act, as well as the position in relation to regulated agreements. Although this chapter will be concerned only with hire-purchase agreements, the practice will be continued, in line with the Consumer Credit Act, of referring to the parties as creditor and debtor rather than owner and hirer, although it is true that many of the

---

[1] ss.140A–140C of the Consumer Credit Act 1974.

creditor's rights derive from the fact that he is the owner of the goods. This is especially so in relation to his rights against third parties.

25–002   This chapter will be devoted to answering four questions, in the following order:

(1) What events cause termination?

(2) After termination, is the creditor entitled to recover the goods from the debtor?

(3) After termination, is the creditor entitled to any further payment from the debtor?

(4) After termination, is the creditor entitled to recover the goods if they have passed to a third person?

EVENTS CAUSING TERMINATION

25–003   Broadly, termination may come about as a result of one of four things: subsequent agreement between the parties; exercise by the debtor of a right of termination; breach of the agreement by the debtor; or, lastly, the occurrence of an event stipulated in the agreement as liable to cause termination. When termination occurs it is not always easy to identify which of these things was the cause. It can, however, be important, for the consequences of termination vary according to the cause.

Mutual Agreement

25–004   It is quite possible for the creditor and debtor to come to a subsequent agreement whereby they terminate the hire-purchase contract. In practice, this will seldom be done except where a new hire-purchase agreement is substituted for the old one. The debtor will hardly wish to return the goods and also to sacrifice the payments which he has already made. On the other hand, the creditor will not usually be too willing to forgo a substantial part of the payments and also have the problem of disposing of the goods. The creditor is more likely to try to persuade the debtor to replace his existing contract with another hire-purchase agreement, spreading the remaining payments over a longer period of time.

The parties may of course decide that it is not necessary to terminate the agreement and substitute a new one and decide instead simply to agree to vary the first one. However, if they do this then the provisions of the Consumer Credit Act will operate as if they had terminated the first agreement and made a new one producing the combined effect of the first agreement and the later variation.[2]

Termination by mutual agreement seldom gives rise to any legal difficulty. The problems with which this chapter is concerned are associated rather with termination which comes about in some other way.

---

[2] See s.82.

Exercise by the Debtor of a Right of Termination

Often a hire-purchase agreement will contain a term expressly allowing the debtor to **25–005**
terminate the contract, although there will usually also be a provision to the effect that the
debtor must, as the price of doing so, make a further stipulated payment (i.e. in addition to
payments falling due before termination). Notice in writing to the creditor will normally be
required. Since the contract expressly allows him to terminate it, the debtor does not commit
a breach of contract by exercising the contractual right. This can be an important point in
relation to whether the creditor is entitled to recover the further payment stipulated to be due
on the debtor exercising his right of termination.[3] It will be important where the agreement
is not a regulated one but not where the agreement is a regulated agreement because in the
latter case the amount of money recoverable by the creditor is governed by s.100.

In the case of a regulated agreement, s.99 gives the debtor a right to terminate the contract
by giving notice in writing to the creditor or any person entitled or authorised to receive
payments under the agreement. The debtor may have both the above rights of termination, i.e.
if the agreement both gives to the debtor an express right of termination and is also a
regulated agreement. If in that situation the debtor exercises his right of termination, the
consequences will be those that are the more lenient and beneficial for the debtor, i.e. those
in s.100 or those stipulated in the agreement. The reason for this is that by s.173 the
agreement cannot increase but can only reduce the debtor's liability as stated in the Act.

Where the agreement is not a regulated one, the debtor will not have a right to terminate
under s.99 but may still have a contractual right of termination. In this case a stipulation for
a further payment may be enforceable even though it is excessive. Thus it might exceed the
actual loss caused to the creditor by the termination. It might mean that he receives in all
more than he would have received if the agreement had never been terminated and had been
fully carried out. To put it another way, it could result in the creditor receiving in all (i.e.
including the sums already paid by the debtor before the termination and the value of the
goods returned to the creditor at the time of the termination) more than the whole of the total
price.[4] This means that where the agreement is not a regulated one, the consequences of the
debtor exercising a contractual right of termination could be very harsh for the debtor. They
certainly could be worse than if he broke his contract (i.e. simply allowed his payments to
get into arrears). For this reason the court will not hold that the debtor has exercised a
contractual right of termination unless it is sure that he was fully aware of the
consequences.

In *United Dominions Trust v Ennis*[5] the subject-matter of the agreement was a Jaguar car **25–006**
and the debtor was a London docker who found he could not keep up his payments when the
dockers went on strike. He wrote to the creditor saying, "I wish to terminate my agreement
with you as I find I cannot fulfil the terms". The Court of Appeal held that the debtor was
not exercising his contractual right of termination but was, in effect, giving the creditor notice
of his breach of contract. Referring to the debtor's contractual right (option) of termination,
Lord Denning M.R. said,

---

[3] See *Associated Distributors v Hall* [1938] 1 All E.R. 511, below.
[4] See *Associated Distributors v Hall* [1938] 1 All E.R. 511, below.
[5] [1968] 1 Q.B. 54.

"A hirer (i.e. debtor) is not to be taken as exercising such an option unless he does so consciously, knowing of the consequences and avowedly in exercise of his option".

Since the debtor had not exercised his right of termination, it was the creditor who had terminated, as he was entitled to do, for the debtor's breach of contract. This meant that the creditor had no right to the stipulated further payment which was excessive and therefore void as a penalty.

Breach of the Agreement by the Debtor

25–007   Not every breach by the debtor will terminate the agreement. Those breaches which may result in termination are:

(i) An act by the debtor wholly repugnant to the agreement, e.g. if he sells the goods or otherwise indicates by acts or words that he repudiates the contract. If the debtor does such an act, the creditor is not bound to regard the agreement as terminated but is entitled to do so. If he does so, the law will regard the termination as having been caused by the debtor's repudiation. This fact will tell against the debtor if the creditor claims damages.[6]

(ii) A breach by the debtor which does not amount to repudiation but which is specified in the agreement as giving to the creditor the right to terminate the hiring. The usual breaches specified in this way are first, failure by the debtor to take reasonable care of the goods and, secondly, the debtor falling into arrears with his payments. Sometimes the contract states that it is automatically terminated on the occurrence of one of the specified breaches. Sometimes it gives the creditor the right of termination after giving notice. When the creditor exercises his right of termination for the debtor's breach then, unless the debtor repudiated the agreement, the law regards the termination as having been caused by the creditor. This fact will be in the debtor's favour if the creditor claims damages.[7]

(iii) A breach of a term which is a condition of the contract. If the contract clearly indicates that a term is a condition (as opposed to a warranty) then any breach of it by the debtor has the same effect as an act by the debtor which is wholly repugnant to the contract. A statement in the contract that a given term is "of the essence" clearly labels it as a condition. Thus where the contract states that punctual payment of all moneys due by the debtor is "of the essence", then, if the debtor is late (even if only by one day) in making one of the payments, he can be treated by the creditor as having repudiated the contract.[8] The damages to be paid by the debtor will be assessed accordingly. Thus there is a fine, but important, line between a contract provision that if the debtor is 10 days late in making any

---

[6] See para.25–024, below.
[7] See *Financings v Baldock* [1963] 2 Q.B. 104, para.25–025, below.
[8] *Lombard North Central v Butterworth* [1987] Q.B. 527.

payment the creditor has the right to terminate the hiring (*Financings v Baldock*)[9] and one which states that punctual payment of all moneys due under the contract is "of the essence" (*Lombard North Central v Butterworth*).[10] Both give the creditor the right to terminate the contract for late payment, but the latter can result in the debtor having to pay greater damages.[11]

If the agreement so specifies, it appears to be possible for the contract to be terminated if the debtor is late with one instalment. However, in the case of an agreement which is a regulated agreement, this cannot happen without the debtor first being given a chance to bring his payments up to date. Section 87 applies where the debtor is in breach of the agreement. It provides that the creditor cannot (amongst other things) either terminate the agreement or treat any right of the debtor's as terminated without first serving a default notice on the debtor. The section applies to regulated agreements and it applies irrespective of whether the debtor's breach was a repudiatory one or not. Default notices were considered in the last chapter.[12] By way of reminder it may be said here that where the debtor's only breach is non-payment of instalments the default notice must make a number of things clear to the debtor, including:

(i) The exact amount required to bring his payments up to date. If the amount is overstated, the notice is invalid.[13]

(ii) Exactly how long (a minimum of 14 days) he has got in which to pay it (i.e. the date of expiry of the default notice).

(iii) The consequences of failure to comply with the notice.

(iv) The provision of the agreement (if any) under which the agreement can be terminated.

(v) That if the breach is duly remedied the agreement will not terminate.

Some of these requirements were not made clear in *Eshun v Moorgate Mercantile Co.*[14] The debtor had paid £115 out of a total hire-purchase price of £405 17s. 3d. The default notice served on him stated correctly that he was £23 3s. 6d. in arrears. It then said:

"... unless we do hear from you with payment within the course of the next nine days after the date on which you would normally be expected to receive this letter, we shall have no alternative but to assume that you do not wish to continue the hiring under the Agreement and are, in effect terminating by repudiation."

The court held that this notice was invalid on three grounds. First, the creditor had no right   **25–008** to assume from the mere non-payment of two instalments that the debtor was in effect terminating by repudiation. The creditor cannot put upon the debtor a repudiation when he

[9] [1963] 2 Q.B. 104.
[10] [1987] Q.B. 527.
[11] See para.25–026, below.
[12] See para.24–009, above.
[13] *Woodchester Lease Management v Swain* [1999] 1 W.L.R. 263.
[14] [1971] 2 All E.R. 402.

has never repudiated. Secondly, the notice did not refer to the provision of the hire-purchase agreement under which it was given and under which the amounts in default were due. Thirdly, it did not clearly state exactly how long the debtor had before the period for payment expired. Since the notice was invalid, the agreement was never terminated and therefore the creditor had no right to recover possession of the goods. The creditor therefore had to pay compensation to the debtor for having done so.

A further interesting point to emerge from the case was that even if the agreement had not been regulated by an Act of Parliament, it still could not have been terminated without a notice of default being served. Lord Denning M.R. said,

> "I think that even at common law a notice of default may be necessary . . . the agreement being a one-sided one with stringent terms, the plaintiff was entitled to a reminder that his instalments were in arrear before it could be terminated".

Other Stipulated Events

25–009 Hire-purchase agreements commonly provide for termination on the occurrence of any one of certain stipulated events (other than breach of the agreement), e.g. on the death of the debtor, on his becoming insolvent or on his being sentenced to a term of imprisonment. Either the contract will provide that it is terminated automatically by a given event or it will give the creditor the right (option) to terminate it on the occurrence of the event. At common law the effect of such an event occurring is as stated in the contract, i.e. either that the contract terminates automatically or that it becomes terminable at the creditor's option.

Where the agreement is a regulated agreement the common law position is modified in two respects. One of these modifications applies where the stipulated event is the death of the debtor. The other modification (the requirement for a non-default notice) applies whatever the stipulated event.

Section 86 applies to any regulated agreement where the debtor dies. This section has already been fully considered in the last chapter.[15] It is sufficient to say here that usually the death of the debtor will not cause the agreement to terminate, notwithstanding anything said in the agreement. The result will be that on the debtor's death, his rights and obligations under the agreement will transfer to his personal representatives, i.e. those responsible for administering his estate.

Sections 76 and 98 apply to regulated agreements where the stipulated event is anything other than a breach of the agreement by the debtor. Their effect is that the creditor cannot (amongst other things) either terminate the agreement or treat any right of the debtor as terminated without first serving on him a notice (a non-default notice) giving him at least seven days' warning. These sections also have already been considered once.[16] However, there are two remaining questions that need answering in relation both to default and also to non-default notices.

---

[15] See para.24–012, above.
[16] See para.24–015, above.

Default Notice and Non-Default Notice

It will be apparent that where termination occurs other than by mutual agreement or by the   **25–010**
debtor exercising his right of termination, one of these notices has to be served. Two
questions arise in relation to such notices:

Exactly When Will Termination Occur?

When the creditor has a right (i.e. option) to terminate the agreement on a breach or other   **25–011**
stipulated event, then termination cannot occur before expiry of the notice served on the
debtor. That (i.e. expiry of the notice) will in practice be when termination will occur—
because the notice will state so. However, sometimes a hire-purchase agreement states that
the agreement is to terminate automatically upon a certain type of breach by the debtor or
upon some other event. At common law, of course, this would mean that termination
occurred as soon as (and at the same time as) the stipulated event. Section 87 (default notice)
or s.76 (non-default notice) prevents the creditor, until the expiry of the notice, from being
entitled to "treat" any right to the debtor as terminated. So we have the position that it is not
until the expiry of the notice that the creditor can treat the contract as terminated. At the
expiry of the notice he can treat the contract as terminated—but, as terminated when? The
answer is that he can then treat the contract as having terminated upon the happening of the
event which was stipulated as causing the automatic termination. This is because the sections
requiring the notice to be given to the debtor do not (with one exception) prevent automatic
termination occurring but only prevent (i.e. delay) the creditor treating the termination as
having occurred. The exception brings us on to the next question.

Can the Notice Requirements Ever Prevent Termination Occurring
Altogether?

In one situation they can. That is where, after a default notice is served and before it expires,   **25–012**
the debtor complies with the notice by remedying his breach or paying compensation as
required in the notice. If he does this, then the debtor's breach is treated as not having
occurred.[17] In this case it follows that the breach cannot give rise to termination (either
automatically or otherwise).

Apart from that one situation, service of a notice will not prevent termination. It does,
however, give the debtor the opportunity to apply for a "time order" and the court then has
power to give the debtor another chance, to allow the debtor to keep the goods, to spread his
repayments over a longer period, etc. However, if the court exercises these powers, that will
not prevent the agreement being technically terminated. It may seem odd that on the one hand
the debtor will in these circumstances be in possession of the goods, paying instalments and
having the ability to exercise his option to buy them, while on the other hand the agreement
has terminated. The explanation is that the debtor is then in possession of the goods under the

---

[17] s.89.

time order made by the court. It is true that he will be "treated" as in possession under the terms of the agreement, but this will not alter the fact that the agreement has technically terminated. It may in these circumstances seem irrelevant that the agreement had, technically speaking, been terminated, and so it is, as between the creditor and debtor. However, as we shall see, it may be an important point in the creditor's favour if the debtor's landlord later seizes the goods from the debtor's possession in order to pay for the debtor's rent. More will be said on this later.

One more thing needs to be said at this stage about time orders. The court's power to make a time order includes the power to allow time (a specified period) during which the debtor can remedy a breach (other than one consisting of non-payment). This will cause a postponement of the time when the creditor will be able to terminate the agreement or to treat it as terminated.

RECOVERY OF THE GOODS BY THE CREDITOR FROM THE DEBTOR

25–013 Whether the creditor is entitled to recover the goods after termination may depend upon whether the hire-purchase agreement is a regulated agreement within the Consumer Credit Act or not. The common law position, i.e. where it is not a regulated agreement, will be examined first.

Common Law

25–014 At common law the rule is that once the hiring has been terminated, the debtor has no right to retain possession of the goods. The creditor is entitled to recover possession. This is so even if the contract does not expressly say so: *Bowmakers v Barnet Instruments*.[18] If on request the debtor refuses or fails to hand over the goods, he commits conversion of the goods. There are two ways in which the creditor can enforce his right to possession. He can either seize physical possession of them or he can commence court proceedings against the debtor for conversion. There may be difficulty in the first method because, if the goods are on the debtor's premises, the creditor may be unable to seize them without trespassing and thus laying himself open to an action by the debtor. For this reason sometimes the hire-purchase agreement will contain a clause expressly authorising the creditor to enter the debtor's premises to recover possession of the goods after termination. If the creditor brings an action for conversion, he is most unlikely to obtain a court order compelling the debtor to return the goods. He will obtain damages instead. The damages will not be the full value of the goods, but only the outstanding balance of the hire-purchase price, i.e. the remaining payments which the debtor would have been liable to pay if the agreement had not been terminated.[19] If the result of an award of damages to the creditor is that he gets payment of the balance of the hire-purchase price earlier than he would have got it if the agreement had not been terminated, then a reduction will be made to take account of this accelerated payment.

[18] [1945] K.B. 65.
[19] *Wickham Holdings v Brooke House Motors* [1967] 1 All E.R. 117.

The Torts (Interference with Goods) Act 1977 allows the creditor, if he wishes, to choose a different judgment in place of a simple award of damages—namely a judgment giving the debtor an option either to pay damages (assessed as just explained) or to return the goods. If the debtor opts to return the goods then the debtor is entitled to receive from the creditor a financial allowance, i.e. a sum equal to the amount by which the value of the goods exceeds the alternative damages awarded.

Regulated Agreements

The position is different in three ways where the agreement is a regulated agreement: **25–015**

    (i) Section 92 provides that the creditor is not entitled to enter any premises to take possession of the goods except under an order of the court. This means that in practice, unless the creditor can persuade the debtor voluntarily to hand over the goods, the creditor will have to bring a court action to recover them. If he does that then the court has power to make a time order.

    (ii) Where the debtor wrongfully retains possession of the goods after termination, the court will normally order the debtor to return the goods to the creditor. The debtor will not be given the option of paying their value instead.[20] The court may, however, refuse to make an order for the return of the goods if a refusal would be "just". Of course, there would be such a refusal or else the operation of the return order would be suspended where the court makes a time order.

    (iii) Where the goods are "protected goods", the creditor is not entitled to recover possession of them without bringing a court action.

It is still the position that where the agreement is terminated otherwise than by the debtor's breach, the creditor is entitled to seize physical possession of the goods without trespassing. The creditor is similarly entitled, even where the agreement has been terminated by reason of the debtor's breach unless the goods are "protected goods". However, no doubt when the court gives the debtor another chance and therefore makes a time order, it will simultaneously deprive the creditor of the right to seize possession while the time order is in force.

PROTECTED GOODS

For the debtor the consequences of termination can be unfortunate in that he may have the **25–016** goods repossessed by the creditor in spite of the fact that he has paid a considerable amount towards them. He may then find that the creditor claims also a further money payment for termination of the agreement. We shall shortly be seeing that the court, by making a time order, can give the debtor another chance of maintaining payments under the agreement. The effect of the protected goods provision is to see that the creditor has not seized possession of the goods before the court has considered whether to give the debtor that second chance.

---

[20] s.100(5).

However, these protected goods provisions apply only where the goods fall within the definition of "protected goods".

The Definition

25-017   Goods which are let under a regulated hire-purchase agreement fall within the definition of protected goods in s.90 if three conditions are fulfilled:

(a)   The debtor is in breach of the agreement.

(b)   The debtor has paid or tendered to the creditor one-third or more of the total price of the goods.

(c)   The property in the goods remains in the creditor.

The last of these will cause no difficulty since property (i.e. ownership) will remain with the creditor until the debtor exercises his option to buy (i.e. until he has paid all the money due under the agreement).

The first condition is satisfied only if the debtor is in breach of the agreement. If the agreement has been terminated for some other reason the creditor will be entitled to seize the goods, providing he does not trespass to do so, or he can sue for their return under s.100(5). Where the debtor falls into arrears, the goods will be protected goods provided one-third of the total price has been paid or tendered.

25-018   The total price is the total sum payable by the debtor under the agreement, i.e. the deposit plus all the instalments plus the option money. The calculation will normally be easy. However, it will be complicated if either the total price includes charges in respect of the installation of the goods or the debtor has more than one regulated agreement with the same creditor.

For the purposes of the calculation, any installation charges have to be separated from the rest of the total price. By s.90(2) the debtor will not be regarded as having paid or tendered one-third of the total price unless he has paid or tendered both:

(i)   the whole of the installation charges, and

(ii)   one-third of the remainder of the total price.

Section 81 applies where the debtor has, in addition to the agreement in question, a further regulated agreement under which he has to make payments to the same person as he does under the agreement in question. The section provides that any payment made by the debtor can be appropriated by him as between the different agreements. If the debtor does not indicate to which agreement any given payment is appropriated, then that payment is appropriated between the agreements proportionately according to the amount of the sums due under each agreement. If on the other hand the debtor has just one agreement under which he owes, both (i) arrears of payments which have already fallen due, and (ii) default interest which has accrued on those arrears, then in the absence of an appropriation by the debtor, there is no automatic appropriation and the creditor can appropriate any payment received to either (i) or (ii).[21] If it is appropriated to (ii) then it will not go towards payment of the one-third of the total price, since default interest is not part of the "total price".

Goods will not be (or will cease to be) protected goods if the debtor exercises his right of termination (i.e. under s.99). Thus where the debtor falls into arrears, it may be much to his advantage not to exercise his right of termination but simply to do nothing and let the creditor, if he wishes, serve a default notice and terminate the agreement. Since in these circumstances it would not be in the debtor's interest for him to exercise a right of termination, the court would be reluctant to find that he had done so, unless he had done it consciously and was fully aware of the consequences.[22]   **25–019**

The Protection

The creditor is not entitled, otherwise than by court action, to recover possession of protected goods from the debtor (s.90). Thus he must not seize physical possession of them. It is not a criminal offence for him to do so. However, if, contrary to s.90, he does so, then the agreement is terminated and all payments made under the agreement are returnable to the debtor who is relieved of further liability under the agreement.[23] There are three significant exceptions to the protection given by s.90, i.e. three situations where the creditor can recover physical possession of the goods without contravening s.90:   **25–020**

(i) If the debtor has disposed of the goods to a third party, the creditor can seize them from the third party without contravening s.90. This is because s.90 prevents him seizing them "from the debtor". If the debtor has not disposed of the goods but has simply, for example, lent them to a friend or left them to be mended by a repairer, the creditor would be contravening s.90 if he seized them. Lord Denning M.R. in *Bentinck v Cromwell Engineering Ltd*[24] was referring to the section of the Hire Purchase Act 1965 which was replaced by s.90 (and which used the word "hirer" instead of "debtor") when he said:

"In the ordinary way, once goods are 'protected goods', i.e. more than one-third has been paid, the finance company cannot recover possession—except by action—from the hirer, nor from any garage or repairer with whom the hirer may have left it. The words 'from the hirer' include all those to whom the hirer has bailed it."

(ii) If the debtor has abandoned the goods, the creditor can seize them without contravening s.90, for he is not then seizing them "from the debtor". In *Bentinck's* case, the debtor paid the deposit and first few instalments before falling into arrears. The car was badly damaged in an accident and he left it at a garage but did not give orders to repair it. Three months later the finance company, the creditor, traced him. He paid none of the arrears, gave a false telephone number and disappeared without trace. After a further six months the finance company

---

[21] *Julian Hodge Bank Ltd v Hall* [1998] C.C.L.R. 14, CA.
[22] See *United Dominions Trust v Ennis* [1968] Q.B. 54, para.25–006, above.
[23] s.91.
[24] [1971] 1 Q.B. 324.

took the car from the garage where it had been left by the debtor some nine months earlier. The court held on these facts that the debtor had abandoned the car and the finance company had not contravened s.90.

(iii) The creditor does not contravene s.90 if the debtor consents to the creditor repossessing the goods.[25] To be effective, the consent has to be given at the time of the repossession. Even then the consent will not be effective unless the debtor knows, or has been informed, what his rights would be if he refuses consent.[26] Those rights would (if the creditor brought legal proceedings to recover possession of the goods) be the right to ask the court to reorganise his repayments and let him retain possession under a time order.

Court Action

25–021   If the creditor wishes to recover possession of protected goods he must bring an action in the county court. Even if he can show that the agreement has terminated he will not automatically be granted a "return order", i.e. an order for the goods to be returned. The court may decide that such an order would not be just and may instead grant a time order. The court's powers will be further considered after we have looked at what money claim the creditor can make.

MONEY CLAIM BY CREDITOR FROM DEBTOR

25–022   When termination occurs, the situation is different according to whether the agreement is or is not a regulated agreement. Regulated agreements will be considered second. Turning first to the position at common law, i.e. where the agreement is not a regulated one, the creditor may have two alternative claims against the debtor. He may be able to claim damages for the debtor's breach of contract or he may be able to claim the amount stipulated in the agreement as being payable upon termination (i.e. the minimum payment).

Damages

25–023   Damages can be obtained for the debtor's breach of contract. Since termination is usually preceded by the debtor falling into arrears, there is usually a reason for claiming damages. The amount, however, will depend upon whether the debtor repudiated the contract or whether he simply got into arrears. If he has simply got into arrears, the amount of damages will depend upon whether punctual payment was of the essence of the contract.

---

[25] *Mercantile Credit Co v Cross* [1965] 2 Q.B. 205 and s.173(3).
[26] *Chartered Trust v Pitcher* [1988] R.T.R. 72.

Damages for Repudiation

These are assessed according to the rule in *Yeoman Credit v Waragowski*[27] where at the time   **25–024**
of termination the debtor had paid only the initial deposit, £72. After termination the creditor
recovered possession of the goods, a car, which was then worth £205. The creditor was
awarded the following damages:

1.	Arrears of instalment due before termination			£60

and

2.	A sum arrived at by taking the total hire purchase price and then deducting certain items:		£434	
	payments already made	£72		
	the amount awarded under (a)	£60		
	the option money in the agreement	£1		
	the value of the goods recovered	£205		
		£338	£338	
			£96	£96
	Total:			£156

When the creditor is awarded damages assessed on the *Waragowski* basis, he is in effect
put in the same position as if the whole transaction had gone through as originally contemplated. Adding up the amounts he receives before termination, the value of the goods he has
recovered and the damages awarded, it can be seen that he receives virtually the whole hire-
purchase price.

Sometimes when termination occurs early on, the creditor gets this sum earlier than he
would have done if the agreement had never been terminated. If it had not been terminated,
he would have had to await payment of the instalments as the months went by. If it does occur
that the creditor receives payment earlier than he would have, the court will make a deduction
from the award of damages to take account of that earlier payment.[28]

Damages Where the Debtor Does Not Repudiate

Where the debtor simply gets into arrears but does not repudiate the contract, the agreement   **25–025**
may give the creditor the right of termination. If the creditor exercises that right then the
termination is caused not by the debtor's breach but by the creditor exercising his right. That
being so, the creditor cannot claim for loss of future payments as damages. He is limited to
a claim for arrears of instalments due before termination. This was decided in *Financings v
Baldock*.[29] The debtor had been in arrears; he had told the finance company (the creditor) that

[27] [1961] 3 All E.R. 145.
[28] *Overstone v Shipway* [1962] 1 All E.R. 52.
[29] [1963] 2 Q.B. 104.

he hoped to pay off the arrears. The finance company later terminated the agreement. It was held that since at the time of termination the debtor could not be said to have repudiated the contract, he was liable only for arrears of instalments up to the date of termination. It is clear then that a debtor who finds he cannot maintain his payment is best advised not to repudiate the agreement, but to indicate that he hopes and intends to make up the instalments. The court's sympathy in these cases tends to be with the debtor rather than the creditor who is normally a finance company. The court will tend, if possible, to find that the debtor's conduct has not amounted to a repudiation and it will not allow the finance company to put upon the debtor a repudiation when the debtor has not in fact repudiated.[30] One clear case of repudiation, however, is where the debtor sells or otherwise wrongfully disposes of the goods, in which case the damages will be assessed on the *Waragowski* basis.

Where damages are assessed on the *Financings v Baldock* basis and the creditor therefore receives only arrears up to the date of termination, there will be added to that amount a sum equal to the creditor's loss caused by the debtor's failure, if any, to take reasonable care of the goods. The hire-purchase agreement will have included a term requiring the debtor to take reasonable care of the goods. If he does not do so then the goods when recovered by the creditor may be worth a certain amount less than if reasonable care had been taken of them. It is that amount which will in the award of damages be added to the arrears due up to the date of termination.

The law as established in *Financings v Baldock*[31] does not apply where the debtor has broken a *condition* of the contract.

Damages Where Debtor's Breach is a Breach of Condition

25–026 In *Lombard North Central v Butterworth*[32] the contract provided that punctual payment of instalments under the contract was of the essence of the agreement. This clearly meant that punctual payment was a condition (as opposed to a warranty). In accordance with the general law of contract, the Court of Appeal held that therefore any lateness in payment, even if it did not amount to a repudiation by the debtor, could nevertheless be treated by the creditor as if it were such a repudiation. This meant that the creditor's damages after termination were to be assessed not on a *Financings v Baldock* basis but on a *Waragowski* basis. This decision may well have resulted in the law in *Financings v Baldock* becoming a dead letter, since many hire-purchase companies have, after *Lombard North Central v Butterworth*, drafted their contracts to state that prompt payment by the debtor is of the essence of the contract. Thus, as Nicholls L.J. said in the *Lombard* case, the conclusion in that case "emasculates the decision in *Financings v Baldock*".

Claim Against a Guarantor or Indemnifier

25–027 As already explained, if, when the debtor has neither repudiated the contract nor broken a condition, the creditor exercises a right of termination, the creditor cannot claim loss of future

[30] *Eshun v Moorgate Mercantile Co* [1971] 2 All E.R. 402, see para.25–007, above.
[31] [1963] 2 Q.B. 104.
[32] [1987] Q.B. 527.

payments from the debtor. He is entitled only to the return of the goods and arrears which were due before termination. That is what happened in *Goulston Discount Co v Clark*[33] where the creditor recovered from the debtor £157 less than he would have recovered if the debtor had repudiated the contract. The question in *Goulston* was whether the creditor, a finance company, could recover that £157 from the car dealer. Under a recourse agreement between the finance company and the dealer, the dealer had, in consideration of the finance company entering into a hire-purchase agreement with W (the debtor), agreed as follows. He had agreed that he would "indemnify" the finance company against any loss that the finance company might suffer by reason of the fact that W did not, for any cause whatsoever, pay all the amounts which he would pay if he completed his hire-purchase agreement. It was held that since this was an indemnity, the finance company was entitled to recover the £157. If it had been a guarantee, the finance company would have failed in this claim because a guarantor is under no greater liability than the debtor. The decision in *Goulston* would be exactly the same if the facts occurred again today. The claim under the indemnity (the recourse agreement) would not be reduced or affected at all by s.113 of the Consumer Credit Act, since the recourse agreement would not be "security" within the definition in the Act.

Minimum Payments

Hire-purchase agreements commonly contain a provision that on termination the debtor must pay a stipulated amount. From the creditor's point of view, one advantage of claiming this minimum payment instead of damages is that no damages can normally be claimed where the termination has occurred not as a result of the debtor's breach of contract, but as a result of some event, e.g. the debtor terminating under a right to do so. Another advantage is that the minimum payment clause will usually provide for a fixed sum, whereas in a claim for damages there may be a dispute about the creditor's actual loss. However, the principal advantage is that the minimum payment clause may provide for a larger sum than the creditor could claim as damages. This last fact has caused neither the courts nor Parliament to look with favour upon minimum payment clauses. Thus a minimum payment clause may either: **25–028**

> (i) be void because of the common law doctrine of penalties, or
>
> (ii) be ineffective because of the provisions of the Consumer Credit Act relating to unfair creditor/debtor relationships (if they apply), or
>
> (iii) be ineffective by virtue of the Unfair Terms in Consumer Contracts Regulations 1999.

Penalties

The common law doctrine of penalties is concerned with a certain type of contractual clause—namely, the sort of clause which stipulates how much will be payable in the event   **25–029**

---

[33] [1967] 2 Q.B. 493.

of a breach of contract. Such a clause is a liquidated damages clause and is void if it amounts to a penalty. It will not be a penalty if it was a genuine attempt by the parties to pre-estimate the likely damages in the event of the breach. It will be a penalty if the stipulated minimum payment is large, out of all proportion to the likely damages.[34] In the words of Lord Dunedin in *Dunlop Pneumatic Tyre Co v New Garage Motor Co*[35]:

> "It will be held to be a penalty if the sum stipulated for is extravagant and unconsciona-ble in amount in comparison with the greatest loss that could conceivably be proved to have followed from the breach."

In *Bridge v Campbell Discount Co*[36] the clause in question required the debtor to pay on termination:

(a) arrears of payments due before termination, plus

(b) an amount which together with payments made and due before termination amounted to two-thirds of the hire-purchase price.

This was in addition to the fact that the creditor was entitled to the return of the goods. The clause was held to be a penalty because, including the value of the returned goods, it would in nearly all cases give the creditor more than 100 per cent of the hire-purchase price, i.e. more than damages assessed on the *Waragowski* basis.

Even a clause where the amount stipulated is the same as would be awarded as damages assessed on the *Waragowski* basis can be a penalty. It will be a penalty if it provides for that amount to be payable where the damages, if awarded, would be assessed on the *Financings v Baldock* basis. In *Anglo Auto Finance Co v James*[37] the clause required the debtor to pay:

1. arrears of payments due before termination, plus

2. the amount by which the hire-purchase price exceeded the sum of:

   (i) payments made and due before termination, and
   (ii) the value of the goods when recovered and resold.

The Court of Appeal held that this was a penalty and awarded damages instead. Since the debtor had not repudiated the agreement the damages were assessed on the *Financings v Baldock* basis.

25–030   The doctrine of penalties applies where an excessive sum is stipulated to be payable on a breach of contract. However, termination can and does sometimes occur where there is no breach of contract, e.g. where the debtor exercises a contractual right of termination or where the contract terminates automatically on some specified event such as the debtor's bank-ruptcy. The Court of Appeal in *Associated Distributors v Hall*[38] held that the doctrine of

---

[34] See, generally, Ch.21, above.
[35] [1915] A.C. 79.
[36] [1962] A.C. 600.
[37] [1963] 3 All E.R. 566.
[38] [1938] 2 K.B. 83.

penalties does not apply where a sum is stipulated payable on a termination which occurs without the debtor being in breach of the agreement. The creditor can sue for the stipulated amount, however great. This decision has proved a controversial one, although it still stands as part of the law. In *Bridge v Campbell Discount Co*[39] the House of Lords was evenly split on the question of whether it was correct. The decision leads to the situation where, if the debtor exercises his contractual right of termination, he may have to pay a larger sum than if he breaks his contract, thus causing termination. It is for this reason that the court will not hold that the debtor has exercised his right of termination unless he did so fully aware of the consequences.[40] Of course it is now possible that a clause providing for a very high sum to be payable on a termination occurring in the absence of a breach by the hirer would be rendered ineffective by the Unfair Terms in Consumer Contracts Regulations 1999.[41]

Regulated Agreements

Where the creditor brings a money claim against the debtor, that is an action to enforce the regulated agreement. That being so, the court will have the power to make a time order which is to be considered in the next section of this chapter. However, what money award could the creditor expect if the court were to make an immediate "return order"? The Consumer Credit Act does not state what size of award should be made. Thus the answer is that the award would equal whatever sum would be obtainable by the creditor as damages at common law—unless the agreement stipulated a different amount. However, it should be added that if the agreement stipulated an excessive amount, the court could reduce that amount. Even if the doctrine of penalties did not apply, the court could reopen the agreement under the unfair creditor/debtor relationships provisions.

25–031

By way of exception to what has just been said, the Act does state in s.100 how much money award should be made where the termination has occurred by the debtor exercising his right of termination under s.99. In that case the debtor's liability is to pay any loss caused by his failure to take reasonable care of the goods, plus all the arrears due before termination, plus whichever is the smallest of the following three amounts:

(i) The amount of the minimum payment stipulated in the agreement. If none is stipulated then the amount under this head is zero.

(ii) The amount, if any, by which one-half of the total hire-purchase price exceeds the total of the sums paid by the debtor and the arrears due before termination.

(iii) The amount of the creditor's actual loss arising from the termination by the debtor (i.e. the amount of damages assessed on the *Waragowski* basis).

Thus where the debtor exercises his right of termination the most that he will have to pay (assuming he took reasonable care of the goods) is the amount required to clear off his arrears due before termination, plus enough to bring up his payments to one-half of the total price.

---

[39] [1962] A.C. 600.
[40] See *United Dominions Trust v Ennis* [1968] Q.B. 54, para.25–006, above.
[41] See Ch.17, above.

In calculating one-half of the total price, difficulties will arise if the total price includes installation charges or if the debtor has a further regulated agreement with the same creditor. For the purposes of the calculation, the installation charges have to be separated from the rest of the total price. By s.100(2) one-half of the total price is to be regarded as equal to the whole of the installation charge plus one-half of the remainder of the total price. Section 81 applies where the debtor has, in addition to the agreement in question, a further regulated agreement with the same creditor.

Powers of the Court in the Case of Regulated Agreements

25–032   Hire-purchase has been picturesquely described as the fertile mother of litigation. The vast majority of this litigation takes the form of an action by the creditor against the debtor in circumstances where the latter has defaulted on paying his instalments. There can be no doubt that the vast majority of hire-purchase agreements fall within the category of regulated agreements. Thus the court's powers, which we are about to examine, are designed to enable the court to deal with the situation where the debtor has defaulted.

A hire-purchase agreement will usually give the creditor the right to terminate it if the debtor becomes a certain amount in arrears. Thus when the debtor gets into arrears the action brought against him by the creditor will be one of two sorts:

(i) The creditor chooses to regard the agreement as terminated and (after serving the necessary default notice) brings an action claiming repossession of the goods and damages or the stipulated payment.

(ii) The creditor chooses not to regard the agreement as terminated and sues simply for arrears.

In the latter case the court will either give immediate judgment to the creditor for the arrears due or it will make a time order under s.129 allowing the debtor extra time to pay.

If the creditor adopts the first alternative and claims repossession, then the court can make a time order or it can exercise its powers under s.133. A time order will have the effect of allowing the debtor another chance of making his payments—perhaps over a longer period. The court's powers under s.133 are to make either a return order or a transfer order. A return order is an order for the return of the goods to the creditor. The court must make a return order unless it would not be just to do so. Such an order would therefore be made if there were clearly no chance of the debtor paying off the debt. In that case the creditor will be likely to ask for damages also. The amount of such an award has already been considered.[42]

25–033   A transfer order is an alternative to making a return order, but one which will in practice be available only occasionally. It is an order that the debtor return part of the goods but which allows him to keep the other part as his own without making further payment. This order can be made only where the court can divide the goods and where the payments already made by the debtor under the agreement are at least equal to a minimum amount. The minimum

---

[42] See para.25–031, above.

amount which he must have paid is a combination of: (i) that part of the total price which is attributable to the goods he is being allowed to keep; and (ii) one-quarter of the rest of the total price. The total price includes the deposit, all the instalments and the option money which were scheduled under the agreement. The reason a transfer order will seldom be available is that the goods cannot very often be divided. It is not common, except perhaps in the case of some items of furniture (e.g. a three-piece suite), for one hire-purchase agreement to embrace more than one item.

Even after a return order or transfer order is made, there may be some delay before the creditor enforces the order. In this situation, if the debtor can find the financial resources to do so, he is still entitled to pay the whole outstanding balance of the total hire-purchase price and thereby become the owner of all the goods. He has this right until the creditor actually recovers possession—s.133(4).

RECOVERY OF THE GOODS BY THE CREDITOR IN THE HANDS OF A THIRD PARTY

We are here concerned with the position where someone other than the creditor or debtor also   **25–034** claims to have an interest in the goods. We have seen that on termination the creditor has a right as against the debtor to possession (subject to the provisions of the Consumer Credit Act). When some third party claims an interest, whose claim takes priority—the creditor's or the third party's?

Sale of the Goods by the Debtor

When the debtor sells the goods before completing his payments, the goods will be in the   **25–035** hands of the purchaser. The general rule is that the creditor is entitled to recover the goods from the purchaser: *Helby v Matthews*.[43] This is the reason that hire-purchase has proved so popular with finance companies. It gives the creditor this high degree of protection even when the debtor wrongfully sells the goods. The reason for the general rule is that the creditor under a hire-purchase agreement remains the owner of the goods until the debtor has paid off all the instalments and exercised his option to buy. He remains the owner even though the debtor sells the goods. It is his ownership that entitles him to recover the goods from the purchaser and he has that right regardless of whether the hire-purchase agreement has been terminated. Of course, if one of the exceptions to the *nemo dat* principle applies (see Chapter 5 above), then the creditor will lose his rights over the goods and the innocent purchaser will acquire good title. From the creditor's point of view the important thing about hire-purchase is that one exception in particular does not apply, i.e. the exception in s.9 of the Factors Act and s.25 of the Sale of Goods Act—because the debtor is not a "buyer" in possession.

The general rule then is in favour of the creditor rather than the innocent purchaser. The rule is the same if, instead of selling the goods, the debtor pledges them with a pawnbroker. The pawnbroker is in the same position as the innocent purchaser.

---

[43] [1895] A.C. 471, see Ch.12, above.

The general rule is very hard on the innocent third party and has been reversed where the subject-matter of the hire-purchase agreement is a motor vehicle which the debtor sells to an innocent private purchaser. In this case the innocent private purchaser acquires good title to the vehicle by virtue of the Hire Purchase Act 1964, Pt III.[44]

25–036   In a case where none of the exceptions to the *nemo dat* principle applies, the creditor may nevertheless not discover that the debtor has disposed of the goods and may therefore do nothing to recover them. If the debtor continues to pay his instalments, eventually completes his payments and exercises his option to purchase, that will operate to feed the title down to the person who acquired the goods from the debtor.[45] If this happens, it follows that, since the creditor under the hire-purchase agreement is no longer the owner, he has no right to the goods.

Even where the creditor under the hire-purchase agreement is still the owner, as in *Helby v Matthews*,[46] it does not follow that he will actually recover possession of the goods. If the third party refuses to hand them over, the creditor can bring a court action, i.e. a claim for conversion. The refusal of the creditor's demand to hand them over is a conversion. However, the court will not order the goods to be returned but will award damages to the creditor. Now, the damages will not necessarily be the full value of the goods at the date of conversion. The debtor has already paid some sums to the creditor (i.e. the initial deposit and perhaps some instalments). If the debtor had not disposed of the goods but had kept them he could have bought them by paying the outstanding balance of the hire-purchase price. Thus, all that the creditor has lost is that outstanding balance. It is that amount which will be awarded to him as damages against the third party.[47] To look at it another way, the debtor, by selling the goods to the third party (albeit wrongfully), has transferred to the third party his (the debtor's) rights—in particular his option to buy the goods for the outstanding balance of the hire-purchase price. The Torts (Interference With Goods) Act 1977 allows the creditor, if he wishes, to choose a different judgment in place of an award of damages—namely a judgment giving the third party (the innocent purchaser) an option either to pay damages (assessed as just explained) or to return the goods. If the third party opts to return the goods then the debtor is entitled to receive from the creditor a financial allowance, i.e. a sum equal to the amount by which the value of the goods exceeds the alternative damages awarded.

There is an important qualification to the rule in *Wickham Holdings v Brooke House Motors*.[48] It is that the creditor cannot recover from the third party any more than the value of the goods at the date of conversion: *Chubb Cash Ltd v John Crilley & Son*.[49] It can happen, for example, that at the date when the third party refuses the creditor's demand to hand over the goods, their value is less than the outstanding balance of the hire-purchase price. The amount recoverable by the creditor from the third party is the *smaller* of the two following amounts: (i) the outstanding balance owing under the hire-purchase agreement; or (ii) the value of the goods at the date of conversion, i.e. the date the third party refused the creditor's demand to hand them over.

---

[44] See Ch.12, above.
[45] *Butterworth v Kingsway Motors* [1954] 1 W.L.R. 1286, see para.7–011, above.
[46] [1895] A.C. 471.
[47] See *Wickham Holdings v Brooke House Motors* [1967] 1 All E.R. 117.
[48] [1967] 1 All E.R. 117.
[49] [1983] 1 W.L.R. 599.

It should be added that an innocent purchaser who is liable in conversion to the creditor   **25–037**
will have an action against the debtor, from whom he bought the goods, for breach of the
condition as to title in s.12 of the Sale of Goods Act.[50]

Suppose that the innocent purchaser to whom the debtor sold the goods has himself resold
them to a sub-purchaser. In that case the creditor may be able to bring a claim against the sub-
purchaser. He will be able to do so provided, again, that none of the exceptions to the *nemo
dat* principle applies. The creditor's claim against the sub-purchaser will be on exactly the
same basis as that (just explained) against the innocent purchaser who has not disposed of the
goods. It is a claim in conversion. Now suppose that such a claim is impossible because one
of the exceptions to the *nemo dat* principle does apply. This might occur where a motor
vehicle is involved. Thus, a debtor who has a car on hire-purchase terms might sell the car
to a car dealer who in turn sells it to an innocent sub-purchaser. Here the innocent sub-
purchaser obtains good title by virtue of the Hire Purchase Act 1964, Pt III.[51] The Act does
not however, protect the car dealer. Thus the creditor has the possibility of a claim against the
debtor or against the car dealer, the latter claim being a claim for damages for conversion. If
the sale by the car dealer was a sale at a car auction, the creditor also has a claim against the
auctioneers for conversion. All of this is because selling someone else's goods without
authority amounts to conversion. The owner (the creditor) can succeed in a claim for
conversion provided that he was either in possession of the goods at the time of conversion
(unlikely) or else had a right, at the time of conversion, to immediate possession (more
likely).

Union Transport Finance v British Car Auctions[52] arose out of facts which occurred before
the Consumer Credit Act 1974 was passed. A hire-purchase agreement required the debtor
not to remove or alter the identification marks on the car and not, without the creditor's
permission, to sell it or offer it for sale. The agreement also provided that, if the debtor made
any default in his monthly rentals or committed any other breach, the creditor had the right
to terminate the agreement by serving a default notice on the debtor. Before completing his
payments under the agreement, the debtor altered the car's registration number and without
authority took it to a car auction where it was sold. Subsequently the creditor learnt what had
happened and brought a claim for conversion against the auctioneers. The auctioneers, in
defending the action, asserted that at the time of the conversion (the auction sale) the creditor
did not have a right to immediate possession because the creditor had not at that time served
a default notice upon the debtor. The defence failed. It was held that the terms of the
agreement allowing the creditor to terminate the agreement by serving a default notice on the
debtor, conferred rights on the creditor *additional* to his rights at common law. The latter
included the right to terminate the hire-purchase agreement without notice if the debtor did
any act wholly repugnant to the agreement. When the debtor put the car into the auction the
creditor therefore had the right to immediate possession, i.e. the right to terminate the
agreement without notice. If the facts of this case were to occur again after the coming into
force of s.87 of the Consumer Credit Act, the result might well be different. Section 87[53]
applies to any breach by the debtor and requires the creditor to serve a default notice giving
at least 14 days' notice before he can be entitled to terminate the agreement or recover

---

[50] See para.7–010, above.
[51] See para.5–031, above.
[52] [1978] 2 All E.R. 385.
[53] See para.25–007, above.

possession of the goods. It thus prevents the creditor having a right to immediate possession unless and until a default notice has been served and has expired.

Debtor Creates a Lien

25–038   At common law a repairer to whom goods are entrusted for repair has a lien over them for his charges. The lien is the right to retain possession of the goods until his charges are paid. A lien does not arise where maintenance alone is involved but only where the work is to improve the goods. Now, it is not uncommon for a debtor to have the goods repaired. This may happen if it is a car that has been in an accident. If the debtor has it repaired and later the hire-purchase contract is terminated, the repairer's lien takes priority over the creditor's right to recover possession. This means that the creditor is not entitled to possession without first paying the repair bill. This is because the essence of hire-purchase is that the debtor shall have the use and enjoyment of the goods and therefore is authorised to have them repaired if need be. It therefore makes no difference that the repairer knows that his customer is hiring the goods on hire-purchase, for the repairer is entitled to assume that the debtor is authorised to have them repaired. This is still so, even if the hire-purchase agreement expressly states that the debtor is not authorised to create a lien. *In Albemarle Supply Co v Hind*[54] the subject-matter of the hire-purchase agreement was a taxi cab. In the agreement the debtor agreed not to create a lien for repairs. The garage where he took it for repair knew that he was hiring it on hire-purchase terms but was unaware of the restriction on the debtor creating liens. The Court of Appeal held that the lien was good even against the creditor. The decision would of course have been different if the garage had known of the restriction in the agreement. In that case the creditor would have been entitled to the taxi free of the lien, i.e. without having to pay off the repair charges.

Another situation where the creditor is entitled to recover the car free of lien is where the debtor deposits it for repair after the hire-purchase agreement has been terminated. This was the position in *Bowmakers v Wycombe Motors*[55] where, since the hire-purchase agreement had been terminated, the debtor had no more authority to use the car or to have it repaired. The garage therefore could not establish a lien against the creditor and this was so even though the garage was unaware that the car was or had been the subject of a hire-purchase agreement. In this case the garage had to surrender the goods to their owner (the creditor) but could of course still sue its customer (the debtor) for the repair charges.

Suppose that at the time the debtor deposits goods for repair, he is in possession of those goods under a time order. Section 130 expressly provides that in such circumstances the debtor "shall be treated as a bailee of the goods under the terms of the agreement, notwithstanding that the agreement has terminated". The position where the debtor deposits the goods for repair after a time order has been made is exactly the same as where he does so during the currency of the agreement before a time order is made.

[54] [1928] 1 K.B. 307.
[55] [1946] K.B. 505.

Debtor's Landlord Levies Distress

A landlord can levy distress on goods in his tenant's premises if the tenant is in arrears with his rent. This means that he can seize the goods in order to sell them to pay the rent. Those goods may well include goods of which the tenant has possession on hire-purchase terms. The Law of Distress Amendment Act 1908 allows others whose goods have been seized by the landlord to serve on the landlord a notice of ownership. If this is done, the landlord is not entitled to continue with distress in relation to those goods. If the law stopped there, the owner (i.e. the creditor) would be in a good position against the landlord provided he discovered that the landlord had seized the goods before the landlord sold them. However, the goods may come within one of two categories in relation to which the creditor is not allowed to serve a notice of ownership. They are: **25–039**

(i) Goods bailed under a hire-purchase or consumer hire agreement or agreed to be sold under a conditional sale agreement—but not where the agreement has been terminated.

(ii) Goods in the tenant's possession with the owner's consent in such circumstances that the tenant is the reputed owner of them.

Goods Bailed Under a Hire-Purchase Agreement, etc.

Normally, therefore, the creditor will not be able to serve a notice of ownership on the landlord because the goods will fall within this category. However they will not fall in this category if, when the landlord seized them, the agreement had already been terminated. Thus it can be vital to decide exactly when the agreement was terminated. A time order being made may not prevent the agreement from being (technically) terminated.[56] We have seen that the requirement for the creditor to serve a default or non-default notice will not generally affect the timing of an automatic termination.[57]   **25–040**

There is one further situation where the goods, even if the agreement has not been terminated, will not fall within this category. That is during the period after a default notice has been served and before it expires or is earlier complied with. If the notice expires and the debtor has not complied with it, the creditor will then be able to terminate the agreement immediately in which case—as we have just seen—the goods will remain outside this category.

Goods in the Tenant's Possession with the Owner's Consent in such Circumstances that the Tenant is the Reputed Owner of Them

We are here concerned only with the situation where either the hire-purchase agreement has been terminated or else a default notice is still current (i.e. has been served and has not   **25–041**

---

[56] See para.25–009, above.
[57] See para.25–012, above.

expired or been complied with). This is because, in the absence of a current default notice or
a termination of the hire-purchase agreement, the goods will in any case be within the
previous category. The point here is that even after termination, the goods, if still in the
tenant's possession, will be assumed to be there with the owner's (i.e. the creditor's) consent
unless the latter has done some act clearly withdrawing that consent. The effective way of
doing this is for him to serve on the debtor a notice expressly withdrawing his consent, at or
after termination. It is not sufficient that the agreement has terminated automatically under
some clause in the agreement which states that upon termination the creditor's consent to the
debtor's possession is automatically withdrawn.[58]

Perdana Properties v United Orient[59] involved goods which were the subject of a hire
agreement (which was not a consumer hire agreement). Before the hirer's landlord levied
distress, the owner had written to the hirer making it clear that the owner's consent to the
continued possession by the hirer was withdrawn, although the owner had not actually
terminated the hiring agreement. It was held that the owner was entitled to have the goods
released to him by the landlord. The goods were not within this second category because the
owner had effectively withdrawn his consent to the hirer's continued possession, even though
he had not terminated the agreement. Of course, if the agreement had been a hire-purchase,
conditional sale or consumer hire agreement, the owner would have been unprotected
because the goods would have fallen within the previous category.

Sometimes goods will not be in the tenant's reputed ownership because of some well-
known custom that people such as the tenant hire goods. Thus it is, or was, apparently a well-
known fact that hotel keepers hire furniture: *Re Parker.*[60]

If the landlord levies distress after the termination of the agreement or during the currency
of a default notice, it seems that the creditor will be able to serve a notice of ownership
provided the goods are not in the tenant's possession with the creditor's consent in such
circumstances that the tenant is the reputed owner of them.

Debtor Goes Bankrupt

25–042   As a general rule when someone goes bankrupt all his property passes to his trustee in
bankruptcy whose task it is to collect in all the bankrupt's assets and use them to pay off the
creditors. This does not, however, affect goods which do not belong to the bankrupt, such as
goods he is hiring on hire-purchase terms.

Sheriff Levies Execution on the Debtor

25–043   When a defendant has a judgment entered against him by a court, the claimant can enforce
that judgment by having the sheriff or court bailiff execute it for him. The sheriff or bailiff
is entitled to enter the defendant's premises and seize his goods so that he can sell them and
use the proceeds to pay the amount of the judgment. The risk is that he seizes goods which

---

[58] *Times Furnishing v Hutchings* [1938] 1 K.B. 775.
[59] [1981] 1 W.L.R. 1496.
[60] (1882) 21 Ch. D. 408.

the defendant is hiring on hire-purchase terms. If he does so unknowingly and sells them, the owner (i.e. the creditor) thereupon loses all rights in the goods and the purchaser acquires good title. However, if the creditor becomes aware of the fact that his goods have been seized, then he can recover possession of them at any time before the sheriff disposes of them. If it is too late and they have been sold, he is entitled to the proceeds of sale.

Chapter 26

TERMINATION OF CREDIT SALE, CONDITIONAL SALE AND CONSUMER HIRE AGREEMENTS

CREDIT SALE AGREEMENTS

Under a credit sale agreement property passes to the buyer before he has paid the instalments **26–001** of the price. If he sells the goods, the person buying them from him will acquire good title. The buyer is free to sell the goods at any time. Some credit sale agreements provide that if he does so, the full outstanding balance of the purchase price shall immediately become payable. This means that the seller can commence proceedings against him immediately for the whole outstanding balance. However, if the agreement is a regulated agreement within the Consumer Credit Act, the creditor (i.e. the seller) will first have to serve a default or non-default notice and the court will also have power to make a time order under s.129, i.e. to allow the debtor (i.e. the buyer) to pay the sum off in instalments.

A credit sale agreement may provide that the whole outstanding balance of the price shall become payable on certain specified breaches by the buyer (e.g. if his payments get more than a certain time in arrears). Here again if the agreement is a regulated agreement within the Consumer Credit Act, then the creditor could not sue for that sum until he had first served on the debtor a default notice. Again, the court would have the power to make a time order.

A credit sale agreement does not give the seller the right to recover possession of the goods on default by the buyer. It will not give the buyer a right to terminate it prematurely and s.100 of the Consumer Credit Act does not apply; so the buyer has no statutory right of termination (other than, in the case of a regulated agreement, to pay off his debt early—s.94). Thus the question of "protected goods" does not arise and the protected goods provisions do not apply to credit sale agreements. From a finance company's point of view, a credit sale agreement is a device for the company to give what in effect is an unsecured loan for the purchase of particular goods.

Conditional Sale Agreements

26–002   A distinction must be drawn between conditional sale agreements which are regulated agreements within the Consumer Credit Act and those which are not. Where the debtor is a company, the agreement will, for example, not be regulated.

Agreements that are not Regulated Agreements

26–003   Under these agreements property does not pass to the buyer until the stipulated conditions are fulfilled (i.e. usually not until he has paid all the instalments). However, the essence of a contract of sale is that the buyer either buys or commits himself to buying, i.e. to acquiring property in the goods. Therefore, as with a credit sale agreement, a conditional sale agreement will not give the buyer a right of premature termination of the agreement. It may, however, give the seller a right to recover possession of the goods and to retain ownership in the event of the buyer's default, death, bankruptcy, etc. If it does, then the common law rules relating to penalties and damages will apply.

If the buyer disposes of the goods before property has passed to him, he may nevertheless confer good title upon the person who buys them from him. Any of the exceptions to the *nemo dat* principle might apply.[1] In particular, the exception in s.9 of the Factors Act and s.25 of the Sale of Goods Act might apply.[2]

Regulated Agreements

26–004   The scheme of the Consumer Credit Act is to make regulated conditional sale agreements the same in effect as regulated hire-purchase agreements. Thus the provisions of the Act apply to regulated conditional sale agreements as they do to regulated hire-purchase agreements. That includes not only the provisions of the Act that apply to regulated agreements generally, but also certain provisions which apply only to hire-purchase and conditional sale agreements. It follows that the following provisions are amongst those that apply to regulated conditional sale agreements:

    (a)   The "protected goods" provisions—ss.90 and 91.

    (b)   The provisions requiring service of default notice or non-default notice—ss.87, 76 and 98.

    (c)   The provision preventing termination upon death of the debtor—s.86.

    (d)   The provision empowering the court to make a time order—s.129.

    (e)   The provision empowering the court to modify the agreement or to make a return order or a transfer order—s.133.

---

[1] See Ch.12, above.
[2] *Lee v Butler* [1893] 2 Q.B. 318.

(f) The provisions giving a statutory right of termination to the debtor and stating the amount payable by the debtor in that event—ss.99 and 100.

The last of these is important because it makes the agreement different in kind from what it is in theory. The agreement involves a commitment by the debtor (the buyer) that he will pay all the instalments and thereby become the owner of the goods. Otherwise it would not be a contract of "sale" at all.[3] The reality is that s.99 gives him (as it does to a debtor under a regulated hire-purchase agreement) a statutory right to terminate the agreement prematurely. As we have seen, this is a right to get out of the agreement without buying the goods which will have to be returned to the creditor.

We come now to the situation where the debtor (the buyer) has disposed of the goods to an innocent third party. The problem arises as to who has the better right—is it the third party or is it the creditor (the seller) under the conditional sale agreement? Remember, the creditor is, until property passes to the debtor, the owner of the goods. Here again, statute makes a conditional sale agreement which is a consumer credit agreement the same, in effect, as a hire-purchase agreement. Thus Sch.4 to the Consumer Credit Act and s.24(2) of the Sale of Goods Act provide that, for the purposes of s.9 of the Factors Act and s.25 of the Sale of Goods Act, a buyer under a conditional sale agreement which is a consumer credit agreement shall be deemed not to be a person who has bought or agreed to buy goods. Thus someone to whom the buyer sells the goods will not acquire good title under either of the two sections mentioned. It should be noted that in the case of a motor vehicle, a "private purchaser" could acquire good title under Pt III of the Hire-Purchase Act 1964 which applies to a purchase from the debtor under a conditional sale agreement as it does to one from the debtor under a hire-purchase agreement.[4]

Buyer's Landlord Levies Distress or Buyer Becomes Bankrupt

These matters are dealt with separately since the relevant law is the same regardless of whether the agreement is a regulated one. We are concerned with the relationship between the seller and the buyer's landlord or trustee in bankruptcy. The position can be put very simply. It is the same as if the conditional sale agreement had been instead a hire-purchase agreement. The seller is in exactly the same position as he would have been if he had let the goods under a hire-purchase agreement instead of agreeing to sell them under a conditional sale agreement. The position in the case where he let them under a hire-purchase agreement has already been explained.[5] **26–005**

CONSUMER HIRE AGREEMENTS

A consumer hire agreement is in one essential respect different from a hire-purchase, conditional sale or credit sale agreement. The difference is that it is not contemplated that the customer (the hirer) will ever buy the goods. **26–006**

---

[3] See Ch.1, above.
[4] See Ch.12, above.
[5] See Ch.31, above.

As in the case of a hire-purchase agreement, termination of a consumer hire agreement can occur in a number of ways—mutual agreement, on breach of the agreement by the hirer, on some other stipulated event or on the hirer exercising a right of termination. Nothing more needs to be said on termination by mutual agreement. After considering the other terminating events in the order just given, consideration will be given to the owner's right to recover possession of the goods and to other rights arising on termination.

Breach by the Hirer

26–007   As with a hire-purchase agreement so here there are three sorts of breach by the hirer, any of which may entitle the owner to terminate the agreement:

(i) A repudiatory breach, e.g. a failure (not mere delay) to make payments over such a period that it seems clear that he is not going to keep the agreement.

(ii) A breach stipulated in the agreement as giving the owner a right of termination, e.g. the hirer becoming more than 10 days late in making any payment.

(iii) A breach of a condition (as opposed to a warranty) of the contract, e.g. late payment when the contract states punctual payment to be of the essence of the contract.

Section 87 applies whenever the owner is entitled to terminate the agreement by reason of the hirer's breach, i.e. it applies to regulated consumer hire agreements just as it does to other regulated agreements. Thus the owner cannot terminate the agreement, cannot recover possession of the goods and cannot enforce any security without first serving a default notice. As with other regulated agreements the serving of the default notice enables the customer to rectify his default within the period of notice and it also enables him to apply for a time order. The court's power to make a time order is restricted to payments that have already fallen due. Thus it cannot alter the future payment pattern and can give the hirer extra time only in respect of payments already due. The court has no power to extend the period during which the hirer is entitled under the terms of the agreement to remain in possession of the goods.[6] It has that power in respect of hire-purchase and conditional sale agreements; for it can make a return order and suspend the operation of the return order for so long as the time order is complied with. Section 135(3), however, prevents the court from doing this so as to extend the period during which the hirer is entitled to possession of the goods under the terms of a consumer hire agreement.

Other Stipulated Events

26–008   The agreement may state that, upon the occurrence of any one of certain stipulated events, the owner can terminate the agreement (or, alternatively that the agreement will terminate

[6] s.135(3).

automatically). Where the stipulated event is a breach of the agreement by the hirer then s.87, which has just been mentioned, applies. We are now dealing with the situation where the stipulated event is something other than a breach by the hirer, e.g. his death, his being sentenced to prison or committing an act of bankruptcy, etc.

Section 86 applies to regulated consumer hire agreements as it does to other regulated agreements, with the result that the death of the hirer under an agreement of specified duration will seldom entitle the owner to terminate the agreement against the wishes of the debtor's personal representatives.

Also, ss.76 and 98 apply in the same way as they do in relation to other regulated agreements. Thus the owner will not be able to treat an agreement of specified duration as terminated upon any stipulated event without first serving a non-default notice upon the hirer. The hirer will then be entitled to ask the court for a time order.

Exercise by the Hirer of a Right of Termination

Section 101 gives the hirer under certain regulated consumer hire agreements a right of **26–009** termination, provided he gives due written notice. Section 101 does not entitle him to terminate the agreement before it has run for 18 months and the hirer must give a minimum period of notice. That minimum period is the lesser of:

(i) three months, or

(ii) the shortest interval between the due dates of the hirer's payments under the agreement.

Thus, if the agreement provides for the hirer to pay rent monthly, then one month's notice is sufficient. The notice can be given to any person entitled or authorised to receive payments under the agreement. Therefore all the hirer need do is to hand the notice to the person to whom he pays his rent.

The agreement can improve the hirer's rights given to him by s.101 but it cannot diminish them.[7] It might improve them, by, for example, allowing him to give a shorter period of notice or allowing him to terminate the agreement before 18 months has expired.

Certain agreements are excluded from the application of s.101. They are: **26–010**

(i) Any agreement under which the hirer's payments are to exceed £1,500 per year.

(ii) Certain agreements involving specialised goods required by the hirer for business purposes.

(iii) Any agreement where the hirer requires the goods so that he in turn can in the course of his business let them out to someone else.

(iv) Agreements, if any, excluded by the OFT from the application of s.101.

---

[7] s.173.

Recovery of the Goods by Owner from Hirer

26–011   The owner under a regulated agreement will not be entitled to enter any premises to take possession of the goods unless at the time he obtains the permission of the occupier to do so. This is because s.92 applies to regulated consumer hire agreements as it does to hire-purchase and conditional sale agreements. Apart from that, however, the owner does have the right, after termination of the agreement, to recover possession of the goods. He has this right as soon as he is entitled to treat the agreement as terminated, i.e. when the default notice expires. This right is enforceable in the courts, or the owner can alternatively enforce it by seizing physical possession. The latter alternative will seldom be very practicable without the hirer's consent, because of the restriction on entering premises imposed by s.92.

Financial Relief for the Hirer

26–012   Where the owner recovers possession of the goods (whether by court action or otherwise) the court can grant the hirer financial relief if it appears just to do so—s.132. The financial relief can take either or both of two forms:

(i) An order that any payment still due from the hirer shall be reduced by an amount stated by the court (even, if the court so decides, reduced to nothing).

(ii) An order that the whole or any part of any sum already paid by the hirer shall be repaid.

The purpose of s.132 is no doubt to enable the court to ensure that when the agreement is terminated the hirer does not end up having to pay or having paid an amount which is equivalent to rent for a much longer period than the agreement actually lasted. Thus in deciding on if and how to exercise its powers under s. 132, the court must have regard to "the extent of the enjoyment of the goods by the hirer".

Hirer Wrongfully Disposes of the Goods

26–013   If the hirer sells the goods then the owner will have a right to recover possession from the purchaser unless the latter acquired them under an exception to the *nemo dat* principle. It will not be very likely, however, that the hirer will sell under any such exception. In particular the hirer is not a buyer in possession and (even if the goods are a motor vehicle) the Hire-Purchase Act 1964 will not apply.[8]

---

[8] For other possible exceptions to the *nemo dat* principle, see Ch.5, above.

Hirer's Landlord Levies Distress or Hirer Becomes Bankrupt

The relationship between the owner and the hirer's landlord or trustee in bankruptcy is **26–014** exactly the same as if the agreement, instead of being a consumer hire agreement, had been a hire-purchase agreement or conditional sale agreement.[9]

---

[9] See Ch.31, below.

Part III

AGENCY

Chapter 27

The Law of Agency

Introduction

The role and importance of agency in commercial law has already been considered in chapter **27–001**
one. What follows in this chapter is an introduction to the law of agency and an analysis of
the two models of understanding the creation and operation of agency law: consent and
authority. This chapter also introduces the various types of authority which will be explored
in the following chapters and are fundamental to the law of agency. Those types of authority
are: express actual authority; implied actual authority; usual authority; apparent authority.

Definition

Agency is a relationship between one person, the principal, and another, the agent, under **27–002**
which the agent will fulfil the intentions of the principal and act on his behalf, generally
through the creation, modification or termination of contracts with a third party. This
relationship is, as a general rule, created through the consent of both agent and principal
whereby the agent is granted the authority (power) to fulfil his principal's instructions. The
relationship may, however, be created through express or implied agreement. Moreover, the
courts may find that the parties have entered into an agency relationship without even
realising it. Clearly therefore, the law of agency involves three possible relationships. First
there is the internal relationship between the principal and the agent. Secondly, there is the
external relationship between the agent and the third party. Thirdly, there is the (possible)
relationship between the principal and the third party.

The law treats these relationships separately and so each has its own legal rules, traditionally imposed by the common law.[1] These relationships are important in defining the authority
of the agent to act on behalf of his principal.

---

[1] See also, however, the Commercial Agents Regulations considered in Ch.32, below.

AUTHORITY

27–003   Clearly crucial to the law of agency is the concept of authority. Authority in this sense refers to the scope of the agent's ability to affect the legal position of the principal. In many situations the agent's authority may be defined in very narrow terms and specific instructions given, e.g. "sell my Vauxhall car for no less than £10,000". This instruction is the express actual authority granted by the principal (the car's owner) to the agent. This type of actual authority is reinforced by a second type of actual authority, that of implied actual authority. Implied actual authority gives the agent the ability to do whatever associated tasks are necessary to ensure that the instructions of his principal are met. So, in the example given above, it would be reasonable for the agent to show the car to prospective buyers. Equally, it may well be necessary to demonstrate the car to them, i.e. take them on a test drive. These activities are not expressly permitted under the principal's instructions and so would not fall within the express actual authority of the agent. They would, however, fall under the remit of implied actual authority since both are tasks reasonably connected to, and necessary for, the fulfilment of the principal's instructions.

There are two further categories of authority which should be mentioned at this point. First, there is the concept of usual authority. This means that an agent will be deemed to have the authority that an agent in his position would normally have. So, for example, a store manager will have the usual authority, amongst other things, to hire staff to work in the store and to purchase stock to sell in the store. Even if the agreement between the principal and the agent does not expressly authorise such actions, the principal will be bound where the court is satisfied that they fell within the usual (or customary) authority of the agent concerned. There is, of course, a clear overlap between usual authority and implied actual authority which will be explored in the next chapter.

Secondly, there is the concept of apparent authority. Apparent authority may at first glance seem very similar to usual authority. It is, however, very different. By virtue of this concept an agent who acts outside his actual authority, will still be able to bind his principal where the principal has made a representation to the third party that the agent is acting within his authority. In such a situation the court is able to use estoppel to bind the principal to the actions of the agent even where the agent knew that he was acting outside his authority.

CONSENT

27–004   The consent model of agency law dictates that the crucial element in the relationship is the voluntary grant of authority from the principal to agent and the voluntary acceptance of such authority by the agent. This fits fairly neatly into a contractual analysis of agency law and as such describes the majority of agency relationships and the concept of authority which underlines them. The difficulty here, however, as will be seen in detail in the following chapter, is that it does not adequately describe every situation where the courts may find an agency relationship to exist. Broadly speaking there are two methods of creating an agency relationship which in turn give rise to two broad categories of authority: those with consent and those without. The consent model describes those agency relationships created by agreement and explains the nature of actual authority (both express and implied). The consent model fails, however, when it comes to the non-consensual methods of creating an agency relationship and the nature of the agent's authority in such relationships. As will be seen, the courts can find that an agency relationship has been created through necessity. Consider the following example: a courier of valuable goods encounters difficulty en route to his destination. Here, the agency relationship between the courier and his employer will be created by agreement and the authority of the agent defined by that agreement. What if however, the goods are in danger of being destroyed by virtue of the courier having encountered difficulties? There will be no agreement between the courier and the owner of the goods as to what actions the agent may take in that scenario. Therefore, a consensual agency relationship will not have been created. Despite this, the courts have been able to find that the courier is an agent of necessity for the owner of the goods, and that consequently the owner would be liable to reimburse the agent's costs associated with the necessary emergency action.

A second illustration of the shortcomings of the consent model of agency is found in what is referred to as "apparent authority". It has been noted above that where a principal makes a representation to the third party that the agent has authority to do a particular act, the principal will be bound by that act. This does not fit with the consensual model of agency law at all, since here the authority (and even the existence of an agency relationship in the first place) is determined by the relationship between the principal and the third party rather than the relationship between principal and agent.

Certainly neither the concept of consent nor that of authority provides an entire description of the agency relationship suitable for every situation. However, both concepts play an important role in the agency relationship and both add to an understanding of such relationships and the rights and duties of all parties involved.

General Reading

- Brown, "Authority and Necessity in the Law of Agency" (1992) 55 M.L.R. 414;   **27–005**

- Brown, "The significance of general and special authority in the development of the agent's external authority in English law" [2004] J.B.L. 391;

- Dowrick, "The Relationship of Principal and Agent" (1954) 17 M.L.R. 24;

- Reynolds, "Agency: Theory and Practice" (1978) 94 L.Q.R. 224.

Chapter 28

THE CREATION OF AGENCY

INTRODUCTION

This chapter examines the different ways in which the relationship of agent principal can be created. This is closely related to the issue of the authority of an agent since the manner in which the relationship is created will clearly impact upon the ability of the agent to act on behalf of his principal. As has already been mentioned, there are various methods through which this relationship can be established but the central difference is that between creation with consent and creation where there is no consent. This distinction is important as it will affect the nature of agent's authority, i.e. the extent to which his acts will bind the principal.

28–001

CREATION WITH CONSENT

Actual Authority

Certainly the most straightforward situation is that where the agency relationship is created by express agreement. In such a case, the agreement will, to some extent at least, dictate the scope of the agent's authority. This is called "actual authority": The agent can properly do anything detailed within the agreement. Whilst this agreement will commonly be a formal contract, there is no requirement under the common law for it necessarily to be so. Thus, a parent sending a child on an errand to the shops is forming an agency relationship even though there is obviously no contract. In that example, the extent of the child's authority as agent would most likely be defined by the instructions given by the parent, e.g. "take this money and buy a loaf of bread".

28–002

The extent of an agent's actual authority depends on the proper construction of the terms of the agreement. Historically much argument turned on ambiguous instructions of the principal. The courts were generally prepared to find that the principal was bound by the acts of his agent where the agent had honestly interpreted those instructions in a manner not intended by the principal. This argument is now much less likely to find favour and it may well be that even in the case of ambiguous instructions, the principal will not be bound if the agent has the opportunity to confirm the meaning of the instructions with the principal before acting on his behalf. This is obviously much more likely in modern times given the ability of speedy, worldwide communications. The nature of "actual authority" is neatly summed up by Diplock L.J. in *Freeman & Lockyer (A Firm) v Buckhurst Park Properties (Mangal) Ltd* in the following terms[1]:

> "An 'actual' authority is a legal relationship between principal and agent created by a consensual agreement to which they alone are parties. Its scope is to be ascertained by applying ordinary principles of construction of contracts, including any proper implications from the express words used, the usages of the trade, or the course of business between the parties."

The words "including any proper implications" is a reference to the second category of authority, implied actual authority, and it is to this issue we shall now turn.

Implied Authority

28–003   In the same way that a contract can be created through implication, so too can an agency relationship. In such a situation the normal rules of contract law will apply. A clear (and important) illustration of both implied actual authority and also the creation of the agency relationship through implication is that of *Hely-Hutchinson v Brayhead Ltd*.[2] The chairman of a company, a Mr Richards, acted as managing director for the company and entered into various contracts on behalf of the company. The board of directors of the company were aware of Mr Richards acting as de facto managing director. One contract Mr Richards entered into on behalf of the company was for the company to act as guarantor for various debts of a third party. The company sought to avoid honouring the guarantee arguing that Mr Richards had no authority to enter into the contract. The Court of Appeal held that the company was liable since Mr Richards had actual authority to enter into the guarantee implied from the conduct of the parties and the circumstances of the case. Lord Denning M.R. explains the matter thus:

> "It is implied when it is inferred from the conduct of the parties and the circumstances of the case, such as when the board of directors appoint one of their number to be managing director. They thereby impliedly authorise him to do all such things as fall within the usual scope of that office."

---

[1] [1964] 2 Q.B. 480 at 502.
[2] [1968] 1 Q.B. 549.

This goes to the root of implied actual authority. Even where there is a formal contractual document detailing the scope and extent of the agent's authority, this will generally not be so detailed as to cover every possible situation the agent may face. The nature of implied actual authority is to confer upon the agent such authority as is necessary to comply with the instructions given by the principal.[3] One important point follows from this understanding. Implied actual authority cannot be employed contrary to the express actual authority granted by the principal. Thus even if the agent's actions are reasonably required by the principal's instructions, if the act is expressly prohibited within the express agreement between agent and principal, the notion of implied actual authority will not be applicable.

A second feature of implied actual authority also stems from the nature of this type of authority and that is that it cannot exist in isolation. That is to say that implied actual authority is an aid to allow the agent to fulfil the express instructions of his principal. It therefore requires there to be an express actual authority in the first place which is then supported by the secondary notion of implied actual authority. This feature was considered by the Court of Appeal in *The Choko Star*[4] where the issue arose as to whether a ship's master was able to make salvage contracts acting as agent for the cargo-owner. It was clear that the ship's master was, at all times, acting as agent for the ship owner, and it was equally clear that he could also be the agent for the cargo-owner where the concept of agency of necessity applied. What was not clear, however, was whether the master had implied actual authority to act on behalf of the cargo-owner in salvaging the cargo in the absence of some compelling and immediate situation which invoked the rules of necessity.[5]

At first instance Sheen J. held that the ship's master was bestowed with an authority to   **28–004**
arrange for salvage of the cargo by implication by virtue of such an authority being implied into the contract of carriage, i.e. that the cargo-owners should reasonably expect that it may become necessary for the cargo to be salved at some point on the voyage, and that thus the ship's master should reasonably have the authority to enter into the necessary contracts in order to secure the salvage of the cargo. The Court of Appeal, however, disagreed and reversed the decision since there was no basis to establish a relationship of agent-principal between the ship's master and the cargo-owners. That being so, it was not possible to consider any implied actual authority of the ship's master since there was no agency relationship or authority by implication or otherwise. This decision would of course have been very different had the Court of Appeal been able to find that this was a situation where the ship's master was an involuntary agent of the cargo-owner as an agent of necessity.

CREATION WITHOUT CONSENT

Apparent Authority

The first situation (termed apparent or ostensible authority) where an agency relationship can   **28–005**
be formed despite there being no express agreement to that effect is that where estoppel is

---

[3] Traditionally known as "medium powers", see for example, *Howard v Baillie* (1876) 2 Hy Bl 618.
[4] *Industrie Chimiche Italia Centrale and Cerealfin SA v Alexander G Tsavliris & Sons Maritime Co, Panchristo Shipping Co SA and Bula Shipping Corp* [1990] 1 Lloyd's Rep. 516.
[5] Agency of necessity is dealt with at para.28–012, below.

established. In short, this means that where an individual (the principal) leads a third party to believe that another person is acting as his agent, the courts can find that there is an agent-principal-third party relationship in effect and enforce the contract between the principal and third party accordingly. It will be recognised immediately that the creation of agency through estoppel has certain distinct features which set it apart from agency created through agreement. First, it applies through the conduct of the principal towards the third party and is not defined by the conduct between the principal and his agent. This is unusual since it appears to run contrary to the general rationale behind agency relationships where the principal will generally have no interaction with the third party, since the agent will have been appointed to fulfil such duties. Secondly, estoppel in this context has two distinct abilities. It can be employed by the courts to discover the existence of an agency relationship. It can also be used, however, in order to expand on the nature of the agent's authority where, for example, the agent's actual authority does not extend to encompass the particular agreement with the third party.

In order for a third party to argue successfully that the principal is bound by the actions of his agent the following requirements must be satisfied:

1. There must be a representation by the principal to the third party that the agent has authority.

2. The third party must rely on the representation.

3. The third party must not be aware that the agent is acting without authority.

All of these requirements must be satisfied and each will now be considered in turn.

Representation from the Principal to the Third Party that the Agent has Authority

28–006   Since the nature of apparent authority is defined by the representation from principal to third party, the requirement for there to be a representation is obviously fundamental. The representation must be such that it indicates to the third party that the agent has authority to act on behalf of the principal. This will be satisfied in the simple case where the principal makes a specific representation to the third party. It will also be satisfied, however, where the principal places his agent in such a position that would usually carry certain powers and responsibilities.[6] Certainly the most straightforward situation is where the principal makes an express representation to the third party. It is clear, however, that a representation can be implied through, for example, the conduct of the principal or through the course of prior dealing between the principal and the third party. An example of the former situation is the case of *Freeman & Lockyer (A Firm) v Buckhurst Park Properties (Mangal) Ltd*[7] where Diplock L.J. stated that[8]:

---

[6] As to the relationship between apparent authority and usual authority, see para.28–009, below.
[7] [1964] 2 Q.B. 480.
[8] [1964] 2 Q.B. 480 at 503–04.

"The representation which creates 'apparent' authority may take a variety of forms of which the commonest is representation by conduct, that is, by permitting the agent to act in some way in the conduct of the principal's business with other persons. By so doing the principal represents to anyone who becomes aware that the agent is so acting that the agent has authority to enter on behalf of the principal into contracts with other persons of the kind which an agent so acting in the conduct of his principal's business has usually 'actual' authority to enter into".

An example of the latter case is that of *Summers v Solomon*[9] where an agent had managed his principal's shop for a number of years. In the course of managing the shop, the agent did, on many occasions, buy goods on behalf of his principal from the third party for which the principal paid. The agent absconded, however, but still purchased goods purporting to do so on behalf of his (old) principal. After absconding, the agent was clearly not acting with any actual authority but the principal was liable on the contract since the previous course of dealing constituted a representation sufficient to clothe the agent with the necessary authority.

Reliance Upon the Representation

This requirement means that where the third party is unaware of the representation made by the principal the third party cannot seek to bind the principal into the contract through apparent authority. It seems reasonably clear that the third party need not act upon the representation to his detriment. This is important since it allows for a claim by the third party against the principal where, for example, the third party did enter into a transaction but suffered no detriment. In *Arctic Shipping Co Ltd v Mobilia AB and Others, The Tatra*[10] Gatehouse J. stated unequivocally "the only 'detriment' that has to be shown in such a case is the entering into the contract by the party relying on that authority".   **28–007**

Third Party Must be Unaware of the Agent's Lack of Authority

It is self explanatory that where the third party is aware that the agent does not have the necessary authority to act on behalf of his principal, the third party cannot raise apparent authority to bind the principal. In many cases this is a natural consequence of the requirement of reliance previously discussed since, if a third party is aware of the lack of the agent's authority, he cannot rely on a representation to the contrary from the principal. This position can, however, be a little complicated. Thus, whilst it may not be possible to establish that a third party had actual knowledge of the agent's lack of authority to act, the third party may, nevertheless, be "put on notice" by the circumstances of the agent's act. In *Lloyds Bank Ltd v The Chartered Bank of India, Australia and China*[11] an employee of a bank was fraudulently drawing cheques on his principal's account and paying them into an account in   **28–008**

---

[9] (1857) 7 E. & B. 879.
[10] [1990] 2 Lloyd's Rep. 51 at 59.
[11] [1929] 1 K.B. 40.

his own name with the defendant bank. It was held that the defendant bank, the third party, was put on notice by the fraudulent cheques since, having regard to the position of the agent, the sums involved were large and also each of the fraudulent cheques was purported to have been signed by the same officer of the principal. This of course, will not protect the principal where the agent is sufficiently deceptive so as to make sure that every fraudulent transaction appears perfectly normal. The issue is not the fraud of the agent, but rather how the transaction appears to the third party.

Usual Authority

28–009   The nature of usual authority has been the subject of much debate in agency law. The debate focuses upon whether usual authority emanates from the other types of authority an agent may possess, particularly actual implied authority and apparent authority, or whether usual authority can exist in its own right as an independent category of authority.

What can be said with confidence is that usual authority is primarily a sub-division of actual, implied authority and it thus emanates from, and enlarges the scope of, the actual authority which exists between the agent and principal. In *Hely-Hutchinson v Brayhead Ltd*[12] Lord Denning M.R. said that when the Board of Directors appoints X as a Managing Director "they thereby impliedly authorise him to do all such things that fall within the usual scope of the Office".[13] It is clear therefore that where an agent belongs to a particular trade or profession he will have the usual authority to do whatever is necessary to fulfil his express authority as agent. This obviously depends upon the interpretation of what is "usual" for an agent belonging to the same business or profession as the agent in question. It is also possible for trade usage to give rise to usual authority whereby the agent will have the usual authority to act in accordance with the lawful usages of that place or trade. This is so even where the principal is unaware of the particular trade usage in question provided that the usage is reasonable. A trade usage will be regarded as reasonable where it is not inconsistent with the principal's express instructions (i.e. the agent's actual, express, authority). This is exemplified by *Robinson v Mollett*[14] where an agent was appointed to buy tallow (processed animal fat) on behalf his principal, a tallow merchant in Liverpool. The agent bought the tallow in his own name and allocated the agreed quantities amongst his multiple principals. Upon discovering that the agent had purchased the tallow in his own name, the tallow merchant refused to take delivery of the goods. The agent sought to rely on the customary trade usage in the London tallow markets whereby agents would buy tallow in their own name. The House of Lords accepted that such a trade custom existed but their Lordships were not prepared to allow it to bind the principal since the nature of the custom was such as fundamentally to affect the relationship between the parties. By buying, and therefore selling, in his own name the agent was in a position of conflict between his position as agent (duty bound to achieve the best price possible for his principal) and as owner and seller of the tallow (whereby he would seek to obtain the highest price possible). This conflict resulted in the conclusion that the trade usage was not reasonable and therefore in order for it to be

---

[12] [1968] 1 Q.B. 549.
[13] [1968] 1 Q.B. 549 at 583.
[14] [1875] L.R. 7 H.L. 802.

effective, the principal must be aware of it. Since he was not, the agent's action for damages failed.

Usual authority is also utilised in apparent authority when the principal's representation involves appointing the agent to a position which carries a usual authority. Thus, in *First Energy (UK) Ltd v Hungarian International Bank Ltd*[15] the Court of Appeal found that, a company, by appointing a man to the role of senior manager within the business of a bank, had given him a position which carried usual authority and consequently the company had clothed him with apparent authority. Steyn L.J. suggested that[16]:

"It seems to me that the law recognises that in modern commerce an agent who has no apparent authority to conclude a particular transaction may sometimes be clothed with apparent authority to make representations of fact".

This is an example of the situation Lord Keith referred to in *Armagas Ltd v Mundogas SA (The Ocean Frost)*[17] as where:

"the ostensible authority is general in character, arising when the principal has placed the agent in a position which in the outside world is generally regarded as carrying authority to enter into transactions of the kind in question".

Whilst the principal has made no representation to the third party that the agent has the authority to perform the specific act carried out, appointing the agent to a role which would usually carry the authority to conduct the transaction in question will be sufficient to bind the principal through recourse to apparent authority.

A further illustration of this aspect of usual authority in the context of apparent authority **28–010** is to be found in *Panorama Developments (Guildford) Ltd v Fidelis Furnishing Fabrics Ltd*[18] where a company secretary hired cars purporting to do so on behalf of the company. In fact, however, the secretary was hiring the cars for his own purposes. When the car hire charges were not paid, the third party (i.e. the car hire company) sued the company, which denied liability. The Court of Appeal held that a company secretary had the usual authority to enter into contracts in respect of the administrative operation of the company and that by appointing a person to such a position, the company had clothed the agent with apparent authority to enter into such contracts. Consequently, the company was bound by the contracts made by the secretary.

The final issue to consider in relation to usual authority is also the most controversial: is there an independent category of usual authority? Put another way, can an agent bind his principal to a contract where the act is outside both express and implied actual authority (for example, where the act is specifically prohibited by the agency agreement) and the principal has not held out the agent to have the authority to act, and so apparent authority is not applicable? The decision of the court in *Watteau v Fenwick*[19] answers these questions in the affirmative.

---

[15] [1993] 2 Lloyd's Rep. 194.
[16] [1993] 2 Lloyd's Rep. 194 at 204.
[17] [1986] A.C. 717 at 777.
[18] [1971] 2 Q.B. 711.
[19] [1893] 1 Q.B. 346.

The facts of the case are deceptively straightforward. The owner of a beerhouse sold it to a firm of brewers who retained the former owner as the manager of the business. The licence was always taken out in the manager's name, and it was his name that was painted over the door. Under the agreement made between the manager and the brewers, the manager had no authority to buy any goods for the business except bottled ales and mineral waters. All other goods required by the business were to be supplied by the brewers themselves. Despite the terms of the agreement, the manager entered into contracts with a third party to supply the beerhouse with, amongst other things, cigars and Bovril. Upon discovering that the manager was not the owner of the business, the third party sued the brewers for payment under the supply contracts in respect of the cigars and Bovril.

28–011   The Court held that the principal was liable under the contracts made by their agent even though (i) they were of a type expressly prohibited in the agreement between the parties and (ii) since the principal was undisclosed there was no apparent authority extended to the agent. Wills J. stated that[20]:

> " . . . the principal is liable for all the acts of the agent which are within the authority usually confided to an agent of that character, notwithstanding limitations, as between the principal and the agent, put upon that authority. It is said that it is only so where there has been a holding out of authority—which cannot be said of a case where the person supplying the goods knew nothing of the existence of a principal. But I do not think so".

Wills J. was very much influenced by the fact that in *Watteau*, the principal was undisclosed. Had the principal have been disclosed, the standard ambit of usual authority previously considered would have applied, and the principal would have been liable on the contracts made by his agent. In order to prevent a "secret limitation" on the liability of all undisclosed principals Wills J. was happy to extend the application of usual authority. This is justifiable on the grounds of public policy, but has been strongly criticised in subsequent cases and has been followed only once.[21] In *Rhodian River Shipping Co SA and Rhodian Sailor Shipping Co SA v Halla Maritime Corp*[22] Bingham J. described *Watteau* as "a somewhat puzzling case" and went on to state that "I would myself be extremely wary of applying this doctrine, if it exists".[23]

It seems likely, therefore, that *Watteau* will not be followed in the future and that its application will be narrowly construed. Nevertheless, at present, it remains a possibility that an agent could bind his principal despite there being no authority whether actual or apparent.

Necessity

28–012   In certain, strictly controlled, circumstances the law will impose an agency relationship or, where such a relationship already exists, extend an agent's authority to act by virtue of an

---

[20] [1893] 1 Q.B. 346 at 348–49.
[21] In *Kinahan & Co Ltd v Parry and Others* [1910] 2 K.B. 389.
[22] [1984] 1 Lloyd's Rep. 373.
[23] [1984] 1 Lloyd's Rep. 373 at 379.

emergency. Thus, for example, where perishable goods are decomposing en route to their intended destination, it is accepted that a courier can, in certain circumstances, sell the goods on behalf of the principal even though he is not an agent of sale.[24] In *Springer v Great Western Railway Co*[25] a consignment of tomatoes was delayed in transit due, in part, to a strike by dock workers which meant that the tomatoes could not be unloaded upon their arrival at the port. This delay meant that the tomatoes were starting to deteriorate and an "agent" sold the entire cargo and sought to rely on his position of agent of necessity in order to effect a sale before the goods became unmerchantable. The Court of Appeal held that whilst the doctrine of necessity could potentially apply to these facts, it did not in fact do so, since the "agent" had the opportunity to contact the owners of the various consignments of tomatoes and take instructions on how to proceed. Scrutton L.J. said[26]:

> "The defendants have sold somebody else's goods, and they have no right to do so unless they establish certain conditions. They are agents to carry, not to sell. To give them the right to sell, circumstances must exist which put them in the position of agents of necessity for the owners to take that action which is necessary in the interests of the owners".

Since the "agent" could have contacted the owners, but failed to do so, he was not an agent of necessity. This will clearly be an important restriction on agency of necessity in modern times since the nature of speedy and effective communications in the 21st century will allow for only a handful of situations where the agent cannot contact the owner of the goods to take instructions on how to proceed.[27] Nevertheless, this case illustrates the sort of situation where a court may be prepared to find agency of necessity.

Lord Diplock in *China-Pacific SA v Food Corporation of India, The Winson*[28] considered a two-fold division of agency of necessity:

(i) where an agent enters into a contract with a third party on behalf on the principal, consequently binding the principal contractually to the third party; and

(ii) where a person acts for another and subsequently seeks reimbursement or an indemnity from him.

Lord Diplock suggested that only in the first scenario would agency of necessity properly arise. The issue of reimbursement could be dealt with by reference to the terms of the nature of the agreement between the parties, e.g. bailor/bailee. Nevertheless, it seems clear that agency of necessity will be deemed to apply in both cases outlined above.

One further point must be made in respect of agency of necessity. That is that the agent must act bona fide in the best interests of the principal. This requirement is exemplified by the case of *Prager v Blatspiel, Stamp and Heacock Ltd*[29] where hostilities prevented the

---

[24] For example, a cargo of grain which was fermenting in *Couturier v Hastie* (1856) 8 Exch. 40.

[25] [1921] 1 K.B. 257.

[26] [1921] 1 K.B. 257 at 267.

[27] It seems that even where the owner can be contacted, but is not in fact giving any instructions to the agent, this will be sufficient to satisfy this requirement of agency of necessity. See *China-Pacific SA v Food Corporation of India, The Winson* [1982] A.C. 939.

[28] [1982] A.C. 939.

[29] [1924] 1 K.B. 566.

sellers from delivering a consignment of furs to their buyer. The sellers resold the furs and argued that the condition of the goods was deteriorating and therefore they were agents of necessity in effecting a resale of the goods. McCardie J. held that (i) there was no commercial necessity to sell the furs since the deterioration was only slight and the increase in the value of the furs more than compensated for this slight deterioration and (ii) the sellers had been dishonest in selling the furs and since they were motivated by the increase in the value of the furs they were not acting bona fide in the best interests of their buyer in effecting a resale. Consequently, whilst agency of necessity could have arisen, on the facts it did not.

RATIFICATION

28–013   Normally, an agent's authority is given to him before he acts for the principal. With ratification the position is reversed and the principal agrees to ratify the agent's conduct subsequently. The concept was explained in the following terms by Lord Macnaghten in *Keighley, Maxsted & Co v Durant*[30]:

> "And so by a wholesome and convenient fiction, a person ratifying the act of another, who, without authority, has made a contract openly and avowedly on his behalf, is deemed to be, though in fact he was not, a party to the contract."

Given the inroad that the concept of ratification (what Lord Macnaghten rightly regards as a convenient fiction) could have on the doctrine of privity of contract, it is not surprising that the courts have imposed fairly restrictive requirements which must all be satisfied in order for ratification to be effective.

These requirements are as follows:

- The principal must be in existence at the time of the agent's act.

- The agent must profess to act as an agent for the principal.

- The principal must have the capacity to act as a principal at the time of the agent's act.

- The principal must have the capacity to act as a principal at the time of the ratification.

Each requirement will now be considered in turn.

The Principal Must be in Existence at the Time of the Agent's Act

28–014   This means that the principal must be a live human being or a juristic person at the date of the agent's act. Thus an agent cannot act for a non-existent principal even if he knows that the principal will subsequently come into existence and then will wish to ratify his conduct.

---

[30] [1901] A.C. 240 at 247.

The rule has caused difficulties where company promoters enter into contracts on behalf of companies which are in the process of formation but have not yet acquired legal status. Both the requirement and the problem it causes in the context of company promoters are evident in the case of *Kelner v Baxter*[31] where there was a contract of sale of some wine. The contract purported to be made on behalf of the Gravesend Royal Alexandra Hotel Company. The problem was that at the time of contracting the company did not exist. When the company had been incorporated, it attempted to ratify the contract of sale. The court held that the newly formed company could not ratify since it had not been in existence at the time the contract was made. The question of liability on the contract was considered by Erle C.J. who stated that "as there was no company in existence at the time, the agreement would be wholly inoperative unless it were held to be binding on the defendants personally".[32]

The Agent Must Profess to Act as an Agent for the Principal

This requirement prevents, for example, a principal from ratifying a contract which his agent   **28–015**
entered into in the agent's own name. This was precisely what happened in the leading case of *Keighley, Maxsted & Co v Durant*[33]: An agent was appointed to buy wheat at a specified price. When he could not find any wheat to buy at the specified price he entered into a contract to buy wheat at a higher price. The contract was made between the seller and the agent in his own name and did not refer to the principal whatsoever. The agent contacted his principal who confirmed that he was happy that the wheat was worth the higher price. When the agent failed to pay for the wheat and take delivery, the sellers claimed that the principal had ratified the contract and was therefore liable under it. The House of Lords, in reversing the decision of the Court of Appeal, unanimously held that ratification was impossible since the contract of sale made no mention of the fact that the agent was acting on behalf of another party. The contract was in the agent's name and thus no other party could be liable under it. Lord Macnaghten, on the question of whether ratification ought to be extended so as to cover such a situation, stated:

> "On principle I should say certainly not. It is, I think, a well-established principle in English law that civil obligations are not to be created by, or founded upon, undisclosed intentions."[34]

The position is the same where the agent forges his principal's signature. In such a case the agent is holding himself out to be the principal and the act is incapable of being ratified by the principal. In *Brook v Hook*[35] an agent forged his principal's signature on a promissory note. The principal did not wish to see his agent prosecuted (since he was his brother-in-law) and agreed to honour the note. The Court held that his attempt to ratify the act of his agent forging his signature was not effective since the act of forgery was illegal and the note void. Therefore, ratification was not possible and the principal was not liable to honour the

[31] [1866] L.R. 2 C.P. 174.
[32] See also Ch.3, below on breach of warrant of authority.
[33] [1901] A.C. 240.
[34] [1901] A.C. 240 at 247.
[35] (1870–71) 6 Ex. 89.

promissory note. This decision can also be explained by the fact that the agent, in forging his principal's signature is not acting as agent, but is purporting to act on his own behalf. This would therefore be incapable of ratification under the principle enunciated in *Keighley*.

The case of *Watson v Swann*[36] makes it clear that whilst the principal need not be named by the agent during his business with the third party, it must be possible for the third party to ascertain the identity of the principal on whose behalf the agent is acting. Thus a general reference to the third party that the agent is acting as an agent will not suffice since it does not allow the third party to ascertain the identity of the person who is to be bound by the contract made by the agent. The ascertainment must be sufficient to identify the individual who can ratify the acts of the agent. If this is not possible, ratification is not possible; therefore, in the case of an undisclosed principal, ratification is not possible.

The Principal Must Have the Capacity to Act at the Time of the Agent's Act

28–016   This requirement is well explained by the nature of ratification already considered. The fiction of ratification is that it artificially deems that the principal himself made the contract. In reality of course the position is that the principal is adopting the transaction. Nevertheless, it follows that if ratification is possible, the principal must have had the capacity to actually make the transaction at the time the agent entered into the transaction. A clear example of this requirement in operation is the decision of the court in *Boston Deep Sea Fishing and Ice Co Ltd v Farnham*[37] where it was held that ratification of acts by the French principal was not possible, since at the time of the acts, the principal was an alien enemy and therefore was "not a competent principal because it could not have done the act itself".[38]

The Principal Must Have the Capacity to Act at the Time of the Ratification

28–017   This requirement is best understood by reference to the reality of the situation where a principal seeks to ratify an unauthorised act made by his agent, i.e. that he adopts the transaction. Consequently, it follows that the principal must have the capacity to enter into the transaction at the time he wishes to ratify it. This rule was effective in *Grover & Grover Ltd v Mathews*[39] where an agent arranged for a factory to be insured without any authority to do so. Unfortunately the factory was destroyed by fire and the principal subsequently sought to ratify the transaction. The court held that ratification was not possible after the subject matter of the insurance policy had been destroyed. The principal would not have been able to make the contract of insurance after the factory had been destroyed and therefore he could not ratify the agent's unauthorised act.

---

[36] (1862) 11 C.B. (N.S.) 756.
[37] [1957] 1 W.L.R. 1051.
[38] [1957] 1 W.L.R. 1051 at 1058.
[39] [1910] 2 K.B. 401.

This decision was based on the earlier case of *Bird v Brown*[40] where Rolfe B. suggested that in order to ratify, the principal must lawfully be able to enter into the transaction which he seeks to ratify. This has been subject to criticism in recent times, particularly in *Presentaciones Musicales SA v Secunda and Another*[41] where solicitors acting without authority issued a writ in April 1988 on behalf of a company in Panama. In May 1991 the company liquidators purported to ratify the solicitor's act (i.e. issuing the writ) but faced the problem that this "ratification" occurred after the expiry of the limitation period under the Limitation Act 1980. Roch L.J. considered the principle of ratification and suggested that "the dictum cited from *Bird v Brown* is not a correct statement of the exceptions to the principles of ratification".[42] Roch L.J. then went on to state that the correct view was that laid down by Cotton L.J. in *Bolton Partners v Lambert*[43]:

> "The rule as to ratification by a principal of acts done by an assumed agent is that the ratification is thrown back to the date of the act done, and that the agent is put in the same position as if he had had authority to do the act at the same time the act was done by him".

Therefore, the Court of Appeal applied *Bolton Partners v Lambert* and held that the ratification was effective. If this position is the law, then it is no longer a requirement of ratification that the principal must at the time of ratification have capacity to enter into the transaction which he is ratifying.

General Reading

- Brown, "Authority and Necessity in the Law of Agency" (1992) 55 M.L.R. 414;   **28–018**

- Brown, "Ratification, Retroactivity and Reasonableness" (1994) 110 L.Q.R. 531;

- Brown, "The Agent's Apparent Authority: Paradigm or Paradox?" [1995] J.B.L. 360;

- Munday, "Salvaging the Law of Agency" [1990] L.M.C.L.Q. 1;

- Reynolds, "Authority, Ratification, Warrant of Authority" [2006] J.B.L. 537;

- Reynolds, "The Ultimate Apparent Authority" (1994) 110 L.Q.R. 21;

- Tettenborn, "Agents, Business Owners and Estoppel" (1988) 47 C.L.J. 274.

---

[40] (1850) 4 Exch. 786.
[41] [1994] Ch. 271.
[42] [1994] Ch. 271 at 284.
[43] (1889) 41 Ch. D. 295 at 306–307.

Chapter 29

THE DUTIES OF AN AGENT

INTRODUCTION

In this chapter we will look at the duties owed by an agent to his principal. This may appear, **29–001** at first instance, to be rather a straightforward investigation. Certainly, where there is an express contract between the parties, the duties of the agent will be defined, in no small measure, by that agreement and any terms which may be implied into it under the normal rules of contract law. Defining the duties of an agent is, however, somewhat more complicated than might have been expected since, the fact that the agency relationship can be created in numerous different ways, coupled with the consequence that the nature and extent of the authority vested in the agent will vary accordingly, dictates that the duties owed by one agent will not necessarily be the same as those owed by another. This is probably made most evident by a comparison of the duties owed by a contractual agent and those of a gratuitous agent. In both cases there is, as we have seen previously, a consensual undertaking of authority by the agent to act in accordance with the instructions of his principal. What if, for one reason or another, the agent refuses to perform his undertaking as dictated by the agency agreement? If the agent is a contractual agent, the position is straightforward and the principal will be able to pursue an action for breach of contract. In the case of the gratuitous agent, however, the agent would not be liable for failing to perform his agreed undertakings; since there is no consideration to bind the agent's promise, enforcement here is impossible. That is not to say, however, that a gratuitous agent owes no duties to his principal. As we shall see in addition to a non-contractual duty of care a gratuitous agent can owe fiduciary duties towards his principal. These are obligations arising out of the voluntary undertaking of authority and power in respect of another person and will apply to both contractual and gratuitous agents. It must also be appreciated, however, that in addition to the nature of the agency created (and therefore the nature of authority granted to the agent) affecting the type of obligations the law will impose upon the agent, the specific requirements of such duties will require will vary from agent to agent. Thus, for example, the contractual duty of reasonable care and the fiduciary duties owed by an agent to his principal are inherently variable.

PERFORMANCE OF CONTRACTUAL UNDERTAKING

29–002 As noted above, where there is an express contract the obligations between the agent and principal will be governed by that agreement. The duty of the agent in this regard is strict. So where the principal's instructions are clear and unequivocal, the agent is duty bound to comply with them precisely. Where an agent fails to comply with such instructions, he will be liable in damages. This rule is exemplified by the case of *Turpin v Bilton*[1] where an agent was instructed to insure a ship. The agent, however, failed to insure the ship and as a result, when the ship was lost, the principal was unable to claim on the insurance. The agent was liable in damages for the value of the lost ship since he had not performed his contractual undertaking. A similar scenario arose in *Bertrom, Armstrong & Co v Godfray*[2] where an agent was instructed to sell certain shares when their value reached a precise amount. The agent was required to sell those shares as soon as the specified price was reached and had no discretion to wait in order that the share price might increase beyond the figure specified by the principal.

It is clear from the authorities, including *Turpin* and *Bertrom Armstrong*, that the agent's duty of performance extends both to cases of non-performance and also to those of mis-performance. It was seen in the introduction that a gratuitous agent will not be liable for non-performance since to hold otherwise would in effect find there to be a contract where there was none. The situation is different, however, where a gratuitous agent mis-performs under the agency agreement. This is exemplified by the facts and outcome of *Wilkinson v Coverdale*.[3] An agent agreed to arrange, without payment, for insurance on behalf of his principal. Due to the agent's negligence in effecting the insurance contract, the principal was unable to claim on the policy when his house was destroyed by fire. The court held that the agent was in breach of his tortious duty in performing on behalf of the principal. This decision raises a clear difficulty since we have already discussed the fact that a gratuitous agent cannot be liable for failing to perform his agreed function. The distinction, albeit a fine one, is said to be that where a gratuitous agent performs (to whatever degree) his functions under the agency agreement, he must carry them out without negligence in order to comply with his tortious duty. Where however, the same agent fails to act whatsoever under the agency agreement, he will not be in breach of his tortious duty. The distinction, therefore, is between misfeasance (performing poorly) and nonfeasance (doing nothing).

The issue of misfeasance by a gratuitous agent will also by definition raise questions over whether such an agent will face liability for breach of a tortious duty of care. This may be contrasted with the contractual (statutory) duty of skill and care which is discussed below. In *Chaudhry v Prabhakar and Another*[4] the plaintiff asked a friend to find a car for her since she knew little about cars. The friend was neither a car trader nor a mechanic but did have some experience in buying and selling cars and had much more knowledge than the plaintiff did.

[1] [1843] 5 Man. & G. 455.
[2] [1838] 1 Knapp 381.
[3] (1793) 1 Esp. 74.
[4] [1989] 1 W.L.R. 29.

The principal stipulated that the car was not to have been in an accident. The friend found a car which he thought was suitable and although he noticed that the bonnet had been either repaired or replaced he did not ask the seller (a car dealer) whether it had been in an accident. After having the car recommended to her by her friend, the principal purchased the car only to discover a couple of months later that it had been in a major accident and had been sold to the car dealer as salvage. The plaintiff argued that (i) the car dealer was in breach of the implied term that the car was of merchantable quality under s.14 of the Sale of Goods Act 1979 and (ii) the agent had breached his duty of care by not taking steps to ensure that he found her a car which met her stipulation that it should not have been in an accident. At first instance, the court easily accepted the first argument. The court also held that agent did owe his principal a duty of care to inquire as to whether the car had been in an accident. The Court of Appeal upheld this decision. Stuart-Smith L.J. stated that[5]:

> "When considering the question of whether a duty of care arises, the relationship between the parties is material. If they are friends, the true view may be that the advice or representation is made upon a purely social occasion and the circumstances show that there has not been a voluntary assumption of responsibility."

The question therefore, is how to determine whether or not the relationship in question was a "purely social occasion" or whether there was something more, i.e. a "voluntary assumption of responsibility". On this point Stuart-Smith L.J. suggested that the relationship of agent and principal "is powerful evidence that the occasion is not a purely social one". This was further supported by the nature of the relationship between the parties, in particular, the fact that the principal clearly relied upon the agent's skill and judgment which was considerably greater than her own. Moreover, the agent knew that the principal was relying upon his recommendation and even told her that she did not need to have an inspection made of the car prior to buying it.

A related issue is the duty of the agent to perform his obligations personally, i.e. not to **29–003** delegate. This duty is easily explained by an understanding of the nature of the agency relationship. Where a principal appoints an agent to act on his behalf, he grants that agent authority to stand in his place. It follows, therefore, that the identity of the agent will be very important to the principal and that the agent may not, without consent, hand over the authority vested in him to another person, a sub-agent, in order to fulfil his obligations under the agency agreement. This is referred to by the maxim *delegatus non potest delegare* which was explained by Thesiger L.J. in *De Bussche v Alt*[6] as preventing two distinct situations[7]:

(i) the ability of an agent to appoint his own agent as principal; and

(ii) the ability of an agent to devolve his responsibilities to another.

This rule, however, has numerous exceptions. Thesiger L.J. in *De Bussche* suggested that the ability of an agent to delegate may well be required due to the "exigencies of business". The Court of Appeal stated that this ability[8]:

---

[5] [1989] 1 W.L.R. 29 at 34.
[6] (1878) 8 Ch. D. 286.
[7] (1878) 8 Ch. D. 286 at 310.
[8] (1878) 8 Ch. D. 286 at 310.

" . . . should be implied where, from the conduct of the parties to the original contract of agency, the usage of trade, or the nature of the particular business which is the subject of the agency, it may reasonably be presumed that the parties to the contract of agency originally intended that such authority should exist".

More recently, the Court of Appeal in *John McCann & Co v Pow*[9] has repeated the general rule that an agent may not, without express or implied authority from his principal, delegate his performance under the agency agreement. Mr Pow wished to sell a flat he owned and appointed John McCann & Co as agents to effect such a sale. The agents sent the details of the flat on to a second firm of estate agents in order that both firms might both advertise the property. The second firm found a willing purchaser, Mr Rudd, and after private negotiations between Rudd and Pow, the flat was sold. After the sale had been effected, John McCann & Co discovered that Mr Rudd had been introduced to the property through the second firm of estate agents. John McCann & Co claimed commission as agreed under the agency agreement on the basis that the second firm of agents were their sub-agents. The court rejected this claim and held that Mr Pow was not liable to pay commission since there was no express authority to delegate and no implied authority could be found to allow the agent to delegate performance. This latter point was explained thus[10]:

> "The reason is because an estate agent holds a position of discretion and trust. Discretion in his conduct of negotiations. Trust in his handling of affairs. It is his duty, certainly in the case of a sole agent, to use his best endeavours to sell the property at an acceptable price to a purchaser who is satisfactory and who is ready and willing and able to purchase the property."

Since these functions required "personal skill and competence" they could not be delegated without express agreement between agent and principal.

Where the functions entrusted to the sub-agent are merely ministerial, i.e. acts which could be done by *any* reasonably competent person, there are two possible views. First, they are sub-agents and are authorised since their role is, for example, purely administrative or clerical. The second view is that such activities are not examples of delegation at all. For example, in *Lord v Hall*[11] an agent gave her daughter the responsibility of endorsing a bill of exchange with the name of her principal. It was held that this was not properly regarded as an example of delegation, since the daughter acted not as a sub-agent, but as her mother's instrument in effecting her function under the agency agreement. In *John McCann & Co v Pow* the agents argued that the functions delegated to the second firm of estate agents were ministerial. This argument was rejected by the Court of Appeal, particularly since the sub-agents were able to draft particulars in respect of the property.

REASONABLE SKILL AND CARE

29–004   An agent owes his principal a duty to fulfil his contractual obligations with due skill and care. In *Keppel v Wheeler and Another*,[12] for example, the Court of Appeal held that an estate

[9] [1974] 1 W.L.R. 1643.
[10] [1974] 1 W.L.R. 1643 at 1647, per Lord Denning M.R.
[11] (1848) 2 Car. & K. 698.
[12] [1927] 1 K.B. 577.

agent was generally employed to effect the sale of the principal's property at the highest price achievable. Consequently, when a higher offer was received by the agents they were under a duty to inform the principal of the new offer even though they had already arranged a sale subject to contract on behalf of the principal. The Court of Appeal awarded damages equal to the amount of the difference between the offer accepted and the higher offer which was not brought to the attention of the vendor as principal. The decision of the Court of Appeal is useful in two other respects. First, the Court of Appeal was minded to accept the proposition that the agents had not wilfully breached their duties in respect of their principal, but rather had "misunderstood their position" in believing that they had fulfilled their responsibilities when an offer had been accepted subject to contract.[13] Secondly, the decision of the court also illustrates that an agent is not prevented from claiming his commission simply by virtue of a bona fide mistake which caused him to be liable in damages for a breach of duty.

The common law duty of an agent to perform his undertakings with reasonable skill and care has been reinforced by the Supply of Goods and Services Act 1982, s.13, which provides that:

"In a contract for the supply of a service where the supplier is acting in the course of a business, there is an implied term that the supplier will carry out the service with reasonable care and skill".

Thus where an agent is acting in the course of a business,[14] he must fulfil his undertakings with reasonable skill and care. Obviously what standard must be satisfied in order to comply with this statutory requirement will vary from case to case and will be judged in the context of the particular type of undertaking carried out.

FIDUCIARY DUTIES

Definition and Application

The concept of "fiduciary" is notoriously difficult to define in precise terms.[15] Nevertheless, **29–005** it is clear that the notion of a fiduciary relationship is an expansion of the law of trusts. Fiduciary obligations are imposed on the agent and principal relationship because the principal reposes confidence in the agent and trusts him to perform his undertaking with honesty and integrity. The position of an agent as a fiduciary is well understood through the Law Commission's attempt to define the relationship[16]:

"Broadly speaking, a fiduciary relationship is one in which a person undertakes to act on behalf or for the benefit of another, often as an intermediary with a discretion or

[13] See, for example, the comments of Bankes L.J. [1927] 1 K.B. 577 at 587.
[14] Defined by s.18 of the Act.
[15] See for example, the observations in Mason, "The Place of Equity and Equitable Remedies in the Contemporary Common Law World" (1994) 110 L.Q.R. 238 at 246.
[16] Law Commission Report, *Fiduciary Duties and Regulatory Rules* (Rep. No. 236 November 1995).

power which affects the interests of the other who depends on the fiduciary for information and advice".

Clearly, an agent is by definition a person who undertakes to act on behalf of another, his principal, and has been vested with authority or power to so act. This position is the same regardless of whether the agent is being paid. Fiduciary relations are thus "founded on the highest and truest principles of morality"[17] and require the agent to work altruistically, i.e. to do what is best for the principal and not what is in the agent's own best interests.

It is important to realise that the labelling of the agency relationship as one which is fiduciary in nature is of little assistance in defining the scope and application of any fiduciary duties which will be placed upon the agent. It merely acknowledges that such an inquiry must be undertaken.[18] This has received support from the judiciary. In particular, Lord Mustill, sitting on the Privy Council in *Re Goldcorp Exchange Ltd*[19] suggested that merely labelling a person as a fiduciary was meaningless. He continued to quote with approval the comments of Frankfurter J. in *SEC v Chenery Corp*[20]:

> "To say that a man is a fiduciary only begins analysis; it gives direction to further inquiry. To whom is he a fiduciary? What obligations does he owe as a fiduciary? In what respect has he failed to discharge these obligations? And what are the consequences of his deviation from duty?"

Such an inquiry, moving away from a purely definitional investigation is certainly a more purposeful charge, and heeds the warning of Fletcher Moulton L.J. against trusting to "verbal formulae".[21] Indeed Fletcher Moulton L.J. summarises the situation well in suggesting that[22]:

> "Thereupon in some minds there arises the idea that if there is any fiduciary relation whatever any of these types of interference is warranted by it. They conclude that every kind of fiduciary relation justifies every kind of interference. Of course that is absurd. The nature of fiduciary relation must be such that it justifies the interference".

Such sentiments have received recent judicial approval, notably through Lord Browne-Wilkinson in *Henderson v Merrett Syndicates Ltd*,[23] who sought to emphasise the fluid nature of fiduciary duties, in observing that such a term was "dangerous", as it leads to the (mistaken) assumption that "all fiduciaries owe the same duties in all circumstances". His Lordship concluded by stating that "this is not the case".[24]

What follows in this chapter therefore is a loose categorisation of the fiduciary duties which may be owed by an agent to his principal.

---

[17] *Parker v McKenna* (1874) 10 Ch. App. 96 at 118.
[18] See, for example, Sealy "Fiduciary Relationships" C.L.J. [1962] 69 at 73.
[19] [1995] 1 A.C. 74.
[20] (1943) 318 US 80 at 85–6.
[21] *Re Coomber, Coomber v Coomber* [1911] 1 Ch. 723 at 728.
[22] [1911] 1 Ch. 723 at 729.
[23] [1995] 2 A.C. 145.
[24] [1995] 2 A.C. 145 at 206.

Conflict of Interests

The general position was stated by Lord Cairns in *Parker v McKenna* that "No man can in   **29–006**
this Court, acting as an agent, be allowed to put himself into a position in which his interest
and his duty will be in conflict."[25] This is exemplified by the facts of *Armstrong v Jackson*[26]
where an agent was instructed to purchase some shares on behalf of his principal. The agent
already owned some shares of the company in question, and, instead of purchasing shares in
the normal manner, he elected to sell the principal his own shares. The court held that the
agent had placed himself in a position where his duty conflicted with his own interest. The
conflict is self evident since the best interests of the principal require the lowest purchase
price possible. The best interests of the agent in selling his own shares, however, are to
achieve the highest possible sale price. McCardie J. suggested that[27]:

> "The prohibition of the law is absolute. It will not allow an agent to place himself in a
> situation which, under ordinary circumstances, would tempt a man to do that which is
> not the best for his principal".

It is irrelevant, therefore, whether the agent sells his shares at the proper market value.
Furthermore, it is not necessary to consider whether the principal has suffered a loss through
the agent's conflict of interest. The court set aside the transaction and required the agent to
repay the payments made under the sale of the shares to his principal.

Where there is a conflict of duty the agent is obliged to make full disclosure of all material
circumstances so the principal with full knowledge can elect whether to consent to the
agent's act. In *Fullwood v Hurley*[28] Scrutton L.J. stated that[29]:

> "No agent who has accepted an employment from one principal can in law accept an
> engagement inconsistent with his duty to the first principal from a second principal
> unless he makes the fullest disclosure to each principal of his interest, and obtains the
> consent of each principal to the double employment".

Where an agent discovers that he has a conflict of interest he must take steps to inform his
principal of the conflict so that either (i) the principal will appoint another agent or (ii) will
give his consent to the agent acting on his behalf despite the conflict. In *Clark Boyce v
Mouat*[30] the plaintiff agreed to mortgage her house in order to secure a loan to her son. The
difficulty was that the solicitor had agreed to act for both the son and the plaintiff. The Privy
Council had to determine the situation of the solicitor in such a position where there was a
clear conflict of interest. Lord Jauncey stated[31]:

> "There is no general rule of law to the effect that a solicitor should never act for both
> parties in a transaction where their interests may conflict. Rather it is the position that

[25] (1874) L. R. 10 Ch. 96 at 118.
[26] [1917] 2 K.B. 822.
[27] [1917] 2 K.B. 822 at 824.
[28] [1928] 1 K.B. 498.
[29] [1928] 1 K.B. 498 at 502.
[30] [1994] 1 A.C. 428.
[31] [1994] 1 A.C. 428 at 435.

he may act provided that he has obtained the informed consent of both to his acting."

Informed consent requires more than simply putting the other party on notice that there is a conflict of interest. According to Lord Jauncey it requires the agent to explain that the conflict may result in him being unable to disclose "to each party the full knowledge which he possesses as to the transaction or may be disabled from giving advice to one party which conflicts with the interests of the other".[32]

Secret Profits

29–007   A secret profit is any financial advantage which the agent receives in the execution of the agency relationship which is over and above the amount to which the agent is lawfully entitled. The agent cannot obtain any such profit unless he makes full disclosure to the principal of all relevant facts and the principal consents to the agent retaining the profit. There are two conceivable situations where a secret profit may arise. First, a secret profit may arise without any active intervention or connivance by the third party. Secondly, a secret profit may arise with the connivance of the third party, e.g. where the third party bribes the agent.

The constituents of a bribe were examined in *Industries and General Mortgage Co Ltd v Lewis*[33] as follows[34]:

- the person giving the bribe (third party) makes the payment to the agent;

- the third party makes the payment knowing that the agent acts in that capacity on behalf of a principal;

- the third party does not disclose to the principal that he has made payment to the agent;

- it is not a prerequisite of the bribe that the principal should sustain any loss and the law will assume the principal has suffered a loss.

This final point was reinforced in *Hovenden & Sons v Millhoff*[35] where Romer L.J. said[36]:

"The Court will not enquire into the donor's motive in giving the bribe, nor allow evidence to be gone into as to a motive ... the Court will presume in favour of the principal and against the [third party] and the agent bribed, ... that the agent was influenced by the bribe; and this presumption is irrebuttable."

In *Anangel Atlas Compania Naviera SA and Others v Ishikawajima-Harima Heavy Industries Co Ltd*[37] Leggatt J. accepted the proposition that the key factor in determining whether or not

[32] [1994] 1 A.C. 428 at 435.
[33] [1949] 2 All E.R. 573.
[34] [1949] 2 All E.R. 573 at 575.
[35] (1900) 83 LT 41.
[36] (1900) 83 LT 41 at 43.
[37] [1990] 1 Lloyd's Rep. 167.

a payment made to the agent is a bribe was whether the making of such a payment gives rise to a conflict of interest. Leggatt J. accepted the following formulation of Anglin J. in *Barry v The Stoney Point Canning Co*[38]:

> "The fundamental principle in all these cases is that one contracting party shall not be allowed to put the agent of the other in a position which gives him an interest against his duty. The result to the agent's principal is the same whatever the motive which induced the other principal to promise the commission. The former is deprived of the services of an agent free from the bias of an influence conflicting with his duty, for which he had contracted and to which he was entitled."

There is, therefore, a clear overlap between the agent's duty to avoid conflicts of interest and the duty not to make secret profits. This relationship was considered by the Court of Appeal in *Hurstanger Ltd v Wilson and another*[39] in the context of a commissioned credit broker. The defendants applied, through a broker, for a loan of £8,000. The lender's standard form pre-contract documents informed the borrowers that a fee would be payable to the credit broker in certain circumstances. The question before the court was whether (i) this declaration negated the secrecy of the commission paid to the broker and (ii) whether the declaration had resulted in the borrowers giving their informed consent to the conflict of interest. The conflict of interest here is straightforward. In acting in the best interests of his principals, the broker must recommend the most suitable loan for his principals with no regard to whether the provider of that loan offers the most profitable rate of commission. The Court of Appeal held that whilst the declaration did negate secrecy, it did constitute a breach of the conflicts of interest rule since informed consent had not been obtained.[40]

Duty to Account

Where an agent receives payments intended for his principal he will be under various duties in respect of those payments. First, he is under a duty to keep such monies separate from his own, unless the agency agreement provides that he may mix such funds with his own.   **29–008**

Secondly, the agent is under a duty to maintain accurate accounts of his transactions, and to produce such accounts to his principal when he is requested to do so by the principal. It is now clear that the duty of an agent in this regard does not cease to exist by virtue of the termination of the agency agreement. In *Yasuda Fire & Marine Insurance Co of Europe Ltd v Orion Marine Insurance Underwriting Agency Ltd*[41] the agents refused to comply with requests to provide records held in respect of transactions entered into on behalf of the principal by the agents. Colman J. was unimpressed by the arguments of counsel acting for the agents that, since the agency relationship had been terminated, the duty to provide accounts had ceased to operate. He said[42]:

---

[38] (1917) 55 S.C.R. 51 at 73.
[39] [2007] 1 W.L.R. 2351. For comment, see (2007) 18 I.C.C.L.R. 365.
[40] This outcome was no doubt influenced by the fact the OFT guidance recommends a clear warning stating that the broker may not be in a position to give unbiased advice, see the comments of Tuckey L.J. at p.2365.
[41] [1995] Q.B 174.
[42] [1995] Q.B. 174 at 185–186.

"Because the agent's duty to provide records of transactions to the principal is founded on the entitlement of the principal to the records of what *has been* done in his name, termination of the agent's authority to enter into further transactions should have no bearing on the continuance of the duty to provide pre-existing records pertaining to the period when transactions were authorised".

Colman J. stated that a continuing right to inspect the agent's records could be excluded by the terms of the contract between the parties, but that on the facts of the case, this had not occurred. The agents were therefore under a continuing duty to allow the principal access to their records in respect of transactions conducted on behalf of the principal.

The need for such an obligation is easily understood by the nature of the relationship between agent and principal. For example, where the agent is instructed to enter into commercial contracts on behalf of his principal, the principal must be able to discover what contracts have been made in his name. In *Yasuda* the rationale was explained thus[43]:

"That obligation to provide an accurate account in the fullest sense arises by reason of the fact that the agent has been entrusted with the authority to bind the principal to transactions with third parties and the principal is entitled to know what his personal contractual rights and duties are in relation to those third parties as well as what he is entitled to receive by way of payment from the agent."

If the agent fails to maintain proper accounts there is a presumption that any funds which the agent cannot prove are his own, will be deemed to belong to his principal.[44] This is an example of what Romilly M.R. in *Gray v Haig*[45] referred to as the court presuming everything unfavourable to the agent. This emphasises both the legal and practical significance of this obligation.

General Reading

29–009
- Bowen, "Principals, Agents and Fiduciary Relationships" (2006) 83 Business Law Bulletin 6;

- Brinkworth, "Gratuitous Agency: Liable or Not?" (1990) Bus. L.R. 111;

- Dowrick, "The Relationship of Principal and Agent" (1954) 17 M.L.R. 24;

- Flannigan, "The (Fiduciary) Duty of Fidelity" (2008) 124 L.Q.R. 274;

- Getzler, "Inconsistent Fiduciary Duties and Implied Consent" (2006) 122 L.Q.R. 1;

- Lowry and Sloszar, "Judicial Pragmatism: Directors' Duties and Post-Resignation Conflicts of Duty" [2008] J.B.L. 83.

---

[43] [1995] Q.B. 174 at 185.
[44] *Lupton v White* (1808) 15 Ves. 432.
[45] (1854) 20 Beav. 219 at 226.

Chapter 30

THE RIGHTS OF AN AGENT AGAINST HIS PRINCIPAL

INTRODUCTION

This chapter explores the position of the agent as against his principal. The common law has **30–001** traditionally taken the view that it is the principal who requires protection from his agent rather than the other way round. This had led to a situation where the rights of the agent as against his principal were somewhat sparse. Nevertheless, there are a handful of areas where the common law has imposed obligations upon a principal. In particular, this chapter will consider the agent's rights of remuneration and indemnification. Moreover, as has already been seen, statute law has recently been active in this area and there is now a general obligation on a principal to "act dutifully and in good faith" towards his commercial agent. The impact of the Commercial Agents (Council Directive) Regulations 1993 on this matter will be considered in Chapter 33. What follows in this chapter is an assessment of the rights on an agent at common law rather than those of a commercial agent under the Commercial Agents (Council Directive) Regulations.

Right to Remuneration

At common law an agent has no automatic right to remuneration. This is so irrespective of **30–002** whether the agency is contractual or non-contractual in nature. It is entirely possible for the parties to enter into a gratuitous agency relationship. At common law, therefore, the agent will have the right to remuneration only where there is an express or implied term to that effect in the agency contract. The relationship between express and implied terms of contract in this context is evident on examination of two leading cases: *Way v Latilla*[1] and *Kofi*

[1] [1937] 3 All E.R. 759.

Sunkersette Obu Appellant v A Strauss & Co.[2] In *Latilla* the House of Lords held that although there was no express term as to the right to remuneration, since the agreement between the parties was one of employment with a clear understanding that the work was not to be gratuitous, their Lordships were able to imply a contractual right to a reasonable level of remuneration for the agent's services. In the *Kofi Sunkersette* case, however, there was an express term in the agency contract detailing the level of remuneration payable to the agent. There was also another term which stated that additional remuneration was available in the form of commission at the discretion of the principal. The Privy Council held that the agent was not *entitled* to any commission since this was clearly available at the discretion of the principal. It was therefore not open to them to impose a reasonable sum of commission payable to the agent since that would be taking a contractual discretion of the principal and placing it in the hands of the court.

The right, or otherwise, of an agent to commission has been a topic upon which there has been considerable judicial consideration. In this context a distinction must be drawn between a salary and a commission. Both are obviously forms of remuneration to which the agent might be entitled, but the distinction is that whereas the right to a salary stems from the contract of employment between agent and principal, the right to commission is not automatic. It is a payment due upon fulfillment of certain conditions. Consequently, it is necessary to interpret the agreement between the parties so as to ascertain what event triggers the right to the commission.

This rule is exemplified by the facts of *Toulmin v Millar*[3] where an agent was employed to find a tenant for a property owned by the principal. The agent found a tenant who went on to purchase the house. The agent claimed that he was entitled to commission as provided for in the agency agreement. The claim failed since he was employed to find his principal a tenant for the house. Since he had found a purchaser for the house, he was not entitled to any commission under the agency agreement.

30–003   More recently, in *Fairvale v Sabharwal*[4] an estate agency was instructed to enter a property for sale at public auction. The contract provided that commission would be payable if the sale was effected within 28 days of the auction. Although the auction was unsuccessful since the reserve price was not reached, the agents introduced the seller to one of the unsuccessful bidders who then went on to purchase the property. The sale was effected more than 28 days after the conclusion of the auction. The Court of Appeal held that since the sale of the house fell outside of the terms of the agreement in respect of the payment of commission, the agents were not entitled to any commission.

In *Luxor (Eastbourne) Ltd v Cooper*[5] an agent was appointed to find a purchaser for a number of cinemas. Under the agreement a minimum sale price was agreed, as was a commission of £10,000 due to the agent upon completion of the sale. Although the agent found suitable buyers at an acceptable price under the terms of the agency agreement the principal company decided not to proceed with the sale. The agent, deprived of the substantial commission payment sued the company for the same amount as damages for breach of an implied term that the principal would not, without just cause, act as to prevent the respondent from earning his commission. Although this argument was accepted by the Court

[2] [1951] A.C. 243.
[3] (1887) 12 App. Cas. 746.
[4] [1992] 32 E.G. 51.
[5] [1941] A.C. 108.

of Appeal it was unanimously rejected by the House of Lords who held that the agent's right to commission must be construed in accordance with the express terms of the contract of agency. On that basis, since the sale of cinemas had not been completed, no commission was due. Moreover, it was not possible to introduce the implied term not to deprive an agent of his commission "unless it is necessary to do so for the purpose of giving to the contract the business effect which both parties to it intended it should have".[6] On the facts of *Luxor* the House of Lords found that it was unnecessary to imply such a term to give commercial efficacy.

The payment of commission to estate agents is still a regular visitor to the courts today. Two recent cases (amongst many) reinforce the point developed above, that the entitlement or otherwise to commission is a matter of contractual interpretation. In *Your Move v Moore*[7] Moore wished to sell her house and entered into a sole agency agreement with Your Move estate agents, The agreement provided that the agent would be entitled to commission "if at any time unconditional contracts for the sale of the property are exchanged with a Person introduced". Your Move successfully found a buyer for the house and contracts of sale were exchanged between the prospective purchaser and Moore. Despite the exchange of contracts the parties never completed the sale. Your Move sued Moore for the commission due on exchange of contracts as dictated in the agency agreement. Moore, however, argued that since the agreement provided for payment in the event completion, the agents were not entitled to any commission. The court found in favour of the agents and followed the principle of the House of Lords in *Luxor*. The agreement between the parties was clear that commission was due on successful exchange of contracts and the clause in the contract providing for payment in the event of completion was designed merely to give the principal more time to pay the commission fee.

The issue of construction was also fundamental to the outcome in *Dashwood (formerly*   **30–004**
Kaye) v Fleurets Ltd.[8] The owner of licensed premises entered into an agency agreement with an estate agent under which the agent had sole selling rights and was thereby entitled to commission where the property was purchased by anyone introduced during the agency agreement. This was so irrespective of whether the agents were the effective cause of the transaction. Since the agreement clearly entitled Fleurets to commission where they had introduced the prospective purchaser it was not necessary to show that they had done anything else to effect the ultimate transaction and the agents were entitled to their commission.

Right to Indemnity

Under the common law a principal must indemnify his agent for losses and liabilities   **30–005**
reasonably incurred through the execution of his obligations as agent. The general rule was stated by Lindley J. in *Thacker v Hardy*[9] in the following terms[10]:

---

[6] [1941] A.C. 108 at 120, per Viscount Simon L.C.
[7] [2002] C.L.Y. 68, CC.
[8] [2007] EWHC 1610, QB.
[9] (1878–79) 4 Q.B.D. 685.
[10] (1878–79) 4 Q.B.D. 685 at 687.

> "Upon general principles an agent is entitled to indemnity from his principal against liabilities incurred by the agent in executing the orders of his principal, unless those orders are illegal, or unless the liabilities are incurred in respect of some illegal conduct of the agent himself, or by reason of his default."

The duty to indemnify also exists in situations where the agent is liable in tort. Thus in *Adamson v Jarvis*[11] where the principal instructed his agent, an auctioneer, to sell goods which he did not own, the principal was under a duty to indemnify the agent for the tortious damages incurred.

Lien

30–006   In order to ensure the principal's performance of, for example, his obligation to pay commission or indemnity, the agent can, of course, commence an action against his principal for breach of contract. It may well be much more effective (and certainly less time consuming) for the agent to exercise his lien over his principal's property. This lien only exists in certain circumstances. First, it is only available where goods belonging to the principal are in the possession of the agent[12] and where those goods are those in relation to which money is owed: *Bock v Gorrissen*.[13] The agent's right to lien does not apply where the existence of the lien would be inconsistent with the terms of the agency agreement. This explains the decision on this point in *Rolls Razor Ltd v Cox*[14] where the agent sought to exercise his lien over some of the principal's goods still in his possession after the agency agreement had been terminated. The court held that since there was a term of the agreement requiring the agent to return all property belonging to the principal upon termination of the agency relationship, no lien could exist after the termination of the agreement, since to find otherwise would run contrary to the terms of the agreement.

---

[11] (1827) 4 Bing. 66.
[12] Actual or constructive possession will suffice, see *Bryans v Nix* (1839) 4 M. & W. 775.
[13] (1861) 30 L.J. Ch. 39.
[14] [1967] 1 Q.B. 552.

Chapter 31

CONTRACTS MADE BY AGENTS

INTRODUCTION

This chapter examines the respective relationships between the principal and the third party **31–001** and between the agent and the third party. We have already looked at the nature of an agent's authority and this will generally explain both the relationship between agent and third party and also that between principal and third party. Thus, generally, where an agent acts within his authority, the principal will be bound to the contract made on his behalf by his agent. Whilst this does explain the normal position between principal and third party, it is not however the full story. There are occasions where, for example, the agent will be liable on the contract made with the third party. Similarly, there are occasions where both the principal and the agent are liable on the contract made with the third party. This chapter explores such issues and begins with the relationship between the principal and the third party. This will depend primarily on the manner in which the agent conducts his dealings with the third party: the agent may name his principal; he may disclose his status as agent (but not name his principal); or alternatively he may not disclose his status as an agent at all.

The Relationship Between Principal and Third Party

Disclosed Principal

The law will generally treat the position of a named principal and that of an unnamed, but **31–002** disclosed, principal in the same way.[1] They are both subject, therefore, to the general position

---
[1] See, however, the comments of Lord Denning M.R. in *Teheran-Europe Co Ltd v S T Belton (Tractors) Ltd* [1968] All E.R. 886 at 889, which appear to blur unnamed and undisclosed principals.

of disclosed principal, which is that the principal may sue (or be sued) on the contract made with the third party. This is so provided that either the contract is within the actual (express or implied) authority of the agent or, alternatively, where the contract is unauthorised, the principal elects to ratify it. This is a relatively straightforward rule whereby the agent effectively drops out of the arrangement, since his function is to effect legal relations between his principal and a third party. It has, however, an interesting consequence in relation to apparent authority. We have already seen that where apparent authority is created, the principal is bound by the acts of his agent and is estopped from denying the contract with the third party, i.e. the third party can enforce the contract against the principal. In order for the principal to enforce the contract against the third party, however, he must first ratify. If this is not possible for whatever reason, the principal will be unable to enforce the contract despite the fact that the third party may well be able to enforce the contract against him.

Where the agent discloses his agency there will be no privity of contract between himself and the third party. It follows, therefore, that the agent cannot be held liable on any contracts he makes on behalf of his principal, i.e. the third party cannot enforce the contract against the agent. This is so even where the agent in fact has no authority.[2] Where the agent is acting without authority he will, however, face liability for breach of warrant of authority.[3] Although this is the normal position it has been qualified so that, in certain circumstances, the agent will face personal liability on the contract.[4]

Undisclosed Principal

31–003 Where the agent does not disclose his status as agent, and the third party is thus unaware that he is dealing with an agent, it might be expected that the principal will not be liable on any contract made by his agent, nor be able to enforce such contracts. This would be a natural consequence of the doctrine of privity of contract. In fact, this is not so. An undisclosed principal can both enforce and be made liable on contracts made by his agent. It follows that the doctrine of the undisclosed principal is restricted to situations where there is actual authority. Plainly, an undisclosed principal cannot make any representation to the third party as to the authority of the agent, since in so doing he would no longer be an undisclosed principal.

That this notion sits uneasily with the traditional rules of contractual privity was noted by Lord Lindley in *Keighley, Maxsted & Co v Durant*[5] where he said that[6]:

> "as a contract is constituted by the concurrence of two or more persons and by their agreement to the same terms, there is an anomaly in holding one person bound to another of whom he knows nothing and with whom he did not, in fact, intend to contract."

[2] *Lewis v Nicholson* (1852) Q.B. 503.
[3] See para.31–010, below.
[4] See para.31–008, below.
[5] [1901] A.C. 240.
[6] [1901] A.C. 240 at 261.

Whilst this anomaly (and the potential inroad into the doctrine of privity of contract) is clear,[7] two points must be made. First, the doctrine of the undisclosed principal was well established at common law long before that of privity of contract. Secondly, there is strong justification for the doctrine on the basis of commercial efficacy since (i) it allows for the collection of payments due under contracts made between agent and third party where the agent was unable to collect and pass such payments on to his principal (e.g. due to insolvency)[8] and (ii) the identity of the principal (or even the fact that the agent is, in fact, acting on behalf of an undisclosed principal) will rarely be of importance to the third party in a commercial contract. This is recognised in contract law generally, and has already been considered in Chapter 5 where the issue of mistake as to the identity of the contracting parties was considered. There may well, however, be cases where the identity of the agent is crucial to the third party in making the contract. This is most likely to be the case where the contract is one where a service is to be provided and that service depends upon the skills and personal attributes of the agent. The courts have been faced with the difficult question, however, of establishing when the identity of the agent is so important that the third party would not have otherwise entered into the contract and where consequently the principal cannot enforce the contract.

In *Said v Butt*[9] an agent was instructed to obtain a ticket for an opening night performance at a theatre. The principal required the services of the agent since he knew that, due to his poor relationship with the third party who managed the theatre, he would be denied a ticket if he attempted to purchase one in his own name. The theatre, not realising that the agent was acting for an undisclosed principal sold the ticket which the principal then attempted to use on the opening night. On being recognised, however, he was refused admission. The principal sought to rely on the doctrine of undisclosed principal, i.e. that he could enforce the contract made between his agent and the third party. The court held that there was no contract between principal and third party since there had been an operative mistake, i.e. that the third party would never have sold a ticket to the principal had he been disclosed and identified. In arriving at this conclusion the court was persuaded by the fact that the ticket was for the opening night, and that it was therefore a special occasion where the theatre would be more selective over admittance to the theatre.

This decision has attracted considerable criticism not least for the fact that it seems to misapply the fundamental doctrine of the undisclosed principal. In such a case the accepted view is that the contract is made between the agent and the third party (and that the undisclosed principal can intervene on that contract which is made on his behalf).[10] It is not correct to say that the principal must establish a contract between himself and the third party. The decision could well have been the same on the facts but it would have required the theatre to establish that the identity of the agent was such that they intended to sell him and only him the ticket in question. It is most unlikely that the theatre manager could have proved this, since the identity of the agent seems to have been irrelevant to his being sold a ticket.

31–004

---

[7] See, for example, the comments of Lord Lloyd in *Siu Yin Kwan v Eastern Insurance Co Ltd* [1994] 2 A.C. 199 at 207.

[8] This is the historical context from which the doctrine originated, see for example, *Burdett v Willett* (1708) 2 Vern. 638.

[9] [1920] 3 K.B. 497.

[10] See, for example, *Welsh Development Agency v Export Finance Co Ltd* [1992] B.C.L.C. 148.

A true reflection of the facts seems to be that the theatre would have sold a ticket to anyone, except the undisclosed principal.

The question of whether identity of the agent was sufficiently crucial to the third party so as to prevent an undisclosed principal from enforcing a contract was more satisfactorily dealt with in the subsequent case of *Dyster v Randall & Sons*[11] where a principal instructed his agent to purchase some land on his behalf as undisclosed principal. As in *Said*, the principal knew that the third party would refuse to sell the land to him (or to his agent where his identity was disclosed). The agent did contract to purchase the land but before completion the third party discovered that the purchaser was in fact acting as agent for the undisclosed principal. Consequently, the third party cancelled the agreement at which point the principal sued for specific performance. The court held that the principal could enforce the contract and awarded specific performance since the contract between agent and third party was an ordinary commercial contract for the sale of land in which the identity of the buyer was unimportant. This is so where the agent does not misrepresent his position, for example, by telling the third party that he is not acting as agent for a principal whom the third party will not deal with. Thus in *Dyster* the court distinguished the earlier case of *Archer v Stone*[12] where such a representation was made. In that case, the court refused to grant specific performance since the third party had made it clear that they would not deal with the principal and the agent had lied about not acting for that principal during the course of the negotiations.

It is possible for the third party to protect himself in the situations above by introducing a term of the contract that precludes an undisclosed principal from intervening on the contract made between agent and third party. Thus, if there is an express term to that effect, the doctrine of the undisclosed principal will not apply and the difficulties of establishing that the identity of the agent was sufficiently important so as to preclude the undisclosed principal from intervening on the contract will not arise. There is difficulty however, where there is no express term but only a term which suggests that the agent is in fact acting as principal. In *Fred Drughorn Ltd v Rederiaktiebolaget Transatlantic*[13] an agent hired a ship and signed the contract as "charterer". The third party argued that this meant that the agent was *the* charterer and that the contract could not therefore be enforced by the undisclosed principal. The House of Lords held that the term "charterer" did not preclude the doctrine of the undisclosed principal and that whether an agent could enter into a contract on behalf of an undisclosed principal was a matter of ordinary business sense. Viscount Haldane sought to emphasise the true nature of a charterparty agreement, i.e. a hiring of a vessel, and the meaning of the term "charterer", i.e. the individual seeking to hire the vessel. The term did not imply that the agent was in fact dealing as principal and was the only person with whom the contract could be made. Neither did the nature of a charterparty agreement result in any assertion being made as to title or ownership of the property. This was important since it allowed the House of Lords to distinguish the previous decision in *Humble v Hunter*[14] where an agent signed a charterparty agreement on behalf of his (undisclosed) principal but signed as "owner". In that case the court held that by signing as owner the agent was contracting as principal and

---

[11] [1926] Ch. 932.
[12] (1898) 78 L.T. 34.
[13] [1919] A.C. 203.
[14] (1848) 12 Q.B. 310.

for that reason the undisclosed principal could not enforce the contract against the third party.[15]

The approach of Viscount Haldane has been supported in recent decisions and it seems **31–005** clear that the courts will make an assessment of the contractual intention in the light of pragmatic "business common-sense".[16] Thus, in *Siu Yin Kwan v Eastern Insurance Co Ltd*[17] the Privy Council held that the insurance contract, properly constructed, did not prevent the doctrine of undisclosed principal from applying where the agent signed in his own name as the "insured". In giving effect to a pragmatic approach, the decision was in no small part based on the fact that the third party was indifferent as to the identity of the "insured" and that, since there was no express term of the contract preventing the principal from intervening to enforce the contract, the doctrine of the undisclosed principal applied.

Merger and Election

Where a third party contracts with an agent acting on behalf of an undisclosed principal the **31–006** agent will be personally liable on the contract. Similarly, where an agent acts on behalf of a disclosed principal but does so in such a way so as to incur personal liability, it is clear that the third party will have two possibilities. First, he may seek to enforce the contract against the principal.[18] Secondly, he may elect to enforce the contract against the agent. Thus liability here is not joint and several but is alternative, i.e. the third party cannot pursue *both* agent and principal but must instead elect which party to sue.[19]

Third Party's Right to Set-Off [20]

There is a general rule that where an agent, acting on behalf of an undisclosed principal, **31–007** concludes a contract with a third party and the principal subsequently intervenes on that contract, he does so subject to any defences and equities which would be available to the third party had the agent himself brought the action.[21]

Therefore, where the third party is sued by the principal he may avail himself of all defences, including set-offs, which he would have possessed against the agent. This is so provided that the third party's right of set-off against the agent existed prior to the third party having notice of the principal's existence.[22]

---

[15] The same logic was applied in *Formby Bros v Formby* (1910) 102 L.T. 116, where the agent described himself as "proprietor" and thus asserted ownership.
[16] [1919] A.C. 203 at 207.
[17] [1994] 2 A.C. 199.
[18] See, for example, *Boyter v Thomson* [1995] 2 A.C. 628.
[19] For criticism of this alternative liability in the case of agent and principal, see *Fowler (LC) & Sons v St Stephen's College Board of Governors* [1991] 3 N.Z.L.R. 304.
[20] See generally, Derham, "Set-off and Agency" [1985] 44 C.L.J. 384.
[21] *Browning v Provincial Insurance Co of Canada* (1873) L.R. 5 P.C. 263.
[22] As to whether the principal's conduct must give rise to an estoppel, see the (much criticised) decision in *Cooke & Sons v Eshelby* (1887) 12 App. Cas. 271.

The Relationship Between Agent and Third Party

Contractual Liability

31–008   It has already been seen that where an agent, having disclosed his authority, effects a contract between a third party and his principal, the standard position is that the agent drops out of the relationship between the parties. Consequently such an agent will face no liability on that contract since it is one between the principal and the third party. This is exemplified by *Wakefield v Duckworth*.[23] A solicitor, acting on behalf of a client, ordered some photographs. The photographer sued the solicitor for the price of the photographs supplied. It was held that he could not succeed since the solicitor was acting as agent on behalf of his client (the principal) and that, since the photographer was aware of this, the action for price should be brought against the principal. This position is not affected by the fact that the agent was acting outside his authority in making the contract with the third party. In *Lewis v Nicholson*[24] Lord Campbell C.J. said that "in no case where it appears that a man did not intend to bind himself, but only to make a contract for a principal, can he be sued as principal, merely because there was no authority".[25] The logic here is straightforward. The fact that an agent acts without authority does not alter the privity of contract between his principal and the third party. However, where an agent acts without authority, he could face liability for breach of warranty of authority (considered below).

Although an agent will not normally face liability under a contract made with a third party there are exceptions to this rule. Where an agent acts on behalf of a non-existent principal, for example, the agent may face personal liability on the contract. This is a particular problem for promoters of a company in the process of formation. This issue has already been considered in respect of ratification and it is the same problem here: where the company is never in fact incorporated, who is liable on any pre-incorporation contracts? It is clear that at common law[26] and under statute,[27] the promoter (agent) is liable. *Kelner* can be contrasted with the decision in *Newborne v Sensolid (Great Britain) Ltd*[28] where there was a contract for the sale of some goods. The contract was signed "Leopold Newborne (London) Ld" and underneath was the name Leopold Newborne. The Court of Appeal suggested that since the signatory to the contract was "Leopold Newborne (London) Ld" and not "Leopold Newborne, by authority of and as agent for the company" it was clear that Mr Leopold was not undertaking personal liability under the contract. If the contract had been signed "Leopold Newborne, by authority of and as agent for the company" the agent would have signed in his own name and would therefore face liability under the contract under the principle in *Kelner v Baxter*. This issue was resolved by s.36C(1) of the Companies Act 1985 and is repeated in s.51(1) of the Companies Act 2006,[29] which provides for personal liability of the promoter on pre-incorporation contracts, but it seems that the issue in respect of the non-existent

---

[23] [1915] 1 K.B. 218.
[24] (1852) Q.B. 503.
[25] (1852) Q.B. 503 at 511.
[26] *Kelner v Baxter* (1866 2 C.P. 174.
[27] Companies Act 1985 s.36C(1).
[28] [1954] 1 Q.B. 45.
[29] Which will replace s.36C of the 1985 Act. The date for the repeal of s.36C has not yet been determined.

principal in other contexts depends upon the form of the signature and whether the agent signs in his own name "on behalf" of the principal or signs in the name of his principal.

An agent will also face personal liability under the contract if, on proper construction of the contract, he has undertaken personal liability under the contract. One example of an agent undertaking personal liability is the decision of *Kelner v Baxter* which we have already encountered. In the case of a written contract the matter will be one of construction: did both the agent and the third party intend that the agent should be personally liable under the contract? The courts have sought to distinguish between words of description and those of representation. Only in the former will an agent be deemed to have undertaken personal liability on the contract. This raises difficulties of interpretation. In *Universal Steam Navigation Co Ltd v McKelvie*[30] the House of Lords held that the signing of a charterparty "as agents" was to be constructed as representative and therefore the agents were not liable to the third party. By way of contrast, the wording "as agent" was held to be descriptive in *Parker v Winlow*[31] since the phrase was used in a commercial, rather than a legal, sense. This demonstrates two things very well. First, it serves as an example against trusting to "verbal formulae"[32] and secondly, reinforces the importance of ascertaining the intention of both agent and third party in making the contract. The difficulties of contractual construction as to whether personal liability was intended are illustrated in the case of *Bridges & Salmon, Ltd v The Swan (Owner)*[33] where the plaintiffs sought to claim for work done to a boat owned by JDR Ltd. The company was formed by the owner of the boat, Mr Rodger, with the purpose of maintaining and repairing the boat. To that purpose, the newly formed company hired the boat from Mr Rodger and entered into contracts with the plaintiffs to effect repairs. The company, before paying for the work completed, became insolvent and ceased trading. The plaintiffs sought payment from Mr Rodger personally and argued that he was personally liable under the contracts made between JDR Ltd and themselves. Brandon J. sought to ascertain the contractual intention (something made more difficult by the contracts having been concluded partly in writing and partly by words) and said:

> "It seems to me that the defendant did not ever contract expressly as agent in the sense of saying either orally or in writing that he was acting 'as agent for', or 'on account of', or 'on behalf of', or 'for' the company. What he did was to describe himself to both plaintiffs at an earlier stage as 'Mr. Rodger, of J. D. Rodger, Ltd.', and later to write the written orders on the company's notepaper and add the word 'Director' to his signature. On the other hand, the plaintiffs' subsequent conduct shows that they understood clearly that the bills for their work were to be sent to the company".

The former point would indicate that in making the contract of repair, Mr Rodger was undertaking personal liability. On the other hand, the latter point, would lead to the opposite conclusion. Brandon J. even suggested that "the present case appears to be somewhat near the borderline, with strong arguments available either way". It was held that, on proper construction of the facts, Mr Rodger had undertaken personal liability since he had not made

[30] [1923] A.C. 492.
[31] (1857) 7 E & B 942.
[32] *Re Coomber, Coomber v Coomber* [1911] 1 Ch. 723 at 728 per Fletcher Moulton L.J.
[33] [1968] 1 Lloyd's Rep. 5.

it clear to the third parties that, although he, as owner, would benefit from the repairs to the boat he was disowning any personal liability to pay for the repairs carried out.

Contractual Rights

31–009   Just as an agent will not normally incur contractual liabilities under any agreements he makes with a third party on behalf of his principal, since he will "drop out" of the picture once he has fulfilled his role, similarly, an agent will generally not incur any contractual rights under such contracts. Thus, generally an agent will not be able to enforce a contract. Where, however, it can be established that the parties intend the agent to be a party to the contract, the agent will be able to enforce the contract against the third party. This is so even though the principal repudiates the contract, again, provided that the third party intends to contract with the agent.[34]

In *Braymist Ltd and Others v The Wise Finance Co Ltd*[35] a solicitor (the agent) signed an agreement to buy some land as agent for an unformed company. The third party seller did not realise at the time of making the contract that the company did not in fact exist and upon realising this he refused to complete the transaction. The solicitor rescinded the contract and brought an action for breach of contract. We have already seen that s.36C(1) of the Companies Act 1985 imposed personal liability on agents who made contracts on behalf of a company which is not yet in existence. The Court of Appeal held that s.36C(1) also entitled the agent to enforce the contract himself unless ordinary common law principles prevented him from doing so.

Liability for Breach of Warrant of Authority

31–010   The situation we are concerned with here is that where an agent represents to the third party that he has the necessary authority but in fact does not. Where the representation of authority induces the third party to take steps that he would not otherwise have done (such as entering into a contract or taking action prior to entering into a contract) then the agent will be deemed to have warranted that he had the authority represented and be made liable for any loss incurred by the third party. The rationale behind this rule is fairly simple: we have already seen that where an agent acts outside his authority the principal will not be bound by the acts of his agent. In order to protect the third party it is necessary to find the agent liable. The liability of the agent in such circumstances stems from a unilateral collateral contract between the agent and the third party under which the agent offers to warrant his authority. This offer will generally be accepted by the third party entering into the contract with the principal, but may also be accepted through the third party taking other action, such as entering into a contract with another party (e.g. to purchase stock etc.).

The existence of an action for breach of warrant of authority was first recognised by the courts in *Collen v Wright*[36] where Willes J. stated:

[34] *Short v Spackman* (1831) 2 B. & Ad. 962.
[35] [2002] Ch. 273.
[36] (1857) 8 E & B 647.

"The obligation arising in such a case is well expressed by saying that a person, professing to contract as agent for another, impliedly, if not expressly, undertakes to or promises the person who enters into such contract, upon the faith of the professed agent being duly authorised, that the authority which he professes to have does in point of fact exist. The fact of entering into the transaction with the professed agent, as such, is good consideration for the promise".

The importance of the decision in *Collen* stems from the fact that it firmly established the strict liability of the agent for breach of warrant of authority. Thus, it does not matter whether the misrepresentation of authority was unintentional, reckless or entirely innocent—the agent is liable to the third party in any event. This is exemplified by the case of *Yonge v Toynbee*[37] where a solicitor continued to act for his principal in defending a legal action after his principal had been diagnosed as suffering from insanity. This ended the agency relationship but the solicitor was unaware of his principal's illness and continued to act on his behalf. He was held liable to the third party for the costs of the legal action since he had (entirely innocently) warranted his authority when in fact he had none since he was no longer an agent at all!

General Reading

- Goodhart and Hamson, "Undisclosed Principals in Contract" (1931) 4 C.L.J. 320;   **31–011**

- Pennington, "The Validation of Pre-Incorporation Contracts" [2002] Comp. Law. 284;

- Reynolds, "Election Distributed" (1970) 86 L.Q.R. 317;

- Reynolds, "Personal Liability of an Agent" (1969) 85 L.Q.R. 92;

- Savirimuthu, "Pre-Incorporation Contracts and the Problem of Corporate Fundamentalism: Are Promoters Proverbially Profuse?" [2003] Comp. Law. 196;

- Twigg-Flesner, "Full Circle: Purported Agent's Right of Enforcement Under Section 36C of the Companies Act 1985" [2001] Comp. Law 274.

---

[37] [1910] 1 K.B. 215.

Chapter 32

COMMERCIAL AGENTS

INTRODUCTION

Traditionally, the relationship between principal and agent has been left as a matter to be dealt **32–001**
with by common law. The approach adopted by the common law has already been con-
sidered. What follows in this chapter is a consideration of the statutory framework which
governs the relationship between principal and agent. The Commercial Agents (Council
Directive) Regulations 1993[1] implement the European Directive relating to Self Employed
Commercial Agents.[2] Broadly speaking, the aim of the Directive is to harmonise the
relationship between principal and agent and to provide protection on certain key issues for
the agent. They do not offer any assistance in detailing the rights or obligations of either party
as against a third party. Such matters being determined solely by reference to the common
law.

COMMERCIAL AGENTS (COUNCIL DIRECTIVE) REGULATIONS 1993

Application and Scope

The regulations deal with the following issues in the relationship between commercial agents **32–002**
and principals:

- rights and obligations of both agent and principal;

---

[1] SI 1993/3053 as amended by SI 1993/3173 and SI 1998/2868.
[2] 86/653/EEC.

- remuneration of agents;
- conclusion and termination of agency contracts;
- restraint of trade clauses.

Clearly of importance is the definition of "commercial agent" since the regulations only impact upon the relationship between a commercial agent and his principal. The term is defined in reg.2 as:

> "a self-employed intermediary who has continuing authority to negotiate the sale or purchase of goods on behalf of another person (the 'principal'), or to negotiate and conclude the sale or purchase of goods on behalf of and in the name of that principal".

This definition serves to immediately restrict the application of the regulations. The regulations do not, therefore, apply to employees acting as agents since a commercial agent here refers to "self-employed". Similarly, the reference to continuing authority must presumably rule out an agent who acts as agent on a one-off basis. The reference to the sale of goods removes agents selling services from the scope of the regulations. In *Mercantile International Group Plc v Chuan Soon Huat Industrial Group Ltd*[3] the Court of Appeal had to determine whether the agreement between CSH (manufacturer of timber products) and MIG (the retailer of such products) was one of commercial agency or resale. The agreement between CSH and MIG was headed "agency agreement" and appointed MIG as "sales and forwarding agents on behalf of . . . CSH". Despite this agreement, however, there were certain features of the commercial relationship which appeared to indicate that the proper construction of the relationship was one of sale and resale. These features included the fact that MIG did not account to CSH for any of the sale proceeds obtained from the purchasers, having always paid CSH before receiving payment for the goods from the customer. In addition, MIG made and retained a substantial mark-up, the amount of which was unknown and uncontrolled by CSH. CSH argued that the agreement was not one of commercial agency.

There is longstanding support for such a position. In *Re Nevill, Ex p. White*[4] Mellish L.J. suggested that:

> "if the consignee is at liberty, according to the contract between him and his consignor, to sell at any price he likes, and receive payment at any time he likes, but is to be bound, if he sells the goods, to pay the consignor for them at a fixed price and a fixed time—in my opinion, whatever the parties may think, their relation is not that of principal and agent."

Moreover, in *AMB Imballaggi Plastici SRL v Pacflex Ltd*[5] the Court of Appeal was persuaded that the relationship was not one of commercial agent and principal, not least because of the mark-up of over five per cent made and retained by Pacflex. Gibson L.J. stated that:

---

[3] [2002] C.L.C. 913.
[4] (1871) L.R. 6 Ch. App. 397 at 403.
[5] [1999] C.L.C. 1391.

"In these circumstances it seems to me plain that Pacflex was never acting as the commercial agent of AMB, on whose behalf it never purported to negotiate, nor did it have a contract or other authority to negotiate a sale on AMB's behalf, still less did it have authority to do so which could be called continuing."

Nevertheless, the Court of Appeal in *Mercantile International Group* decided that the agreement in that case was one of commercial agent and principal, and that therefore, the Commercial Agents Regulations 1993 did apply to the agreement between the parties. The key distinction between this case and, for example, that of *Pacflex*, was that in the present case there was a written agreement between the parties which was clearly drafted in agent and principal terms. Rix L.J. held that MIG had continuing authority to act on behalf of CSH, its principal, and that it was therefore within the meaning of "commercial agent".[6]

These two recent cases demonstrate that there are still considerable difficulties in distinguishing an agency relationship from other analogous relationships and that, most importantly in our present context, the regulations are of application only where there is a genuine relationship of commercial agent and principal.

Regulation 2 continues further to restrict the definition of "commercial agent" by stating **32–003** that it does not include any of the following:

   (i) a person who, in his capacity as an officer of a company or association, is empowered to enter into commitments binding on that company or association;

   (ii) a partner who is lawfully authorised to enter into commitments binding on his partners;

   (iii) a person who acts as an insolvency practitioner.

The first category would obviously rule out the managing director of a company from the scope of the regulations since a managing director has the authority to enter into commitments binding on the company. The second category imposes the same restriction in relation to members of a partnership. Regulation 2(2) also specifically removes certain other types of commercial agents from the remit of the regulations, including unpaid commercial agents and commercial agents working in commodity exchanges or markets.

The regulations are of no application to commercial agents whose activities as a commercial agent are considered to be "secondary".[7] The Schedule to the regulations defines "secondary activities" as meaning where the primary purpose of the agency agreement does not meet both of the following requirements[8]:

"(a) the business of the principal is the sale, or as the case may be purchase, of goods of a particular kind; and

(b) the goods concerned are such that—

   (i) transactions are normally individually negotiated and concluded on a commercial basis, and

---

[6] Rix L.J. did raise the possibility that the mark-up may well constitute a breach of the fiduciary obligations owed by an agent to his principal.

[7] reg.2(4).

[8] para.2.

(ii) procuring a transaction on one occasion is likely to lead to further transactions in those goods with that customer on future occasions, or to transactions in those goods with other customers in the same geographical area or among the same group of customers, and

that accordingly it is in the commercial interests of the principal in developing the market in those goods to appoint a representative to such customers with a view to the representative devoting effort, skill and expenditure from his own resources to that end."

The Schedule offers the following indications that an agreement falls under the requirements above[9]:

(a) the principal is the manufacturer, importer or distributor of the goods;

(b) the goods are specifically identified with the principal in the market in question rather than, or to a greater extent than, with any other person;

(c) the agent devotes substantially the whole of his time to representative activities (whether for one principal or for a number of principals whose interests are not conflicting);

(d) the goods are not normally available in the market in question other than by means of the agent;

(e) the arrangement is described as one of commercial agency.

Where these indications are not met by the agreement in question, it is an indication that the agreement is secondary, and not therefore covered by the regulations. Moreover, the Schedule also lists the following as specific indications that the agreement will be secondary[10]:

(a) promotional material is supplied direct to potential customers;

(b) persons are granted agencies without reference to existing agents in a particular area or in relation to a particular group;

(c) customers normally select the goods for themselves and merely place their orders through the agent.

This is clearly a very complicated assessment and has unsurprisingly given rise to considerable litigation as to whether an agent's activities are properly regarded as primary (and therefore regulated) or secondary (and therefore unregulated). Indeed, in *AMB Imballagi Plastici SRL v Pacflex Ltd*[11] Waller L.J. suggested that the test for ascertaining whether the agent is engaged in secondary activities was "an almost impenetrable piece of drafting".

32–004   In *Tamarind International Ltd & Others v Eastern Natural Gas (Retail) Ltd & Anor*[12] the court had to determine whether Tamarind International, sales agents for a gas and electricity

[9] para.3.
[10] para.4.
[11] [2000] E.C.C. 381 at 383.
[12] [2000] C.L.C. 1397.

supplier, were engaged in secondary activities and not therefore subject to the Commercial Agents Regulations 1993. The agents' job here was to use Eastern Natural Gas' promotional material to persuade existing customers of competitor suppliers to sign up with Eastern for their future gas requirements. It was clear that the agents were effectively operating exclusively on behalf of Eastern Natural Gas since Tamarind's employees were devoting between 85–98 per cent of their time to Eastern Natural Gas. In finding that the activities of Tamarind were not secondary for the purpose of the regulations, Morrison J. stated that the proper approach in this matter was to:

> " . . . look at the nature of the commercial bargain between the principal and agent. Was it in the principal's commercial interests that this agent should be appointed to develop the market in the particular goods by the agent's expenditure of money and his own resources?"

In adopting this test, Morrison J. rejected the submission of counsel that a "horizontal" approach should be preferred. The "horizontal" approach would suggest that the issue of whether the commercial agent's activities are primary or secondary is determined by assessing how much time and effort is expended in respect of that agency agreement as compared with the other activities of the commercial agent. It seems reasonably clear that the approach required through the construction of reg.2 with the guidance and indicators in the Schedule supports the conclusion and approach of Morrison J. Given the complexities of reg.2 and the Schedule in determining when commercial activities are deemed secondary, it is perhaps unfortunate that the Directive did not clarify the matter by adding a definition of "secondary activity" to be adopted by the Member States.[13]

Despite the complexities shown above it is clear that there are substantial restrictions on the definition of "commercial agent" and also on the scope of the regulations. It should be made clear here that where the regulations do not apply, the rights and obligations of both agent and principal will be governed by the agreement between the two and the relevant provisions of the common law.

Obligations of a Commercial Agent to his Principal

The duties of a commercial agent to his principal are detailed in reg.3. The duties of the commercial agent are broadly similar to those dictated by the common law.[14] The obligations are that, generally, there is an obligation to "look after the interests of his principal and act dutifully and in good faith". In addition the commercial agent must[15]:   **32–005**

    (a) make proper efforts to negotiate and, where appropriate, conclude the transactions he is instructed to take care of;

---

[13] See further, Gardiner, "The EC (Commercial Agents) Directive: twenty years after its introduction, divergent approaches still emerge from Irish and UK courts" [2007] J.B.L. 412.
[14] See, for example, *Cureton v Mark Insulations Ltd* [2006] EWHC 2279 where the failure of a commercial agent to disclose the practice of selling insulation as agent and windows as principal during the same home sales visits constituted a breach of both reg.3(1) and the common law.
[15] reg.3(2).

(b) communicate to his principal all the necessary information available to him;

(c) comply with reasonable instructions given by his principal.

It was noted above that the duties of the commercial agent are broadly similar to those dictated by the common law. This is true, but does not take into account one crucial fact, namely that under the principles of common law, both the rights and duties of an agent can be restricted or excluded under the normal contractual rules we looked at in Chapters 29 and 30. Under the Commercial Agents Regulations the duties imposed on commercial agents cannot be restricted or excluded by agreement between the parties.[16]

Obligations of a Principal to his Commercial Agent

32–006 These are covered by reg.4 which imposes a general obligation upon the principal to "act dutifully and in good faith" and more specifically to:

(a) provide his commercial agent with the necessary documentation relating to the goods concerned;

(b) obtain for his commercial agent the information necessary for the performance of the agency contract, and in particular notify his commercial agent within a reasonable period once he anticipates that the volume of commercial transactions will be significantly lower than that which the commercial agent could normally have expected.

A principal is also under a duty to notify his commercial agent (within a reasonable time) of the outcome of any transaction which the agent has procured on his behalf, i.e. whether the proposed transaction was accepted, rejected or not-executed. Similarly to reg.3, the obligations of a principal cannot be restricted or excluded by agreement between the parties by virtue of reg.5.

Remuneration

32–007 Part III of the regulations deal with the remuneration of commercial agents, although the parties are free to make whatever agreement they wish in respect of remuneration where there is no remuneration through commission. Where, however, they do not make any agreement in respect of remuneration, reg.6 dictates that the amount of remuneration payable is that which would customarily be payable under such an agreement. This will obviously be determined by: the nature of the transaction; the type of goods sold; and the country of business. Where there is no customary practice to determine the remuneration payable, the courts will make an assessment of what is reasonable in all the circumstances of the transaction.

---

[16] reg.5.

Where a commercial agent is to be remunerated either wholly or in part through commission, the regulations impose certain mandatory requirements. "Commission" is defined in reg.2 as meaning "any part of the remuneration of a commercial agent which varies with the number or value of business transactions". Thus it applies not only to the standard model of commissions where the agent secures payment upon completion of a particular transaction but also to various incentive schemes such as loyalty bonuses, yearly bonuses where they are paid by virtue of achieving a predetermined number of transactions. Where a commercial agent is paid in some part by commission, the regulations entitle the agent to commission in three distinct situations where the principal and commercial agent relationship is in operation:

(i) Where the transaction has been concluded as a result of the agent's actions.[17]

(ii) Where the transaction is concluded by a customer introduced by the agent.[18]

(iii) Where the agent is appointed sole agent in a particular geographical area or to a particular group of people and a transaction is concluded with either someone from that geographical area or with a person from within that particular group.[19]

The regulations also dictate that commission is payable in certain situations even though the agency relationship has been terminated. Under reg.8, commission is payable, even after termination of the agency agreement, where:

(a) the transaction is mainly attributable to the agent's efforts during the period covered by the agency contract and if the transaction was entered into within a reasonable period after that contract terminated; or

(b) the order reached the principal (or the agent) before the agency relationship was terminated and commission would be due under one of the three situations detailed in reg.7.

What constitutes a "reasonable time" is a question of fact to be decided on the facts of the case and the regulations offer no guidance on this issue.[20] One further question is answered by the regulations: what is the position if an order from a customer in England (a) is received by the principal before the agreement with the exclusive agent for the principal in England is terminated and a new agent appointed to replace him, and (b) is processed and concluded after the new agent is appointed. To whom will the commission be payable? This is dealt with by reg.9 which provides that, generally, the commission in such circumstances willl be payable to the original commercial agent and not to the replacement.[21]

[17] reg.7(1)(a).
[18] reg.7(1)(b), e.g. "follow-up" sales would obviously be covered by this provision.
[19] reg.7(2).
[20] By way of illustration, in *Tigana Ltd v Decoro Ltd* [2003] E.C.C. 23 the court held that nine months was a reasonable period in respect of a year-long agency agreement.
[21] reg.9(1) allows for the sharing of the commission in such circumstances where that would be the most equitable solution.

32–008   Regulation 10 deals with the issue of when commission will become payable to the commercial agent and states that as a general rule it becomes payable:

(a) when the principal has executed the transaction; or

(b) when the principal should, according to his agreement with the third party, have executed the transaction; or

(c) when the third party has executed the transaction.

Once commission becomes payable by one of the above events occurring, the commission must be paid no later than the last day of the month following the quarter in which it became due.[22]

In order to ensure that the commission paid is in fact that which is owed by virtue of the regulations, the commercial agent has the right to be provided with any information necessary to confirm the amount of commission payable to him. This includes the right to inspect the principal's accounts, or an extract thereof.[23] In addition, the principal is under a duty to provide the commercial agent with a statement of commission due.[24] This statement must also demonstrate the method of calculating the sum of commission payable. Neither of these obligations may be excluded or limited by agreement between the parties.[25]

Termination

32–009   Part IV of the regulations deal with the conclusion of agency agreement. Somewhat curiously it begins with something which ought, as a matter of good practice, to be done at the very start of the agency agreement: the right of both commercial agent and principal to receive a signed written document laying down the terms of the agreement, which may well include a term detailing the requirements for termination of the agency agreement.[26]

The regulations provide for the situation where the agency agreement is for a definite period of time but both the commercial agent and the principal continue to perform their obligations under that contract (e.g. the agent continues selling goods on behalf of the principal and the principal continues to pay the agent) after the expiration of that date. Regulation 14 states that in this situation the agency agreement will be converted into an agreement for an indefinite period. The significance of this becomes clear upon reading reg.15 which allows for indefinite agency agreements to be terminated by notice from either party to the other. Regulation 15(2) lays down minimum mandatory periods of notice which must be given. They are:

- one month during the first year of the contract;

- two months during the second year;

---

[22] Any attempt to exclude or restrict this position to the detriment of the commercial agent shall automatically be rendered void, see reg.10(4).

[23] reg.12(2).

[24] reg.12(1).

[25] reg.12(3).

[26] reg.13.

- three months during subsequent years.

Where an agency agreement for a definite period has been converted into one for an indefinite period under reg.14 above, reg.15(5) makes it clear that (i) the above notice periods apply and (ii) the period of the definite period of the agency agreement should be taken into account when assessing the appropriate notice period under reg.15(2).

The regulations allow for termination without notice in three distinct situations: **32–010**

    (i) Where the agency agreement is for a definite period of time and is not converted into an agency agreement for an indefinite period as detailed above.

    (ii) Where one party fails, either in part or otherwise, to perform his obligations under the agency agreement.

    (iii) Where "exceptional circumstances" apply. Sadly the regulations do not specify what would constitute "exceptional circumstances".

Where an agency agreement is terminated reg.17 lays down the framework for either compensation or an indemnity to be payable to a commercial agent. Unless the parties agree otherwise in the agency contract, the agent is entitled to compensation rather than an indemnity.[27] Regulation 17(6) states that "the commercial agent shall be entitled to compensation for the damage he suffers as a result of the termination of his relations with his principal." In particular, damage suffered includes the loss of commission which could have been earned through the proper performance of the contract.

Where the agency contract provides for the commercial agent to be indemnified rather than compensated, the approach is somewhat different and is based upon the extent to which the principal's business has benefited from the agent's activities. Regulation 17(3) provides that the agent shall be entitled to an indemnity where:

"(a) he has brought the principal new customers or has significantly increased the volume of business with existing customers and the principal continues to derive substantial benefits from the business with such customers; and

(b) the payment of this indemnity is equitable having regard to all the circumstances and, in particular, the commission lost by the commercial agent on the business transacted with such customers."

The amount of the indemnity is controlled by reg.17(4) which dictates that any indemnity payable shall not be more than the agent's annual remuneration as calculated by averaging the remuneration of the agent for the previous five years.[28] It now seems clear that the use of the word "termination" in reg.17 does not preclude a claim for compensation or indemnity where a commercial agency agreement has expired, rather than being "terminated" by the principal.[29]

---

[27] See reg.17(2).

[28] Where the agency agreement has not existed for five years at the time of termination, the maximum indemnity payable shall be the yearly average over the period of the agency agreement.

[29] See the purposive approach of Davies J. in *Tigana Ltd v Decoro Ltd* [2003] E.E.C. 23 at [71] onwards.

The rationale behind both indemnity and compensation as protective measures on behalf of commercial agents was clearly stated in the recent decision of the House of Lords in *Lonsdale (trading as Lonsdale Agencies) v Howard & Hallam Ltd (Winemakers' Federation of Australia Inc intervening)*[30] where Lord Hoffman stated[31]:

> "They are both ways of dealing with the unfairness which it was thought might arise if the termination of the agency leaves the agent worse off and the principal better off than if the agency had continued."

32–011   Despite this seemingly straightforward aim, the failure of the regulations (and indeed the Directive) to give any indication as to how properly to calculate the amount of compensation due to the commercial agent (in contrast to the same issue in respect of an indemnity) has caused difficulty for English courts. This difficulty is, in part, caused by the fact that compensation under the regulations is due where there is no fault on the part of the principal. As has been seen, under the traditional approach of the common law damages are only available to the agent where the principal by terminating the agency relationship was acting in breach of contract.

In *Lonsdale* the House of Lords adopted a two-part approach in assessing the proper award of damages under reg.17 following the termination (with reasonable notice) of a commercial agency relationship. Since the parties had not made any agreement as to whether to choose indemnity rather than compensation the default position of compensation was applicable. The two-part approach was to ask:

1. What should the agent be compensated for?

2. How should the compensation be determined?

Lord Hoffman dealt with the first question fairly quickly in referring to the Directive[32]:

> "On this first question the Directive is explicit. The agent is entitled to be compensated for 'the damage he suffers as a result of the termination of his relations with the principal'. In other words, the agent is treated as having lost something of value as a result of the termination and is entitled to compensation for this loss."

The second question, however, is much more problematic. It might have been expected that, since the compensation regime in reg.17 is based on French Law whereby an agent is compensated for the deprivation of the commercial agent's business[33] the House of Lords would adopt the jurisprudence of the French courts in assessing compensation under the regulation. Indeed, this is the approach which has been adopted by the Scottish courts.[34] The approach favoured by the House of Lords was to assess the level of compensation due through a valuation of the agency business. His Lordship supported the earlier approach of

[30] [2007] 1 W.L.R. 2055.
[31] [2007] 1 W.L.R. 2055 at [5].
[32] [2007] 1 W.L.R. 2055 at [8].
[33] By way of contrast, the indemnity option is based heavily on the position in German Law.
[34] See, for example, *King v T Tunnock Ltd* (2000) S.L.T. 744, strongly doubted by the House of Lords in *Lonsdale*.

Bowers J. in *Barrett McKenzie & Co Ltd v Escada (UK) Ltd*[35] where it had been suggested that it was a matter of compensating for the notional value of the agency on the open market. On that basis, the House of Lords affirmed the decision of the Court of Appeal in awarding compensation in the amount of £5,000. This was considerably less than would have been awarded if the French system of valuation had been adopted, since that system values agencies at twice the gross annual commission paid to the agent over the previous three years. In the Court of Appeal, Moore-Bick L.J. approved of the approach at first instance where it had been found that the *net* commission of the agent was around £8,000 a year, observing that[36]:

> "[The judge at first instance] pointed out that the agency was producing a modest and falling income in a steadily deteriorating environment and doubted whether anyone in those circumstances would have been willing to pay as much as two years' gross commission based on historical figures in order to acquire it. There was no evidence that anyone would have paid anything to buy it or that Mr Lonsdale could realistically have expected to be able to sell it. In the end [the judge] assessed compensation at £5,000."

It would appear that until there is a determination at a European level on the specific method to be adopted in calculating compensation for termination of a commercial agency agreement such difficulties and divergences of approach are likely to continue.

Payment of either compensation or indemnity can be excluded only in certain situations laid down in reg.18.[37] Those situations are: **32–012**

(i) the agency agreement was terminated by the principal because of a default by the commercial agent which justifies immediate termination under reg.16, discussed above; or

(ii) the agency agreement is terminated by the agent; or

(iii) the commercial agent, with the agreement of his principal, assigns his rights and duties under the agency contract to another person.

However, where the agency agreement is terminated by the agent, an indemnity or compensation shall remain payable where the termination is justified:

(a) by circumstances attributable to the principal, or

(b) on grounds of the age, infirmity or illness of the commercial agent in consequence of which he cannot reasonably be required to continue his activities.

Restraint of Trade Agreements

Regulation 20 deals with restraint of trade agreements. It inserts various controls into the use of such an agreement: **32–013**

---

[35] [2001] E.C.C. 50.
[36] [2006] 1 W.L.R. 1281 at [56], CA.
[37] There is a prohibition on the derogation from both regs 17 and 18 by virtue of reg.19.

- It must be concluded in writing.

- It must refer to the same type of goods dealt with under the agency agreement.

- It must refer to the same geographical area or group of customers as the agency agreement.

- It must not be of application for a period greater than two years following the termination of the agency agreement.

General Reading

32–014
- Gardiner, "The EC (Commercial Agents) Directive: Twenty Years After its Introduction, Divergent Approaches Still Emerge from Irish and UK Courts" [2007] J.B.L. 412;

- Saintier, "A Remarkable Understanding and Application of the Protective Stance of the Agency Regulations by the English Courts" [2001] J.B.L. 540;

- Saintier, "Final Guidelines on Compensation of Commercial Agents" (2008) 124 L.Q.R. 31;

- Saintier, "New Developments in Agency Law" [1997] J.B.L. 77;

- Saintier, "The Principles Behind the Assessment of the Compensation Option under the Agency Regulations: Clarity at Last?" [2007] J.B.L. 90;

- Sasse and Whittaker, "An Assessment of the Impact of the UK Commercial Agents (Council Directive) Regulations 1993" [1994] I.C.C.L.R. 100.

Chapter 33

TERMINATION OF AGENCY

INTRODUCTION

In this chapter we will examine the various means by which an agency agreement can come **33–001** to an end. We will then assess some of the effects of the termination of the agency relationship. It should be recognised at this point that just as agency law generally involves the relationships between three parties, the principal, the agent and the third party, so too does the termination of an agency agreement. We must consider therefore, not only the ability of principal and agent to terminate their internal relationship, but also the impact of that termination on the external relationship, i.e. upon third parties dealing with the agent. Note that the special position of "commercial agents" under the Commercial Agents (Council Directive) Regulations 1993 in respect to termination (e.g. notice period required etc.) has already been considered in Chapter 32 and will not be repeated here.

THE TERMINATION OF THE AGENCY

Termination by Agreement

Just as an agency agreement may be created by agreement between agent and principal, so **33–002** too, the agreement can similarly be terminated. In that respect an agency agreement is no different from any other contract. Where the agency agreement is non-contractual, the position is the same and either party can end the agreement at any time. Where the agency agreement is contractual, that contract may well specify that the agreement is to take effect only for a limited time, e.g. one month, one year etc. In such a case, the agreement will be regarded as automatically terminated upon the lapse of that period of time. Similarly, the agreement may be silent as to how long the agency agreement will continue to operate. In such a situation there are two possibilities. First, it may be possible to imply an automatic expiration date into the agreement, e.g. by trade custom.[1] Thus in *Danby v Coutt & Co*[2] the court held that the principal was not liable for the fraudulent acts of his agents which were committed after he returned from time abroad. Here the principal appointed two agents with power of attorney prior to going abroad. Although the power of attorney did not express any duration for the agreement to remain in place, it was accompanied by a recital stating that the principal was going abroad and wanted the agents to act on his behalf. The court implied from this that the power of attorney was only effective whilst the principal was abroad and so the principal was not liable.

The second possibility where the agency agreement has no express duration is that it may be terminated by reasonable notice. In *Staffordshire Area Health Authority v South Staffordshire Waterworks Co*[3] (not an agency case) a dispute arose between a hospital and a water company over an agreement made in 1929 concerning the cost of water supplied to the hospital. The agreement fixed a price for the supply of water and included the words "at all times hereafter". The hospital sought to rely on those words to bind the water company to the contract in perpetuity (and therefore pay for the water at the rate agreed in 1929!). The Court of Appeal held that the agreement was determinable by reasonable notice. Cumming-Bruce L.J. stated that[4]:

> " . . . the words 'at all times hereafter' mean that the obligations granted and accepted by the agreement were only intended to persist during the continuance of the agreement; and the agreement, in my view, was determinable on reasonable notice at any time".

The water company was therefore allowed to terminate the 1929 agreement in order to renegotiate a new price for the water supplied and were not to be bound by the old agreement in perpetuity.

Termination of Principal's Business

33–003 The courts have on many occasions been faced with claims from disgruntled agents where the agency agreement has a fixed duration but the principal's business has, for one reason or another, ceased to exist prior to the expiration of the agency agreement. The answer as to whether the agent is entitled to damages in such an event is not entirely clear since the courts have decided the issue in both ways.

In *Rhodes v Forwood*[5] the House of Lords refused to imply a condition into the agency agreement that the business itself shall continue to be carried on during the period specified. In *Rhodes* the plaintiff had been appointed as sole agent for the sale of the respondent's coal in Liverpool for a period of seven years. After around three and a half years the principal sold the colliery and thus the agent could sell no more coal in Liverpool. This obviously caused

---

[1] See, for example, *Seton v Slade* (1802) 7 Ves. Jr. 265 (customary for a broker's authority to expire at the end of the day).
[2] (1885) L.R. 29 Ch. D. 500.
[3] [1978] 1 W.L.R. 1387.
[4] [1978] 1 W.L.R. 1387 at 1405.
[5] (1875–76) L.R. 1 App. Cas. 256.

the agents to (i) lose out on future commission to be earned in the three and half years which the agreement had left to run at the time of the sale of the colliery and (ii) lose various expenses incurred in setting up as the sole Liverpool agent in anticipation of the agreement lasting for the full seven year period. The House of Lords found that there was no express term of the contract requiring the principal actually to send any coal to Liverpool to be sold by the agent. The plaintiffs had argued that there was an implied condition that the principal was to send coal to Liverpool for sale by the agent and that this implied condition had been breached by the principal's sale of the business. The House of Lords declined to accept this argument.

In *Turner v Goldsmith*,[6] however, the Court of Appeal arrived at the opposite conclusion by finding that an agent was entitled to maintain an action against his principal who did not resume his business when his factory burnt down two years into the five year agency agreement. The court based this decision on the fact that the principal had agreed to employ the agent for five years and that in not resuming his business the principal had not met his obligation to supply the agent with the samples necessary for the agent to fulfill his role as agent. At first glance, it appears that the facts are remarkably similar to those in *Rhodes*. The Court of Appeal distinguished *Rhodes*, however, on the basis that in *Rhodes* there was no express agreement actually to send any coal to the agent in Liverpool. In *Turner*, the Court of Appeal determined that there was an express agreement to employ the agent for five years, and that in order to fulfill that agreement, the principal was to send the agent a reasonable amount of samples in order to enable the agent to earn his commission.

The distinction appears to be difficult to sustain. In *Rhodes v Forwood* there was an   **33–004** agreement to employ Forwood as Liverpool sales agent for a period of seven years. Surely by the logic of the Court of Appeal in *Turner* in order to fulfill that agreement, the principal was to send the agent a reasonable amount of coal to enable him to earn the agreed rate of commission? This logic cannot apply however, since in *Rhodes* the agreement expressly stated that the principal was not bound actually to send any coal at all to Liverpool. *If* coal was sent to Liverpool, the agreement did oblige the principal to send it to Forwood as the sole agent in Liverpool. The key point therefore is the clause in the contract in *Turner* which stated that:

> "The said A. S. Turner shall do his utmost to obtain orders for and sell the various goods manufactured or sold by the said company as shall be from time to time forwarded or submitted by sample or pattern to him at list price to good and substantial customers".

Thus by not continuing his business following the fire, the principal was in breach of his contractual obligation to forward samples of the goods manufactured or sold by the principal. Perhaps surprisingly, there was no equivalent term in the contract between agent and principal in the *Rhodes* case.

Death of Principal or Agent

The death of either principal or agent will suffice to terminate the agency agreement. This is   **33–005** whether or not the surviving party has notice of the other's death. Thus, in *Campanari v*

---

[6] [1891] 1 Q.B. 544.

Woodburn[7] the agent was not entitled to claim a commission earned on the sale of a painting made after the death of the principal. Similarly, in *Pool v Pool*[8] a solicitor was prohibited from recovering costs incurred after the death of the client. This is a natural application of the rule that an agent cannot enter into contracts on behalf of a principal who is incapable of entering into the contract.

Insanity of Principal or Agent

33–006   In the same way as the death of either party will terminate the agency agreement, so too will the insanity of either party. In contrast to termination through death of the principal however, where the principal becomes incapable by reason of mental illness although the agency agreement between the principal and the agent is terminated, the agent can continue to bind his principal through apparent authority. This is so only where (i) the requirements of apparent authority have been met and (ii) the third party is unaware of the mental illness of the principal. In *Drew v Nunn*[9] the court had to determine to what extent the authority of an agent was terminated by the insanity of the principal. Brett L.J. searched for general principle within various authorities, but found none before stating[10]:

> "I think that the satisfactory principle to be adopted is that, where such a change occurs as to the principal that he can no longer act for himself, the agent whom he has appointed can no longer act for him."

However, by virtue of the principal having made representations to the third party as to the authority of the agent to act on his behalf, the third party was entitled to enforce the contract since the agent's apparent authority was binding upon the principal.

IRREVOCABLE AUTHORITY

Irrevocable Powers of Attorney

33–007   The Powers of Attorney Act 1971 amended the common law position regarding the ability to revoke a power of attorney. Under the common law such a power would be revoked, for example, by the death of the principal (the donor). This is now not the case by virtue of s.4 of the Act which provides:

> "(1) Where a power of attorney is expressed to be irrevocable and is given to secure—
>
> (a) a proprietary interest of the donee of the power; or

---

[7] (1854) 15 C.B. 400.
[8] (1889) 58 L.J.P. 67.
[9] (1878–79) 4 Q.B.D. 661.
[10] (1878–79) 4 Q.B.D. 661 at 666.

(b) the performance of an obligation owed to the donee,

then, so long as the donee has that interest or the obligation remains undischarged, the power shall not be revoked—

(i) by the donor without the consent of the donee; or
(ii) by the death, incapacity or bankruptcy of the donor or, if the donor is a body corporate, by its winding up or dissolution."

Thus where a power of attorney is stated to be irrevocable and is given to secure the interest of the agent (the donee) that power will be irrevocable whilst the interest remains. Moreover, it will remain despite the death, incapacity or bankruptcy of the principal (the donor).

Authority Coupled with an Interest

Where the authority given to an agent is coupled with an interest, the authority is irrevocable. **33–008** The interest of the agent here must be one which exists independently of the agency relationship. Therefore, the fact that by performing under the agreement the agent can earn fees or a commission is not enough to be an interest sufficient to render the authority irrevocable. In *Clerk v Laurie*[11] it was explained that[12]:

"What is meant by an authority coupled with an interest being irrevocable is this—that where an agreement is entered into on a sufficient consideration, whereby an authority is given for the purpose of securing some benefit to the donee of the authority, such an authority is irrevocable."

The authority would be irrevocable, therefore, where A owes B some money and authorises B to sell goods in order to satisfy that debt.[13] The pre-existing debt which the authority is designed to protect constitutes an interest and the authority will be irrevocable until the goods have been sold and the debt paid. In *Re Hannan's Empress Gold Mining and Development Co, Ex p. Carmichael's*[14] a man by the name of Phillips promoted a company in order to buy a mine from him. Mr Carmichael agreed to buy those shares in the company, which were not sold to members of the public, and granted Phillips the authority to apply for those unsold shares on his behalf. In the end Mr Carmichael was contractually bound to buy 980 shares but sought (prior to the purchase going through) to revoke the authority of Phillips to purchase the shares on his behalf. The Court of Appeal upheld the decision at first instance and held that since the authority was designed to protect an interest of the agent it was irrevocable. The interest of the agent here was that, as the principal was aware, if the shares were not all sold, the agent would not be able to use the company to buy the mine (and therefore receive the purchase price).

[11] 2 H. & N. 199.
[12] 2 H. & N. 199 at 200.
[13] See for example, *Spooner v Sandilands* (1842) 1 Y & C 390.
[14] [1896] 2 Ch. 643.

Personal Liability of Agent

33–009   The principal cannot revoke the agency where the agent has incurred a personal liability through the exercise of his authority under the agency agreement. This rule is designed to protect the agent from acting under the agency agreement, incurring liability (e.g. to pay for goods etc.) only to be left to carry the liability where the principal revokes the agent's authority. Where the agency agreement is revoked in such circumstances, therefore, it follows that the agent will be indemnified in respect of his personal liability.

In *Read v Anderson*[15] the Court of Appeal was required to decide whether a principal could revoke an agent's authority to pay losing bets. The agent in *Read* was employed as an agent to place bets on behalf of his principal. The principal therefore gave the agent the authority to pay and receive money on those bets. It was already well established that where an agent incurs a legal liability, the agent cannot revoke the agent's authority so as to avoid indemnifying the agent for his loss. At the time of *Read*, however, gambling debts were unenforceable at law, and so therefore, the agent faced no legal liability by failing to honour the bets placed (and lost). The agent however, as a professional turf commission agent (someone who places such bets for a living) would face substantial financial loss if he failed to honour the bets since he would lose his professional reputation.[16] A majority of the Court of Appeal held that the principal was not able to revoke the agent's authority to honour the debts since, although the agent had not incurred any legal liability, he would incur a financial loss if he failed to honour the bets placed on behalf of his principal.

---

[15] (1884) 13 Q.B.D. 779.

[16] This was irrelevant to Brett M.R. who in his dissenting judgment stated that "the plaintiff's business, although it may not be illegal, is directly objected to by the law", at 782.

INDEX

This index has been prepared using Sweet & Maxwell's Legal Taxonomy. Main index entries conform to keywords provided by the Legal Taxonomy except where references to specific documents or non-standard terms (denoted by quotation marks) have been included. These keywords provide a means of identifying similar concepts in other Sweet & Maxwell publications and online services to which keywords from the Legal Taxonomy have been applied. Readers may find some minor differences between terms used in the text and those which appear in the index. Suggestions to *sweet&maxwell.taxonomy@thomson.com*.

(All references are to paragraph number)

Acceptance
  conditional sale agreements, 22–002—22–003
  credit cards, 22–017—22–018
  credit-sale agreements, 22–002—22–003
  hire purchase agreements, 22–002—22–003
  other credit agreements, 22–015—22–016
  sale of goods, 2–002—2–004
Action for price
  generally, 12–003—12–004
Actual authority
  generally, 28–002
  introduction, 27–003
Advertisements
  auctions, 15–002
Advertising (consumer credit)
  canvassing off trade premises, 21–008—21–010
  categories, 21–008
  circulars to minors, 21–006
  controlled advertisements, 21–008—21–009
  'health' warnings, 21–011
  quotations, 21–011
  regulations, 21–010
  unsolicited credit tokens, 21–007
Agency
  actual authority
    generally, 28–002
    introduction, 27–003
  agent's duties
    account, to, 29–008
    conflict of interests, and, 29–006
    fiduciary duties, 29–005—29–008
    introduction, 29–001
    performance of contractual undertaking, 29–002—29–003
    reasonable skill and care, 29–004
    secret profits, 29–007
  apparent authority
    consent, and, 27–004

Agency—*cont.*
  apparent authority—*cont.*
    generally, 28–005
    introduction, 27–003
    reliance upon representation, 28–007
    representation from principal to third party, 28–006
    third party unaware of lack of authority, 28–008
  authority, 27–003
  commercial agents
    application of regulations, 32–002
    definition, 32–002—32–003
    introduction, 32–001
    obligations of principal, 32–006
    obligations to principal, 32–005
    Regulations, 32–002—32–013
    remuneration, 32–007—32–008
    restraint of trade agreements, 32–013
    scope of regulations, 32–002—32–004
    termination of agency, 32–009—32–012
  conflict of interests, 29–006
  consent, 27–004
  contractual relationships
    agent and third party, between, 31–008—31–010
    breach of warranty of authority, 31–010
    contractual liability, 31–008
    contractual rights, 31–009
    disclosed principal, 31–002—31–005
    introduction, 31–001
    merger and election, 31–006
    principal and third party, between, 31–002—31–007
    set-off, 31–007
  creation
    actual authority, 28–002
    apparent authority, 28–005—28–008
    implied authority, 28–003—28–004
    introduction, 28–001

Hire purchase—*cont.*
sale by description, 23–011
title to goods, 23–008—23–010
termination
  breach by debtor, 25–007—25–008
  damages, 25–023—25–027
  default notice, 25–010—25–012
  events of termination, 25–003—25–012
  exercise of debtor's right, 25–005—25–006
  further payment from debtor, 25–022—25–031
  introduction, 25–001—25–002
  minimum payments, 25–028—25–030
  mutual agreement, 25–004
  non-default notice, 25–010—25–012
  other stipulated events, 25–009
  protected goods, 25–016—25–021
  recovery of goods from debtor, 25–013—25–015
  recovery of goods from third party, 25–034—25–043
  time orders, 25–032—25–033
  unfair relationships, 25–002
time orders, 25–032—25–033
unfair contract terms, 10–031
unfair relationships, 25–002

Implied authority
generally, 28–003—28–004
introduction, 27–003

Implied terms
contracts for transfer of goods, 8–002
contracts of hire, 8–008
contracts for services, 8–009
correspondence with sample, 7–028
fitness for purpose, 7–024—7–026
introduction, 7–009
quality
  fitness for purpose, 7–024—7–026
  introduction, 7–016
  relationship between terms, 7–027
  satisfactory quality, 7–017—7–023
sale by description, 7–013—7–015
satisfactory quality, 7–017—7–023
title to goods, 7–010—7–012
unfair contract terms
  'deals as consumer', 10–018—10–020
  introduction, 10–017
  non-consumer deals, 10–021—10–024

Importers
product liability, 9–014—9–015
product safety, 9–023

Incorporation
exclusion clauses
  displayed notices, 10–006
  introduction, 10–002
  oral agreement between parties, 10–003
  overriding oral warranty, and, 10–009
  previous course of dealing, 10–007
  signed document, 10–004
  trade usage, 10–008
  unsigned document, 10–005

Indemnities
agency, and, 30–005
consumer credit, and, 18–015

Inertia selling
See **Unsolicited services**
Innocent misrepresentation
And see **Misrepresentation**
generally, 6–003
Instalments
delivery, 11–009—11–010
Insurance contracts
cancellable agreements, 2–015
linked transactions, 19–026
Interest
late payment, 24–005
International contracts
applicable law, 16–026
branch or agency, 16–021
Brussels Regulation, 16–019
claim by consumer, 16–023
claim relating to land, 16–024
country of performance, 16–022
enforcement of foreign judgment, 16–027
introduction, 16–019
jurisdiction, 16–020—16–025
Lugano Convention, 16–019
non-European connection, 16–025
Internet sales
See **Electronic commerce**
Invitation to treat
generally, 2–002—2–004
Jurisdiction
cross-border contracts, 16–020—16–025
Late delivery
measure of damages, 14–009
"Lease purchase"
generally, 18–003
Licensing (consumer credit)
agreements rendered unenforceable
  agreements for services of unlicensed ancillary credit trader, 20–010
  introduction, 20–007
  regulated agreements made after introduction by unlicensed credit broker, 20–011
  regulated agreements made by unlicensed creditor, 20–008—20–009
businesses requiring licences, 20–003—20–004
categories, 20–003
doorstep sales, and, 20–001
exclusions, 20–004
group licences, 20–001
introduction, 20–001—20–002
Office of Fair Trading, and
  generally, 20–001
  powers, 20–012—20–013
partial exclusions, 20–005
purpose, 20–002
standard licence
  categories, 20–003
  generally, 20–004
unlicensed trading, 20–006
Liens
agency, and, 30–006
generally, 12–007—12–010